KILLIE

CONFIDEMUS

KILMARNOCK F.C.

1869 - 1994

KILLIE
The Official History

125 Years Of Kilmarnock F.C.

By David Ross

Published by:
YORE PUBLICATIONS
12 The Furrows,
Harefield, Middx.
UB9 6AT.

Printed by:
THE BATH PRESS

ISBN 1 874427 75 5

Published by:
Yore Publications
12 The Furrows, Harefield,
Middx. UB9 6AT.

....

British Library Cataloguing-in-Publication Data.
A catalogue record for this book
is available from the British Library.

ISBN 1 874427 75 5

ACKNOWLEDGEMENTS

A book of this nature inevitably requires assistance from many sources. I list below those who have helped this publication see the light of day:

For offering, and in many cases loaning, much-valued items for purposes of illustration, I would like to thank (in no particular order) James Strathearn, Scott McKenzie, Tam McDougall, Maureen Trodden, Gordon Allison, Billy Galloway, James McIlwraith, Wing-Commander Don Devine, KFC's long-standing scout James McIntosh, John Ferrol, Walter McCrae, Kevin Collins, Andrew Black, Alan Sutterfield, Alex Milligan, Gordon Simpson, Douglas & Iona Stevenson, David Mawson, William Clark, Arthur Walls, Alan Brown, Mr & Mrs A.A. Rannachan, Campbell Coupland, Gordon Robb, Graham Rankin, J. Stewart McLauchlan and William Paton.

For letting me use their statistical records and for double-checking my own, I am grateful to Gordon Allison, Richard Cairns and John Livingston, whose painstaking research has been well known to Killie fans for many years. In particular I would like to thank Gordon Allison for giving me access to his horde of memorabilia.

Similarly, Alex Milligan and Gordon Robb of the *Kilmarnock Standard* were of immense assistance and the reception staff at the *Standard* office deserve thanks for collecting material on my behalf.

Robert Fleeting, Tommy Burns, the directors, and all staff at Rugby Park were enthusiastic supporters of the book. Kevin Collins and Walter McCrae turned the ground into an Aladdin's cave on my behalf when I visited them. Nothing was too much trouble and no effort was spared in retrieving material which had been locked away for years. I am in their debt.

I am grateful to the London and South-East England Supporters Association, Phil Hall, and Gordon Simpson in particular for a steady flow of up-to-date information. And to the Ayrshire Districts Supporters Association for many enjoyable journeys to watch Killie in action. Also to the Dundonald Members for some memorable post-match Saturday nights.

The staff of the National Newspaper Library in Colindale, North London deserve credit, particularly for the stoical way in which they adapted to my requests for some of the more obscure 19th Century Scottish titles.

I would also like to thank *Yore Publications* for their faith in this book. To Dave Twydell, steeped in football lore, in particular but also to Fay for her hard work too, and to Kara Matthews who drew the short straw and had to type up the statistical section.

The Scottish Football League were also very accommodating, as were the Scottish Football Association.

Then there were those other books, without which this one would never have been written: the 1898 Cup Final booklet, the 1912 *Kilmarnock Standard* Portrait Gallery, the 50th anniversary book by Charles Smith and, of course, Hugh Taylor's centenary book, *"Go Fame..."* There was also John Livingston's excellent booklet published in 1990 to mark the 25th anniversary of the League Championship success. For a detailed history of the players I would point the reader in the direction of Bill Donnachie's superb *"Who's Who of Kilmarnock FC"*, published by Mainstream in 1989.

In what may be seen as reverse nepotism, I wish to thank my Uncle, Richard Ross, for ferrying car-loads of scrapbooks back and forth and also my parents, David and Elizabeth Ross for storing so much for so long. My thanks wouldn't be complete without placing on record the help given to me by my wife Josephine. Not just for her unerringly analytical journalistic eye, but for the support and encouragement she gave me right from the start. It has been greatly appreciated, especially at the beginning when it looked like I had taken on too much and that this book would never appear. Her faith never faltered.

Finally, although I've already mentioned him, I would again like to thank my father, David Ross. He is, after all, the true progenitor of this book. For if he hadn't taken a very small boy along to Rugby Park one day in the early 1960's, then I doubt very much if this book would ever have been written. Thanks, Dad.

Dedication

This book is dedicated to all those who have supported Kilmarnock Football Club over the past 125 years. And to those who will do so over the next 125.

David Ross July 1994

Contents

Dust Jacket Illustrations:

Front:

An amalgam of Kilmarnock F.C. items reflecting the Club's past 125 years, including a portrait of Bob Templeton, and the Ayrshire Cup.

Rear:

(Top) Left, John Wallace - founder and first secretary. Centre, 1869 membership card. Right, Player/manager Tommy Burns.
(Centre) The 1964/65 season Championship winning squad.
(Bottom) Left, 1938 Scottish Cup Final ticket. Centre, Windsor Hotel, Montreal reception - 1930 North America Tour. Right, 15 May 1993, a pitch invasion - Killie are promoted to the Premier Division.

FOREWORD

My first game for Kilmarnock was a Second Division match at East Fife where the team bus broke down, the players put on their strips in taxis, and the game - played in monsoon conditions - was abandoned with some players at risk of hypothermia. Less than five years later, Kilmarnock are a Premier League side, have tasted the atmosphere of a Scottish Cup Semi-Final and are aiming for a return to European football in what will shortly be an all-seater stadium.

This total transformation in the club's fortunes can be attributed to several factors. The players have performed with pride, effort and ability to take the club back into the higher echelons of the Scottish League. The Chairman and the Board's progressive outlook has greatly assisted Billy Stark and myself in our endeavours to bring success to Rugby Park. And, of course, there are the supporters.

Playing for Celtic - as I did - or for Rangers, there is a tendency to assume that 'Old Firm' fans are the most passionate in the game. But within a month of my arriving at Kilmarnock I realised just how dedicated the club's supporters were. Their commitment at home and the fervent backing they give on our travels has played no small part in the club's revival.

I realise that the will for success and the appreciation of the club's traditions are as strong at Kilmarnock as at any club in the country. So I am delighted that Kilmarnock FC - the oldest professional club in Scotland - are having their illustrious history related in this book. It is my fondest hope that Killie's most glorious chapters are still to come.

TOMMY BURNS

INTRODUCTION

As the world fast approaches a new millennium, football's dominance as the global game is complete. The sport which had conquered Europe and South America in the early days of this century has reached new peaks in the same epoch's fading years. The World Cup is decided on U.S. soil and the lure of the Yen finds top players Tokio-bound. And in the years in between, every country in every continent has fallen under the spell of *"the beautiful game"*.

Yet the origins of this most fascinating of sports remain determinedly obscure. The earliest games probably involved the kicking around of a severed head on some distant battlefield. However, these nascent international matches between, say, Greece and Persia, must remain the subject of conjecture - in those times the keeping of casualty lists was deemed more important than any record of 'goals' scored.

What is certain is that a form of football was played in Roman Britain. The annual Shrove Tuesday match at Ashbourne in Derbyshire has been traced back as far as AD 217. Though it is difficult to visualise exactly what transpired, the image of a legionary's helmet being booted between such rudimentary goalposts as a pair of togas may not be all that fanciful. In Scotland, similar games came to be played on the same occasion - although known by its Christianised title of Fastern E'en.

Despite repeated royal bans - medieval Scots Kings preferred to concentrate on establishing superiority over their southern rivals at archery rather than football - this primitive game survived into the 19th Century, where no less a luminary than Sir Walter Scott can be found lamenting the passing of the game from friendly rivalry between villages into bitter, local enmity. An early example of the tendency of the older generation to bewail to those younger that the *'game's not what it used to be'*.

But while Sir Walter worried that the ancient game was going into terminal decline, it was actually being taken up - and transformed with vigour - by students in those inappropriately named institutions - the English public schools. Their own version of football increased rapidly in popularity throughout the first half of the 19th Century, culminating in the establishment of the Football Association in 1863.

The second half of that century witnessed an explosion in the game's popularity as it became adopted by the working class. The era of huge paying crowds and professional players was but a short step away from the winter pastime of the Victorian gentry.

But it is to that earlier time of *'gentlemen'* rather than *'players'* that we must travel if our story is to unfold; to the middle years of the reign of Queen Victoria. William Gladstone has just become Prime Minister for the first time. On the continent - a strange place that can still be *"cut off by fog"* as one famous newspaper would have it - mastery is being striven for by the twin colossi of Bismarck and Napoleon III. In far-away America, civil war not long ended, a hero of that conflict - Ulysses S Grant - is about to assume the Presidency.

But in Scotland, an old pursuit has taken new shape. The Queen's Park Football Club has been formed in Glasgow and it is looking for others to play. For our story to begin, we must travel south-west of that city. To Ayrshire. To that county's largest town. To the place where the works of Scotia's national Bard first saw the light of day. To a town where our ears can detect the sound of a new-born football infant.

To Kilmarnock ......

The first mention of Killie in print. From the Kilmarnock Standard, 2nd January 1869

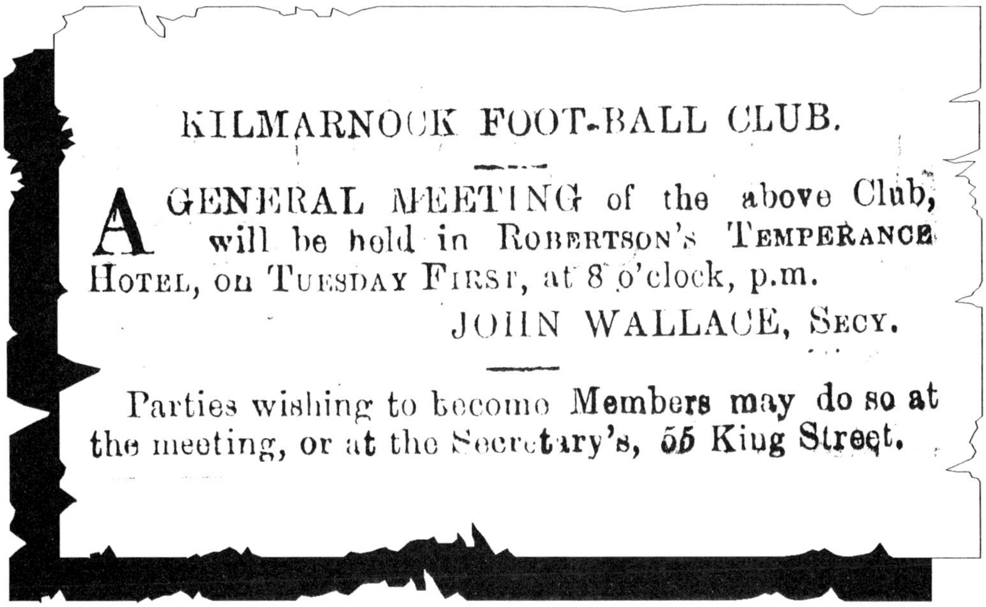

KILMARNOCK FOOT-BALL CLUB.

A GENERAL MEETING of the above Club, will be held in ROBERTSON'S TEMPERANCE HOTEL, on TUESDAY FIRST, at 8 o'clock, p.m.

JOHN WALLACE, SECY.

Parties wishing to become Members may do so at the meeting, or at the Secretary's, 55 King Street.

Chapter 1
BORN KICKING: 1869 - 1884

We can't be exactly sure of the year we have arrived in - either 1868 or 1869. In the former year there is plenty of sporting activity in the town of Kilmarnock. Cricket, in particular, is popular with young, bourgeois gentlemen. The Kilmarnock Cricket Club has been established since 1852. Its Secretary is James Dickie - a figure who will become prominent in the new winter sport. The Kilmarnock Shaw Cricket Club is another strong local body. John Wallace, the 19 year old Secretary, is a phenomenally busy young man, also being Secretary of the Young Men's Literary Association.

Other cricket teams abound in the town - Portland, Thistle, Wellington, Stewart and Newfield to name but a few. They play on the Barbadoes Green, now known as the Howard Park. But these games are for participating in - the concept of spectator sport is unknown in these times. To our eyes it is a strange society indeed, as an advertisement in the local newspaper intimates: *"DUNG FOR SALE"* it proclaims, going on to add: *"A Quantity of excellent farm yard dung, **to be seen** at the farm of Gateside, 2 miles from Stewarton Station"*. If that was typical of the sort of thing that could be viewed publicly, then it is little wonder that the locality was ready for alternative pleasures.

The cricketers were keen, but even the boldest of such knows that their sport is one which is not suited to the winter months. John Wallace was one of those attracted to the growing activity of football. So he with some fellow scholars from the Kilmarnock Academy, took to the 'new' game with alacrity. That games of some kind took place from October 1868 onwards is not in doubt, but the level of their organisation remains debatable.

There was undoubtedly an upsurge in the popularity of the sport - some of the cricketers joining the schoolboys. By the beginning of 1869, the redoubtable John Wallace was attempting to establish the game. An advertisement appeared in the *Kilmarnock Standard*, dated January 2nd 1869.

A membership card was issued for 1869 showing Wallace as both Secretary and Treasurer. The President was Robert Rankin - 'Old Bob' - as he was better known. The first in the long illustrious line of Kilmarnock goalkeepers. One of the committee members was James Dickie, proof that the cricketers had become enthusiastic about football.

But the type of game played would mystify today's followers. It was in reality a mixture of what we know as football and rugby. Hence the name of the club's ground - Rugby Park. The original ground lay at right angles to the present stadium. Access was via Dundonald Road with South Hamilton Street, replete with trees, in the middle of the ground. There were thirteen rules for play. The ball could not be *picked* up while in play, but if *caught*, above knee height, a player could either take a free kick or run carrying the ball. The dimensions of the pitch would have taxed even the most herculean of performers - 200 yards long, 100 yards wide. Mercifully, there was no limit on the number of players in a team.

It is impossible to envisage an eleven-a-side match in such circumstances. Goals could only be scored by *kicking*. Of the remaining rules, the two most interesting are rule 7 which stated: *"Any player may hold, push with his hands, or trip any player of the opposite side, when within 4 yards of the ball"*. And Rule 8: *"Though it is lawful to hold a player with the ball, this holding does not include attempts to throttle or strangle, which are, of course, opposed to all the principles of the game"*. Any modern spectator can cite instances when Rule 7 appears to be still in effect and where Rule 8 has been ignored completely. It is, though, an indication of the rough-and-ready nature of the game at this time that it was felt necessary to elaborate on the 7th rule by the introduction of the 8th.

As to their foes, well, they didn't exist. Games were played between members. And of these, nothing is recorded. The *Kilmarnock Standard* in its pages for 1869 makes reference to: Cricket, Bowls, Horse Racing, Billiards, Curling, Quoits, Golf, Athletics and even Rounders, as extensive a list of sports as can be found anywhere at the time. But of football - zero. It seems almost inconceivable that the erudite John Wallace can have made no record of events - he was after all, Secretary of the Literary Association. Unless, that is, his many social and sporting activities left him no time to do so. Another explanation for the lack of recorded detail is that the papers of the time may not have been happy to carry accounts of what they felt to be a 'ruffians' game. Credence is lent to this theory by a comment in the *Standard* more than 20 years later that they would *"pay gold"* for accounts of football matches that would have hitherto gone unreported.

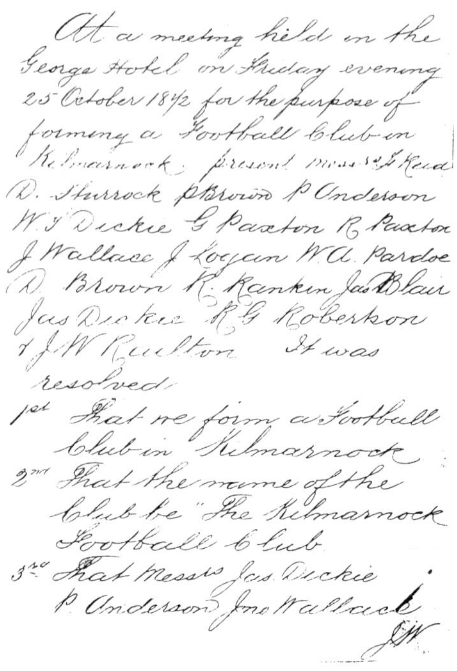
At a meeting held in the George Hotel on Friday evening 25 October 1872 for the purpose of forming a Football Club in Kilmarnock; present Messrs J. G. Reid D. Sturrock P. Brown P. Anderson W. J. Dickie G. Paxton R. Paxton J. Wallace J. Logan W. A. Pardoe D. Brown R. Rankin Jas Blair Jas Dickie R. G. Robertson & J. W. Poulton It was resolved

1st That we form a Football Club in Kilmarnock

2nd That the name of the Club be "The Kilmarnock Football Club"

3rd That Messrs Jas. Dickie P. Anderson Jno Wallace

JW

An extract from the minute book relating the re-formation of the club in 1872.

Whatever the reason, the first written record of the club stems from October 1872. On the 25th of that month, at a meeting in the George Hotel, the sixteen assembled gentlemen resolved *"to form a football club"* and that its name be *"The Kilmarnock Football Club"*. This has led some historians to suggest that the club's foundation should be dated from this point. Indeed, this date was given as the year of formation when the club played in its first Scottish Cup Final in 1898, when there were still some active in its affairs who could have contradicted such a notion. This theory must be discounted. For no fewer than four of the 1872 committee - James Dickie, John Wallace, Bob Rankin and Peter Brown - are all listed as committee members on the 1869 membership card.

Another advert for recruits was placed in the *Standard*, a further committee was set up to *"look after a field for the club"*, and the Secretary was instructed to obtain copies of other clubs' rules. Having done so, the next meeting agreed that the club would abide by *Rugby* rules. And it was under those rules that the first recorded 'match' took place - a 0-0 draw with a Kilmarnock Cricket Club XI. Note that there were *eleven* players on each side. Killie's historic team was:- R. Rankin (capt.) J.W. Railton, G. Paxton, C. Cowie, D. Sturrock, D. Brown, J. Wilson, P. Brown, J. Blair, J. Dickie, W.A. Pardoe.

Games after a fashion were played in March and April of 1873. A 15-a-side 0-0 draw at Paisley - the first 'away' match. That was followed by a defeat at home to the same team by *"0-1 and three tries"*. Fifteen Kilmarnock men played twenty from Ayr Academy with the result unrecorded. There was a game consisting of four periods of twenty minutes against Ayr followed by a ninety minute match against the same team a week later.

Yet even while these games were being played, the club was making a fundamental change to its rules. The doyen of Scottish football - Queen's Park - had written to Kilmarnock in December 1872 asking for a match under F.A. rules. Killie replied that, as a rugby club, they could not oblige. ButQueen's were persistent. In March 1873 they again wrote to Kilmarnock informing them of a scheme to establish a Scottish Cup and asking if they would subscribe £1 towards a suitable trophy. The recorded minute states: *"As the rules of the club are at present rugby, the proposal could not be at first entertained, but it was agreed that next season the rules of the Association should be adopted. The Secretary was then instructed to intimate the club's willingness to subscribe"*. The club also decided to join the newly formed Scottish Football Association. In an attempt to preserve the unity of the club, it was agreed that rugby could be played in the second half of the season.

Attempts were made to reverse the decision but the die was cast. Football enthusiasts were signed up as members on the eve of a meeting; ensuring the upper hand against the rugby men. A decision was taken in December 1873 to *"play no other than Association rules"*. This prompted a walk-out by some rugby followers. Some still adhered to both codes. And two months after the December meeting, Killie played a rugby game in Paisley. But that was a one-off. From now on, the winter game was football only. It had been the establishment of the Scottish Cup that had determined which way Kilmarnock would go in the 'code war'. And, appropriately, that is where our season-by-season account of their history starts.

1873-74

Shortly before the first proselytising approach fromQueen's Park, Kilmarnock had decided to adopt a blue jersey as their uniform. And it was these blue shirts of Kilmarnock who stepped out ontoQueen's Park's Crosshill ground - the original Hampden Park as it became - beforeQueen's had played on it themselves. Their opponents were the Dunbartonshire side, Renton. It was the very first match in the first ever Scottish Cup competition. Although another tie was played the same day, reports of it are difficult to come by. But, at any rate, it is unlikely to have taken place before Killie's game which kicked off at ten minutes to three.

Of the four clubs in action that day, only Kilmarnock are still in existence. Indeed, Killie rank alongside Dunbarton andQueen's Park as the only clubs to take part in that initial tournament who are still alive today. Posterity has accorded them such achievement. Sadly, their playing performance was not so memorable. The *Ayrshire Argus and Express* reported the match so:

"Football. Kilmarnock V Renton. This match, the first tie for the Association Cup, took place on the Queen's Park on Saturday, and after an hour and a half's stiff play, resulted in favour of the Dumbartonshire players by two goals. The play on both sides was rather wild at first, but improved greatly before the game closed".

Just like the game, football writing was in its infancy too. So perhaps we can forgive the rather spartan approach in the *Argus*. A longer account was related in the *Glasgow News* which mentions that Killie played with only ten men, that they were persistently penalised for using their hands (understandable in the light of the club's fortunes to that date), and that both halves were of 40 minutes duration. But the date - October 18th 1873 - goes down in history, not just as the start of the Scottish Cup, but also as the day when Kilmarnock as a 100% *football* club made their debut.

Killie's formation in that Cup tie was what a modern fan would call 0-2-7. For their first home match as an Association side, they played 2-3-5. That line-up, so beloved of those who call themselves 'traditionalists', was - for the time - highly unusual. Two full-backs, two half-backs and six forwards was the conventional approach. Alas, Kilmarnock's tactical ploy failed to protect them from a 9-0 defeat at the hands of Queen's Park. But the famous Glasgow team had yet to lose a goal to any opponent, far less a match.

More practical opponents were old foes, Paisley. They travelled to Ayrshire on December 27th 1873 to play their first match under the Association rules. Killie triumphed 1-0, their first victory. To Peter Brown falls the honour of scoring Kilmarnock's first goal. There were other notable matches too. A 1-0 win over the Third Lanark Rifle Volunteers was the first in a series of games against that club which continued until the 1960's. Clydesdale - who reached the first Scottish Cup Final - were held to a 0-0 draw. Queen's Park were held to a more respectable 4-0 on their own ground.

The Kilmarnock
FOOTBALL CLUB.
SEASON, 1873-74.
PRESIDENT,
JAMES DICKIE.
VICE-PRESIDENT.
P. BROWN.
CAPTAIN.
ROBERT RANKIN.
VICE-CAPTAIN.
G. PAXTON.
SECRETARY and TREASURER.
J. W. RAILTON, Deanside House.
COMMITTEE.
W. DRENNAN.
F. REID.
J. WALLACE.
W. THOMSON.
D. STURROCK.

RULES
OF THE
Kilmarnock Football Club.

I.
That this Club shall be called the "KILMARNOCK FOOTBALL CLUB.

II.
The following Office-Bearers shall be chosen annually, viz.:—President, Vice-President, Captain, Vice-Captain, and Secretary and Treasurer.

III.
That the management of the Club shall be in the hands of a committee of Five Members in addition to the Office-Bearers who shall be members *ex-officio;* and this committee shall be empowered to fill up such vacancies among its members as may from time to time occur. Five Members shall constitute a quorum.

IV.
Office-Bearers shall be elected and Members admitted to the Club by ballot of Committee.

1873/74 Members Card (Killie entered the inaugural Scottish Cup this season)....

KILMARNOCK FOOTBALL CLUB FIXTURES—SEASON, 1874-75.

DATE.	PLAYED AT	CLUB.	CLUB.	RESULT.	REMARKS.
1874.					
Sept. 26	Kilmarnock	Kilmarnock	Ardrossan	Won by 2 Goals to nil.	
Oct. 10	Glasgow	Queen's Park	Kilmarnock		
,, 10	Kilmarnock	2nd Do.	2nd Do.		
,, 17	Do.	Kilmarnock	Vale of Leven Rovers		
,, 24	Do.	Do.	Bellahouston Wanderers		
,, 31	Do.	Do.	Alexandra Athletic		
,, 31	Glasgow	2nd Do.	2nd Do.		
Nov. 14	Kilmarnock	Kilmarnock	Standard		
,, 14	Glasgow	2nd Do.	2nd Do.		
,, 28	Kilmarnock	Kilmarnock	Barrhead		
Dec. 5	Do.	2nd Do.	Oxford, Glasgow		
,, 12	Do	Kilmarnock	Clydesdale		
,, 12	Glasgow	2nd Do.	2nd Do.		
1875.					
Jany. 1	Kilmarnock	1st Kilmarnock	2nd Kilmarnock		
,, 16	Barrhead	Barrhead	Kilmarnock		
,, 23	Kilmarnock	Kilmarnock	Queen's Park		
,, 23	Glasgow	2nd Do.	2nd Do.		
Feby. 27	Do.	Alexandra Athletic	Kilmarnock		
,, 27	Kilmarnock	2nd Do.	2nd Do.		
March 6	Glasgow	Standard	Kilmarnock		
,, 6	Kilmarnock	2nd Do.	2nd Do.		
,, 20	Glasgow	Clydesdale	Kilmarnock		
,, 20	Kilmarnock	2nd Do.	2nd Do.		

On OPEN Dates games will be played on the

KILMARNOCK
FOOTBALL
CLUB
FIXTURES.
SEASON, 1874-75.

..... and the fixture list for the following season.

And, as the new craze spread across Scotland, local rivals emerged. Kilmarnock played and beat fellow town side Portland, 3-0.

By now the difficulties of playing on a pitch with trees in the centre of the park became apparent. Killie sought a new ground. Holm Quarry was used for one game before decanting to the Grange, located on Irvine Road. Bob Rankin told how the farmer agreed to let them use his field, claiming that the grass was *"a' the better for being trampit a bit"*. And that after receiving a bag of meal for his trouble, the farmer asserted that *"Thae fitba players are fine laddies"*.

1874-75

By now Kilmarnock were well-enough organised to produce a fixture list at the start of the season. Although some adjustments were made as the year progressed, most of the matches listed were played. Among them was Killie's first-ever Scottish Cup victory, a 4-0 home win over Vale of Leven Rovers. Cup success was short-lived however, Killie losing to Glasgow side, Eastern, in the second round. The highlight of the term was a visit from the still-invincible Queen's Park. This was billed as:

"THE GRAND MATCH OF THE SEASON".

The club were alive to the new-found prospect of paying customers and admission for this game was 3d. A curiously-worded advert also promised "Ladies Free". It was some time before the unintended *double entendre* was noticed and even then such adverts remained common at Scottish football games.

Rules still needed clarifying. In a game at Ardrossan, the width between the posts was only just over half the regulation size but this didn't prevent Kilmarnock from winning 3-0. Other teams were now playing in Kilmarnock as football continued on its upward curve. Apart from Portland, Killie now had to contend with teams like St. Andrew, Dean, Shewalton and Winton all vying for the townspeople's support.

1875-76

Kilmarnock won their opening Scottish Cup tie against Ayr Eglinton, 8-0, aided, no doubt, by the fact that the Ayr side fielded only ten men. This match was advertised as a *"friendly contest"* in the press, but it is clearly marked as a cup tie in the match list for the season belonging to Killie player, Andrew Ferguson. Mr. Ferguson noted on his list that he "kicked one" of the goals - the only record of any of the eight scored.

In the second round, it was Killie's turn to play a man short as they crashed out of the tournament to Clydesdale. At 2-0 down it was reported that with *"A heavy shower falling, the Kilmarnock men were minded to give up the match"*. Perhaps they should have, as the final score was 6-0.

Only four of the listed eight friendlies were played. Other Saturdays continued to be taken up with the old practice of the first footballers - inter-club games. New Year's Day was set aside for an early form of the 'derby' game - a match between the 1st and 2nd XIs. There were few other diversions on a weekend. The likes of the "Auchinleck Cheese Show", featured prominently in the local press, was hardly going to entice people away from the Grange. Oddly enough, although this pitch was still used, the Holm Quarry was also named as a home ground in Andrew Ferguson's Match List.

1876-77

Kilmarnock moved to the cricket club's ground at the Holm Quarry. But the harmony between the two sports broke down over a move by the cricketers to raise the rent paid by the footballers to such an extent that cricket could be played rent-free. This was a blatant attempt to exploit the popularity of football and the players refused to stand for it. There was a breakaway. Some players tried to stay loyal to both sports, but the split was permanent. Kilmarnock FC departed once more to the Grange where the rent was now substantially more than a single bag of meal - the farmer there being as keen as the

KILMARNOCK FOOTBALL CLUB.

GROUND,.....................HOLM QUARRY AND GRANGE.

President, DAVID STURROCK | Vice-President, PETER BROWN | Captain, ROBERT RANKIN | Vice-Captain, J. B. WILSON.

JOHN WALLACE, Match Secretary, 55 KING STREET,

MATCH LIST FOR SEASON, 1875-76.

WILLIAM DRENNAN, Treasurer, 2 KING STREET.

FIRST ELEVEN.

Dates.		CLUB.	Ground.	Total Goals. For	Total Goals. Agst.	Results. Lost by	Results. Won by	Remarks.
Oct.	2	Queen's Park	Glasgow					
,,	9	Ayr Eglinton (Cup Tie)	Grange	8	/	/		Kicked 1
,,	16							
,,	23	Ayr Thistle	Ayr					
,,	30							
Nov.	6							
,,	13							
,,	20							
,,	27							
Dec.	4							
,,	11							
,,	18	Ardrossan	Ardrossan					
,,	25							
Jan.	1	1st and 2nd	Holm Quarry					
,,	8							
,,	15	Alexandra Athletic	Glasgow					
,,	22							
,,	29							
Feby.	5							
,,	12							
,,	19	Ayr Thistle	Holm Quarry					
,,	26	Queen's Park	Holm Quarry					
March	4							
,,	11	Ayr Eglinton	Ayr					
,,	18							
,,	25							
April	2	Alexandra Athletic	Holm Quarry					
,,	9							
,,	16							
,,	23	Closing Game	Holm Quarry					

SECOND ELEVEN.

Dates.		CLUB.	Ground.	Total Goals. For	Total Goals. Agst.	Results. Lost by	Results. Won by	Remarks.
Oct.	2	Queen's Park	Grange					Did not join
,,	9							
,,	16	St. Andrews	Hillhouse farm	2			2	Kicked 1
,,	23	Ayr Thistle	Grange					
,,	30							
Nov.	6							
,,	13							
,,	20							
,,	27							
Dec.	4							
,,	11							
,,	18							
,,	25							
Jan.	1	1st and 2nd	Holm Quarry					
,,	8							
,,	15	Alexandra Athletic	Holm Quarry					
,,	22							
,,	29							
Feby.	5							
,,	12							
,,	19	Ayr Thistle	Ayr					
,,	26	Queen's Park	Glasgow					
March	4							
,,	11	Ayr Eglinton	Holm Quarry					
,,	18							
,,	25							
April	2	Alexandra Athletic	Glasgow					
,,	9							
,,	16							
,,	23	Closing Game	Holm Quarry					

On Vacant Saturdays sides will be chosen on the ground by the Captain and Vice-Captain. A good attendance of the Members is urgently requested.

Fixture list for 1875/76 season. Belonging to Kilmarnock player Andrew Ferguson

cricketers to exact his pound of flesh - while a new team called the "Kilmarnock Cricket and Football Club" stayed at the Holm Quarry. Protests by Killie forced this new outfit to change their name to Kilmarnock Athletic and for a number of years they were a power in the land.

This last season with the cricketers was marked by a controversial Scottish Cup defeat by Mauchline - a potent team at the time. Their second goal in a 2-1 win was protested against by the Killie players, whose pleas were heeded by the Referee. But, on appeal to the SFA, the goal - and the tie - was awarded to Mauchline. Kilmarnock had to console themselves with the burgeoning popularity of their sport. A crowd of 500 attended a game against Caledonian from Glasgow while the gate for a 'derby' with Kilmarnock Winton was reputed to be in excess of that figure.

1877-78

Despite the continued presence of men from 1869 on the committee, the rules card for this season stated that the club was constituted in October 1872. Dan Gilmour took over as President and he would remain a central figure in the club until limited company status was adopted nearly 30 years later. The club colours were listed as Oxford Blue Jersey and White Knickers. The badge on the jersey was similar to the town's coat of arms. It consisted of a hand-index and second fingers upright, thumb outstretched, other fingers enclosed over palm. The hand rested on a bar over a ball marked KFC.

John Wallace and Dan Gilmour had played leading roles in forming an Ayrshire Football Association in 1876 and now that body instituted its own knockout competition - the Ayrshire Cup. This magnificent trophy is one of the most beautiful in football. It stands thirty inches high, surmounted by a figure representing victory holding a palm leaf in her right hand and a laurel wreath in her left. Under this are two shields bearing the arms of Kilmarnock and Ayr. On either side are two figures in football costume and between them is a portrait of Robert Burns. In the centre are a series of figures playing football. Underneath this come the arms of Lord Eglinton and at the base of the Cup are two lions serjeant: one bearing the arms of Scotland, the other the arms of Bruce.

Designed by John Cameron and Son, a Kilmarnock Jewellers and Silversmiths, the solid silver trophy cost over £100 - a massive figure for the time. Now played for by just three teams; Kilmarnock, Ayr United and Girvan Amateurs, in its heyday, over 40 clubs fought over this splendid trophy. In this first season there were 27 entrants, including such long-forgotten luminaries as Burnfoothill Ramblers, Rankinston Mountaineers and Kilmaurs Floors.

Although drawn away, Kilmarnock's first game was actually played at their new home, the *"fine new ground of the former Rugby Park, Dundonald Road"*. A 5-1 win over Dalry Rangers marked Killie's return to the improved Rugby Park. The old nemesis of Mauchline eliminated them 4-0 on the same ground in the second round, and went on to become the first winners of the Ayrshire Cup, beating Portland 4-3 in the Final at Holm Quarry, watched by 5,000. In the Scottish Cup, Killie beat Hurlford 5-1 but succumbed to Ayr Accies away from home.

1878-79

The splits with the Rugby and Cricket players allied to the passage of time and the proliferation of clubs, meant that Kilmarnock were no longer as strong as before. This was reflected in a 2-0 Scottish Cup defeat by Kilbirnie and a 7-0 hammering by Mauchline in the Ayrshire Cup. Kilmarnock Athletic won 5-1 at Rugby Park as well. On the Friday evening of November 8th 1878, there was a most unusual game. Billed as the *"Grand Match Under Electric Lights"* Killie played host to local rivals, Portland.

A London firm supplied three lights, one of 6,000 candlepower and the others of 1,200 each. Although the main light worked well enough, the others faltered, throwing huge shadows over the pitch, confusing spectators and resulting in serious injury to two Kilmarnock players. One of these was J.B. Wilson who had played in the first Cup game against Renton, as well as the inaugural game against the Cricket Club. He never played again but went on to become Provost of Kilmarnock. The match was won by Portland 3-0 but the experiment had proved too costly, in terms of injury, to be continued. It would be 75 years before floodlit football was again played at Rugby Park.

The victors that evening, Portland, were the most popular of all the Kilmarnock clubs at this time and it was reported that many spectators often left Rugby Park and climbed the fence to the adjoining Hamilton Park where Portland played. Portland returned to Rugby Park to contest the Ayrshire Cup final again - that ground's first representative final - but were beaten by Kilmarnock Athletic in a replay. The host club's sole contribution was to supply the Referee - the ubiquitous John Wallace.

With Wallace no longer playing, the injury to Wilson and the retiral this season of Bob Rankin, there were now no survivors at Rugby Park of those early games. New blood was needed if the team was to survive. The St. Andrews and Hawthorn clubs had already folded, but their loss was Killie's gain; many of their best players joining up with the Rugby Park outfit.

1879-80

Impressive-sounding victories over the likes of Irvine (10-0), Catrine (11-0) and Stewarton (8-1), the latter two away from home, couldn't disguise the fact that Killie were often found wanting when faced with more serious opposition. A 6-2 Scottish Cup thrashing at Mauchline, a 1-0 away defeat at Portland in the Ayrshire Cup and a dreadful 5-1 Rugby Park loss to Hurlford demonstrated that they were some way behind the leading teams in Ayrshire - let alone Scotland.

Action to correct this state of affairs was taken at the end of the season with the appointment of Robert Russell. Known as the 'Cutler' on account of his profession, Russell took charge of the 2nd XI and for many years he was the man responsible for ensuring that a suitable supply of fresh blood found its way through the ranks. But his talents didn't end there. Often, over the next eight years, he would turn out for both 1st and 2nd XI's, usually as a goalkeeper but sometimes outfield as well. The 'Cutler' went on to become one of the most famous characters associated with Killie in their pre-League days.

1880-81

Killie made some progress in the Scottish Cup this season. They had a first round walk-over when Stewarton failed to turn up for a tie. An *"ungentlemanly practice"*, according to the *Standard*. A fine 6-3 win over Ayr sent them into yet another meeting with Mauchline. The first tie was watched by 'only' 2-3,000, most Mauchline fans expecting Killie to be easy meat for their favourites. But this time, in a protest-ridden tie, it took three games before Killie were beaten. Was the tide beginning to turn at last? Apparently not. For, in the newly-instituted Kilmarnock Charity Cup, Mauchline easily beat Kilmarnock 4-1 at the Holm Quarry. This new competition was one of several founded around this time with the aim of distributing the takings from matches to local charities. It continued in one form or another until 1939 and the Charity Cup is now in the possession of the Dick Institute in Kilmarnock.

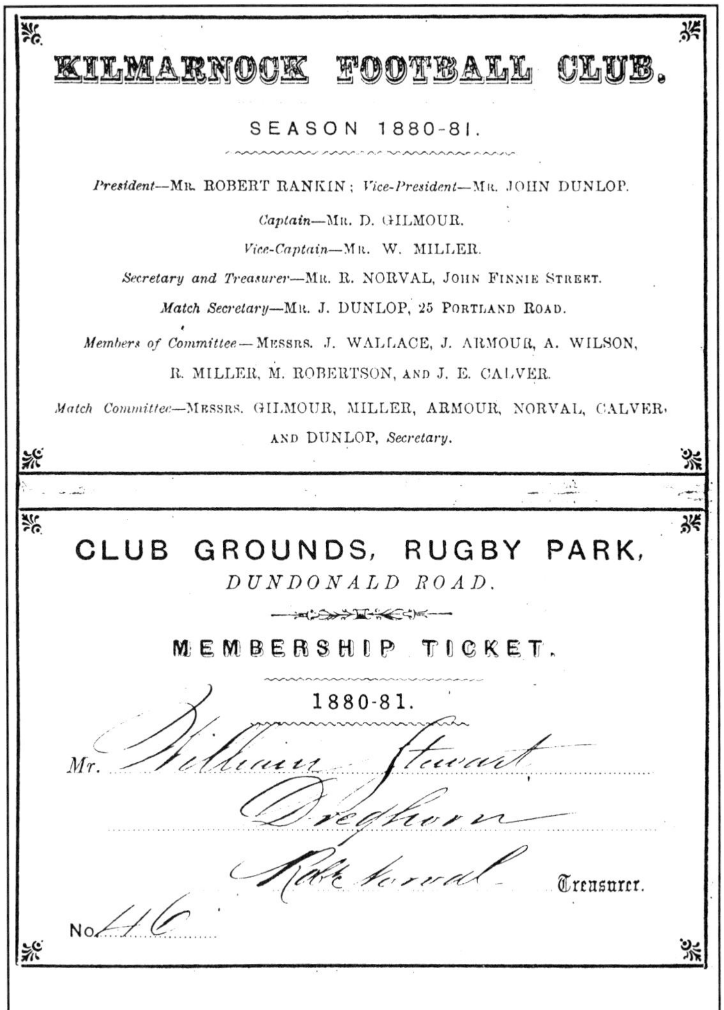

KILMARNOCK FOOTBALL CLUB.

SEASON 1880-81.

President—MR. ROBERT RANKIN; *Vice-President*—MR. JOHN DUNLOP.

Captain—MR. D. GILMOUR.

Vice-Captain—MR. W. MILLER.

Secretary and Treasurer—MR. R. NORVAL, JOHN FINNIE STREET.

Match Secretary—MR. J. DUNLOP, 25 PORTLAND ROAD.

Members of Committee—MESSRS. J. WALLACE, J. ARMOUR, A. WILSON, R. MILLER, M. ROBERTSON, AND J. E. CALVER.

Match Committee—MESSRS. GILMOUR, MILLER, ARMOUR, NORVAL, CALVER, AND DUNLOP, *Secretary*.

CLUB GROUNDS, RUGBY PARK,

DUNDONALD ROAD.

MEMBERSHIP TICKET.

1880-81.

Mr. William Stewart

Dreghorn

Robt Norval Treasurer.

No. 46

By 1880 football was becoming increasingly popular. For the first time Killie issued a hardback membership card.

Administratively, things were changing. This was Bob Rankin's last year as President. He emigrated to New Zealand later in the year. Sadly, he died there shortly after his arrival. Robert Norval took over from John Wallace as Secretary, but the club's founder remained as a committee man. As President of the Ayrshire FA, he also edited the Ayrshire Football Annual, one of the earliest publications of its kind. John Wallace was destined to take the migratory path south as well. He sailed to Australia in 1883, becoming a well-known flour merchant. Even in Sydney, he remained a sportsman, this time in a bowling club. Needless to say, he was the Secretary. When John Wallace died in 1917, his obituary described him as *"the father of Ayrshire football"*, and *"the patron saint of football in the county of Ayr"*. Sentiments applauded by all connected with Kilmarnock F.C.

1881-82

A much-improved Kilmarnock enjoyed good runs in both the Scottish and Ayrshire Cups. In the national tournament they reached the last 16, scoring heavily on the way. But some of their opponents were not rated too highly. Our Boys from Dundee were beaten 9-2 at Rugby Park and described in the *Standard* as *"not being able to play the game much better than eleven old ladies"*. Arthurlie, from Barrhead, proved too strong for Killie in the next round.

In the county competition, Killie marched all the way to their first Cup Final, beating Kilbirnie, Rankinston, Beith Thistle (after another protested match) and Lanemark. Alas, in the Final, Portland demonstrated that Killie were far from being the best in the town, never mind the County, winning a one-sided match 4-0 at the Holm Quarry. The usual residents of that ground - Kilmarnock Athletic - were doing even better. They reached the Semi-Finals of the Scottish Cup before losing 3-2 to a Queen's Park side on their way to their 6th Cup win. If Kilmarnock were to prosper they would have to match - then eclipse - their powerful local rivals.

1882-83

At last Kilmarnock beat Mauchline, winning their 1st round Scottish Cup tie 2-0. But they found another village team too good for them in the next round, losing 6-2 at home to Hurlford in a match which was described as the *"wildest and most rough game ever played in Ayrshire"*. Rough the games may have been, but the after-match 'Football Supper' was still something to be savoured. *"Good beer and good music have a charm only equalled by that of rich mutton and rare eloquence"* wrote one scribe after participating in one of these events.

One such supper most likely occurred after Killie's furthest venture to date. On November 2nd 1882 they travelled to England for the first time to face Carlisle. The Scottish side returned in triumph after a *15-1* slaughter of their Cumbrian hosts. But the Ayrshire press were rather less than generous in their praise, preferring to describe Carlisle as *"poor exponents of the manly game"*. The public were also sceptical about this result.

Kilmarnock's next home match was played before their lowest recorded attendance. Three men, two boys and a reporter who failed to classify himself into either category watched the match against Thornliebank in conditions akin to a hurricane. But at least Killie kept playing. Just along the road, neighbours Portland, playing Third Lanark, walked off the pitch as the weather got too much for them.

Once more it was Kilmarnock Athletic who made the running. They won the Ayrshire Cup and again reached the last four in the Scottish. They drew their Semi-Final with the famous Vale of Leven before losing the replay 2-0. Athletic's success was having an obvious effect on their rivals in the town and it is no exaggeration to suggest that, had they reached the Cup Final, it may have been the defining moment in the battle for football supremacy in the town, with the red shirts of the Athletic taking pride of place today and their Rugby Park rivals naught but a faded memory on a yellowed page.

1883-84

If ever there was a time when success was a must then this was the season. Players were leaving Scotland in droves as illegal payments by English clubs became commonplace. And clubs were struggling to survive. Portland failed to appear this year while others such as Beith, Kilbirnie and Mauchline maintained a precarious hold on existence. But the Mauchline club were still capable of giving Killie a hard time, their games being described as *"hand-to-hand and heel-to-head encounters"*.

Other matches were just as rough. After defeating Hurlford in the Scottish Cup, Killie faced Thornliebank - a team labelled as *"most unmanly and brutal"*. Four Kilmarnock players needed medical treatment after the Ayrshire side's defeat in the protested Cup-tie. That loss apart, Kilmarnock were a much-improved team. Full-back James Lucas and centre-forward Sandy Higgins - 'The Demon Dribbler' - were the star men in an outfit which gained an infusion of fresh blood by picking up the best players from defunct Portland.

Ayr were beaten 10-0 and Kilmarnock Athletic 8-2 as Killie stayed unbeaten at home all season - the first time they had achieved this distinction. But it was in the Ayrshire Cup that they excelled. A walk-over versus Portland was followed by a narrow 4-3 win away to Maybole.

Then Lugar Boswell were edged out 3-2 at Rugby Park before Killie took the short trip to play rivals Athletic in the Semi-Final. The Rugby Parkers emerged triumphant 3-1 but Athletic protested that Lucas should not have played as he was not resident in the County. A secondary protest from the Holm Quarry club charged that the match referee - Mr. M. Browning from Stewarton - displayed a *"want of knowledge of the rules"*. Their protests were dismissed but Lucas was transferred south before the *"Final tie for the Ayrshire Cup and badges"* against Hurlford.

The game took place at the Holm Quarry with this eleven representing Kilmarnock: McCall; Plumtree, Young; Burnett, Grier, A. Black; Walker, Higgins, Wallace, Wark,G. Black. Killie went a goal down in 30 minutes of a game reputed to have *"kicking and tackling of the highest order"*. In a much rougher second half, with the wind behind them, Killie equalised through Higgins with 25 minutes to play. *"Wire in Kilmarnock"* shouted their supporters, *"their pipe's oot"*. Such cries served only to galvanise Hurlford into action. They took the lead again and were only a few minutes from victory when former Hurlford player Allan Black scored for Killie.

In the replay, Killie again fell a goal behind. But Jeb Wark and Sandy Higgins put them ahead before the break to give Killie a lead which they clung onto until the final whistle. At last, the magnificent Ayrshire Cup was on its way to Rugby Park. Even now Killie had to wait until a Hurlford protest had been debated and rejected by the Ayrshire FA before they could finally claim the Cup as theirs. The long-overdue success was not only just reward for years of effort though. It was also the moment when Kilmarnock became the undisputed number one team in the town as well as the County.

Kilmarnock F.C. 1879. The earliest known team picture.
Back: A.Robertson, J.Dunlop, J.Black, R.Rankin, M.Robertson, R.Norval, J.Wallace.
Front: J.B.Wilson, W.Millar, D.Gilmour, R.Millar.

Chapter 2
FROM HURLFORD TO HAMPDEN: 1884-1899

1884-85

Hopes of a good Scottish Cup run were raised thanks to a 6-1 thrashing of Hurlford at Rugby Park, only to be dashed by a successful protest. Killie lost the rematch 3-1 but this time their own protest - submitted before the kick-off - was successful. So, despite having 'lost', Kilmarnock reached the second round. Protests were common in football at this time and usually took the form of a rule infringement concerning players registrations. But no complaints were forthcoming after Killie lost their next tie at Annbank on a pitch which was a *"mysterious-looking incline"*. Just off the field was an area *"resembling a jungle, a most useful spot for diverting the leather into"* when on the defensive.

THE AYRSHIRE CUP

The Ayrshire Cup was retained, enhancing Killie's reputation as the County's premier team. A crowd of 2,000 saw a 5-2 home win over Ayr in the Semi-Final, the same number as attended the Final, again against Hurlford and again at the Holm Quarry. And, in a further echo of their previous success, their scorers in the Final were Wark and Higgins once more, as Killie's 2-0 triumph confirmed their pedigree status.

Killie undertook their first tour of England this year. But they found the opposition more daunting than on their hop over the border to Carlisle. Yet they returned undefeated, having beaten Burnley 3-1 and drawn against Bolton teams, Great Lever and Halliwell, 2-2 and 1-1. A return to the same territory at season's end in April was less satisfactory, going down to a strong Bolton team 8-1 and to Great Lever by 3-1. These English teams all had a fair number of Scots in their ranks, and these players were looked down upon by the press who described the life of a professional footballer as *"degrading"*. Further insisting that *"wiser youths"* would stay at home, thus avoiding the inevitable *"indolent habits"* of the pro.

In fact the exact opposite was true. Scots players rushed south, and now that professionalism had been legalised this year, that torrent was about to become a flood. If offered the choice between playing football for a living, supplemented by a guaranteed job, there were few about who were prepared to stand on their dignity. One who did just that though was Killie's Sandy Higgins. Notwithstanding the hardships faced in his life as a miner, Sandy eschewed all blandishments aimed at securing his signature for another club. His career was undoubtedly harmed by his stance as the selectors of the Scotland team tended to look at the big city clubs or the 'anglos' when picking the national side. But in March 1885, as Scotland prepared to play Ireland, he was given his chance.

It was the first game in Scotland between the two countries and the first international to be played at the Second Hampden Park. Higgins was superb. Although played out of position on the left wing, he rattled in four goals as Scotland won 8-2. Yet he was never picked again. Even in those days, there were dark mutterings as to how many more caps Sandy would have achieved had he worn the colours of a Glasgow or English club. But four goals on his only appearance is a fine record for the man who was the first Kilmarnock player to wear the Blue of Scotland.

1885-86

Killie gained Scottish Cup revenge over Annbank with a 7-1 home win but their second round tie with Hurlford became a marathon affair. Dogged by protest, abandonment and non-appearances,this bad-tempered clash was finally resolved in Hurlford's favour by 5-1. The Ayrshire Cup was a different story. For the third year in succession, they lifted the trophy. By now Kilmarnock were the undisputed kings of Ayrshire football and rivals Athletic were struggling to survive. Killie's standing can be gauged from their results against some of the most powerful teams in the country. They drew 5-5 with Third Lanark at home and narrowly lost 4-3 away to Rangers.

At home to the latter side, Kilmarnock pulled off a remarkable 4-1 triumph - their first win over the Glasgow club. Inspirations in that team were the McPherson brothers - representatives of a remarkable footballing family. The father - John Q. McPherson - was Kilmarnock's trainer. Apart from also editing football annuals, he would go on to become trainer to Newcastle United and **both** the Scotland and England national teams. His sons who played in this match, were James and John, a half-back and a forward. Both would later play for Cowlairs. John - 'Kytie' as he was known - also went on to play for Rangers and Scotland, becoming a director of the Ibrox club. Watching his big brothers was young Davie McPherson, another who would play for Kilmarnock and Scotland one day.

1886-87

Killie's hold on the Ayrshire Cup was broken by a 2-1 defeat at Hurlford, but their long grip on the trophy had contributed heavily to the decline of Kilmarnock Athletic. 5-0 and 7-0 victories over this side showed how far they had fallen since the heady days when they had reached the last four of the Scottish Cup. Athletic folded this season and though revived after a couple of years, they were never again a threat to Killie's supremacy.

Indeed, for the first time, Kilmarnock themselves made a determined assault on the Scottish Cup. A walk-over versus Cumnock followed by 10-2 and 7-2 home wins against Lanemark and Lugar Boswell respectively, took them into the 'all-in' stage of the draw. They received a 4th round bye, then beat Dunblane 6-0 at home to set the scene for another Rugby Park tie - this time against Queen's Park.

2,500 watched the Quarter-Final match but Queen's demonstrated that they were still at the forefront of the Scottish game by winning 5-0.

The journey south was again undertaken as Killie lost 3-2 to Burnley on New Year's Day, then beat Fleetwood Rangers 3-0. A Kilmarnock man's sister, resident in England, wrote to the *Scottish Athletic Journal* before the tour, bemoaning Killie's prospects. While admitting that the Scots were superior footballers, she was of the opinion that the team would lose their matches as *"Scotch people are such whisky gluttons that it would be almost impossible for them to turn up sober"*. The honour of the players was defended in the same publication by Dan Gallacher. Writing under the pen-name of *'Horatio'*, he was an avid supporter of the club and his column in the *Kilmarnock Standard* was one of the best and most informative of its kind. For over a decade, until his death, he was the acknowledged expert on events at Rugby Park.

1887-88

This was one of the best teams to have represented Kilmarnock since their foundation. Ayr Thistle were trounced 8-2 in the Scottish Cup and after drawing away to Dykebar, a long-running complaint in football generally was addressed by 'Horatio' in the *Standard* when he wrote that the replay was *"likely to woo many back who have for a long time forsaken football"*. Those who did witnessed a splendid 9-1 victory. But Cup hopes were ended by a result which was a Rugby Park first but - alas - not a last, a replay win for Partick Thistle.

By the end of the season though, a formidable outfit had emerged. Arthurlie and Queen of the South Wanderers were beaten by 8-3 and 8-0. Scottish Cup winners Renton were held to a 1-1 draw, although the side they had beaten in the Final - Cambuslang - who were also holders of the Glasgow Cup, won 5-2 at Rugby Park. But it was against Preston North End - *"the greatest football combination in the world"*, as the *Standard* labelled them, that Killie made their mark. Led by the English-born but Kilmarnock-raised John Goodall - the most feared forward of his time - Preston were put to the sword as Killie triumphed 4-1. Shortly afterwards, Renton beat Preston in a match for the *'Championship of the World'*. But just how good Preston really were can be shown by their record the following season when they won the inaugural Football League without losing a game and took the F.A. Cup without conceding a goal. Truly, Kilmarnock's victory over such a talented team established them as one of Scotland's top sides.

But it was a team that was destined never to reach its potential. Its apotheosis was reached with the selection of 'Kytie' McPherson to play in Scotland's 5-1 win over Wales at Easter Road. When the team lined up for the start of the following season, both McPhersons' would be gone. As would right winger and prolific scorer, John Smith, who joined Sunderland. But the hardest loss of all to take was that of Sandy Higgins. After years of resistance, the lure of English gold finally proved too great. Higgins had been badly burned in a pit accident in August 1887 and that no doubt played a large part in his decision to sign for Derby County. He would go on to become the highest paid player in England but would return to Rugby Park for one last glorious season. That players such as Higgins were subject to constant 'tapping' was well-known. Most Scottish clubs had trouble with 'professional agents' who would make illegal approaches to players. Often, English-based players, back home on 'holiday' would make the approach themselves. Football was becoming a business and there were voices raised, querying how long it would be before Scotland too was forced to march down the path of professionalism.

'Horatio' was adamant that it was inevitable and that the bigger Scottish clubs were already paying their players. But he was certain that Kilmarnock could not afford to take this path. So were the club officials who were resolutely behind Queen's Park in opposing the introduction of professionalism into Scottish football.

1888-89

Inevitably, it would take time for Killie to regain their previous position. And this was demonstrated in the Scottish Cup when a 5-0 win at Lugar was followed by a home loss to Kilbirnie. A trip to England ended in disaster with all three matches being lost (albeit narrowly) to Bootle, Accrington and Bury. The re-born Kilmarnock Athletic provided renewed local competition but in the county cups Killie had lost their former advantage. Hurlford despatched them from the Ayrshire Cup and Kilbirnie repeated their Scottish Cup triumph in both the Kilmarnock and Ayr Charity Cups.

In a dismal season, there was just one shaft of light. This came in the form of James 'Bummer' Campbell, a 20 year old local lad signed from junior club Kilmarnock Thistle. Taking the place of Higgins during the pre-season Glasgow Exhibition tournament, the youngster's enthusiasm was evident. And although he would take time to be accepted by the supporters - he was, after all, replacing a local legend - the 'Bummer' was destined to create a legend of his own.

1889-90

Another poor year saw Kilmarnock eliminated from Scottish, Ayrshire and Kilmarnock Charity Cups by the same opponents - Annbank. A curious addition to the fixture list was the Kilmarnock Ornithological Society Competition with time-pieces for the winners. Kilmarnock players had to buy their own watches after losing to Hurlford 3-1 at home. 'Bummer' Campbell - still not accepted as a forward - played most of his games in the half-back line where he was joined by a newcomer destined to become equally as famous. This was the diminutive John 'Jocky' Johnstone. At just 5ft 5ins and weighing around the 10 stone mark, the slightly-built Johnstone was a tenacious midfield warrior who injected some welcome 'bite' into the side. But even Johnstone couldn't prevent Killie's English tour from being their worst ever. They faced Bury, Bootle and South Shore (Blackpool) over the New Year period, going down to 7-2, 6-2 and 5-1 defeats respectively. The gulf between professionals and amateurs was growing wider each year. In an attempt to stem the flow of talent from the game, leading Scottish sides in Glasgow, Paisley, Dunbartonshire and Edinburgh got together to form a League. The English version of League football had been a tremendous success in its two years of existence and it was hoped that a Scottish League would do likewise north of the border. Kilmarnock - one of Scotland's leading teams just a few years earlier - wern't even considered for the new competition which would commence the following season.

1890-91

"How I do detest that League" wrote 'Horatio'. His dislike of the new combination lay in the fact that Ayrshire (by which he meant Kilmarnock) was excluded from it. He argued, perfectly logically, that the end result would be an ever-increasing gap in quality between the League and the rest of Scottish football and that League clubs would raid counties like Ayrshire for talent, depriving local clubs of the best players. 'Horatio's' anxiety seemed to be justified. Kilmarnock played two League clubs in friendlies and lost both games - 3-1 away to Rangers and 5-1 at Paisley's Abercorn. Yet Killie were a much-improved side this season. Their annual trip was more successful. A narrow 1-0 defeat at Rossendale was followed by 2-1 wins over Southport Central and Rotherham Town. And although there was another Scottish Cup exit at the hands of Annbank, the Ayrshire Cup returned to Rugby Park.

A closely-fought 3-2 away win over Athletic in the Semi-Finals was the precursor to a glorious 7-1 triumph over Hurlford at the same venue in the Final. Scoring five goals that day was Andrew Kelvin, one of the fresh batch of players intent on bringing renewed success to Rugby Park. Among the others were Davie McPherson, the youngest scion of that illustrious family, winger Robert Tannahill, John Brodie - 'Bummer' Campbell's brother-in-Law and a player who flitted between clubs but always ended up back in Kilmarnock - and James 'Duster' Orr, small for a full-back but such a good player that he forced his way into the Scotland team the following season - no mean achievement for an Ayrshire-based player.

Yet for all their success, one massive problem remained for Kilmarnock and clubs like them. How to respond to the success of the Scottish League? Clearly, competitions like the Ornithological Society one or this season's debutante - the Quoiting Association Competition - where Killie lost to the old nemesis of Annbank - weren't enough to attract increased crowds to Rugby Park.

1891-92

The answer was devastatingly simple. Form your own League. The great success of the Scottish League's first season saw the spawning of lesser imitations all over the country. An Ayrshire League brought together most of the county's smaller outfits. Then there was the Scottish Federation which Kilmarnock Athletic and Hurlford joined. This also contained well-known names like Motherwell and Albion Rovers. But the best-known - and highest in standard - of the new combinations was the Scottish Alliance. This was the body which Kilmarnock - and county rivals Ayr - started this season in.

The opposition was strong. Airdrieonians, East Stirling, Morton and Partick Thistle were all members. As were long-forgotten names - but powerful at the time - like Thistle (Glasgow), Port Glasgow Athletic, St. Bernards (Edinburgh), Northern (Glasgow), Linthouse (Govan), and Kings Park (Stirling). Every side in the Alliance later went on to become members of the Scottish League, eight of its twelve sides eventually playing in Division One.

Yet Kilmarnock found the initial going easy. They won their first four matches, scoring 21 goals in the process. Their home record remained excellent. Only Port Glasgow - with a 0-0 draw - left Rugby Park with as much as a point. 8-1 versus Morton and 7-0 against Ayr were among the highlights as Killie piled on 48 goals in their 11 home games. But away from home it was a different story.

Kilmarnock are acclaimed as Champions of Ayrshire after winning the Ayrshire Cup in 1891. John O.McPherson is wearing the Scottish cap and his son Davie is second from the left in the middle row. Other Killie legends in the group are: 'Bummer' Campbell (top, second from left) and Jocky Johnstone (middle, extreme right).

Killie won their first two matches but took just one win and two draws from the rest of the programme. Still, second place behind Linthouse was ranked as a successful start in their new surroundings. And the Govan team were a good side. They brought over 300 supporters with them to Rugby Park. Had it not been for the close proximity of another team in Govan they may well have gone on to greater things.

There was still room in the programme for friendly matches. One such game - a charity affair against Annbank which Killie won 4-0 - saw the first penalty kick scored at Rugby Park. Jocky Johnstone being the scorer under the newly-introduced law. Killie's games with Queen's Park were close affairs, the Glasgow side winning 5-3 at Rugby Park and by only 4-3 on their own ground. Scottish League members, Third Lanark, were beaten 3-1 by Killie. One week later, Rugby Park was witness to a thrilling 2-2 draw with a major new force in Scottish football - Celtic. Interestingly, the Parkhead side wore stripes in this first meeting of the two clubs.

And the English tours continued too. There were defeats at Rotherham Town (3-2) and Bolton Wanderers (6-1) but beforehand Kilmarnock achieved a splendid 1-1 draw away to Everton - one of the best sides in England - before a crowd of around 7,500. But, as always, it was the Scottish Cup which really enthused the supporters, although some half-dozen Killie diehards travelled south to follow their team.

A crushing 6-1 victory away to East Stirling gave Killie a trip to Ibrox in the 2nd round. They held the reigning joint-champions of Scotland to a 0-0 draw and also drew 1-1 - at Rugby Park in the replay. So it was off to Westmarch, St. Mirren's ground, for a second replay. Here the favourites emerged triumphant but only by 3-2 as Kilmarnock proved again that they could match the best of what the Scottish League has to offer. International Caps awarded to 'Bummer' Campbell and Davie McPherson emphasised Killie's strength.

1892-93

Sadly, the same could not be said of Kilmarnock this season. Brodie had gone a-wandering again. Kelvin had gone to Liverpool and Orr to Darwen. Although 'shamateurism' was rife in Scotland by now, professionalism was still illegal and Kilmarnock would have nothing to do with it. As in the late 1880's they were forced to watch the break-up of a fine team. The replacements were not as good as the men who had departed although one newcomer to the side - Charles Smith - would prove an invaluable acquisition. Smith was an administrator without peer. He became Secretary of Kilmarnock and, ultimately, Chairman. It was he who wrote the club's first history in 1919 - an indispensable guide to Killie's early days.

At one stage it was even thought that 'Bummer' Campbell had left for Third Lanark but, happily, his differences with Killie were resolved and he missed only the first match in the Alliance. The addition of former Scottish League teams Vale of Leven, Cambuslang and Cowlairs strengthened an already tough contest and after a good start Kilmarnock slumped. They ended up 9th out of 10. Killie found time to further their horizons, travelling to Ireland for the first time where they played Glentoran in Belfast, opening that club's new ground with a 1-1 draw. Other friendlies were less successful. English champions Sunderland, led by former Killie star Tom Porteous, won 7-1 at Rugby Park. In the Scottish Cup came an even worse home humiliation. After beating Albion Rovers away, Killie were annihilated 8-0 on their own soil by Queen's Park.

Kilmarnock decided they could no longer thrive in the Alliance and took the retrograde step of joining the newly-formed Ayrshire Combination, stronger than the Ayrshire League but much weaker than the body Killie left. As the last Alliance games were played, the SFA took the momentous decision of legalising professionalism. Then the Scottish League announced the formation of a Division Two with half its members coming from the ranks of the Alliance. While their erstwhile opponents marched forward, Kilmarnock prepared for the insular encounters of the Ayrshire Combination.

1893-94

Although referred to as the 'Mother Club', Kilmarnock cut a poor figure indeed this season. With the loss of another fine player - Tannahill to Bolton Wanderers - they found it difficult to hold their own against their Combination foes - Ayr, Stevenston Thistle, Kilbirnie, Hurlford, Ayr Parkhouse and Annbank. The return of Kelvin was some consolation but they finished a disappointing 5th out of 7.

Opposition in friendly matches was of a poor standard with the exceptions of Queen's Park, Rangers and Sunderland. Killie still couldn't beat Queen's Park but they pulled off a superb 3-1 win over Rangers and held Sunderland to a 2-2 draw. The Scottish Cup presented new problems. Since the tournament had been restructured at the behest of the Scottish League in 1891, Killie had always been one of the clubs granted exemption into the competition proper. This year they had to qualify.

They did so in some style, beating Morton 5-3 at home, Newmilns 1-0, also at home and Motherwell 3-1 away after a 3-3 draw at Rugby Park. But in the First Round proper they were beaten 3-1 at home by St. Bernards. 'Horatio' lamented that he had always been for professional football but that as long as Kilmarnock Athletic existed, Ayrshire would *"Never have a professional team"*.

But the bold scribe was, for once, wrong. At last Kilmarnock recognised that to continue on the same path invited the fate which had already befallen the likes of Portland, Hawthorn and the others on the once thriving local scene - extinction. The game was up with amateurism. Even Queen's Park - those haughty corinthians of old - were struggling to keep abreast of the new powers in Scotland - Rangers and Celtic. Of course no other club could even come close to the drawing power of these two clubs, but Kilmarnock folk would turn out for football if it was of a sufficiently high standard. This was proven in March 1894 when 12,000 attended Rugby Park to see the first full International game played there when Scotland - with Jocky Johnstone in the team - beat Wales 5-2.

That match provided the impetus for the biggest decision the club had made since the split with the cricketers. From now on Kilmarnock would pay their players.

1894-95

Of course professionalism at Rugby Park wasn't on a par with Ibrox or Parkhead, let alone England. But it was in the hope of deterring local players from taking the trek south that the decision was made. The reasoning was that if **some** money was forthcoming for their labours on the pitch then it may be sufficient to prevent players from uprooting themselves and their families. In an era when travel was much more difficult - before the motor car - there was more than a grain of truth in this theory.

But if part-time professionalism was going to be a success, Kilmarnock would have to play in a higher sphere than the Ayrshire Combination. That body welcomed new teams this season in Monkcastle (Kilwinning), Saltcoats Victoria and old foes Kilmarnock Athletic. But the best news for Killie was the return of Sandy Higgins. A hero at both Derby County and Nottingham Forest, Higgins returned home to play one final season with his old club. The sight of Sandy and 'Bummer' Campbell in the same side drove fear into the hearts of defenders everywhere but brought rapture to Kilmarnock's supporters.

Kilmarnock stormed past most opposition in the Combination, but a double defeat against Ayr and a 7-4 loss away to Athletic proved fatal to their chances to taking the title. Hit by a three-point deduction for playing the ineligible Peter Maxwell against Annbank, they found that ruling prevented them from at least a share of the honours as the final table shows;-

	P	W	D	L	F	A	Pts
1. Ayr	16	12	0	4	37	21	24
2. Kilmarnock	16	11	2	3	56	29	21*
3. Kilmarnock Ath.	16	10	1	5	65	36	21

*= 3 pts. deducted

It was the last time that Killie and Athletic competed on anything like level terms. The Holm Quarry amateurs were still capable of causing the odd upset, but their second incarnation had only a few years of life left. By the beginning of the 20th Century, they would be dead and buried. Henceforth, Kilmarnock would have to look to the county town to provide local rivalry.

This season the Ayrshire Cup was played over two legs from the first round onwards but Killie marched effortlessly to the Final. Both they and opponents Annbank resented the choice of venue - Stevenston. They felt, not unnaturally, that the small North Ayrshire town would not attract a good crowd for the match. Equally, the denizens of Stevenston were horrified at this display of what they considered to be greed by the Finalists. The Ayrshire FA refused to budge. It was Stevenston or nowhere. Killie and Annbank took matters into their own hands by playing for the unofficial 'Ayrshire Championship' at Rugby Park. The first match ended all-square at 2-2 with Annbank winning the return - also at Rugby Park - 4-2. But this result was never accepted by the Ayrshire F.A. Hence the curious affair went into the annals as the 'Cupless Final'.

Again, Killie had to qualify for the Scottish Cup. Their first opponents - Pollokshaws - scratched. Carfin were beaten 4-2 at Rugby Park after a 4-4 draw away. Dykehead were beaten 3-1 away and a bye in the next round enabled Killie to keep their appearance record in the Cup intact. In the competition proper they hammered East Stirling 5-1 at Rugby Park before losing again to St. Bernards by 3-1 - this time in Edinburgh.

But the season's record had been good. Taking all first-team games into account it read:-
P 40 W 26 D 6 L 8 F 140 A 72.
This doesn't include an unofficial match in aid of striking miners in which Killie beat Athletic 3-0.

Kilmarnock decided to make a bid for the big time. They applied to join the Scottish League. As the rules stood, there were three places up for election. Including those clubs who had finished near the bottom, there were seven teams vying for the three spots in the League's lower division. No-one could be quite sure what chance Killie had.

While the League's verdict was awaited, Rugby Park was the setting for two totally different types of football occasion. First, Sandy Higgins played his last match for Kilmarnock in a friendly against Rangers which Killie lost 4-2. Then came a charity match played by two womens sides - the first all-female game at Rugby Park. This match serves as a wonderful example of how quickly the meaning of a language can change. The *Scottish Referee* in their account of proceedings refers to the *"Gay Queens"* who took part. A century later that phrase has an altogether different meaning!

On June 3rd, 1895 the voting took place at the Scottish League AGM. Kilmarnock and Linthouse received 24 votes each, Abercorn 22, Raith Rovers 10, Wishaw 6, Dundee Wanderers and Northern 3 each. Ayrshire's 'Mother Club' left her children behind and embarked upon a voyage of discovery into the Scottish League.

Dan Gallacher who wrote under the name 'Horatio in the 'Kilmarnock Standard' and other Scottish papers and was, to a great extent, responsible for popularising the game.

1895-96 DIVISION TWO

Kilmarnock's Scottish League career started away to Leith Athletic on August the 17th, 1895. Leith were powerful opponents, having spent the previous four seasons in the First Division. So it was no great surprise that Killie's debut ended in defeat. Even so, impressive form at home showed that Killie could easily hold their own in this company. Away was a different matter. Heavy reverses at Port Glasgow and Renton offset some convincing Rugby Park triumphs and by the time Killie visited Morton they had one solitary point, from a visit to Partick Thistle, to their credit from four away outings. Thus, when a local reporter suggested that Killie could triumph at Cappiel ow if they played more of a passing game, one supporter prompted the rejoinder that *"they can't win after they pass Kilmaurs"*.

They did win at Cappielow, and at Motherwell in a game which lasted just 73 minutes when play was stopped due to bad light. Victory in Govan against Linthouse brought three away successes out of four. With six of their last seven matches at home, hopes were high that Killie would make the top three; this would allow them to put their name forward for election to the First Division. Alas, it was not to be. Abercorn, destined to win the Second Division that season, became the first side to lower the colours at Rugby Park, then, in an ugly match, so did Partick Thistle. Contemporary reports of this match fail to record the goal-scorers, preferring to point out that after the match some 40-50 men and boys pelted the Thistle players with a *"shower of stones, sand and mud"*.

Football in the 1890's was a hazardous game indeed. At least proceedings at Rugby Park never got out of hand to the same extent as in England, where two men were shot, one fatally, in a Jarrow pub over an argument about football. Even more tragic was the case of the 8 year-old-boy in Glasgow who died from injuries sustained in a kickabout in Firhill Park. Kilmarnock, too, witnessed the dread hand of fate in action. Peter Maxwell, a 22-year-old defender of great promise, died of the ravages of the then common scourge of typhoid. His untimely demise cast a pall over the entire town.

The season ended with a final defeat, at the hands of Renton, in a play-off for that precious 3rd place. There was to be no consolation in the Cup either. Despite taking 700 fans with them, Kilmarnock were bundled out of the tournament by the proud villagers of Annbank. Still, 4th place in the League was a satisfying conclusion to a season which had proved that Kilmarnock belonged in the Scottish League. There were some who thought that Killie should aspire no higher; worried that the team may not be able to cope with superior opposition. They were about to be proved wrong.

MATCH OF THE SEASON

August 24th 1895.
Kilmarnock 7 Motherwell 1

"Will the public of Ayrshire support sixpenny gates?". That was the question posed by the local press prior to this match - the first ever League game to be played at Rugby Park. They were worried that crowds heading for the match might stop off in the Howard Park and watch the amateur games in progress there instead of handing over their hard earned 'tanners' to the League new boys. The other fear was whether or not Killie would be good enough for this level of competition? They had lost at Leith and Motherwell had finished runners-up in the Second Division the previous year.

As the press themselves reported, by kick-off at 4.00 p.m. the first fear had been allayed and by 5.30 p.m. the second had been dispelled also. Yet it was Motherwell who had scored first! Stung by this audacity, Killie roared into action and soon made the Lanarkshire side suffer. Watson equalised from a 'scrimmage' and then a beauty of a drive by McAvoy put Killie ahead at half-time. At the re-start, Killie looked confident; their foes had an air of defeat about them. Just two minutes into the half, Cox shot the home side further ahead. The one-way traffic which followed saw the ball defeat the 'Well goalie four more times. McPherson and Fisher put their names on the score-sheet while Cox scored twice more to record Killie's first League hat-trick. League football had come to the town of Kilmarnock and was joyously christened with seven goals.

(Top) James 'Bummer' Campbell. Possibly Kilmarnock's greatest ever centre-forward. Records were not kept efficiently in the 19th century and the standard of opposition varied, but the 'Bummer' notched up at least 186 goals for Killie, and in all probability exceeded the 200 mark, if not 300!
(Lower) Tom Busby who played in Killie's first ever League match.

1896-97 DIVISION TWO

Killie had to take part in the Qualifying Cup this season, which, coupled with bad weather, played havoc with their League programme. Just one League fixture was completed between mid-October and March, but what a game it was. Only seven Kilmarnock players took the field at Airdrie. All eleven had boarded the train at Glasgow Central but four of them had entered a carriage which separated from the train and the unlucky quartet found themselves alighting at Coatbridge.

Meanwhile, the seven on the pitch at Broomfield were struggling. Winger McLean, in goal, retrieved the ball from the back of the net on three occasions before the cavalry, in the shape of the lost foursome arrived. With equality in numbers Killie showed their mettle, rescuing two goals before half-time and going on to score a further three in the second half to pull off an epic 5-4 victory.

But this was a year when the talk at Rugby Park was of Cups. Killie dismissed the local Qualifying Cup opposition with ease. Lugar were beaten 6-2 on their own ground. In the second round, Saltcoats Vics were thrashed 13-2, a result which stands to this day as the record score by a Kilmarnock team. At the time it was not very highly regarded, the local press commenting that *" 'twould be a waste of space detailing a game so one-sided"*, 'Bummer' Campbell notched up eight of the thirteen.

Ayr were the next sacrifices, 7-1 at Rugby Park. Hurlford were beaten there too, 4-2. Away from home there was a satisfying 5-2 success over Partick Thistle. A scrappy 1-0 home win over Dunblane set Killie up for their first Hampden Cup Final.

The Scottish Cup proper carried on where the Qualifying competition had left off. Motherwell were easily beaten after a replay and Falkirk were disposed off without difficulty. Or so it seemed. For the Bairns protested over the pitch markings and size, claiming that they were entitled to a replay and at Falkirk as well. The SFA granted the replay but ordered that it go ahead at Rugby Park. Falkirk were taught a lesson. The crowd was twice as big as for the original match and the angry supporters roared their team on. By half-time the ball had been plucked from the Falkirk net on six occasions. Killie eased up in the second half but they had done enough to ensure that Falkirk - or any other team - would think twice before protesting again.

First Division Third Lanark were the next to fall. Just as the game seemed to be heading for a draw, Killie delivered a double knockout blow. The semi-finals had been reached for the first time and as Killie travelled to Dumbarton's Boghead they were strongly fancied to make the Final. It wasn't to be. Killie were below form and were 4-1 down mid-way through the second half, two late goals giving Campbell his hat-trick and making the score more respectable. Now it was Killie who protested. Dumbarton had not worn their usual outfits. The two teams had clashed. Their appeal was unsuccessful. Despite great public sympathy there would be no re-match, Kilmarnock would have to wait before they played in a Scottish Cup Final. What they wouldn't have to do was to wait for long.

The Cup runs took their toll on both side and spectators. Five home league games had to be played in the course of nine days, no extension to the season being permitted. Turnout was poor and results were patchy. At the game against Airdrie, just £3.18s.9d. (£3.94p) was taken at the gate, representing just over 150 paying spectators. Club members brought the total up towards respectability. The League record was almost identical to the previous season which, considering the number of Cup ties and the changing side, was a good performance.

MATCH OF THE SEASON

December 5th, 1896
Kilmarnock 4 Motherwell 1

500 fans left a rain-sodden Ayrshire by special train to see the Scottish Qualifying Cup Final. They joined a surprisingly strong total of over 4,000, more than £100 being taken in gate money, a fine sum considering both the rain and the fact that the Scottish League refused to cancel League games in Glasgow that day. The Hampden crowd saw Killie score almost immediately. Motherwell equalised before half-time and the game was well balanced until Killie took the lead again. Another soon followed then a fourth, from McPherson, and the first trophy contested by teams other than from Ayrshire was on its way to Rugby Park.

The perspective was different in those days. A club official said of the Cup the *"although a fine piece of silverware, it is not to be compared with the Ayrshire Cup"*. Whether he was talking about its beauty, importance, or both was not recorded. When the victorious eleven of Ralston, Busby, Brown, McPherson, Paterson, Johnstone, Watson, McAvoy, Campbell, Richmond and McLean returned with the trophy they were given a reception which was said to be the *"Most enthusiastic since Kilmarnock Bowling Club won the Scottish Rink Competition"*.

1897-98 DIVISION TWO

Six straight League victories marked the start of this season. Even when that run was broken, it seemed to have little effect on this confident Kilmarnock side; four more wins and a draw taking them up to the New Year. They had won three times away from home by early November - as many as they had won in each of the previous two seasons. At Rugby Park they were well-nigh invincible, scoring at least FIVE goals in every game bar one. So, by the time the Scottish Cup came round, Killie, were in a positive state of mind.

The goals continued to flow in the Cup-ties. The hapless 6th GRV from Dalbeattie were summarily dismissed. Despite going behind to Leith, Killie piled on nine goals against what had been assumed to be difficult opposition. An even more awkward looking tie against the amateurs of Ayr Parkhouse was their reward. Parkhouse's Beresford Park was besieged by a record crowd. Again, Killie fell behind. They had to recover from a two goal deficit and did it in style, scoring five times in the first half and twice more in the second to take the club into their second successive Semi-Final.

A rare defeat at Airdrie was poor preparation for their Semi-Final game against First Division Dundee. Even so, the largest assembly ever seen at Rugby Park awaited them. Yet again,

Killie did things the hard way, coming from behind to defeat their Tayside rivals and clinch a place in the Scottish Cup Final for the first time.

This season, Kilmarnock did not allow their Cup Success to affect their League form. They won all three games played between the Semi and the Final. Still, after their return from Hampden, the Second Division title had yet to be won. Only Port Glasgow Athletic could overtake them and the two outstanding League fixtures were against that Renfrewshire side.

It was a nervous ninety minutes and the closest fought home game of the season before Kilmarnock emerged victorious, securing the flag and making the dangerous trip to Port Glasgow academic. Now, Killie looked forward with confidence to election to the First Division. After all, had not the three previous Second Division Champions been so rewarded? And none of them had made the Scottish Cup Final as well.

Kilmarnock received a lesson in power politics. Only seven clubs - Celtic, Rangers, Hibs, Hearts, Third Lanark, St. Mirren and Dundee had a vote. They had to choose three from those finishing at the foot of the First - Partick Thistle, St. Bernard's and Clyde - and the top three from the Second - Kilmarnock, Port Glasgow and Morton. St. Mirren were known to be hostile to their local rivals and rumoured not to want Killie as well. Pledges of support from the Glasgow clubs turned out to be worthless. Partick and St. Bernard's were re-elected easily, leaving Killie and Clyde to fight it out for the final place.

The *Standard* listed ten points in Kilmarnock's favour: Scottish Cup Finalists, Second Division Champions, Ayrshire Champions, Kilmarnock Charity Cup Winners, Gate-drawing power, Season's record, no First Division club within 20 miles, a 'superior football nursery', 'financially happier' and 'better prospects' than Clyde, who had just won one match all season. In Clyde's favour the paper sarcastically noted that they had *"had a ground in Glasgow"*. Clyde were duly re-elected.

Charles Smith, Killie's Secretary told that year's AGM that *"It was an injustice"* that there was *"no club more deserving"* .... that *"Scottish football had been shamed"* and, prophetically, Killie would show the League *"how ridiculous (it was) to be excluded"*. Club President Dan Gilmour said that the First Division had *"covered themselves with dishonour"*. The record for the season including local cup-ties and friendlies was:
P43 W34 D2 L7 F170 A74.

MATCH OF THE SEASON
March 26th 1898. Rangers 2 Kilmarnock 0

Although the 'Kilmarnock Herald' took the view that with 15 Ayrshire-born players taking part in the Scottish Cup Final, that this was proof that the county was the "nursing ground of the cream of Scottish players", the Glasgow-based 'Scottish Referee' condescendingly hailed Kilmarnock's arrival at the pinnacle of the game by describing their achievement as being only the third time that a team of such stature had reached the Final. The other two being "the model villagers of Thornliebank and Cambuslang".

Similar sentiments were expressed in the Glasgow and Edinburgh press. Most suggesting that the Final would be a waste of time. Rangers, apparently, only had to turn up to be presented with the trophy. This, and the weather, may have helped keep the attendance down, but thousands travelled from Ayrshire with defiant hope outweighing cold reason. Kilmarnock were first out, led by McPherson (whose brother was in the Rangers side) and despite an icy blast and persistent snowfall which made ball control difficult, proceeded to give Rangers a hard time. It seemed to contemporary on-lookers that it was boys against men - many in the Killie team were in their early twenties and Muir and Maitland were both just nineteen.

Their opponents were seasoned professionals and players of International standing. Yet all through the first half it was Killie who did the attacking. Only Dickie, in the Rangers goal, keeping his side in the game. Even, after the break and with the wind behind them, Ranger's shooting was poor. Midway through this period though, a suspiciously offside-looking score was allowed to stand and, four minutes later, a defensive lapse allowed a second goal. Even now, Killie attacked as though the match had just started. But to no avail. It was never a classic Final - conditions saw to that - and both sides displayed a tendency towards the physical, Rangers being the guiltier of the pair; although it must be noted that even the Ayrshire press said of Killie's left back, Brown, that he was "rather sore" on Miller, the Rangers outside right, and that Brown "might well have left that player little oftener on his feet". No wonder that Rangers greeted the final whistle with relief.

Monday's editions of the Glasgow papers were happy to admit that they had been wrong and that this Kilmarnock team was one which all Ayrshire could be proud of.

1898-99 DIVISION TWO

Killie set about their task with a vengeance. Again, the first six League games were won, including a bruising battle with Port Glasgow, which was described as one of the roughest encounters ever seen at Rugby Park. Closest rivals, Leith, were beaten in an enthralling match. Leith's winger, Walker, was one of the earliest black players in Scotland. Happily, there were no reports of racial taunting at this game. Support was growing rapidly and the fans were losing interest in the local - now regarded as minor - competitions. At an Ayrshire Cup game against Monkcastle, many were heard asking if anyone knew the score from the first leg of the tie. They would have been relieved to hear that Killie were 5-2 up. Some even lost count of the score during this match. Not surprising, really, since it ended in a 10-0 triumph for the Rugby Parkers - an indication of the gap in class between Kilmarnock and their county rivals.

The first dropped point came at Airdrie. Undaunted, Killie replied by putting eight goals past Linthouse, a result which saw much celebration in the town. Ayr deprived them of another point and, in truth, (though it could only be whispered about in Killie's hostelries) deserved to win. The Killie goal machine took no notice. Hamilton were played twice within a week. In both games Killie won 7-1. The second of these matches producing a goal direct from a corner by Bobby Muir, Kilmarnock's brilliant right winger. When Killie won for the first time at Port Glasgow, a ground they had lost fifteen goals at in their three previous games, and gave Ayr a hammering for their presumption in the earlier match, they could almost smell the First Division.

There were to be no Scottish Cup heroics this year. It took three games to get past East Stirling. A new record attendance was set at the Quarter-Final tie with St. Mirren but a poor first half left Killie with too much to do. Killie returned to the League programme, finishing the season undefeated. It was an incredible record but one which never received its due. This was mainly thanks to Rangers, who were not only undefeated in the League but, actually WON all their First Division matches.

The elections to the First Division had been altered. Now, only the top and bottom two respectively would fight it out. There were already three Edinburgh sides in the top flight, so that meant that there was little chance of success for Leith. On the other hand, the League was determined to maintain first class football in Dundee, then the most northerly League side, so their re-election looked a formality. So of the four clubs in the ballot, it looked a straight fight between Kilmarnock and Partick Thistle. Mindful of the shenanigans of the previous year, the Kilmarnock committee took no chances. They wrote to every voting club, outlining their claim. The playing record was even better than before:
P42 W31 D8 L3 F153 A53.

This time their claim was unanswerable. The result of the ballot was: KILMARNOCK 15, DUNDEE 10, PARTICK THISTLE 5 and LEITH ATHLETIC 2. Just four years after joining the League, Kilmarnock were in the First Division. Annbank, Kilbirnie and Hurlford lay in the past. Hampden had been tasted twice. The future lay at Ibrox and Celtic Park.

MATCH OF THE SEASON

April 15th 1899.
Leith Athletic 3 Kilmarnock 3

As unbeaten Killie walked out for this match, they knew that they still had not won this Second Division title for the second successive year.

The League table looked like this:-

	P	W	D	L	F	A	Pts.
Kilmarnock	*16*	*13*	*3*	*0*	*65*	*22*	*29*
Leith Athletic	*16*	*12*	*2*	*2*	*59*	*32*	*26*

A point would clinch the flag. Defeat would mean the race going right to the wire. Leith attacked from the off. After just five minutes Killie conceded a soft goal. Busby went to clear the ball, missed it altogether and it rolled past Craig. Some fierce end-to-end play followed before Campbell headed the equaliser. Next, Killie's Howie saw an open goal appear in front of him, only to be desperately blocked as he was about to shoot. At the other end, Anderson was giving away too many free kicks. From one of them, he contrived to head the ball past his own keeper. 2-1 down.

Again, it was 'Bummer' Campbell to the rescue with another header. 2-2. Reid 'scored' what looked like a perfectly good goal, only to see it disallowed. Then, disaster. Leith's Fotheringham went past Anderson, evaded McPherson, past both Busby and Brown. Ignoring Craig's despairing lunge, he scored a brilliant goal. 3-2 down. It was now that Killie had to call on all their reserves, their skill, ingenuity and - as it happened - their sheer bare-faced cheek.

They assaulted the Leith goal, Muir grazing the bar, still a goal refused to come. Was it asking too much for them to equalise for a third time? Bob Findlay provided the answer. The Galston-born winger moved inside to receive the ball from Muir. Once in possession, he let fly, shouting at the Leith players "Let it come". Amazingly, they did precisely that. They stood, bemused, as the ball sailed into the net for the vital third equaliser. There was no time for Leith to attack again. What had been a truly superb match was over. And Kilmarnock - again - were the Second Division Champions.

John Q.McPherson.
Father of a footballing dynasty. His three sons all played for Killie (two of them also for Scotland) and John Q., trainer of the 1898 Cup Final team, went on to become trainer of Newcastle United and both Scotland and England.

Chapter 3
UP WHERE WE BELONG
1899 - 1919

1899-1900 DIVISION ONE

The pressure of a top division of ten is nothing new in Scottish football. That was the number making up the First Division when Kilmarnock took their place there. Nor was a computer a pre-requisite for drawing up a difficult fixture list. Killie's first two home games were against Celtic and Rangers, either side of visits to Paisley and Easter Road for good measure. Still, this was what Killie had wanted and in this first season in the big time they gave as good as they got. They never looked in danger of having to apply for re-election, despite the fact that their forwards obviously found the going a lot harder in this class. Killie's rock-solid defence ensured that, with one exception, they were never beaten easily.

There were odd incidents too. At home to Clyde, only eight of the selected eleven had turned up by kick-off. Despite this, Killie recorded their only two-goal victory of the campaign! At Ibrox, in the only really poor performance, Bobby Findlay netted a goal that gave Killie a shock lead. Rangers equalised with an effort so outrageously offside that even their own supporters were astonished that it was allowed. Findlay, the obvious playmaker, was constantly kicked by Rangers' Gibson until, eventually, the Killie man retaliated with a punch. Incredibly, both stayed on the pitch. Findlay was scythed down repeatedly after this and Rangers went on to win easily.

At home to St. Mirren, the roof flew off the new stand and landed in the middle of the pitch, but not before three spectators were injured by the flying metal. In an incredible game, at Celtic Park, three times Kilmarnock took the lead, only for Celtic to equalise every time, thus denying Killie what would have been an historic victory. Away to Clyde, reserve centre-forward, Young, who had scored in his only previous first-team outing, hit a hat-trick. Amazingly, he was never to play for the first eleven again!

On January 2nd 1900, Kilmarnock staged a benefit match for one of the true heroes of this era, the incomparable 'Bummer' Campbell. Celtic (admittedly not at full strength) were thrashed 6-0 and the then huge sum of £120 was raised for the 'Bummer'. 5000 fans had braved the incessant rain to pay tribute to the man of whom the *Standard* said *"Killie without Bummer is like Hamlet without the Prince of Denmark".*

The season ended with only the 'Old Firm' and Edinburgh's top two ahead of Killie. Where other 'new boys' had struggled, Killie had made themselves right at home. The Cup had brought a massive victory against Orion but disappointment at Celtic Park. Club finances were looking healthy too. That year's AGM heard that members tickets had brought in £292-2-6d, an increase of £70 on the previous year and almost three times as much as in 1897. Gate receipts at home League games produced £1,075-7-0d., more than the four Second Division seasons put together. Some things then are still familiar today. More than half the cash had been taken from the two visits by the Glasgow giants.

MATCH OF THE SEASON
August 26th 1899.
Kilmarnock 2 Celtic 2

What an occasion. Kilmarnock's first-ever home game in Division One. The Second Division flag unfurled. A 'new' ground - Rugby Park had been extended and a new grand-stand built. A huge crowd. Glorious sunshine. The Scottish Cup holders as visitors. Who could ask for anything more? Well, the home support would have liked a victory over their illustrious opponents. The team did their best to oblige them. Kilmarnock welcomed the top Divison with a flurry of corner kicks, three in rapid succession. Nothing came of this early pressure and Celtic gradually took over. Divers scored their opener, then calamity. An indirect free kick. No danger. Or there wouldn't have been but for the ball just grazing the hair on Jocky Johnstone's head on its way to the net. Celtic weren't satisfied with two. Until half-time they relentlessly bore down on the Killie goal. Fortunately, without success.

The second half started as the first had ended. Cletic pressing forward, ever forward. Killie held firm. Slowly, they began to pull themselves back into the match. Howie, from the most awkward of angles, slotted home a goal. Johnstone, making amends for his misfortune, provided Howie with the pass which brought the equaliser. A goal, which the 'Standard' reporter at the game described, with understandable hyperbole, as making "even the horses of the mounted police dance with joy".

Now it was all Killie. Howie hit the crossbar. Campbell unleashed a powerful shot which was saved but rebounded to Findlay. The winger joyfully netted, only to see the Referee signal a free kick. Celtic were happy to hear the whistle blow. They knew that Kilmarnock were worthy members of the First Division.

1900-01 DIVISION ONE

This was very much a transitional season for Kilmarnock. Old favourites like 'Baker' Brown, 'Bummer' Campbell and Jocky Johnstone bade their Rugby Park farewells, to be replaced by new faces such as William Agnew and James Mitchell, men, who in time, would carve out as illustrious a name for themselves as the giants they took over from.

With only five of the eleven who played in the first League game of the season also taking part in the last, performances were bound to be a little uneven; as heavy defeats at Ibrox and Tynecastle show. All the same, it wasn't a bad year. Killie were unlucky to lose at Celtic Park and, the following Saturday, exacted their revenge. They took on, and beat, a Celtic side which was the only unbeaten team in Britain and which was five points clear at the top of the table. Once again the side finished in a healthy fifth place in the League and once again, Parkhead proved to be their Scottish Cup graveyard.

The new boys had slotted in well, experienced hands like Craig and Muir (who along with new boy Andrew Reid) were ever-presents, providing a steady link between the old and the new. A reminder of the amateur era was provided this year by the occasional presence in the side of Dr. William Crerar, an Ayrshire GP, who scored four times in his six matches.

Attendances were pretty stable, as was reported at the AGM but club membership had taken a sharp fall, down from 800 to under 500. No doubt the novelty of the First Division was wearing off. It had been just five years since many had questioned whether Killie were capable of surviving in the top class. Now, it was assumed that this was their natural habitat.

MATCH OF THE SEASON
December 15th 1900.
Queen's Park 5 Kilmarnock 5

From the youngest to the eldest, every Kilmarnock supporter knows all about the night that Killie came back from four goals down to defeat Eintracht. Few will know about this match, when a similar thing happened - only in reverse. Killie had been humiliated 7-0 at Tynecastle the previous Saturday, so little was expected of them when they trooped out at Hampden. This was their first visit to the National Stadium on League duty, Queen's Park having finally abandoned their gallant efforts to stand alone, had joined the League this season.

In the first half, Killie produced their best form of the season, overrunning Queen's down the left flank. After 20 minutes Maitland opened the scoring. He was followed in quick succession by Reid, Graham (twice) and Reid again. Five goals up and still Killie attacked, almost securing a sixth before half-time. Unsurprisingly, the Hampden defence was said at this stage to be "playing a very slack game and displayed bad judgement in defending their goal".

The second half was the mirror image of the first. Queen's Park, with the wind behind them, rained shots down on the Kilmarnock goal. Ten minutes into this half and they pulled one back. Almost immediately, the famous R.S.McColl got a second. Still, Killie looked certainties to win and they pressed forward seeking a sixth. Queen's Park were having none of it and they counter-attacked, scoring a third. A minute later and it was R.S. McColl again. A brilliant solo run saw him score the fourth. Thankfully, no-one described it as a 'sweet' move! Even while their supporters were still cheering, Queens' McGhee nipped in for the equaliser.

That was how it stayed, 5-5. To be five goals ahead at the interval and still fail to win was a bitter blow to the Killie faithful but, it must be said, the fighting response shown in the second half by Queen's was reminiscent of their halcyon days. In the end the points were deservedly shared.

1901-02 DIVISION ONE

Lack of firepower up front hindered Killie this season. The defence was even more solid than usual - and it had to be. There were six ever-presents in the side, Craig, in goal, the two full-backs and all three half-backs. Muir had departed to Bristol Rovers, so there was a constant re-arranging of the wing pairings only Hugh Morton, a gem of a discovery, providing any real continuity in this vital part of the team.

After beating Rangers in the opening match, the forwards struggled. It would be eight games later before they managed to score in the first half of a match. The old away problem returned as well; not until their final match did Kilmarnock secure two points other than at Rugby Park. It might be thought that the biggest victory of the entire season - 4-0 at home to Dundee - would be a cause for rejoicing, but no. That game was immortalised by a headline reading:-
"POOR GAME - KILLIE WIN BY FOUR GOALS"
Imagine reading that today! I dare say that the Kilmarnock supporters of the Edwardian age would have been content to see a few more poor games if the result was the same.

The Cup brought renewed hope. League form was left in the locker room as Partick Thistle and Dundee were both comprehensively beaten. At Ibrox, Killie fought hard, eventually succumbing to a powerful Rangers side.

One of the brighter notes of the season occurred on November 30 when the sum of £65 was presented to Jocky Johnstone as reward for thirteen years loyal service. In celebrating a great servant of the past, however, there was no anticipation of the future. When asked about the decline in playing fortunes at the AGM, the official reply was that the Division contained one fewer side than the previous year and that side was Partick Thistle, whom Killie had taken four points off. If those four points were added to the total, then things were not so bad. Such complacency was dangerous.

MATCH OF THE SEASON
August 17th 1901.
Kilmarnock 4 - Rangers 2

Strong winds and heavy rain kept the attendance down at this, Kilmarnock's opening League game. The conditions were reckoned to favour a Rangers team strongly fancied to win their fourth successive League title. In the early stages of the game, Rangers did indeed take control, but they hadn't reckoned on ten wonderful minutes of Rugby Park riotousness.

First, Graham eluded the defence to put away a splendid goal. Then, Reid crossed to Norwood for the second. The Killie fans could scarcely believe what was happening when Geordie Anderson thumped a free kick from 40 yards out which was headed home by Howie for number three. Kilmarnock stayed on top until one minute from the interval, when one of those suspiciously 'offside' goals that Rangers seemed to specialise in was allowed by the Referee.

There was still some trepidation amongst the home support. Twice previously they had met Rangers at Rugby Park in a League game. Twice previously Kilmarnock had led at half-time. And twice previously Rangers had won both points. The 'Gers opened well against the wind and rain but Killie looked composed. Rangers full-back Drummond was so intent on watching Reid that he failed to notice Graham coming in from behind. The Killie centre-forward stole the ball, circled round both Reid and Drummond and shot on the turn. The ball cracked off the bottom of the bar and into the net. 4-1. There was no way back for Rangers now. They did manage to score a second but the game was well and truly over by then. For the first time ever, in the League, Kilmarnock had beaten the mighty Rangers. It would be a long time before a Rangers side set foot on Rugby Park expecting two easy points.

1902-03 DIVISION ONE

Rugby Park was a confusing place to be around in 1902-03. There were two players called Young, (not related) two Findlays, (brothers), two Hugh Morton's (both from the Irvine Valley, but not related) and John Wyllie was the brother of former player James Wyllie. Sadly, this confusion did not translate itself to the opposing teams. From the first match, when Partick Thistle repaid the Killie committee's presumption of the previous AGM by defeating Kilmarnock 2-1, it was always going to be a struggle. Killie may have regretted Thistle's return to the First Division but they were glad to renew acquaintances with Port Glasgow Athletic. They, along with Morton (to whom, even more confusingly, Hugh Morton, the winger, would eventually end up with) provided Killie with four of their six League victories.

Good players, like Agnew and Howie, had been sold in acrimonious circumstances and their replacements were nowhere near the same quality The defensive backbone of the side began to slip; just one player - Geordie Anderson - taking part in every League match. Nor was the Scottish Cup to bring any consolation. For the fourth successive year Kilmarnock were drawn away to one of the 'Old Firm', Rangers following in Celtic's path by removing Killie from the tournament for the second year running.

The 1903 AGM witnessed some angry scenes. The Committee revealed that the club's balances had been eaten up by a loss of £260 over the year despite a profit of over £600 in transfer fees. The premier team in the County had even been forced to scratch from the Ayrshire Cup. The Kilmarnock Charity Cup, too, was held in abeyance. No new signings had been made, yet long-service players of proven calibre, such as Tom Bushy and Bobby Findlay had not been offerred terms for the following season. Angry club members demanded to know why Agnew and Howie had gone. The answer was simple - money. In the case of Howie, the Committee pleaded that he had been offerred the best terms ever laid before a Kilmarnock player but they still couldn't compete with English gold. Some members accused the existing players of not trying. Others branded both players and Committee a disgrace. The harmony and bright hopes of the infant Century had not taken long to collapse. The atmosphere at Rugby Park was full of foreboding. Those present sensed that there was worse to come.

MATCH OF THE SEASON
August 23rd 1902.
Kilmarnock 4 - Morton 2

This was the first home game of the season and Kilmarnock found it hard going initially. They were under the cosh, right from the moment the game started. A dreadful first-half performance saw them trail by two goals, with scarcely an attempt of their own to speak of. The second period started the same way as the first. Killie desperately defended in a bid to keep the score down. Then, in the space of fifteen minutes, the game changed.

Tom Findlay found himself in space. He fired in a speculative shot which surprised the Morton 'keeper totally. Killie were back in the match. The Morton defence, hitherto utested, collapsed. Winger Hugh Morton twice spurned easy opportunities to score against his namesakes, before finally landing on target from a more difficult position. The Greenock defenders now formed a line in front of their goal, blocking everything that Killie threw at them, until, unbelievably, they simply watched as Matthew Mair literally walked the ball past them and into the net. A mad quarter of an hour had seen Killie transform what was a hopeless situation into a 3-2 lead.

The game wasn't over yet though. Morton (the team) took a corner. Up went the Killie defence. Up too, went Geordie Anderson's arm, striking the ball. Penalty! Voices hushed all around the ground as the kick was taken. Softly. Right into Craig's waiting arms. Kilmarnock sensed that Morton had blown it. Off went Bob Findlay on a sparkling run which ended with the ball in the back of the Morton net and cheers ringing out from the Rugby Park crowd. Findlay's goal capped an amazing fightback. The Killie fans were right to cheer. There would be precious little else for them to celebrate in the season which lay ahead. This second-half performance was a rare gem in what was a very poor season.

1903-04 DIVISION ONE

Attempts were made to strengthen the team by introducing some promising Juniors but it quickly became apparent that this wasn't going to work. After an opening victory over Queen's Park, Killie struggled badly. A humiliating 4-0 defeat at home to Port Glasgow, all the goals coming in the second half, seemed to be the final straw. Proceedings were initiated to call a Special General Meeting of the Club. The popular Bobby Findlay was restored to the side and a mini revival took place. Findlay hit three goals in four games. Victories were recorded away to Airdrie and at home to St. Mirren. Third Lanark, destined to finish as Champions, were lucky to take the points at Rugby Park.

The change of fortunes didn't last. Kilmarnock managed a solitary win from their last sixteen matches. After a 6-1 thrashing at home to Celtic, Killie found themselves in the position they had dreaded - bottom of the League. The special meeting took place in early December, called by 50 members of the Club. There were two subjects discussed - the possibility of establishing a limited company and the urgent need for new players.

Many clubs were now forming themselves into limited companies. Those in favour argued that such a move brought smaller - amd more professional - management to the club and it was agreed to set up a group to inquire further and report back to the members. As far as the playing staff was concerned, the demand from the body of the meeting was that new players had to be secured before the onset of the Scottish Cup.

Frustration with the present management was intense but, nevertheless, the Committee won a vote of confidence from the meeting.

The Cup duly arrived, with only Davidson, one of soccer's nomads, arriving on loan to augment the squad. Killie struggled through three games before eliminating Nithsdale Wanderers. The non-League side earned the praise of the Ayrshire press, whose verdict on the cup marathon was *"Sanquhar (where Nithsdale played) Plucky, Killie Lucky!"*. It took a further two matches to remove Albion Rovers. To no avail. Killie were easily beaten at Cathkin in the Quarter-Finals.

The AGM was held in March, with two League games still outstanding. The Committee felt complacent enough to declare that the present condition of the team was due to *"ill-luck"* rather than *"inability"*. Membership had increased to 538 and there was some money in the bank. Why grumble? The final two games showed why. A 2-1 lead away to the Champions-elect, Third Lanark, was thrown away after the interval and, in the last match. Celtic notched up another 6-1 scoreline. Amazingly, Killie had been level at half-time.

That match witnessed two significant events. James Gunzeon became the only ever-present of the season, playing in all six cup matches as well as 26 League games. Gunzeon had never played for Kilmarnock before the start of the season and he would never play for them again. It was also the last time that Davie McPherson would pull a Killie jersey over his head. He had been on the books since 1891 and was the last surviving member of the team that had played in that first League game in 1895. With justification it can be said that McPherson's going did indeed mark the end of an era.

There was a real fear that Killie would lose their hard-won First Division place. Especially when the League AGM voted not to increase the number of top-clubs. Of the clubs in the running, Falkirk, East Stirling and Clyde were generally discounted. Rightly so, as they failed to muster a single vote between them. The dangers were Aberdeen - not even in the Second Division but well supported by the big clubs who sensed the potential of the Dons - and Hamilton. The latter were handicapped by the fact that both Airdrie and Motherwell had recently achieved First Division status and Motherwell like Killie, were having to apply for re-election. The Killie committee wasted no time in pointing out to voting clubs what an injustice it would be to have three Lanarkshire teams in the top grade and none from Ayrshire. An audible sigh of relief could be heard all over the county when the result was announced; Motherwell 10, Kilmarnock 8, Aberdeen 4 and Hamilton 2.

Killie were safe. Aberdeen did take some sort of revenge though. They were admitted to the Second Division at the expense of the amateurs of Ayr Parkhouse.

MATCH OF THE SEASON
December 5th 1903.
Kilmarnock 2 Rangers 2

Even die-hard Killie fans feared that this match with the League leaders would result in a heavy defeat. After all, the last six League games had all been lost, four of them at Rugby Park. Yet after weathering the initial Rangers storm, Killie held firm. They they went on the offensive themselves. Half-an-hour had elapsed when Findlay got away from the defenders and crossed to provide Gibson with an open goal, a chance the inside-right tucked away with relish. Rangers equalised with a well-struck shot from a free kick twenty yards out. Bolstered by this goal against the run of play, they proceeded to give the Kilmarnock defence a torrid time. Killie, though, were resolute. At half-time it was still 1-1.

The second half was almost a mirror image of the first. For the first five minutes, Rangers attacked furiously, then Killie took control. Drummond, the Rangers defender, left the ball for his 'keeper, Dickie, to collect. In nipped Willie Banks to put Killie in front again. Now, Rangers were riled. "No team on Rugby Park this year had played so unfair", noted one reporter. The Glasgow side were "continually shoving and holding". Drummond, in particular, employing tactics "unworthy of a sportsman". Rangers anxiously sought to level affairs. They forced four successive corners, the last of which brought them the equaliser. The table-toppers were lucky to return from their visit to the bottom side with a point. This was far and away Kilmarnock's best performance of the season. Every commentator thought that they were unlucky not to win. In a season of despair at Rugby Park, this was one small symbol of hope for the future.

1904-05 DIVISION ONE

Kilmarnock acted quickly to avoid a repeat of the previous year's disasters. Fresh blood was drafted into the side for the opening game against Hearts. Local talent in the shape of Aitken, from Ardeer, and Johnstone, from Darvel, was supplemented by the experienced Currie, from Queen's Park, and the famous Barney Battles, signed from Celtic. The result was a fine win, three Killie players getting their names on the scoresheet for the first time in two years. The blend of youth and experience would be continued throughout the season; 'keeper Willie Monteith, also from Queen's Park, and veteran, McQueen, from Gainsborough Trinity played alongside Sandy Graham from Clydebank Juniors and Patna's splendidly named Fairfoul.

The team took some time to settle down after their initial success and results were poor until the start of October when Hibernian were beaten at home. Hibs had been Killie's bogey team - the only side they had failed to beat at least once since joining the First Division. There were other notable performances too. A 1-1 draw at Airdrie may not seem to rank highly but, at the time, Airdrie were three points clear at the top of the table.

This season had its low moments too. The side lost six League games in a row in November and December. In the cup, there was humiliation at the hands of Beith. The experience of Nithsdale had taught Killie nothing. They struggled to draw with the North Ayrshire side at home and were well beaten in the replay. That setback ended a promising New Year run which had started with Willie Banks firing in a second-half hat-trick against Partick Thistle after Killie had been two down at the interval.

Tragedy struck this year with the sad death of Barney Battles. Barney went down with influenza after playing in the 6-2 defeat at Ibrox. He felt well enough to watch the first game against Beith but less than a month later, he was dead - the 'flu having developed into pneumonia. The hugely-popular Battles had a wife and young daughters and was probably unaware that his wife was pregnant again. This child, a boy named after Barney, would emulate the father he never knew by growing up to play for Scotland. His father's memory was honoured by the estimated 40,000 who lined the route of his funeral in Glasgow.

A slight decline in membership to 507 was not a serious cause for concern at the club's AGM. The committee considered that the season, notwithstanding the shock at Beith, had been a satisfactory one. That the number of points garnered was a record for the club, was pointed out. That the side now played eight more games than when they debuted in Division One was not. The question of forming a Limited Company appeared to have been forgotten - at least for the moment. The more perceptive members worried if one season's temporary revival had encouraged complacency to set in once more.

MATCH OF THE SEASON
January 7th 1905.
Hearts 1 Kilmarnock 3

It had been fifteen months and twenty League matches since Kilmarnock had last lifted both points away from home. Since they had never won at Tynecastle, that depressing run seemed unlikely to end here. Killie were in a confident mood though. Three days earlier Banks had performed his one-man rescue mission against Partick Thistle. Against Hearts, however, with Johnstone and Crichton both unavailable, Killie were forced to play Banks at right-half. Into his place at centre-forward, came Sandy Graham, signed less than a month previously from Clydebank Juniors.

Graham's debut proved to be unforgettable. The Edinburgh side's defenders just couldn't handle this unknown quantity. He burst through the middle to put Killie ahead and repeated the trick shortly afterwards. Hearts managed to scramble a goal just before the break but the game was lost for them when left-back Orr was forced to leave the field through injury, early in the second-half. Hearts then played a spoiling, offside game, content, it appeared, to keep the score down and hope for something on the break. It didn't work. For a third time the bold Sandy strode through the middle. For a third time the ball found the back of the Hearts net. A hat-trick away from home. Sadly for Sandy, his subsequent career never hit such heights again. For Killie, this first victory at Tynecastle was a moment to savour, as well as a portent of greater triumphs to come.

1905-06 DIVISION ONE

Some people would have you believe that teams meeting each other more than twice in a season is a modern-day phenomenon. Yet, in this season, Kilmarnock played Port Glasgow Athletic on no fewer than seven occasions in the League and Cup, unfortunately winning just once. That sad statistic sums up what was a depressing time for Killie and their followers.

The improvement of the previous year turned out to be a temporary reprieve. Some hard facts needed to be faced up to. When Kilmarnock entered the First Division they had finished fifth out of ten clubs. This season they ended up fifteenth out of sixteen, only the amateurs of Queen's Park finishing below them.

Admittedly, having to play both Rangers and Celtic in the two opening games meant that an uphill struggle awaited should Killie fail to take anything from these initial fixtures. They lost both, despite relatively strong performances. From then, things went from bad to worse. One solitary point - from a draw at Airdrie - was all that Killie could muster from fifteen games away from home. One notably bad performance was at Motherwell, where, after drawing 0-0 at half-time, Kilmarnock were slaughtered 5-1; the damage being wreaked upon them by the Findlay brothers - both released by Killie - Tom because he wasn't considered good enough, and Bob because he was reckoned to be too old.

Constant team changes didn't help the cause. A total of 32 players saw first team action in League and Cup. Of the eleven who lined up against Rangers on the opening day of the season, only left-back Aitken took part in the last game against Port Glasgow. The AGM took place even earlier than usual, in February. Club finances were fairly healthy, over £1,300 had been taken in the fourteen home League fixtures completed since the previous year. Willie Banks, a player capable of filling any role on the pitch, had been transferred for the sum of £450 - a huge sum at the time when the world record fee was £1,000. Still, the dissenting voices within the Club would not be silenced. A motion to dissolve the present Club and refloat it immediately as a Limited Company was passed unanimously. Whether the new administrative set-up would produce greater success on the pitch, only time would tell.

MATCH OF THE SEASON
November 11th 1905.
Kilmarnock 7 Queen's Park 0

There was one side worse than Killie in 1905-06 and that side was Queen's Park. The famous amateurs of old had struggled to cope with the demands of playing against professionals each week and they found themselves on the receiving end of what was Kilmarnock's record First Division victory to date.

Only the "strongest superlatives" could describe Killie's performance, according to the 'Standard', perhaps forgetting the quality of the opposition. The slaughter started with ten minutes gone, when Young took a backheel from Fairfoul to put Killie one up. Galloway scored a second shortly after. Young was brought down twice in the box by the less than gentlemanly amateurs, the second offence bringing a penalty which Young himself converted.

Not to be outdone, Galloway added his second and Kilmarnock's fourth before the interval. On resuming, Queen's fought hard and the game was evenly balanced until the last twenty minutes, when Galloway netted from a rebound for his hat-trick. Young followed suit, with a cleverly taken goal, eluding the Queen's defence totally. Willie Banks rounded off the afternoon with a seventh, near the end.

As welcome as rain in the desert, this win provided Kilmarnock with a rare cause for celebration. The press went into rapture at the result, one description rather flatteringly describing the undoubtedly talented centre-forward Jock Young as being "the finest since the days of Bummer".

1906-07 DIVISION ONE

The First Division was extended to eighteen clubs, so Killie were re-elected without any difficulty. The problem for the new Kilmarnock F.C. Ltd. lay in the need to rebuild the team while retaining supporters loyalty. The faith shown in the existing staff was not rewarded, as Killie made a desperately poor start to the season. After about a dozen matches, changes were made, but these, at first, had no effect. The *Standard* wrote that "Defeat after defeat is lessening the prestige of the club, imperilling its position as a First League team, driving away support, making members despondent, ruining prospects of the new Limited Company". The paper pointed out that there had now been three years of this, that players wages were higher than ever before but still results were no good.

On the 29th December 1906, Killie faced Celtic at home. With just seven points and two wins from nineteen matches, Killie were bottom of the table. Celtic, with twenty nine points from seventeen games, were effortlessly coasting to a third successive title. Kilmarnock upset all the predictions by turning a two goal interval deficit into a fighting 2-2 draw. Appropriately enough, the final match of the old year saw the club finally turn the corner. Killie averaged just under a point a match from then on. At Hamilton they recorded their first away League win in over two years and after over thirty matches. At home, only Dundee left with both points.

The Cup was witness to an oddity. The Rugby Park pitch was declared unplayable by both a local and the match referee on the morning of the game against Clachnacuddin from Inverness. Yet because the Highlanders had travelled the day previously, a friendly was allowed to go ahead. Such confusion abounded in Scottish football at this time. Killie won the friendly 1-0 and the real thing, the following week, 4-0. Two tough matches with Cup-holders, Hearts, followed before Killie made their exit from the competition.

The new Committee had shown some deft touches when it came to signing players. Old stalwart, Geordie Anderson, a survivor of the days in the Second Division, was brought back in early November. Also returning was full-back Willian Agnew, who, like Anderson, had been part of the line of defensive ever-presents in 1901-02. Adding to the 'old-fashioned' look was Davie Howie, younger brother of the inside-right of the turn of the Century team and also an inside-forward. By the season's end, the team had been completely transformed. Not a single one of the eleven who played in the first game of the season took park in the last.

The improvement had come too late however, to stop Killie from finishing in a three way tie with Hamilton and Port Glasgow at the foot of the table. The Scottish League didn't recognise goal average as a means of differentiating between sides and had a potentially tricky problem on their hands when it came to re-election. They eventually decided not to have a series of play-offs (which might have left the situation unresolved if each side won two games) unless the League AGM adopted a resolution from Hearts to cut the number of First Division sides to 16. Happily, the League refused to do so and, as the AGM also threw out a motion for automatic promotion/relegation, all three clubs were easily re-elected. The first year of the limited company ended with a worrying loss of £500 but balances were still healthy (over £1500 was taken in receipts at home league games) and for the first time in years, there was an air of optimism about the future.

MATCH OF THE SEASON
January 1st 1907.
Kilmarnock 1 St. Mirren 0

A doubly significant affair. Immediately so because Killie ended a depressing run of fourteen games without a win, capitalising on their success in holding Celtic three days previously. In the long term, because this was the first ever Ne'erday derby with the Paisley side. There had never been any love lost between them, Killie suspecting that Saints had conspired to keep them out of the top League. But the competitive edge with which this fixture is associated can be traced back to this game.

It was a keen contest. The pitch had thawed quickly since the Celtic match and both teams played some fast, clever football. There was no sign of a goal though, until Killie winger Barton crossed to Maxwell. The resulting shot was going wide until St. Mirren's right half, Greenlees, deflected the ball into his own net. In the second-half, St. Mirren attacked, only to be repelled by the cool pairing of McCallum and Angnew in defence. Then the Killie half-backs took control, Crichton in particular having a marvellous game. Killie ended on top but without adding to their score. It was, declared the press, a Kilmarnock performance which gave "unbounded satisfaction". So began what would rapidly develop into a tradition.

1907-08 DIVISION ONE

This was a crazy season. By common acclaim, Kilmarnock were one of the finest sides in Scotland, yet they struggled woefully in the League. After the opening game against Hearts, they were faced with the oddity of their next six matches all being against Glasgow sides. Once again, they drew with Celtic and came within three minutes of taking a point from Ibrox for the first time. They were thrashed 6-1 at home by Falkirk - a sad Rugby Park debut for Bobby Templeton - and it took until their twelfth match, away to Motherwell, before a win was chalked up. At home, supporters had to wait until December before Killie took both points - a win over Hamilton finally doing the trick. The Celtic match was also notable in that Killie recorded their best League takings to date and it was the first time this season that Celtic had failed to win both points.

The Board certainly couldn't be accused of lack of ambition. Hugh Wilson, a winner of Championship medals in both England and Scotland had arrived at the end of the previous season. Wilson, the greatest inside-left of the day, was joined by wing partner Bobby Templeton, fresh from appearing in Celtic's first-ever 'Double' winning side. Veteran Wilson, 38, and Templeton, 28 and at his peak, were both Ayrshire born and bred. They joined such talented team-mates as Anderson and Agnew, as well as James Mitchell, now back to his best after serious injury. Indeed, the London-based *Football Star* went so far as to say that Wilson and Templeton were *"two of the most remarkable footballers the world has ever seen"*. With half the side having played for Scotland at one time or another, it was an ever greater accolade that came Killie's way when three of them, Agnew, Mitchell and Templeton line up together for their country against Ireland.

Such a talented combination couldn't stay struggling for long. Gradually, Kilmarnock began to improve their position and although they only finished fifteenth, they were a good seven points clear of the re-election zone. There was greater continuity in the side too. Seven of the players featuring in the last League match had also taken part in the first. And, just to emphasise that Killie were well on the road to recovery, they recaptured their Cup form of old. They disposed of stuffy opposition in Hamilton, before demonstrating that they had learned their lesson as far as non-leaguers were concerned, by comfortably beating Dunblane. The Quarter-final was a different proposition althogether. No-one really expected Killie to win at Easter Road. In nine outings away to Hibernian in the League, they had lost seven and drawn two.

Few, however, had heard of John McAllister, who had made his League debut, ironically, at Easter Road earlier in the season. John would have three spells with Killie, never establishing himself as a regular. He scored fewer than a handful of goals in Killie colours but the one he got in this game was a screaming shot, from a distance, and it put Killie into the last four in the Cup, after a ten year absence. Sadly, the Semi-final was a disappointment. Until shortly before the First World War, there were no neutral grounds for Semi-finals, so it was that Rugby Park saw a new attendance record when 15,000 turned up for the visit of St. Mirren, beating the previous best (also in a cup-tie against St. Mirren) by a good three thousand. They witnessed a dull, dreary affair, neither side scoring. The replay was watched at Love Stree by a massive 20,000, who saw Saints triumph with a goal in each half. No Final for Killie, but proof positive that they were back as a force to be reckoned with.

The AGM was the happiest for some time. The club had made a profit of £224-15-6d and had taken just short of £2,500 at home League games. Taking members into account, this meant that League gates at Rugby Park totalled over 100,000 for the first time. Evidence, if it were needed, of the popularity of the new signings and of the quality of the team's play. There was an indication of a growing trend in football reaching Ayrshire when a motion to appoint a team manager was ruled out because it was submitted too late, but a guarantee was given that the Directors would carefully consider the issue.

MATCH OF THE SEASON
January 4th 1908.
Port Glasgow Athletic 4 Kilmarnock 1

This has to be one of the weirdest matches Kilmarnock FC have ever been involved in. By kick off time, just seven Killie players had turned up for the game. After waiting in vain for 25 minutes, the seven were ordered to play against their full-strength opponents. Port Glasgow, like Queens Park, were amateurs, but there was nothing gentlemanly about their approach to this match. They insisted it went ahead and proceeded to attack the Killie goal which was defended by left-half Shaw. Port scored quickly and were awarded a penalty shortly afterwards. They missed. Suddenly, one of Killie's valiant seven, Howie, broke away to score an equaliser. Ayrshire joy was short-lived as Port regained the lead before half-time. In the second half, Barton took over from Shaw in goal as Port scored twice more. Many fans left before the end, less than pleased at having to watch what the 'Scottish Referee' described as a "burlesque" which had "just one side in the game". A rather obvious statement, really. Killie's seven had performed well in the circumstances to lose by just three goals. Those players who arrived at Port Glasgow, Mitchell, Anderson, Shaw, Barton, Howie, Walker and Alex Wilson have gone down in history as the smallest recorded number to start and finish a first class football match.

The missing foursome, Agew, Halley, Templeton and goal-keeper Strachan claimed that they had arrived in Glasgow in good time to make the connection for the match but that fog had prevented them from doing so. They said that they had been informed at Glasgow Central that they would only be able to get as far as Greenock by kick-off and that there was no way they could have been in Port Glasgow before the match ended. What their seven colleagues - forced to play into near darkness - thought about it all is unrecorded. There was press clamour for an SFA inquiry but no-one could prove that the players hadn't done their best to reach the ground. The matter simmered awhile before being quietly forgotten. The bare facts are all that the record books have shown of this most extraodinary match.

1908-09 DIVISION ONE

Off the pitch, it was a sensational start to the season. The club were forced to publish a letter appealing to the supporters for good behaviour; a consequence of having been find £50 after the Referee at the Rangers game the previous season, had the windows of his train carriage smashed and Rangers officials had been attacked in the street. Then, Bobby Templeton struck a bet which saw him enter the lions den at a visiting circus. Luckily the beast had been well doped beforehand; the press recording that it lay *"quiet as a St. Bernard dog"*, as the bold Bob crawled under its belly before patting, stroking and turning the tail of the jungle king.

Early performances were poor - ex-Evertonian left-half William Black having such a bad game in his only appearance for Killie that he was described as being *"practically a convalescent"*. Calls were made for a player-manager, a refrain that would be heard again more than eight decades later. Results began to improve and even in some seemingly bad performances there were hopeful signs. A 5-0 beating at Dundee provoked the headline:-

"SPIRITED GAME AT DUNDEE.
KILLIE PLAY WELL BUT FAIL TO SCORE".

Such equanimity would not be forthcoming nowadays. Killie hit a purple patch around the turn of the year. When Celtic were beaten 3-1 on January 2nd, it was only the second such triumph ever. It was, said the *Standard*. an *"historic struggle"*. This match set a new record for receipts at a League game - over £320 being taken at the gate. Two days later, Killie lost heavily at Cathkin in a match which rang down the curtain on one of the club's legendary figures.

Geordie Anderson, almost 32, played his last League game for Kilmarnock that day. He had been granted a testimonial earlier in the season but the game - against St. Mirren - was played the night before Killie's League match at Shawfield. Only 1,000 turned up to see what was the reserve team receive a 6-0 thrashing from St. Mirren's first XI. Although hopes were expressed that many tickets had been sold other than to those who turned up, it seemed a sad way to end the career of this magnificent servant. As far back as 1901 the *Scottish Referee* had said that it would be a *"sad, sad day"* for Kilmarnock when Geordie had to retire. Geordie had returned to Rugby Park after a spell in the South and his retiral severed the last playing link with the team that won the Second Division twice and reached the Cup Final.

There were some notable successes this season. Falkirk, then riding high in the table, were beaten by a Killie side which was reduced to nine men for most of the match. The side's performances as a whole were said to be *"so much in advance of past years"*. Only a late losing run at the end of the season prevented them from averaging a point a game for the first time since their initial season in Division One. The final defeat - at Port Glasgow - being orchestrated by the nomadic Findlay brothers, continuing to haunt the club which had written them off.

Surprisingly, home gates were down by £132 and the early exit in the cup, after an exciting tussle at Tynecastle, meant that the year was not a success, financially. At the AGM, John Greenway, a perennial scourge of first Committee, now Board, moved that a Manager be appointed. The resolution was lost by 78-63.

MATCH OF THE SEASON
December 19th 1908.
Rangers 1 Kilmarnock 1

With two successive wins under their belt, Kilmarnock travelled to Ibrox with rather more optimism than was usual. Playing in a dense fog, they gave their illustrious opponents a hard time. Templeton, revelling in the conditions, dribbled through the Rangers defence, winning a corner. He took it himself, floating the ball into the box, where inside-right Aaron Ramsay, only 5ft 6ins tall, out-jumped the entire defence to head Killie into the deserved lead. Rangers sneaked a lucky equaliser, when Kilmarnock 'keeper Aitken slipped in the Ibrox mud.

In the second-half, Killie piled on constant pressure for over twenty minutes. Templeton hit the ball over the bar from ten yards out. Howie, from just six yards, and with only the goalie to beat, kicked the ground instead of the ball. Near the end, Rangers were awarded a penalty kick. Bennett promptly despatched the ball into the net whereupon the brave Referee instructed him to take the kick again, as he had not blown his whistle when the first shot was hit. The kick was re-taken, Aitken redeeming himself with a wonderful save. For the first time ever in the League, Kilmarnock left Ibrox undefeated.

1909-10 DIVISION ONE

The steady improvement in form was further consolidated this year. And the supporters found a new hero to cheer. After opening with two defeats, Killie drew 3-3 at home to Airdrie. Opening his scoring account with a pair of goals that day was Andy Cunningham, playing in only his second match for Kilmarnock. The tall 18-year old was starting out on a magnificent career which would see him adorn the famous grounds of Ibrox and St. James Park. Cups, caps and medals would be in abundance for this supremely talented and confident inside-come-centre-forward. At the age of 38, Cunningham would play his first English Division One match, but for the next six years he would be the darling of the Rugby Park faithful.

The other Killie goal against Airdrie was a real oddity. Standing off the pitch, David Chalmers headed the ball back into play and watched, bemused, as the wind blew it into the net. The unsighted referee gave the goal - Chalmers' only score for Killie. The Ayrshire team was turned over in the next match, against Third Lanark to the tune of 7-0. After that though, Killie started dishing out the same punishment themselves. Six goals against Queen's Park in the very next game and another half-dozen against Clyde exacted revenge for the drubbing Killie had taken against their fellow Glaswegians. Hibs were beaten 4-0 at Rugby Park as were Port Glasgow. Cunningham, amply assisted by Howie, doing most of the damage in these games.

King Tailors ran an early form of sponsorship with an 'Overcoats for Goals' competition. His brace against Motherwell earning Cunningham a coat as well as one for a lucky spectator, one Charles Thomas of Grange Street, Kilmarnock being the presumably grateful recipient. Sadly there is no record of how long the competition ran for. At the rate Cunningham was scoring there must have been an awful lot of well-dressed, snugly wrapped-up citizens in the town that winter. Disaster struck at Brockville when a telegram arrived shortly before kick-off stating baldly *"STRANDED AT STRATHAVEN"*.

Club Secretary, Barrie Grieve, had been ferrying the colourful Cunningham to the game at Falkirk via the latest invention of Edwardian technology - the motor car. Breakdown and the failure of alternative transport to materialise forced Andy to sit around as his team-mates lost 4-0. Barrie Grieve, who had been Secretary since the limited company had been formed, left the club this season to become Manager of St. Mirren. Killie thought about obtaining a Manager of their own. The man they were after was Andy 'Daddler' Aitken. On offer was a wage of £4 per week and an undisclosed signing-on fee. Aitken was already a successful player-manager with Middlesbrough and Leicester and Killie offered that latter club £300 as a transfer fee. Leicester insisted on Aitken honouring his contract and the proposed move fell through.

A new crowd record was set at Rugby Park when 18,000 watched Scotland beat Wales 1-0, James Mitchell playing in the Scotland team. Mitchell's selection for two International matches prevented him from equalling Dan Armour's achievement of the previous year of playing in all 34 League games - no question of postponements in those days. Mitchell's first match after his Scotland duties were over was away to Aberdeen. Kilmarnock, the most southerly of the First Division sides, won away to the most Northerly team for the first time. A result which the *Standard* called a *"pleasant surprise"*. This game had been scheduled for December when, after 55 minutes of playing in a blizzard, the Referee had abandoned the match. The Aberdeen fans rioted at this decision and it took some time for the police to disperse them. There had already been trouble at Killie games and the notorious Scottish Cup Final of 1909, when 'Old Firm' fans set payboxes alight, gives the lie to those who pretend that hooliganism is something which first happened in the 1960's.

Finishing in mid-table may be a better performance than struggling to avoid re-election but it is nowhere near as exciting. Home League gates fell by a massive £503 this year, the total loss for the season being £444-6-0. It was not a busy time in the transfer market, just £5 being spent in transfer fees. One event of interest at the AGM was the election - after years of trying - of vociferous critic, John Greenway, to the Board of Directors.

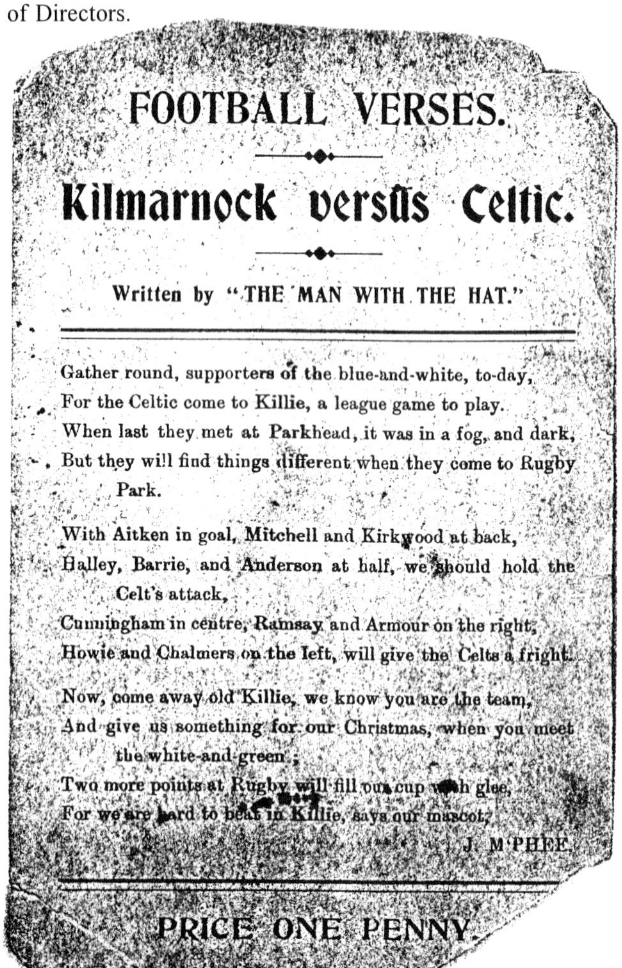
FOOTBALL VERSES.

Kilmarnock versus Celtic.

Written by "THE MAN WITH THE HAT."

Gather round, supporters of the blue-and-white, to-day,
For the Celtic come to Killie, a league game to play.
When last they met at Parkhead, it was in a fog, and dark,
But they will find things different when they come to Rugby Park.

With Aitken in goal, Mitchell and Kirkwood at back,
Halley, Barrie, and Anderson at half, we should hold the Celt's attack,
Cunningham in centre, Ramsay and Armour on the right,
Howie and Chalmers on the left, will give the Celts a fright.

Now, come away old Killie, we know you are the team,
And give us something for our Christmas, when you meet the white-and-green;
Two more points at Rugby will fill our cup with glee,
For we are hard to beat in Killie, says our mascot.

J. M'PHEE.

PRICE ONE PENNY.

A postcard poem dedicated to Kilmarnock's home match with Celtic on Christmas Day 1909. Unfortunately, the hat-wearing rhymster was better with verses than versus. Celtic won 1-0!

MATCH OF THE SEASON
February 12th 1910.
Hamilton Academical 1 Kilmarnock 7

The Press noted, rather sarcastically, that Kilmarnock usually managed to win at least one game away from home each season. Six months into this one, they were still searching for an away triumph. They also went into this match not having scored in their four most recent games, during which time they had been knocked out of the Cup by Third Lanark. It was time to make amends.

Early in the match, Hamilton took the lead. Undaunted, Killie replied within a minute through the irrepressible Cunningham. The same player scored again. Then, Hamilton's centre-forward was carried off injured, unable to take any further part in the match. All this, and only fifteen minutes played. Cunningham continued to set the pace. His cross provided McAllister with Killie's third before the interval. The second period was reportedly "pretty much a farce", Howie scoring twice, McAllister notching his second and Andy Cunningham recorded another goal to give him his first hat-trick for the club. More significantly, as he stepped off the Douglas Park field, Andy had the satisfaction of knowing that he had broken the club's League scoring record. The Evening Times summed it up when they said of Andy that he could shoot "from any angle" and was in possession of those three great strikers attributes, "power, accuracy and direction".

1910-11 DIVISION ONE

A poor start was compensated for by victory at Rugby Park over six-in-a-row title winners Celtic. Killie began to put some solid performances together - on only two occasions were they beaten easily. The first of these was a controversial home defeat by Third Lanark. Killie were already certain of losing when a Thirds player scored with an early-century 'hand of God'. The blatant handball was witnessed by the entire crowd, press included, except for one man - the Referee. There were angry scenes as the crowd invaded the pitch at the end of the match, the *Glasgow Herald* reporting *"Not for the first time, Kilmarnock was the scene of temper, not so much inside the ground, as outside"*, as the trouble spilled over into the streets.

To lose 5-1 at home to Third Lanark was a bad result. The 5-0 reverse away to Hearts was more excusable. Killie also had an Ayrshire Cup tie against Beith the same day, so the term was 'split', four first-team regulars taking part in the local competition with reserves taking their place at Tynecastle. Coming out of retirement for one last hurrah against Beith that day was Geordie Anderson, more than two years after he had played his last League match.

But this season was also a time of some memorable triumphs. Killie won at Easter Road for the first time, a match where the attendance was lower than expected on account of the presence of Lloyd George in Edinburgh at a political rally. Revenge was gained against Third Lanark when a first ever victory at Cathkin was achieved. Just before that triumph, Mattha' Shortt introduced himself to Kilmarnock fans with an explosive debut at Broomfield.

The game was barely thirty seconds old when Mattha scored - or did he? The Airdrie players were adamant that the ball never crossed the goal-line. Despite furious protests, the goal stood. Even without the aid of a Russian linesman, the Referee held firm. Mattha' made only a few appearances this year but he would become one of the Rugby Park immortals thanks to another one of his rare goals, just after the First World War.

The season ended with Killie averaging a point per game for the first time since their inaugural year in Division One. A cause for modest celebration? Perhaps. But one poor soul went about it the wrong way. This miscreant attempted to evade the Sunday liquor laws by claiming that he was a professional footballer recently transferred to Kilmarnock. He partook - as a bona fide traveller - of some liquid refreshment in a local hotel, only to find himself before the courts where he was fined £1 with the alternative of tens days in jail. For 1911, that was a very expensive price for a pint.

MATCH OF THE SEASON
November 19th 1910.
Kilmarnock 5 Clyde 2

Clyde sat proudly at the top of the League when they met Killie on this day. Twenty points from thirteen games and with just seven goals conceded, they looked a good bet to beat a Kilmarnock side lying eight points and eleven places beneath them.

Killie had other ideas. Both teams struggled to cope with the early snow which lay all around the pitch when Killie got a lucky break. Howie's header looked harmless. Twice the Clyde 'keeper looked to have held it and twice it slipped from his grasp, eventually ending up just over the line. On the balance of play, the leaders were unlucky to be behind. Clyde spent the rest of the first half playing like prospective champions but without success. Half-time arrived with Killie still a goal in front.

The second period was enthralling. From eighteen yards out, Howie went past three men, leaving them all on the ground, then shot past the advancing goalie to put Killie two up. It was, declared the press, quite a sight to see the Clyde defence "helpless in the snow and with their heels in the air". Clyde fought back though. Soon, they had scored and were again threatening, when Killie's left-half 'Swifty' Anderson cracked the ball home from thirty yards to make it 3-1. Still, Clyde weren't beaten. Again, they pulled one back. The game still hung in the balance when Cunningham's shot restored Killie's two-goal advantage. Finally, in a goal-mouth melee, Howie grabbed his hat-trick - and Killie's fifth. The leaders had lost almost as many goals in one match as they had in the rest of the season. For Killie, it was the best home win since putting six past the same side a year previously.

1911-12 DIVISION ONE

This season marked a return to the bad old days. Killie lost two of their best players - George Halley and Davie Howie - to Bradford Park Avenue and struggled to replace them. Eight different players were fielded at right-half during the season. In total, **thirty-six** different players took part in League and Cup. Little wonder that there was no cohesion in Kilmarnock's performances.

Early defeats saw the remaining star players - Andy Cunningham and Bobby Templeton - take the brunt of the criticism. Home performances were particularly poor, five of the first six League games at Rugby Park were lost. In amidst the gloom, there were moments to savour though. Goalkeeper Smart was knocked unconscious when hit by the ball before the match at Aberdeen. Mattha' Shortt took over in goal and proceeded to give a superb showing as Killie pulled off an unexpected 2-1 win. The 'Overcoats for Goals' competition returned. Against Dundee at home it was announced that there would be a pair of coats for each goal scored. Andy Cunningham - who must have been able to open a tailor's shop by now - hit the only goal of the match. Stung by criticism that the competition offered little chance for defenders, the company stated that they would give the entire defence a coat each if they kept a clean sheet against Third Lanark. The match finished 0-0, part of Killie's best run of the season, when they went four games without conceding a goal; winning three times.

The threat of re-election was staved off thanks to two fine victories near the end of the season. Aberdeen were beaten 3-0 in the final match and, before that, there was an excellent 3-2 win over Rangers; a game that marked the debut of Willie Culley at Centre-Forward. Willie would go on to become Killie's all-time top scorer in League and Cup but he never once scored in his few outings this season and it would take some time before the sceptical Rugby Park crowd would become convinced of his worth.

MATCH OF THE SEASON
February 24th 1912.
Kilmarnock 1 Clyde 6

Killie's Cup form was in marked contrast to their struggles in the League. Hamilton - losing Finalists the previous year - were ousted in a tough Rugby Park encounter. Then Leith were beaten on their own ground. Clyde were expected to fall in the Quarter-Finals. After all, in the two previous seasons, Killie had smashed eleven goals against the Shawfield club. A more recent home defeat - when Clyde won 3-1 at Rugby Park two days before Christmas - was either forgotten, or discounted totally.

The biggest crowd yet assembled at Rugby Park watched a fairly even opening fifteen minutes till Clyde opened the scoring. Killie saw a good penalty claim turned down. Unlike last season's League game, there was no luck going Kilmarnock's way. Ten minutes from the interval, Clyde scored again. Killie, if anything, had been slightly the better side. Two down at half-time was rough justice indeed. Still, the match could be saved. Or so the home fans thought. Five minutes into the second-half and Killie were struck by a body blow.

The ever-reliable left-back, Davie Kirkwood, went lame in one leg and had to leave the field. Reduced to ten men, Killie clawed their way back into the game, a header from Alex Logan making it 2-1. Briefly, hopes were raised. Only to be dashed as the defence watched a soft goal enter the net for Clyde's third. The game was up for Killie now. When the fourth went in, the crowd started to leave. 1000's were spared the further agony of watching Clyde's final two goals.

The only consolation lay in the takings from the hugh attendance. 18,888 had paid at the turnstiles. Coupled with season ticket holders and members, a grand total of 19,564 had watched the match. Not for the last time, disgruntled supporters were heard to comment that whenever there was a big crowd, Killie would let them down.

1912-13 DIVISION ONE

Goals were hard to come by this season as Kilmarnock clawed their way back into mid-table. Myth would have it that defensive football was born some time in the 1960's but a homegrown form of catenaccio was second nature to Scottish defenders at a time when the three-man offside rule was in operation. Killie played no fewer than than six 0-0 draws in League games this season and, after the 1-1 draw with Morton in mid-September, the next time they scored in the first 45 minutes was against St. Mirren on New Years' Day seventeen matches later.

Aitken, the man once sought as Manager, finally made a return to Rugby Park as player, some thirteen and a half years after his two previous appearances, guesting for Killie in two Cup games in 1899. Sadly, at 35, the years had taken their toll. He managed just eight games before being forced to retire - a groin injury received against Third Lanark just before Christmas doing most of the damage. Also returning was James Maxwell. He too was no longer the force he once was, playing just five games. James was destined to be killed in the coming global conflict. In January 1913 his wife gave birth to a son who would one day equal his father's achievements with Kilmarnock.

Andy Cunningham went one better than the legendary 'Bummer' by finishing as top scorer for the fourth season in a row. Otherwise, it was a season where little happened. Ther was a stirring fightback at home to Raith Rovers, Killie winning 4-3 after trailing 3-1 at the break. The most interesting thing about the away visit to Dundee, where Killie got a 0-0 draw, according to the local papers, was that the quality of the team singing had improved!

The revolving door policy was once again in operation. Twenty-seven players took part in the campaign, including Alex Logan, goalscoring hero of the previous year, now scapegoat-in-chief when things went wrong. Logan was sold to Partick Thistle, probably glad to be away after one scribe had memorably described him as being unwilling to use his *"super-abundance of avoirdupois"* to any good effect.

The small profit of £77 of the last season became a worrying loss of £368 this time round. Players wages were responsible as gates increased by a healthy £385, equivalent to an extra 900 spectators per home game.

MATCH OF THE SEASON
February 8th 1913.
Kilmarnock 5 Abercorn 1

This Second Round Scottish Cup match was earmarked by the 'experts' as a possible upset. Abercorn were going strong in Division Two - they were, in fact, the only unbeaten team in Britain at the time - and they had won the Qualifying Cup. But Killie too were on a run of good form - unbeaten in their last eight League and Cup games. The scene was set for a tough game. It didn't materialise. True, the Paisley side did shock Killie. Despite being reduced to ten men for fifteen minutes, Abercorn were first to score. It took this goal to galvanise Kilmarnock into action - Dickie equalising before the break.

At 1-1 there was still a chance of an upset. Killie, however, had other ideas. They took control early in the second-half. Andy Cunningham scored with a penalty. Dickie scored again, then Maxwell got into the act, scoring the fourth. Dickie grabbed his hat-trick to round off a comfortable victory.

Killie faced Hearts in the last eight and, in a disappointing performance, were beaten 2-0 before 16,000 at Rugby Park. For Abercorn it was the end of the road. Three times Semi-Finalists in their day, their appearance at Rugby Park was their last ever in the Scottish Cup proper. They went into hibernation during the War and failed to re-awaken after it.

1913-14 DIVISION ONE

Kilmarnock made their now traditional poor start but picked up strongly around the turn of the year to once again secure a place just below the middle of the table. Just three wins were recorded away from home but these were at Pittodrie, Tynecastle and Easter Road. When Dumbarton were beaten 6-0 at Rugby Park, two players - Andrew Neil and William Whittle - each scored a hat-trick, the first such double since Young and Galloway against Queen's Park eight years earlier.

The gifted Templeton had gone - sold to Fulham for just £50. At 34 he was nearing the end of his career, but the Board had let him leave without knowing who would be his replacement. Seven players tried out the outside-left position but by the end of the campaign, the question of replacing Templeton had still not been settled.

There were fewer goals from Cunningham this year. He failed to finish as top scorer - the first time he had not done so since joining Killie. The general lack of excitement in the air was reflected at the turnstiles. At just under £2000 for the season, there was a drop in takings of over £150. Considering that there were two more home fixtures - Division One now had twenty clubs - this was a hefty loss. Nearly all the extra spectators gained the previous year had vanished. Even so, the AGM reported a modest profit of £15 for the year. These meetings were now tame affairs. The rebellion of a decade ago had long since been extinguished. Now, questions were politely asked and generally prefaced with a word of congratulation to the Board. Directors were usually re-elected, either easily, or unopposed.

MATCH OF THE SEASON
September 13th 1913.
Kilmarnock 0 Ayr United 1

There had been Ayrshire 'derbies' in the League before this match. Kilmarnock had faced Ayr FC in their Division Two days and Ayr themselves had played local rivals Parkhouse in the same Division. This one was different though. It was the first League meeting between clubs from Ayrshire's biggest towns for fourteen years. It was the first encounter between Killie and the infant Ayr United (Ayr and Ayr Parkhouse had merged in 1910) and it was the first meeting in Division One - Ayr, along with Dumbarton, benefitting from the decision to have twenty clubs.

Sadly, for Killie, it was not an auspicious occasion. The match itself was said to be a good one. "Fast, clever, clean and keen" were words commonly used to describe the affair. Certainly the excitement of the event was evident throughout. Yet, Kilmarnock lost. Killie had attempted to play their traditional close passing game. United chose to be more direct. The simple approach paid off, Ayr's first-half goal securing both points. Killie, it was averred, had beaten themselves. Most 'neutral' onlookers felt that Kilmarnock had been desperately unlucky to lose. The 'Standard' saw it differently. It was, they said, "A deep humiliation". The County's premier team for a generation had lost to the upstart newcomers.

1914-15 DIVISION ONE

The outbreak of war threw a shadow over domestice sport. How, people asked, could football matches go on while young men were being slaughtered daily in Flanders? The answer was, that at the start of the conflict at any rate, the fighting was not expected to last for long. Even when it became clear that it was going to be a long war, it was argued that events such as football matches were a welcome distraction from the conflict - evidence that life continued as usual. Of course, many players joined up to fight - Queen's Park and Hearts both saw their entire first elevens volunteer - but, nevertheless, the Scottish League continued to function right throughout the war. The Second Division was scrapped after one season and the Scottish Cup was suspended for the duration.

The clubs did their best to aid the services. Killie Secretary, James MacDonald, wrote to the *Standard* after a 'Tobacco Day' at the home game against Celtic, saying that 106 pipes, 252 packets of cigarettes, 111 packets of Woodbine, 4lbs of tobacco, 8 pouches, various cigarette cases and cash to the value of £12-10-0d (£12.50) had been collected at the match for despatch to troops in the front line.

The football itself was less than enthralling. A poor start saw Killie having to struggle to catch the field. There were some auspicious moments - a first-ever win at Dens Park for instance, and Andrew Neil's four goals against Dumbarton - but, overall, it was a disappointing time. Neil was the first Kilmarnock player to hit four goals in a Division One game and the first to do so in any major competition since Maitland scored five against Orion in a 1900 cup-tie. The most passionate incident involved Mattha' Shortt's 'goal' against Rangers which was disallowed. Even the Rangers players were preparing to kick-off and could not believe what had happened. Rangers further infuriated the Killie faithful by signing Andy Cunningham just before the end of the season. For at least the past three years, Andy's name had been linked with Ibrox and Kilmarnock had turned down four-figure bids twice. Now, he was sold for just £800 - on account of his scoring being no longer quite as prolific - and went on to give Rangers fourteen years of service before being transfered on to Newcastle for three times the fee they had paid for him! The season ended with Killie having made sufficient recovery as to finish in 12th spot. A loss of £177 was recorded but - against all expectations and trends - games were up by £214; 450 spectators per match.

MATCH OF THE SEASON
September 26th 1914.
Airdrieonians 0 Kilmarnock 2

The omens were not good this game. Killie had won just twice at Broomfield in fifteen League outings - in sharp contrast to the seven times the Diamonds had triumphed at Rugby Park - and the Ayrshire team's last away success here had been as far back as October 1903. Kilmarnock were rock-bottom of the League, played six, lost six. Airdrie were 4th top and had won all their home games.

Yet Killie tore into their 'bogey' team with gusto. Willie Culley missed two 'sitters'. Then Goldie narrowly missed, as did Cunningham, twice. Five attempts on goal and no joy when, suddenly, the ball was in the back of the Kilmarnock net. This time it was Airdrie who were chagrined by the refereeing decision as 'no goal' was signalled. That was the turning point. From close in, Vickers netted to give Killie an interval lead. After the re-start, Airdrie played an offside game and seldom threatened to equalise. Still, the result remained in doubt until the last minute, when Armour pounced on a rebound to give Killie a worthy - and much needed - 2-0 victory. The jinx had been broken. Not only had Kilmarnock won at last on their 'bogey' ground, this was the first time that they had left Airdrie with a clean sheet.

1915-16 DIVISION ONE

Kilmarnock made one of their best starts to a season, lying in second place after six games. Lack of a scoring partner for Willie Culley meant they couldn't keep such a high position for long; eventually finishing 10th. Culley hit 23 goals - a new record - three more than Neil's tally of the previous season. Neil himself had gone to Third Lanark, and although brought back to Rugby Park in January 1916, didn't reach the heights of his previous effort. Other than Culley, no player scored as many as a handful of goals this season. For war-time, there was a welcome solidity to the side. Two players missing just one game and another pair missing only two. Nine players who took part in the opening game also played in the closing one and it would have been ten had centre-half, Dickie, not been called away on active service.

The experience of war forced football to alter its rules. Some games lasted just 35 minutes each half, Killie away to Clyde for example.

One ninety-minute match which stirred up controversy was the home game with Morton, then lying in third place. During the game Killie were reduced, through injury, to nine men. Inside-left Armstrong hit the bar with a shot which saw a goal awarded, much to the delight - and astonishment - of the home support. A draw in these circumstances was a good result, even if the goal was decidedly dodgy. The same game witnessed an incident in which Killie inside-right Fulton, as the press rather delicately put it, let his *"hand collide rather heavily with the proboscis of his antagonist"*. Or, to put it another way, he punched him on the nose!

Killie played their final home game at Somerset Park - Rugby Park being used for an agricultrual show. This decision didn't help crowd figures which were beginning to show the effects of what was now recognised as a long war. 80% of season ticket holders (who would have bought for 1914-15 before the conflict started) didn't renew this year and, at the turnstiles, the fall in revenue was huge. Almost £500 fewer was taken in, representing a loss of 1,000 spectators per home match. The war effort was aided substantially by the playing staff. Six were in uniform and eleven more were working in munitions. Two of the club's Directors were also in the Army.

MATCH OF THE SEASON
August 21st 1915.
Kilmarnock 5 Aberdeen 0

What a glorious start to a season. The opening game saw Killie destroy Aberdeen. No-one could quite believe it. The press, both local and national, found this an altogether surprising result. Willie Culley, now accepted by the fans as continuing in the tradition of the 'Bummer' and Andy Cunningham, had hit 26 goals in 82 League contests prior to this match. He gave notice that his strike rate was about to go into overdrive with his first hat-trick. Culley scored twice in the first-half, with a goal from Goldie sandwiched between. The blistering performance convinced the supporters that the one thing the war hadn't done was to diminish the standard of football in any way. In the second-half, Culley's powerful header earned him that elusive third goal. A superb drive from Armstrong gave Killie their fifth against an Aberdeen side which was simply overwhelmed by this strong, yet skilful, Kilmarnock eleven.

1916-17 DIVISION ONE

Signings from the Junior ranks in the shape of Henderson, Rutherford and Mattha' Smith made a favourable impression this season. There was the usual slow start, beaten early on by an Ayr team which hadn't scored a goal let along collected a point before visiting Rugby Park. But with the return of Fulton and Mackie from injury, plus the increasingly impressive Malcolm McPhail on the left wing, Killie had the nucleus of a fine side. Blair, in goal, Tom Hamilton at right-back and the menacing Culley up front added the experience necessary to make a good showing. Revenge was gained with a 2-0 win at Somerset, Killie's first success there and also the first goals they had netted on that ground. To Mattha' Smith falls the honour of being the first Killie scorer at Ayr.

The team had to cope with some terrible conditions. Against Hearts, there was a torrential thunderstorm which left captain, Jamie Mitchell, saying that if he won the toss, he would elect to *"play with the tide"*. Killie won that game and others too. By the turn of the year they were in the unaccustomedly high position of 4th, with 26 pts from 20 games. Having won five successive matches to reach that lofty spot, the team proceeded to lose the next five. They ended that dismal run with a 7-0 win over Aberdeen. Unbeaten Celtic were four minutes away from losing their proud record at Rugby Park before scrambling a draw. Rangers were demolished 4-1 with Willie Culley netting three. Despite a penny increase in admission, there was a slight improvement at the gate. With a new Division One high of 69 goals and 43 points, the future seemed bright. The air of optimism was dashed against the rocks of sombre reality at the AGM where it was reported that messages of sympathy had been sent to the families of the late Sergeant McCurdie and Lance-Corporal Maxwell, two players killed in the Hell that was the Western front.

MATCH OF THE SEASON
April 21st 1917.
Celtic 0 Kilmarnock 2

Celtic were not only unbeaten as they went into this, the final match of the season. They hadn't lost at home since October 1915, nor away since November of the same year. All told, this would be their 63rd League game since defeat and their lead in the table stretched to double figures. Yet Killie had led 2-1 at Rugby Park with just four minutes left of the clock. They knew what to expect and weren't afraid of their awesome opponents.

A huge - for war-time - crowd of 18,000 saw Kilmarnock make a confident start. Slowly, Celtic threw off their lethargy and attacked the Killie goal. Blair, however, was equal to the task and defied everything flung at him. Utilising what the papers said was "sheer clever, calculating and sparkling footwork". Killie took a shock lead through Culley. Before the break, Smith had scored a second. The second period saw more of the same. Killie could easily have won by more but, even this 2-0, result was sensational. Hailed, even by the Glasgow press, as the "outstanding result of the season", Kilmarnock served notice that their days of making up the numbers were over. From now on they would be at the forefront of Scottish football, challenging for honours themselves. This was a performance and result which saw Kilmarnock enter the record books.

1917-18 DIVISION ONE

A memorable season. Kilmarnock ended their dismal home run against Ayr United (they had lost every Rugby Park match) with a 2-0 win which could have been greater. The first 'double' against the old enemy came with a 3-0 victory at Somerset, a game in which Killie had three 'goals' disallowed in the second-half.

Just as in the previous year, 69 goals were scored and 43 points amassed. But this was a better performance. Three clubs - Aberdeen, Dundee and Raith Rovers - had dropped out of the League and only Clydebank had been admitted, so there were four fewer fixtures to fulfil. There were just two defeats in the first three months and Killie were never out of the top placings, eventually finishing 3rd, their best position to date.

MATCH OF THE SEASON

October 13th 1917.
Celtic 2 Kilmarnock 3

Celtic were in their usual position. Top of the table. They had won all six League games before this clash. Killie, though, after their historic triumph at the end of the previous season, were also going strong. The match opened with Celtic forcing corners. Kilmarnock retaliated, Culley and McPhail both going close. The nearest thing to a goal in the first half-hour was a Celtic shot which rasped off the post. Then nine minutes from the interval, McPhail nipped in to put Killie ahead. Immediately, Celtic hit back. From just outside the penalty area, Celtic's McLean headed superbly into the net. The excitement wasn't over yet. In 41 minutes, Mattha' Smith took a pass from McPhail and shot Killie back in front. Half-time came with Killie defending their 2-1 lead.

The second period was barely a minute old when Killie sensationally scored again. Celtic failed to clear their lines, McPhail pounced and Kilmarnock led 3-1. Killie defended in depth after that, relying on the odd break to ease the pressure. It worked. Their defence was breached successfully just once. For the second time in their history and for the second year in succession, they had beaten Celtic at Parkhead. In their last ***seventy*** *League games Celtic had been mastered by only one side - Kilmarnock.*

Yet the true significance of this success could only be gauged by looking at the League table which read:-

	P	W	D	L	F	A	Pts
1.Kilmarnock	9	6	1	2	22	9	13
2.Celtic	7	6	0	1	17	7	12
3.Morton	9	5	2	2	17	11	12
4.Rangers	7	5	1	1	16	7	11

For the first time in their history, Kilmarnock were top of the Scottish League.

The Glasgow press hailed Kilmarnock. It was, averred in 'The Bulletin', a *"triumph of youth"*. The 'Daily Record' stated that Killie's *"position is no mystery"*. And the *Glasgow Herald* went as far as to hope that Killie would win the League!

Killie didn't win the League. They did stay at the top for almost two months, their defeat at Tynecastle on December 8th knocking them off the top spot. However, no-one now harboured any doubts about Killie's ability to live with the top clubs.

1918-19 DIVISION ONE

The end of the war brought great jubilation everywhere. It also meant that many potential footballers returned home. The glut of players meant that clubs could - and did - pick and choose. In total, thirty-eight players pulled a Killie jersey over their heads in 1918-19.

There were bound to be uneven results. Killie lost by a record 8-0 at Ibrox but three weeks later, they beat Rangers at Rugby Park. 4-1 successes were achieved at both Easter Road and Tynecastle. For the players too, fortunes varied. Malcolm McPhail played for Scotland, albeit in an 'unofficial' International against Ireland. His erstwhile team-mate, Walter Rutherford, struggling to recover from serious injury was awarded a benefit game against Celtic; some 3,000 paying tribute to a talented player who would never be quite the same again.

Peace brought a great celebration to Rugby Park. In April 1919 there was a 'Grand Victory Show' with Cart and Van Horse Parades, Pony Gallops, a Handicap Trot and a match between the first elevens of Killie and Ayr. 6,000 paid their eightpences (3p) to watch Killie win. But it wasn't a joyous time for everybody. The great Spanish Influenza epidemic swept across Europe. Killie's inside-forward, Sandy Goldie, died. As did Willie Culley's wife. Culley himself was fortunate to survive.

A curious affair took place on October 26th 1918 after the home game with Partick Thistle. A small invited group of Scottish football officials met to celebrate Kilmarnock's Jubilee, lending credence to the theory that the club had been founded in 1868. Club President, Charles Smith, outlined Killie's history, while Dan Gilmour unveiled a tablet bearing the names of past Presidents, announcing his intention to make Kilmarnock the *"Mecca of Ayrshire football"*. Queen's Park, Partick Thistle and Rangers all had guests present who responded with kind words for Killie. The evening was rounded off by John Ferguson, who had captained Vale of Leven in their great days and played for Scotland too. Now 70 years old, Ferguson (who worked in Kilmarnock), led the assembled party in a lusty rendition of *"Will Ye No' Come Back Again"*.

MATCH OF THE SEASON

September 7th 1918.
Kilmarnock 7 Hibernian 1

Culley put Killie ahead after just three minutes. A chance to increase the lead was squandered when Hamilton's penalty was saved. At the other end, Hibs also got a penalty and they made no mistake. Right from the kick-off, Killie attacked, the tragic Sandy Goldie heading them back into the lead. From a Turner cross, Goldie scored again. 3-1 at the break. Hibs came back at Killie early in the second-half. The storm was weathered though. Guthrie broke away to score Killie's fourth.

Hibs simply collapsed. Another of Turner's crosses floated into the box, this time Culley was the grateful recipient; tucking away the fifth. Culley, having an outstanding game, scored twice more to mark up four for himself and seven for Kilmarnock.

Chapter 4

TWIN PEAKS - A DOUBLE CUP TRIUMPH 1919-1929

1919-20 DIVISION ONE

The first full post-war season saw several changes at Rugby Park. John Greenway - the poacher turned gamekeeper - had returned from the Army and now became Club President. James MacDonald relinquished his position as Secretary in order to take over as Ayr United's Manager. Hugh Spence, formerly assistant to William Wilton at Rangers, became the new Secretary/Treasurer. Admission, which had been 6d (2½p) for twenty years and had risen during the War to 8d, was now One Shilling (5p). 25% of this went to the Government in Entertainment Tax. However, this meant that the price at the gate had doubled in four years. Yet there was a rise in attendances all over Britain. Those young men who had survived the carnage were determined to enjoy the pleasures of life once more.

Kilmarnock endured some awful results early on; in three successive matches they lost 1-7 to Rangers at Rugby Park, then 0-5 away to both Ayr and Rangers. After the game at Ayr, Jamie Mitchell was presented with that most typical of retirement gifts - a gold watch. Jamie had made his debut against Hearts in December 1900 (still technically the 19th Century) and played his last game for Killie at Firhill in September of this season. All in all, Mitchell had played in 410 League games and 23 Scottish Cup-ties. Considering that he spent two years away from Rugby Park after a bad injury, his record is even more impressive.

Sadness gripped the town with the news of the death of the great Bob Templeton. After watching Killie at home against St. Mirren, the legendary winger (who was known to have a week heart) dropped dead the following day. He was just 40 years old. At his funeral, the streets were lined with sympathisers.

Postponements were rare at Rugby Park but one of the oddest such cancellations took place this season. Dundee called off from playing because of a railway strike. It was the only Scottish League game affected even though the stoppage was a national dispute. Presumably the ominbus had yet to arrive on Tayside. More seriously, Killie's home defeat by Morton, in October, left them bottom of the League.

Things improved with the return of Culley and Mattha' Smith to the side after injury. With a promising new striker in J.R. Smith, the prospects for 1920 looked better.

In the early part of the new year, Killie played **seven** League games in succession at Rugby Park. They lost the first of these, to Celtic, but proceeded to win the other six, shooting up the table. It was in the Cup though, that Killie excelled. The first proper Scottish Cup competition since 1914 attracted huge crowds. After receiving a bye in the first round. Killie travelled to Alloa, where a record 10,000 gate saw them triumph 2-0. The next round brought Queen's Park to Rugby Park. A new record for the ground of 20,000 saw Killie score three times in the second-half after a dour first 45 minutes had ended one apiece. The Quarter-finals sent Killie on a tricky visit to Armadale. The local side were the giant-killers of the season, having beaten both Clyde and Hibernian at home and then eliminated Ayr at Somerset. Kilmarnock were made of sterner stuff though. Culley and J.R. Smith both scored in the first-half to kill the game off. An Armadale goal after the break made the score look tight but Killie were never in any real danger.

The Semi-Final clash with Morton was more difficult, Killie going two goals down early on. Nerves were showing and at half-time most commentators thought that Killie looked a beaten side despite having retrieved a goal. The second period was the complete opposite of the first. Tenacity and determination were the watchwords as Killie clawed their way back into the match, eventually running out worthy 3-2 winners. After 22 years, Kilmarnock were back in the Scottish Cup Final. Only one man on the staff was less than euphoric. For, as Jamie Mitchell pointed out, he had been just too young for Killie's first Final and now, he was just too old for their second.

MATCH OF THE SEASON
April 17th 1920.
Kilmarnock 3 Albion Rovers 2

Albion Rovers were Killie's opponents at Hampden in the Cup Final. Surprise Finalists maybe but deservedly there, for they had overcome Rangers after two replays in the Semi-Final. Those games had taken their toll and Rovers were missing a couple of first team regulars at Hampden. Killie were at full strength and with the conditions perfect, were the overwhelming favourites. The authorities reckoned that, with the two Finalists both being provincial clubs, a gate of 50,000 would be the most that would attend. Instead, Hampden witnessed a record Cup Final crowd. There were 95,000 inside the ground when the gates were closed, with several thousands more outside.

The huge Kilmarnock contingent present were alive with expectation of a comfortable victory. A roar as mighty as at any International match greeted Kilmarnock as 'keeper and captain, Tom Blair, led his team out first. Any illusions as to the difficulty of the task in hand were shattered after just five minutes play, as Rovers snatched a shock lead. Killie refused to let this setback affect them. Nine minutes later, Mattha' Smith passed to Willie Culley who levelled the scores. For a time it was end-to-end play but gradually Killie got the upper hand. The 'Evening Times' reported that Killie "piled up points" in this half. Football isn't Boxing though and the half ended with the sides still level at 1-1.

The second period saw Rovers resort to their 'kick and rush' style as Killie's forwards asserted their authority on the match with some clever play. Mattha' Smith again was the provider as Mattha' Shortt put Killie ahead two minutes after the restart. Three minutes later and against the run of play, Rovers equalised. Killie's superiority had to find a way through and, with half an hour remaining, J.R. Smith sent a superb shot into the net to put Killie 3-2 ahead. Rovers tried, but failed, to get back into the match and when the final whistle sounded, it was Killie who were on the attack, seeking to improve their lead. The end of the game saw jubilation amonst the Ayrshire crowd. Of all the entrants in that initial Scottish Cup in 1873 who were still playing football, Kilmarnock were the only ones not to have their names engraved on the trophy. Until now.

The club arrived back in the town at 8.30 on Saturday evening to scenes of unrestrained celebration. The crowd - said to be bigger than on Armistice Day - cheered the players on a procession which saw them parade through the streets to the Town Hall for a civic reception followed by a party in the George Hotel. It was here that Jamie Mitchell lauded them. Present too, were those heroes of the 1898 side, 'Bummer' Campbell and 'Baker' Brown. Sportingly, they recognised the achievement of the current team and hailed them as better than the side they had played in. The celebrations were, however, tinged with sadness. Archie Mackie, a splendid servant, had been badly injured in the Cup-tie at Alloa and had missed out on a richly deserved chance to play in the Final. Sandy Higgins, who also played only in the Alloa match, had worse tidings for his team-mates. His father, also Sandy, that superb player of the 1880's and the first Kilmarnock player to play for Scotland, had died on the very morning of the Final.

The 1920 Final spawned one of Scottish football's longest-runing 'trick' questions. The one about which Cup Final saw both teams play a man short. The answer being of course that Mattha' Shortt was Killie's centre-half and John Short was the Albion Rovers 'keeper. But, in the spate of matches Killie had to play after the Final, they did indeed play a man short. Only ten players took the field against Morton at Cappielow. Despite this, Killie held the Greenock team for 70 minutes before eventually being over-run, losing 4-0. With 42 Divison One games, the season then was as crowded as it is now. Killie played seven League games in April, in addition to the Cup Final, and ended the campaign on May 1st with another win over Albion Rovers, this time at Coatbridge.

The Cup success helped produce a profit for the season of £860-11-2d. Drawings at home games amounted to £7757-4-11d. and season tickets added another £560 to the coffers. It was an auspicious moment for Charles Smith to retire from the Board. After more than a quarter of a century's service as a player, Secretary, Treasurer and Chairman, there could be no finer time to bow out. That famous old player, Jocky Johnstone, tried, unsuccessfully, to gain election to the Board this year.

Kilmarnock's success drew praise from all corners of the football world. At Ayr United's AGM, their Chairman was unstinting in his congratulations to Killie. He did note though, that if Kilmarnock could win the Scottish Cup, then so could Ayr United. *"At some future date"*. He was astute enough not to specify how far into the future he was referring to. More than seventy years later, Ayr still await that promised success, their lack of concrete triumphs providing Kilmarnock supporters with ample opportunity to remind Ayr fans that their team has never really won anything of note and forecasting, in terms too indelicate to print here, that they had little hope of success *"at some future date"*.

1920-21 DIVISION ONE

The euphoria generated by the Cup success saw attendances improve dramatically this year. Five figure crowds turned out for the games with Rangers, Celtic, St. Mirren, Motherwell and Ayr. Reserve games were also well attended. The 4,000 who watched the second eleven play Forfar not being untypical. Only the proliferation of benefit matches seemed unattractive to the fans. There were just too many of these largely non-competitive affairs. Mitchell had received £150 from his benefit but Willie Culley picked up only £100 from his, and Mattha' Shortt would get about the same amount in early January 1921.

Despite the improved financial situation, Killie still struggled to hold on to their top players. Right-back Tom Hamilton was sold to Preston during the season and Killie's offer to J.R. Smith couldn't even match that of Cowdenbeath, so the prolific striker parted company with the club at the end of the season. Two years later, Smith scored the second goal in the first Wembley Cup Final, making him the first player to score in Finals both there and at Hampden.

There must have been money available. Entertainment tax to the tune of £2624-3-8d. was handed over to the Exchequer, meaning that Killie must have topped £10,000 in gate revenue for the first time. Yet the club was actually turning fans away! Worried about rowdyism from visiting fans, Kilmarnock took the matter up with the SFA. They announced their intention to deny entry to Rugby Park to any supporter - home or away - carrying flags or using 'ricketties'. There would have been precious few Killie fans flaunting either at the away game at Cappielow where Morton won 9-2, the largest number of goals ever conceded by a Kilmarnock side in a League match. There were a couple of 5-0 home wins - over Dundee and Hamilton - to compensate, but after 1920's champagne, this season was small beer indeed.

MATCH OF THE SEASON

February 5th 1921.
Kilmarnock 1 Aberdeen 2

The holders had started their defence of the Cup with a win at Arbroath and a 12,000 crowd gathered at Rugby Park to see this Second Round tie. Killie started strongly yet it was the Dons who scored first. Hamilton delayed his clearance and the Aberdeen inside-right, Connon, dispossessed him and scored. Hamilton saved his blushes by converting a penalty before the break. Aberdeen were the better side in the second-half but Killie looked like holding out for a replay until two minutes from time the Dons' No.9, McDonald, beat the offside trap to score the winner. Kilmarnock's reign as Cup holders was over.

1921-22 DIVISION ONE

Automatic promotion and relegation was introduced this season, three teams going down. Although never out of the lower half of the table, Killie managed to keep just above the bottom three places. They showed occasional flashes of form, continuing to cause Celtic trouble. When Killie won 4-3 at

Rugby Park in November 1921, it was the first time for six years that a Celtic side had lost as many goals. The same month saw a benefit game of a different kind take place. The Provost's Fund for the Unemployed receiving the takings from an afternoon's event at Rugby Park. Track and field events such as pole vaulting and a ½ mile race were among the attractions, chief of which was a football match between two teams of 'old-timers'. A Hurlford XI, sprinkled with ex-English League players, beat a Killie side 3-2. The Kilmarnock team was:-
J.Baillie, J.Orr, R.Brown, D.McPherson, G.Anderson, J.Johnstone, A.Armour, R.Richmond, J.Campbell, H.Wilson and A.Smith (ex-Rangers). Killie's two goals were scored by the indefatigable 'Bummer' who was jokingly asked if he would turn out for the Killie first team. He said no, he was considering a better offer from an English First Division club! Even the youngest present that day will be in their late seventies by now but it is not inconceivable that there are still people alive today who saw that match and thus constitute a link with those players from the 19th Century.

Unemployment was biting hard and gates were affected. Just 2,000 saw Mattha' Smith's benefit game against Ayr in January 1922. The same figure attended a Saturday afternoon League game against Hamilton. The post-war boom was over and dissatisfaction returned to Killie's AGM, two directors failing to be re-elected. Ironically, one of them was John Greenway. The one-time arch-critic found himself the victim of the same sort of dissent he himself had revelled in almost twenty years earlier.

MATCH OF THE SEASON
January 28th 1922.
Inverness Caledonian 1 Kilmarnock 5

This First Round Scottish Cup tie was the furthest that a Kilmarnock side had travelled in the competition. For 25 minutes, the gutsy Highlanders held out against a Killie team who had a strong wind in their favour. Then, Killie took control. Gray's goal was followed by the luxury of a penalty miss but fine combination play saw Scott put Killie two up at the break. Watson scored just after the interval and Culley had added a fourth before Caley pulled one back. Culley got Killie's fifth, to cap what the 'Evening Times' called an "excellent display from start to finish". But for the heroics of Bowden in the Caley goal, this could have been a record win for Killie. Apart from their 'keeper, the Inverness side were best served by the almost-appropriately named Dr. Finlayson.

There was to be no more Cup glory this year, however. A big crowd turned out to see St. Mirren comprehensively win at Rugby Park in Round Two.

1922-23 DIVISION ONE

Scandal gripped Rugby Park. First, there was the case of John Goldie, Killie's centre-half. He had been involved in bribery during a spell playing in England. John would see this season out before the cumbersome machinery of the FA caught up with him. Before the start of the following year, he would be suspended sine die. Of much more immediate consequence, was the Willie Culley affair.

Kilmarnock were knocked out of the Cup, in a replay, by Division Two club, East Fife and, commenting on Culley's performance at Methil, the *Standard* noted that he was *"in one of his lackadaisical moods and appeared not to care whether his team won or lost"*. The rumour machine worked overtime. Three players, Culley, Ramsay and Marshall were supposed not to have tried to win the game. Marshall was immediately exonerated, accused of nothing worse than playing poorly, but not deliberately so. Still, he never played for Killie again. Ramsay was a more difficult case. The Board decided to investiagate further after he appeared before them. Within six weeks he was back in the first team but was transferred a year later. (He would return as a player to Rugby Park after a couple of years). The Board's wrath was reserved for Culley.

He was found quilty of breaching Clause 3 of his contract which stated *"every member of the team shall use his utmost endeavour to win"*, and suspended sine die. The accusation was harsh, the verdict damning and the sentence astonishing. This was the man who had scored more goals for Kilmarnock than any other player. With over 300 appearances, he was the longest serving player at the club. Yet the 'inside' view from Rugby Park was that, drastic though the punishment was, it fitted the crime. The *Standard* noted how sad it was that such a *"talented, popular servant for 12 years should end his career that way"*.

Fortunately, a compromise was arrived at and Culley was sold to Clyde. It was the worst moment of a traumatic season. Killie had lost 6-0 at home to Motherwell and, a fortnight later, saw five goals go past them in the second half at Aberdeen. Killie were thankful to discover in winger, Walter Jackson, a player who revelled in being switched to centre-forward. Jackson hit four in the 1st Round Cup game with Broxburn and did the same in a 7-0 win over Albion Rovers. But not even his prodigious feats could have saved Killie at Alloa where they were losing 5-2 with eight minutes left, when fog came down and forced an abandonment.

Amazingly, the Scottish League ordered the entire ninety mintues to be played again and this time, Killie returned with a 3-3 draw.

Gates dropped below the £10,000 mark and a worrying loss of over £900 was recorded. The future looked uncertain, at best.

MATCH OF THE SEASON
February 2nd 1923.
Kilmarnock 4 Celtic 3

In the hour of their great adversity, Kilmarnock pulled off one of their finest-ever victories. This match took place just three days after the defeat at Methil. Killie had an early penalty appeal turned down and followed up with two wild shots nowhere near the goal. When the legendary Jimmy McGrory left Killie 'keeper, John Morton, floundering in the mud after ten minutes play, to put Celts ahead, another disaster seemed on the cards. Killie confounded, not only all their critics, but most of their supporters as well. Two minutes after McGrory had scored, debut boy Rattray took a cross from Killie's Irish International winger, Lyner, and hit it first time past Charlie Shaw in the Celtic goal. The Celtic defence looked wobbly, unable to cope with this surprise reversal.

In 20 minutes, Jackson shot Killie into the lead. It was John Morton's turn to come under pressure and he made three fine saves in under ten minutes before conceding the equaliser. Half-time arrived with the score 2-2.

Killie attacked right after the break. Lyner's shot was tipped over the bar by Shaw. From the corner, Jackson headed narrowly over. Lyner, having a superb game, hit the bar, McCulloch headed in the rebound to make it 3-2 with just five minutes of the half gone. Five minutes later and John Morton mishit a clearance, turning the ball into his own net. 3-3. Then, Mattha' Smith took a pass from McCulloch and hit a fine shot past Shaw. 4-3. Morton made up for his error by making several fine saves. In defence, Dunlop was outstanding and of the forwards, Lyner was simply brilliant. Killie held out for a most remarkable - and totally unlikely - victory. This was the second year in succession that they had beaten Celtic 4-3 at Rugby Park and, coupled with an earlier win at Parkhead, it meant that this scandal-ridden, supposedly dejected Kilmarnock side had just accomplished the 'double' over the mighty Celtic for the very first time.

1923-24 DIVISION ONE

Malcolm McPhail played his last few matches this season, leaving only Davie Gibson and Mattha' Smith from the 1920 Cup-winning side still active at Rugby Park. The year was spent on the fringe of the relegation struggle, just two wins coming from the last twelve games. Not surprisingly, crowds slumped. 17,000 turned out at the opening match to welcome Queen's Park back into Division One but only 1,000 watched the midweek game with Morton, four days after Killie's Scottish Cup exit. There were some successes on the playing front. The accomplished veteran, Bobby Brown, from Morton, added style to Killie's play. Centre-forward Alex Gray had a good year, briefly banishing memories of Culley; and in Jock McEwan, nicknamed 'Tarzan' by the fans, Killie unearthed an excellent left-half who would go on to serve the club with distinction for a dozen years. Surprisingly, for a team in Killie's position, the club made a handsome profit of over £1,000.

Andrew Herron, who kept goal expertly in the early 1920's.

MATCH OF THE SEASON
February 9th 1924.
Ayr United 1 Kilmarnock 0

Killie had played spectacularly well to eliminate Celtic in their opening Scottish Cup-tie. Now they travelled the well-worn path to Somerset Park to meet local rivals, Ayr United in the Second Round. The two League games between the clubs had both been drawn and their League positions were similar so another tight match was expected. This was also the first 'true' Cup derby match. Killie had played teams from Ayr in the competition before, even the ancestors of the present Ayr club, but they and United had never met.

In a disappointing game, Ayr 'scored' in the first half, only to see the 'goal' disallowed. Defences were well on top and according to a contemporary report, fouls were numerous. What little skill was on show came from Kilmarnock who were desperately unlucky not to score, hitting the bar twice. A replay looked on the cards until five minutes from time, when Ayr's Harry Cunningham fired in an unstoppable shot from twenty yards out. The 'Evening Times' said that Killie had enjoyed cruel luck and a draw would have been a fair result in a match which had "too much vigorous kicking with little purpose behind it". The 'Standard' was straight to the point: "AYR'S LUCKY VICTORY" was their headline.

Ayr eventually lost after a four match marathon to this year's Cup Winners, Airdrie, in the Quarter-Finals. It was to be their first - and last - Cup win over Kilmarnock. Four times since then the two teams have clashed, Killie winning the lot. This defeat even did Killie a big favour. For it brought Harry Cunningham to Rugby Park's notice. And Harry - 'Peerie' as he became known - would more than make up for the day he put Killie out of the Cup.

1924-25 DIVISION ONE

The flirtation with relegation grew more serious this season. By December 13th, Kilmarnock were second bottom of the table. The League was so tight that, even in their perilous position, they were only four points away from 5th place. At this stage of the season, it was perm any two from sixteen for the drop. It was an exciting time for the youngsters coming to the fore, chief among these being Joe Nibloe, who would go on to become Killie's most-capped player.

Undeterred by their League placing, Killie put together a decent Cup run. Non-League Arbroath Athletic were disposed of easily, then Hearts were beaten in a rousing Rugby Park tie. The next visitors to Rugby Park were Dykehead, of the short-lived Third Division. They held Killie to 0-0 at half-time before losing five goals after the break. Dykehead tried to protest their way into the last eight, claiming that Killie's right-half, Willis, had been guilty of a close season infringement. The days of protest victories in the Cup were long over and Dykehead withdrew before the SFA considered their appeal.

Killie's fourth successive home draw in the Cup brought Rangers to Rugby Park. In a tremendous game, Kilmarnock took the lead and held it until mid-way through the second half.

Rangers' winner, fifteen minutes from the end, came from former Killie hero, Andy Cunningham. A grand total of 31,502 watched this match - a new Rugby Park record. The Cup exit focused attention on the League struggle where Killie still needed to clamber to safety. Two wins in the last two matches - over Celtic and St. Johnstone brought relief to Kilmarnock. The table was still as close as at Christmas. Those two wins propelled Killie up from second bottom (19th) to 12th place, an apparently respectable slot.

There was a flourishing end to the season when Killie travelled to play Everton in a match played under the forthcoming new offside rule, winning 3-2 in front of 15,000 at Goodison. The club made a profit of over £700 and took a record £12,000 plus in receipts but, after a lull of some years, the thorny question of appointing a Manager was raised again at the AGM. This time, the shareholders would not be fobbed off and action was promised by the Board.

MATCH OF THE SEASON
January 1st 1925.
Kilmarnock 4 Ayr United 1

It was a windswept and rain-soaked Rugby Park which saw Ayr United enter as the first foots of 1925 - the first Ayrshire derby to be played on a New Year's Day. Both sides were deep in the relegation zone and, as the match kicked off at 1.55 p.m., a dour contest was expected. Maybe it was even tougher than the team anticipated as, according to the 'Evening Times', Ayr escaped losing an early goal, only because their 'keeper "was interfered with"!

In desperation, Ayr fired in shots on goal from up to 40 yards out, but with no effect. It was Killie's Bobby Brown who orchestrated play, his pass to Lindsay resulting in a cross which Gray converted in fifteen minutes. On the half-hour mark, Brown's own shot was stopped by Ayr's 'keeper but he couldn't hold on to it and the ball came off his shoulder into the net to put Killie 2-0 up. Ayr put on the pressure up to the interval but couldn't find a way through the Kilmarnock rearguard. In the second half, Ayr now had to play against the gale and Killie were well on top. After 65 minutes, Brown's free-kick found Dunlop's head and Killie were three up. Harry Cunningham briefly rallied Ayr with a goal but Alex Gray scored a fourth for Killie to round off an important and - in the end -easy victory. Not only was this ample revenge for the previous year's Cup defeat, it moved Killie up to 12th and pushed Ayr to bottom of the table.

At the end of the season, Ayr United were relegated, having lost both Ayrshire derbies. Had they taken just one point from the four on offer, they would have survived. Had they won both games then Killie, not Ayr, would have gone down. Some were sad at the demise of the old foe, it would be two good gates less in the season ahead. *"Aye, and four easy points as well"*, more than one Killie fan commented. If there was genuine sorrow in Kilmarnock, then it was more likely to be on account of the news of the death of the last surviving grand-daughter of Robert Burns - representing the passing of an era - than over the tribulations.

Of the 'Honest Men' - as the Bard once famously described the citizenry of Ayr.

1925-26 DIVISION ONE

The new offside law - requiring a player to have only two defenders in front of him to be onside as opposed to three previously - meant an upsurge in goalscoring; Killie being no exception. They notched up a new record 79 League goals in what was their best season for five years. New faces emerging this season included Harry 'Peerie' Cunningham, rescued from playing Second Division football with Ayr. Cunningham scored on his debut against Morton, coming into a team which had just lost 6-1 at Falkirk. Indeed, Falkirk also won at Rugby Park this season. It would be the last time for nearly **sixty** years that they would do so.

Another making his first appearances this year was Sam Clemie. The 'keeper put in some outstanding performances, none more so than at Parkhead, where he single-handedly earned Killie a 0-0 draw. Killie took three points off Celtic in the League but were destroyed 5-0 at Rugby Park in the Cup, a game which brought another huge crowd. Some estimates reckoned that close on 40,000 people attended that day but the official figure was given as 24,174. Clemie - not in goal for the Cup-tie - was making people take note of his ability, and his name, for, in this first season, many reporters persisted in referring to him as *Climie*. Another player making headlines this year was Jimmy Weir. His 26 League goals constituting a new record. The all-round improvement was reflected in another profitable season, the club finishing almost £1,000 to the good and a long-standing bone of contention appeared to be over when the AGM heard that Hugh Spence had been appointed Manager.

MATCH OF THE SEASON
September 22nd 1925.
Hibernian 8 Kilmarnock 0

Along with similar results at Ibrox and Parkhead, this is Killie's heaviest losing margin in a League game. In an evenly fought opening half, Killie were unlucky to find themselves two down at the change-over. Hibs' third goal looked like going over the bar when a gust of wind blew the ball underneath. Two minutes later, Hibs outside-left, Walker, scored a cracking solo goal then had another chalked off before a defensive lapse let in number five. At this point Killie attempted their only shot of the half - with no success. Hibs scored a further three times in the last twenty minutes.

The papers reported that, despite the scoreline, Killie had been unlucky and that everything Hibs attempted came off. That was the Rugby Park assessment too, just two changes being made for the next match.

1926-27 DIVISION ONE

In a depressing year, Kilmarnock were ravaged by injuries to leading players and won only four of the first 22 League games. The aftermath of the General Strike and the continuing Miners strike also took a heavy toll on crowd figures. The situation improved dramatically in the New Year. New players like Jim Thomson and John Murphy, aided by the returning prodigal, Ramsay, helped lift the side. 'Peerie' Cunningham hit a purple patch, scoring eleven goals in seven matches. With just two defeats in thirteen games since the turn of the year, survival was assured and the team eased up in the last few contests. The accumulated problems showed up in the balance sheet though, there being a loss of close on £1,200 over the year. The club had financed the new signings with the help of a £5,000 overdraft - a lot of money at the time. It was, however, worth it, the Directors informed the AGM. The new players had achieved the task required of them; to keep Kilmarnock in the top Division.

MATCH OF THE SEASON
August 14th 1926.
Kilmarnock 2 Celtic 3

The troubles looming ahead were unthought of when Killie opened the new season with a fixture against the League Champions. Rugby Park had a new wall, turnstiles and gates and 20,000 fans passed through to watch Killie start promisingly with Mattha' Smith in the unusual role of outside-right. Smith hit a belting shot which was fisted clear, only for McEwan to net the rebound. Four minutes into the season and Killie were a goal ahead. Celtic equalised after fifteen minutes play but, undaunted, Killie kept up the pressure. Nothing came of it. Then Jimmy McGrory stepped in. For the first time in the game, he got the better of Killie's centre-half, Jake Dunlop. Once was all McGrory needed. He scored to give Celtic a 2-1 lead.

20 minutes into the second half and disaster struck. Mattha' Smith collided with Celtic left-back, Hilley, and was carted off the pitch with a broken leg. It would be over a year before he graced Rugby Park again. Taking advantage of Smith's absence, Celtic scored a third. With ten minutes remaining, Cunningham scored to give Killie renewed hope. Alas, the injury-prone Jake Dunlop also had to leave the field shortly after this. Try as they might, nine-man Kilmarnock couldn't equalise. They lost, but in circumstances which had the Glasgow press singing their praises.

1927-28 DIVISION ONE

A much-improved performance by Killie, albeit not without some occasional disasters along the way. There was an inexplicable 7-1 home defeat by St. Johnstone, for instance. Before that the side lost 6-0 and 7-0 in successive weeks away to Falkirk and Dundee. Those defeats prompted the return of Clemie into goal. Mattha' Smith also made his long-awaited comeback and scored against Airdrie on his re-appearance. The main talking point of this season though, was 'Peerie' Cunningham, who rattled in 34 goals, a new record. For a shot time there were two Harry Cunninghams in the team, the other being a short-term loan signing from Celtic.

Among the better games were victories at Tynecastle and Pittodrie, which, along with Celtic Park, were visited in the opening month. The fixture list was every bit as demanding in the 1920's as it is now. Another epic was the series of meetings with Queen's Park, three clashes in seven days, at the end of which, Killie had been removed from the Cup and lost in the League as well. More than 20,000 watched an incredible 4-4 draw in the Cup-tie at Rugby Park. Several thousand turned out to watch a very special reserve fixture. 'Bummer' Campbell was suffering ill-health, so the Club agreed to donate the proceeds of the game with Rangers reserves on November 26th, to their old stalwart. More than £140 was raised as a result. The club still made a loss, although the figure this year was a more respectable £332-9-2. One sad event was the decision of the Supporters Club to disband on account of what was described as *"unpleasantness"* from the Board.

MATCH OF THE SEASON
December 24th 1927.
Kilmarnock 5 Hearts 0

Although Cunningham scored exactly half Killie's League goals, others could get in on the act as this match showed. Killie swamped the Hearts defence from the kick-off, 'Peerie' himself scoring in four minutes. Ten minutes later, Ramsay scored with a blistering shot from 30 yards and in 18 minutes, Smith hit number three. Clemie destroyed any hopes of a Hearts fightback with one of his speciality penalty saves early in the second half. Midway through this period, Morton, one of the stars of the game, grabbed Killie's fourth and, with seven minutes left, Murphy got the fifth. Five different players had scored and Hearts - who had been going strongly - saw their Championship hopes, not for the last time, extinguished by Kilmarnock.

1928-29 DIVISION ONE

High scoring was the main feature of the League campaign. An enthralling match at Love Street ended with Killie losing 5-4. Incredibly, press reports of this match heavily criticised both sides for their *"poor finishing"*. Mattha' Smith hit four at home to Queen's Park, a match in which Killie were 5-0 up after 30 minutes, eventually winning 7-4. Mattha' was awarded his second benefit match this season but only 2,000 turned up to watch Killie play a strong Rangers XI, proving that the non-competitive nature of such games were a serious turn-off for the fans. These games now went into abeyance for some time, something which would create friction between Kilmarnock and some of their best servants over the next decade.

The two fixtures with Raith Rovers bagged the largest aggregate of goals, sixteen in all, eight in each game. Killie won 7-1 at home but, at Starks Park, surrendered a three goal interval lead, losing 5-3. Other notable events included the end of Joe Nibloe's long run of consecutive League games. Since taking the field against Dundee United on October 24th 1925, Joe had played in all 132 Leauge matches up to and including the away game to Third Lanark on February 9th 1929. He had also taken part in all ten Scottish Cup ties over the same period and played in an eleventh the week after the Thirds game, giving him a grand total of 143 consecutive competitive appearances. Joe's record could have been even better if he had not been as good a player as he was. For the reason he missed the game on February 23rd against St. Johnstone was that he travelled with the Scotland team to Belfast. He didn't play that day but made his international debut two months later in a 1-0 win over England at Hampden. Joe would go on to become Killie's most capped player with 11 appearances for his country.

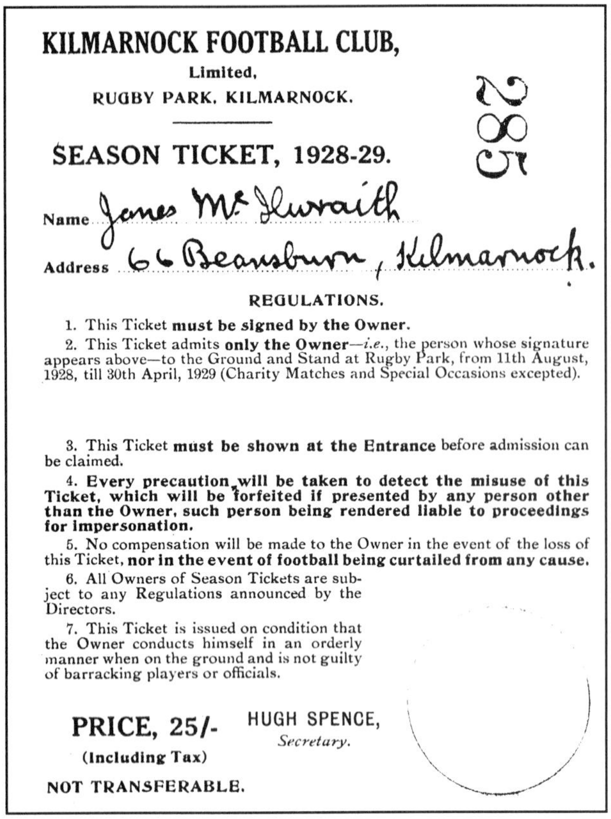

KILMARNOCK FOOTBALL CLUB,
Limited,
RUGBY PARK, KILMARNOCK.

285

SEASON TICKET, 1928-29.

Name James McIlwraith

Address 66 Beansburn, Kilmarnock.

REGULATIONS.

1. This Ticket **must be signed by the Owner.**
2. This Ticket admits **only the Owner**—*i.e.*, the person whose signature appears above—to the Ground and Stand at Rugby Park, from 11th August, 1928, till 30th April, 1929 (Charity Matches and Special Occasions excepted).
3. This Ticket **must be shown at the Entrance** before admission can be claimed.
4. **Every precaution will be taken to detect the misuse of this Ticket, which will be forfeited if presented by any person other than the Owner, such person being rendered liable to proceedings for impersonation.**
5. No compensation will be made to the Owner in the event of the loss of this Ticket, **nor in the event of football being curtailed from any cause.**
6. All Owners of Season Tickets are subject to any Regulations announced by the Directors.
7. This Ticket is issued on condition that the Owner conducts himself in an orderly manner when on the ground and is not guilty of barracking players or officials.

PRICE, 25/- (Including Tax)

HUGH SPENCE, *Secretary.*

NOT TRANSFERABLE.

Season ticket for 1928/29 season.
Ticket-holders were not allowed to barrack players or officials upon pain of removal of their ticket. In the cup-winning year of 1929 there wasn't much booing of the Rugby Park side.

The League season ended with the previous highest total of 79 goals being equalled as Killie settled for a reasonable 10th place. A new record attendance - for a League match - had been set at the game with Rangers on December 29th 1928, when approximately 30,000 turned up. That helped push total gate takings up to a new high of £14,320-4-2d. with profits of £2,694-9-5d.. The Rangers game apart, most of this money had been made from the Scottish Cup.

The draw for the Cup was kind to Killie - in the early stages at least. Glasgow University visited Rugby Park and were walloped 8-1. Bo'ness provided sterner opposition in the next round but they too were beaten, 3-2 at Rugby Park. Round Three saw Killie travel to Coatbridge where a dourly defensive Albion Rovers were eliminated 1-0. The Quarter-Finals entailed a visit to Kirkcaldy. Raith Rovers were the first Division One opposition Killie had met, but their card had been marked for relegation since early in the season. Nevertheless, they put up a strong fight, particularly in the latter period of the game, before Killie emerged triumphant by 3-2.

Ibrox was the venue for the Semi-Final against Celtic where, against the odds, Jimmy Weir in his only Cup outing of the year, gave Killie a first-half lead which they tenaciously clung on to, winning by that solitary goal. Killie were back in the Final. Now all they had to do was to beat Rangers.

MATCH OF THE SEASON
April 6th 1929.
Kilmarnock 2 Rangers 0

*Rangers were the Scottish Cup holders - having ended a 25 year "hoodoo" with their 1928 victory. They were about to receive the Scottish League Championship for the third year in succession. They were a massive **sixteen** points clear of Celtic in 2nd place in the table. In short, they were considered unbeatable. Certainly unbeatable by Kilmarnock. Killie were a mid-table team who had enjoyed the luck of the draw, turning in one good performance to beat Celtic and deprive the Final of its 'glamour'.*

Consider the players: for Rangers there were such names as Duggie Gray at right-back, then 24 but so fit and strong that he would turn out for the first team at the age of 40. There were Buchanan and Craig, international wing-halves, with the great Davie Meiklejohn, the outstanding Scottish pivot of the inter-war years, in the middle of defence. A strong centre-forward in Fleming, with the best inside-forwards in the game alongside him - Tommy Muirhead and Bob McPhail, younger brother of Killie's 1920's hero, Malcolm. On the wings were Archibald, yet another international and Alan Morton, nearly 36 but still the peerless "Wee Blue Devil", the greatest left-winger of his - and some would claim any - era. Of the eleven wearing Rangers shirts, just one, left-back R. Hamilton, would never wear a Scotland jersey.

Contrast that with Kilmarnock. Not a single Cap amongst them (Nibloe's debut was a week after the Final). Not only that but they were an injury-ridden outfit too. Not so much in defence, Clemie, Robertson, Nibloe, Morton and McEwan were all regulars. The exception here was McLaren, signed on loan from Aberdeen to replace the luckless Dunlop who, yet again, was out of action. It was in attack that Killie were considered to be weak. The right-wing pairing of Connell and Smith was the usual one (Mattha', of course, being the sole survivor of the 1920 side). Cunningham, at centre-forward, was as powerful, if not so prolific, as ever. But on the left, Killie were devastated. The normal pairing of Ramsay and Paterson was unavailable. Ramsay out through injury, Paterson by illness. In their places came Jimmy Williamson and John Aitken. Williamson was a natural inside-right moved in desperation to the left. He had played in just ten League games over two seasons in addition to the Cup Semi-Finals. Aitken was considered to be a veteran at 31. He had a varied, if undistinguished, career behind him when he joined Killie in late 1928. He had only five outings in a Kilmarnock strip before the Final and this was his first Cup appearance for the club. How could this team of no-hopers, containing three players with less than twenty appearances between them for the side, hope to beat an outfit described as the 'best in Britain'? It was billed as a contest between a team which cost £800 and one assembled at a huge (for the time) cost of £10,000.

The first sign that 'unbeatable' Rangers might be falliable after all, came when they lost a Leauge game, at Hamilton, ten days before the Final. It had been more than a year since they had tasted defeat and this reverse, even if it didn't affect them, certainly gave Killie confidence as the Final approached. On the morning of April 6th, Ayrshire experienced an Exodus, as trains, buses and cars ferried thousands to Glasgow. The good wishes of the heroes of 1920, Blair, Shortt and Gibson, arrived via cable from the USA where they all now played. Hampden was packed, 114,708 waiting in anticipation, as Mattha' Smith led Kilmarnock out to do battle with their mighty foes.....

Killie were forced to play against a strong breeze and blinding sunshine and were soon forced onto the defensive as Rangers pitched camp around the Kilmarnock penalty area. With sixteen minutes gone, just as Killie thought that they had weathered the Ibrox storm, Hugh Morton was adjudged to have brought down Buchanan. Referee Tom Dougray consulted both linesmen before pointing to the spot. Penalty. Tully Craig stepped up to deliver a blistering shot into the top left corner of the net but the roars in the throats of the Rangers supporters lay stillborn as Sam Clemie leapt, salmon-like, into the air and returned to earth with the ball safely in his arms. Killie's ace penalty-saver had proved himself in the hardest arena of them all. If he saved another 100 penalties in his career, none would be as important as this.

Rangers resolve was undaunted by the save. From a corner, McPhail headed narrowly over the bar. Then, the light blues appealed for another penalty, this time against Nibloe. Dougray waved play on. Clemie, called into action again, fisted a shot away. The ball fell to the unmarked McPhail who, with the goal at his mercy, missed by a foot. The half-time whistle saved Killie from further punishment. They were relieved to be still on level terms. Rangers restarted strongly but now conditions were in Killie's favour and, at last, the Ayrshire team took the initiative. Connell fired in a shot which Tom Hamilton, in the Rangers goal, could only try to kick clear.

He mishit totally, the ball never reached above knee-high, as it sliced to the left where Aitken stood. The winger hit it first-time, right into the back of the net. 48 minutes played and Killie were 1-0 ahead. Connell, again, tried a shot. This time he hit the post. Mattha' Smith also narrowly missed scoring. With twelve minutes to go, Connell once more, instigated proceedings, sending a pass to Williamson which the youngster despatched with aplomb, to put Killie two up. In the dying moments of the game, Buchanan's frustration with the way things had gone, boiled over, as he received his marching orders from Tom Dougray. He was the first player to be sent off in a Scottish Cup Final. The whistle blew, to be met with scenes of Ayrshire ecstasy. The Cup was again winging its way to Kilmarnock, and deservedly so. As the 'Evening Times' reported, "Superior tactics beat the Rangers".

The homecoming was tremendous. People formed a *"human avenue"*, said the *Standard*, from Beansburn to Portland Street. At the Grand Hall there were 2,000 inside and many times that number outside as the civic dignitaries tried to make themselves heard. The Provost was howled down by cries of *"Good old Sam. Give us the man who saved the penalty"*, and *"Gie's wee Mattha'"*. The only one of the civic party who was heard in silence was Ex-Provost Wilson. He had played in the Killie side which had met Renton in that very first Scottish Cup tie in 1873. At length, the supporters got their way and Sam Clemie addressed them. In words, which are often misquoted, but which retain their potency today, he made what must be the best, and the shortest, speech ever heard in the town. *"I can save penalty kicks but I canna mak' a speech"*. With that, he sat down as the celebrations continued long into the night. Heroes all, but in particular, Clemie, Mattha' Smith, the ingenious Connell and the goalscorers, Aitken and Williamson. The two reserves had won the Cup for Kilmarnock.

114,708 spectators look on as Kilmarnock captain Mattha' Smith, Referee Tom Dougray and Rangers skipper Tommy Muirhead get the 1929 Scottish Cup Final under way.

Chapter 5
MORE FINAL FLINGS 1929 - 1939

Following their 1929 Scottish Cup win, Kilmarnock made a good start to the following League campaign. Although the Rangers defence are comfortable on this occasion, Killie won the Rugby Park game 1-0 in September, which kept them near the top of the table.

1929-30 DIVISION ONE

Cup success brought improved League form as Killie made an excellent start. They lost just three of the first fourteen League games and it was the fifteenth match before they failed to score. Like the previous year, goalscoring feats were numerous. Jimmy Weir hit six in the 11-1 slaughter of Paisley Academicals in the Cup but there was to be no repeat of the glory of 1929, Killie losing at Hamilton in Round 2.

Bobby McGowan, a loan signing from Rangers, scored five in a 7-2 win over Morton - the first Killie player to do so in a League match. He also hit four in a 7-1 win against Airdrie, his season's record standing at 18 goals in 15 appearances. Overall though, inconsistency let the team down. At one stage there was press speculation that Killie might succeed where Airdrie and Motherwell had narrowly failed, and smash the 25 years old 'Old Firm' monopoly on the Championship. But the team lost too many games they should have won, like going down 6-4 at Tannadice after being 4-2 up at half-time. Even crazier was the match at Pittodrie where Killie recovered from a 2-0 interval deficit by scoring three times in five minutes, only to lose 4-3.

There were moments of sadness this season. John Ferguson, that grand old stalwart of the early Vale of Leven sides, who had long been associated with Killie, died at the age of 82. It was said that this remarkable man had never even seen a football until he was 25.

Tragedy struck the town of Paisley with the death of scores of children in a cinema fire on Hogmanay. Despite appeals to the League for cancellation, the Ne'erday fixture at Love Street was ordered to be played. It took place in an atmosphere of unreality, the grimmest game Killie have ever taken part in.

The flat end to a season of high hopes was reflected at the gate, takings were down by over £3,000 but a modest profit of £102 was still made. The players represented Kilmarnock abroad for the first time, going on a tour of North America, playing 17 times (one of which was arranged at short notice and not counted as 'official'). The record read:

P 16 W 11 D 2 L 3 F 47 A 12.

It gave the team a chance to meet up with those Killie 'exiles' in Canada and the USA like Blair, Shortt and Gibson. As their ship was about to arrive in Newfoundland, a bottle (empty, of course) of Johhnie Walker's Black Label was thrown into the Atlantic with the promise of a *"real guid dram"* for its finder. Months later, the club heard from a Donegal fisherman who claimed - and received - his prize.

MATCH OF THE SEASON
September 7th 1929.
Kilmarnock 2 Ayr United 0

With Killie unbeaten in the League and holders of the Scottish Cup, Rugby Park was not a happy place for any Ayr United supporter at this game.

Killie demonstrated their superiority in a one-sided affair, Connell and McEwan ran the show and when Connell was fouled in the box, Cunningham scored from the spot. With three minutes left, 'Peerie' scored a second against his old team.

They lost the following week to Morton but Killie then beat Rangers to keep up their challenge. Although their title bid faded, the strength of their early results can be gauged from a look at the League table as it stood after the win over Ayr.

	P	W	D	L	F	A	Pts
1. Rangers	6	5	1	0	12	1	11
2. Kilmarnock	5	4	1	0	12	3	9
3. Cowdenbeath	5	3	1	1	7	4	7

1930-31 DIVISION ONE

Again, League form was average, Killie reserving their best for the Cup. Goals were a lot harder to come by as defences had finally adjusted to the two-man offside law. One oddity of this term was Killie's solitary counter in a 3-1 defeat at Firhill. The Partick Thistle 'keeper took a free-kick which hit Killie's No.9, John Irvine, on the head and cannoned off him into the net. Irvine was a reserve centre-half, playing up front for the first time. It was the only Killie goal he ever scored.

With 'Peerie' Cunningham nearing the end of his career, it was fortunate for Killie to have a new goalscoring hero to hand. This was James 'Bud' Maxwell, son of the winger killed in the First World War. 'Bud' scored regularly in the League but his first hat-trick came in a Cup-tie away to Inverness Citadel. Killie disposed of the Highland team 7-0 before knocking out Hearts in a Hard-fought tussle, 3-2 at Rugby Park. They successfully negotiated another trip north - this time to Montrose - winning 3-0, but the Cup dream almost perished at Bo'ness (then a League club) in the last eight; Aitken once more being the hero with an 87th minute equaliser. Killie easily won the replay 5-0 before going on to meet Celtic at Hampden in the semi-final. Although beaten by Celts 3-0, Killie were not disgraced. They suffered bad luck - a good-looking penalty appeal being turned down, for example. And they had the misfortune to run into the Celtic 'keeper, the legendary John Thomson, at his very best.

There was a further £500 decline at the gates and a loss of £464 was declared. Life membership was conferred on Mattha' Smith at the AGM. Mattha' had announced his intention to retire (although he would briefly play for Morton and Ayr). For fifteen years, Mattha' had been an inspiration to all around him. It was a sad occasion for all Kilmarnock fans.

Programme from Killie's tour of North America in Summer 1930.

MATCH OF THE SEASON
November 15th 1930.
Kilmarnock 5 East Fife 1

Injury to Maxwell gave a rare first-team outing to Abraham Wales. In Killie's first attack, he opened the scoring. When the Fifers 'keeper fumbled a long shot from Nibloe, Wales grabbed a second goal. From a Mattha' Smith pass in 33 minutes, the reserve hit his third.

Seven minutes into the second-half, Wales capped a remarkable day by heading home for his, and Killie's fourth goal. Connell scored a fifth for Killie and East Fife pulled one back before the finish but the day belonged to the previously unsung, and latterly unheard of, Abraham Wales.

1931-32 DIVISION ONE

A superb start, an opening win over Airdrie, defeat by Hearts, followed by six straight wins, two draws and another victory. Killie were one of only two teams (Rangers being the other) to inflict defeat upon the eventual Champions, Motherwell.

Although the team faded, winning just once in two months, recovery came in style. Dundee United were thrashed 8-0 with Aitken scoring five from the wing. Even more sensational was the home game against Leith Atheltic, where Killie fought back from 3-0 down to win 6-3 **and** they missed two penalties! After that win came a depressing end to the League campaign, losing the last six matches to finish 9th.

The loss in League form can be accounted for by the fact that, yet again, Killie had embarked upon a thrilling Cup run. Again, the draw was kind. Division Two opposition in the shape of East Fife and Albion Rovers were accounted for, before relegation certainties Dundee United held up proceedings by forcing a draw at Tannadice. Once they were safely despatched in the Rugby Park replay, it was the turn of another lower League outfit, Dunfermline, to face elimination at Kilmarnock's hands. Killie's luck held in the Semi-Final draw, being paired with Airdrie, the lowest placed of the four survivors. They were beaten 3-2 at Firhill and, for the third time in a dozen years, Kilmarnock were off to Hampden for the Scottish Cup Final.

The Cup had brought much-needed revenue into the Killie coffers. Season tickets sales had been declining but a profit of almost £4,000 was attained, gate money exceeding £15,000 for the first time. The AGM was a happier occasion than in the last two years. The one sad note was the death of rebel-turned-director-turned-Club President-turned-rebel again, the colourful John Greenway. In addition to his interventions at AGMs, he had also, for a number of years, written the football column of the now-defunct *Kilmarnock Herald* under the pseudonym, 'Evergreen'.

MATCH OF THE SEASON
April 16th 1932.
Rangers 1 - Kilmarnock 1

Jock McEwan had taken the captaincy over from Mattha' Smith and he led Kilmarnock out for the Scottish Cup Final to a crowd of 111,982. Apart from himself, McEwan had Nibloe, Morton, Connell and Aitken of the 1929 winners in the team so, for once, inexperience was a charge unable to be levelled at Kilmarnock. Sam Clemie nearly made it too. The out-of-form 'keeper was brought back against Cowdenbeath the week before the Final. Sadly, for both Sam and Killie, he picked the ball out of the net on no fewer than seven occasions, so Willie Bell returned for the final. The excellent Tom Smith was at centre-half and the new hero, Maxwell, at centre-forward. Three 'Jimmies', Muir and Duncan the inside-forwards and Leslie at right-back, completed a line-up which truly was that most beloved of cliches, a blend of youth and experience.

It was a confident Kilmarnock who took the game to Rangers. First, Duncan, then McEwan went close. For Rangers, Sam English was the main danger and Bell, Smith and Nibloe all saw plenty of action, Nibloe, in particular, making a number of crucial interceptions. The game was well-balanced and looked to be heading for a scoreless first-half when, in a goalmouth melee three minutes from the break, Maxwell scrambled the ball into the net. 1-0 to Kilmarnock. The early stages of the second period saw Killie continue to give as good as they got until the 53rd minute, when Bob McPhail tried a shot from 20 yards. Bell reacted tardily and Rangers had equalised. Now it was Rangers who were in charge, swarming around the Killie goal. Bell redeemed himself with a point-blank save from English. McPhail netted, only to be given offside, an unusual development for Rangers; particularly in a Cup Final. Bell was forced into a number of good saves before Killie counter-attacked, Maxwell's shot being kicked off the line by Gray. Rangers returned to the offensive, forcing corner after corner but to no avail as Killie held out to earn a replay the following Wednesday.

Unfortunately for Kilmarnock their chance had gone. The replay, watched by 105,695, belonged to Rangers. Scoring in ten minutes, the Ibrox men were always in command. Even so, at 1-0 Killie still had a chance. It wasn't until 20 minutes from the end that McPhail added to Fleming's opener. Five minutes later, English wrapped things up with a third. The same eleven, who had fought so heroically on the Saturday, just couldn't rise to the occasion a second time.

1932-33 DIVISION ONE

When the season opened, Joe Nibloe was missing from the Killie ranks. Joe was adamant that he was due a benefit game, a demand the Board refused to accept. He kept in trim by training at Cathkin and, after a month, accepted new terms. Or so it seemed. Supporters read one week that Nibloe would be back in the side and the next, incredulously, that he had been transferred to Aston Villa. The fee, at £1,875, was a record for a Kilmarnock player. His place in the side was taken by a local 19 year-old, Freddie Milloy. Milloy would, in time, become one of the most popular players ever to wear a Killie shirt. As would another youngster who made his debut near the end of this season, the 17 year-old Bobby Beattie.

On the field the hero of the hour was 'Bud' Maxwell. 'Bud' hit hat-tricks in both opening games, missed the third through injury then returned to score in each of the next five matches. With eight games to play, he had scored 30 goals and seemed certain to beat 'Peerie' Cunningham's record. Injury then forced him to sit out four games on the trot and he ended on 32, two short of 'Peerie's total. It seemed that a nickname was *de rigeur* for Killie strikers. First, 'Bummer', then 'Peerie', now 'Bud'.

Poor defending cost Killie dear, 86 goals, a new high (or low) were conceded and the side slid to 14th. Season tickets fell again and gate income slumped by almost £4,000. Despite this, a profit of over £1,000 was recorded, the Nibloe fee avoiding a worrying loss.

MATCH OF THE SEASON
February 18th 1933.
Kilmarnock 1 Rangers 0

Once more, the Cup appeared to be Kilmarnock's forte. Non-League Lochgelly were disposed of with little difficulty and Killie emerged triumphant, by a single goal, after a hard game away to St. Mirren. Their reward was this Third round tie with Rangers. The opportunity for revenge over their conquerors in the 1932 Final brought a new record attendance at Rugby Park. 32,745 watched the customary Rangers cavalry charge fail to produce results. Killie took time to settle though and the biggest danger posed to Rangers in the first half-hour came when their own centre-half, Simpson, (father of Lisbon Lion, Ronnie) almost scored an own goal; Jerry Dawson, the 'Gers 'keeper, pulling off a fine save.

In 37 minutes, Jock McEwan shot across the goal and in dashed winger Liddell, replacement for the injured Willie Connell, to score. The Stand rose to their feet. The terraces roared and, contrary to those who would have you believe that in the 'good old days', players were content to shake hands with the scorer and retire to the centre circle, Liddell was smothered in congratulations by his team-mates. Killie held the lead until the break and started the second-half well. From 18 yards, Aitken's shot produced a marvellous save from Dawson.

Rangers tried to get back into the match and English fired a header narrowly past the post. But, as time dragged on, the light blues became increasingly desperate and it was Killie who returned to the attack, McEwan bringing out another superb save from Dawson. As the final whistle signalled a famous victory, the Kilmarnock supporters, "delirious with joy" according to the 'Standard', invaded the pitch in their thousands.

Revenge over Rangers didn't proved to be the key to Cup success. The other outstanding team in Scotland at this time were Motherwell and it was they who visited Rugby Park in the Quarter-Finals. A crowd of 20,658 were witness to a thrilling 3-3 draw and, in the replay, Killie again found the net three times. Regrettably, their opponents did so on eight occasions to end Kilmarnock's Cup hopes for another year.

1933-34 DIVISION ONE

With a new goalkeeper in Jem Miller, Milloy - with a year's experience under his belt - the ever-reliable McEwan, the return of Hugh Morton, and Tom Smith in such superb form as to merit selection for Scotland, the defence was on a much sounder footing this year and 22 fewer League goals were conceded. There was just one erratic spell, when a 4-3 away win over Queen's Park was followed by 4-1 and 5-2 defeats by Queen of the South and Hearts respectively. The game at Hampden was notable in that Killie were leading 4-0 at one stage and if Miller had not 'done a Clemie' and saved **two** penalties, Killie might well have lost.

For once, a good start wasn't spoiled later in the season. Killie finished in 7th spot, aided by winning at Parkhead and drawing at Ibrox, the first time they had been undefeated at both these venues in the same season. The low points were provided by exit from the Cup away to lower Division Albion Rovers and a loss of £1,439 on the season.

MATCH OF THE SEASON
September 23rd 1933.
Kilmarnock 7 Airdrieonians 1

This match marked the returned of Willie Connell after a year on the injury list. Although Killie started well, it was Airdrie who scored first. Killie retaliated through Williamson who crossed the ball the width of the field where it was met by left-winger, John Keane, who slammed the ball home for the equaliser. A free-kick from McEwan took a deflection off an Airdrie defender to put Killie ahead at the end of the half.

The second-half saw Connell pass to Maxwell, who lost the ball, regained it, sped past two defenders and rifled home Killie's third. Two minutes later, Maxwell, unchallenged, shot home the fourth, then repeated the trick for number five. A hat-trick for 'Bud' within the space of five minutes. Showing himself not to be greedy, Maxwell provided the pass which allowed Keane to score the sixth. With a minute to go, Willie Connell capped a memorable comeback by scoring himself to make it 7-1 at the close.

1934-35 DIVISION ONE

The season opened ominously with the news that 'Bud' Maxwell had been transferred to Preston. His replacement, Jimmy Robertson, was a Scottish international, who cost Killie £1,000 (a large sum for Kilmarnock) from Birmingham. Following Maxwell was always going to be a tough act and Killie experienced some anxiety at the start of the season. The first four matches were lost and **twenty** players had been used when Killie met Ayr at Rugby Park. A 6-3 win over the old enemy marked the turning point and the side settled down somewhat (although a further seven players were fielded) to finish 9th, averaging a point a match.

The excitement of the Cup campaign concerned an 'Ayrshire Derby' match, but not against Ayr United. Kilmarnock found themselves drawn away to play Galston. The Irvine Valley team played, alongside Killie Reserves, in the Scottish Alliance and, until shabbily axed from that set-up a few years later, they, and Beith also, took part in the Qualifying Cup. The tie was a curious affair. The Kilmarnock players stripped at Rugby Park, put on overcoats and travelled to Galston's Portland Park. Afterwards, they returned to Rugby Park for a bath. The game itself saw Galston, with a number of ex-Killie players in their ranks, give Kilmarnock some frightening moments and it wasn't until the 71st minute that Killie took the lead through outside-right, Black. Even then, Galston put on a storming finale which left Killie grateful to hear the final whistle. A record 4,211 watched the game and it is to Galston's credit that they refused to countenance what many small sides did at the time and transfer the match to the ground of their opponents. The crowd at Galston was nothing though when compared to the 36,863 who turned up at Tyne castle to see Hearts beat Killie 2-0 in the next round.

MATCH OF THE SEASON
December 15th 1934.
Rangers 2 - Kilmarnock 3

The 'Standard', on the day of this game remarked how odd it was that Kilmarnock had won on every other ground but never at Ibrox. "Perhaps that great event is reserved for today's meeting", it added, prophetically. This was Killie's 36th visit to Rangers' ground on League business. The previous 35 had seen just 3 draws and 32 defeats. Rangers were top of the table, on course for their 8th Championship out of the last 9. It had been three years since they had last tasted defeat on their own ground, October 17th 1931, to be exact. What chance did Kilmarnock have? Those who thought that way had forgotten the 1929 Cup Final.

They had forgotten that Killie were also the only team to have beaten Rangers in a cup-tie since 1931, (it would be 1937 before Rangers lost another cup game). In short, they had forgotten Killie's fighting spirit.

The game started sensationally. Killie's Black shrugged off the challenging defenders to score with just thirty seconds on the clock. Rangers didn't allow themselves to be upset by this shock opening - plenty of teams had taken an early lead, holding on to it was the difficult part - they hurled themselves forward in a mass assault on the Killie goal. With no success. Only seven minutes had elapsed when Killie broke out of their own half and Williamson, that tormentor of Rangers of old, found space for himself in the Rangers penalty area and cracked home Killie's second goal. Two up at Ibrox and Kilmarnock were in a position they had never experienced before. The Rangers attacks intensified but Miller and his defence stood firm. Just once was the Killie rearguard breached, Alex Venters scoring in 26 minutes. Come the interval, Killie were ahead 2-1.

Rangers continued to press in the second-half but Killie did some attacking of their own. From a corner, Keane received the ball. Trapped in a penalty area full of defenders and with little room to manoeuvre, he somehow managed to turn and smash the ball between the crossbar and the upright to put Killie into a 3-1 lead. There was little time to celebrate. One minute later, the Referee missed a defensive handball in the Killie penalty area. Surrounded by furious Rangers players, he consulted both linesmen before awarding a penalty kick. Up stepped the renowned Torry Gillick to take the kick. Any Kilmarnock supporter, afraid to look, could tell by the eerie Ibrox silence that Gillick had placed the ball on the wrong side of the post.

With five minutes left, Gillick did get the ball into the net but the Killie defence refused to surrender again. After 35 years of trying, they had finally beaten the Rangers on their own ground, and deservedly so. As Glasgow's 'Evening Citizen' put it, there was "no fluke about the result". Kilmarnock were "deserving of great praise". The astonishing aftermath was that Ibrox went from being the one ground Killie couldn't win at to the only one they ***could****. Killie lost their next four matches and, Galston apart, it was ten games before they won again!*

1935-36 DIVISION ONE

Killie had two really poor spells during the season. They won only one of the first seven in the League and one out of the last eight. Perhaps they should have consulted Mr Z. Abba. This gentleman operated out of Bank Street, Kilmarnock and advertised himself, on the sports page of the *Standard*' as an "African Medicine Man", able to cure all ills. It is doubtful though, whet her the redoubtable Mr Abba could have done anything to assuage the hurt experienced by Killie supporter, George Hodge, a 19 year-old apprentice joiner, who complained that after the 2-0 home win over Hearts on November 9th 1935, he was assaulted by having mud thrown at him by the Edinburgh club's Scottish international, Alex Massie.

The upshot was a court case in which Killie Manager, Hugh Spence, took the witness stand to be queried about the state of the Rugby Park pitch. Another celebrated witness was Hearts goalkeeper, Jack Harkness, who averred that it was common practise for players to divest themselves of mud at the end of a game and that he had no doubt that was what his team-mate had been doing. Massie was found not guilty.

Whatever the state of the pitch, the ground itself was in excellent condition. There was a new covered enclosure behind the west goal (the 'Johnnie Walker' terracing) and a car park was built at the Dundonald Road end. These decisions had been approved by the 1935 AGM which had lasted all of fifteen minutes, a far cry from its stormy predecessors. The Maxwell transfer fee being the obvious source of income. It was just as well that this money was spent as the 1936 AGM heard that gates were down by over £800 and a loss was declared of £2,389. Six Saturday matches had been lost to the weather and, in the era before floodlights, midweek attendances were often scanty, particularly so when played on an afternoon.

The club ended a nondescript season with an early Cup exit, beaten by Falkirk, and in a respectable 8th place. Casting a pall over Rugby Park though was the tragic death of right-half, Andrew Kelvin. This promising young player - the only ever-present the previous year - died suddenly after an appendectomy. A bright future, extinguished by fate.

MATCH OF THE SEASON

January 2nd 1936.
Kilmarnock 7 Ayr United 2

If Killie had been going through a poor spell then neighbours Ayr were doing even worse. They arrived at Rugby Park for this holiday clash in the not entirely unusual position of foot of the table. Killie were in the middle of their best run of the season (seven games undefeated) and took Ayr to the cleaners. They mounted a seige of United's goal, forcing three corners in succession. The breakthrough came with a Robertson header after 15 minutes. Four minutes later, Robertson scored again. A brilliant shot on the run from left -winger, Sammy Roberts, after 30 minutes gave Killie their 3-0 half-time lead. Ayr came storming back at the start of the second-half. Within a minute they had reduced the deficit and five minutes later, added a second.

At 3-2 and with nearly 40 minutes remaining, the pendulum appeared to be swinging United's way. That was before Jimmy Williamson put Killie 4-2 ahead and Bobby Beattie restored the three goal margin shortly afterwards.

Ayr folded completely at 5-2 down, their promising second-half started to reduce to a shambles as first, Robertson, then Roberts, added to their misery with further goals for Kilmarnock. It finished 7-2, Killie's biggest ever League win against Ayr (or equal with the 6-1 Premier Division in 1976-77, depending how you look at it). At any rate, it left Ayr firmly anchored at the bottom of the League. They were relegated this season, left to reflect ruefully, that, just as in 1925, if they had won both games against Kilmarnock instead of losing them, they would have stayed in the top flight.

1936-37 DIVISION ONE

A fine 4-2 win away to Celtic, all the goals coming in the second half, heralded a promising season, but inconsistency riddled the side and the Celtic Park performance proved to be the highlight of the year. There were some entertaining moments; against St. Johnstone, winger Roberts ran half the length of the pitch, carrying the ball in his armpit. He let it drop, crossed, and forced the 'keeper to concede a corner. Such occasions were few and far between.

The transfer of Tom Smith to Preston didn't aid stability. Eighteen months later, Tom would captain the Lancashire club to victory in the F.A. Cup Final. He would have been glad to have gone before the humiliating 8-0 defeat at Ibrox, a game which saw Jimmy Williamson, the last of the 1929 Cup winners, play his final match for Kilmarnock. A sad affair to bow out on.

The Ibrox debacle sparked off controversy over who was responsible for team selection. There were suggestions that Hugh Spence was only Secretary, not Manager, despite an announcement to that effect at the 1926 AGM.

The official position was that Spence would make recommendations but the final say on selection was in the hands of a three-man sub-committee of the Board. As one shareholder remarked, *"Hugh Spence is the Manager all right - whenever we lose"*.

MATCH OF THE SEASON

January 30th 1937.
Kilmarnock 1 Brechin City 2

A contender for the title of worst Rugby Park result of all time. The 'Standard' was once again in a prophetic mood when it welcomed the first visit of Brechin, fifth bottom of Division Two, to Rugby Park, in these words; "This match should offer no serious opposition to Kilmarnock, but football is such an uncertain game that it is wise never to take anything for granted". How true. With light snow covering the bone-hard pitch, Killie spent the first quarter of an hour camped around the Brechin goal but with nothing to show for their efforts.

In a rare excursion into Killie's half, Brechin's No.8, MacDonald, took advantage of incredible slackness in the Killie defence to give his side a shock lead. Worse was to come. Four minutes later, Killie 'keeper, Miller, collected the ball from a Brechin free-kick. Before he could kick clear, Brechin's inside-left, Bollan, knocked the ball out of his hands into the net. Nowadays this would result in a free-kick for the defending team and maybe a booking for the aggressor, but in 1937 it merited a goal.

For the next hour, Brechin solidly defended their two-goal lead, helped by some really awful finishing from Killie. A Robertson header with nine minutes remaining, offered some hope as Killie mounted a last-ditch offensive in search of the equaliser, but it never came. A team with one of the finest Scottish Cup pedigrees had been beaten by a side which wasn't even in the League the last time Killie won the Cup.

1937-38 DIVISION ONE

For drama, tension, excitement and sheer, nail-biting nervousness, only 1964-65 can compare with this season. There were some good early results. Ayr and Celtic were beaten in the first two home matches, always welcome occurrences. But four successive defeats in September sent the team plunging down the table.

Then came a surprising win at Dundee. The Dens Park club had won their first six matches and were still top of the League when Killie came back with both points. It shows what kind of season this was when Dundee - managed by former Killie star, Andy Cunningham - could make such a fine start, falter, recover to hammer Rangers 6-1, only to end up relegated.

Killie still couldn't climb out of second bottom position. Against Clyde, their problems were compounded when 'keeper Brown broke a leg, never to play again. Meanwhile, Bobby Beattie followed the same road to Preston as Smith and Maxwell before him, the club was £4,000 better off as a result but impoverished beyond repair in terms of quality on the pitch. The Board thought they knew what the problem was. They wrote to Hugh Spence, asking him to resign, because of the *"unsatisfactory manner in which you have conducted your duties as manager"*, asking also that he make sure that *"the keys should be returned to Rugby Park at once"*. At least they didn't give him the, now-traditional, eve-of-sacking vote of confidence!

Hugh Spence, not unnaturally, refused to reply. Perhaps he reasoned that two Scottish Cup wins wasn't all that "unsatisfactory" a record. The fans, the press and some of the shareholders were outraged. Common opinion was that the three Directors who formed the selection committee were at least as much to blame as Spence for the position the team was in. *"Kilmarnock are suffering today for their doubtful policy of transferring players"* was one newspaper comment. The Board would not be deterred though. They promptly terminated Hugh Spence's contract and, with Christmas approaching, acted in the same vein as Ebenezer Scrooge by paying Spence just one month's salary in lieu of notice. Scant reward for almost two decades service.

The Board had one trick up their sleeve which no-one anticipated. Supporters dissent and adverse press criticism was quelled in one swift move when the name of the new manager was announced - Jimmy McGrory. The greatest goalscorer in Scottish football. Over 400 in the League, 550 in total. McGrory had scored his first goal for Celtic at Rugby Park and now, with rich irony, his first game in charge of Killie would be at Celtic Park, on Christmas day. There was little of the festive spirit to be found among his former team-mates though. Killie were demolished 8-0 and four days later they were beaten 3-0 at Rugby Park by Hibs.

McGrory went back to his old club to sign inside-right George Reid and he made his debut against St. Mirren at Love Street on New Year's Day. Much to everyone's surprise, Killie won 2-0. Now, at least there was a chance of staying up.

Kilmarnock hit a golden spell of form in early 1938. Benny Thomson scores the winner, watched by Alan Collins, against Rangers in the League - just seven days after beating Celtic at Parkhead in the Cup.

McGrory made just one more signing, Felix McGrogan, a winger from Falkirk. He made his debut in a 4-2 defeat at Motherwell but after that reverse, Killie started to climb the table. They won six of the next seven League games, drawing the other. The sequence included wins over Hearts and Rangers as well as a crucial one over Clyde, who were below Killie in the League but with games in hand. There were so many teams separated by less than a handful of points however, that safety was still some way off. In the meantime, there was also the Scottish Cup to play for.

Killie had beaten lower division Dumbarton and then drew the only bye available, to land themselves with an away visit to the holders, Celtic. Just over two months after their 8-0 drubbing, Killie went back to Parkhead and knocked Celtic out of the Cup. Goals from Collins and McGrogan in the first-half being enough for a 2-1 victory which rocked Scottish football. It was the following week that they beat Rangers in the League. They then returned to Cup duty. Hollywood couldn't have produced a better script. First, Celtic, next, Rangers, now Ayr United. Killie's neighbours were the Quarter-Final visitors to Rugby Park.

They too were struggling in the League but, thanks to the luck of the draw, they now had a chance to reach the last four for the first time.

This match was watched by the largest crowd ever assembled at an Ayrshire derby match, some 27,442 being present. The Kilmarnock revival appeared to have come to a standstill when they couldn't hold on to a first-half lead, a 1-1 draw sending them to Somerset where Ayr fancied their chances. Nothing daunted, Killie astonished the 23,785 who watched the replay by again taking a first-half lead and then ran riot after the break to crush their county rivals 5-0. With their potential Semi-Final opponents to be drawn from Division Two clubs, East Fife and St. Bernards, or the mighty Rangers, there was only one team destined to come out of the hat against Killie. Inevitably they drew Rangers.

In a pulsating Semi-Final at Hampden which swung first one way, then the other, Killie again confounded expert opinion by triumphing 4-3. It was now the raw nerves of this amazing season began to show. They picked up just one point from three League games after the Semi-Final and relegation was still a distinct possibility as they faced East Fife in the Final.

A Dramatic end to one of Kilmarnock's most tempestuous season's.

(Top right) From Junior football to the Scottish Cup Final inside a season. That was the remarkable achievement of John Hunter - Killie's goalkeeper.

(Left) Another member of the Final team - Sammy Ross.

A disappointing game ended 1-1, bringing both clubs back to Hampden the following Wednesday. More worrying for Killie, the Scottish League had decreed that they fulfil their League engagements on the Friday **and** the Saturday. Facing three tough matches in under 72 hours, the players steeled themselves for one last gargantuan effort.

MATCH OF THE SEASON

April 27th 1938.
East Fife 4
Kilmarnock 2

Good luck messages poured in for the replay from former players. Sadly, there would be none from 'Bummer' Campbell. The Killie legend of old had died just four days before the first game at Hampden. Killie would need performances reminiscent of his fighting qualities if they were going to emerge triumphant over the next few days.

PRESENTED WITH THE SUNDAY POST. MARCH 13, 1938.
SOUVENIR OF A FAMOUS VICTORY
CELTIC 1
KILMARNOCK 2
SCORERS · CELTIC, McDonald
KILMARNOCK, McGrogan Collins

The 'Sunday Post' brought out a special souvenir to mark Kilmarnock's success at Parkhead in the Scottish Cup in 1938, and mighty pleasant reading it made too. For it was contained in the issue of the paper that also reported on Killie's home League win over Rangers.

After fifteen minutes, it appeared that the tide had finally turned against Killie when, against the run of play, East Fife took the lead. Four minutes later, Benny Thomson, Killie's outside-right, was brought down in the box. Benny insisted on taking the resulting penalty himself and promptly levelled the scores at 1-1. In 25 minutes, the inspirational Felix McGrogan ran through on his own and evaded the challenging 'keeper, to put Killie ahead for the first time in the tie. It stayed that way until half-time. Throughout the second period, it became apparent that too many Killie players had picked up injuries which prevented them from playing their full part in the match. Collins, McAvoy, Milloy and Ross were all hobbling so it was no great surprise when East Fife fought back to 2-2 to take the match into extra time.

Killie held out for the first part of the extra half-hour but, in the second fifteen minutes, tiredness and injury caught up with them as East Fife scored twice to become the only lower League side to lift the Scottish Cup. It had been a performance of Herculean proportions by Kilmarnock but, sadly, it had not been enough. Despite defeat the players were rightly give a heroes welcome when they returned to the town.

The 'Standard' remarked that, in the end, they were beaten because they were "crippled, dispirited, exhausted".

There was still the matter of securing Division One status to be attended to. Killie knew that, as Ayr played Dundee on Saturday, one of those teams had to finish with no more than 32 points. Killie had 31. So one win, or two draws, would be enough.

They had the chance to clinch things on the Friday night when Morton were the visitors to Rugby Park. No-one wanted to have to go to Tynecastle on the Saturday needing to draw, or win. The injury list was so long that only six of the eleven who had played at Hampden could take part and some of them were carrying knocks.

So it was a side of jaded players and raw reserves who took the field before an encouraging crowd of 8,000 to play Morton. And it was the reserves who were the heroes.

Gallacher, playing at inside-right for the first time, Henry, in his third appearance and his first since November, and Gillespie in his fifth game as centre-forward and his first since the slaughter on Christmas Day scored the goals, which enabled the team to relax at Tynecastle the following day and let the relegation drama be played out at Somerset Park once more. Perhaps buoyed by Killie's example, Ayr got the point they needed and it was the one-time leaders, Dundee, who went down.

The drama had been good for the bank balance. The Directors reported a record profit of £8,452-19-10 for the season. Gates, which had averaged 7,000 up until the New Year, had increased with the advent of McGrory and the change in the team's fortunes. From January onwards, the average crowd was 10,000 at League games, 12,000 if the Cup was included as well. McGrory had brought in just two players and moved inside-forward Allen Collins to centre, suggesting that whatever else Hugh Spence had got wrong, he had bequeathed to his successor a fine bunch of players.

Alan Collins heads home Kilmarnock's fourth goal in the cup Semi-final against Rangers in April 1938. Killie won 4-3.

1938-39 DIVISION ONE

The season started sensationally when Killie took the lead after just three minutes at Parkhead in their opening game. The prospect of another glorious success over Celtic soon evaporated as the League Champions proceeded to thrash their Cup conquerors 9-1. Perhaps this was Killie's worst defeat. This author would argue that, having at least scored a goal, it was not quite as disastrous as those 8-0 hammerings at Celtic Park, East Road and Ibrox (twice). The opening game apart, it was a pretty mundane year. There was an excellent home win over Rangers and very nearly a 'double' when Killie narrowly failed to hold on to a 2-0 interval lead at Ibrox, settling for a draw.

It was, declared the Chairman, Norman Robinson, *"the calm **after** the storm"*. There was never any danger of repeating the previous year's struggle as Killie finished in 10th place. Money had been made available to strengthen the side and this was responsible for the loss for the year of £3,667-1s.-1d.

MATCH OF THE SEASON
December 10th 1938.
Queen's Park 1 Kilmarnock 5

Both teams displayed poor finishing in the first twenty minutes until Benny Thomson received the ball from a free-kick and crossed for Sammy Ross, a left-half converted by manager McGrory into a centre-forward, to score the opener. A long pass from Reid enabled Thomson to put Killie two ahead, five minutes before half-time. According to contemporary reports, Killie could have been five ahead at the break. Reid gave Ross an easy chance to make it 3-0 after 52 minutes. Queen's grabbed a goal back which gave them some brief encouragement, but this was snuffed out when Ross hit Killie's fourth. Ross squandered two more easy chances before Thomson made it five before the close. A sad day for Queen's Park's Egyptian 'keeper, Mustapha Mansor, but a hat-trick for the converted wing-half, Sammy Ross.

Tom Smith, 'Bud' Maxwell and Bobby Beattie,
the three ex-Kilmarnock players who won
F.A.Cup winners medals with preston North End in 1938

Chapter 6

ADOLF HITLER - HIS PART IN KILMARNOCK'S DOWNFALL 1939-1952

1939-40 DIVISION ONE

War was less than a month away when this season opened and the atmosphere was unreal. When, after five games had been played, the inevitable happened, the SFA acted quickly. Fear of air raids on heavily-attended grounds brought about the suspension of all football, four days after the outbreak of war. As the blitzkrieg failed to develop, there was a consequent softening of this stance. First, friendlies outside designated 'dangerous areas' (those near military installations or munitions and shipbuilding areas) were permitted. On September 22nd, the ban on competitive matches was lifted. Killie played an Ayrshire Cup tie at Somerset on September 30th but only 3,000 attended; a far cry from the thousands who rolled up in August, hoping against hope that the war might be averted. The first war-time game at Rugby Park was a friendly with Clyde on October 7th 1939, which ended in a 5-5 draw and was watched by 3,000.

The tragic Benny Thomson. A superb winger in the late 1930's, he was the only Killie player to lose his life in the War, when his merchant ship was sunk.

In October, two Regional Leagues came into operation, Kilmarnock being one of sixteen clubs in the Western League. Interest was poor and attendances seldom rose above the 5,000 mark. The new conditions meant that many players were on the move, often turning out for clubs near where they were stationed, if serving in the forces. The popular St. Johnstone centre-half, Frank Moulds, an Ayrshire man, turned out for Killie. So too did an old favourite, 'Bud' Maxwell. The Scottish Cup, as in the First World War, was suspended and a 'War' Cup took place. This was a success with the fans, as the attendances show. The two ties played at Rugby Park totalling over 16,000 as opposed to the two top League gates which came to just 10,500.

Killie performed averagely in the new set-up, coming 8th of the 16. The final game was a disaster, Killie were five goals down to Airdrie at half time. With the last shot of the match, Felix McGrogan scored a consolation goal. Little did he, or anyone else, know that it would be the last ball kicked at Rugby Park for over five years. At the time the club was in mourning for the death of R.B. Russell, 'The Cutler', the last link with the pre-League days of the 1880's.

The slump in gates was reflected in annual takings which were down from almost £12,000 in 1938-39 to just over £5,000 this year. There was a loss for the year of £528 but the club had given the Government a £1,000 interest-free War loan.

By the end of the season, no fewer than nine Kilmarnock players were on active service.

Killie signed up for what was now called the Southern League for 1940-41, but, one week later they withdrew, citing the loss of their ground as a reason. Everything was hush-hush. When the withdrawal was questioned at the AGM, the reply was that Rugby Park had been taken over for *"national purposes"*, and the matter should not be pursued any further. What had happened was that the ground had been requisitioned as a fuel dump by the Army and it would remain in their possession until April 1945.

Those five years out of football would hurt Kilmarnock considerably but, at the time, people had things other than football on their minds. When Rugby Park was closed down, Denmark, Norway, Belgium and the Netherlands had just been overrun by the Nazi war machine and France was on the point of collapse. Invasion of Britain seemed imminent. When football re-opened in Kilmarnock, Hitler would be dead in his bunker and Japan would be on the verge of surrender. Yet, given the problems post-war Killie would have to face, there is a case for arguing that it was the demented actions of Adolf Hitler which played a large part in Kilmarnock Football Club's wilderness years.

MATCH OF THE SEASON

September 2nd 1939.
Arbroath 1 Kilmarnock 2

Injuries and National Service call-ups forced Killie to make five changes for this game and a train delay on the way to Arbroath meant an undignified dash to the ground in time for the kick-off. In an even first-half, Killie were unlucky to retire a goal down, Arbroath's 30th minute opener giving them the lead. After the break, Killie's Collins shook off the Arbroath centre-half, Gavin, for once, to slam in a shot from off the bar.

The game appeared to be heading for a draw until the 85th minute, when McGrogan's cross found Reid, who headed home to give Killie their first ever win at Arbroath. It would also be the last game played under the auspices of the Scottish League for six years. Less than 24 hours later, Britain was at war.

Rugby Park in 1945 - after five years in the hands of the British Army.

1945-46 DIVISION ONE

Handicapped by the wartime closure, Kilmarnock were not in good shape for the re-start of organised football. The Scottish League had decreed that there would be no promotion or relegation in 1945-46, to allow clubs to re-organise after the hiatus. However, they had altered the set-up. Now there were only sixteen clubs in what was re-named the 'A' Division. Almost without exception those clubs had been playing football continuously throughout the conflict. Killie and Queen of the South were the only teams starting from 'scratch'.

Killie had operated aeserve side in 1944-45, playing their home games at Hurlford's Blair Park. Rugby Park - handed back to the club in April 1945 - was badly in need of repair. The stand had been used for storing crude diesel oil containers, the terracing needed concreting, a new drainage system had to be built. Right up until kick-off, German POW's were busy erecting new turnstiles at the Dundonald Road end. Then, on the eve of the new season, Rugby Park was hit by a metaphorical bombshell. A small snippet tucked away in a corner of a newspaper read *"Watch Jimmy McGrory. He will make a sensational move soon"*. He did. Killie's boss announced that he had been appointed as manager of Celtic. The Board acted quickly, securing the services of Tom Smith. The former player, now a policeman in Preston and coach with the North End, leapt at the chance to take over at Rugby Park.

With only two of Killie's pre-war players - Turnbull and Dornan - immediately available, Smith had a difficult job trying to mould Killie into an effective force and the makeshift side took some real pummellings. 6-1 at Cappielow. 7-0 at home to Rangers. It was November before the team won at home - beating St. Mirren 6-4 in a real thriller.

Despite achieving some creditable results - taking three points off Celtic, scoring four times in the second half at Tynecastle and hammering Falkirk 6-2 - the team of slowly demobbed veterans, young hopefuls and locally-barracked guest players lost far more than they won, finishing second bottom; thankful that there was no relegation, but apprehensive about the future.

Probably their best performance was in beating the highly rated Hibernian in the Southern League Cup - forerunner to the Scottish League Cup. Killie won a hard game 1-0. During the match, Freddie Milloy was forced to leave the pitch with a nasty-looking injury. *"I think he's off for good"* muttered Tom Smith, no mean judge of such matters. Sat beside him was Jack Harkness, who replied wryly *"Then he must be dead"*. Sure enough, the indomitable Milloy returned to spur Killie on to a rare - but deserved - victory.

MATCH OF THE SEASON
August 11th 1945.
Queen's Park 2 Kilmarnock 3

Kilmarnock wasted no time in celebrating their return to football after an absence of more than five years. After just seven minutes 'Swig' Turnbull beat 14-year old 'keeper, Ronnie Simpson, to put Killie ahead. Eight minutes from the interval, inside-left McLaren beat two defenders, passed to Walsh, accepted the return and shot Killie into a 2-0 lead. In the second half, Turnbull added a third while Killie were temporarily down to ten men. Although Queen's scored shortly afterwards and added a second just before the end, the Killie performance in this opening game was good enough to have the 'Sunday Post' enthusing that they "arrived as an unknown quantity, (and) left as a team likely to trouble the best". Ah, if only.... The paper had forgotten to take the quality of the opposition into account.

The Amateurs were destined to struggle as badly as Killie in the year ahead and the 'Post's confidence in Kilmarnock was sadly misplaced.

Three days later, Japan surrendered and after six long years, the war was over at last. As people all over the globe celebrated what they hoped would be a new era of eternal peace, in a small corner of Western Scotland, Kilmarnock Football Club's darkest hour was just about to strike......

1946-47 DIVISION ONE

Close on 50 players had turned out the year before. This was cut to more manageable proportions this term but there was no improvement on the pitch. The season opened with grandiose talk of a Super League in the air and the word was that Killie would be invited to take part. By mid-November they were again second last, struggling to hold their own in the current set-up, let alone the Premier League paradigm that was being bandied around. An unbeaten December saw Killie move two points above Queen's Park, giving the Rugby Park crowds - at record levels in the post-war attendance boom - something to cheer at last.

The New Year witnessed the same old story though. Killie didn't win a game in January or February, their only consolation being the new record League crowd of 32,325 who watched Rangers win 2-0 on January 2nd. This was a harsh winter and Killie, fearing that the road might be impenetrable, arrived for the vital fixture away to Third Lanark by train. An hour late.

The crowd turned angry during the delay, demanding their money back, pelting police and photographers with snowballs, booing a hastily improvised seven-a-side match; a pitch invasion was narrowly averted. When, at 4.15, the game finally kicked off, Killie were a team transformed. They routed their Glasgow opponents 4-1, their first League win in three months.

The following week Killie beat Motherwell 2-0 before 16,000 jubilant Rugby Park fans. Now they were fourth bottom with 21 points and three games remaining. St. Mirren were two points behind but with three games in hand. Queen's Park, with only two games in hand, were languishing six points behind Killie and bottom-placed Hamilton were already doomed.

No wonder the *Sunday Post* reported *"Relegation gloom practically cleared"* from Rugby Park. Then Killie lost to Celtic, St. Mirren were beaten also but Queen's Park won away to Hearts, forcing the 'Post' to revise its opinion of Kilmarnock who were now in *"parlous relegation straits"*. Forget politics, a week is an eternity in football. Killie's position worsened 7 days later when they were demolished 5-1 at home to St. Mirren who virtually guaranteed their own safety in the process. Queen's Park had an idle Saturday. They were still four points adrift but now had three games to spare over Killie.

MATCH OF THE SEASON
April 12th 1947.
Partick Thistle 5 Kilmarnock 2

Killie travelled to Firhill for their final League game in reasonable spirits. Three times this season they had played Thistle. Three times they had beaten them. When McAvoy scored in 32 minutes, number four - and potential safety - looked on the cards.

Then the Firhill air was rent by two mighty roars. The first celebrated the news that Scotland had scored at Wembley. The second that the Jags had practically walked the ball into the net for the equaliser. Killie were not playing particularly well but fate appeared to be smiling on them when Turnbull's free kick from 20 yards took a deflection, the ball landing in the net. Half-time arrived with Killie holding on to their precious 2-1 lead.

Foolishly, Kilmarnock decided to defend their lead. After fifteen minutes, the otherwise immaculate centre-half, Bob Thyne, conceded a penalty which Thistle's Sharp promptly converted. 2-2. After this Killie simply collapsed. Four minutes later, Thistle were ahead. They scored twice more in the last ten minutes to leave a dazed Kilmarnock eleven scurrying to the dressing room to find out how their rivals had fared.

It was bad news. St. Mirren had got the draw they needed to make them absolutely certain of staying up, and Queen's Park had beaten Queen of the South. Now they were only two points behind with three games still to play.

Kilmarnock fans consoled themselves with visions of the Amateurs failing to catch them. Seven days later, Queen's Park beat Hamilton to move above Killie on goal average. Still, the die-hards convinced themselves that Queen's might lose their last two games heavily and Killie could yet survive. One more week and Queen's Park took a point off Aberdeen.

Even now there were those who would not accept the inevitable. There was (as always) talk of League reconstruction. Perhaps the League would increase the top flight of 18 teams, meaning no relegation! Alas for Kilmarnock, that only seems to happen when Motherwell are one of the bottom pair. A few even hoped that the much-talked of Super League would be formed with Killie in its ranks. It was not to be. After 48 years Kilmarnock were relegated.

They were, said one paper, *"a war casualty"*, a reference to the tribulations faced by Killie after their enforced idleness. A casualty of a different sort was Tom Smith. Unable to attend to his duties since January, as a result of illness, his contract was terminated in May 1947. At the same time it was announced that £7,000, raised in no small part by a record near-14,000 average home attendance, had been spent on players in the forlorn fight to stay up. The lone crumb of comfort came from the fans. In preparation for the renewed clashes with their county rivals, Kilmarnock supporters took on Ayr fans over ninety minutes, winning 8-1.

1947-48 DIVISION TWO

Despite relegation the club had made a profit of over £2,700, gate money coming to almost £20,000 and season tickets accounting for just under £2,000. Indeed, with 900 season tickets available for the first Second Division campaign for nearly half a century, Rugby Park was swamped with 2,000 applications for them, such was the loyalty of the supporters. Appointing a new manager played a part in creating an air of optimism for the coming season. Tom Mather was the new boss. Formerly in charge at Southend, Stoke, Newcastle and Leicester, he brought with him three decades of experience - a complete contrast from the tyros McGrory and Smith. Mather was the man who had signed Stanley Matthews for Stoke and great things were expected of him at Rugby Park.

At first such expectations appeared to be justified. Despite an indifferent League Cup campaign, the League saw Killie get off to a flying start. They put seven goals past Raith Rovers and won at Somerset Park. After four games unbeaten Kilmarnock were top of the table and looked good for a quick return to the top flight. October shattered this fond illusion. On their first-ever visit to Ochilview they were beaten by humble Stenhousemuir. Despite reclaiming top spot by beating Hamilton, they lost away again - this time to Leith - where, in contrast to Stenhousemuir, they were playing for the very last time. Double defeats in early November by the Fife pair of Cowdenbeath and East Fife increased dissatisfaction amongst the support.

Killie hung on to the leading pack until the end of January. They revenged their early defeats by crushing both Stenhousemuir and Leith at Rugby Park - 7-2 and 6-2 respectively. Tom Mather, though, had seen enough. Unable to find a house in the area, fed up with staying in a hotel and worn out by the strain of travelling back and forth to Lancashire to take care of his ill wife, he announced his intention to resign. Again, double defeats by Fife teams - this time Cowdenbeath and Dunfermline - plus an unwanted 'hat-trick' through dismissal from the Cup by East Fife, left the team with nothing to play for. They won just twice, both away from home, after January. In May, a special general meeting of the club was called, where shareholders vented their wrath on the Board. The shareholders elected their own committee, almost a 'shadow' Board. The Directors attempted to placate the criticism by recognising that the club was at its lowest ebb in fifty years and announcing Mather's successor - Alex Hastings. The former Scotland half-back was untried as a manager but he had a reputation as one of the deepest thinkers in the game.

Change took place at the AGM. Club Chairman, John Herries, resigned. He was off to work in Australia where he would be reasonably safe from the army of disgruntled Kilmarnock fans. The disaster of lower grade football was made clear in the financial statement. For despite the increase in season ticket sales, the club had lost over £6,000. Gate receipts had been halved to under £10,000 for the season. Questions were asked, but unanswered, about severance payments to Tom Smith. Bill McIvor, later to become Chairman, wanted to know if the Board had interfered with selections. Alex Hastings won support for this assurance that the day any director tried to pick the team would be the day he walked out of Rugby Park.

With the co-option of Frank Moulds to the Board and the election of Andrew McCulloch as Chairman, a position he had held at the time of the 1929 Cup triumph, the shareholders left hoping that the bad days were over at last. Such thoughts were premature.

MATCH OF THE SEASON

February 28th 1948.
East Fife 1 Kilmarnock 3

Killie travelled to face their cup conquerors of 1938 and now of 1948 also. East Fife were undoubtedly the team of the season in this division. In the League they had lost just once all season. At home they had won all eight games played. The only side to lower their colours at Bayview had been Killie - in the League Cup. Killie repeated that triumph. Leading 1-0 at the break, they grabbed two goals inside a minute to take a commanding lead. It was then that East Fife threw "everything but the grandstand" at Kilmarnock while in return Killie "put everything but the main gates across their citadel", if one press report is to be believed. The Fifers hit the post, had a penalty saved and saw Killie clear off the line twice. Three times East Fife's Aitken shot narrowly wide. Killie 'keeper Murdoch pulled off a string of remarkable saves. Even when East Fife did score, it was at the fourth attempt and too little too late. Killie had proven that they could rise to the occasion. Their problem lay in trying to consistently reproduce the form they displayed at Methil.

1948-49 DIVISION TWO

Alan Collins had been transferred to Raith Rovers and 'Swig' Turnbull to Queen of the South. Such was the extent of Killie's decline that these two veterans had actually moved to better clubs. With their going and the retiral of Freddie Milloy, the last of the pre-war players left Rugby Park. A reminder of happier times came with the appointment of Jimmy Williamson, hero of the 1929 Cup Final, as assistant manager.

Jimmy had been working as a sports writer for the *Evening Times* and his return to Rugby Park was warmly welcomed by the fans. One of his first duties was to present what was described as a *"well-filled wallet of notes"* to Freddie Milloy on behalf of the Supporters Association. *"Kilmarnock never had a more whole-hearted or loyal servant during all the years of its existence"* said Jimmy, a sentiment warmly endorsed by all those present.

It was an unhappy time on the field though. A 5-0 defeat at Airdrie and a humiliating 6-2 reverse at Stenhousemuir demonstrated how far Kilmarnock had fallen. It might even have been worse. Away to bottom of the table East Stirling, a team destined for the footballing netherworld of the 'C' division, Kilmarnock were beaten 3-0. Killie escaped with such a relatively mild defeat owing to East Stirling's inability to convert more than one of the **four** penalties they were awarded during this match. Just once in their last twelve matches did Kilmarnock taste victory and that, amazingly, was against Division Two champions Raith Rovers.

MATCH OF THE SEASON
January 3rd 1949.
Kilmarnock 8 Arbroath 0

Killie did have one outstanding player in their side. This was the gifted Hugh McLaren who operated on the left, either as winger or inside man, with great skill. In this game he scored twice in the first twenty minutes, from crosses provided by Sinclair and Fitzsimmons. Centre-forward Clive added a third before half-time. Allan Sinclair, only occasionally a first team player, scored two shortly after the re-start, the second being the culmination of a four-man move. With nine minutes remaining, Clive bagged his second and Killie's sixth. One minute later and Sinclair got his hat-trick. McLaren, who had ran the entire show and even afforded himself the luxury of missing a penalty, scored the eighth - and his own hat-trick - with five minutes to go. Coming on top of a 6-0 win over Alloa in their last home match and with draws at Hampden and Somerset in between, this was the pinnacle of Killie's best run in what was a dreadful season. It had been more than seventeen years - December 1931 to be exact - since Kilmarnock had last scored as many goals in a League game. On that occasion they had beaten Dundee United 8-0. And you have to go back to 1914 to find the last time that two Killie players notched up 'hat-tricks' in one League game, when Neil and Whittle did so against Dumbarton.

1949-50 DIVISION TWO

A huge clear-out took place amongst the playing staff. Of the eleven who lined up for the first League game of the previous season, only left-back Jimmy Hood, centre-half Bob Thyne and McLaren on the wing took part in this term's opening match. Twenty five players appeared in the first seven games. There were three different goalkeepers in the first three games and 'keeper number four, Benson, appeared in the fifth match. Killie's poor start was not really surprising therefore. After four games they were rock-bottom. The club was also in desperate financial straits. These were the boom years in British football yet Kilmarnock contrived to actually lose money despite the fact that they were, potentially at least, the best supported club in the division.

At this time of crisis the club did the unthinkable. They sold Hugh McLaren to Derby County for £7,000 plus inside-left McGill, who had played for the Derby first team just eight times and had been in their reserves for over two years. Fortunately, some of the transfer fee was invested in fresh blood which transformed the situation. Benson, in goal, had already solved that problem position. McKay, from Largs Thistle, looked promising on the right wing. But the two master strokes were the signings of Ralph Collins and Tommy Johnston. Right-back Collins cost £1,000 from East Stirling and would serve Killie superbly for a decade. Johnston, signed from Peebles Rovers, was a prolific goalscorer.

After finally winning a League match - at the seventh attempt - Killie went on a largely successful run. Johnston scored in all of his first five outings, eight goals in total and the supporters filled Rugby Park once more. 23,000 enjoyed the 4-0 drubbing of Ayr on January 2nd and almost as many turned out to see Killie beat Morton - the only unbeaten team in Britain - five days later. 22,000 turned up for the first Scottish Cup tie to be played at Rugby Park for eleven years, only to be disappointed with a 2-2 draw with Stirling Albion, Killie losing the replay 3-1. By the end of February when Killie travelled to Airdrie, they were in third place, just three points behind their opponents that day. The first real hope of promotion since 1947 was snuffed out at Broomfield that afternoon as Killie lost 2-0. Morale was affected and the team won only one more match this season. Not for the last time, the expectant Killie support saw their dreams dashed.

Notwithstanding the surge in support - 17,900 watched a friendly against Derby (part of the McLaren transfer deal) which Killie lost 5-1 - a loss of over £2,000 was recorded. How much worse it would have been without their incredible fans is open to conjecture. But it would not be an outrageous statement to suggest that, but for their loyal supporters, Kilmarnock could have been bankrupted this year. Instead, the AGM heard that, such was Killie's pulling power, that they were in effect subsidising the rest of the division to the tune of £1,000, based upon sums paid to visitors to Rugby Park and contrasted with what Killie received when they played away. A complaint made at the AGM that year would find an echo down the years when one brave soul took the directors to task over the inadequate lavatory provision at the ground. While improving the toilets' was the Board's consideration, team matters were in the hands of yet another new manager. The disappointed Alex Hastings had resigned, to be replaced by former Killie player Malcom McDonald. At 35, McDonald quit his job as coach at Brentford to embark on what would be a long - and ultimately successful career.

MATCH OF THE SEASON
January 14th 1950.
Queen's Park 1 Kilmarnock 3

Both teams were well in the hunt to accompany Morton into the big time. Killie, playing with what the press called "revivalist enthusiasm" took the lead in ten minutes when McKay's corner was back-headed by Tommy Johnston to allow yet another new face in the side, left-winger Alex Donaldson, to hook a right foot shot into the net. The game was finely balanced, even when Johnston headed Killie two ahead in 57 minutes, Queen's were still in with a chance and three minutes later they pulled one back. Right on the final whistle, Killie's Sam Cowan netted to end Queen's Park's unbeaten home record and put Killie fourth in the table with a game in hand of those above them. The following day, a special feature appeared on Kilmarnock in a Sunday paper under the heading "Killie's two-month miracle", describing the fightback from near oblivion to playing for promotion before massive crowds. It noted the atmosphere at Hampden as being similar to a Cup Final or International match. How true. More than 10,000 had travelled from Ayrshire for this game and the attendance of 27,205 was, and still is, a record crowd for a non-Division One/Premier League match.

1950-51 DIVISION TWO

McDonald's first year in charge was nothing short of disastrous. The previous season's promise was unfulfilled. A League Cup game at Dunfermline illustrated the frustrating inconsistency of this Killie side. Two goals down inside thirteen minutes, they scored four times in the next quarter of an hour yet lost the match 5-4. Also in the League Cup, there were amazing scenes at Somerset Park when hundreds of Killie fans, already angered by having to pack together like sardines on the train to Ayr, were still queueing outside as Kick-off approached. They lifted one of the entrance gates off its hinges and swarmed into the ground free of charge to see their team draw 2-2.

If the League Cup was disappointing then the League was worse. Far from pushing for promotion, Killie appeared to be heading in the opposite direction - towards the 'C' Division. The team won just three home matches, waiting until October 7th for their first Rugby Park success and then until January 2nd for another. Injuries forced manager McDonald to play himself - two years after he had 'retired' - and he even scored in one of his two outings, against Queen's Park. Killie finished in 12th place with just four teams below them. It was their worst season ever.

Off the pitch, matter were no better. Gates were down by over £4,500 and the club lost nearly £4,000 over the season. Andrew McCulloch resigned as Chairman and launched a savage attack on the Board at the AGM. He branded their annual report as *"fatuous, futile and inept"*, demanding that the 9,000 shares lying unissued be made available to supporters forcing the Board to report back early in the next season with proposals for playing and financial success. Frank Moulds also resigned. Former player Hugh Morton was elected to the Board but ex-manager Alex Hastings was unsuccessful in his attempt to before a Director.

MATCH OF THE SEASON
January 27th 1951.
East Stirlingshire 2 Kilmarnock 1

Killie travelled for this First Round Scottish Cup tie confident of recording their first post-war success in the tournament. After all, their opponents played in the 'C' Division, the same League as Kilmarnock Reserves and, averaging a point a game, were of roughly the same standard. Yet, after only three minutes, Killie were a goal down. Shire's number seven, Kemp, put over a low cross which inside-right, Craig, pounced on to score. Killie, with Tommy Johnston in fine form, did fight back but it was three minutes into the second half before they equalised through outside-right, McKay. Fifteen minutes later, East Stirling's own McKay, their centre-forward, out-jumped the entire defence to head the winner. Perhaps the most damning indictment of Kilmarnock was that defeat was not entirely unexpected. Even so, the 'Standard' felt moved to comment that it w - the "blackest day in the history of the club and the sorriest a..play ever given by a Kilmarnock eleven". Near the end of the season, Kilmarnock Reserves, playing with ten men for 45 minutes, beat East Stirling 2-1 in a 'C' Division match. Further comment would be superfluous.

1951-52 DIVISION TWO

Although much improved, Killie still lacked the consistency required for a promotion bid. New players helped the side rise to 5th place by the season's end. Henaughan, from Queen's Park, Mathie, from Motherwell and Willie 'Puskas' Harvey from junior side Bridgeton Waverley all made a favourable impression, but it was one of the 'old guard', Bob Thyne, that the fans warmed to; 16,000 turned out to watch his benefit match when a Killie side strengthened by the inclusion of Sammy Cox and George Young from Rangers lost 2-1 to the Celtic first eleven. After a twenty year gap, benefits were back at Rugby Park and Thyne's was so successful that other players all over Scotland rushed to cash in.

The re-convened AGM duly took place, the result being a less than earth-shattering decision to recommend going back to nine directors as opposed to five. Quite how that would revolutionise playing fortunes was not explained. At least 1952 opened brightly for Killie. Ayr were beaten 4-0 and that was followed up with a 5-3 win over Dunfermline, Killie's highest since they put eight past Arbroath three years previously. After a midweek draw at Coatbridge, Killie beat Stenhousemuir away 2-1. Willie Harvey scored the winner in unusual circumstances. He had married the night before and the club promised that if he turned out on the Saturday they would fly him to London on the Saturday night to join his bride on their honeymoon.

Killie played six League and Cup matches in January and remained unbeaten but their inconsistency returned to haunt them the next month when, following their elimination from the Cup, they lost 6-2 at home to Dundee United, after drawing 2-2 at half-time. Crowds had dropped from their peak and some of the midweek games were watched by so few that many clubs were on the edge of bankruptcy. Killie's first four away games of 1952 totalled less then 4,500. So when East Fife tabled a motion to reconstruct the League by taking the top four into the top division and abandoning promotion and relegation for at least one, maybe two seasons, Killie were outraged. They saw a future where they would be stranded permanently as the biggest fish by far in what would be more of a puddle than a pool. Fortunately, East Fife's resolution failed at the League AGM.

MATCH OF THE SEASON
January 20th 1952.
Kilmarnock 2 Stenhousemuir 0

A Scottish Cup win at home to Stenhousemuir does not, on the face of it, appear likely material for a season's outstanding result. But Stenhousemuir were a fair side in the early 50's and had an excellent record in the Cup which was more then could be side for Kilmarnock. Killie had already lost to the Larbert side in the League, former Rugby Park hero, Alan Collins, scoring on that occasion, so nothing was being taken for granted in the Cup tie.

Wing halves, Russell and Middlemass, prompted Killie forward from the start and after thirteen minutes, winger Anderson's free kick was met by recent signing Willie Jack who clipped the ball home to put Killie ahead. Five minutes later, Anderson's drive was parried by the keeper and Harvey tucked the ball away for the second goal. The snow-covered pitch gave both teams problems but Killie - with Collins and Russell wearing continental-style rubber boots - coped better. They held on to celebrate something special - their first Scottish Cup win since 1939. There was to be no glory but a fighting display at Pittodrie in the next round, where Aberdeen snatched a late goal to win 2-1, augured well for Killie's future.

Chapter 7

BLUE AND WHITE SHOOTS OF RECOVERY 1952-1957

1952-53 DIVISION TWO

The forward line was strengthened by the addition of Matt Murray from Queen's Park and the experienced Gerry Mays from Dunfermline. The revamped formation worked immediately, Killie qualifying from their League Cup section for the first time, winning five of their six games. St. Johnstone were turned over in the Quarter-Finals but Cup success was bought at the price of a poor League start. Coupled with the fact that Killie had played fewer games than their rivals, they found themselves in the incredible position of preparing for a Cup Final while lying bottom of the League.

Gradually, Killie climbed up the table, a seven match unbeaten run culminating in a New Year's Day win away to Ayr. Three successive defeats followed, to end any hope of promotion. There were some impressive performances in the second half of the season. Stirling Albion, who ended up champions, were thrashed 6-0 and the other promoted side, Hamilton, fared nearly as badly as Killie beat them 6-1. That latter result was part of a run of six wins which saw Killie rise to third place but a long way behind the two teams they had so recently humiliated.

Forced to make several changes for a midweek match at Forfar, Killie lost 6-0 at Station Park and had to settle for fourth place. Still, this was easily their best season since relegation and the League Cup run helped the club achieve a modest profit. The revival was tinged with sadness at the news of the death, at 55, of double-cup winner Mattha' Smith.

Goalkeeper John Niven, who had played in every match in his two years with the club, was freed at the end of the season and the AGM was told that 'Malky' McDonald was negotiating for the signature of Jimmy Brown from Hearts but had not yet received a reply to his offer.

The question of floodlighting was raised; the Board considered it too expensive but McDonald intimated that he was in favour, considering that the benefits of evening training and the ability of the system to pay for itself via midweek matches far outweighed the costs involved. Almost unnoticed, the first foundation of a new era was laid in March of this year with the signing of an eighteen year old forward from Lugar. Bertie Black was the first of the class of 1965 to arrive at Rugby Park.

MATCH OF THE SEASON
October 4th 1952.
Kilmarnock 1 Rangers 0

15,000 Killie fans left Ayrshire, bound for Hampden Park, hopeful in their hearts that they would witness an historic triumph, but mindful that the odds against their team winning this League Cup Semi-Final were 6-1 against. Killie - the 'B' Division outsiders - were meant to be lambs to the slaughter against a formidable Rangers eleven. Somehow it didn't turn out that way.

The entire Rugby Park defence was outstanding. In particular, Bob Thyne was in dominating form at centre-half and John Niven, in goal, was faultless. But Killie didn't just defend. Henaughan headed into the side-netting early in the game to show that they meant business. Grierson actually had the ball in the net for Rangers but the alert officials detected the use of his hand in so doing. Sammy Cox flashed a shot just past the post from 30 yards but the Killie support swore that Niven had it covered anyway. Grierson brought out a superb save from the Killie 'keeper then Rangers appealed - in vain - for a goal when Middlemass cleared a shot off the line. Half-time arrived with the match still goalless.

Rangers went on the rampage early in the second half. Grierson, twice, Hubbard, Paton, Waddell and Hubbard again all saw their efforts saved by the brilliant John Niven. Killie had their moments too; George Young having to head the ball clear off his own goal-line and the Rangers and Scotland skipper was consistently beaten by Matt Murray.

With two minutes left, Murray crossed the ball, and Rangers full-back, Little, in attempting to clear, saw the ball hit off the on-rushing Willie Jack and land up in the back of the net. Lucky? Maybe, but there were few who would deny that Kilmarnock were due some good fortune. Be that as it may, the 'B' Division side had humbled Rangers and put themselves into a major Cup Final for the first time since the War.

In the Final itself, against the holders, Dundee, the luck ran the other way. Killie were well on top, 13 corners to Dundee's 9 and 19 free kicks to the Dens men's 8 testify to that. But a combination of good goalkeeping and shot-shyness from the Killie front line kept the scoreline blank until Dundee's Bobby Flavell nipped in to score twice in the last eight minutes.

Afterwards, there was precious little of the traditional victory celebration in the Dundee dressing room. They were, as was reported, *"11 men only too conscious of their narrow escape"*.

OFFICIAL PROGRAMME

SCOTTISH FOOTBALL LEAGUE CUP 1946

SCOTTISH LEAGUE CUP

RANGERS versus **KILMARNOCK**

3D

Sensation! Kilmarnock, near the foot of the 'B' Division, knock mighty Rangers out of the League Cup in one of Scottish football's biggest-ever shock results......

......Unfortunately they couldn't repeat their shock Semi-Final result over Rangers, and lost to the holders Dundee 2-0.

```
                    DUNDEE
                      1
                   HENDERSON
         2                           3
        FOLLON                      COWAN
         4            5              6
       ZIESING       BOYD           COWIE
  7         8          9         10         11
TONER   HENDERSON   FLAVELL     STEEL     CHRISTIE

   Referee—                    Linesmen—F. SCOTT, Paisley
   J. MOWAT, Glasgow                     S. K. THOMSON, Glasgow

  MURRAY    JACK        MAYS      HARVEY    HENAUGHAN
    11       10           9          8          7
         MIDDLEMAS      THYNE      RUSSELL
            6             5           4
              HOOD              COLLINS
               3                   2
                      NIVEN
                        1

                    KILMARNOCK
```

1953-54 DIVISION TWO

Again, Killie stormed through their League Cup section, winning five out of six. Against Partick Thistle in the Quarter-Finals, they fought back from a 3-1 interval deficit to win by the odd goal in seven. At Firhill it was a different story, Killie losing 4-0 over the 90 minutes and 7-4 on aggregate. The League campaign got off to a dreadful start, however. Killie lost the first three matches, failing to score in the process. The third of these defeats, against Albion Rovers at home, marked the first-team debut of Bertie Black. Playing on the right wing it was reported that he *"seldom got a decent pass"*. Missing from the team through injury was left-back, Jimmy Hood. Jimmy was the longest-serving player at Rugby Park and he was rewarded with a benefit against Hibs. The Edinburgh club fielded a reserve side, causing much ill-feeling in Kilmarnock and on a rain-sodden night just 4,000 turned up - a far cry from Bob Thyne's successful benefit two years earlier.

October 1953 marked a significant watershed in the history of Killie. On the 17th, Hugh Spence, the architect of the two cup-winning sides, died. It was reported that he had severed his connections with the club when he left its employ in 1937. Perhaps out of consideration for his family, no mention was made of the unhappy circumstances in which he had left. As one hero departed the stage, others were about to make their entrance. October also saw a new face at Rugby Park when it was announced that *"Kilmarnock have signed a new inside forward - a big 'un. He is Frank Beattie, the 19 year old inside-left of Bonnybridge Juniors. He stands 5ft 10½ins and tips the scale at 11½ stone"*.

Frank was a useful signing in more ways than one. For, as a miner, he was exempted from National Service, an important consideration in the 1950's. It was frustrating for clubs to unearth potentially good players, only to see them vanish into the Forces for two years. It is also a mark of how quickly a society can change that just over 40 years later, no-one would seriously describe a player of Frank's dimensions as 'big'. Indeed, this author is within half an inch and a couple of pounds of Frank's reputed size and feels positively small when watching some of the modern players. Perhaps it is distance lending its vaunted enchantment but those who grew up watching Frank Beattie in action felt that they were looking at a giant of a man, a veritable Olympian on the field of play.

But Frank's position in the pantheon of Kilmarnock heroes lay far in the future when he made his debut for the Reserves against East Stirling on October 10th 1953. A trialist full-back failed to turn up and, by sheer good fortune, the Killie party spotted a 17 year old in St. Enoch station in Glasgow carrying a pair of football boots. He was on his way to play for Kilmarnock Amateurs but readily agreed to turn out for Killie reserves at Firs Park instead. Even more fortuitously, the lad was a full-back. His name? Matt Watson. No-one could ever have suspected that the two raw youths - Beattie and Watson - would make 1,000 Killie first team appearances between them, nor that the young Black - having his brief run in the first eleven would add over another 300 to that total.

October also saw the opening of the floodlight system that the board thought too expensive and which McDonald thought vital. Before 16,000 spectators, Killie lost 3-0 to a full strength Manchester United team. Coming on as substitute for an injured player in the English side, was a young man named Duncan Edwards. It was his first appearance for United in a career which was destined to be glorious but brief; his life was one of many lost in the tragedy of the Munich air crash in 1958. Strangely, the debut boy Edwards was the only one of the United side familiar with Rugby Park, having previously played there for England in a Youth International.

The First Eleven also played their part in making October such an eventful month. On the third, they finally not only scored a League goal and won a match, but did so in some style, leading Morton at Cappielow 4-1 at half time, eventually winning 6-4. They then beat Dundee united 3-2, having been two down at the break. A 1-0 reverse at Alloa was offset by thumping home victories over Forfar (6-0) and Arbroath (4-0). Alas, November opened badly when Killie lost 2-0 away to Third Lanark, their chief tormentor that day being a player described as *"amazing"* in the Sunday press, one Alastair McLeod. It wouldn't be the last time that Killie fans would wish they had never heard of the bold Ally. The defeat at Cathkin left Killie in 10th place with 8 points from 9 matches. Promotion seemed as far away as ever.

Then came a run of five straight wins, followed by two draws. Victory over Motherwell by 2-0 at Fir Park establishing Killie's credentials as genuine promotion aspirants. The game was heading for a goalless draw until Willie Harvey shocked the League leaders by scoring twice within a minute as full time drew near. Having pegged back Motherwell, Killie were now in a position to launch their own challenge. 'Well still led with 20 points from 14 games. Stenhousemuir and Albion Rovers both had 18 from 14, Dunfermline had 17 from 12 and in fifth spot, Killie had 16 from 13. The following week, Killie - a goal down at the interval - crushed Stenhousemuir 6-2 to go third. After draws with Dunfermline and Queen's Park, Killie were shocked by a 3-0 Rugby Park defeat at the hands of Ayr United. When they could only draw with Albion Rovers in their second New Year fixture, Killie had dropped to 7th, but such was the competitive, cut-throat nature of this season, that they were only two points behind 2nd place St Johnstone.

Killie took up the challenge again with three successive 2-0 wins, over Morton at home, Dundee United away and Alloa at home - the Tannadice triumph putting them into 2nd place. For the first time Killie were in a promotion position. January 1954 closed with an almost unbelievable result. Killie lost 6-0 away to Cowdenbeath. Yet, paradoxically, that result reinforced the desire to succeed. Narrow wins were carved out away to the two Angus teams, Forfar and Arbroath. Sandwiched in between these was an epic cup tie with Rangers. Killie took a first half lead at Ibrox, fell behind then equalised to bring the Ibrox side to Rugby Park where 33,545 watched the replay, Killie giving a good account of themselves before succumbing 3-1. The attendance was a new record for Rugby Park, being 800 more than assembled for the 1933 cup tie against the same opposition. Round about the same time, Ayr United also announced a new record attendance. A record low. Only 600 watched their home League fixture with Alloa. Ayr had faded after a bright start and not even doing the 'double' over Killie seemed to enthuse their support.

With the Cup out of the way, Killie could now, in the words of one of football's oldest cliches, 'concentrate on the League'. This they did with devastating effect. Dumbarton were destroyed 7-2 at Rugby Park. St. Johnstone's now fading promotion hopes were extinguished when Killie put five past them without reply in another Rugby Park goal feast. The home fans joy increased when Motherwell were the next victims. A 4-2 win being the third time in four fixtures this season that Killie had beaten the side who had already booked their promotion slot. Then came a nail-biting game away to Stenhousemuir. The Larbert side were still very much in the frame themselves until Gerry Mays struck with just two minutes left to play to give Killie victory by a solitary goal. It was their sixth successive League win. Now only Third Lanark could prevent Killie from ending their seven year exile from the big time and they were Kilmarnock's next opponents.

MATCH OF THE SEASON
April 17th 1954.
Kilmarnock 1 Third Lanark 1

Killie had 39 points and two games remaining. Thirds had 33 with four to play. If Killie lost, they and Thirds were effectively on level terms, providing the Glasgow club won their games in hand. A draw kept Killie as favourites to go up but a home win would have settled the issue there and then. Kilmarnock would be promoted. A massive crowd of 21,600 turned up, most of them expecting nothing less than a Killie victory.

From the outset it was clear that the tension had got to the Killie players. Their nerves were showing. Thirds, by contrast, were much calmer, almost serene in their approach. Killie's high ball down the middle approach was easily lapped up by the big Thirds' defenders. Midway through the second half, disaster struck. Bob Thyne handled the ball in his own penalty area. From the resultant spot kick Third Lanark took the lead. Now Killie could see their long-awaited prize slipping away from them. They bombarded the Thirds goal, skill became an idle luxury as they forced their way through. In a crowded penalty area, Gerry Mays scrambled the equaliser with thirteen minutes to go. The celebrations on the terracing were still in full swing when it was Killie's turn to be awarded a penalty. In a hushed ground and with the weight of seven years expectations on him, Jimmy Middlemass stepped up to take the kick - and blasted the ball wide of the goal. The final whistle sounded only for the expected party to fall into limbo.

A frantic forty eight hours followed as Killie fans awaited the news of Third Lanark's match with Dunfermline at Cathkin on the Monday afternoon. In a town and surrounding area fraught with nervous excitement, the calmest person around was Killie boss, Malky McDonald. He pottered about in his garden until late afternoon, then nonchalantly picked up the phone and rang a Glasgow newspaper to find out the result from Cathkin - 1-1. Kilmarnock were back in the top flight of Scottish soccer. The last match against Queen's Park rendered meaningless other than as the occasion for the party delayed from the previous week. Word spread quickly and McDonald received congratulatory telegrams and phone calls at his home as the fans started celebrating at last. The years in the wilderness were over.

12,000 saw Killie confirm their status with a 2-0 win over Queen's Park. In amidst the push for promotion, Killie had also found time to invite continental opposition to appear at Rugby Park for the first time. This was the Austrian side, Admira Wien, who were thrashed 5-0 under the lights before 12,500 curious supporters.

Gates were up by £2,000, income from season tickets, the car park and programme sales had risen by nearly £700. After deductions to visiting sides, the floodlights had earned another £1,100 yet the overall profit (probably because of the costs of installing the lights) was small, just £232. Killie's re-emergence as a power in the land was recognised when Tommy Henaughan was named in the provisional squad of 40 from which Scotland's World Cup pool would be picked. And this despite the fact that there was doubt over whether the USA-born Henaughan would be eligible for the full Scottish side. He was the only player from the 'B' Division to do enough to catch the selectors eyes.

At the AGM, Malky McDonald savagely rounded on his critics. He condemned those who had wanted him to field *"hammer-throwers and bulldozers"* in the team. He taunted those who said that the team was too old and too light to go up. In words that could have been repeated nearly forty years later, he vowed that if the players were skilful enough then age and physique were secondary considerations. He promised that his team would continue to play attractive football and pledged that, if he was given 7 or 8 years, then he would give Kilmarnock *"a team to be proud of"*. The season ended on a praiseworthy yet light-hearted note when McDonald and skipper Ralph Collins attended a ceremony where they were presented with an outsize key as they were awarded the 'Freedom of Moscow'. Of course, the Moscow they were entitled to enter at their leisure was the small village in Ayrshire and not its larger namesake in the East.

1954-55 DIVISION ONE

The great day dawned on August 14th 1954 when a crowd of 18,000 assembled at Rugby Park to see Killie taken on Raith Rovers in the League Cup. The first League match was still a month away but huge crowds turned up to see 'A' Division opposition in the sectional stage of the League's own knockout competition. Killie won that opening game 3-2 and 19,500 watched them draw 2-2 with St. Mirren. 22,000 saw Motherwell win 1-0 at Rugby Park. In total, over 100,000 watched the six League Cup games and with five points Killie felt reasonably confident about their League prospects.

The actual League start was a disappointment. 15,000 watched a 0-0 draw with East Fife. McDonald gave the players who had gained promotion the opportunity to show what they could do in a higher sphere and that meant that Jimmy Hood and Bob Thyne, the sole survivors of the side relegated in 1947, lined up against East Fife just as they had done against Partick Thistle on that fateful day seven years ago. It soon became apparent that the team was just not good enough to cope with the superior level of opposition. After three games Killie were without a goal to their credit. When they did score, they managed to do so three times, and at Parkhead too. Sadly, Celtic put six past Jimmy Brown. The following week saw Frank Beattie score on his League debut against Partick Thistle

(Big Frank had also scored in his inaugural first team outing against St. Mirren in the League Cup) but Killie lost 2-1.

They had played 5 games for the paltry return of 1 point, the same as Stirling Albion. It was Albion's Annfield ground that was the next port of call and Killie broke their Division One duck by winning 2-1. Those who thought the corner had been turned were given further ammunition for their belief when, in their next game, Killie were leading 2-1 at Easter Road, only for Hibs to steal the points by scoring twice in the last two minutes. A 6-0 defeat at Ibrox was a stark reminder of the task facing Kilmarnock if they wished to survive. After 12 games Killie had just 4 points, less than they had accumulated in the League Cup. The dismal record read: P12 W1 D2 L9 F13 A25 Pts4. Only Stirling Albion were below them in the table.

McDonald had reluctantly concluded that some players had to go. Right-half John Russell had already been dropped. Now his midfield partners, Bob Thyne and Jimmy Middlemass - outstanding in the lower League - were axed, as were Hood and Beattie. Frank would return of course, but of the others only Russell would appear in the first eleven again and that would be on only half a dozen occasions. Alistair Mackay was promoted from the reserves and McDonald splashed out over £4,000 to secure the transfer of centre-half Bobby Dougan from Hearts. Dougan was a former Internationalist and his experience would prove to be invaluable. McDonald also persisted with playing forward man Davie Curlett at right-half to link up with Dougan and Mackay. With Ralph Collins returning to action to partner Alex Rollo (a shrewd signing from Celtic in the close season) at the back, Killie had a more solid look about them.

The new look paid immediate dividends as Killie raced into a 4-1 lead at home to Queen of the South in just 32 minutes. The score remained just that as Killie celebrated their first home victory in the top flight since March 1947, seven years and nine months previously. More importantly, they climbed above Queen's in the table. Those critics who had Killie written off as certainties to go down had an uncomfortable time during December and early January as the Ayrshire team put together a decent run. After the Queen of the South game, Killie drew away to Raith Rovers and then ran riot against fellow strugglers, East Fife, at Bayview, winning 5-1. Next, a massive 28,000 crowd saw a 1-1 home draw with St. Mirren on New Year's Day; a match which saw the debut of another famous name.

Bobby Flavell, an experienced Internationalist and one of those who had sampled life with Millionarios of Bogota in the illegal Colombian League, alongside the likes of Alfredo Di Stefano, had been signed from Dundee. The man whose goals had beaten Killie in the League Cup Final two years beforehand was now charged with the responsibility of keeping them up. Two days after his first game, he took a starring role as Killie humiliated his old team, winning 5-2 away to Dundee.

The unbeaten run came to an end with defending champions Celtic winning 2-1 at Rugby Park as 24,500 watched on, but Killie bounced back to win away to Motherwell and climb three places to 11th. Shortly afterwards, Matt Watson made his first appearance in the League game at Palmerston Park. Killie lost that day and they still weren't certain of survival with just two games to play. They had 22 points and below them were: Falkirk, also on 22 but with a game in hand, Motherwell and East Fife, both on 21 but both having played a game less than Killie, Queen of the South on 20 and with two games left, Raith on 19 with three to play and Stirling Albion with a record low of 6 points, already seemingly doomed. Once again, Firhill was the fateful venue which awaited Kilmarnock.

This time there was no repeat of that disastrous day in 1947. Killie stormed into a 2-0 lead and, spurred on by a good section of the 18,000 crowd, added another in the second half to ensure their survival. Victory over Stirling Albion in the last match gave Killie their only 'double' of the season and allowed them to finish in the comparative luxury of 10th place. It was now that the Scottish League stepped in, the number of clubs in the top Division being increased to 18 and relegation suspended. All the worry, all the sweating, all the fear had been for nothing.

With an average of nearly 16,000, gates were at an all-time high. £28,462 was taken at the turnstiles, nearly £10,000 more than the promotion-winning season, yet the club had lost £2,715. This was due to spending £7,590 in transfers, principally on Dougan and Flavell. A satisfied AGM was over in 20 minutes, scarcely time to pause and remember those stalwarts freed by the club this summer, Thyne, Middlemass and Hood.

MATCH OF THE SEASON
February 26th 1955.
Kilmarnock 1 Rangers 0

This was the culmination of a terrific week, the kind that Killie fans had waited so long to see. The previous Saturday, 31,000 excited spectators had seen Killie draw 1-1 with holders, Celtic, in the Scottish Cup. On the Wednesday, Killie had put up a superb fight before losing the replay 1-0 before 41,000 at Parkhead.

Now, 24,000 witnessed a Kilmarnock side, still deep in the relegation zone, put Rangers to the sword. Bobby Flavell ran the show, dominating the game like "Cagney used to dominate his pictures" according to one star-struck reporter. Bustling, positioning, distribution, ball control, he was reckoned to be the complete centre-forward. And it was Flavell who sent the Ayrshire contingent in the crowd into ecstasy. Beattie beat two men and sent Matt Murray away with the ball. The wing er's cross was blocked but the ball spun to Flavell, who accepted the chance with alacrity and scored. Killie's lead was deserved and they clung on with tenacity, especially in the last ten minutes of the game, described in the press as the "Siege of Jimmy Brown". Brown was aided by his defence, both Rollo and Mackay making crucial goal-line clearances.

The final whistle signalled a remarkable Killie triumph and proof positive that they were back as a force in Scottish football. And although not ending relegation worries it gave Killie a five point advantage over second from bottom East Fife.

1955-56 DIVISION ONE

Killie's second season back at the top ought to have been quieter than 54-55 but it opened sensationally when Malky McDonald dropped the entire forward line after a terrible performance against St. Mirren in the League Cup, bringing in four reserves and moving Davie Curlett back up front. With Bobby Dougan a long-term injury victim and Ralph Collins also out of the side for a lengthy period, the team had a distinctly youthful, if unsettled, feel about it. The injury problems were compounded when Gerry Mays collided with a corner flag during training, breaking his nose.

Bertie Black

On October 8th 1955, Beattie, Watson and Black all lined up together for the first time, a triumvirate which would last for a decade. Gradually, the more experienced players returned to action and, from late November onwards, Killie showed a marked improvement. They fought their way into mid-table and stayed there. Frank Beattie, often *"criticised and barracked"* according to the *Standard* won over the fans and *"silenced the loudmouths"* with an outstanding performance against East Fife in January, scoring twice in a 3-0 win. A month later, Bobby Flavell registered the first hat-trick by a Killie player in a Division One game since August 1946 when he netted all Killie's goals in a 3-2 win over Stirling Albion. The season ended with some good results, a 2-0 win away to a Hearts side which had just lifted the Scottish Cup being the most notable. Killie averaged a point a game and finished in 8th position, their highest for twenty years.

There had been a slight decline in attendances, gates dropping to just over £25,000 and £1,850 was lost over the year. Some familiar and well-loved faces departed on free transfers. Chief among them being John Russell, Willie Jack, Matt Murray and Bobby Flavell. Trainer John Brown left too and the AGM heard that a new trainer had been appointed in Walter McCrae. This year's annual meeting heralded the arrival on the Board of Bob Thyne and heard manager McDonald proclaim his belief that Kilmarnock were *"on the threshold of something big"*. The shareholders, satisfied with progress on the pitch, turned their complaints on to the state of Rugby Park. There was a clamour for a new stand. The old one, holding just 2,000, was recognised as being obsolete but the old bogey - money - prevented the construction of one more in keeping with the club's renewed stature.

MATCH OF THE SEASON

December 10th 1955.
Celtic 0 Kilmarnock 2

Killie supporters couldn't believe that the team they had watched struggle up to this point was the same one they saw at Parkhead. Celtic, the League leaders, were unbeaten at home but were rocked by a Davie Curlett goal in just four minutes. Jimmy Brown then made two fine saves before Beattie and debutant Chris Fletcher took charge of midfield. Alex Rollo and Willie Toner - converted to centre-half from centre-forward by McDonald - were also playing out of their skins against their old club. In 38 minutes, Fletcher, on the left, passed to Harvey who, in justification of his 'Puskas' nickname, beat no fewer than four Celtic defenders before squaring the ball for Curlett to score his, and Killie's, second goal. Killie kept up the pressure after the break and they were as likely to score a third as Celtic were to pull one back. The 2-0 result was Killie's first League victory at Celtic Park since September 1936. They followed up seven days later by beating reigning Champions Aberdeen, to claim a mid-table slot which set them up for a solid second half of the season.

1956-57 DIVISION ONE

McDonald's bold declaration looked premature, to say the least, when the team opened with one solitary win in their League Cup section. Even in the early part of the League campaign Killie looked distinctly ordinary, despite occasional flashes of brilliance such as when they recorded what was only their second League victory at Ibrox; a game in which they could have scored six by the interval yet had to settle for Curlett's lone strike. Rangers performed better in the second half but, as the *Sunday Post* put it, *"like the spectator who was carried bodily from the terracing by four policemen, they were always struggling"*. Another fine win was the 4-1 thrashing of Ayr United in the first Division One Derby match since the war, but by December when Rangers arrived, looking for revenge at Rugby Park, Killie had averaged just a point per match.

In this one game Kilmarnock emerged as a side not only capable of troubling the best, but one which could live with the elite on their own terms. Every player was a hero. From the bandaged Jimmy Brown in goal - hastily returning from injury - to Bertie Black on the wing. And of them all, none was bolder or braver than Gerry Mays - scorer of two goals - whose performance was dubbed in the press as his *"finest hour*". Killie beat the 'Gers 3-2 to record a league 'double' over the Glasgow side for the first time. Even more importantly, they now embarked upon a run which would see them go 14 games without loss and which stretched into March 1957.

There were some excellent performances. A gallant draw at Celtic Park after being a goal down - Mays again saving the day. Five games in a row without losing a goal - the origins of Killie's famed 'Iron Curtain' defence. Victory - and another 'double' - at Somerset, followed by a Cup win over Ayr at Rugby Park the following week. A spirited triumph over a tough Airdrie side which saw Killie enter the semi-finals of the Scottish Cup for the first time since 1938. When the run came to an end - with a midweek defeat at Falkirk - few thought it was a portent of the immediate future. Killie simply carried on as if they had never lost. They won their next three League games, including a 4-1 success over a Hearts side seven points clear at the top of the table. In the Cup, the final was just six minutes away when Celtic - going for a fourth final in succession - equalised to please the majority of the six-figure crowd. The replay was a different story as Killie cantered to a 3-1 win and prepared to face relegation-haunted Falkirk in the Final.

MATCH OF THE SEASON
April 24th 1957.
Falkirk 2 Kilmarnock 1

Killie approached the Final under a threat of disciplinary action. Forced to play a League game at Kirkcaldy on the Monday prior to the Final, the Ayrshire team responded by putting out what was virtually a reserve side - only Gerry Mays of the eleven who lost 4-2 at Starks Park would walk on to the Hampden pitch five days later. There were many who thought that Killie could have played their first eleven and won both matches, for Falkirk were a poor team. They had struggled all season to avoid relegation. Yet they had taken three of the four points on offer in the League clashes between the teams. That should have served as a warning to Killie. It didn't. Prentice's penalty gave Falkirk a deserved lead against a disappointing Kilmarnock team. Curlett's volley just before the break giving Killie an equaliser they scarcely merited. In the second half the Rugby Park forwards were atrocious - only Black playing well. Lucky to obtain a replay, the general opinion was that Killie couldn't possibly play as poorly again.

The answer to that was that they could play a whole lot worse. Again, the forwards just couldn't get going, Curlett and Mays in particular looking sluggish. The defence was little better and it was no great surprise when all-round slackness was punished by Merchant's header in 24 minutes. At last Killie woke up. Black, Rab Stewart and Mays all went close. Eventually, Curlett scored from a Burns corner to take the game into extra time where a mix-up between full-back J. Stewart and centre-half Toner allowed Falkirk's Moran in to score. Killie had lost, yet in a way it was a triumph. Just three years previously they had been a 'B' Division side. Now, they (and Falkirk) had confounded every know-all pundit in the country by playing before 160,000 spectators over the two games. Just as in 1920, Killie proved that you didn't have to be a big city club to have thousands of loyal fans.

When Killie finished their season by playing two matches less than 72 hours after the replay and taking three points, they had reached 3rd place, equalling their previous best of 1918. McDonald's comments at the previous year's AGM no longer seemed so far-fetched. With the club's deficit entirely wiped out, a 'token' £20 SFA fine for fielding the reserves at Kirkcaldy, and some promising youngsters like Joe McBride, Pat O'Connor and Bobby Kennedy signing on, the future appeared to be bright indeed. Just at this point the man credited with the turnaround in the club's fortunes - manager Malky McDonald - handed in one month's notice.

Dave Curlett equalises for Killie on the stroke of half-time.
Killie lost the 1957 Cup Final replay versus Falkirk, 2-1.

So tactics were invented in the late 60's were they?

Manager Malky McDonald sets his stall out for the 1957 Cup Final.

Reverberations and recriminations were both instant and intense. Supporters wondered why McDonald, after seven years in which he had transformed Kilmarnock into one of the best teams in Scotland, would wish to leave to join Brentford - a team in the English Third Division (South). The Board came in for ferocious criticism at what should have been a celebratory AGM. Why hadn't they kept McDonald? What, if anything, had they done to try to keep him? Who would be the new manager? The questions were fired in without mercy as the beleaguered directors seemed unable to come up with anything which would placate the wrath of the supporters.

The fans were astounded to learn that McDonald had worked all these years without a contract. That no contract had been offered and no improvement in salary considered. Money, it appeared, was the answer. Brentford had made McDonald an offer which - to use the cinematic jargon of a time yet to arrive - he couldn't refuse. The Board had simply accepted the situation and that was that. As far as a new manager was concerned, they had no intention of advertising. They would approach candidates as they saw fit. That only led to a bout of feverish speculation which swept across the town. Ex-Rangers hard-man defender Willie Woodburn, said one rumour. Bob Shankly, said a second. No, it would be Scotland trainer and former Killie player, Dawson Walker, said a third. None of these were even asked.

Two who were - Walter Galbraith and Willie Thornton - turned the job down flat. With the new season less than a fortnight away Killie were still without a manager.

The optimism of April had been but the precursor to an uncharacteristically gloomy July. In a bid to stave off the relentless criticism at the AGM, Chairman George Barr tried to announce some good news. Matt Watson had been released from the forces after just a few weeks. *"Apparently"* said the Chairman, *"the armed forces don't like his feet but they will do for us"*. The joke fell as flat as poor Matt's feet.

Chapter 8
CHAMPIONS - WADDELL, EUROPE AND GLORY 1957 - 1965

1957-58 DIVISION ONE

On August 1st 1957, Willie Waddell, the 36 year old former Rangers and Scotland winger took over as Kilmarnock manager. Once again, an inexperienced man was at the helm of the club - it was Waddell's first managerial appointment. With the new season just six days away, there was little time for the fans to form an opinion of the new boss before events on the field got under way. One change was noticeable though - Waddell would be in charge of the football side of affairs only. The secretarial/administrative role carried out by all former managers was eschewed by the new man as he strove to prove that the modernity of his ideas would be the recipe for continued success.

It was an unsettling time; several senior players were due benefits and, clearly, they could not all be accommodated at once. Skipper Ralph Collins was at the head of the list and over 8,000 saw McDonald's Brentford belie their status by winning 2-0 in Collins' testimonial. The team qualified from an all-Division One League Cup section for the first time, the three points taken off Hearts would be exactly half as many as that team were destined to lose in the entire League campaign. A close fight with Rangers in the last eight saw Killie maintain an aggregate lead in front of 66,000 at Ibrox until less than a quarter of an hour from the end before narrowly losing.

There was a good start in the League too. Henaughan, back after two years in the army, was in good form as was Gerry Mays who, at 36, was as old as the manager. Mays hit 14 goals in as many games. Yet some fans still weren't satisfied. The Mauchline branch of the Supporters Club complained that there was too much barracking of players at Rugby Park.

The barracking got worse as winter arrived. Throughout December and January Killie won just one of the ten League games played. Indeed, from the end of November until March 15th, the only team they beat in the League was Queen of the South (twice) yet, ironically, the Dumfries side knocked Kilmarnock out of the Cup for the second time in three seasons to dash any hopes of further Hampden glory. The one bright spot was the emergence of Joe McBride who made his debut in a Christmas Day defeat at Dundee. His two goals in the 3-3 draw with Rangers at home proving he had the skill to play against the best. Killie won again at Ibrox this year, by 4-3 and with victories at Easter Road and Pittodrie as well, the poor winter run was a puzzling failure. The team recovered well enough to finish in 5th place but the crowd at the final home game, versus Raith Rovers, was just 4,478 - the lowest since the war. It was an indication of two things. Firstly, that football's great hold on the populace was beginning to weaken as the age of television dawned, and that the Kilmarnock support in particular now expected so much of their team that a position, which only a few years beforehand would have been seen as cause for celebration, was now regarded as nothing special.

At the time the powers-that-be wrote off the poor crowd as being due to wintry weather and a clash with the Cup Final.

Another modern innovation was the creation - by the Supporters Association - of a *'Player of the Year'* award, the first recipient being Willie Toner. There was sadness too with the death of two of the club's truly great players. Jock McEwan, stalwart of the 20's and 30's was only 55 when he died in October 1957. In April 1958, that legendary figure of the Edwardian era - Jimmy Mitchell - passed away, aged 78. Their memory was honoured at an AGM which saw a return to in-fighting as Hugh Morton - recently appointed a Scotland selector - lost his place on the Board to Tom Lauchlan.

MATCH OF THE SEASON
April 5th 1958.
Kilmarnock 1 Hearts 1

Since being outclassed by Killie in the League Cup, Hearts had been a team transformed. They were so far ahead of the rest of Scottish football as to render the Championship meaningless well before Christmas. They arrived at Rugby Park having lost just five points out of the sixty on offer and with 122 goals scored in their 30 League games - an average of more than four per match. They were ***eighteen*** *points clear of their nearest rivals and two points from Killie would allow them to officially celebrate the formal accomplishment of their first League Championship of the 20th Century.*

Not for the last time, Killie were determined to spoil the Jambos flag day. After 30 minutes of solid pressing, the Edinburgh side took a deserved lead as a 30 yard shot screamed into the Killie goal. 10 minutes later, Hearts looked to be two up before the linesman spotted an infringement unseen by 22 players and 15,865 supporters. The let-off inspired Killie in the second half. On the hour mark, Burns' corner was side-footed goalwards by Bobby Kennedy and in a desperate bid to clear, the visitors left-half, Thomson, put the ball past his own keeper as Hearts dropped their sixth - and last - point of the season.

1958-59 DIVISION ONE

Waddell's second season in charge was marked by another good League Cup campaign as Killie qualified from a difficult group, then easily beat Dunfermline in the Quarter-Finals, only to lose 3-0 to Hearts at Easter Road in the Semi-Finals. Yet the League was a different story. With only one win from the first seven played and supporters, already angry at a rise in admission from 2/- to 2/6, beginning to stay away, Waddell swapped around inside-right Beattie and right-half Rab Stewart for the fixture at Palmerston Park. It worked. Stewart justified his elevation to the forward line by grabbing a hat-trick as 4th-bottom Killie thumped Queen of the South 5-0, yet in the long run the significance of the occasion lay in moving Frank Beattie into the half-back line.

The same month - October - saw Willie Toner become the first Kilmarnock player to turn out for Scotland since Tom Smith, when the centre-half played against Wales. Yet that didn't deter Waddell from dropping Toner and bringing back Bobby Dougan. In the mythology which has grown up over the past thirty years it is difficult to imagine a time when Willie Waddell was ever treated with less than reverence by Kilmarnock fans, let alone booed by them, but in ditching their idol, Toner, the supporters vented their feelings on Waddell in no uncertain terms. Peace - of a kind - was restored when Toner was brought back into the side. But, with a characteristic show of determination, Waddell played him as a right-back, keeping Dougan as pivot.

Gerry Mays became the latest old-stager to receive a benefit but fewer than 3,500 watched the strange match with Brentford. The English side's fog-bound flight left late and ended up diverted to Edinburgh. By the time they arrived, both teams agreed to play 40 minutes each half. Even so, it was 9.45 before the teams left the field, Brentford having won 3-0. As the old stars took their leave (Ralph Collins was freed this season) Waddell sought fresh blood. Pat O'Connor was given a few games this year and Vernon Wentzel, the Rhodesian who had figured occasionally the previous year, enjoyed an extended first-team run during which he scored all four goals in a win over Airdrie. But it was another old favourite - Jimmy Brown who took over Toner's mantle as Player of the Year.

Waddell now put his plans in gear for Kilmarnock's most ambitious move. As part of a long-term policy, he started offering full-time contracts. At £20 per week this compared very favourably to the wage of the average spectator and was rumoured to be only £2 less than that available at Ibrox. It was also hoped that, with England still having a maximum wage (something which had never applied in Scotland), players would be encouraged to stay at Rugby Park rather than travel South of the border. The snag was that the current part-time wage was £15 per week and in order to make the full-time set-up more attractive, the part-time scale was reduced to £12. Needless to say, this was not viewed in an entirely good light by those players happy to remain part-time. Still, it was an indication of the progressive outlook at Rugby Park that despite a £2,000 drop in gate money and a loss of over £700 for the season that such moves were put into motion.

MATCH OF THE SEASON
February 14th 1959.
Dumbarton 2 Kilmarnock 8

This Scottish Cup second round tie was Killie's version of the St. Valentine's Day massacre. Yet the lower League Sons controlled the opening stages of the match until the fifteenth minute when Wentzel, facing a goal "as wide open as his native veldt" as one scribe put it, shot Killie ahead. In 32 minutes Burns added a second and when the Dumbarton 'keeper brought down McBride five minutes after that, Mays netted from the spot for the third. Dumbarton pulled a goal back a minute later but McBride restored Killie's three goal lead 30 seconds from the interval. In 51 minutes it was Mays' turn to be brought down in the box and McBride returned the earlier compliment; his penalty making it 5-1. Wentzel got the sixth in 65 minutes with Dumbarton scoring immediately afterwards. McBride got his hat-trick after 73 minutes and Wentzel completed the scoring with his own third, and Killie's eighth, twelve minutes from the end; completing a satisfying afternoon for Kilmarnock in which it was reported that Black was the outstanding player. Ironically, he was the only forward who failed to score.

Killie hit another purple patch in the next round. Away to Hamilton they were lucky to be still on level terms after 68 minutes yet ended up winning 5-0! Another away tie - at Aberdeen in the Quarter-Finals - ended Killie's Cup interest when they lost a tough game 3-1.

1959-60 DIVISION ONE

This season didn't start as if it was going to be the best in Killie's history to date. After a poor League Cup campaign, the League got under way with two opening defeats, including a 5-0 thrashing at home by St. Mirren. After seven games Killie were fourth bottom but, aided by the return of Willie Toner, four games later were fourth top. Even so, they didn't look like title contenders and when they suffered another 5-0 pasting - this time at Ibrox - Killie were heading for mid-table obscurity. Matters were compounded by the sale of Joe McBride to Wolves and Killie struggled to replace their centre-forward. The club's ambition was demonstrated by attempts to sign Willie Bauld and Jackie Mudie. Both Scotland internationals, both proven goalscorers and both reluctant to come to Rugby Park. One former Scotland men who did sign was Andy Kerr. The £6,000 fee it cost to bring him from Manchester City being a record for Kilmarnock.

Kerr joined a team which was starting to show some consistency both in selection and in performance. Bobby Kennedy was back from injury and Jim Richmond a £4,000 signing from Falkirk proved to be a wise investment at right-back. Richmond's debut - against Raith Rovers in December 1959 - marked the start of a remarkable unbeaten run. For four months Killie beat every team they played in the League - fifteen matches in all. With a good Cup run as well, Kilmarnock played 21 games during this spell of which they won 20 and drew the other. There were some outstanding results. The earlier humiliation by St. Mirren was reversed with a 3-0 win at Love Street, much-fancied Dundee were routed 4-0 at Dens Park, and big Jackie McInally scored his first hat-trick in a 5-1 home slaughter of Partick Thistle. Yet the press were slow to praise Killie. 12 of their 20 victories were by the odd goal and eight League games and one cup tie saw Killie score the winner in the final five minutes of the game, leading some to suggest that an element of luck was involved in this marvellous run. A similar suggestion to golfer Gary Player met the withering riposte *"It's funny. The harder I practice the luckier I get"*. That reply could well have been Killie's motto as they kept on winning, against the odds.

A wonderful week in February summed up the determination of this Kilmarnock side. On Monday 22nd, they fought back from a 1-0 half-time deficit to force a Cup replay with League leaders Hearts. Wednesday 24th saw them eliminate the Edinburgh club at Rugby Park with an 86th minute winner from Bobby Stewart. And on Saturday 27th a brace from McInally saw Killie emerge triumphant over a highly-rated Motherwell side in the next round of the Cup.

Now the press had to consider a very real possibility; Killie could become the first team apart from the 'Old Firm' to win the 'Double'. The next cup tie on the agenda was of an entirely different complexion to the thrillers against Hearts and Motherwell. More than 30,000 had watched the match at Tynecastle. Nearly 25,000 witnessed the replay. And Killie's crowd against Motherwell - at nearly 30,000 - was the largest ever assembled on Rugby Park for the visit of anyone bar Rangers and Celtic. Yet fewer than 3,000 were permitted to watch their Quarter-final clash against the fishing village team Eyemouth United.

The non-League club had deservedly fought their way into the last eight by beating Albion Rovers and Cowdenbeath and they provided a few anxious moments, pulling a goal back after Killie had gone two up. Although Killie dominated the match, the result was always in doubt right up until the final whistle blew, their 2-1 win putting them into a semi-final clash with Clyde - twice cup winners in the previous five years. Killie rattled up consecutive League wins numbers 12, 13, 14 and 15 between the time of the draw and the semi-final. One of these, a victory over Hearts, opened up the League race. The press changed tack. Now Killie were accused of 'ruthlessness', a laughable allegation. It may seem unthinkable now, but not one Rugby Parker had been so much as booked during the season and they were the only team in Scotland that could boast such a record.

Killie safely disposed of Clyde in their Ibrox semi-final and their thoughts returned to the League. They had 47 points with four games to play, three behind Hearts who had played a game more. On the Monday after the semi-final, Killie were expected to close the gap to a single point by winning at East End Park Dunfermline. Alas, nobody had told Dunfermline. The Pars were in the midst of a dour relegation fight and they battled gamely that evening. In the second half, a shot from Ron Mailer from all of 40 yards screamed past Jimmy Brown in the Killie goal. The run was over and the title dream ended. Hearts beat Clyde the following evening and confirmed that the flag was Edinburgh bound when they drew at Love Street on the same day as Killie were held at Rugby Park by Rangers in a Cup Final 'rehearsal'. Killie did emerge with some consolation. They had taken a record points haul - 50 - and they had achieved their highest ever League position by finishing runners-up. If they had failed to enter the new arena of European football, they had the consolation of being nominated by the Scottish League to take part in the International Soccer Tournament in New York. It was a surprise therefore, when a section of the support slow-handclapped and booed the team during the last League game of the season against Clyde. The *Standard* - correctly - berated the fans for their poor memories. A side which not so long ago had languished in the backwaters of 'B' Division, was now flying overseas to represent their country against the cream of World football.

Killie set off for America minus the injured Bertie Black. In his place came Tommy Bryceland - on loan from St Mirren. They left Scotland happy in the knowledge that a new stand, indicative of their higher status, had been given the go-ahead. Manager Waddell was busy right up to almost departure time. He snatched the signature of Rangers free transfer man Brian McIlroy, wanted by several clubs, but about to become a key component of the brilliant team Waddell was assembling at Rugby Park.

In the USA Killie got off to a sound start. They beat Bayern Munich and Irish side Glenavon. The big test was against Burnley - Champions of England. Killie won with ease, Andy Kerr and Vernon Wentzel scoring the goals which shocked English football. Burnley moaned and complained about the result. Killie were lucky, it was a fluke, the Burnley players weren't accustomed to playing in the heat. Perhaps a summer holiday on the Ayrshire coast would have disabused them of the notion that Killie gained any advantage from the sun. In turn, Waddell attacked the English team's attitude. They weren't happy with their luxury hotel, they whinged about not getting steak every day. Indeed, said Waddell, *"The Shah of Persia wouldn't get the treatment Burnley were looking for"*.

Killie won their section by drawing with Nice of France and beating the host side New York Americans. Almost two months later - and just a week before the start of the Scottish season - they crossed the Atlantic again to play the Final against Bangu of Brazil. The match was lost 2-0 but Killie had triumphed with the public. The Scottish players applauded the Brazilians off the pitch and raised the Bangu captain up on their shoulders. The Americans loved it. Before a ball was kicked in the 1960-61 season the New York organisers were pleading with the Scottish League to enter Kilmarnock in the next year's tourney. Back home, a belated AGM heard that the season ended was the most successful in the club's history. There was a profit of nearly £3,000. Gates were up by over £4,500 to a total of £37,350. And Willie Waddell continued to make some shrewd signings. Local lads called up for the new season included goalkeeper Sandy McLaughlan from Ardeer Recreation, centre-half Jackie McGrory from Kilmarnock Amateurs and a promising pair from the Saxone Youth Club, Eric Murray and Andy King. One item from the 'B' Division days remained unresolved as the condition of the Rugby Park toilets was again criticised at this meeting.

MATCH OF THE SEASON

April 23rd 1960.
Rangers 2 Kilmarnock 0

It isn't often that Killie are favourites to beat Rangers. Even less so when the match in question is the Scottish Cup Final, as this one was. But that was the scenario. Killie were greatly improved from the eleven who lost 5-0 at Ibrox in the League. One week before the Final the honours had ended even in a 1-1 draw at Rugby Park and while Killie had been climbing the League to challenge for the title, Rangers had slipped back to third and a long way behind Hearts and Killie.

But an early injury to Willie Toner seemed to disrupt Killie's pattern in what was, in truth, a poor game. The long-ball approach failed to unsettle Rangers and winger Davie Wilson and half-back Ian McColl put Killie under severe pressure. Four times in the first twenty minutes Jimmy Brown saved his team. Then, in 22 minutes, McColl slipped the ball to Wilson who beat Richmond and crossed the ball into the penalty area. Jimmy Millar beat Brown to the jump and Rangers were a goal ahead. Killie did attempt to come back into the game - a McInally header was well saved by George Niven - but half-time arrived with Rangers holding their precious lead.

The last occasion when Kilmarnock played in front of a crowd in excess of 100,000.

The second half opened sensationally when Matt Watson bumped Alex Scott outside the area and the Rangers man fell inside it. Penalty, said referee Bobby Davidson. The feared Eric Caldow stepped up to take the shot but memories of 1929 were revived and justice was done as Cadlow belted the ball over the bar. Beattie and Kennedy took up the pace for Killie but little of note occurred until, once again, the 22nd minute of the half. And once again it was Jimmy Millar. Again he fired in a header. Again, the ball landed in the net. 2-0 to Rangers and the match was effectively over. Killie did fight back but to no avail. They trooped off the Hampden pitch as 'Double' runners-up.

One of the saddest players must have been Jackie McInally. Just twelve months earlier he had scored twice for the victorious Crosshill Thistle side at the same ground in the Scottish Amateur Cup Final. His hopes of a notable 'double' dashed. McInally had played in front of 2,500 that day. Now he watched as the stadium disgorged 108,0 17 from its portals. It would be the last time that a Kilmarnock side appeared before a six-figure crowd. The team returned home where they were welcomed by thousands lining the streets. The good people of Ayrshire were determined to pay tribute to their heroes. Kilmarnock - the revelation of the season - deserved every single cheer.

No, not a new strip. Killie happily pose for the camera in the latest Gannex rainwear prior to the 1960 U.S.A. trip.

1960-61 DIVISION ONE

An excellent League Cup campaign was followed by an unbeaten six match start to the League programme. Even when Killie did lose a game - at Dundee - they responded with another fine run - seven matches without loss. And in contrast to 1959-60 this was achieved with a changing side. Five different players played on the right wing. 'Keeper Jimmy Brown was transferred to St. Mirren, Killie receiving £5,000 plus Campbell Forsyth. Sandy McLaughlan took over in goal. Beattie was switched from right to left-half where it was reported he was *"not at ease on the left side of field"*. A statement guaranteed to raise eyebrows among Killie fans under the age of 40. Brown's last match - against Airdrie - also marked the debut of a young centre-half who would go on to become one of the finest ever to appear in a Kilmarnock strip. Injuries to Willie Toner and Bobby Kennedy plus a National Service call-up for Pat O'Connor meant that the name of Jackie McGrory appeared on the team-sheet for the first time.

That another title challenge was in the offing was confirmed with a tremendous win at Ibrox. Two down in 35 minutes, Killie were level by half-time. Hugh Brown's winning goal sparked off celebrations among Kilmarnock supporters which would not be seen again on that ground for over thirty years. Following up with a 5-3 win over Motherwell in which Andy Kerry grabbed four goals, Kilmarnock could content themselves by looking at the League table which read; Rangers P13 Pts 22, Kilmarnock P14 Pts 21, Third Lanark P14 Pts 18. 1960 ended as the most successful calendar year in the club's history. 57 competitive matches had been played in the League, Cup, League Cup and the New York Tournament. Of these, 38 had been won, 10 drawn and only 9 lost.

The New Year seemed to wreck Kilmarnock's title hopes though. Three successive defeats sent the team plummeting down to 4th place, nine points behind leaders Rangers. Then, just as in the previous season, Killie embarked on a long unbeaten run, starting with a 5-1 demolition of Ayr United and followed by a resounding 6-0 victory over Raith Rovers. But gaining ground on Rangers was hard work. With eight games remaining they were still eight points adrift, albeit with a game in hand. Killie kept plugging away at the gap and showed themselves to be no fools by comprehensively beating Rangers 2-0 on April 1st, a result which left the top of the table looking like this:-

	P	W	D	L	F	A	Pts
1. Rangers	31	21	5	5	79	37	47
2. Kilmarnock	31	18	5	8	66	41	44

Now there was a chance that Kilmarnock might just catch the favourites. The next week saw Killie win 3-1 away to Motherwell while Rangers were - incredibly - trounced 6-1 at Aberdeen. The 'Gers squeezed a nervous 1-0 win over Hibs in midweek to leave the situation like this:-

	P	W	D	L	F	A	Pts
1. Rangers	33	22	5	6	81	43	49
2. Kilmarnock	32	19	8	5	69	42	46

Killie were forced to endure two agonizingly blank Saturdays as the annual England-Scotland match and the Cup Final were given precedence over League fixtures. They offered to play Dunfermline the night after the Scottish Cup Final replay but Pars boss Jock Stein refused.

In 1960, Killie played Bangu of Brazil in the Final of the International Soccer League in New York

His side had just won the Cup for the first time by beating Celtic and he had no intention to aid Killie's dream of overhauling the other half of the 'Old Firm' by letting Kilmarnock take on a tired Fife outfit and grab the two points which would increase the pressure on Rangers.

Killie did have one important game during this period. They played the side who had beaten them in America - Bangu - at Rugby Park in a friendly and won 1-0 in front of over 18,000 jubilant fans. The crunch arrived on April 29th. Kilmarnock entertained Partick Thistle at Rugby Park and had to win while at the same time hope that county rivals Ayr United could beat Rangers at Ibrox. Ayr's relegation place had already been booked but they had upset Rangers earlier in the season by winning at Somerset Park. Killie raced ahead in their match and amassed a 4-1 lead by the interval.

Spectators anxiously awaited the news from Ibrox. There was to be no joy. Rangers too were 4-1 up. Reality dawned on the Kilmarnock support. It was asking too much to expect a team at the foot of the table - especially deadly local rivals - to beat Rangers at Ibrox. The flag was Glasgow-bound. There were no more goals against Thistle and Rangers ran out easy 7-3 winners over Ayr. Killie duly beat the new Cup holders at East End Park to finish just one point behind Rangers and were left to ruefully reflect on those three defeats in a row at the New Year. Victory in just one of those games would have made Kilmarnock the Champions.

Once again Kilmarnock were selected to represent Scotland in America. They flew off in good heart. Andy Kerr - scorer of 34 League goals - had equalled the record held by 'Peerie' Cunningham and he now succeeded Billy Muir as Player of the Year. Willie Waddell and Walter McCrae's efforts were rewarded with new five-year contracts. And they long-awaited new stand finally got the go-ahead.

In the States, Killie were not as successful as in 1960, finishing 5th in their group. There were some who thought that they were playing on the wrong continent. Having finished twice runners-up in the League they had a case to compete in the Inter-Cities Fairs Cup but the SFA decided which teams to select for this tourney and merit seemed to play little part in their considerations.

In 1960 they had entered 7th place Hibernian and now they again put forward the Easter Road team (7th again) and 8th-placed city rivals Hearts as the Scottish entries. Their somewhat specious argument was that they wanted clubs who would attract big gates to represent Scotland. However, Dunfermline were now going into the Cup-Winners Cup and their drawing power was certainly no better than Kilmarnock's.

Killie returned home to find they had recorded a profit of £9,385 for the year and to local headlines which pronounced that Bobby Kennedy would not be sold to either of the two clubs after his signature - Manchester City or Everton. As is often the case, such a firm denial of any intention to transfer a player was merely the prelude to his eventual sale. In July 1961 Kennedy was sold to Manchester City for £45,000 - a record for a player from a Scottish League side. With no obvious replacement, supporters were distinctly doubtful about Killie's chances to maintain their record of the past two years.

MATCH OF THE SEASON
October 29th 1960.
Rangers 2 Kilmarnock 0

Killie's League Cup form was exemplary. They had rattled through their sectional matches, losing only after they had already qualified. Clyde were easily disposed of in the two-leg Quarter-Final and Hamilton were brushed aside at Ibrox in the Semi-Final. Now they met Rangers in the Final at Hampden. It was a quick opportunity for revenge after the Cup Final defeat six months previously. And it was a better match too. Rangers had players like Alex Scott and Davie Wilson on top form in attack, the incomparable Jim Baxter in Midfield and the best full-back in Scotland - Eric Caldow -in defence. Yet Killie opened more lively as Muir hit the side-netting in five minutes. Beattie clashed nastily but innocently with Jimmy Millar which resulted in both players needing treatment. Rangers team-work was superior but Killie's tackling was stronger. Brown made a diving save from Davis. At the other end, Andy Kerr forced George Niven to his knees to bring off a good save. Then Millar passed to Ralph Brand who left Beattie trailing in his wake, took the ball clear of the advancing Brown and angled it home to put Rangers ahead eight minutes from the interval. Brown had his work cut out, making fine saves from Millar and Ian McMillan, to keep the score to 1-0 at the break.

The second half opened with Wilson hitting the bar before Killie struck back - Bertie Black shooting wide from a good position. Kerr headed narrowly past the bar. Scott almost forced a second for Rangers - Toner having to fall to his knees to ***head*** *clear. McMillan lashed a shot off the post. Scott saw Brown off his line and sent over an in-swinger. Brown back-pedalled furiously only to see the ball hit off the post and fall over the line. Rangers had won the League Cup for the first time in twelve seasons. Yet this had been Killie's best performance for some time and those who expected a massacre went home disappointed. Left to ponder that following the League, Cup and New York tournament, this was Kilmarnock's* ***fourth*** *runners-up prize in six months, many of their fans wondered just what they had to do to actually win something.*

1961-62 DIVISION ONE

By their own recent high standards this was a disappointing season for Kilmarnock. Yet it started promisingly. After winning their first three League games Killie were top of the table and had unearthed a promising new find in 16-year old schoolboy Ronnie Hamilton who scored twice on his debut against St. Mirren. But they didn't have a 'general' in the middle of the park to replace Kennedy. After months of speculation, Waddell finally signed Davie Sneddon from Preston for a club record of £17,000. But it would take time before Sneddon's ability would make its mark on the field - and even longer before it became apparent to many supporters.

Successive home defeats by Motherwell and Rangers in December pushed Killie down to 6th and they never got back into the title hunt, finishing in 5th spot. Off the pitch the new stand was progressing nicely. It would have over 4,000 seats - twice as many as the old one.

When complete, Rugby Park would have cover for 25,000, meaning all but the very biggest attractions could be watched in the dry. Doubts were expressed as to how often anyone would get wet as attendances fell. An increase in ground admission from 2/6 (12½p) to 3/- (15p) was partly responsible as was the heightened expectations of the supporters. Chairman George Barr reckoned that a home average of 12,000 was needed if Killie were to compete at the top. One pleasing note was the election of club captain Jim Richmond as Player of the Year.

MATCH OF THE SEASON
March 10th 1962.
Kilmarnock 2 Rangers 4

Kilmarnock had an easy ride in the early stages of the Scottish Cup. A 1st round bye was followed by a trip to Brechin where the humiliation of 25 years ago was assuaged with a 6-1 win. A 7-0 stroll over Highland League Ross County set the scene for this Quarter-Final tie. For the third year in a row Killie's most important game was a cup tie. For the third year in a row their opponents were Rangers. Interest in the game was immense. Rangers received 7,000 tickets which they sold easily. All the others were quickly snapped up in Kilmarnock. 36,500 tickets were printed and every one of them was accounted for by the time the game took place, although the actual numbers passing through the turnstiles totalled 35,995. It was the largest crowd ever seen at Rugby Park and, owing to modern safety factors, will remain the ground record in perpetuity. There was a sensational start to the match. In just eight minutes, Hugh Brown dispossessed the acclaimed Jim Baxter and crossed to Andy Kerr whose diving header gave Killie the lead.

Kerr passed up chances to bury Rangers after that, heading over the bar from a McIlroy cross then shooting harmlessly when a pass to Sneddon might have been more productive and was certainly more obvious. Others spurned opportunities too; right-half Ian Davidson shooting high and wide from a good position. In an exciting contest Rangers came back into the game; McLaughlan making two good saves near half-time. Just when it looked that Killie would make the dressing-room with their lead intact, disaster struck. Sneddon (who was having his best game in a Kilmarnock jersey) tackled McMillan on the edge of the box. As the Rangers man went down, a penalty was awarded. Caldow sent McLaughlan the wrong way as be blasted home the equaliser.

In 61 minutes Ritchie, the Rangers 'keeper, punted the ball up to Brand who swiftly passed to Wilson. He, in turn, laid it off to McMillan who belted the ball into the net from 20 yards. An object lesson to those who think the 'long ball' approach was patented in Wimbledon in the mid-1980's. But Killie weren't finished yet. With twelve minutes remaining, Sneddon passed to Black who shot past the advancing Ritchie to make it 2-2. Just seven minutes were left on the clock when McMillan changed the nature of the game. He went on a long solo run, dodging, dummying and dribbling before despatching a dynamite drive to put Rangers ahead once more. Brand added a fourth two minutes from time to give the score a more uneven look than the game deserved. For the third year running Kilmarnock had lost their most crucial match to Rangers. Yet, in defeat, they had served up a performance in keeping with their status as one of Scotland's top sides. This had been a game worthy of the vast crowd which had witnessed it.

£45,000 was a record sum for a midfield player in 1961. That's what it cost Manchester City to obtain the services of Killie right-half Bobby Kennedy. He returned to Rugby Park when with Grimsby Town to play in Frank Beattie's testimonial ten years later.

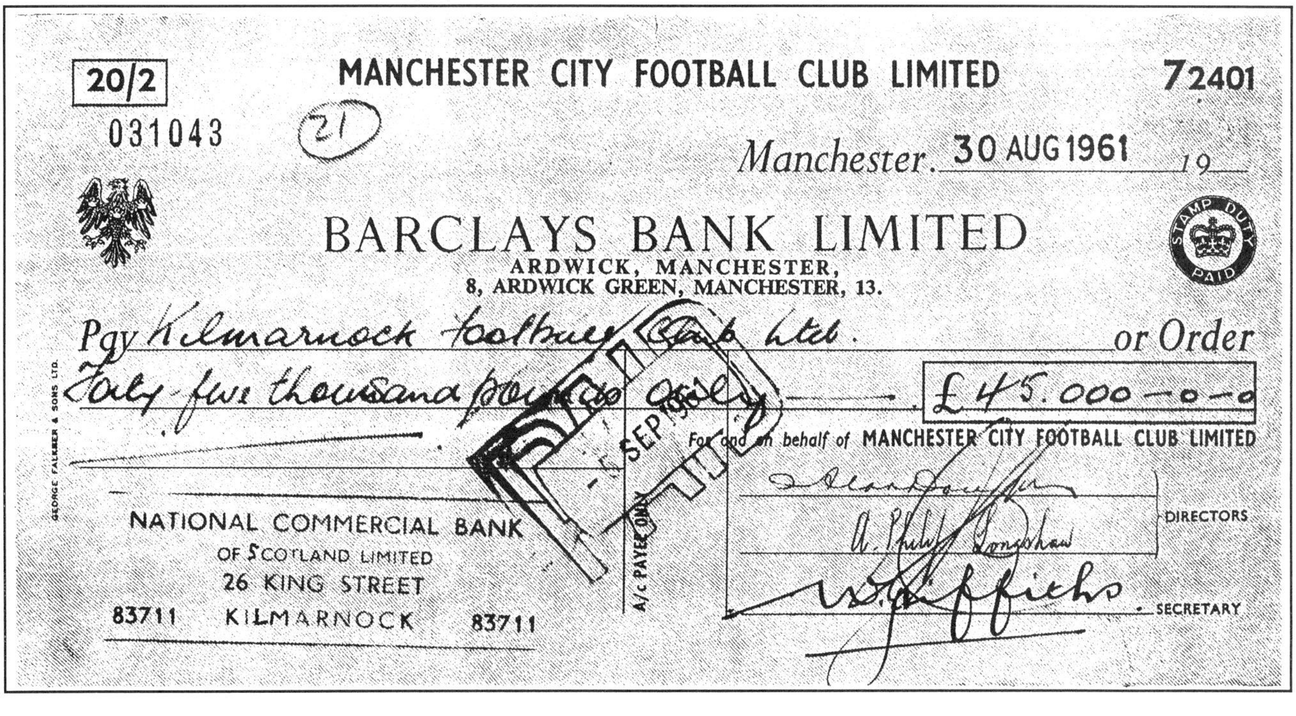

1962-63 DIVISION ONE

Kilmarnock were one of nine Scottish clubs who applied for the three Fairs Cup places on offer and the reaction from Rugby Park was furious when the SFA selected 3rd placed Celtic, and 4th placed Dunfermline, then leap-frogged past 5th place Killie to enrol Hibernian (who had finished 8th the previous season) for the last place. Killie director Bob Thyne had protested in person - but in vain - demanding that teams should be selected on merit only.

The team set about sorting out the injustice in the best way possible - winning on the pitch. By mid-October they had lost just once in sixteen League and League Cup outings, scoring in every game. When their run came to an end they immediately picked themselves up and started knocking in the goals again. The results this season give the lie to those who asserted that Killie were primarily a defensive side. They took on an Airdrie team fresh from an 8-1 win over Raith Rovers and showed the Broomfield outfit what it felt like to be humiliated, winning 8-0. They put seven past Queen of the South without reply but failed to score even once against the same team in the Cup three weeks later, as the Palmerston Park hoodoo continued to hold sway.

Motherwell were beaten 7-1 in a game which saw seven different Rugby Parkers get on the scoresheet. They made sure that Celtic winger Jimmy Johnstone would never forget his debut game, hammering Celts 6-0 for what was Killie's eighth win in succession. And they could dish it out away from Rugby Park too; as both Clyde and Falkirk - beaten 5-0 on their own grounds - would testify.

The European disappointment was also forgotten when Moscow Torpedo played in a memorable friendly at Rugby Park. The Russians led 2-0 and 3-2 before Killie emerged triumphant 4-3 in front of nearly 17,500 spectators; many of whom invaded the pitch in celebration of a glorious victory. Meanwhile, manager Waddell refused to rest on his laurels.

Forever seeking out promising youngsters, he signed three future Scotland players inside a month. First came Billy Dickson, a full back from Birkenshaw Amateurs. A week later, he returned to the same Lanarkshire side for Dickson's team-mate and best pal, Tommy McLean. Waddell persuaded the outstandingly talented winger to append his signature to a Kilmarnock contract while - at the same time - Rangers boss Scot Symon was sat downstairs waiting to speak to young Tommy. A fortnight after that, young goalkeeper Bobby Ferguson joined up to complete a remarkable treble.

But while Waddell was busy securing the future, the present took several turns for the worse. Killie's title challenge faded after a 6-1 rout at Ibrox, which left them six points behind Rangers. Then the AGM heard that the club had traded at a profit thanks only to transferring players. It was now claimed that an average gate of 13,000-14,000 was needed, something that had rarely been achieved at Rugby Park and, with gates falling all over Scotland, was highly unlikely to ever be realised. The same meeting affirmed, though not without dissent, that the team's new blue and white stripes were here to stay.

The worst news of all though concerned the weather. Heavy snow had fallen as early as the beginning of November and, by January, blizzards had become the norm. Killie, two months without a game, were lightly treated compared to some. The last match before the great shutdown was a 0-0 draw with Queen of the South in the Cup, the first scoreless game at Rugby Park since April 1957. It would be 44 days before the replay took place, only for Killie to take what was now an accustomed Palmerston Park knockout. In the League, nine long weeks elapsed without Killie kicking a ball. They did manage one game near the end of the big freeze, a friendly which they lost 4-1 away to English Champions-elect Everton. It was the worst disruption of sport in British history and its legacy can still be seen today in the form of the Pools Panel which made it's bow this year. Another feature of this winter readily recognisable to the modern ear, is the demand for a mid-season break. *"Support growing for winter shutdown"* read the headlines in early 1963, a call which has been parroted throughout the years by those who possess a power beyond the reach of we mere mortals, the ability to forecast accurately, when a British Winter will arrive and depart, and arrange sporting fixtures some months in advance, to coincide with their prognostications.

With the arrival of the thaw, came the revival of Kilmarnock's fortunes. They consolidated on the three wins they had enjoyed before the shutdown, extending the winning run to eight. Indeed, they lost only once in their final sixteen League games. They battled with Partick Thistle for second place and qualification for yet another American trip, ensuring success thanks to the 5-0 Brockville win, as Thistle lost at home to Aberdeen. Second in their own right and Atlantic bound again, Killie were four points behind Rangers, but the Glasgow club had so many games in hand as to render thoughts of the title meaningless.

The team still had something to play for. The Falkirk match also saw them beat the previous best total of League goals by a Kilmarnock side and they finished with a total of 92, two fewer than Rangers. So much for the defensive tag. Two players who weren't around for the end of season, were Andy Kerr and Willie Toner. Kerr was sold to Sunderland for a (for the time) huge fee of £25,000 while Toner, nearing the end of a fine career but unable to dislodge Jackie McGrory from the first team, departed to Hibs for a more modest £750. His first match for the Easter Road team was a European one, a prize again denied to his former colleagues. Astonishingly, the names of Partick Thistle and Hearts were put forward for the Fairs Cup. Thyne's protest and the fact that Killie, again, had finished runners-up in two of the three domestic competitions failed to sway the Scottish FA. This was an injustice crying out to be righted.

Killie narrowly failed to win their section in the States and had to put up with the strange behaviour of Italian side Mantova. They claimed that Jim McFadzean, who had scored against them, was an impostor. This preposterous assertion was later withdrawn but not before Willie Waddell had witheringly shrugged it off by asking: *"Who did they think he was ? Pele?"* without wishing to disparage the versatile McFadzean, this was a case of mistaken identity which few Kilmarnock fans were ever likely to make.

HEART OF MIDLOTHIAN
SCOTTISH LEAGUE CUP FINAL
KILMARNOCK
PRICE 6D.
Kick-off 3 p.m.
SATURDAY 27th. OCTOBER, 1962
HAMPDEN PARK · GLASGOW

MATCH OF THE SEASON
October 27th 1962.
Hearts 1 Kilmarnock 0

People need heroes and heroes need villains. It has been ever thus. Beowulf and Grendel, Wallace and Edward I, Holmes and Moriarty, Batman and the Joker. This was the match which finally saw Frank Beattie enter the pantheon of Kilmarnock heroes and also provided the supporters with an arch-enemy - a Joker if you like - for years to come in the unmistakable, bulky figure of Tom 'Tiny' Wharton, the match referee. The controversy arou sed by Wharton still stirs emotion to this day among those who were there when little else remains in the memory of the match itself.

At first sight it appears remarkable that so much passion surrounded the fixture. For this was the weekend when the world held its breath. The Cuba crisis was at a peak and few could say with certainty that the threat of nuclear oblivion would be averted. In these circumstances it might appear odd that over 50,000 people should choose to spend what may have been their last day on Earth, watching twenty-two men hump a leather sphere around a park. Be that as it may, almost half of those present had resolved that if the end of the world was truly nigh then they were going to see Kilmarnock finally win some silverware first.

Killie's achievement in reaching the League Cup Final for the third time in a decade had been superb. They had banged in 20 goals in their qualifying section, dropping only one point. Partick Thistle (then at the top of the League) had been shrugged aside with ease in the Quarter-Finals. But when the Semi-Final draw had paired Killie with Rangers, even their most fervent supporters had groaned. Since their victory as a 'B' Division side over Rangers in this competition, they had been drawn to play the Ibrox men five times in the two Cups, losing each tie; three times in the Scottish Cup and twice in the League Cup.

This time was different. Beattie outshone his Rangers opposite number - Jim Baxter. Jackie McGrory came of age in repelling the star-studded Rangers attack and Matt Watson - despite being injured - held off the threat of the precocious Willie Henderson. 76,000 saw McIlroy head Killie in front after 16 minutes only for Rangers to score twice in the next eight minutes. Following a neat one-two with McIlroy, Kerr equalised just before the break. With only ten minutes remaining, Black rose above the entire defence to meet Sneddon's corner and nod home the winner, ending an enthralling match described by the late Hugh Taylor as the "greatest ever game in League Cup history".

So Killie took the Hampden field confident of repeating that success against Hearts. Bertie Black failed to repeat his Semi-Final heroics, twice not being sharp enough to take the chances which came his way. Killie were the better side early on but Hearts looked more threatening coming forward. Their most dangerous player was Willie Hamilton and Hamilton it was who advanced menacingly, midway through the first half. He beat Richmond, centred the ball beyond McGrory and there was Norrie Davidson running in to put Hearts in front. Killie tried to fight back. Near the end of the first period, Beattie let go a belter which forced Marshall into making an incredible save. Hearts dominated the early stages of the second half but in the last twenty minutes, Killie played as if the world really was going to end any second. They piled forward in waves. But attack after attack ended fruitlessly until there were just thirty seconds of the match remaining. Richmond punted a free kick into the penalty area and Frank Beattie soared above everyone in the crowded box to majestically head home the equaliser. Or so it seemed....

There were scenes of jubilation among both players and supporters until Wharton ignited a fuse of hatred by signalling a free-kick to Hearts. What for? The linesman's flag had stayed studiously down, not a single Hearts player had protested that anything was untoward. Killie players surrounded the referee (no mean task, given his girth) and eventually Wharton walked over to consult the linesman. That conversation has never been revealed but it was enough for the referee to stand by his decision. The conclusion among the support was that he must have felt that Beattie had handled the ball. Once again, Killie were forced to accept second prize.

But the furore didn't finish there and then. Fans asserted that the only time the referee had been up with play had been at corner kicks. Most felt that he had been nowhere near the area when the alleged handling took place. Beattie denied handling the ball. Waddell thought it a fine goal. It was said that the truth would never be known, but if 'Tiny' Wharton saw Frank Beattie handle the ball then he witnessed something which was not seen by 51,280 spectators, twenty-two players, both linesmen, the two benches, a whole bemused press box and TV crew, and very probably the ball-boys, the St. Andrews Ambulance and the vendors of the half-time pies.

In a gesture of Corinthian vintage, Kilmarnock asked the SFA to appoint Wharton as the referee for their friendly with Moscow Torpedo. Wisely, the SFA appreciated the gesture but declined the offer. Wharton became the object of the Killie fans wrath from that day until the end of his career, with even those too young to have been there joining in the crescendo of booing which greeted him at every Rugby Park game he ever officiated at. Beattie, after years of trying to prove himself, became lionised by the supporters. He was a worthy choice as Player of the Year. In denying him that equaliser, Wharton helped create the legend that Frank Beattie became. For that, at least, Kilmarnock supporters owe him their thanks.

1963-64 DIVISION ONE

For so long this looked like it might be the season when Kilmarnock won that long awaited trophy, perhaps even the Double. They hit the top of the League early on and with players like Davie Sneddon and Campbell Forsyth finally winning over the fans, prospects were good. There was still some discontent amongst the support, who felt that the money received from transfers should have been spent on strengthening the side. And, despite the team's form, crowds were down again. Eric Murray had briefly assumed the captaincy, Jim Richmond had lost his place to Andy King and was transferred to St Johnstone, but when Rangers arrived at Rugby Park on November 16th, Frank Beattie led the side for the first time. The table when the teams emerged for this match read:

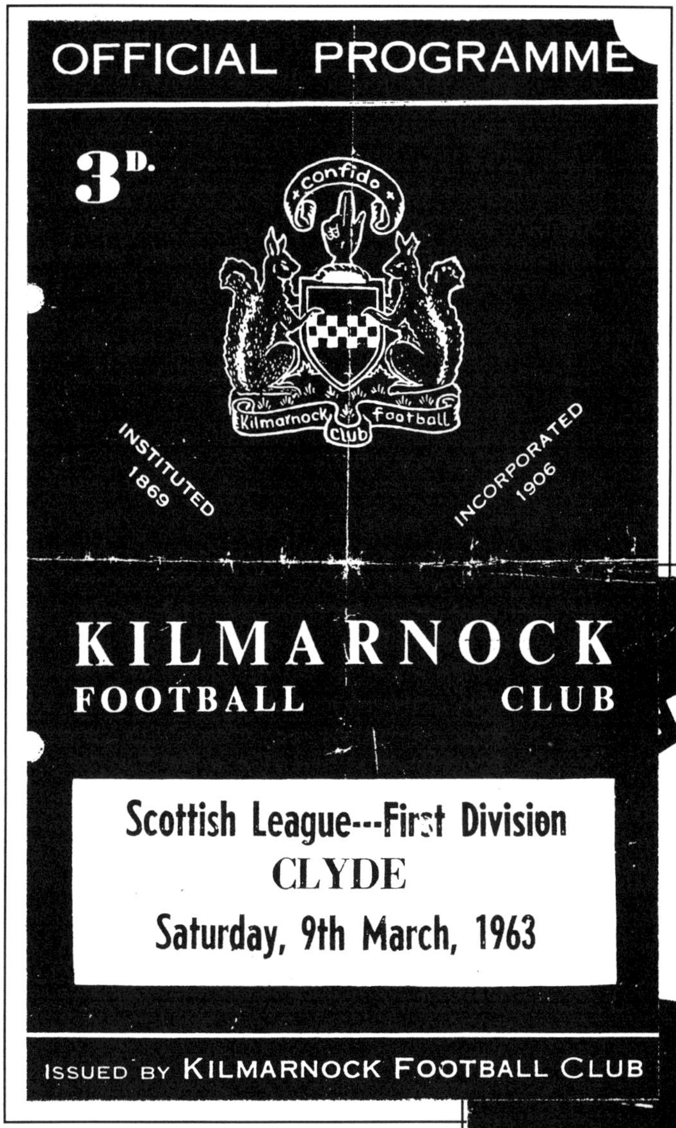

Rugby Park seldom falls foul of the weather, but the winter of 1963 was horrendous. This game against Clyde was the first action on the Ground in **nine weeks.**

Killie returned to the U.S.A. in 1963. Although playing German side Preussen Munster, the programme cover features one of Killie's other opponents in the group - West Ham - with a young Geoff Hurst in action against Leicester City!

	P	W	D	L	F	A	Pts
1. Rangers	11	9	2	0	32	3	20
2. Kilmarnock	11	9	1	1	26	9	19
3. Dundee	11	7	2	2	28	12	16

McIlroy's 57th minute goal looked to be enough to put Killie back on top until one of those 'soft' penalty decisions which Rangers seem to attract in abundance, gave them a lucky equaliser. Killie lost their next match 5-0 to Celtic and the fans waited to hear what Waddell's plans were. The manager, plus Walter McCrae and Dunfermline boss Jock Stein had been the only representatives from Scotland present at a 'teach-in' by the legendary Helenio Herrerra, coach of Inter Milan and High Priest of catennacio. Although Waddell thought that there was much to learn from the Italians, he was to tell the Rugby Park AGM that in modern football, *"coaching swamped individual talents"* and that there were *"fewer personalities allowed to express themselves"* in the modern game. Statements which have issued forth from countless lips from that time to this.

When Rangers sensationally lost to St Johnstone, it allowed Killie's 2-1 win at Third Lanark to propel them back to the top at Christmas:

	P	W	D	L	F	A	Pts
1. Kilmarnock	17	12	3	2	37	19	27
2. Rangers	17	11	4	2	45	16	26
3. Dundee	17	10	4	3	43	21	24

Killie had embarked on a run of nine successive wins, seven in the League, two in the Cup which saw them safely overcome the New Year period, a time when they had been undone in the past. Yet all was not entirely well. They had struggled to beat non-League Gala Fairydean and Division Two Hamilton in the Cup and the straight run in the League had not shaken Rangers challenge any, though it had eliminated the rest from contention as the table showed:

	P	W	D	L	F	A	Pts
1. Kilmarnock	22	17	3	2	53	25	37
2. Rangers	22	16	4	2	55	21	36
3. Hearts	23	12	7	4	50	26	31

February opened with Killie losing 2-0 at Firhill, a game in which Partick could have scored another four but for the brilliance of Campbell Forsyth in goal. Niven, his Thistle counterpart, didn't have one difficult save to make all afternoon. Kilmarnock recovered sufficiently well to take six out of the next eight points, but a midweek defeat at Tannadice meant that they had 43 points with six matches remaining, while Rangers, also with six to play, had 45.

Within two weeks, the Killie season collapsed. The two table toppers met in the League at Ibrox on March 14th 1964 and the scoreline of 2-0 in Rangers favour, hides the fact that Killie were well beaten. They bounced back the following Saturday by beating Celtic 4-0, but seven days later, they were beaten out of sight, going down 4-0 to Dundee in the semi-final of the Scottish Cup at the same Ibrox ground which had buried their chances in the League. Any faint hope of landing the flag was dispelled by a 2-0 defeat at Motherwell four days after the second Ibrox fiasco.

Having lost three of their first twenty seven League games and then four of the next five, Killie had slipped to fourth. They partially redeemed themselves by winning their last two games to claim runners-up spot for the fourth time in five seasons. Yet the altered attitudes of the support and the gravity of their slump was reflected in the attendances for these last two games, both at home. 4,321 and 3,672 respectively, the worst since the War. The high points at the end of the season came when Campbell Forsyth, the new Killie Player of the Year, made his debut for Scotland and performed well in a 1-0 win over England. Also, came news that, at long last, Kilmarnock would play in Europe for the first time, as League placings were used to determine the Fairs Cup entrants.

A new competition, the Summer Cup, conceived in the aftermath of the dreadful winter of 1963 began. All Division One sides entered except the Old Firm, who stood aloof and thus became responsible for it's failure, after two years. Killie were red hot favourites to win it, but after qualifying from a section which saw the number of times they defeated their erstwhile bogey team, Queen Of The South rise to six this season they lost to Hibs in the semi-final. There were many who thought that Killie's good days were over and that the end of season slump presaged a return to mid-table mediocrity at best. If those critics had seen the two youngsters, Dickson and McLean,in their Summer Cup outings, they may have been forced to change their minds. Killie finished? No way. The best was yet to come.

MATCH OF THE SEASON

February 8th 1964.

Kilmarnock 9 Falkirk 2

A riot of a day. Killie could have beaten anyone in Scotland and most of the rest of the globe too on the form displayed here. Having lost the League lead at Firhill the week before, this was the answer to the critics. The game was scarcely a minute old before Stuart Layburn, in a rare First Team appearance, passed the ball to Brian McIlroy who crashed it past Willie Whigham to open the scoring. McIlroy tried again in the 4th minute, with a shot which Whigham could only parry to the waiting Beattie who notched the second. Neat inter-passing between Hugh Brown and Jackie McInally resulted in 'Big Jake' grabbing the third. Ten minutes later, it was McInally again from an opening supplied by McIlroy. Then, in one of those 'death or glory' runs which were a feature of his play, McInally ran right through the Falkirk defence on his own and dribbled round Whigham. With Jackie, it was still only an even money bet that he would score, but this time there was no mistake as he netted his hat-trick. Time: 32 minutes, just thirteen minutes after his first. Right on the interval mark, Sneddon rolled a short corner to Beattie who stroked the ball back to McIlroy for the prolific Brian to score from an impossible looking position on the bye-line. Half-time, Kilmarnock 6 Falkirk 0.

Killie resumed, still bent on destruction. In 47 minutes, Whigham failed to hold Sneddon's cross and Brown was on hand to first-time the ball home for number seven. Three minutes later, an Eric Murray pass helped McIlroy to his hat-trick, and in 54 minutes, McIlroy out-paced the defence to rifle an unstoppable shot past Wigham to make it 9-0. In 61 minutes, McInally was brought down, but McIlroy spurned the chance to put Killie into double figures and net his own fifth, by shooting weakly at Whigham. Killie eased up now and Falkirk came forward to score a couple of late goals which, in view of what had gone on before, it would have been st retching credibility too far to describe as any sort of consolation. As Kilmarnock left the pitch to the cheers of their fans (and as rumour has it, one or two disgruntled about 'slack defending') they heard the news that Rangers had been surprisingly beaten by St Mirren. Killie were back on top of the League. One week after this performance, Killie drew 0-0 at Aberdeen. It was their first goalless draw in the League since November 1958!

1964-65 DIVISION ONE

Admission charges had been raised for the ground to 4/- (20p) from 3/- (15p) for adults and to 2/- (10p) from 1/6 (7½p) at the boys gate, but the club held the season ticket price at £6 in an attempt to prevent any further erosion in support. On the field, Waddell's faith in the 4-2-4 system he was deploying, was tested by some poor results in the League Cup. However, the final three sectional games were won as was the opening League game against Third Lanark and the team travelled to Germany for their European baptism in good heart.

A new era opens as Killie enter Europe for the first time with a daunting visit to the famous Eintracht Frankfurt.

Their opponents were Eintracht Franfurt, who had played in the 1960 European Cup Final at Hampden Park in what was almost universally regarded as the best club match ever. They still had four or five first-team regulars who had taken part in that wonderful exhibition of football against Real Madrid. Killie held their own after a nervous start and were starting to get on top when Eintracht opened the scoring. Inexperience showed as Killie lost a further two goals to leave the tie seemingly lost, with Waddell facing a barrage of criticism over his tactics.

Killie won three League games without losing a goal before facing Eintracht in a return leg which was viewed as a forlorn cause. Forced through injury to reshuffle his side, Waddell brought in 17 year old McLean, who had yet to make his League debut and, after less than two minutes, the task facing McLean and his fellow forwards was made even more difficult when a shot from more than 20 yards flew past Forsyth into the Killie net. Fans still entering the ground might have been tempted to walk right back out again upon finding that Killie were now four goals down.

4-2-4 was forgotten as Killie adopted an approach more like 1-1-9. In thirteen minutes Ronnie Hamilton scored from a Sneddon pass and four minutes later, McLean sent McIlroy through to make it 2-1 on the night. Now there was real hope but Killie's non-stop attack failed to reap any further dividends before half-time. They weathered an early second half flurry by the Germans but a McGrory free-kick which was headed home by McFadzean sent the home crowd into a frenzy.

One goal behind and more than half an hour to play. McIlroy got the ball into the net but it was chalked off. With nine minutes remaining, and just as it looked that Eintract were going to survive, McIlroy's cross was met by McInally's head and Killie were level. Jubilant supporters swarmed onto the pitch, unable to contain their delight. But the drama wasn't over yet. McLean tormented the German defence until he was brought down with just two mintues to go. Sneddon touched the free kick to Ronnie Hamilton who let fly and his shot took a deflection into the net. Again the pitch was invaded by ecstatic supporters. When the final whistle eventually sounded it was the signal for the third field invasion of the evening as Kilmarnock's first night in Europe ended in a magnificent victory which few could have hoped for and fewer still predict.

Yet as so often seems to happen, triumph was tinged by tragedy. Watching the Eintracht game was Davie Gibson, who played in the 1920 Cup-winning side. Four days later, at the home game against Dunfermline, he collapsed and died; leaving only Mattha' Short, Malcolm McPhail and John McNaught from the first trophy-winning side still alive. Killie won the game, ending Dunfermline's unbeaten start and the following week, forced to give Bobby Ferguson his first-team debut, (McLaughlan had gone to Sunderland and Forsyth was playing for Scotland in Wales) the young keeper was inspiring in a 2-1 away win to Hibernian which left the table reading:-

	P	W	D	L	F	A	Pts
1. Kilmarnock	6	6	0	0	11	2	12
2. Hearts	6	5	1	0	26	9	11
3. Morton	5	4	1	0	10	4	9

An impeccable start was blemished by a goalless draw with Partick Thistle the next week, but with Hearts also drawing, Killie stayed top.

McGrory's excellent performances saw him gain international recognition and both he and Forsyth played in the Scotland team which beat Finland 3-1 in a World Cup Qualifier in October 1964. Days later, Willie Waddell stunned the football world by annoucing that he intended to retire from soccer management and go back to journalism at the end of the season. Waddell would not be shaken from his intent. If his team ever needed any incentive to win the title then his announcement provided it. They went out and promptly took apart a Celtic side which had five future European Cup winners in it 5-2, having been 5-0 up in under an hour. Victory away to Dundee United meant that October ended with things looking like this:-

	P	W	D	L	F	A	Pts
1. Kilmarnock	10	9	1	0	20	5	19
2. Hearts	10	7	3	0	33	12	17
3. Hibernian	10	8	0	2	24	14	16

Killie wobbled in November, successive draws with Motherwell, Rangers and Aberdeen, wrapped aroung a double defeat by Everton which ended their Fairs Cup interest, but they still led Hearts on goal average. Oddly enough it was when they won at Clyde that they lost the lead. But the situation at the top was so close that when Killie won the next week against Falkirk, they returned to the top, again on goal average. Then came disaster. With Jackie McGrory missing through injury, Morton took Killie apart, winning 5-1. Now Hearts were the only unbeaten side in the League and they visited Rugby Park next. Despite losing an early goal, Kilmarnock stormed back to a 3-1 win, but Hearts still led - again, on goal average.

With emphatic 4-0 wins over Third Lanark and St. Mirren following, Killie were happy to see in 1965. But January proved to be as miserable this year as it had so often in the past. An astonishing defeat at relegation-bound Airdrie was followed by three goalless games, a draw with St. Johnstone and defeats at Dunfermline and Partick. The month ended with the fight for the flag now a four-way affair:-

	P	W	D	L	F	A	Pts
1. Hearts	24	16	4	4	65	31	36
2. Kilmarnock	23	14	5	4	40	19	33
3. Hibernian	22	15	3	4	51	27	33
4. Dunfermline	21	14	2	5	46	22	31

February was little better. Killie beat lower League opposition in the Fife pair of Cowdenbeath and East Fife in the Cup but their unbeaten home League record was ended when Dundee came to Rugby Park and won 4-1. Killie had amassed just one point from their last five games. Then came a welcome return to form with a stirring win over title rivals Hibs, but even this was almost lost, Killie leading 4-1 with three minutes to go and hanging on to win 4-3 in a game which saw Billy Dickson make his League debut and Bertie Black play his first League match of the season. Alas, the next game was Killie's fifth loss in the last seven played when they went down 2-0 away to Celtic. The misery was compounded when they returned to Parkhead the following Saturday and were beaten 3-2 in the Cup.

The strain was beginning to tell on all the contenders. On the day Killie lost the League match at Parkhead, Hearts had been beaten **7-1** at home by Dundee. It was a result which would have tremendous significance for the finale. But when Killie prepared to meet Dundee United in a midweek home game, they appeared to have blown all hope of the Flag. The *Standard* which had almost written them off after the Dundee defeat, said that *"Only a winning run can now keep Kilmarnock in with a chance of honours"*. The League table seemed to bear that out. Killie had slumped to 4th and looked to have difficulty even staying in that position. With a win at Firhill the previous evening, Dunfermline now headed the pack, and were installed as 9-4 favourites with Rangers. Hearts were quoted at 7-2, Hibs 9-2 and Kilmarnock were 25-1 outsiders.

	P	W	D	L	F	A	Pts
1. Dunfermline	25	17	3	5	59	26	37
2. Hearts	26	16	5	5	67	39	37
3. Hibernian	25	16	3	6	58	34	35
4. Kilmarnock	26	15	5	6	45	28	35
5. Rangers	23	12	7	4	58	23	31

Waddell, it appeared, was destined to finish his career a loser once again. Black returned against Dundee United and, just as he had done against Hibs, hit a brace as Killie won 4-2. Then Waddell made his most audacious move. He dropped International goalkeeper Campbell Forsyth. The out of form custodian had conceded 14 goals in his last five League and Cup appearances. In against Motherwell came Bobby Ferguson, so impressive in his one match earlier in the season, but untried beyond that. With the retention of Black, it was just the fillip the team needed. Killie beat Motherwell 2-0 at Fir Park, then drew 1-1 at Ibrox, a game they would have won but for that Rangers speciality, the 'doubtful' penalty. At any rate, this destroyed the fading Ibrox hopes, leaving Killie to slug it out with the Edinburgh pair and Dunfermline. A hard fought home win over Aberdeen meant that Kilmarnock left March in far greater spirit than they had entered it. The old adage was reversed. Killie had come in like lambs and gone out like lions.

Meanwhile, what of their rivals? Dunfermline had boosted their goal average with an 8-0 win over doomed Third Lanark, but they too had encountered trouble from Dundee, drawing 3-3 at home to the Dens club and losing, also at home, to Dundee United. The dog-eat-dog situation at the top got more complicated when they lost 1-0 away to Hibs. The Easter Road side had enjoyed a good month, beating Motherwell at home in addition to Dunfermline. Away, they had beaten both Third Lanark and Celtic and drawn at St. Mirren. But Hearts had performed best of all... Falkirk and Motherwell at home... Clyde and Morton away... they had won the lot. So, although Killie had gained ground on Dunfermline they had actually fallen behind the Edinburgh sides and games were running out, as the table shows:-

	P	W	D	L	F	A	Pts
1. Hearts	30	20	5	5	82	45	45
2. Hibernian	30	20	4	6	67	36	44
3. Kilmarnock	30	18	6	6	54	32	42
4. Dunfermline	29	18	4	7	70	31	40

True, Killie had to visit Tynecastle on the last day of the season, but, if Hearts kept on winning, that match would be meaningless by then.

But within a week of entering April, one of the contenders threw in the towel. While Killie clung on for a nervous home win over Clyde and knew that Dunfermline and Hearts had also both won at home, Dundee, yet again, crushed the aspirations of one of the leaders when they beat Hibs 2-1. The following Wednesday (7th) saw Killie scrape a 1-0 win at Falkirk while Hibs were sensationally beaten 4-0 at home by Celtic. These matches had been brought forward to avoid clashing with the Scotland-England clash at Wembley on the 10th and Killie knew that both Hearts and Dunfermline would now be looking nervously at the renewed Rugby Park challenge. The table now read:-

	P	W	D	L	F	A	Pts
1. Hearts	31	21	5	5	86	46	47
2. Kilmarnock	32	20	6	6	57	33	46
3. Hibernian	32	20	4	8	68	42	44
4. Dunfermline	30	19	4	7	72	32	42

Kilmarnock enjoyed a Saturday with the pressure off as their rivals sweated. Dunfermline laboured to a 2-1 win at Third Lanark and Hearts could only draw with Dundee United. That was the result Killie needed. They were now two points behind and could go to Tynecastle on the last day still in with a chance. But Dunfermline - Cup finalists hunting the 'double' - could still achieve their dream. They played their game in hand on April 14th and beat Rangers 3-1. Goal average might well prove to be decisive and in the days before the pocket calculator amateur mathematicians all over Scotland were frantically scribbling on bits of paper to show how the rivals stood:-

	P	W	D	L	F	A	Pts	G. Av.
1. Hearts	32	21	6	5	87	47	48	1.8510
2. Dunfermline	32	21	4	7	77	34	46	2.2647
3. Kilmarnock	32	20	6	6	57	33	46	1.7272
4. Hibernian	32	20	4	8	68	42	44	1.6190

The logic was clear. Hibs were out of it. The others would have to lose and Killie would have to beat Hearts while Hibs win their last two games, scoring heavily, to have any chance. If Killie beat Hearts then they might have a chance but not if Dunfermline won their games. Their goal average was far superior to all the rest. Hearts were favourites. Three points would clinch it. Two might be enough. That was why the air at Pittodrie was rent with cheers on April 17th 1965. Hearts had beaten Aberdeen 3-0. They now had 50 points. Hibs - despite a 5-1 win over Airdrie couldn't catch them. And the strain had finally told on Dunfermline. They had drawn 1-1 at home to St. Johnstone and were also out of the reckoning. That left only Kilmarnock. The side written off by many of their fans and by the press after their disastrous start to the year had kept plugging away while first Hearts, then Hibs, then Dunfermline were talked of as prospective Champions. Now Killie had battered Morton into submission by way of revenge for their Cappielow collapse. Three second-half goals, including another Bertie Black brace had pushed them back up into their accustomed second place. Quick calculations revealed that they would have to beat Hearts by two goals at Tynecastle if they were to collect that precious Championship flag.

"Noo's the day and noo's the hour" wrote one famous Ayrshireman, referring to an altogether different kind of battle. But Burns could hve penned those words for this most dramatic of matches. Thousands travelled from the Bard's county to see if Kilmarnock could snatch the title with a two-goal victory which would make them Champions by 0.04 of a goal. Back home, thousands more sat around their radios which frustratingly switched back and forth from Tynecastle to the Cup Final at Hampden between Celtic and Dunfermline. From the youngest to the oldest, all knew the significance of the occasion. Although the odds were stacked against Kilmarnock, there were few willing to wager that they would ever have another chance to become Champions. For, in its entire history, only twice previously had a team from outwith the four large cities of Glasgow, Edinburgh, Aberdeen and Dundee, taken the title. And one of those teams was Dumbarton whose triumphs were recorded at the very dawning of the League in the 1890's. The other, the fine Motherwell team of the 1930's.

But if Hearts were overwhelming favourites, they still had reasons to make them pause and ponder. There had been that 7-1 thrashing by Dundee. A less heavy scoreline that day would have made Kilmarnock's task even more difficult, if not impossible on this one. And Hearts had played Killie three times this season, losing twice, including a 1-0 defeat in the League Cup. That had been Killie's first away win of the season. Would today be their last? If so then the Edinburgh team would settle for a 1-0 defeat, for that would give them the flag. A further warning had been posted in a Sunday paper the previous week when the headline screamed

"HEARTS - CHAMPS OR CHUMPS?"

Today would provide the answer.

Waddell kept faith with the team which had beaten Morton. That meant the two talismen, the tyro Ferguson and the veteran Black - Killie's longest-serving player - neither of whom had tasted defeat in the League this season would play. So too would young Tommy McLean, fast becoming the most talked about winger in the country. The others picked themselves. The immaculate Andy King, along with Matt Watson, the new Player of the Year. The iron middle three of Murray, McGrory and Beattie. The scheming, skilful Sneddon, the razor-sharp Brian McIlroy and the all-action Jackie McInally. Others who had played such a valiant part in the campaign were destined to sit this match out. Ronnie Hamilton, the leading scorer; Jim McFadzean, the play-anywhere stalwart; Campbell Forsyth, until recently Scotland's Number One. A handful of others - Pat O'Connor, Hugh Brown, Frank Malone, Joe Mason and Billy Dickson had also performed when called upon. All now hoped - and some doubtless prayed - for those two precious goals.

MATCH OF THE SEASON

April 24th 1965.

Hearts 0 Kilmarnock 2

The match started with Hearts pressing forward, determined to snatch an early goal which would leave Kilmarnock facing a task of almost Eintracht proportions. Their Norwegian winger Jensen, left the defence trailing, drew Ferguson out of his goal and shot goalwards....... Breath swelled in thousands of Ayrshire lungs, sweetly exhaling as the ball cannoned off the post. Hearts drove forward again but Killie's defence, buoyed by the early let-off, adopted the motto of the French at Verdun.

The great day dawns.
The programme for Kilmarnock's epic match.

They shall not pass. And with Murray, McGrory and Beattie displaying all the resolve they were renowned for, they did not pass. Attack after attack foundered on those three immovable rocks.

Slowly, Kilmarnock began to match their opponents in attack as well. Hearts early storm had blown itself out midway through the half when Killie surged forward. McInally, surprisingly agile for his size, took a pass from McIlroy and sent the covering defender the wrong way as he darted along the bye-line to cross to Tommy McLean, waiting just outside the box. The youngster quickly fired over a cross and Davie Sneedon sped in to head the ball downward into the goal as Hearts defenders stood bemused. 1-0 to Kilmarnock.

Less than three minutes later, Bertie Black took the ball out on the left. Bertie waded his way across the pitch and past a series of defenders before releasing it to the advancing Brian McIlroy. Calmly, as if he was on the practice gound, McIlroy struck his shot firmly, but low, past Hearts 'keeper Cruickshank into the left corner of the net. 2-0 to Kilmarnock. Killie's dominance continued for the rest of the half and they retired easily holding that vital two-goal lead.

Hearts began the second half exactly as the first. Pouring men forward in an attempt to break down the Killie defence. They bombarded the goal but Ferguson was immaculate. Although Hearts occasionally looked dangerous, the entire Kilmarnock defence was resolute. The roars in the supporters throats grew ever louder as the ninety minutes elapsed but still play went on. Back home the radio announced a late goal that was heralded as the winner. Relief spread all over the county as it transpired that this goal was for Celtic in the Cup Final, not at Tynecastle. The radio commentary returned to Edinburgh where over three minutes of injury time had been played and Hearts were attacking once more, desperately seeking the goal which would give them the Championship. Beattie, for once, was beaten as Alan Gordon received the ball. He hit a belting shot to Ferguson's right hand side which looked like it was going all the way, but Ferguson threw himself toward the post and pushed the ball clear. Hearts had a corner though which was frantically cleared as the final whistle sounded. The long years of second prizes were over.

Kilmarnock were the Champions and Willie Waddell sprang from the bench like an Olympic sprinter to embrace and dance with his players. Celebrations continued long into the night as supporters, both at Tynecastle and at home, wept joyously, sang, chanted and jigged with delight. Evening papers, confirming the triumph were bought by the barrowload as Killie fans everywhere revelled in reading and re-reading the League table which now read:-

	P	W	D	L	F	A	Pts
1. Kilmarnock	34	22	6	6	62	33	50
2. Hearts	34	22	6	6	90	49	50

The press hailed Killie's success, *"a truly glorious effort"* said the *Sunday Mail*. Even the 'Times' in London, still a paper with only 'hatches, matches and dispatches' on its front page, found room to congratulate Kilmarnock even if its use of language was in the more sedate style expected of it. *"Kilmarnock snatch title by 0.04 of a goal"* it truthfully, if somewhat prosaically, reported in an article 'From Our Glasgow Correspondent.' as if Scotland were some imperial outcrop. Still, it wasn't every day that Killie made headlines in the 'Times'.

The following Monday, the League Championship Trophy was paraded around Rugby Park in front of the 5,673 dedicated supporters who braved the West Scotland monsoon to watch the occasion and also the Ayrshire Cup Final being played that night. Killie were still hungover - whether physically, metaphorically, or both was impossible to discern - from Saturday's triumph, and inexplicably lost the match to their Division Two opponents. For once, no-one cared. The season wasn't offically over. There was still the Summer Cup and another American trip to undergo, but for every Kilmarnock supporter, no matter where in the world they were, the curtain on 1964-65 rang down gloriously at 4.44 pm on Saturday 24th April at Tynecastle Park.

(Above) Davie Sneddon scores Kilmarnock's first goal in the crucial Tynecastle encounter.
(Below) Bobby Ferguson makes the save of his career in the dying seconds - allowing Killie to win the title.

At last. Kilmarnock are the Champions of Scotland and Willie Waddell is the first to congratulate his troups, hugging Sneddon and McInally. Bobby Ferguson is embraced by Bertie Black. Andy King (with arms raised) is congratulated by a jubilant fan.

For Hearts, Willie Wallace looks wistfully on, while Roy Barry slumps to his knees.

Homecoming. The night of April 24th 1965. As the triumphant Kilmarnock XI arrive back, a delighted populace takes to the streets to welcome the conquering heroes home.

Monday April 26th 1965.
Those supporters who braved the elements to watch the Ayrshire Cup Final see something really special
For only the third time the Scottish League Championship has been won by a team outwith Scotland's big four cities.
(Left to right): Black, Beattie, McGrory, Sneddon, Watson, McIlroy, King, McInally, Ferguson, Murray, McLean.

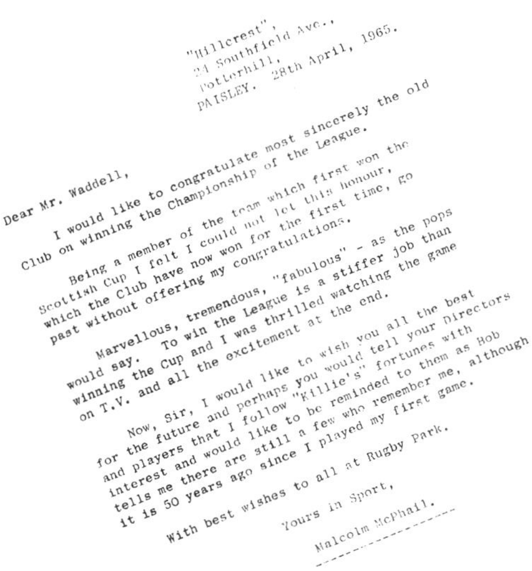

"Hillcrest",
24 Southfield Ave.,
Potterhill,
PAISLEY. 28th April, 1965.

Dear Mr. Waddell,

I would like to congratulate most sincerely the old Club on winning the Championship of the League.

Being a member of the team which first won the Scottish Cup I felt I could not let this honour, which the Club have now won for the first time, go past without offering my congratulations.

Marvellous, tremendous, "fabulous" - as the pops would say. To win the League is a stiffer job than winning the Cup and I was thrilled watching the game on T.V. and all the excitement at the end.

Now, Sir, I would like to wish you all the best for the future and perhaps you would tell your Directors and players that I follow "Killie's" fortunes with interest and would like to be reminded to them as Bob tells me there are still a few who remember me, although it is 50 years ago since I played my first game.

With best wishes to all at Rugby Park.

Yours in Sport,

Malcolm McPhail.

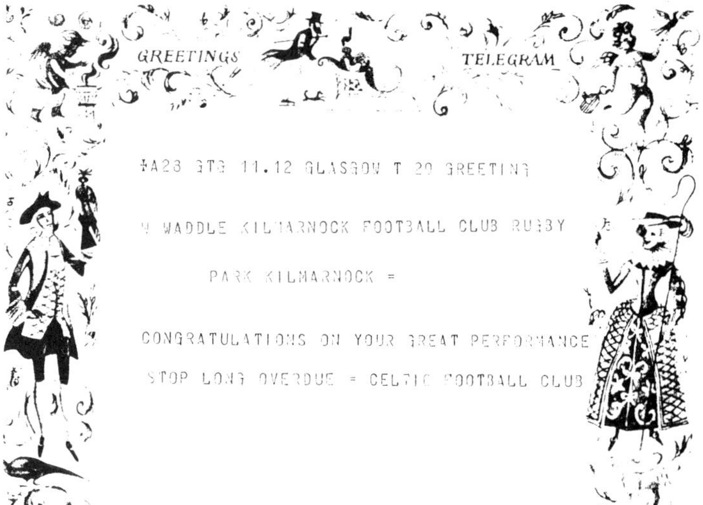

GREETINGS TELEGRAM

+A23 GTG 11.12 GLASGOW T 20 GREETING

W WADDLE KILMARNOCK FOOTBALL CLUB RUGBY

PARK KILMARNOCK =

CONGRATULATIONS ON YOUR GREAT PERFORMANCE

STOP LONG OVERDUE = CELTIC FOOTBALL CLUB

Two of the many letters and telegrams of congratulation.

Chapter 9

DECLINE AND FALL - FROM EUROPEAN ELITE TO RELEGATION

1965 - 1973

1965-66 DIVISION ONE

The close season didn't exist in 1965. The Summer Cup in May was followed by an experimental game under relaxed offside rules with Hearts in June; this match was Willie Waddell's last in charge of the side as his predecessor, Malky McDonald, became his successor for the trip to America in July. The eleven players who took part in the epic at Tynecastle played as a team on just six occasions; the last two League games, the Ayrshire Cup Final and three Summer Cup ties. When McDonald and his charges returned to begin the defence of their title and launch a new European challenge, the glorious memories of the recent past - the medals given to every player who took part in the campaign, the lumps in the throats at the sight of 1920 Cup-winners, Shortt and McPhail, toasting the success of the class of '65 - had to be put behind them.

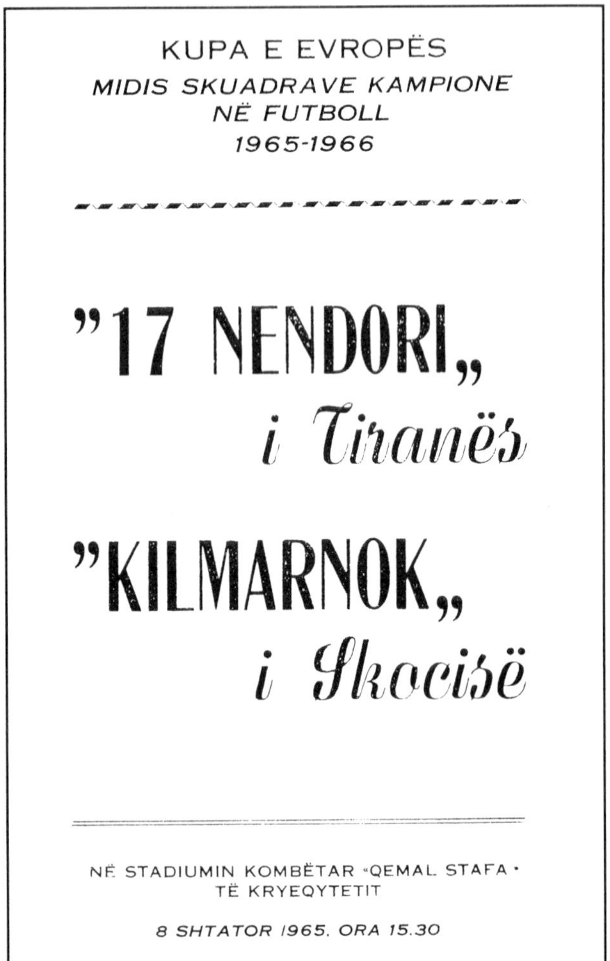
KUPA E EVROPËS
MIDIS SKUADRAVE KAMPIONE
NË FUTBOLL
1965-1966

"17 NENDORI"
i Tiranës

"KILMARNOK"
i Skocisë

NË STADIUMIN KOMBËTAR "QEMAL STAFA"
TË KRYEQYTETIT

8 SHTATOR 1965. ORA 15.30

A real rarity. The match programme from Killie's first European Cup-tie - in Albania. The first visit by any British club to that mysterious country.

But the League Championship flag, fluttering proudly in the Rugby Park breeze, was a constant reminder of what had been achieved, of what the support now expected and a yardstick by which future Killie sides would be judged. The team made a good start despite contract problems with Jackie McGrory which saw the centre-half ruled ineligible for Europe, and quickly went top. Then came a dismal run of five defeats out of six which put paid to hopes of retaining the Championship. When they lost 5-0 at Ibrox in November, they were seven points behind Rangers and out of the running. The Glasgow side had also ended Killie's League Cup hopes in an amazing semi-final which saw Killie trailing 6-1 with 20 minutes to play, yet saw them claw their way back to 6-4 by the final whistle.

The AGM heard that a profit of £21,401 had been made on the title-winning season and that there had been a modest rise in attendances - the first for several seasons. Willie Waddell had declined an offer to join the Board and a satisfied meeting concluded with a pledge from Chairman Bill McIvor that full-time football was essential to the club and that they would never go part-time again. That set the scene for a successful start to 1966 in which Killie enjoyed a run of 14 League and Cup games (including six straight League wins) in which they lost just once, between mid-December and March.

The most memorable game during this time was an incredible New Year's Day match at Love Street where Killie led 5-1 at half-time, finally beating St. Mirren 7-4. Rumours flew to the effect that perhaps more than a small Ne'erday dram had been indulged in by both sides prior to kick-off but this foul calumny on the dedicated athleticism of the Scottish footballer was never proven. Nor, it must be admitted, was it disproven either. Playing for St. Mirren that day was Gerry Queen whom McDonald promptly signed for £4,000 plus Ronnie Hamilton in part exchange. Queen was the most successful of McDonald's signings suring his second spell at Rugby Park and, later in his career, when playing for Crystal Palace, Gerry found himself the subject of one of the most famous newspaper football headlines ever. Sent off for fighting with an opponent, he (and thousands of others) turned to the sports pages the next day to see these immortal words emblazoned across the breakfast table:-

"QUEEN IN BRAWL AT PALACE"

Trophy hopes ended with a Cup Quarter-final defeat at Dunfermline and this prompted another signing by McDonald - the Danish international striker Carl Bertelsen arriving from Dundee for £8,000. He helped Killie finish the season strongly, ending up in 3rd place, behind the resurgent Celtic and Rangers, and qualifying for Europe once more. McDonald opened the cheque-book again, buying Craig Watson from Morton for £8,000 and off-loading Joe Mason in the process. The profits from the title had been spent on fresh blood. Whether they were up to the job remained to be seen.

The night it rained goals! The two allegedly best defensive sides in Scotland conceded 10 goals as Rangers beat Killie in the memorable League Cup Semi-Final.

When Killie made their first serious title bid in 1960, a Sunday newspaper mocked the very idea of a team like Kilmarnock ever playing the likes of Real Madrid. It came true, and the Spaniards left Scotland relieved with a lucky 2-2 draw. Alas they proved too strong in the 2nd leg.

One player who seemed certain to be on his way from Rugby Park was 'keeper Bobby Ferguson, whose outstanding form had merited selection for Scotland and who had been watched by several English clubs. Despite his international recognition, Bobby was not this season's choice as 'Player of the Year'. The coveted award going to the ever-reliable Eric Murray.

MATCH OF THE SEASON

November 17th 1965.

Kilmarnock 2 Real Madrid 2

Kilmarnock's foray into the European Cup saw them become the first British team to visit Albania where they earned a 0-0 draw in hostile conditions. Bertie Black's late winner at Rugby Park saw them safely into the last 16 where they were drawn - appropriately enough - against Real Madrid, the most famous club side in the world. Appropriately, because their Albanian foes rejoiced in the name of 17 Nentori, which means 17th November - the date for the clash with Real. And also since having played one of the teams who took part in that wonderful 1960 European Cup Final - Eintracht - it seemed apt that they now face the winners of that legendary contest - Real.

The Spanish side that visited Rugby Park hadn't won Europe's club competition since that historic Hampden final but they still had players from that eleven in their side. Puskas - the Hungarian genius and architect of the 1960 triumph stepped on to Rugby Park. As did Santamaria, who had won three European Cup winner's medals with Real. So too did Gento, the left-winger who had played in all five of Real's European Cup wins. There were new stars as well; players like the dangerous Grosso and men like Amancio and Zoco who had played starring roles in the Spanish national team which had won the European Championship the previous year. All in all it was a line-up which suggested that perhaps the Kilmarnock players would be better off staying indoors. After all, hadn't the great Real humiliated Rangers 7-0 on aggregate in 1963?

Yet when the match got under way, Killie treated Real in precisely the correct manner - with respect but not with fear. In just eight minutes Brian McIlroy had Rugby Park cheering to the rafters as he slipped the ball into the Spanish net. Shouts of joy metamorphosed into yells of anger as the supporters realised that McIlroy's 'goal' had been adjudged offside. Kilmarnock would not be denied though. In 20 minutes McInally was brought down in the box. Up stepped Tommy McLean - just 18 years old but already battle-hardened in Europe - to coolly slot home the resultant penalty and put Killie ahead. Four minutes later, Puskas - who up to this point had looked lethargic and even more on the portly side than in his 'Galloping Major' heyday - belied his apparent nonchalance by revealing a still-dazzling burst of speed which saw him shake off the defence and pass to Martinez who, in turn, rounded Matt Watson before crashing an unstoppable shot into the roof of the net. 1-1.

Play was evenly balanced when, in the 53rd minute, McInally was decked by Zoco inside the area. Perhaps fearful of awarding two penalties to one team, the referee waved play on as Killie fans howled for a spot-kick. Losing concentration briefly as a result, Killie found themselves behind two minutes later; Amancio scoring from Gento's cross. In 60 minutes came restored hope. Ronnie Hamilton's cross was met by Jackie McInally's head. Before he could be brought down a third time, McInally had firmly nodded in the equaliser. Kilmarnock continued to press, McLean in particular tormenting the Spaniards as if he was one of their own ancient Grand Inquisitors. Even the great Gento was reduced to fouling young Tommy, earning himself a caution in the process. But there was no further scoring and a crowd of nearly 25,000 roared with delight at the end of 90 minutes; proud that their team had proven themselves the equal of the magicians from Madrid.

The second leg was no mere formality for Real. McIlroy missed a sitter before stunning the crowd in the Bernabeau Stadium by putting Killie ahead in 27 minutes. After that the roof fell in. Within four minutes, Real - through Grosso and Ruiz - had scored twice. But, in a move which saw him at his best, McInally got possession and rounded the 'keeper. Then, Dr Jackie turned into Mr Hyde as he missed the open goal. Grosso added a third for the Spaniards before the interval. Gento scored a 4th in the second-half before Tommy McLean - on a night when nothing went right for Killie - missed a penalty kick for the first time. Grosso's 5th for Real gave the game a final scoreline which was at odds with the run of play. Kilmarnock were out of the European Champions Cup. But they had the comfort of knowing that they had made the Spanish maestros fight all the way. The Real Madrid side which eliminated Kilmarnock may not have been on a par with the team of 1960 but they were good enough to go on and win the European Cup, the sixth time they had done so.

1966-67 DIVISION ONE

It was a time of innovation at Rugby Park. Jim McFadzean replaced the injured Gerry Queen away to Clyde in September - the first Killie player to come on as a substitute in a first-class match. The home win over Hibs in October was recorded on video and used as an aid to training. McDonald doubled up briefly as caretaker manager of Scotland and a new country - Belgium - was visited as Killie won a bad-tempered Fairs Cup game against Royal Antwerp 1-0. On a sadder note, Bertie Black - after thirteen years - left the club. He was the first of the eleven who won the League to do so. Within six years they would all be gone.

Antwerp were slaughtered in the second leg - Killie winning 7-2. They accounted for another Belgian team, La Gantoise, in the next round. Leading 1-0 from the Rugby Park first leg, Killie were thirteen minutes away from victory when the Belgians were ludicrously awarded a free-kick (the referee ruling that Beattie had handled the ball when he was actually placing it for a Killie free kick) from which they scored. Two Belgians were sent off as Killie won in extra time. But the Rugby Parkers also had Jim McFadzean sent off for fouling an opponent who then pole-axed him. At least McFadzean went quietly. When McInally was sent off against Antwerp, Walter McCrae had to come on the park and order him to obey the referee's decision.

The League wasn't as successful; even a 0-0 draw with all-conquering Celtic (the first time Celts hadn't scored all season) was met with a chorus of boos. McDonald's tactics were too negative for many supporters.

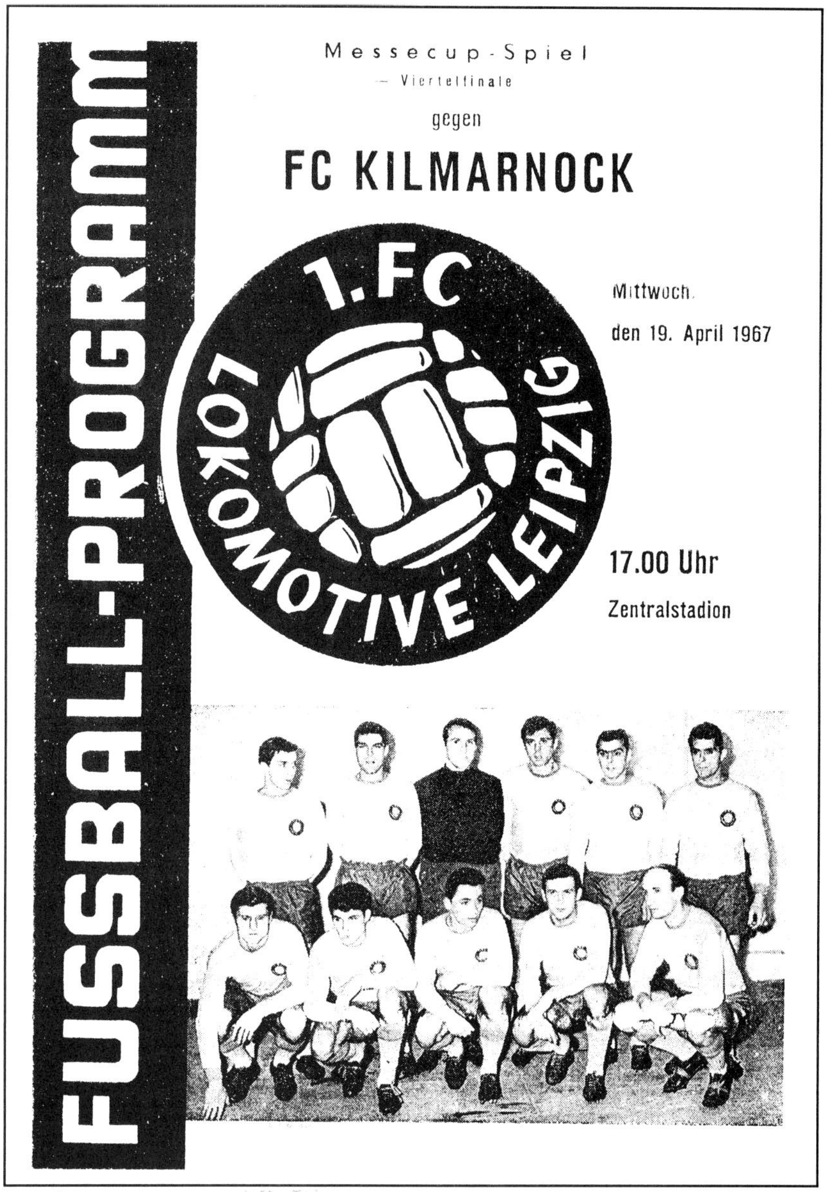

Voraussichtliche Aufstellungen der Mannschaften

(Änderungen vorbehalten)

FC Kilmarnock — Trainer Mc Crae

Ferguson 1

King 2 — Mc Fadzean 3

O' Connor 4 — Mc Grory 5 — Beattie 6

Mc Lean 7 — Mc Nally 8 — Berthelsen 9 — Queen 10 — Mc Ilroy 11

1. FC Lokomotive Leipzig — Trainer: Studener

Löwe 11 — Naumann 10 — Frenzel 9 — Engelhardt 8 — Berger 7

Drößler 6 — Faber 5

Zerbe 4 — Geisler 3 — Franke 2

Weigang 1

Kilmarnock travelled to the then East Germany to face Lokomotiv Leipzig in the Quarter-Finals of the Fairs (UEFA) Cup. They lost 1-0, but a 2-0 triumph in the return leg set them up for an enthralling Semi-Final with Leeds United.

The manager himself stated that qualifying for Europe was the aim if the club was "to make ends meet" as he told the AGM which also heard that there had been a lost of £21,298 over the year. McDonald faced some criticism but insisted that his first season back in charge had been a success.

Injuries forced him to give debuts to two young players ahead of schedule, against Hibs at Easter Road. One was Brian Rodman, inadvertently called 'Rothman' at the time of his signing and the other was an 18 year old from Port Glasgow who had only signed for the club two weeks previously, after scoring twice for the reserves as a trialist. Within four minutes of walking onto the Easter Road turf though, Eddie Morrison had scored for Kilmarnock - a sight which would become familiar to Killie fans for the best part of a decade.

KILMARNOCK
INSIDE-LEFT
EDDIE MORRISON

Killie's record post-war goalscorer. Clever, powerful, determined, brave, unselfish. It is easy to run out of adjectives to praise Morrison. Suffice to say that those who saw him in his prime were privileged indeed.

The following week provided another of those 'trick' questions which infuriate football supporters. Which King and Queen stood to attention under the Soviet flag? The answer being Andy **King** and Gerry **Queen** as the Kilmarnock players were introduced to the Prime Minister of the Soviet Union - Alexei Kosygin - as he attended Killie's game with Rangers. A huge crowd greeted the Russian guest by chanting his name football-style, as the hammer and sickle flew over Rugby Park for the day. Kosygin - a keen football fan - had insisted on seeing a football match during an official visit to Scotland and picked a cracker which Killie lost narrowly 2-1.

Kilmarnock won the next five after that and reached 3rd place with three games remaining but with only one point from that trio of matches, they slipped to 7th and missed out on European qualification by one place. In order to play on the continent next season they would have to win the Fairs Cup.

After a four-month gap, they returned to duty in that competition, narrowly losing their Quarter-Final first leg 1-0 to Lokomotiv Leipzig; a match in which 'keeper Bobby Ferguson excelled. Ferguson - the new 'Player of the Year' was also in outstanding form in the second leg as Killie pulled off a tremendous 2-0 win with goals in each half from Murray and McIlroy inspiring emotional scenes as Rugby Park witnessed another European pitch invasion. The men from Ayrshire had reached the Semi-finals of the Fairs Cup.

MATCH OF THE SEASON
May 24th 1967.
Kilmarnock 0 Leeds United 0

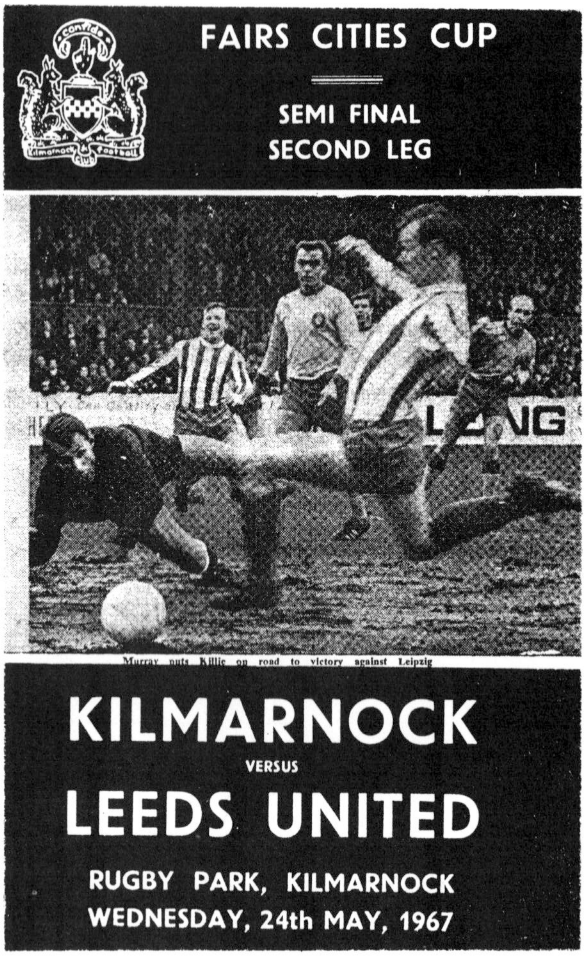
FAIRS CITIES CUP
SEMI FINAL
SECOND LEG
Murray puts Killie on road to victory against Leipzig
KILMARNOCK
VERSUS
LEEDS UNITED
RUGBY PARK, KILMARNOCK
WEDNESDAY, 24th MAY, 1967

*1967 was Scottish football's **annus mirabilis**. Celtic became the first British team to win the European Cup (the night after this tie). Rangers reached the Final of the Cup-Winners Cup and Scotland not only humbled World Champions England on their own Wembley turf, their fans carted most of it back over the border with them. Set against this backdrop it is hardly surprising that Killie's great achievement should have gone little recorded outside Ayrshire. But make no mistake, it was a great achievement. This was a tournament where the winners scroll contained the names of Barcelona, Valencia, Real Zaragoza, Ferencvaros, Roma and no others. Now Kilmarnock had the chance to reach the Final where they might again meet Eintracht, who played Dynamo Zagreb in the other Semi-final.*

To do that they would have to beat Leeds United, one of the top teams in England. A side with iron men like Norman Hunter, Jack Charlton and Billy Bremner in midfield plus Paul Reaney and Terry Cooper in defence, yet which also possessed flair and skill, exemplified by Eddie Gray and Peter Lorimer in attack.

The first leg had been played on Friday 19th May and a mad first half, in which both teams reputedly sound defences were repeatedly torn to shreds, left the score at 4-2 in Leeds favour after 45 minutes. The defences reverted to type and no more goals were added, leaving Killie with a difficult, but not impossible, task at Rugby Park. For this was the first year of the 'away goals' rule. If Killie were winning 2-0 or 3-1 after extra time, they would go through.

But Leeds had a reputation as well as a lead to protect and they did it tenaciously. "Rough, tough and crude" they may have been but they were also the most determined and adept side in Britain at holding on to their advantage. They packed all eleven players into their own half, "sometimes" said the 'Standard' "the penalty box". It helped too that their goal-keeper Gary Sprake, who could have his 'off-days', was on top form. McIlroy's shot, deflected by Sprake, was the best effort of the first half for Killie while Gray and Lorimer both went close in Leeds sporadic breakways. A blatant penalty was denied in the second half when Terry Cooper downed Tommy McLean in the penalty area. Killie never gave up fighting to the end but there was to be no more European joy. Leeds achieved the 0-0 draw they had come for. Eintracht too missed the Final, losing 4-3 on aggregate to Dynamo Zagreb who then did to Leeds what Leeds did to Killie, taking a two goal lead to Elland Road and forcing a goalless draw there. For Bobby Ferguson, it was the end of his Kilmarnock career. In a move concluded months beforehand, he was transferred to West Ham United for a fee of £65,000 - a world record for a goalkeeper.

The late Sandy McLaughlan.

1967-68 DIVISION ONE

Sandy McLaughlan returned to take Ferguson's place and other new faces included prolific scorer Kenny Cameron, a £10,000 signing from Dundee, free transfer man Jimmy Cook, from Hearts and another of those players who took ages to win over the fans but once he did became venerated by them, John Gilmour, from Hamilton. Departing during the season were Jackie McInally to Motherwell and Davie Sneddon, who returned with lowly Raith Rovers to inspire his new side to a victory at Rugby Park which saw the home team leave the pitch to the jeers of their own supporters. And those supporters were fewer in number as the dual effect of a ground admission price rise to 5/- (25p) and in season tickets from £6 to £7 took a heavy toll. Performances on the pitch also contributed to the alarming decline in support. The transfer of the team's main asset - Tommy McLean - would have hurt even more. But - buoyed by profits of £36,758 thanks to the Ferguson move - the Board felt able to reject an offer of £70,000 for McLean from Chelsea boss Tommy Docherty. On the pitch, the bad run ended with a late winner from Morrison at Fir Park; the start of a six goals in four games spell from the young striker who now staked a claim to the regular first-team place. His double in a 3-2 win over Hearts in December helping the side to their first home win since the opening day of the season and lifting them away from 6th bottom position.

The New Year brought little change. Crowds would still come out for big matches - almost 14,000 had watched Killie flop against Morton in a League Cup Quarter-final - but after a disappointing Scottish Cup exit at the hands of Partick Thistle at Rugby Park, fewer than 2,500 watched the next home game versus Falkirk. A 6-0 home defeat by Celtic demonstrated how far the team had fallen. Stuck in mid-table with 28 points from the same number of matches, Malky McDonald was sacked with two years of his contract still to run. Perhaps he never really had a chance - inheriting a side which had just won the League - but with the gate at his last match in charge, against Motherwell, coming to just 2,333, something had to be done. It was McDonald's misfortune that he failed to realise the extent to which supporters expectations had changed during his time away. They were no longer happy with mid-table and the odd Cup run. They wanted European football and trophies in the boardroom.

Trainer Walter McCrae took charge on a caretaker basis for the final six games and although there was no immediate improvement in results, amazingly, for the second year running, Killie missed out on Europe by just one place. But the decline was there for all to see in their points total. 50 in 1965, 45 (1966), 40 (1967), 34 (1968). McCrae was appointed Manager on a permanent basis at the end of the season and his first job (apart from appointing his own successor as Trainer/ Physiotherapist, Hugh Allan) was to sever further the links with the title-winning team; Matt Watson receiving a free transfer and Eric Murray going to St. Mirren. Only five of the eleven Tynecastle heroes were still at Rugby Park; King, McGrory, Beattie, McLean and McIlroy. Of the eight others who took part that season, just McFadzean and Dickson remained. The 'old' favourites were still highly regarded by the fans and it was 21 year old 'veteran' McLean who narrowly beat 26 year old McGrory for the title of 'Player of the Year'.

MATCH OF THE SEASON
January 20th 1968.
Dundee 6 Kilmarnock 5

An amazing free-for-all which mystified those - including their own supporters - who thought that Killie were a defensive side. A George McLean penalty in five minutes put Dundee ahead. But Eddie Morrison replied with Killie's equaliser five minutes after that. Then, in fourteen minutes, Tommy McLean chipped a free kick over the defensive wall. 'Keeper Donaldson palmed the ball away but only as far as the waiting Morrison who gratefully accepted the chance to put Killie 2-1 ahead. Dundee's Bryce levelled affairs three minutes from the break.

Beattie's half-time substitution by Gilmour saw Killie's defence collapse. Alex Stuart's free kick put Dundee in front once more. Then, George McLean's 30 yard run ended with him passing to Kinninmonth, who returned the ball to McLean for the Dens side's fourth goal. McIlroy reduced the leeway, but twice within three minutes, Dundee's Irish International, Billy Campbell, scored to put Dundee 6-3 up. Kenny Cameron - who had been quiet all game - burst into life against his old team-mates with a late brace of goals to make it 6-5. And it was Kilmarnock who were on the attack in a desperate search for the equaliser when time ran out on a match which it was said would "live in the memory for years to come".

1968-69 DIVISION ONE

The optimism engendered by having a new manager and trainer, coupled with a new-look programme and revamped local press coverage was dissipated by half-time on the opening day of the season when Kilmarnock were 4-0 down at Dundee. The entire League Cup campaign was disastrous, not a single match being won. But once the League started, Killie were a different proposition. They took a 2-0 lead at Ibrox, fell 3-2 behind and rallied to earn a point. The early leaders - Dundee United - were thrashed 3-0 at Rugby Park. Credit for the improvement went to McCrae's shrewd signing of Jim McLean, Tommy's older brother. He was the playmaker so badly missed since Sneddon left.

But it was Tommy who was involved in the most amazing fightback of the season. Down 4-0 at home to Raith Rovers at half-time, the younger McLean, aided by Beattie, inspired a tremendous Kilmarnock revival culminating in McLean's last minute equaliser. In the next home game - versus Falkirk - Kilmarnock again hit the net four times in the second half. McCrae's publicly proclaimed commitment to attacking football was paying off. The following home match saw only one Killie goal but what a goal it was. Dundee were the visitors and defending competently until Tommy McLean crossed the ball to Brian McIlroy. The winger, stood near the post, back-headed the ball to Eddie Morrison. With his back to the goal, Morrison let fly with a terrific scissors-kick into the corner of the net. For many in the crowd it was the most spectacular goal they had ever seen.

Meanwhile the club had lost £37,891 on the previous year and McCrae launched a campaign aimed at attracting supporters back to Rugby Park. Acting more like a politician than a football boss, he stomped the county, speaking at factory gates and town and village halls. Special deals were on offer: half-price season tickets with more than half the season to run, reduced rates for families. Every effort was made to convince the lost thousands to return to Rugby Park. The team played their part too. A splendid draw with the well-nigh invincible Celtic at Parkhead helping the cause.

Kilmarnock performed well after the New Year but they drew too many matches to stay in contention for the title. Easy draws in the early stages aided an advance to the last eight of the Cup but after a fighting 0-0 draw at Aberdeen, Killie lost the replay 3-0. For many of the supporters it was a bitter defeat. More than 18,000 had turned out, expecting to see at least a contest, not the woeful surrender they were forced to endure. Yet this Kilmarnock side lost just five League matches, one fewer than the team that won the flag. Finishing 4th ended the downward slide and earned a European place again. The team was invited to America once more but this time it was little but a stunt whereby U.S. cities adopted British clubs to play under their names. It was more of an end-of-season tour than a competitive tourney, with strange rules which saw Killie finish last in their group but with (supposedly) 26 points from their eight games.

The League campaign had ended with Killie again drawing with Celtic, thus maintaining their unbeaten record against the 'Old Firm' this season. But some Celtic fans took exception to the flying of the 1965 League flag and purloined it, leaving it in a locker at Glasgow's Queen Street railway station from where it was recovered by grateful Killie officials. In a bid to offset their losses, Gerry Queen was sold to Crystal Palace but a new star was born. Although he had been around for a few years, this was the season which saw Billy Dickson hit the headlines and the full-back was a deserved winner of the 'Player of the Year' award.

The talking point off the pitch was the club's Centenary. 1969 marked the 100th anniversary of Kilmarnock F.C. and the Board prepared to make it an unforgettable time. The focal point of the celebrations was a match against Eintracht. The Germans were still a formidable side and Huberts, scorer of their Rugby Park goal, was one of their star attractions as were newer players like Holzenbein and Grabowski who would destroy England in the 1970 World Cup. In advance of the match came a special publication, *"Go Fame...."* a history of the club written by Hugh Taylor, the foremost football writer in Scotland and a Killie fan since childhood. At a civic lunch, a copy of the book was presented to the Provost by the club, while in turn, the Provost gave the club a plaque to celebrate the Centenary. Kilmarnock MP and Secretary of State for Scotland, Willie Ross, looked on approvingly as the ball-boys for the match received a tie, a badge, a copy of 'Go Fame....', and an autographed team photo. They then had their photographs taken with Walter McCrae and captain, Jackie McGrory, as the rest of the players applauded the youngsters.

On the field, Scottish Television's Bill Tennent introduced dozens of former players to the crowd. Invitations had gone out to all ex-Killie players who had either five years service or played for the club in a Cup Final. From the 1920 side came Shortt, McNaught and McPhail.

Action from the Centenary match v. Eintracht Frankfurt in April 1969.
At just over 10,500, the crowd was considered poor for this prestigious match which finished 1-1.

The 1929 winners were represented by Williamson and Cunningham. On came Connell, Milloy and McAvoy from the thirties, Mays and Henaughan from the post-War era. Hamilton of the 1965 side and many, many more. The match itself was rather a tame affair, a 1-1 draw being about right. But afterwards came the criticism of the fans. The press were unanimous. *"Ayrshire doesn't deserve a team of Kilmarnock's calibre"* said one paper. The reason for the adverse press comment was the size of the crowd. Just over 10,500 turned up for a once-in-a-hundred-years event when McCrae had hoped for 18-20,000. Perhaps the press had a point and more could have turned up but a valid comment too came from the supporters who wrote to the local paper pointing out that over 18,000 had witnessed the feeble performance against Aberdeen a month earlier. At any rate it was a disappointing postscript to a series of events which had been run with precision and style.

MATCH OF THE SEASON
January 4th 1969.
Kilmarnock 3 Rangers 3

McCrae's appeals were working. 12,000 had watched the New Year's Day game with St. Mirren and Rangers - fresh from victory over Celtic - brought a huge support with them for this game. The attendance of 32,893 was - and will remain - a record for a League game at Rugby Park. The reason for this spectacular crowd can be seen from the League table which looked like this as the teams took the field:-

	P	W	D	L	F	A	Pts
1. Celtic	19	12	5	2	44	13	29
2. Dundee United	19	13	3	3	38	24	29
3. Dunfermline	19	12	3	4	43	27	27
4. Rangers	18	11	4	3	40	18	26
5. Kilmarnock	19	10	5	4	33	19	25
6. St. Mirren	19	8	8	3	24	24	24

At this stage, the League race was the most open since 1965 with all the top six fancying their chances. Killie's appeared to have been obliterated after just seven minutes of the match when Andy Penman shot Rangers ahead. But that free kick specialist, Tommy McLean, floated the ball to the unmarked Billy Dickson for the defender to notch a 15th minute equaliser. Another dead-ball move saw Rangers' Johansen try to find Willie Johnston but Johnston was challenged by Frank Beattie who had the misfortune to knock the ball past McLaughlan to put Rangers back in front in the 26th minute. Nearing half-time, Rangers skipper, John Greig, blatantly brought down Eddie Morrison in the box then had the temerity to argue against the penalty which ensued. Tommy McLean made no mistake from the spot, so Killie reached the dressing-room level at 2-2.

The match continued to enthral the support, first one side, then the other, gaining the upper hand until Orjan Persson restored Rangers lead after 61 minutes. For the third time, Killie were asked to respond and for the third time they rose to the occasion.

A Tommy McLean corner found Gerry Queen whose header was cleared only as far as the menacing McIlroy. The winger didn't miss many chances like that and he tucked the ball away with pleasure as Kilmarnock made it 3-3. After this, came the incident which nearly threatened a full-scale riot. Colin Stein, most expensive player in Scottish football and darling of the Ibrox legions, assaulted Tommy McLean, hero of the Kilmarnock crowd. Incensed at the attack on his team-mate and friend as much as he was appalled by a big guy belting a little one, Billy Dickson waded into Stein. As bottles and cans reigned onto the pitch and the unsegregated supporters started fighting on the terracing, Stein was sent off for the third time in just over year and Dickson accompanied him. Ironically, Stein would end his playing days at Rugby Park and McLean would serve out his time with Rangers.

McLean had been too quick and clever for Rangers and Stein had been policed out of the game by Jackie McGrory but this excellent match, which presaged the start of a 12 match unbeaten run in the League by Kilmarnock, was overshadowed by the violence both on and off the pitch, by the sudden death of a spectator and by the complaints made afterwards about the poor crowd control by both police and stewards. A sorry aftermath to what had been a terrific game of football. The offenders must have made up quickly though as McLean (who was an entirely innocent party) played alongside Stein for Scotland in Wales four months later, both scoring in a 5-3 win. McLean's goal was the first by a Kilmarnock player for Scotland since Sandy Higgins hit four back in 1885. A year later, Dickson too would play alongside Stein and McLean for the national team.

1969-70 DIVISION ONE

Thirteen players - virtually the entire first-team squad - stunned Rugby Park at the start of the season by demanding a transfer. The players claimed that they had been promised a bonus for qualifying for Europe which had not been paid. McCrae's response was to strip Jackie McGrory of the captaincy and give it to newcomer Hugh Strachan. Although McGrory was later re-instated, the dispute rumbled on into October before an undisclosed settlement was reached. The bitter atmosphere took its toll on performances and the promise of the previous year evaporated - the team struggling to climb above mid-table. The one bright spot was the discovery of an ace striker in Ross Mathie, who teamed up with Eddie Morrison to form a free-scoring partnership.

In December, the AGM heard that despite an increase of over 50% in attandances, the profit for the year was just £5,875. And that was after taking into account the £35,000 received from Gerry Queen's transfer. Crowds this season had dipped again. European matches in particular had failed to attract enough supporters to make Killie's Fairs Cup campaign profitable. If gates didn't improve in the second half of the season then the Board intimated that they may be *"compelled to alter their present policy"*. A clear reference to the possibility of going part-time, even if no-one would yet utter those dreaded words.

So, as the most successful decade in Kilmarnock's history drew to a close, the future seemed less than secure. And, by a tragic twist of fate, the very last match of the 1960's appeared to have ended the career of a Rugby Park icon. After 15 minutes play at Celtic Park, Frank Beattie and Celtic's Jimmy Johnstone raced for the ball. In a genuine accident they clashed into each other. Beattie lay motionless on the pitch. He was helped off the park, his face contorted with unbearable agony. His right leg was broken. At 36 it appeared that Beattie's playing days were over. But Walter McCrae, acting with commendable loyalty, declared that Beattie would be "signed up again for 1970-71", adding that the Board had agreed to a testimonial match for their longest-serving player but stressing that this should not be taken as a sign that Frank was finished as a player.

1970 opened with Killie in 9th place with 18 points from as many matches. A replacement for Beattie was signed in the shape of Alan MacDonald from Hearts. Nicknamed "Chopper" by the fans, he was an instant success. His first match saw Killie losing 2-0 away to Raith Rovers with just six minutes left on the clock when MacDonald scored (his only goal for Killie) to inspire a winning flourish, goals from the dynamic duo of Morrison and Mathie conjuring two points from a match where defeat appeared inevitable.

Beattie hobbled into Rugby Park on crutches to see a 3-0 win over Partick Thistle in the Scottish Cup as Killie embarked on their best run in that competition for six years. Hearts were beaten 2-0 in the next round - a pulsating game in which Kilmarnock supporters demonstrated their elephantine memories by keeping up a non-stop barrage of abuse at referee 'Tiny' Wharton. In the Quarter-Finals, Killie survived a torrid first-half at Motherwell before turning on the style to win thanks to a Ross Mathie header midway through the second period. The venue for the Semi-Final with Aberdeen - St. Johnstone's Muirton Park - was a controversial choice. Aberdeen said they were sick of travelling to Glasgow for Semi-Finals and wanted fairer treatment from the SFA. Some bright spark worked out that Perth was almost equidistant from Aberdeen and Kilmarnock so the match was awarded to a ground which had never hosted a Semi-Final before, never would again, and is now the site of a supermarket! Although there was some sympathy for Aberdeen, many Killie fans observed that they never carped too much about playing in Glasgow when there were 100,000 plus crowds attending matches against the 'Old Firm'.

The Perth match was a disgrace in more ways than one. Killie fielded Ross Mathie, despite the after-effects of the previous week when the brave striker had dived to head the only goal of the game against Dunfermline and smashed head-first into the goal-post. Aberdeen won a poor game 1-0. Crowd trouble marred what little spectacle there was and supporters of both sides could be seen hanging off floodlight pylons or sitting on top of turnstile roofs in an attempt to get a glimpse of the rare moments of action in the game. Aberdeen's goalscorer, McKay, was their cup saviour this year and he scored again as they beat Celtic in the Final. He was never heard of again. In the aftermath of the Perth defeat, Walter McCrae declared that.... *"the club's financial state has never been worse"*, yet Killie finished in 6th place, qualifying for Europe again. Still on the transfer list was Jackie McGrory, yet his oustanding form over many years was finally recognised when he became the 'Player of the Year'.

Killie's controversial Scottish Cup Semi-Final at Perth.

Aberdeen insisted on a venue that was geographically 'neutral' yet they never complained about playing the Old Firm in Glasgow if there was the prospect of a cut from a 60,000 plus gate!

Desperate for cash from any source, the club agreed to undertake a tour of Rhodesia. This was a country in rebellion against Britain, shunned by the rest of the world, recognised only by their fellow apostles of apartheid in South Africa. Yet despite the outcry from most political parties and from local churches, cash-strapped Kilmarnock went ahead with the tour. They were even happy to send back messages saying how lovely the country was and how friendly the people were. Like those England footballers who had given the Nazi salute in pre-war Berlin, Kilmarnock allowed themselves to be duped by a philosophy of evil. It was an inglorious episode in their chiefly illustrious history.

MATCH OF THE SEASON
November 19th 1969.
Kilmarnock 4 Slavia Sofia 1

Killie's renewed assault on the Fairs Cup had already produced one thrilling tie. They held a 2-0 lead in Zurich before losing 3-2, and in the return game won 3-1 at Rugby Park, a match in which Jackie McGrory scored for the only time in over 400 first-team appearances. Now they faced this Bulgarian team who had caused Rangers problems in a Cup-Winners Cup Semi-Final two years beforehand.

Kilmarnock had the best start imaginable. Mathie's shot from the left opened the scoring and Jimmy Cook, following a defence-splitting pass from Tommy McLean, hit a second. Just ten minutes had elapsed since the kick-off. Killie took a bad blow when the influential Jim McLean was forced to retire injured after 28 minutes but brother Tommy kept up the pressure, hitting the bar before half-time. After the break, supporters were treated to the rare sight of the diminutive Cook heading into goal but Mathie was adjudged to be offside so 2-0 it stayed until fifteen minutes from the end when Eddie Morrison's shot was parried away to Mathie who pounced to put Killie three up. The fans were still singing Mathie's praises thirty seconds later, when a bad clearance from the Slavia 'keeper was seized on by John Gilmour who punted the ball over the goalie's head from all of 40 yards to make it 4-0. With two minutes to go, Shalamanov kept the tie alive by scoring for Slavia.

Billy Dickson captained Killie in Sofia where they lost a goal in the first minute and were two down after 24 minutes. One more goal and they would have been out on the away goals rule but Dickson marshalled his men superbly to keep the opposition out. Killie could only draw at home to Romanians Dinamo Bacau in the third round and on a rutted surface covered with ice and mud, they lost the away leg 2-0 to end their European hopes for another season.

Kilmarnock's controversial tour of Rhodesia (now Zimbabwe) in 1970.
Here, Tommy McLean shows off his skills to local youngsters.

The Teams
KILMARNOCK
From
ALASTAIR HUNTER
BOBBY KENNEDY
JIMMY WHITE
FRANK BEATTIE
JACK McGRORY
ALAN MacDONALD
WILLIE HENDERSON (Rangers F.C.)
TOMMY McLEAN
COLIN STEIN (Rangers F.C.)
ALEX. INGRAM (Ayr United F.C.)
GERRY QUEEN (Crystal Palace F.C.)
ANDY KING
JIM COOK
ALEX. McLAUGHLAN
Referee:
Mr R. K. WILSON, Glasgow
Linesmen.
Mr H. ALEXANDER, Kilmarnock
Mr A. McCRIRICK, Kilmarnock.
Ball donated by
Miss J. McInnes and friends.
ACKNOWLEDGMENTS
Frank Beattie wishes to express his thanks to the Directors, Manager Walter McCrae and Staff of Kilmarnock Football Club, the Celtic Football Club, Rangers Football Club, Ayr United Football Club, Crystal Palace Football Club, the Match Officials and all who have assisted in organising his testimonial.
CELTIC
From
EVAN WILLIAMS
JIM CRAIG
TOMMY GEMMELL
BOBBY MURDOCH
BILLY McNEILL
JOHN CLARK
TOMMY CALLAGHAN
HARRY HOOD
WILLIE WALLACE
LOU MACARI
BOBBY LENNOX
VIC. DAVIDSON
KEN. DALGLISH
FRANK BEATTIE
THE DEDICATED PROFESSIONAL - BY THE MANAGER
It is very gratifying for me to be able to participate in and contribute to this testimonial for Frank Beattie

Frank Beattie received a testimonial game in 1971 after 18 years at Rugby Park.

A Select XI, featuring several guest players, was beaten 7-2 by a strong Celtic team.

A youngster named Dalglish netted six goals for the visitors!

1970-71 DIVISION ONE

The inspirational Jim McLean hung up his boots and departed for a coaching job at Dundee - the first step on his successful managerial career. Brother Tommy was locked into a re-signing dispute. Admission charges were raised to 6/- (30p). McLaughlan, Gilmour and McGrory were all on the injured list and Ronnie Sheed broke a leg six minutes into the start of the League campaign. All in all, Kilmarnock did not have their troubles to seek. Yet the club insulted a substantial section of their support by withdrawing - at two weeks notice - the Rugby Park catering contract from the Supporters Association who had held it for 20 years. Even worse, the new caterers failed to turn up at one reserve match, an occasion when the old problem of poor toilet facilities was subject to a unique solution. They were closed for the duration of the match!

Killie's off field problems were mirrored on the park by their worst start for years. The team were struggling near the foot of the table come October, when Eddie Morrison and Robin Arthur were hospitalised as a result of a car crash on their way to the home game against Dundee United. Two youngsters from Bellfield Boys Club were hurridly recruited to take their place and both played their part in a fine 2-1 win. That (plus the fact that neither Morrison nor Arthur was seriously hurt) was the first bit of good news of the season. Other hopeful signs arrived, including the opening of a new club, the 'Killie Club' underneath the stand and the unanimous election of Frank Beattie by his fellow pros in the Scottish Professional Footballers Association as their 'Player of the Year', despite the fact that he hadn't kicked a ball throughout 1970. It was a touching gesture.

With a loss of nearly £43,000, the financial outlook was bleak, but Chairman McIvor denied press speculation that the club would go part-time. The supporters were sceptical, especially as the results showed no sign of improving. A home defeat by Airdrie in the Cup marked the last appearance of 'keeper Sandy McLaughlan in the First Team. He was blamed for the Cup exit which saw Killie three down at half time. It was a sad end to his career but the restoration of Alastair Hunter in goal saw Killie pick up at last. A fine away win over 3rd placed St Johnstone and a 4-1 home win against Hibs, took the club clear of the danger zone.

A novel way of finishing a tied game occurred at the end-of-season Ayshire Cup Final when Killie lost to Ayr on penalty kicks. It was the first time any Scottish game had been decided in this manner.

Shortly after this match came the benefit game for Frank Beattie. 8,727 turned out on a Friday evening to see a Killie side minus McLean and Dickson (away on international duty), but plus old favourites Bobby Kennedy and Gerry Queen - augmented by guest stars, Alex Ingram of Ayr and the Rangers duo Colin Stein and Willie Johnston - take a 7-2 hammering from a Celtic team which included "one of Celtic's brightest young starlets". This was Kenny Dalglish who scored six of his team's goals that evening. Murdoch notched the other while Stein and Ingram countered for Killie. After the match, the players rushed to attend the 'Player of the Year' dinner being held in honour of the latest recipient of that award, John Gilmour. Big John's feelings must have been mixed as he, along with McLaughlan, Cook and Mathie, had just been offered a part-time contract despite the Chairman's previous pledges. On this occasion, it was withdrawn, but not before McLaughlan turned his back on the senior game, signing for Troon Juniors.

Hopes that the traumatic 1970-71 season might prove to be a one-off aberration, were dashed in July when Tommy McLean, the one undoubted star in the team, was finally sold. Rangers acquired his services for a fee estimated to be between £60-£70,000. The supporters were angry. Most recognised that McLean couldn't be kept at Rugby Park any longer, but to sell an experienced International player for less than had been on offer from Chelsea four years ago, seemed foolish to say the least. To sell him to Rangers rather than to England, compounded the folly in the eyes of many.

MATCH OF THE SEASON
September 29th 1970
Kilmarnock 2 Coleraine 3

Killie had drawn the first leg of this Fairs Cup 1st round tie 1-1 and the fans turned up expecting to see a comfortable victory over the Irish part-timers. Tommy McLean in the 16th minute and Eddie Morrison in the 22nd, provided the goals which appeared to presage a blitz on Coleraine. Even when John Gilmour was denied a third goal, courtesy of a weird offside ruling, nothing seemed amiss. Half-time came with Killie still two ahead and coasting to victory.

Thirteen unlucky minutes of madness destroyed that illusion. Two minutes after the restart, Coleraine's no.9 Des Dickson, charged through the middle, shrugging aside a challenge and blasted the ball past Hunter. Five minutes later, he grabbed the equaliser, and when the ball was headed down to him from a corner in 60 minutes, Dickson confidently struck it into the net for Coleraine's (and his) third.

Shell-shocked Killie just couldn't get back into the match and the Irish side rarely looked troubled in the half hour that remained. For Coleraine it was a result that they could have only dreamed of, but for Kilmarnock it was a night of humiliation. The European curtain rang down at Rugby Park on a performance which would haunt the club for years to come.

1971-72 DIVISION ONE

Nearing his 38th birthday, Frank Beattie made a triumphal return to action. But despite scoring a cracking 25 yard goal against Hibs in the League Cup, it was soon apparent that Frank's comeback was of a sentimental, and strictly limited, nature. The expected struggle didn't take long to materialise. The first three League games were lost, indeed, Killie won only one of their first nine, then came a welcome hat-trick of League victories which helped take some of the pressure off. Between mid-November and January, six successive home games ended in triumph, taking Killie up towards the middle of the table.

Off the park, the pressure increased. A profit of £31,000 was a direct product of the McLean transfer and the Board had decided that the time had come to revert to part-time status. They announced that this would be phased in - all existing full-time contracts would be honoured - but any new signings would be on a part-time basis only. *"To the theorist or purist, this may appear a retrograde step"*, said Chairman Bill McIvor at the AGM. But he attempted to justify it on the grounds of economic necessity. No mention was made of the now-forgotten pledges to stay full-time. And no-one explained why talented youngsters would sign for a part-time club in preference to a full-time outfit. After 12 years, Kilmarnock could no longer live with the elite.

The team slipped back in the League, failing to win any of their final five games, but at least the spectre of relegation didn't haunt Rugby Park this year. And in the Scottish Cup, the side put together a useful run. They beat Alloa easily enough, then travelled with some trepidation, to Elgin. Killie had lost their last four League games and Elgin City had a deserved reputation as the giant-killers of Scottish Football. But Kilmarnock performed like true professionals, a 4-1 win satisfying the large number of fans who undertook the arduous journey to the far North of Scotland. In the Quarter-Finals, Killie were ahead 2-1 away to Raith Rovers but were coming under attack from the Fife team when Morrison let loose 20 yards from goal with a powerful shot shich scythed every blade of grass on its way to the corner of the net, moving Walter McCrae to comment that it was *"one of the finest goals I have ever seen a Kilmarnock player score"*. This clinched the tie to set Killie up for another Semi-Final.

MATCH OF THE SEASON
April 12th 1972.
Celtic 3 Kilmarnock 1

The team who stood between Kilmarnock and a place in the Cup Final were Celtic. Heading for their seventh League title in succession, in the last four of the European Cup again, Scotland's top team had won 3-1 in a League match at Rugby Park just four days before this Semi-Final and there were few who gave Killie any sort of chance. Yet for almost the entire first-half, Killie kept the marauding Celts at bay. Hunter was at his best in tipping a 25 yarder from Murdoch over the bar. Twice he stopped good efforts from Jimmy Johnstone, whose wing wizardry in this match was on a par with any performance in his celebrated career. But, just as the more optimistic supporters were on their way to the pie-stand, 'Dixie' Deans struck to give Celtic the interval lead.

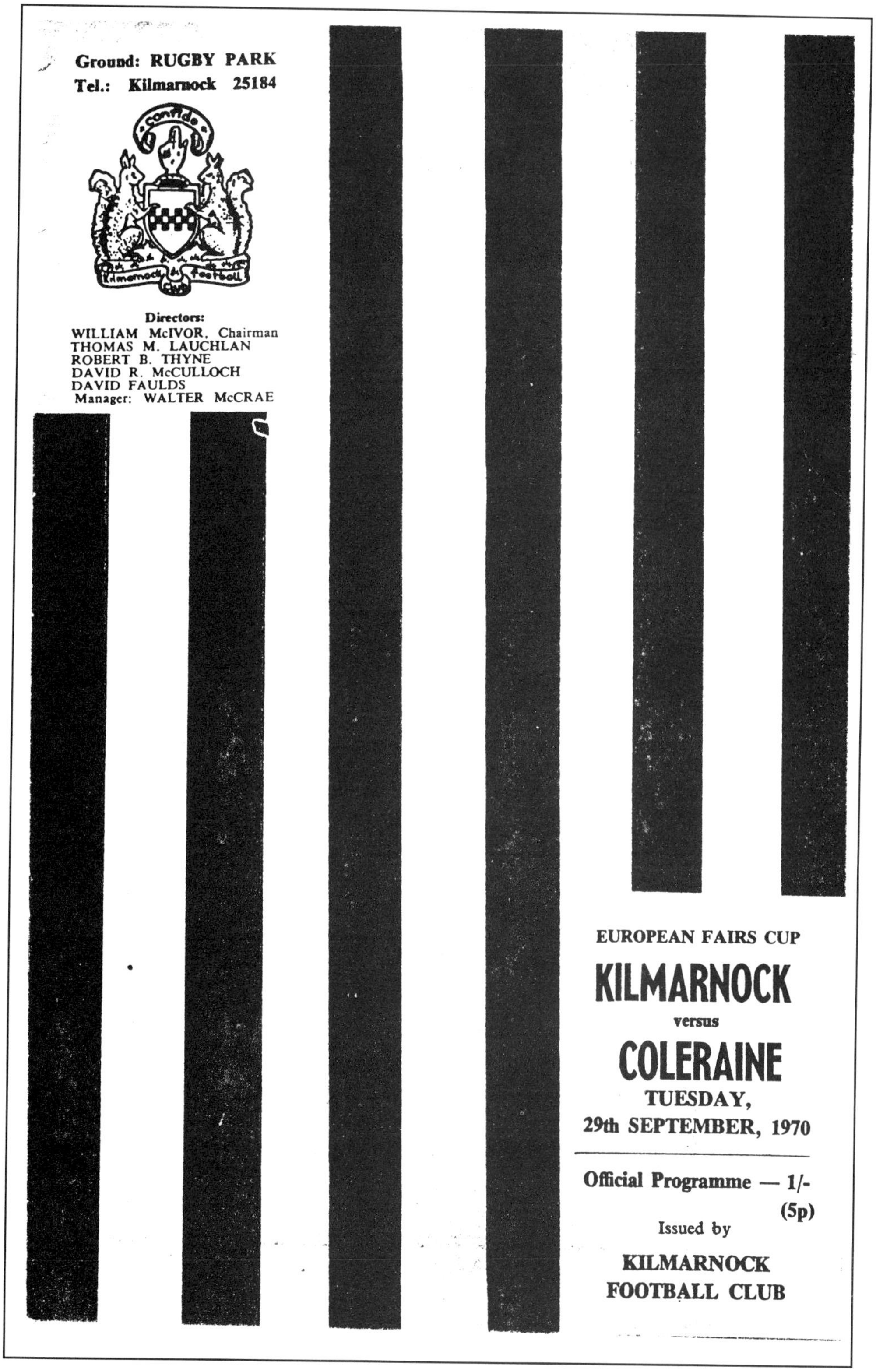

A tragic night.
Kilmarnock were bundled out of the Fairs Cup by Northern Irish part-timers Coleraine after leading 2-0 at half-time. A sad end to Killie's European days.

Kilmarnock fought back determinedly after the break. A pass from George Maxwell split the defence and found Jimmy Cook. Just to prove that there was more than one wee winger called Jimmy who could work magic with the ball, Cook blasted home a terrific equaliser from the edge of the box. That was the signal for a hail of bottles, cans, pennies and assorted sweets and toffees to come raining down on the Kilmarnock supporters occupying the front of the 'neutral' terracing,as the Celtic fans above showed their displeasure at the turn of event. The barrage stopped only when Celtic regained the lead through Deans again, in the 59th minute. Killie kept fighting but when Macari scored after 77 minutes, another Cup campaign had ended in failure at the penultimate stage. Hunter's superb showing in goal meant that he returned to Hampden two weeks later, making a successful debut for Scotland in a 2-0 win over Peru. The latest addition to the conveyor-belt of International 'keepers at Rugby Park was recognised by Killie supporters as well when he picked up the award for this season's 'Player of the Year'.

But if Ally Hunter was at the peak of his Kilmarnock career, for others their time at Rugby Park was over. Among the free transfers were 'Chopper' MacDonald, Andy King and the great Frank Beattie.

1972-73 DIVISION ONE

The League Cup provided a foretaste of what lay ahead when Kilmarnock failed to finish in one of the two qualifying spots in the new-look competition, being pipped by Stenhousemuir. A 6-2 defeat by Celtic in the opening League match prompted the headline:-

"ARMCHAIR FANS ARE FORECASTING THE 'DROP' FOR KILLIE".

Jackie McGrory had been injured in this match and although he later played a few times for the reserves, further injury prompted him into retirement in November 1972. He was the last of the Championship-winning side to leave Rugby Park.

The first four League games were lost, leaving Killie rock-bottom. Changes were badly needed. Goalkeeper Jim Stewart and defender Alan Robertson came in against Wolves in the second leg of a Texaco Cup tie which saw Killie keep a clean sheet for the first time this season. The 0-0 draw was of little consequence - Wolves having won the first leg 5-1 - but it produced a suitable metaphor for the club's predicament when the lights failed, leaving the ground in darkness for twenty minutes.

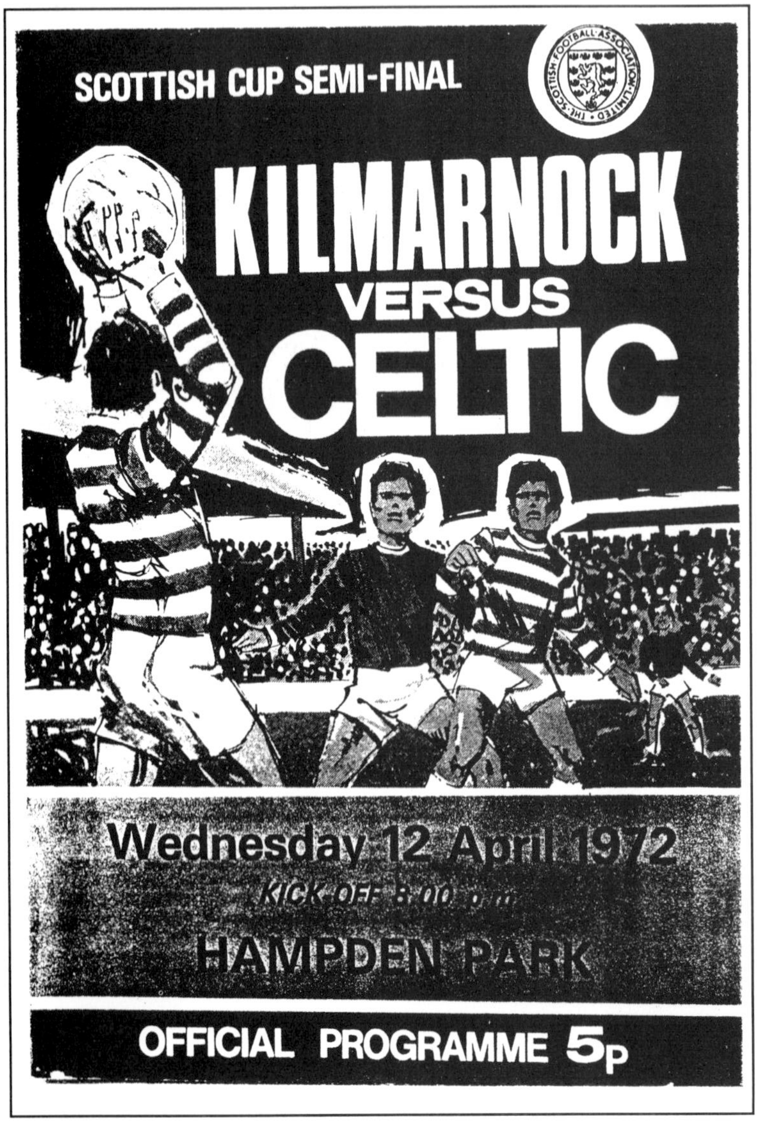

McSherry and Cook returned for the next game, at home to Rangers and for the first time, Kilmarnock showed some spirit in their game - coming back from a goal down to beat the Ibrox team with two Eddie Morrison goals. But it was only a temporary respite. In the next home game, Killie held a one goal half-time lead against St. Johnstone, only to lose four goals in the second half. Those supporters who still turned out were now praised for their loyalty by Walter McCrae after - as he himself admitted - years of criticism. But the fanaticism of the hardcore wasn't enough to lift the struggling side - especially when poor performances were coupled with dreadful luck. On November 11th (by cruel irony, Armistice Day) Jackie McGrory pulled on a Kilmarnock jersy for the last time before retiring injured in a reserve game and John Gilmour broke a leg playing for the first team against Dumbarton.

At least the financial outlook wasn't as bad as it might have been. The club had lost £13,162 - the Cup run having helped to keep the loss down. Chairman McIvor told the AGM that.... *"talk of relegation with more than half the season to go is nonsense".* His optimisim was shared by few. Having lost his place to Jim Stewart, Ally Hunter was sold to Celtic, but the £40,000 fee for an International was a poor return. Even worse was the decision to transfer Ross Mathie - out of the first team picture - to fellow strugglers Dumbarton for a derisory £5,000. One month later, Mathie scored twice for Dumbarton as they beat Killie 4-2, a game which had a vital bearing on the final table.

Kilmarnock's last attempt at glory before their fall. An excellent game sees Jimmy Johnstone in top form as Celtic go through to the final.

That defeat galvanised Kilmarnock into action. They beat Morton and Hearts, drawing away to Partick Thistle in between - their best run of the season. Even when they lost to Dundee United, their fate was still very much in their own hands. With one game to play, the foot of the table looked like this:-

	P	W	D	L	F	A	Pts	GD
15.Falkirk	33	7	11	15	37	54	25	-17
16.Kilmarnock	33	7	7	19	38	69	21	-31
17.Dumbarton	33	5	11	17	39	71	21	-32
18.Airdrieonians	33	4	8	21	34	74	16	-40

MATCH OF THE SEASON
April 28th 1973.
Kilmarnock 2 Falkirk 2

It was a straight fight between Kilmarnock and Dumbarton to see who would accompany Airdrie into Division Two. Kilmarnock had a slender one-goal advantage on goal difference and both teams faced home games on the final day. Unless Dumbarton got a better result than Killie then the Ayrshire team was safe. Supporters were optimistic too. Dumbarton had to play Dundee United - sixth top - while Killie's opponents were Falkirk - fourth bottom.

The first half against Falkirk saw Kilmarnock..."play like Champions" according to one report". McSherry's cross to Stevenson was headed down to Morrison. The striker - as prolific as ever despite playing in a struggling side - struck the opening goal in 13 minutes. After 27 minutes, a Dickson throw-in found Sheed who took the opportunity to put Kilmarnock 2-0 ahead. Kilmarnock stayed well on top without adding to their score. The team was cheered back to the dressing room at half-time. Even the news that Dumbarton were also winning - 2-1 - didn't perturb the Killie fans. All that meant was that Killie were now two goals better off than their rivals and now there were only 45 minutes of the season left.

No-one knows what happened during the break. Were Killie instructed to try to protect their lead? McCrae denied this afterwards, saying such a move would have been "suicidal". But something happened to upset the team's rhythm. They emerged for the second half looking and playing nervously. The ball was treated like a hot potato, no-one was willing to hang on to it. Falkirk got the message and panicky Kilmarnock paid the price when Somner reduced the leeway on the hour mark. Now Killie were just a goal to the good. And that was only if Dumbarton hadn't scored any more. Nobody knew what was happening at that game. The security blackout at Boghead would have made MI5 envious. Then with only three minutes remaining came the moment Kilmarnock had feared when Cattenach equalised. At 2-2, the bemused players left the field while stunned spectators huddled around transistor radios to learn their team's fate.

Maybe Dumbarton had drawn too? In which case Killie were safe. Nails were bitten down to the quick and cigarette ash carpeted the Rugby Park car park as the fateful radio announcement was awaited.

Finally, came the voice from the ether, *"Kilmarnock have been relegated after 19 years...."* The voice trailed away. No-one needed to know more. Grown men wept alongside their children and grandchildren. Youths not even born when Killie last played in Division Two cast aside all pretence of acne-fired machismo as they too broke down in tears. It had been just eight years and four days since Kilmarnock had been crowned Champions of Scotland.

If there can be such a thing as a silver lining in relegation then it was there in the form of Jim Stewart. The young 'keeper - only just turned 19 - had played for little more than half a season but it was enough to earn him the 'Player of the Year' award. More fittingly, the end of an era was formally marked in June when the last full-time contracts - those of McSherry, Gilmour and Dickson - expired.

Already 24 when he joined Killie from Junior football, Ross Mathie was pitched straight into the first team and was an immediate success.

A superb header of the ball, he was asonishingly transferred to Dumbarton and helped relegate Kilmarnock in 1973. Now part of Scotland's coaching set-up, he can still be seen regularly at Rugby Park.

Chapter 10

WHAT DIVISION IS IT ANYWAY? THE YO-YO YEARS 1973-1983

1973-74 DIVISION TWO

Rebellion was in the air as a new Shareholders Association was formed, allying with the Supporters Association in a bid to make changes. Killie won their League Cup section, but only after a struggle. In the League, they made a poor start. They lost three of their first seven fixtures, the third of which was a home defeat by Berwick Rangers, a match which sealed the fate of Walter McCrae. After seventeen years at Rugby Park, the last 5½ as manager, McCrae was dismissed. With experienced players like Cook, Dickson, McSherry, Rodman and Morrison available, the team should have been doing better. Yet McCrae left knowing that there was a crop of young players at Rugby Park who would serve the team well for years to come. Ian Fleming was a natural goalscorer. Ian McCulloch was tipped for greater things. Gordon Smith was one of the classiest players in Scotland. Jim Stewart was on the fringes of the Scotland side. Others like Maxwell, McDicken and Robertson, were solid club performers who would have been welcome in any team. And with youngsters like 'keeper Alan McCulloch and defender Stuart McLean knocking on the First Team door, there was plenty of talent at Rugby Park.

The task of bringing the best out of this squad was entrusted to Willie Fernie. The former Celtic and Scotland player was a novice to team management but his attacking approach would win him plaudits before long. He took over a team which temporary boss Davie Sneddon had instilled some pride back into, having eliminated St Johnstone after extra time in the League Cup. Fernie's first match saw his charges beat Division Two leaders Airdrie 4-0.

Kilmarnock went on a 17 game unbeaten stretch in the League, overcoming all obstacles in their way. And the difficulties they faced were of a more unusual kind, for this was the time of the three day week. Floodlights were banned. Kick-offs were arranged early. Killie's League Cup match with Albion Rovers started at 1.45 p.m. That game saw them reach the semi-finals where they met Dundee, a game which could go on under lights as Hampden Park had it's own generator. But, at the onset of a severe winter, the match was twice postponed before it went ahead in a ghost-like atmosphere. Just over 4,500, most following Killie, turned up at the vast arena to see the Division One team scrape a lucky victory. Eddie Morrison had the ball in the net for Killie, but an offside decision denied them the chance to emulate the team of the early 50's by reaching the League Cup Final as a lower League side. Tommy Gemmell scored the winner for a Dundee team who went on to beat Celtic in the final.

Hunter's transfer meant that a small profit of £5,911 was achieved, good news as Kilmarnock knew that they couldn't afford to stay in the bottom Division for long. Crowds at some away matches failed to reach four figures. The lack of atmosphere at such games didn't seem to inhibit free-scoring Killie however. They scored five against Forfar at home and away. They hit four away from home on three other occasions. And at home, they had their biggest win for years, beating Alloa 8-2. Even when they eventually lost a game, at Raith Rovers, they promptly went out and won the next ten on the trot. As the season neared it's end, Airdrie had already booked a promotion place and the other was fought over between Killie and Hamilton Accies.

MATCH OF THE SEASON.
April 27th 1974.
Kilmarnock 2 Stirling Albion 1.

An edgy 1-0 midweek win over Queen of the South had been Killie's 9th in succession and had pushed them to the very brink of promotion as the table showed:

	P	*W*	*D*	*L*	*F*	*A*	*Pts*	*GD*
1. Airdrieonians	34	27	4	3	99	23	58	+76
2. Kilmarnock	34	25	5	4	92	41	55	+51
3. Hamilton Ac.	34	23	6	5	65	36	52	+29

Killie's goal difference was so superior that one point would be enough to take them back up. But if they slipped up against Stirling Albion then they could be in trouble, for their last match was away to Hamilton. Remembering the Falkirk game of a year ago, every Kilmarnock supporter wanted to settle things against Albion.

But, six minutes into the game, Stirling's Lawson took advantage of Killie's nerves to put his side ahead; a lead which they comfortably held until half-time. With the news that Hamilton were ahead at Alloa, the nightmare scenario of missing out at the last flashed across the minds of everyone at Rugby Park. Midway through the second half, and with Killie still trailing, Fernie sent on Ian McCulloch as substitute. He provided the shake-up the team needed, challenging for every ball going. Three minutes after McCulloch's arrival, Smith crossed from the corner flag for Fleming's head to connect with the ball and Killie were level. The game proceeded at an even pace and Killie were always aware that one blunder could still ruin everything, until 87 minutes had elapsed. Then, Eddie Morrison, with the style which made him this season's Player of the Year, smashed home the winner. As the final whistle blew and Kilmarnock celebrated promotion, hundreds of joyous fans gathered behind the stand to chant the names of their heroes and also that of Willie Fernie.

Fernie had done as he promised; gained promotion with attacking football. The 96 League goals scored this season constituted a new club record as did the 58 points amassed. (Killie drawing in the now meaningless game at Hamilton). The defence played their part in the success too, Jim Stewart being selected for the Scotland World Cup Squad which performed so nobly in West Germany.

Killie made an enterprising League Cup run while stuck in Division Two in 1973-74.

This Semi-Final which they lost 1-0 was eventually played after the third attempt - seven days after the date on the programme. The ghastly cover is typical of big Cup games at the time.

Also with Jim was Killie's trainer Hugh Allen, carrying on in the tradition of McCrae as the Scotland trainer. One defender who, a few years previously, might have joined them was Billy Dickson. But the sadly out of form Dickson was given a free transfer at the end of the season. He was the last of the squad of 1965.

A sadder occasion was the death of Mattha' Shortt, the hero of the 1920 Cup Final, who passed away in June 1974, at least knowing that his beloved Killie were back in the big time. And they took with them a new song. One which would be their own, which no other set of fans would even dare think of expropriating. For this was the year that the strains of 'Paper Roses' was first heard at Rugby Park. The exact origin, like all best legends, cannot be too accurately traced. Was it after beating Hamilton in January? Or after winning promotion? No-one can be sure. The one certainty was that no-one else would steal the song from Kilmarnock; the only football supporters in Britain content to adopt a country and western tear-jerker, alter not a single word yet turn it into a paean of praise for their team.

If supporters, sociologists, psychiatrists and psychologists from that day to this, have been unable to fathom out the reasons for a song of **Marie** Osmond's becoming a Rugby Park anthem, then the followers of Scottish Football have given thanks for Killie fans for at least not choosing one of **Little Jimmy's**!

1974-75 DIVISION ONE

Having scaled what they thought was a mountain to gain promotion, Killie found that they were still on the foothills of Everest as the new season opened. For, after years of talk, Scottish Football had decided to embark upon the most far-reaching reconstruction in it's history. The top ten Division One teams at the end of this season would form a new Premier Division. The rest would join the top six from Division Two in what was euphemistically called the 'First Division'. To finish in the top ten would be a difficult task for a newly promoted side. Of the 77 sides who had gone up since automatic promotion was introduced in 1922, only 20 had finished 10th or higher in their first year.

Fernie's team was determined to give it their best shot. Strengthened by the arrival of centre-forward Ian Fallis and winger Davie Provan, they knew that each match would have a cup-tie atmosphere about it, supporters would have an interest right up to the end of the season. And that was an important consideration as inflation took its effect on prices. Stand season tickets rose from £8 to £11 and ground admission was up to 40p.

Killie romped through their League Cup section and gave title-challenging Hibs a hard fight in the Quarter-Finals before a flurry of late goals at Easter Road killed off their challenge. Late goals ended their efforts at Parkhead too, in the first League game. Losing 1-0 with 10 minutes to go and harbouring hopes of sneaking a point, Killie were beaten 5-0. Wins over Ayr United (3-0) and Aberdeen (1-0) at home, either side of a 1-1 draw away to Hearts gave hope that Killie would be up to the mark, but a humiliating 6-0 Rugby Park troucing by Rangers pushed them down the table. They won just one of the next eleven in the League but the demands of the new set-up produced a keenly fought season, even in December there were only six points separating 5th top from last place. Fernie - who had earlier maintained that only full-time teams could hope to compete in the Premier - told the AGM that he didn't think full-time football would ever come back to Rugby Park, citing the attendance of shareholders at the meeting - just 26 - as one example of the problems facing Killie. The club had lost £23,237 and the Chairman - Bob Thyne - admitted that after nearly two years of holding the line, players may have to be sold.

Killie's first away win didn't arrive until four days before Christmas when they played Dundee United. They astonished even their own fans by taking a 4-0 lead and holding it until thirteen minutes from the end before having to hang on for a narrow 4-3 victory. But that result was followed by another bad run in which Killie slumped to 15th place with hopes of the top ten fading fast. Until they went to Ibrox, that is. Kilmarnock avenged their earlier defeat by three times taking the lead against a Rangers side on their way to their first League title in 11 years. Although the game ended 3-3, it was the boost Killie had been looking for. They struck a rich vein of form, a nine match unbeaten run producing four wins and five draws which saw them climb to 9th with three games to play. Alas, the dreaded nerves got the better of them. A defeat by Dumbarton and a draw with Airdrie sent Killie into their final game knowing that they needed to win to have any chance of making the Premier League.

MATCH OF THE SEASON

April 26th 1975.
Kilmarnock 2 Dundee United 4

Kilmarnock enjoyed a good opening ten minutes, coming close to scoring on several occasions before the roof fell in on them. In 11 minutes, defensive lapses allowed Andy Gray to score for United. Five minutes later, with the defence askew again, Sturrock put the Tayside team two in front. And when Killie lost a third goal just two minutes later, their Premier dream was in tatters. Throwing caution to the wind, Killie decided to launch attack after attack in the hope of salvaging something from the wreckage. In 30 minutes, Fleming's shot was pushed away by United 'keeper McAlpine, but Fallis swooped in with a diving header to reduce the deficit. A Fleming header three minutes from half-time made it 3-2.

McLean, Morrison, Fallis and Fleming all brought the best out of McAlpine in the second half but there was no further scoring until six minutes from time when United's McDonald ran through the Killie defence to leave Sturrock with the easiest of chances to make it 4-2. Kilmarnock were consigned to the middle Divison. Some consolation emerged when they learnt that thanks to Motherwell and St. Johnstone both winning that they would have had to have beaten Dundee United by nine goals to qualify for the Premier Division. Still, Killie's valiant attempt had earned them credit and they could look ahead to the new League with confidence.

Brian Rodman's displays earned him the 'Player of the Year' award and a call-up into the Scotland squad on several occasions. Brian never played for the National team though, sitting on the bench, perhaps fortunately, as England won 5-1, was the nearest he ever got to a cap.

1975-76 FIRST DIVISION

Fernie refused to alter his attacking principles despite a poor League Cup campaign and the team responded with a high-scoring burst in the League. Hamilton were beaten 4-2 at home, Airdrie 4-3 away and East Fife 4-2 away as Killie surged to the top of the table. But the manager's forays into the transfer market left something to be desired. Under no pressure to sell, he let new Aberdeen boss, Ally McLeod, snap up Ian Fleming for just £15,000 and spent £12,000 replacing him with Rikki Sharp from Morton. Fleming had averaged more than a goal every two games and was later sold to Sheffield Wednesday for £50,000. Sharp never scored a goal during his time at Rugby Park.

The club made a profit of £13,000 this season - *"from turnstile receipts, not transfer fees"*, as Chairman, Bob Thyne, pointed out; claiming this justified the decision to go part-time. But with another price increase - to 50p - and no big name opposition, promotion was an absolute imperative if the club was to continue in the black. But the team struggled around the New Year, a defeat at Partick Thistle ending their hopes of winning the title. The points banked in the early part of the season were invaluable as Kilmarnock stuttered their way to the Premier Division.

On the brink of stepping up, Fernie caused a stir among the support by selling - for a modest fee - Eddie Morrison to Morton. Letters appeared in the press contrasting Morrison with his replacements, to the detriment of the latter. A tribute to him appeared in the *Standard* saying.... *"although every individual fan has his own favourite, you have to be something rather special to appeal to the crowd en masse. Eddie Morrison was such a player"*. How true. Morrison was the spectator's ideal player. He never shirked a tackle, he fought for every ball, he played each minute as if it was the 90th in the Cup Final and his team a goal down. And he scored goals. Spectacular goals, mundane goals, but always plenty of goals. He was going to be impossible to replace.

MATCH OF THE SEASON

February 21st 1976.
Kilmarnock 1 Falkirk 0

Killie needed a drew to fend off the late challenge of Montrose and ensure their place in the Premier Division. Having beaten Falkirk in a cup-tie the previous week, there should have been little difficulty in achieving their aim. When Ian Fallis latched onto a Billy Murdoch pass to put them ahead after just six minutes play, it should have been a signal to relax and enjoy the proceedings. But that wasn't the case. Fallis, Sheed and Smith all missed chances when scoring looked easier. In the second half, Falkirk took the game to Killie but, fortunately, their finishing was every bit as woeful as the home team's. As the final whistle blew it was greeted by "a roar, perhaps more of relief than acclaim" as the 'Standard' said. Kilmarnock were in the Premier but, already, fears for their future in that set-up were being expressed.

Those fears were given credence by the rest of the season. Killie were knocked out of the Cup at Dumbarton - despite newsreader, Angela Rippon, informing the nation that they had reached the Semi-Finals. A mistake which must have seen many stay-at-home fans celebrate prematurely. In the Spring Cup - a competition for teams outside the Premier - Killie won only one of six games played. And in a friendly match which Clyde, the attendance numbered just 526. Among them were several scouts from English clubs who were watching Ian McCulloch, the new 'Player of the Year'.

1976-77 PREMIER DIVISION

Premier Division football didn't come cheap. Ground admission this season showed a 40% increase to 70p and matches worth watching were few and far between. Fernie's original dictum, that a part-time team couldn't survive in this company, was sadly borne out, as his later optimism proved to be a mirage. Kilmarnock struggled from the word 'go', they were never out of a relegation place after the third game and never off the bottom from Mid-November onwards. Three times they had losing sequences of five in a row. They won only four games out of thirty six played.

Yet, early on, there had been some good performances. Motherwell were beaten 4-0 in the Anglo-Scottish Cup, a result which saw Killie face English Second Divison team, Nottingham Forest, in the next round. And it took extra time in the second leg before Brian Clough's team emerged victorious. Considering that, with basically the same players, Forest would lift the English title and the European Cup within 2½ years, it was no mean performance from the Rugby Park team. And they took three points from their four games with Rangers. But no amount of gloss could cover over the fact that this Kilmarnock team were nowhere near the standard needed to survive in the Premier Division. £30,000 had been spent on upgrading the floodlights to the level required for colour television transmissions, but relegation meant that there would be little call for the cameras to come visiting. This outlay contributed to the loss of £40,774 incurred during this year. Iain McCulloch retained his 'Player of the Year' title, now sponsored by the Killie Club, but in truth, he had little competition for the award. One player definitely not in the running was Rikki Sharp, who was given a free transfer. Jim Stewart's herculean efforts in goal did not go unrewarded, as he finally made his Scotland debut during the close season.

MATCH OF THE SEASON

October 30th 1976.
Kilmarnock 6 Ayr United 1

This was the one game which showed Killie fans what it ***could*** *be like in the Premier. With seven games played, Kilmarnock were bottom of the League and still looking for their first win. But local rivals Ayr were only one place above them. Playing for Ayr was Brian Rodman, bought from Killie a month earlier. By the time the game was over, Rodman must have wished he had never moved, for in this game, old fashioned wing-play was at its best.*

The rout started in 11 minutes when Provan's cross was headed into goal by Sheed. Just two minutes later, Smith, on the left wing, also crossed into the area, where McDicken climbed above the entire Ayr defence to head in the second. With half an hour gone, Fallis shot home the third goal from outside the box. And four minutes later, the same player notched his second goal, and Killie's fourth. There was to be no respite for United after the interval. In 53 minutes, right-winger Provan beat two defenders and sent over another perfect cross which Fallis headed home for his hat-trick. At 5-0, Killie eased off and Ayr pulled a goal back with two minutes to go. They weren't even allowed to celebrate this as another Provan cross was flighted over for Billy Murdoch to head in number six before the final whistle blew.

It was one of those rare days in football when, for one team anyway, nothing can go wrong. Kilmarnock achieved their first win in the Premier Division, and against old rivals at that. Even sweeter, was the fact that this win lifted Killie off the bottom and put Ayr there instead. Kilmarnock had *"unchallenged control from first moment to last"* was how one report summed it up. For a brief period, Killie had renewed hope in their ultimately futile battle to survive in this League. The sweet taste of victory was marred for older supporters though, when they heard that Joe Nibloe, Kilmarnock's most capped player, had died at his Sheffield home.

1977-78 FIRST DIVISION

Hopes of a quick return to the Premier were soon dashed. Kilmarnock lifted just one point from their first five games and sold Gordon Smith to Rangers for £65,000 in acrimonious circumstances. A deal for a similar sum, but also throwing in two Ibrox reserves, had already been turned down and the sale now went ahead without the knowledge of the Chairman, Bob Thyne, or the Honorary Secretary, David McCulloch. They had been on holiday and both promptly resigned from the Board when they found out what had happened. Tom Lauchlan took over as Chairman, with Bill McIvor becoming Hon. Sec. Lauchlan's brother, Bob, joined the Board.

Fernie was given only £15,000 of the Smith fee to spend and he bought two players from St. Mirren - Donnie McDowell and Jackie McGillivray - neither of whom exactly sent the home supporters into raptures. One player who did was the bustling Ian Fallis and the club was dealt a devastating blow when the popular 23 year old was killed in a road crash on his way to work. Immediately, arrangements were made to organise a benefit match to assist Fallis' 19 year old widow - Rangers agreeing to play as soon as a suitable date could be fixed up. The Glasgow team's willingness to help didn't end there. Ibrox General Manager, Willie Waddell helped out his old charges by sending Colin Stein on loan to Killie. Just as it looked as though the corner might have finally been turned - a win at Alloa giving Killie their first two points away from home since November 1975 - the Board stepped in. A midweek home defeat by St. Johnstone at which the crowd dipped below 2,000 saw Willie Fernie sacked. As before, Davie Sneddon stepped into the breach and his first game in charge provided an away win against hitherto unbeaten Morton.

The Board received a shock indication of the club's standing in the game when they opened up the applications for the manager's job and found that one of the aspirants was a lady called Doreen Nicholl; a former winner of the 'Miss Scotland' beauty contest and currently part of a comedy double act with her husband! All good, risible stuff for the press, of course, and proof that Killie were fast becoming cannon fodder for the jokers on the club circuit.

But the team had only lost once since Sneddon took over and it was no surprise when he was confirmed in the job. What did raise a few eyebrows was that he would be a part-time boss. The attitude was, that if the players were part-time, then the manager might as well be too!

Davie Sneddon was supposed to spend a couple of nights and a Saturday afternoon every week putting together a team which would challenge the best in Scotland. For the Board knew that the Premier Division must still be their aim. They had made a profit over £8,000 on their year at the top - unthinkable in the First Division.

Of course, Killie were too far behind to make up much leeway during this campaign. And the prospects for the next term looked bad before this season was even over. Iain McCulloch was sold for £80,000 to Notts County in March 1978, and in May, Jim Stewart filled the Rugby Park coffers to the tune of a further £110,000 when he signed for Middlesbrough. With Smith, McCulloch and Stewart gone, plus the tragic death of Ian Fallis, and a manager who worked for the club only two nights and weekends, promotion would require something in the order of a minor miracle.

MATCH OF THE SEASON
March 6th 1978
Kilmarnock 1 Celtic 0

Sneddon's revitalised team had already taken one Premier scalp, that of St Mirren, when they were drawn away to Celtic in the 4th round of the Scottish Cup. Owing to postponement, the draw for the Quarter-Finals had already taken place before Killie travelled to Celtic Park and with the winners due to face Rangers away, the bookmakers decided that Kilmarnock were no obstacle to an 'Old Firm' cup clash. They quoted the Ayrshire team as 500-1 to lift the Cup; rank outsiders along with Cowdenbeath. But Killie almost had the last laugh at Parkhead, McDowell's first-half goal looked like creating a major upset until Celtic equalised six minutes from time. The teams were forced to reassemble at Rugby Park on the Monday prior to the Quarter-Finals.

Although Celtic, 'Double' winners the previous year, had been having a lean time, they could hardly be expected to give the First Division side another chance of a shock win. And, with players in the green and white line-up like Tommy Burns and George McCluskey, men who could win a game with an extravagant display of skill, Killie looked to have little hope of further cup progress. Why, the tickets for for the Rangers-Celtic Quarter-Final had already been printed and were due to go on sale on Tuesday morning; once the formalities had been observed. Ah, but perhaps the mighty Glasgow duo had forgotten that it was an Ayrshireman who had written that "the best laid schemes o' mice an' men gang aft a-gley".

In the first half, Kilmarnock pounded the Celtic goal in the manner of the first day of the Somme offensive. But just like that unhappy day, their attack bore little fruit. Peter Latchford in the Celtic goal, was in tremendous form, saving everything that came near him. Half-time arrived with the game still goalless. Celtic resumed with renewed vigour. At last, they began to look like a Premier Division side. Three times in the first five minutes, they carved out good chances and three times they spurned them. Then, came the incident that changed the game. In 57 minutes, Killie's George Maxwell was fouled by Roy Aitken. In itself, it merited a booking, but, as the 19 year old Parkhead captain had already been shown one yellow card, the referee had no option but to send the Ayrshire-born Aitken off the pitch.

Now it was Kilmarnock who seized the moment. Wave after wave of blue-and-white shirts poured down the park, but still Latchford remained unbeaten. With thirteen minutes to go, Colin Stein unleashed a vicious shot straight for the top corner of the net, only to look incredulously away as Latchford one-handedly tipped the ball over the bar. There were only eight minutes of play left when Killie forced a corner. Like so many before, it was cleared, but only to Killie's Derek McDicken. Waiting 25 yards out, Big 'D' drove the ball furiously towards the target. His shot lashed off the post and into the net. 1-0 and Killie were ahead.

There was little time to celebrate as Celtic launched an immeadiate counter-attck. Their Icelandic International 'Shuggie' Edvaldsson, fired in what looked like the equaliser until, again, it was McDicken to the rescue; heroically clearing the ball off the goal-line. As the final whistle blew, Rugby Park was invaded by success-starved fans, happily celebrating what the 'Standard' described as Kilmarnock's best Cup win "since Eintracht". Celtic hadn't lost a Scottish Cup tie to opposition from a lower league since 1949. Perhaps, thought the Killie faithful, Davie Sneddon really could work miracles after all.

Unfortunately, the games with Celtic exerted a heavy toll on the part-time team and they were beaten easily, though not disgraced, 4-1 at Ibrox the following Saturday. But no-one would ever be able to take away the memory of the night when the no-hope First Division side knocked the holders out of the Scottish Cup and gave a Glasgow printers some unexpected overtime the very next day.

1978-79 FIRST DIVISION

There was still a solid backbone to the team despite the sale of so many stars; men like George Maxwell, Alan Robertson, Stuart McLean, Derek McDicken and Paul Clarke gave Sneddon the base with which to build a side capable of challenging for promotion. And the manager was busy in the transfer market too. Ian Gibson, signed from Aberdeen for £17,500 was a potetial first-teamer who would soon get his chance. Joe Cairney, a prolific scorer with Airdrie, was a £35,000 acquisition. Jim Clark, a dyed-in-the-wool Killie fan, arrived from Stirling Albion for a fee of £25,000. Bobby Street, a dual broken leg victim, was given a chance to rejuvenate his career at Rugby Park, and from the Reserves came two outstanding prospects, Alan McCulloch, who had waited a long time to emerge from Jim Stewart's shadow and Ally Mauchlen, an enthusiastic teenager with ability to match.

Ironically, Sneddon's signings broke the long-standing club transfer record which had been paid for his own services back in 1961. But the club could afford it as the transfer cash kept rolling in. Davie Provan was sold to Celtic for £125,000, a record for a Scottish player. Kilmarnock had taken in just under £400,000 in transfers in a year, and even when Sneddon shelled out again, buying striker John Bourke from Dundee United for a new record fee of £40,000, the net profit in buying and selling was more than £250,000. Amid the frenetic pre-season atmosphere, time was still taken to honour the pledge to Ian Fallis's dependants. The benefit game with Rangers and other fund raising activities helped raise the total handed to his widow to over the five-figure mark.

The much-changed side, unsurprisingly, took some time to gel together and after fourteen games, Killie were only 7th in the table, but so tight was the fight for promotion, they were just two points off second place. A 5-0 home win over Stirling Albion and a 4-0 away triumph at Montrose, hoisted then up to 4th. Meanwhile, the Board announced profits of over £90,000, but any euphoria this might have generated was soon dissipated by the chilling news that gates had slumped by £34,000. The average home League attendance for the previous season was quoted as being just 2,838.

A new ground safety limit of 18,500 had been placed on Rugby Park and it looked to be more than sufficient. As the team headed into the most vicious Winter since 1962-63, they heard the comments of their manager ringing in their ears. For Davie Sneddon had responded to a December defeat at Arbroath by informing the assembled press that the match had indeed been *"a game of two halves"*, thus giving the lie to those who claim that football's most famous cliche is a work of fiction.

Kilmarnock played only three League games in two months but they were part of a run of seven successive wins (including a fine 5-1 away success to Clyde in the Cup) which allowed them to overtake their rivals and perch proudly on top of the table. Others had games in hand, but Killie had the priceless asset of points in the bag. In the Cup, they nearly caused another sensation by holding Rangers at Ibrox, only to lose narrowly at home in a replay which stretched the new safety regulations to the limit - and beyond.

The fixture pile-up meant that one third of the season had to be crammed into the two months of March and April. Not surprisingly, the positions at the top altered rapidly and often. But as neighbours Ayr faltered and with Dundee overwhelming favourites to go up, it became a battle between Kilmarnock and Clydebank for the second promotion spot. So when Killie won 2-1 away to Clydebank, that looked like being the clincher. But Kilmarnock never do things the easy way. They contrived to lose for the first time in nine matches, at Hamilton, to throw it all back into the melting pot again. Four days later, they beat title favourites Dundee 2-1 at Rugby Park. So when they travelled to Dumbarton for their final game, there was still everything to play for.

MATCH OF THE SEASON
April 28th 1979.
Dumbarton 1 Kilmarnock 3

As the team took the field, the League table read:

	P	W	D	L	F	A	Pts	GD
1 Kilmarnock	*38*	*21*	*10*	*7*	*69*	*34*	*52*	*+35*
2 Clydebank	*37*	*23*	*5*	*9*	*75*	*48*	*51*	*+27*
3 Dundee	*34*	*22*	*6*	*6*	*61*	*29*	*50*	*+32*

No-one expected Dundee to lose three of their last five so it was all down to what Killie and Clydebank would do. If the 'Bankies won their last two games, then they would go up. Kilmarnock had to win and hope that Clydebank would slip up. But for the first fifteen minutes of the match at Boghead, it appeared to be all academic, as Dumbarton took control of the match. Their forwards' failure to capitalise on the defensive nervousness of the Ayrshire team, let Killie off the hook.

On the quarter hour mark, Cairney scrambled a goal for Kilmarnock, a lead which they held till half-time. During the interval came news that Clydebank were leading Arbroath 1-0. The eerie silence which gripped the Killie fans was broken by the arrival of the teams for the second half and, within six minutes, the blue and white legions were shouting the praises of their heroes; as Bourke headed the ball down for Gibson to put Killie two in front.

With twelve minutes to go, a fine four man move ended with Mauchlen cutting inside to pass to Bourke, whose first time shot flew into the net for Killie's third. Two minutes later, the 'Sons' pulled a goal back, but that didn't deter a couple of Kilmarnock fans behind the goal from embarking on a victory jig there and then. At the final whistle, the players disappeared under a sea of blue-and-white, as jubilant fans swarmed all over the field. Then came a tannoy announcement which sent the already delirious supporters into greater paroxysms of ecstasy; Arbroath 1 Clydebank 1. A few amateur mathematicians may have calculated that Clydebank could still have gone up if they won their final match by ten goals, but the vast majority of Killie fans knew that their team was back in the Premier League. Champagne corks were popped, songs were sung and players' jerseys were strewn to the crowd. Sneddon, the part-time boss, and his part-time team had achieved the miracle.

Sure enough, Clydebank won their last match by only 2-1 and Dundee, though dropping points at random, managed to secure one more than Killie and thus win the flag. By yet another of those tragic ironies of fate, the edition of the *Standard* which reported on the Boghead victory, also carried the sad news of the death of that great stalwart of the 1930's, Freddie Milloy. Fittingly, it was a long-serving defender in the Milloy tradition, Stuart McLean, who was this season's 'Player of the Year'.

1979-80 PREMIER DIVISION

Kilmarnock's second venture into the Premier Division was awaited with greater optimism than their first. For, as the *Standard* pointed out in a pre-season supplement, *"big names may have departed for pastures new, but this is a far better team".* And they had the chance to prove it even before the official start of the season. Killie's promotion entitled them to play in the Drybrough and Anglo-Scottish Cups. They defeated Aberdeen in the former, then lost to Rangers and were eliminated by Dundee in the latter, on away goals after two drawn matches. In between these tournaments, Killie took part in an invitation contest for the Tennent-Caledonian Cup at Ibrox. Ostensibly there to make up the numbers, Kilmarnock shocked their hosts by returning to Ayrshire with the trophy. They defeated English First Division side Brighton, then Rangers themselves; winning both games on penalty kicks. More importantly, they had played six very competitive games and had lost just once.

It was the springboard they needed for a good start to the League campaign. Rugby Park was turned into a veritable fortress, six of the first seven home League games were won, including victories over both Old Firm sides, and the other drawn. Although life was more difficult away, there was only one really bad result, a 5-0 defeat at Celtic Park. And the draws Killie earned at Love Street, Firhill and Easter Road meant that with just over a third of the season gone, they were comfortably placed indeed, as this table shows:

	P	W	D	L	F	A	Pts
1 Morton	13	8	3	2	30	17	19
2 Celtic	13	8	3	2	25	12	19
3 Kilmarnock	13	5	4	4	15	21	14

Yet when Killie lost their next three games, they plunged from third top to second bottom! Just as it looked as if they might go into a tailspin, Sneddon's battlers astonished the football fraternity by embarking on a run of ten League games without defeat. Three wins and seven draws hoisting them to fourth place. The victories included a win over Hibs in which Bobby Street's hat-trick eclipsed the skills of George Best in the Edinburgh side. The away problem was solved with successes at Cappielow and Pittodrie. Then, when it looked like the part-timers had achieved safety, the roof fell in. Six defeats in succession meant that when Killie travelled to Easter Road in April, they had now played ten since their last win and had plummeted to 8th in the table, with relegation still possible. A battling 2-1 win against the already doomed Hi-bees on the Monday, set Killie up for the visit of Rangers on the Wednesday. Bobby Street's first-half goal not only handed Killie their second home win over the Glasgow team, it also virually assured them of safety. They travelled to Dundee - now certainties for the drop - and beat them 2-0. Despite losing at Ibrox in their last game, 8th place and a satisfying seven point cushion over Dundee meant that the part-timers could be well pleased with their season's work. Never had Premier football had been more vital. The 1979 AGM had heard that, although a profit of £44,515 had been made (thanks to transfers) the average home League gate in the promotion winning season had been just 3,033. This term, that figure rose to a much-healthier 6,990.

MATCH OF THE SEASON

November 24th 1979.
Kilmarnock 3 Morton 2

Killie had lost 3-2 at Cappielow in the first leg of this League Cup Quarter Final tie and faced a difficult task to overcome a Morton team which sat proudly at the top of the League. Despite having the bulk of the first half play, Kilmarnock were unable to force a way through the strong Morton defence. Indeed, the ball ended up in Killie's net but, fortunately, the 'goal' was disallowed. The second period followed the same pattern and time appeared to be running out when, with 71 minutes gone, Paul Clarke surged forward with the ball. Pausing near the penalty spot, Clarke smashed the ball into the net to send the game into extra-time.

The additional period was less than two minutes old when Clarke found Cairney with a long pass. With no hesitation, the striker lashed the ball home to put Killie ahead. The cheers were still ringing from the terracing three minutes later when Morton won a corner. The mercurial Andy Ritchie's superbly placed kick reached Roddy Hutcheson who headed powerfully past McCulloch to level the tie again. One minute into the second extra quarter hour and Jim Tolmie took on Killie single handed. He beat five defenders before ramming home an unstoppable shot to give Morton the lead once more. But Killie weren't finished yet. A cross from Doherty gave Gibson the opportunity to make it 3-2 for Killie on the day and 5-5 on aggregate. After 210 minutes of football over both legs, the game went to penalty kicks.

Miller scored for Morton, as did Gibson for Killie. Ritchie for the Greenock men and McLean for the home side both converted their kicks. As did Hutcheson and Cairney. Nothing, it seemed, could separate the sides. Tolmie performed his club another service by scoring with his penalty. Up stepped Killie's Bobby Street who unleashed a terrific shot - which crashed against the crossbar. Morton duly converted their fifth kick and Kilmarnock were out, the unlucky losers in a titanic struggle, the reward for which, suggested the 'Sunday Post', should be "knighthoods at the very least". The 'Standard', more prosaically, but with no less justification, called it "the best game at Rugby Park for years". Few among the 8,407 present would have dissented from that view.

1980-81 PREMIER DIVISION

A wage dispute rocked Rugby Park before the start of the season. The board upped the previous year's weekly pay by £10 to £50 and offered £15 per point, a £5 improvement, but the players weren't happy and although all eventually re-signed, the lingering resentment made for an unhappy atmosphere. Another notable change was the return of Walter McCrae as Secretary/General Manager. While this brought order to the club's administration, McCrae had no say in events on the pitch and it was here that the club was in dire need of assistance.

After taking three points from visits to Tannadice and Firhill, Killie sunk to the foot of the table. The first **six** home games were lost, including a catastrophic 6-1 defeat by St Mirren which sparked off a spontaneous demonstration, demanding the resignation of the Board. It was November before a point was gained at Rugby Park, in a 1-1 draw with Airdrie. Yet, in the knockout competitions, the team fared rather better. They were eliminated from the League Cup in a Third Round penalty shoot out with Dundee, having been unbeaten in six games in this tournament and losing only one goal. In the Anglo-Scottish Cup, Kilmarnock reached the Semi-Final, before losing to a promotion-chasing Notts County side containing internationalists Avramovic of Yugoslavia and O'Brien of Ireland, as well as the Scots trio of Eddie Kelly, Don Masson and ex-Rugby Parker Iain McCulloch.

Floodlit action as Kilmarnock beat Hibernian in the 1979-80 season League Cup.

A loss of £38,268 was attributed to the club being net spenders in the transfer market. But the player pool still wasn't up to the rigours of this division. A slight improvement in results, home draws coming against Aberdeen, Morton and Rangers wasn't enough to save Davie Sneddon and after a 7-0 trouncing away to Dundee United, he was dismissed. With typical chivalry, Sneddon requested that the news be withheld for 24 hours until he had the chance to inform his family and the players himself. He spent the next day talking to the press without letting anything slip and courteously informed the papers afterwards why he had done so.

Speculation as to the identity of the new boss was intense; names as diverse as Ally McLeod, Tommy Gemmell and Bruce Rioch were bandied around. Meanwhile, reserve team coach, Rab Stewart, took charge and Kilmarnock finally won at home in the League, 2-0 against St. Mirren on January 10th. Stewart also picked the team which sent the supporters home happy after a 2-1 win against Ayr United in the Scottish Cup. After that match, the Board made an audacious attempt to speak to Ayr boss, Willie McLean, regarding the Rugby Park vacancy. An approach which was firmly rebuffed by United's directors.

From the 27 existing applications, Jim Clunie was selected as the new manager. It was the first time that Kilmarnock had appointed an already experienced manager since McDonald's second stint. Clunie had been Southampton coach when they won the FA Cup and had taken St. Mirren to their highest League position for 87 years and into Europe for the first time. Although he made all the right noises about not surrendering to relegation until it was mathematically impossible to stay up, he was essentially preparing for the following season. Remaining games showed a marked improvement. Less than a goal a game was conceded and ten points were gleaned from his fourteen games in charge, one more than from the first 22 played. Aberdeen were beaten both home and away and a point was taken from Celtic Park.

Clunie also cleared out the playing staff. Seven players were freed, including five who had played in the first eleven this term; the most prominent of these being Joe Cairney who had cost £35,000 three years previously and now returned to the junior ranks. Unlike his predecessor, Clunie was a full-time manager and he brought in a new part-time assistant in Davie Wilson, the former Rangers and Scotland winger.

But it would have taken a lot more than this duo to save Kilmarnock from the inevitable drop. Crowds fell by over 38%. Just over 80,000 watching the home League programme with the average dipping under 5,000. Of those who still attended regularly, more than a few were heard to suggest that divine intervention was necessary to stop the rot at Rugby Park.

Yet, Kilmarnock were better placed than most to seek a favour from the Almighty. For, speaking to the General Assembly of the Church of Scotland, the Archbishop of Canterbury, the Right Reverend Dr Robert Runcie, informed those present that he was a Kilmarnock supporter. He reminisced about the 1929 Cup winners and spoke warmly about this boyhood idol of the 1930's, 'Bud' Maxwell. Perhaps if the Archbishop had given his old favourites a special prayer?

MATCH OF THE SEASON
September 20th 1980.
Kilmarnock 1 Rangers 8

It would certainly have taken a miracle to save Killie this day. It was, said the 'Standard', "Clydesdales against racehorses". It was certainly an unforgettable Premier Division debut for 'keeper Jim Brown - for all the wrong reasons. Yet Kilmarnock didn't start too badly. They recovered from the loss of a third-minute goal to Rangers' McAdam by equalising through John Bourke in 14 minutes. Parity was short-lived though. Three minutes later, Killie's defence was posted missing as McDonald beat Brown with a header to put Rangers ahead again. A belting shot from Redford just before the break gave Rangers a 3-1 half-time lead.

The second half was one long procession of tragedy. Sandy Jardine's speculative 25-yarder was fumbled over the line by Brown. A McDonald volley also beat the rookie then Bett made it six with a ferocious shot. Jim Clark's handball conceded a penalty which Redford converted. Then McDonald notched his third and Rangers' eighth with a header which slipped under Brown's body. The third in a run of nine consecutive defeats, this match summed up the nightmare season which lay ahead.

1981-82 FIRST DIVISION

A determined effort was made to regain Premier status. Brian Gallacher was signed from Dumbarton for £40,000. The same club also transferred midfielder Ally McLeod to Killie, but, as the clubs failed to agree on a fee, the matter was referred to the transfer tribunal. Killie had offerred £30,000. Dumbarton wanted £75,000. As usual, the tribunal hit on a sum between the two, but what was odd about their verdict was the precise value they placed on McLeod. £54,625 was the figure Killie were ordered to pay. With season tickets reduced from £47.50 to £38 and ground admission down from £1.50 to £1.30, plus a staggering loss of £106,720 on the previous year, it was clear that if Clunie wanted to recruit any more players, then he would have to do so much more cheaply. And he did. Sammy McGivern, from Glenfield Boys Club, made his debut, as did Ian Bryson, from Hurlford. And promising centre-half, Kenny Armstrong, promoted to the first team the previous season, played throughout this campaign.

So it was a team very much of Clunie's own making which played this season. The first seven games were played without loss when Killie were victims of a 2-1 upset away to East Stirling - the man scoring both 'Shire's goals was Rikki Sharp, thus notching two more than he ever did in Killie colours. The team kept near the top but performances were disappointing - especially at home. There were too many low-scoring, drawn matches, for the fans liking. When revenge was gained with a 2-0 Rugby Park triumph over East Stirling at the end of November, it was the first home win since the opening match. Yet Kilmarnock were in 3rd place!

Postponements forced Killie into a series of friendlies and it was during one of these - against Rangers - that young defender Albert Morrison saw his career ruined. With his first touch of the ball, after coming on as a substitute, he was the victim of a dreadful tackle by Rangers 'hatchet-man' Gregor Stevens. The offender was given a six-month suspension. Morrison, leg broken and heart-broken as well, never played senior football again.

After a dull few years, Killie enjoyed a promising Scottish Cup run. They actually led away to Aberdeen in the Quarter-Finals before losing 4-2 in controversial circumstances, the Dons scoring twice from penalties and Stuart McLean being sent off. But it was the League which worried the fans most. Away form was magnificent - East Stirling apart, only runaway leaders Motherwell lowered Killie's colours, winning twice at Fir Park. But those home draws looked like denying them promotion. When second-place Hearts lost at home to Dumbarton, hopes were revived, but in the second last game of the season and before a near-10,000 crowd, Killie and Hearts contrived to play out a boring 0-0 draw at Rugby Park. It was Kilmarnock's **twelfth** home draw in the League and it appeared to have blown their hopes of promotion as the table confirmed:-

	P	W	D	L	F	A	Pts	GD
1.Motherwell	38	25	9	4	91	36	59	+55
2.Hearts	38	21	8	9	65	36	50	+29
3.Kilmarnock	38	16	17	5	54	29	49	+25

If Hearts lost their last match then Killie had to win but if Hearts even drew, then Killie had to win by five clear goals to overtake them. A tall order for a team that had scored just 19 goals in as many home matches. But Killie's final opponents were doomed bottom club, Queen of the South, while Hearts were at home to Motherwell.

MATCH OF THE SEASON
May 15th 1982.
Kilmarnock 6 Queen of the South 0

Gates had dipped below 2,000 at times this season and even the prospect of a promotion finale failed to rouse the punters. Fewer than 2,500 were in the ground when the teams kicked off. In 6 minutes, Armstrong had a header blocked, but the ball fell to the handily-placed Gallacher, who opened the scoring. There was no sign of nerves from Killie - after all few expected them to take advantage of any Hearts slip - and just two minutes later, it was Gallacher again; this time from a McGivern cross. Killie were two goals in front with less than ten minutes gone. With 28 minutes played, Queen's defender, Robertson, turned a McLeod cross past his own 'keeper and now the Killie fans sensed that promotion might be back on the agenda. Armstrong had another header blocked in 38 minutes but this time he forced home the rebound himself. With a minute of the half remaining, McDicken ran on to a McLean free kick, to score Killie's fifth, capping a magnificent 45 minutes.

The news from Tynecastle sent the Kimarnock fans wild. Motherwell were leading 1-0. Once again the Edinburgh ground was a scene of last day drama for Killie. John Bourke scored a sixth for a more subdued Kilmarnock in the second half, always alive to the possibility that one careless mistake could undo the work of a season. And it nearly happened. With only 11 minutes left on the clock, Bryson pulled down Queens' Miller in the penalty box. The crowd were silent....before erupting into a roar of joy as McCulloch saved the spot kick. There were no more goals, nor was there any further scoring at Tynecastle. Against all expectations Kilmarnock were back in the Premier.

Even in the moment of triumph, Clunie sounded a cautionary note by claiming that there was no money available to strengthen the squad. Indeed, the manager was more concerned with shedding staff. Gordon Cramond, signed for a record £50,000 by Davie Sneddon, shortly before he was sacked, was given a free transfer. As was George Maxwell, that old warhorse from the days when Kilmarnock entertained notions of doing more than simply surviving in the top flight. Maxwell was the last player with European experience at Rugby Park, having made his debut as far back as New Year's Day 1970.

Sadder news emerged about players from an even more distant era. Jimmy Williamson, scorer in the 1929 Cup Final, died. Shortly afterwards, a team-mate from the game, Willie Connell, also passed away. Connell may have been the last of the class of '29 to go, the fate of McLaren who emigrated to South Africa in the 1930's being uncertain. And the club Chairman at the time of the 1965 Championship win, Bill McIvor, retired from the Board of Directors, having served continously since 1949.

1982-83 PREMIER DIVISON

Kilmarnock's third attempt to live with the elite was doomed almost immediately. The injury-hit side struggled from the start and an indication of the lack of depth at Rugby Park came in the second game of the season when the reserve game with Hibs had to be called off as Killie were unable to field two teams on the same day. Worse was to come at the hands of Rangers. In less than three weeks, the Ibrox eleven, no great shakes themselves, handed out a trio of drubbings to the Ayrshire hopefuls; 5-0 at Ibrox in the League, 6-1 at Rugby Park in the League Cup and 6-0 at Ibrox, also in the League Cup.

To make matters worse, Killie sold Ally Mauchlen to fellow strugglers Motherwell for £35,000, a deal reminiscent of the mistake made over Ross Mathie a decade beforehand. While Clunie pondered over how to avert looming relegation, came the sad news that Jimmy McGrory, who had saved the club in similar circumstances before the war, had died. One week later, Killie finally won a League game, beating Morton 3-1 at home. It was the 10th match of the season.

The bad news kept coming. Gate receipts from the season in the First Division were down by over £78,000 on the previous year, a clear indication of what lay in store if the club went down again. The total loss for the season was a staggering £191,919, but Chairman Tom Lauchlan declared that the club was in no imminent danger of collapse, although he emphasised that greater support was necessary. Just how the fans were to be enticed through the Rugby Park portals was anyone's guess.

More disastrous results hardly helped swell the crowd figures. 1-0 down at half-time at Tannadice, Killie collapsed in the second half, losing 7-0. When Motherwell won at Rugby Park on New Year's Day, a result which virtually sealed Kilmarnock's fate, even Jim Clunie was compelled to admit that the players at his disposal were simply not good enough for the Premier Division. He asked for money for new blood. The Board responded by permitting him to sign players on loan. Even this was a disaster. He pitched Jimmy Simpson straight from Muirkirk Juniors into the first team, failed to borrow Gordon Dalziel from Rangers and Ian Clinging from Motherwell lasted just three games. Hardly fair exchange for Mauchlen.

Clunie, never the most eloquent of bosses, issued cliches which were meant to inspire his team. *"It won't be a day for football. I'll be looking for a team of battlers."* Such terminology did little for morale. At Easter Road, six goals were conceded in the second half as Killie lost 8-0 to Hibs. The *Standard* spoke for most supporters when it declared *"relief will surely come when the season ends."* It ended with just three League wins, only 28 goals scored and 91 conceded. In their hearts, Kilmarnock's supporters knew that this time there would be no automatic return to the top flight. Even so, it is difficult to believe that anybody could have predicted just how long it would take to reach the Premier Division again.

MATCH OF THE SEASON
February 9th 1983.
Kilmarnock 0 Partick Thistle 1

When a club is in the doldrums, it's supporters often indulge themselves in the luxuriant fantasy of a glorious Cup run. Such was the case with Killie's fans this year. And briefly, it looked like it might come true. At Firhill, Ian Bryson's second-half goal looked good enough to send Killie into the fourth round of the Scottish Cup until Partick Thistle equalised with only four minutes to go. In the replay at Rugby Park, the fans witnessed 120 minutes of tedium with neither side looking likely to score.

That was followed by a better match in the second replay when Thistle's third minute opener was cancelled out by Gallagher's 48th minute reply. Again, the game went into extra-time and Killie struck almost immediately; McGivern's 91st minute goal once again bringing a Firhill victory within sight. To no avail, McDowall rescued the Jags in the 100th minute. So, to Rugby Park again, where, after 45 minutes, the teams were still level. Then, a budding young striker called Maurice Johnston, who had netted two of Thistle's three previous goals in the tie, struck, to give the Maryhill men an advantage which proved decisive. Little over a year later, Johnston would play in the FA Cup Final at Wembley, but for now he was the villain of the piece at Rugby Park; the man who ended the deadlock, sending Partick through to the next round after seven hours football, and in doing so, extinguished the last small flicker of hope that something might be salvaged from Kilmarnock's disastrous season.

Rugby Park from the air.

An 'Old Crocks' match at Rugby Park featuring the stars of yesteryear.

Back: F.Beattie, M.Watson, E.Morrison, J.McFadzean, J.McInally,
R.Stewart, E.Murray, R.Hamilton, W.McCrae.
Front:J.Cook, W.Muir, D.Sneddon, R.Lennox (Celtic),
A.McLaughlan, A.King, T.McLean.

How much at present-day values for that squad in their prime?

Chapter 11

THE TWILIGHT ZONE
KILLIE REACH ROCK BOTTOM 1983 - 1989

1983-84 FIRST DIVISION

An audacious attempt to finance a return to full-time football was floated pre-season. The idea was for 7,000 people to covenant £30 per annum to Kilmarnock F.C. In September it was announced that the response was *"in several hundreds rather than thousands"* and the scheme was shelved. It never stood a chance. No incentives were offered to potential subscribers and, since one of the object of the ambitious plan was to keep star players at Rugby Park, then the transfer of Kenny Armstrong to Southampton weeks beforehand was bad timing to say the least.

Initially though, results were good. Particularly at home where Killie spent the first three months unbeaten despite playing to fewer than 1,500 most weeks. There was reasonable success in the (yet again) revamped League Cup. Kilmarnock went into their last section match needing to beat Celtic to reach the Semi-Finals. That match was narrowly lost, setting off a chain reaction of catastrophe which continued to the end of the season. The unbeaten home record, broken in the League Cup, was shattered again in the League and the team began to slide out of the promotion hunt. Influential midfielder Jim Clark broke a leg against Clydebank in December and was never adequately replaced.

The Board announced a modest loss of £13,909 but admitted that *"results taxed loyalty of supporters to the utmost"*. When Partick Thistle won at Rugby Park on Hogmanay, they were the fourth visitors in succession to triumph at the hitherto imppregnable fortress. One small ray of hope for the future emerged from that match however. For the first time Kilmarnock secured shirt sponsorship and the team that day wore the logo of A.T. Mays on their jerseys.

A fighting display over two games with Aberdeen in the Cup served only to delay the bitter realisation that this was a team in severe decline. Disillusion and cynicism amongst the support hardened into anger and, after the home game with Meadowbank in early April, there were ugly scenes as a small demonstration gathered outside the ground. Two players - Brian Gallacher and John Walker - were involved in scuffles with supporters and Walker was charged with assult - later pleading guilty but being admonished by the court.

As the season meandered to a close, the *Standard* ran a series of articles on the club's predicament and a questionnaire in the paper revealed the level of dissatisfaction felt by the fans when 89% of those who responded stated that Killie's future lay in the First Division - or worse.

The dismal term drew to a close with news of the deaths of two former players, Jimmy Weir - goalscoring hero of the 20's - and Bertie Black, that magnificent forward of the 50's and 60's. He was just 49 years old.

MATCH OF THE SEASON
April 28th 1984.
Kilmarnock 2 Alloa Athletic 0

This, the second last home game of the year, was a typical end-of-season affair. A speculative Robert Clark shot was diverted past the Alloa 'keeper shortly before the break and Lawrie McKinna headed a second after good work by Stuart McLean in 57 minutes. Killie could, and should, have scored more but the real significance of this otherwise meaningless affair lay in just how few supporters were bothered to turn up to watch it.

Crowds had been poor all season. The New Year period apart, Killie had failed to attract as many as 1,500 fans to the League game. Interest was still there - as crowds of over 6,000 for Aberdeen in the Scottish Cup and nearly 9,000 for Celtic in the League Cup showed - but few were bothered to watch the poor fare on show in the First Division. It wasn't a problem unique to Kilmarnock - as a look at attendances at other grounds will show - but the decline was particularly steep at Rugby Park.

Dropping out of the promotion race brought three figure gates on a regular basis, but this was the worst of all. A grand (sic) total of four hundred and sixty watched this match. That figure included season ticket holders, Children and complimentaries. Only a couple of hundred actually paid full cash at the turnstiles. How could the club have expected a regular supply of cash from 7,000 when they couldn't get one tenth of that number to watch the team? Those who did still attend consoled themselves with the thought that at least things couldn't get much worse. Sadly, they were wrong.

1984-85 FIRST DIVISION

Cash-strapped Killie sold Brian Gallacher to St. Mirren for £40,000 plus John McEachran in exchange. Six players had still to re-sign at the start of the season, including Derek McDicken. The Board had previously turned down a transfer bid by West Ham for his services and now it was rumoured that three English First Division clubs and one Scottish Premier team were interested in the big defender. Yet by the end of the campaign, McDicken had asked for - and received - a free transfer.

Tom Lauchlan was succeeded by his brother Bob as Chairman. But the change at the top did nothing to influence events on the park. *"Never in living memory has the club's fortunes been at such a low ebb"* was the press comment which followed a terrible 5-0 defeat at Clydebank. Two weeks later, after a similar scoreline at home to Airdrie, Jim Clunie resigned. Amazingly, there were still plenty of people who wanted to be a football manager - thirty-two applications being received for the position, including names like Pat Quinn and Bertie Auld. Eventually, the Board selected former goal hero Eddie Morrison. Killie's record post-war goalscorer was a popular appointment but he had never previously held the reins at a club,having been boss of Morton on a caretaker basis only.

Eddie's return saw an immediate improvement in results, but this needed to be sustained if the club were to avoid relegation. The new boss quickly recognised the dearth of ability in front of goal and resolved to sign centre-forward Blair Millar from Airdrie. The Board swithered. Augmented by the presence of former player and now chartered accountant, Ronnie Hamilton and cheered by the relatively small loss of £24,934, after such a poor season, the signing of Millar on a permanent basis should not have been too difficult. But they refused to pay the £25,000 Airdrie were asking. Instead, while Millar continued on loan, they offered the paltry sum of £8,000 and even asked if it could be paid in stages!

After two months of dithering, they finally came up with £22,000 which secured the player's transfer. But the team still faced a struggle to survive. They took points off the leading pair of Motherwell and Clydebank but were left staring relegation in the face after a 3-0 home defeat by Falkirk - that club's first League victory at Rugby Park since 1925! Then, in one week, the situation altered dramatically. First-half goals from McKinna and Cuthbertson gave Killie a 2-0 win over Partick Thistle.

It was just two weeks short of 15 years since they had last beaten the Jags at Rugby Park (a game in which Eddie Morrison had scored a hat-trick). Since then they had drawn three times and lost nine in the League and drawn once and lost another three in the Cups against their bogey team. The message was; if Killie could beat Thistle they could beat the drop. Away victories over East Fife and St. Johnstone quickly followed and when Killie beat Clyde 2-0 at Rugby Park, safety was assured with one match still to play.

The winning run came to an end in that final game at Rugby Park - Airdrie winning 4-1. But Morrison showed a commendable commitment to footballing principles by giving a debut opportunity to Rashid Sarwar, thus ignoring those who felt that the player - of Asian decent - might come in for the sort of racist chanting which was now common in football. It was rumoured that when Sarwar signed for Kilmarnock, he was told to spell out his place of birth so that the registration form could be filled in correctly. No doubt the young Rashid took pleasure in watching the bemused looks on the Killie officials faces as he intoned the letters;

P-A-I-S-L-E-Y.

MATCH OF THE SEASON

February 9th 1985.

Inverness Thistle 3 Kilmarnock 0

Away trips to Highland League clubs in the Scottish Cup are always regarded with a degree of wariness. But, even strugglers like Kilmarnock were expected to beat an Inverness Thistle side which lay second bottom of their League and hadn't won any of their last six home games. And for the first half-hour of this 3rd round tie, it seemed to be only a matter of time before the Ayrshire side opened the scoring.

But, in 36 minutes, a Thistle corner found the unmarked Milroy who promptly shot the Inverness men ahead. In the second half, Killie failed to make much impression - a Bryson shot which hit the post before being cleared was the nearest they got to goal. Then, with nine minutes remaining, Hay's header beat McCulloch to put Thistle two up. In 87 minutes the humiliation was complete when substitute Fraser scored a third. A "shattered" Eddie Morrison declared that he could "understand the anger felt by the fans who travelled all that distance in the poor weather conditions". They had "sung their hearts out" until defeat became inevitable. All this was scant consolation to the supporters, many of whom surrounded the team bus and vented their wrath on the Directors; only two of whom had watched the match. The police were forced to provide an escort out of Inverness for the bus. The result was described, accurately, in the 'Standard' as "one of the worst in the 116-year history of the club".

1985-86 FIRST DIVISION

Stung by accusations that they were content with the club's standing in the game, the Board called a special meeting to approve a new share issue. Although sanctioned, raising £55,000, there was still criticism of the Directors. One shareholder went as far as to exclaim that there was no hope for the club unless they had *"someone like Robert Maxwell on the sidelines"*. Fortunately for Kilmarnock, this plea fell on deaf ears. But certainly, more needed to be done. The past twelve months had produced the not-so-grand total of £535 in sponsorship.

On the field, although form could be patchy, Morrison's team was putting in a promotion bid. Unbeaten at home, they dethroned leaders Brechin City 3-1 at Rugby Park at the end of November and assumed the crown themselves, as the table shows:-

	P	W	D	L	F	A	Pts
1.Kilmarnock	16	8	5	3	26	15	21
2.Brechin C.	16	9	3	4	29	19	21
3.Dumbarton	16	8	5	3	28	18	21
4.Hamilton A.	16	7	6	3	30	16	20

For the first time since 1981, Kilmarnock were top of the Division but, with two points separating the top six, it was going to be a closely fought contest. Killie managed to win 1-0 away to Falkirk the next week but then came an inexplicable collapse. They lost 4-1 three times in succession, followed by a New Year's Day home defeat by Ayr United.

When Killie did start to win again, they were hampered by injury to Blair Millar, forcing Morrison to buy Jimmy McGuire from Stranraer for £8,000. That was the most the club could afford, having lost £135,814 over the previous twelve months. The AGM took that news stoically, the meeting lasting just 40 minutes. But the days of the docile annual meeting were over. There were 147 in attendance this year - the highest number for over 25 years. Clearly, once the new shareholders found their feet, then more serious probing would be done.

Stuart McLean scores from the penalty spot against Partick Thistle in 1985-86.
Note the sparsely populated terracing. Fewer than 2,000 watched the match.

Killie fared better in the Scottish Cup this year. They reached the last sixteen and drew at Tannadice, forcing Dundee United to a Rugby Park replay where the Tayside team narrowly triumphed in front of more than 9,000 fans. Crowds were up in the League too, by 44%. That looks a massive jump but the actual figures tell another story. The 27,078 who watched in 84-85 rose to 38,981 this term. In other words, the total for the season was only slightly more than used to watch just one big match.

Narrow away defeats undermined the promotion bid and Killie had to settle for 3rd place. What could have been a last-day thriller against Ayr at Rugby Park turned out to be a disappointing finale for both teams - Killie's promotion chance gone and Ayr already doomed for the drop.

Nevertheless, it had been a massive improvement on the previous year and, having come so close, the supporters would expect promotion in 1987. Even if the team would be missing one of their most whole-hearted players - popular forward Lawrie McKinna having decided to emigrate to Australia.

MATCH OF THE SEASON

September 7th 1985.
Kilmarnock 5 Partick Thistle 0

Killie's good start to the season had been spoiled by a dreadful 3-0 defeat at Somerset Park the week before this match. What better way to get the promotion bid back on the rails than by beating Thistle. With the 15 year jinx smashed in February, this Killie team was the most confident outfit to have faced Partick for some time. And it showed. With only six minutes played, McGivern sent McKinna away on the left. His cross was met by Bryson who scored the opener. Cockburn's pass allowed Cutherbertson to make it 2-0 in 21 minutes. Eight minutes after that, Mackin handled the ball in the penalty area. McLean cooly converted the spot-kick for Killie's third goal. With a minute to go before the interval, Clarke's low cross was seized on by McGivern, who smashed the ball into the net for the 4-0 half-time lead. The team left the pitch to a deserved standing ovation.

Killie eased up in the second half. Clarke's 78th minute header from a McKinna cross was the only addition to the score. But, if any remnant of that long Thistle bogey still existed in the minds of players or supporters, then this game finally dispelled it. Furthermore, the comprehensive thrashing dished out, was a real boost after the defeat against Ayr and gave genuine belief that Killie would be up there fighting for promotion for the rest of the season.

1986-87 FIRST DIVISION

Activity of a 'clerical' nature marked the beginning of this term. Robert Clark returned to Rugby Park, as did namesake Jim. The latter was ostensibly there to help the reserves but was soon forced into first-team action. Meanwhile, Paul Clarke, after donning a Kilmarnock strip more than 450 times, retired from football to join the Strathclyde Police. He was still only 29 years old - a serious loss for Killie to bear.

But other long-servers like McCulloch, McLean and Robertson were still around. And it was one of these - Alan Robertson - who broke Frank Beattie's League appearance record when he turned out against Brechin City on September 20th 1986. It was the 422nd time Robertson had started a League match in Killie colours - a magnificent achievement.

Harkness had made an explosive introduction when signed from amateurs Hurlford Thistle at the age of 24, scoring in each of his first three outings.

But, as a poor season drew to a close, the most exciting affair at Rugby Park was the all-Ayrshire Scottish Junior Cup Final, which saw Auchinleck Talbot triumph over Kilbirnie Ladeside after two games which attracted a total of well over 20,000 spectators. Both teams contained a sprinkling of ex-Killie players and, sadly, one of them - Derek McDicken - received such a bad double leg fracture, that he was forced to retire from playing football together. One of the most poignant photos of the season showed McDicken being visited in hospital by Albert Morrison - his Auchinleck team-mate - whose senior career had been ended by a broken leg before it had properly began.

John Kerr, on behalf of the supporters, makes a presentation to Alan Robertson in recognition of the player's record-breaking achievement.

Sadly, it was the only achievement worth of mention this season. The expected promotion push failed to materialise and the 160 shareholders who attended the AGM voiced their displeasure at the turn of events. Another big loss - of £84,884 - was announced. Hungry for cash, Sammy McGivern was sold to Falkirk for £25,000. Some of this money was utilised in the acquisitions of Joe Reid and John McVeigh. Reid's goals in particular came in useful just when the goal supply of promising ex-junior Colin Harkness dried up.

July 1987 witnessed the death of Hugh Taylor at the age of 70. Hugh had written for both the *Standard* and the now-defunct *Kilmarnock Herald* before going on to become Scotland's premier football writer. The 'Daily Record', *Evening Times* and *The Times* being but three of the diverse publications which enjoyed his unique journalistic style. But he had also been a great Kilmarnock supporter all his life. He had edited the club programme for thirty years and, of course, he had written 'Go Fame....', the club's Centenary history, in 1969. The press had lost one of their finest wordsmiths, but Kilmarnock had lost one of their greatest fans.

MATCH OF THE SEASON

February 9th 1987.
Kilmarnock 1 Hearts 3

Once again, Killie's best performances were reserved for the Scottish Cup. And, in this 3rd round tie against a Hearts side which had narrowly been deprived of a 'double' triumph in 1986, they showed the kind of skill and enthusiasm which could still draw big crowds to Rugby Park.

The first match at Tynecastle was watched by 15,227, more than 2,000 of them cherring for Kilmarnock. And it was so nearly a great success. Both Cook and Bryson had chances to score what would have been a famous victory while Alan McCulloch - in immaculate form - kept the Hearts forwards at bay. The first half of the replay at Rugby Park also looked like ending scoreless until Hearts' Whittaker was sent off for a bad tackle on Harkness.

Momentarily rocked by this dismissal, Hearts conceded a penalty which Ian Bryson scored to give Killie a deserved lead. But in the second half, the ten-man Edinburgh side fought tenaciously and Wayne Foster's 66th minute equaliser sent the game into extra time. Try as they did, Killie just couldn't find a way through a determined Hearts rearguard, and both sets of fans among the 14,932 present left, not knowing what it would take to win the tie.

Another massive crowd of 14,146 turned up at Rugby Park - Killie having won the toss for venue for the second replay. They saw Bryson and McGuire both go close for Killie in the opening minutes and Harkness earned himself a 5th minute booking for a 'revenge' tackle on Whittaker. Another Bryson attempt - a header - forced Henry Smith into a good save. But, in 25 minutes, Killie full-back, Graham Millar, lost possession to Sandy Clark, who cut the ball back to Gary Mackay to score from 12 yards. Killie surged forward in search of the equaliser. Bryston saw a shot beaten away by Smith's legs. A Robert Clark shot took a deflection and went past the post. Harkness was blocked in the box but no penalty was given. Half-time arrived with Killie still a goal down.

The second period was only a minute old when Killie's Cockburn lost possession to John Colquhoun. He floated the ball over McCulloch where it fell off Black's head into the net. Still, Killie refused to surrender. Paul Martin's 73rd minute header reduced the leeway and in desperate attempts to equalise, McGuire had a shot blocked, Harkness hit the post, and Robert Clark had a 20 yarder saved by Smith.

With almost the entire Killie team camped in their opponents half, Hearts broke away in the 89th minute, Foster scoring a third. It certainly didn't reflect the way the game had gone. And the Kilmarnock supporters made their feelings known by giving the team a rousing reception as they left the field.

Defeated they might have been, but this series of games showed Killie what they could achieve and demonstrated that there was still support for a team that played well and with passion. Eddie Morrison summed it up perfectly when he said; *"Both the players and the fans were brilliant".*

1987-88 FIRST DIVISION

After an opening 2-0 defeat at home to Hamilton in the League which was described as a *"gutless performance"* by Morrison, worse was to follow. A 6-1 pasting at Tynecastle ended Kilmarnock's League Cup hopes and after another home League defeat - by Queen of the South - there was a demonstration outside the stand. The beleaguered Board said that they would welcome financial assistance if anyone was interested and held an open meeting which attracted over 300 supporters in an attempt to improve relations with the fans.

Gordon Wylde was signed for £12,000 from East Fife in order to put some steel into the side. In his first match he provided a touch too much - lasting just 30 minutes before being sent off. After 9 games, Killie were rooted to the foot of the table with just three points. Then came a mini-revival, with six points being taken from the next four games. A bad defeat at Forfar was countered by a fine win away to second placed Raith Rovers. But then came a home defeat by Clydebank which Eddie Morrison described as the worst he had ever seen a Kilmarnock team play at Rugby Park. Another bad home defeat - by Meadowbank - prompted yet another demonstration behind the stand. By the end of November the team were stuck in second bottom position, level on points with Partick Thistle. Somehow though they had managed to beat high-flyers Airdrie and Hamilton, giving hope that all not yet be lost.

The loss for the year was contained to £25,841 and Bob Lauchlan told the AGM that an approach had been made to Robert Maxwell but that he wasn't interested in buying Kilmarnock. One shareholder told the Board that it was a *"sad indictment"* that the club could no longer compete with the likes of Meadowbank and Forfar. But Killie did compete against Motherwell in the Scottish Cup, cheered on by over 2,000 travelling fans, they drew 0-0 with the Premier Division side before the now alomst-traditional home replay defeat.

In the League though, matters went from bad to worse. A 2-0 loss at home to Forfar was responsible for the headline in the *Standard*: **"BLACKEST MOMENT IN THE CLUB'S HISTORY"**.

There had been a few contenders for that unwanted title recently. The Forfar loss was one of four in succession, without a goal being scored by Killie, which left the Rugby Parkers three points adrift of third bottom Dumbarton with ten games remaining. Morrison called in the cavalry in the shape of the 34 year old John Bourke, brought in, like an aged gunslinger, for one last hurrah.

It worked too! Killie started snatching points to keep them in touch. Then they beat Dumbarton at Rugby Park, 3-1, in a game which aptly fitted the description of a 'four-pointer'. News of the death of Dougie McAvoy - who had starred in that 1938 Cup Final and relegation-defying outfit - may have brought back memories for some old-timers, but in the here and now, a similar great escape was being carried out. A draw away to Clyde, followed by a 4-1 home win over Airdrie meant that Killie looked a good bet for safety as the table confirmed:-

	P	W	D	L	F	A	Pts	GD
10th Kilmarnock	42	12	11	19	53	57	35	-4
11th East Fife	42	12	9	21	57	74	33	-17
12th Dumbarton	42	10	12	20	44	68	32	-24

Killie's next foes were East Fife at Rugby Park. Given the Ayrshire side's overwhelming goal difference advantage over both the bottom pair, then one point would suffice. The largest home crowd apart from at New Year - 2,488 - were shocked into silence as the Fifers scored three times in the first 14 minutes. Killie could only score once in response. So, instead of being content with a home point, Killie - now level on points with East Fife and only one ahead of Dumbarton who had won at Meadowbank - had to look for two from their final away fixture.

MATCH OF THE SEASON
May 7th 1988.
Partick Thistle 0 Kilmarnock 1

Firhill was probably the last place many Kilmarnock supporters would have wanted to go to needing a win to guarantee First Division survival, but that was what was required this day. Alan McCulloch was in superb form during the first half, as a nervy Killie team took time to settle. Gradually, Kilmarnock came more into the match and made one or two chances themselves, but the first 45 minutes closed without a goal.

News from the other games was favourable. East Fife were drawing and Dumbarton winning. If things stayed as they were then Killie were safe. But it Killie drew and East Fife won ... or Killie lost and Dumbarton won ..... Those thoughts were torturing the large contingent of Kilmarnock supporters at Firhill when it looked as if their worst nightmare was about to come true. "Penalty" roared the Thistle supporters. And there was little appeal made by the Kilmarnock players as the Jags case looked good. But the referee not only refused to award a spot-kick, he sent off Partick's Eddie Gallacher for protesting against his decision.

Now Killie sensed that the day was theirs. From a free kick in 66 minutes, Jimmy Gilmour drove his shot low and hard past Thistle 'keeper, McLean. A mighty roar of relief emanated from the Killie support. It didn't matter what happened elsewhere. Dumbarton won their match and East Fife only drew but Kilmarnock could gaze with contentment as they studied the final table of the season:-

	P	W	D	L	F	A	Pts	GD
10th.Kilmarnock	44	13	11	20	55	60	37	-5
11th.East Fife	44	13	10	21	61	76	36	-15
12th.Dumbarton	44	12	12	20	51	70	36	-19

When the euphoria gave way to sober reality, there was a recognition amonst the support that, if changes were not made soon, then the whole process would be undergone again in 1988-89.

Two who wouldn't be taking part in any more relegation struggles were Jim Cockburn and Robert Clark, the most prominent names among the list of free transfers.

There were rumours that an approach was to be made to David Murray asking if he would like to get involved with the club. Murray had already seen his overtures rejected by Ayr United, but, unbeknown to anyone at the time, he had his sights set on a much bigger fish altogether. As the football world found out later that year when he took control of Rangers.

1988-89 FIRST DIVISION

John Bourke's illustrious career was almost over and forward strength was further depleted by the sale of Ian Bryson to Sheffield United for £40,000. For a player with over 200 first-team appearances behind him and not yet 26, the fee represented a bargain - for the buying club. One significant new face in the Killie line-up was Ray Montgomerie, a £12,000 signing from Dumbarton.

Ray Montgomerie

But the main pre-season activity surrounded Alan Robertson, whose testimonial season this was. A full-strength Rangers outfit won 3-1 in Robertson's benefit game in early August, before an excellent attendance of 9,649. Eventually, a total of over £25,000 was raised. But no amount of money could adequately reflect nearly two decades of sterling service.

An early victory over the resurgent Ayr United in a match which attracted the first 5,000+ League attendance since relegation in 1983 proved to be a false dawn. It was one of only two wins in the first thirteen games, by which time Kilmarnock were third bottom. The result was depressingly familiar. This time it was Eddie Morrison who became the sacrificial lamb. He was sacked, confessing that he had found the transformation from hero to villain difficult. *"The cheers I had received as a player turned to jeers and I found that hard to deal with"* said the refreshingly honest Morrison. No-one, he maintained, felt worse about the situation the club were in than he did. He left without any of the rancour which often accompanies the axing of a boss, going so far as to declare *"It's a great club"*, it was *"an honour to have been manager"* and hoping that the next boss *"would take Killie back to the top"*. Such dignity was magnificent to behold as one of the legends of the post-war era departed from the Rugby Park scene.

Manager Eddie Morrison celebrates a win against Clyde. Sadly, such victories were to be all too rare during his time as boss.

Meantime there had been a takeover bid. Largs businessman, Hugh Scott, put in a £½m. offer for control of the club. One of his schemes was to build a small hotel on what was the club car park. There were suggestions that football might not be guaranteed at Rugby Park under Scott's regime. Not so, said the would-be buyer. Maybe, said the Board. Shareholders were confused. Over 400 attended a meeting with Scott and half resolved to boycott the next home match. The Board's doubts won out. A special meeting of shareholders resolved unanimously to reject the bid.

But confusion remained the order of the day. Morrison, with the axe hanging over him, was allowed to spend as the Board finally decided to speculate to accumulate. He broke the club's transfer record by signing Dave McFarlane from Rangers for £100,000. At the same time, powerful defender Paul Martin was allowed to leave, joining Hamilton for £60,000.

Jim Clark took charge until a new manager was appointed and the purse strings were loosened during his brief tenure too, as he signed the experienced Robert Railly from Meadowbank for £8,000. It was unusual for a caretaker-manager to make a signing but Rugby Park was gripped by desperation and panic. There were more than 20 applications to fill the vacancy and the eventual appointee - Jim Fleeting - was something of a surprise.

Sandy Jardine's had been the name most mentioned but Fleeting had taken Stirling Albion to the top of the Second Division during his short spell there. Fleeting - once turned down by Kilmarnock as a player - said that he would be the *"fullest part-time manager in the country"* and brought former Killie player Jim McSherry plus Frank Coulston with him as his assistants. Another ex-Rugby Parker returning was Jim Stewart as specialist goalkeeping coach.

The new boss wasted no time trying to sort things out. **Nine** players left by Christmas, among them Alan Robertson. One who remained, but who was out of action nonetheless, was Gordon Wylde, victim of a savage tackle by Billy Abercromby of Partick Thistle which put him out of the game for over a year. Sadly, when he did return, he was never as effective again. Among the players Fleeting brought in were Paul Flexney, a £35,000 purchase from Northampton who had been an oustanding centre-half with Clyde, and Willie Watters, another former Clyde man who cost £20,000 from St. Johnstone and who had a good track record in front of goal. Fleeting's determination to stamp his authority on the team was demonstrated after a 3-0 defeat at St. Johnstone when he stated that, of the thirteen players used, *"only three wanted to win"*.

When Killie were eliminated from the Scottish Cup by Queen of the South (in yet another home replay), Fleeting led the press into the home dressing room and announced before the collection of startled, partially-dressed, dripping wet, towel-clad players: *"These gentlemen are the people I have to talk to after each match. Tonight, you can do the talking for yourselves"*. The astonished players, questioned about the result, could only mumble words like *"rubbish"*, *"disappointing"* and *"dreadful"* to describe their own performances.

His point made, the manager promised the assembled scribes that he would repeat the exercise after a victory! But the surest indication that Fleeting would run things his way, came not in the more flamboyant gestures, but with the decisiveness he showed over Kenny Brannigan.

The central defender head-butted former Killie colleague Derek Cook after only three minutes of the League game with Queen of the South and was sent off with a chorus of boos from the **Killie** support ringing in his ears. When Fleeting was asked if he was considering disciplinary action against Brannigan, he replied *"The player has been sacked and has been told he's been given a free transfer"*. Although some supporters disagreed, arguing that a transfer fee at least could have been obtained, Fleeting stuck to his guns and the majority appeared to back him as a welter of letters and phone calls demonstrated. With the memory of the sickening attack on Gordon Wylde fresh in their minds, most fans applauded the manager's bravery in insisting that thuggery had no place at Rugby Park.

With so much taking place on the pitch it would be easy to forget events off-field. Easy, but remiss. It should be recorded that club surgeon, Gavin Ralston, retired after 36 years loyal and outstanding service and he received an appropriate presentation. Gordon Cramond, once Killie's record signing, died of a heart attack at the tragically early age of 39 and the club was represented at his funeral.

The financial situation continued to worsen. Gates for 87-88 were down by £48,500, a major factor in the loss of £74,806 this year. February 1989 saw the name of Fleeting again in the headlines but this time it was Jim's brother, Robert, who was making the news. He was heading a consortium aimed at taking over the club and, at first, it seemed that things were running smoothly. At the time no-one was aware that they were witnessing the beginning of the saga that would run until almost the end of the calendar year.

On the field, a defeat at Ayr was the only setback in eleven matches as the team looked to have clawed their way to safety. With five games to go, Killie were four points ahead of second bottom Clyde.

Two successive defeats reduced this advantage to two points and when Kilmarnock could only draw 0-0 with Partick Thistle in their last home match, they were only a point to the good. Despite a large support, aided by the provision of free buses by the *Standard* and the Western SMT, they squandered an interval lead at Clybebank, losing 3-2. Clyde came back from a goal down at Dunfermline, to earn a draw and climb above Killie on goal difference. With one game left the table looked like this:-

	P	W	D	L	F	A	Pts	GD
11th.Ayr Utd.	38	13	9	16	56	71	35	-15
12th.Clyde	38	8	16	14	38	52	32	-14
13th.Kilmarnock	38	9	14	15	41	60	32	-19
14th.Queen of Sth.	38	2	8	28	38	93	12	-55

MATCH OF THE SEASON
May 13th 1989.
Queen Of The South 0 Kilmarnock 6

If Clyde won then Killie would have to win by a margin of five more than Clyde to stay up. It was a daunting task, hopeless, reasoned many. After all, just a few weeks ago, Killie looked certain to beat the drop. Their own folly had brought them to this pass. The players seemed to think it was beyond them too. In the first 45 minutes Kilmarnock scored just once, Watters capitalising on a poor back pass in 39 minutes to keep some hope alive.

The news that Clyde were drawing 0-0 at half-time galvanised Killie into action. Early in the second period, Watters prodded the ball through the 'keeper's legs to make it 2-0. After a 15 yard run, the same player hit his hat-trick in the 54th minute. Robert Reilly broke up Watters goal monopoly with a fourth for Killie in 61 minutes.

In 69 minutes a Queen's defender hesitated as Watters pounced on a loose ball to make it 5-0. Watters had the ball in the net again shortly afterwards but this effort was chalked off for offside. But word was filtering through that Clyde were a goal up. 5-0 wouldn't be enough.

Amazingly, with just three minutes to go, Watters burst away to score his fifth and Killie's sixth. That made their goal difference the same as Clyde's but the Ayrshire side had scored more goals - the determining factor when teams are otherwise level.

The final whistle at Palmerston Park saw scenes of jubiliation as hundreds of Kilmarnock supporters invaded the pitch. They sang and danced and shouted for their hero - Willie Watters.

Then cheers turned to tears as the unbelievable truth came through. Clyde had been awarded a penalty seven minutes into injury time and they had scored! Both teams had 34 points but Clyde now had a goal difference of minus 12, compared to Killie's minus 13. The evil day, averted so narrowly the year before, had now arrived. Kilmarnock - once hosts to Eintracht and Real Madrid - would now be taking on Stenhousemuir and East Stirling in the depths of the Scottish Second Division. The unthinkable had happened:-
RELEGATION.

Off the park, events were more confused than ever. The Board rejected - by four votes to two - the takeover bid from the Fleeting consortium. At a meeting of supporters to hear what was on offer, a massive 1,136 turned up and gave unanimous backing to Robert Fleeting, Laurel Chadwick and John Moffat of A.T. Mays when they heard that, relegation notwithstanding, the consortium were committed to ground improvements and the return of full-time football as the first step towards the rebuilding of Kilmarnock into a power in the land. The *Standard* wryly remarked that the removal of four directors from Rugby Park would do little harm whereas the loss of over a thousand supporters would be infinitely more damaging.

At an Extraordinary General Meeting of shareholders on June 19th 1989, there was a massive turn-out as the Fleeting bid was backed on a show of hands by 344-22. In a poll vote of shares held, there was still a comfortable majority for acceptance of 40,656 to 32,320 or 55.7% to 44.3%. But, with a 75% acceptance vote constitutionally required, the bid was deemed to have fallen.

Robert Fleeting made an impassioned plea to those assembled in the stand - the meeting having been switched from the Killie club owing to the unprecedented turnout - that he would *"go down on my knees"* if the Board would accept the offer. No reason was given for the *volte-face* by the directors beyond vague mutterings about "unsuitability". But, the shareholders - who had been four-square behind the Board in their rejection of the Scott offer - were left no wiser as to why the Fleeting bid had been fine in February but jilted in June. One thing was manifestly clear. That with Kilmarnock - once Kings of Scotland - about to kick-off as one of the fourteen lowest placed teams in the League, the issue had to be resolved for good. And it had to be resolved soon.

Chapter 12

BACK TO THE FUTURE - KILMARNOCK REDIVIVUS

1989 - 1994

1989-90 SECOND DIVISION

The club's problems were temporarily laid aside as a massive crowd of 11,333 attended Alan McCulloch's testimonial game which a strong Rangers outfit won 3-0. But the boardroom power struggle took a new, machiavellian twist with the resignations of the pro-Fleeting directors Ronnie Hamilton and Jim Thomson and the announcement of a bid from a rival consortium headed by ex-Ayr United striker Alex Ingram. This group offered £250,000 for control of the club - some £200,000 less than the Fleeting bid. The Ingram group would also keep two of the present directors on the Board if they were successful.

Yet the new group were far from harmonious. One of their backers, John Paton, a former Chairman of Rangers, switched sides, joining the Fleeting consortium. Even so, another Ingram backer - hotelier Bill Costley - felt confident enough to declare that he was *"100% certain that the future of this club is decided"*. Others were less sure. Ingram faced hositility from the supporters, his presence at matches being greeted with resounding booing; no doubt on account of his former playing allegiance. More disturbing was the attitude displayed by one of his backers - Glaswegian businessman John Kerr. In a question-and-answer session, he demonstrated an almost total lack of knowledge about Kilmarnock F.C. and, worse still, a profound inability to understand why this was resented by supporters.

On the field, the team took just one point from the first three games. There had been plenty of contenders for the unwanted title of lowest point in the club's history over the past few years but the morning of Sunday 27th August 1989 must have a strong claim to that particular 'prize'. For, on that day, supporters of the crisis-ridden Killie scanned their Sunday newspapers to find their team lying third bottom of the Second Division - ranked 36th of Scotland's 38 clubs. Several hundred supporters staged a boycott of the next home game, holding a rally in the Howard Park instead. The nadir had truly been reached.

Those who did attend Rugby Park that day witnessed not just the first win of the season - 2-0 over East Stirling - but the start of a record breaking run by veteran 'keeper McCulloch. This game was the first of seven in succession - six wins and a draw - where he kept a clean sheet. His heroics in goal helped Kilmarnock to the top of the table. A late goal at Stranraer put an end to this run but Killie won the next two to stay top. After a goalless first half away to East Stirling, the players retired to the dressing room content in the knowledge that this - their 14th match of the season - was also the 14th in which their foes had failed to score in the opening 45 minutes.

But the second half at Firs Park was disastrous as the bottom club beat Killie 2-1 to knock them off the top. The next week saw an end to that first-half record as Jim Fleeting's former club, Stirling Albion, scored twice during the period, eventually winning 2-1. And after that came a truly dreadful 45 minutes as Killie went three down to Berwick Rangers in a game switched at short notice to Tynecastle, owing to Berwick's failure to obtain a safety certificate for their stand roof. A second half recovery wasn't good enough - Killie losing 3-2. Suddenly, promotion looked a long way away.

The battle for the boardroom was reaching its finale as these events unfolded on the field. Hugh Scott re-emerged, briefly, before being discounted as a contender. At an EGM in October the Ingram offer was the only one put forward and was expected to succeed. But the meeting degenerated into a shambles, amid allegations of unconstitutionality and prior knowledge of the bid being available to some shareholders. Just **one** of the 400 present declared that the Ingram offer was acceptable. With the legality of the whole meeing in dispute, the Chairman adjourned to a later date. The re-convened meeting fared no better. It too was adjourned but not before it became apparent that the Fleeting offer was back under serious consideration.

Pressure from the banks was building up and the intense opposition shown by shareholders in particular (the largest individual shareholder Richard Thomson came out strongly against the Ingram group) and supporters in general, resulted in the Ingram-Costley-Kerr group agreeing to sell their shares to the Fleeting consortium. A further meeting was again adjourned after it was intimated that the Fleeting bid would finally be recommended for acceptance. The final meeting took place on Thursday 30th November 1989 when the Fleeting offer went through. Ronnie Hamilton rejoined the Board which now consisted of Laurel Chadwick - the only woman director in British football -, ex-Ibrox boss John Paton, Jim Moffat from A.T. Mays (who the old Board had assiduously tried to woo away from Fleeting) and Robert Fleeting himself as Chairman. The battle had raged for almost a year. At times it had degenerated into farce as the old guard tried to find an injection of capital which would allow them to retain control.

The overwhelming majority of supporters backed the Fleeting team, believing that here, at last, was a group which would take Kilmarnock in an upward direction. Proof that this was indeed the case wasn't slow in arriving. Within days of his brother being installed as Chairman, manager Jim Fleeting signed a man he described as the *"biggest player ever to sign for the club"*. Tommy Burns, a Celtic stalwart for 15 years, rocked Scottish football by joining Kilmarnock.

Burns had won every domestic honour available and his collection of eight Scotland caps was regarded as scant reward for a player who had long been viewed as one of the most skilful and intelligent in the country. At 33 he was no longer guaranteed a regular first team place at Parkhead but it was still an astonishing move to make. Four Premier Division clubs had been after his services, but Killie - helped by a commitment to involve him in coaching and in business management - secured his signature. The boost the club received from his signing was immeasureable. It also sent a clear message to others. If Kilmarnock was a big enough club for Tommy Burns to join, then it was big enough for anybody.

Days later Burns may well have doubted his decision. He made his debut at a rain and wind encrusted Bayview, after the team bus broke down, the players arriving in taxis. With eleven minutes remaining and Killie losing 2-1, the referee abandoned the match as hypothermia posed a real threat to those on the pitch. It is difficult to envisage a worse welcome to the lower reaches of Scottish soccer than that.

The new Board met with over 700 fans in the Grand Hall in Kilmarnock and repeated their pledges to fund ground improvements and re-introduce full-time football. An additional commitment - and one which could have come straight from the 1940's - was made to improve the state of the Rugby Park toilets! This time - to much surprise - the promise was kept. Other innovations helped to increase crowds. Shares in the club could be won as raffle prizes and a new car was won at one home match. Signings continued as well. John Sludden - Ayr United's prolific scorer - arrived for £50,000. The loss for this year was £130,043, over £55,000 more than the previous season. But no-one was really bothered. The AGM lasted all of six minutes.

Stuart McLean

While new boys Burns and Sludden made their Rugby Park bows in a 3-0 win over Arbroath which kept Killie on the fringes of the promotion race, a more familiar face received a well-deserved tribute. Stuart McLean wore the Number 9 shirt in his testimonial game against the Ranger XI. It was the only outfield jersey he hadn't previously worn in the 15 years since he first appeared at Rugby Park. A respectable crowd of 4,371 turned up in January 1990 to salute a magnificent club servant.

The change of regime wasn't reflected by any great difference in the Scottish Cup. Once again Kilarmock were eliminated in a home replay. It was, in one sense, historic though. The 4-3 penalty shoot-out defeat by Stranraer was the first time ever that this method had been used to decide a Scottish Cup tie. Meanwhile, in the League, Jim Fleeting's 'revolving door' policy was beginning to be discerned as players arrived and departed Rugby Park with alarming frequency.

Following Burns and Sludden through the 'in' door were Tom Spence, Michael McArthur and Ian Porteous among others, while Bobby Geddes arrived on loan to replace the injured McCulloch. Gordon Wylde made a welcome return from his horrendous injury but he was not as effective as before. Already, nine players were full-timers.

Results took some time to improve but a 4-2 away victory at Arbroath was the launch pad for a run of five wins. Berwick were beaten 4-1 at their roofless ground and home wins over East Stirling, Stirling Albion and Queen's Park took Killie to 3rd place. Defeats by Queen of the South and Stenhousemuir threatened the promotion push but the team recovered well. Two away wins at Dumbarton, with a home draw against leaders Brechin sandwiched in between, helped Kilmarnock to joint second spot with Stenhousemuir.

When East Fife were beaten 2-1 at Rugby Park in a game Killie had been losing with just six minutes to go, things were looking good. Then came another defeat at the hands of Stranraer and Kilmarnock dropped to 3rd. At the same time news arrived of the sad and untimely death, at 53, of Sandy McLaughlan, that great goalkeeper of the 1960's.

With three games remaining, Killie had no room for error and had to rely on their rivals slipping up. Brechin were going through a bad patch but their lead looked unassailable. Second place Stirling Albion lost at home to 4th placed Stenhousemuir and this clash between their two antagonists meant that Killie's 4-1 demolition of Queen of the South allowed them to regain that precious second promotion spot. The next week, while Stirling kept their hopes alive by winning at Dumbarton, Stenhousemuir lost at home to East Fife. Killie's 3-1 win at Montrose kept their noses in front as the last match approached:-

	P	W	D	L	F	A	Pts	GD
1.Brechin City	38	19	10	9	59	44	48	+15
2.Kilmarnock	38	21	4	13	65	38	46	+27
3.Stirling Albion	38	19	7	12	71	50	45	+21
4.Stenhousemuir	38	18	8	12	59	49	44	+10

MATCH OF THE SEASON

May 5th 1990.

Kilmarnock 2 Cowdenbeath 1

A draw would take Killie up unless Stirling won their last match by six goals and, bearing in mind Killie's own win at Palmerston on the last day of 1988-89, that was something which couldn't be ruled out. Victory, it had to be. The scene awaiting the players as they took the field resembled the Rugby Park of old. There were 8,526 paying spectators present - the largest crowd ever seen in this Division since reconstruction. In addition the club had shrewdly distributed 1,500 free tickets to local schoolchildren.

If the opposition were over-awed by the presence of such a large crowd then they didn't show it. The first attack came from Cowdenbeath and Killie were fortunate to survive. But, with only four minutes played, Tommy Burns took a free kick which Paul Flexney headed home to give Kilmarnock a vital lead and soothe fraying nerves both on the pitch and on the terraces. Reilly, Watters and Sludden all had chances to add to the lead but failed to do so. Near half-time, Sludden headed narrowly over the bar but at the break Killie were still only a goal in front.

News that Brechin were drawing came as a disappointment. For if the long-time leaders lost and Killie won, then the Championship as well as promotion would by Ayrshire-bound. Of more immediate importance was the fact that Stirling Albion were leading East Fife 1-0.

There was no room for complacency in the second half and Killie appeared to be coasting to victory when they were caught out by an equalising goal from Cowdenbeath's Malone in 77 minutes. Stirling, meanwhile, were two ahead but before Killie fans had time to pontificate on the possibility of a late goal rush from their rivals, drama unfolded at Rugby Park.

Four minutes after the shock equaliser and with just nine minutes to play, Paul Flexney headed what appeared to be a certain second goal for Kilmarnock until the ball was handled on the line by a Cowdenbeath defender. 'Penalty', roared the crowd. The Referee agreed. Club skipper Dave Mackinnon was entrusted with the responsibility of the spot kick. Watched by thousands of anxious eyes he stepped up to the mark and confidently blasted the ball past the 'keeper into the net. The cheering from the terracing hadn't died down when the final whistle sounded. Brechin got the draw which gave them the title. Stirling had won 2-0. But no-one at Rugby Park cared about either of those results. The crowd swarmed all over the pitch, returning to the ground to allow the players to take a bow. After a year in the twilight zone of Scottish Football, Kilmarnock had gained promotion as the table confirmed:-

	P	W	D	L	F	A	Pts	GD
1.Brechin City	39	19	11	9	59	44	49	+15
2.Kilmarnock	39	22	4	13	67	39	48	+28
3.Stirling Albion	39	20	7	12	73	50	47	+23

Aerial view of Rugby Park in the late 1980's.
(The old half-time scoreboard is still visible on the uncovered terrace)

The celebrations didn't end there. There was an Ayrshire Cup win over Ayr United at which Bobby Geddes signed before the game. And despite the £100,000 outlay involved, Jim Fleeting asserted that he still had money available for new signings.

A mini-business boom took place in the town itself. Not just in the pubs on the night of promotion but in the sports shops; as sales of Killie gear at last began to match that of the 'Old Firm'. And, it was reported, the most popular sales were of Kilmarnock strips in sizes 38-42. It wasn't just children who wanted to dress like their idols. Crowds had risen by 37% over the season. Only two **First** Division clubs averaged gates better than Kilmarnock's. Killie's home crowds were more than four times bigger than any other club in the Second Division. Indeed, those home figures accounted for **one-third** of all Second Division attendances. That division had never seen a club with the drawing power of Kilmarnock in its ranks, and Falkirk, St. Johnstone, Ayr and Dunfermline had all played there at some time. Little wonder that the minnows didn't want to see Killie go up, pulling out all the stops whenever the Rugby Park roadshow hit town.

This memorable season was rounded off by a dinner in honour of the 25th anniversary of the League Championship success. But one of the Board members of the time - Tom Lauchlan - died shortly beforehand, aged 77. In addition to his Kilmarnock duties, he had also served as President of the Scottish Football League. Also passing away at the same age was 'Bud' Maxwell, the goalscoring hero of the Archbishop of Canterbury. But, sadness at these deaths aside, the club faced the future with an optimism unknown for years.

1990-91 FIRST DIVISION

More than 8,000 turned up to the club's Open Day, underlining the potential that existed at Rugby Park. That day was the first chance the fans got to see the new family enclosure, an all-seated area replacing the old enclosure in front of the stand. Another innovation was the transferable season ticket. The Board decided, correctly, that if someone had paid out £100, they were entitled to give their ticket to a friend any time they felt like it.

Sponsorship was on the increase too. The name of A T Mays returned to the team jerseys. And Player of the Year, Tommy Tait, received a brand new Peugeot 405 for the duration of the season. Another ex-Celt, Billy Stark, was signed at a cost of £50,000. An equally famous name, Gary Shaw, who had played in the Aston Villa side which won the European Cup, also arrived at Rugby Park. But the injury-plagued striker didn't stay long.

Another testimonial marked the opening of the season. This time the recipient was Walter McCrae. As Trainer from 1956-68, Manager 1968-73 and Company Secretary from 1980 onwards, he had been a loyal servant of Kilmarnock F.C. In addition, he had also been trainer to the Scotland team for many years; a position he was succeeded in by Hugh Allan. Although often coming under fire latterly from the supporters - a classic case of failing to observe the old Greek maxim of refusing to shoot the messenger - for his public utterances of the Board's deliberations, the genuine esteem Walter McCrae was held in was marked by the attendance of 5,499 who saw Rangers win 3-1.

Walter McCrae served the club as Trainer, Manager and General Manager for 30 years.

The early days of the season saw Killie lose their first three League matches but put up a terrific fight at Ibrox in the League Cup before succumbing to Mo Johnston's late goal. At length, the League results improved, a seven match unbeaten run culminating in a fine 3-1 win over Ayr United. But a stuttering run after that game saw Jim Fleeting open the cheque-book again as £100,000 obtained the signature of Bobby Williamson from Rotherham United. He was an instant success, providing the goals which Watters and Sludden found harder to come by this season. Later, he was joined by Gus McPherson, a £30,000 bargain from Rangers and Calum Campbell, a £65,000 acquisition from Partick Thistle. Others departed the scene, including the popular Gordon Wylde, sold to Queen of the South for just £5,000.

The commercial side of the club continued to grow. A new shop, in the centre of the town, attracted £60,000 worth of custom in just five weeks. And a new supporters club for children was established. With the unlikely name of the KGB (Killie Girls and Boys), it was launched appropriately enough in the village of Moscow.

One of the most welcome 'innovations' of them all was a win in the Scottish Cup. Victory over Arbroath put Killie into the last 16 for the first time in five years. Defeat at Dens Park was a bitter pill to swallow but at least it ended the run of home replay defeats. Amazingly, it was the first time Killie had lost away in the Cup since their trip to Inverness.

In the League, the team were always just that little bit behind the front-runners to really inspire hopes of a second successive promotion. But they finished a respectable 5th, giving rise for optimism for a more sustained challenge in 1991-92. Near the end of the season, Kilmarnock played, and beat, a side representing the Irish League 2-1 in a match to commemorate that body's Centenary. It was also significant as the last time Alan McCulloch pulled the goalie's jersey over his head. He played for the first 45 minutes before quietly retiring from the action. Another leaving at the end of the season, was Stuart McLean. Both he and McCulloch had been Kilmarnock players for almost two decades. Also leaving on a free transfer was Dave MacKinnon, the hero of just 12 months previous. A year of effective consolidation ended on a respectful note in the Ayrshire Cup Final when both Killie and Ayr agreed to hand over the proceeds from the match to the family of the late Gordon Cramond who had been a player for both clubs.

MATCH OF THE SEASON

April 10th 1991.
Meadowbank Thistle 1 Kilmarnock 8

Just over a thousand fans, most supporting Killie, gathered in the Commonwealth Stadium to see this end-of-season game on a Wednesday evening. "Killie to win a close one" was the 'Daily Record's' prediction. It was close too, for the first seven minutes. That was the time that had elapsed when Bobby Williamson rounded Meadowbank 'keeper McQueen, to let Calum Campbell notch the opener. Four minutes later, another defensive error allowed Billy Stark to grab the second. And when Campbell got the third in 14 minutes, there must have been a sheepish expression on at least one face in the Press Box.

Bobby Williamson got into the act himself, grabbing the fourth and fifth goals before Trevor Smith made it six just before half-time. Tommy Burns produced a superb seventh goal in 58 minutes, but Meadowbank raised ironic cheers when they pulled a goal back with 14 minutes to play. Since the fourth goal went in, the electronic scoreboard had constantly reminded the crowd of how long it had been since Meadowbank had lost first five, then six then seven in a home game. Now it proclaimed that they had ***never*** *lost eight. That had to be altered as Tommy Burns scored the goal that sent Killie fans home arguing over just how many their team had scored.*

Among those supporters were some who reckoned that Killie had eased up in the second half and that the defence had been "a bit slack" in allowing Meadowbank to score. The opposite perspective was taken by the fanzine 'Killie Ken' which greeted this record away League victory in true historical fashion by asking it's readers:

WHERE WERE YOU WHEN?....
John F Kennedy was assassinated?
Man walked on the Moon?
Nelson Mandela was released?
Thatcher resigned?
Killie scored eight at Meadowbank?

1991-92 FIRST DIVISION

Jim Fleeting was busy in the transfer market in the run-up to the new season. Winger Ally Mitchell arrived from East Fife in a complex deal which saw John Sludden and Tom Spence head in the opposite direction. If Mitchell made a certain number of appearances, the value of the transfer could reach £100,000. Left-sided defender Mark Reilly, unable to command a First Team place at Motherwell, was signed for a small fee. Shaun McSkimming, a speedy left-winger or full back, cost £40,000 from Dundee and Centre-forward Ross Jack, left Dunfermline for £45,000.

Robert Fleeting's stated aim was not just to take Kilmarnock back into the Premier Division, but also to return to Europe. The players got some taste of this with a pre-season tour to Malta and a four-team tournament at Rugby Park involving Rangers, Coventry City and Sparta Rotterdam in which Killie beat the Dutch team before losing to Rangers in the Final.

But despite a good performance against Hibs in the League Cup, the goals Kilmarnock scored in the 3-2 defeat at Rugby Park were the only ones Hibs conceded on their way to lifting the trophy, the League start was again poor. Just one win in the first eight games. More changes needed to be made. Billy Stark left in a straight swap for Hamilton's Hugh Burns. Out-of-contract Craig Paterson was signed from Motherwell. A tribunal decision eventually ordering Killie to pay £50,000 for the vastly-experienced defender - less than one-third of Motherwell's valuation. Six players were transfer-listed in a bid to reduce costs. And, in what proved to be a highly significant move, Tommy Burns was appointed Assistant Manager - Jim McSherry staying on the staff and Frank Coulston leaving.

Other departures included Ronnie Hamilton. He resigned again from the Board, but this time in amicable circumstances. Walter McCrae finally stepped down. The man whose boyhood ambition had been to sell chocolate bars at Rugby Park and ended up being blamed for everything down to the cold pies, handed over to new Secretary Kevin Collins.

Robert Fleeting put forward an ambitious scheme for a new ground on the site of the Scott-Ellis playing fields. A £12m., 20,000 all-seater stadium was the idea. It was to be funded by including housing and a supermarket on the site plus the sale, for housing, of Rugby Park. It was estimated that this would leave only a £1½m. shortfall to be raised by the club, whereas to refurbish Rugby Park to an acceptable European standard would cost a prohibitive £6m.

Unfortunately these proposals ran counter to local authority structure plans and the planning application was 'called in', meaning it would be determined by Strathclyde Region rather than the more sympathetic local council.

The club lost £498,054 this year, compared to £463,317 the year before. Reasons for these huge amounts weren't hard to find. The new Board had done what the old regime had been criticised for not doing. Spent money. Transfer fees and the return of full-time football bore the bulk of the costs. Indeed, had it not been for transfers, there would have been an operating profit of £100,000, Roberts Fleeting told the AGM. The growth of the club's commercial income meant that it could stand the current overdraft, he assured shareholders.

Back on the park a run of just one defeat in eleven games put Killie into contention. A home loss to Dundee soured the picture but there was some compensation as the crowd that day (7,137) was larger than the rest of the First and Second Divisions combined! Another run without loss - this time of four games - kept them challenging near the top. In mid-December this was the way the table looked:-

	P	W	D	L	F	A	Pts
1.Dundee	24	15	5	4	49	27	35
2.Hamilton Aca.	24	12	9	3	45	27	33
3.Kilmarnock	24	12	7	5	37	22	31
4.Partick Th.	24	13	5	6	38	26	31

But Killie had a dreadful New Year. After 1991's aberration, there was a home replay defeat in the Cup against Meadowbank. The Ayrshire side lost on penalties. The League saw another run with just one win in eight games. It was virtually impossible to gain promotion in such circumstances but a six match unbeaten run almost brought them back into the frame until they were beaten at Stirling. The following week, Killie were 2-1 down to Partick Thistle with 16 minutes to play when Referee, Brian McGinlay, ignored a clear offside decision from his linesman which allowed the Jags to secure a third goal. Less than 48 hours later, the two Jims, Fleeting and McSherry, accepted the inevitable price of failing to gain promotion and both resigned.

It is unusual for a manager to lose his job when his club is in a better position both in a playing sense and financially than when he found it. But the Kilmarnock fans expected Jim Fleeting's big-name signings to take them up this season. Anything else was failure. Fleeting had been a flamboyant character whose main failing had lain in spending too much too soon and in off-loading many players for a lot less than he paid for them. At the same time, it is undeniably true that Kilmarnock FC was a much healthier club on the day he left than it had been on his arrival.

Tommy Burns took over as caretaker until the end of the season. An unbeaten run then ensued which restored much of the optimism of the fans. In the end the team finished 4th, just three points behind 2nd placed Partick Thistle. And when they thought of the **eight** points lost to the Maryhill club and mused on what might have been....

For many years Kilmarnock supporters have enjoyed the work of Scotland's foremost cartoonist - Malky McCormick - in the programme, fanzine and local paper.

But there was little time for such idle dreams. Kilmarnock supporters were actually sorry to see the season's end. Most couldn't wait for the new one to start, such was their belief that Burns was the man to lead them back to the big time. The Board showed that they shared those sentiments by confirming Burns as boss. He brought Billy Stark back, primarily as his assistant, but still registered as a player too. Burns himself stated that he intended to play as often as possible in the coming campaign.

Alas, one stalwart who would not see that battle was Freddie Milloy, son of the great full-back of the 30's, and a stout worker behind the scenes at Rugby Park for many years - as indeed was his wife Jean, officially a secretary but in reality a general factotum par excellence. Freddie's death was mourned by all with the club's welfare at heart.

MATCH OF THE SEASON

November 2nd 1991.
Ayr United 0 Kilmarnock 3

Ayrshire derbies are always fraught affairs and this one was no different. Kilmarnock were seeking to improve their dismal record of just two wins in eighteen games at Somerset Park over the past 22 years. But they were almost caught out in the game's frantic start when Ayr's George shot just over the bar. Killie quickly countered, with Williamson nearly getting on the end of a flick from Campbell.

In 14 minutes, Jack saw his shot cleared by 'keeper Duncan who had come out well off his line. The ball broke to Tommy Burns, 35 yards out - a range beyond the wit of most but which often sees Burns at his deadliest. So it was here, as he calmly lobbed the ball over the stranded Duncan and into the net. Five minutes after that, a bad pass back let in Ally Mitchell to score Killie's second. The Kilmarnock fans were in ecstasy. Hugh Burns tried to imitate his namesake but saw his effort saved. With 35 minutes on the clock, Geddes brought off a save from ex-Killie player, Tommy Bryce. It was the first time the Kilmarnock 'keeper had been called into action. Two minutes from half-time, a Tommy Burns drive was saved by Duncan. Sixty seconds later, a Mitchell corner was headed on by Paterson and Williamson soared above Duncan to head in the third goal.

The second half was a much quieter affair as Killie coped easily with the seldom-threatening Ayr forwards. At 3-0 it was the "highlight of the season so far" said the 'Standard' as it hailed Kilmarnock's "flash finishing on the park" and "people power on the terracing". It was Kilmarnock's biggest away win over Ayr since November 1917. The experience was so enjoyable that Killie returned to Somerset later in the season and won again, this time by 2-0. They had confirmed that their period in the doldrums was over and that, as far as the supporters were concerned, there was indeed only 'one team in Ayrshire'.

1992-93 FIRST DIVISION

Scottish football was thrown into turmoil at the start of the season as the big city clubs attempted to break away from the Scottish League and form a 'Super League'. At first it looked like Killie were going to throw in their lot with them but after careful study it became apparent that proposals which increased the wealth of the few to the exclusion of the many were not quite as revolutionary as the scheme's apologists asserted. Kilmarnock announced that they would stick with the Scottish League.

Football was getting more expensive to watch: stand season tickets now cost £145 but renewals, could be obtained for the previous price of £130 if purchased early enough. Ground admission also rose - by £1 - to £5. But those attending Killie's games were given value for money as the Rugby Park side got off to a good start. They also gained a 'revenge' victory over Hibs in the League Cup - knocking the holders out of the tournament in a 3-1 thriller after extra time. But when Killie lost at home to Dunfermline in the League, they found one pressman already writing them off as promotion candidates - with **forty** games to play!

Two of the giants of days gone by died early in the season. Rab Stewart, aged 59, who had played for the club between 1951-60, had been reserve team coach from 1973-89 and had also filled in as caretaker manager twice, was first to go. Rab had also been coach to the fine Stewarton ladies team of the early 70s and had turned out for Killie reserves at the age of 53 when the team was a man short. The second to pass away was Willie Waddell, aged 71. As Killie manager, Waddell had *"moulded what was probably the most consistent side in British football during the 60's"* said Walter McCrae.

Although Waddell's Ibrox career as player, manager and director meant that he would enter the history books as one of Rangers' all-time greats, McCrae averred that he would be remembered in Kilmarnock as *"one of the greatest Killie men of all time"*. McCrae's tribute to the man who brought the League flag to Ayrshire was echoed by Kilmarnock fans all over the world.

While Killie were well in contention for promotion, they were dropping some points carelessly. Playing away to runaway leaders Raith Rovers, the Ayrshire team were so superior that even Rovers boss Jimmy Nicholl had to admit that his team were lucky to scrape a 1-1 draw. The next week, playing Clydebank at home, Killie fans were privileged to watch two absolute gems of goals. First, Shaun McSkimming took the ball from the half-way line past four defenders before cracking home a shot from 25 yards. Then, George McCluskey, flat on his backside on the grass, spectacularly hooked the ball into the net. Yet Clydebank snatched a 3-3 draw.

Next, another draw. This time at Meadowbank where Killie's fans were forced to watch the match in freezing cold conditions from the uncovered terracing. Officially, a cat show under the main stand (the only part of the ground officially used for football) was the reason for this. The suspicion that this was a pretext was hard to shake off though. Two weeks later, Edinburgh was the venue for the summit meeting of European Community Governments and Meadowbank was converted into a vast media centre for the occasion. That Kilmarnock supporters shivered in Arctic conditions while MI5 took over Meadowbank was a rumour easily believed by the frozen faithful.

Raith Rovers ran away with the First Division in 1992/93, but they were no match for Killie, who put eight goals past them in two games within the space of three weeks in January. George McCluskey proved to be a master signing in the Kilmarnock promotion bid. Here the Raith Rovers defender can only watch, unsure as to what trick George will pull next!

Whatever the truth, Chairman Robert Fleeting abandoned the area of the stand where officials were allowed to congregate, to mingle with the supporters on the cold terraces. A move applauded by the spectators.

Another defeat by Dunfermline - this time away from home - saw Killie slump to 4th. Then came an invigorating 3-0 win over Ayr United which set the promotion train back on the rails. Especially pleasing for manager Burns must have been the performances in this match of the two Marks, Skilling and Roberts. These two youngsters were outstanding, belying the 'Dad's Army' tag bestowed upon the team by a press eager to point out the high number of *thirty-somethings* in the side. One man who could laugh off the media jibes was George McCluskey. Signed, reputedly, at the cost of a few packets of sweets for his children, McCluskey was still displaying the skills and vision that had made him one of the most talented ball players of his time. Though not as quick as in his days at Celtic, Leeds and Hibernian, the forward was proving to be the experienced player Kilmarnock had needed up front. Not just for his goals, but for his ability to hold the ball and for his lethal, precision passing.

The win over Ayr was the first of six consecutive triumphs which allowed Killie to reach the half-way mark in one of the promotion positions:-

	P	W	D	L	F	A	Pts
1.Raith Rovers	22	14	7	1	48	19	35
2.Kilmarnock	22	12	6	4	32	18	30
3.Hamilton Aca.	22	10	6	6	36	23	26
4.Dunfermline A.	23	12	2	9	37	25	26
5.St. Mirren	23	10	5	8	30	30	26

But that comfortable looking cushion over their rivals soon vanished as Killie lost for the third time to Dunfermline, bringing back haunting memories of the defeats against Partick which had seen promotion denied in 1991-92. There was another bad defeat at Greenock, where Morton won 2-0 in a game played on a Tuesday afternoon. A win away to Ayr helped stabilise things but Killie were now just three points clear of Hamilton and Dunfermline, with the Accies having a game in hand.

The loss for the year was £361,426, bringing the total deficit to £2,041,033. But turnover was up by 15% to reach over the £1 million mark. Club souvenirs accounted for sales of over £200,000 compared to £8,500 when the old Board had been in charge. The Top Ten lottery attracted over 11,000 members at 50p per week, as well as envious eyes from rival teams.

After the New Year win at Ayr, Kilmarnock embarked on a superb start to 1993. Raith Rovers were hammered 5-0 at Rugby Park in the Scottish Cup, with Bobby Williamson grabbing a hat-trick. Seven days later, in a League match, it was the turn of Meadowbank Thistle to receive a 5-0 thrashing. Then, the District Council in Kilmarnock decided unanimously to recommend acceptance of the new stadium proposals to Strathclyde Region.

Promotion rivals Hamilton were beaten 2-1 on their own Douglas Park turf. Kilmarnock's *mensis mirabilis* ended with another home win over Raith Rovers. Iain Porteous scored twice (taking his total to five from the last four League games) in a 3-0 success which saw some Killie fans harbour hopes that their team might yet overtake the long-time leaders:-

	P	W	D	L	F	A	Pts
1.Raith Rovers	29	17	10	2	59	27	44
2.Kilmarnock	28	16	6	6	45	24	38
3.Dunfermline A.	29	17	3	9	47	29	37
4.St. Mirren	29	15	6	8	42	35	36

"February made me shiver" sang Don McLean in 'American Pie', *"Bad news on the doorstep. I couldn't take one more step"*. And how Kilmarnock must have empathised with those lyrics as their season appeared to crumble beneath their feet. First, there was the pain of a narrow - and unlucky - Cup defeat away to St. Johnstone after 210 minutes of proud performance but no Killie goals. That was followed by a late goal defeat at Dumbarton. Late, in the sense that there were only a few minutes to play, and late also in the sense that it was scored well after 5 o'clock - the game's start having been delayed for 40 minutes by a fire in the Dumbarton stand. Fortunately, the blaze was only a small one and no-one was hurt.

Three days later, came a dreadful 2-0 loss at Clydebank. Then, with 90 minutes on the clock, Killie were a goal down at home to relegation certainties Cowdenbeath, before an injury-time equaliser from Calum Campbell saved some face as well as ending the four-game goalless run. It was the last match of the month before Kilmarnock re-discovered their form - beating St. Mirren narrowly, 1-0, in a game which should have been won with ease. That win took them clear of the Paisley side but the promotion pairings were now filled by two Fife teams:-

	P	W	D	L	F	A	Pts	GD
1.Raith Rovers	32	19	11	2	64	28	49	+36
2.Dunfermline A.	32	19	4	9	54	34	42	+20
3.Kilmarnock	32	17	7	8	47	28	41	+19
4.St. Mirren	32	16	7	9	43	36	39	+7

But hopes that the win over the Saints marked a return to promotion form proved to be illusory, as March became as disastrous a month as it's predecessor. There was a 2-0 defeat away to Stirling Albion - ex-Killie striker Willie Watters scoring both goals. That was followed by a scrambled 2-2 draw at home to Morton. Then came a 2-0 loss away to a Raith team now so far in front that it seemed madness to think that just six weeks beforehand, Killie had entertained thoughts of catching them. Then Ayr United took a point from Rugby Park in a 1-1 draw. At Dunfermline the following week, Shaun McSkimming produced another wonder goal; picking the ball up midway in his own half, he ran through the defence, rounded the 'keeper and slotted the ball into the empty net. But Killie let slip a 2-0 lead, settling for a 2-2 draw. At least they had taken a point from the Pars for the first time this season.

Against Clydebank, in the first match in April, it all suddenly clicked together. McSkimming scored within 90 seconds and McCluskey put Killie two up after three minutes play. There were no more goals for the next 40 minutes then Killie ended the half as spectacularly as they had started, with a McPherson penalty and curling shot from McCluskey sending them into the dressing room 4-0 up. Two late goals from sub Ally Mitchell in the second half rounded off a terrific 90 minutes, as Killie confirmed that the race for promotion wasn't over yet.

Killie had a blank Saturday as the water-logged Meadowbank pitch was unplayable and all their rivals lost ground. Hamilton were beaten at Ayr, St. Mirren lost away to Stirling and Dunfermline dropped a point at Clydebank. So it was all the more galling when Killie passed up on the chance to move to within a point of the Fifers by drawing at Meadowbank on the Wednesday evening, despite another early score from McSkimming; this time in just 30 seconds. The news that Kilmarnock's match programme had been voted best in the Division was a well-deserved honour but at this stage of the season - with five games to play - it looked like it might be the only award coming Rugby Park way:

	P	W	D	L	F	A	Pts	GD
1.Raith Rovers	39	23	14	2	75	31	60	+44
2.Dunfermline A.	39	21	7	11	61	41	49	+20
3.Kilmarnock	39	18	11	10	59	38	47	+21
4.Hamilton Aca.	39	17	11	11	60	39	45	+21
5.Morton	39	18	8	13	58	47	44	+11
6.St. Mirren	39	18	8	13	52	44	44	+8

But Killie disposed of Stirling Albion easily, winning 3-0 at home while St. Mirren revived their fading hopes by beating Dunfermline away. Now Killie were back in 2nd place with four games to go, ahead of Dunfermline on goal difference. If they won these four games then they would go up. Unless Dunfermline won all of theirs and scored more in the process. By half-time the next Saturday, - April 24th, 28 years to the day since Killie landed the League flag - Kilmarnock supporters were celebrating. Ally Mitchell had given their side the lead at Love Street, Paisley and the team looked Premier-bound. But this amazing season still had a few tricks to play. Killie folded against the young Saints team after the break, losing 2-1. A result which allowed Dunfermline to regain 2nd and brought St. Mirren to within a point of Killie.

Kilmarnock entered May, scraping a nervy 1-0 win over Dumbarton but, suddenly, the cheers rang out at Rugby Park once more. The one result no-one expected had happened. Cowdenbeath - with only one win from their previous 41 League games - had beaten their neighbours Dunfermline at the latter's East End Park. Once again, Kilmarnock were in the driving seat. And with only two games left to play, surely this time there would be no mistake.

	P	W	D	L	F	A	Pts	GD
1.Raith Rovers	42	24	15	3	81	35	63	+46
2.Kilmarnock	42	20	11	11	64	40	51	+24
3.Dunfermline A.	42	22	7	13	63	45	51	+18
4.St. Mirren	42	21	8	13	58	47	50	+11

The next port-of-call for Kilmarnock was Cowdenbeath. Grateful as they may have been for the favour done them the previous week, Killie were in no charitable mood as they romped home 3-0, to leave Cowdenbeath in the unenviable situation of having completed their home programme without a solitary victory to their name. The news from their rivals was good. Dunfermline had only drawn at Dumbarton and Ayr United had done their neighbours a great turn. Their draw with the fast-rising St. Mirren, coupled with the respective goal differences, had all but eliminated that team from the race. As the teams entered their final games, the table stood like this:-

	P	W	D	L	F	A	Pts	GD
1.Raith Rovers	43	25	15	3	84	37	65	+47
2.Kilmarnock	43	21	11	11	67	40	53	+27
3.Dunfermline A.	43	22	8	13	63	45	52	+18
4.St. Mirren	43	21	9	13	61	50	51	+11

Unless Dunfermline won their last match by nine goals then a draw would take Kilmarnock up.

MATCH OF THE SEASON

May 15th 1993.

Kilmarnock 0 Hamilton Academical 0

The week before this game saw a build-up of an intensity not experienced since 1965. Thousands of posters, drawn by Malky McCormick - Scotland's foremost cartoonist and a Killie fan of long-standing - urged the people of Ayrshire to come along and "JOIN UNCLE TAM'S BLUE AND WHITE ARMY". And they did. Long before kick-off it became apparent that the crowd limit would not be enough, for the most important match played at Rugby Park for a least a decade.

Hundreds were locked out as the First Division's biggest crowd of the season - a splendid 12,830 assembled to watch their heroes in action. But it was Hamilton who shot straight out of the traps, intent on spoiling Killie's hopes in much the same way as the Rugby Parkers had extinguished the Lanarkshire side's promotion chances twelve months previously. Player of the Year Bobby Geddes was forced into making an early save, as Paul McDonald opened up the Killie defence to shoot. The same player had another attempt on goal which Geddes brilliantly blocked. But the ball broke to Hamilton's Napier who smacked a fierce shot goalwards, only to see it crash off the underside of the bar. The ball rebounded safely for Killie, only the man from the 'Sunday Post' thought it had crossed the line, no Hamilton player made such a claim.

After those opening minutes, Kilmarnock began to recover their composure. George McCluskey and Shaun McSkimming doing most to take the game to Hamilton. A McCluskey cross which fooled the entire defence dropped invitingly into the box but there was no-one there to take advantage. Next, George decided to have a go himself but this shot took a deflection off a defender, falling just wide of the post. Hamilton hadn't come to lie down though, and Geddes again had to be alert to save from Cramb.

Ally Mitchell attempts to break the deadlock in the tense encounter with Hamilton.
This game took Killie back into the Premier Division after a 10 year absence.

By now, Rugby Park was a wall of noise as the singing and dancing spectators reacted to the welcome news that Dunfermline were losing to Morton. Some of that confidence percolated through to the pitch where McSkimming took off on one of his runs close to the break, forcing 'keeper Ferguson into a fine save. Immediately after the restart, it was McSkimming again. This time he beat the 'keeper but watched, agonisingly, as the ball bounced off the crossbar to be cleared by the Hamilton defence.

That was the closest Kilmarnock came to a goal and, as it became apparent that Dunfermline were definitely heading to defeat, the cheers and celebrations of the supporters gathered momentum as they waited for the historic moment to arrive.

At last, Hugh Williamson, the referee, blew for time up on Killie's only goalless draw in the League. The players made straight for the dressing room "with most of the crowd in hot pursuit", said the reporter from 'Scotland On Sunday'. The pitch was awash with blue and white. There were thousands of supporters celebrating, in scenes which were "mad, glad and glorious" as the 'Ayrshire Leader' put it.

Tommy Burns gives thanks
for his prayers being answered

And those fans had every right to celebrate. It had been ten long years since they had last sampled top-class football. Many of those caught up in the rapture were too young to remember the glory days. The problems which Kilmarnock would face in the Premier Division and the talk of yet another reconstruction of the Scottish League could wait awhile. For now, all the fans wanted to do was to express their elation that Killie were going up.

The strains of 'Paper Roses' could be heard long into the night in every town and village in the county. Killie were back and their supporters wanted the world to know it. For this famous old club the depression years were over, at last. Tommy Burns, unable to play through injury summed it up perfectly. When asked to compare this triumph to his many successes at Celtic, the Killie manager replied that this was "the greatest moment of my career".

FINAL TABLE 1992-93

	P	W	D	L	F	A	Pts
1.Raith Rovers	44	25	15	4	85	41	65
2.Kilmarnock	44	21	12	11	67	40	54
3.Dunfermline A.	44	22	8	14	64	47	52
4.St. Mirren	44	21	9	14	62	52	51

Back where they belong.
Jubilant fans invade the pitch.

(Above) Players and fans celebrate promotion, and ....
(Below) the achievement did not go unnoticed by the Solomon Islands.
News of Killie's triumph is greeted with smiles by the Solomon Islands Kilmarnock Supporters Club.

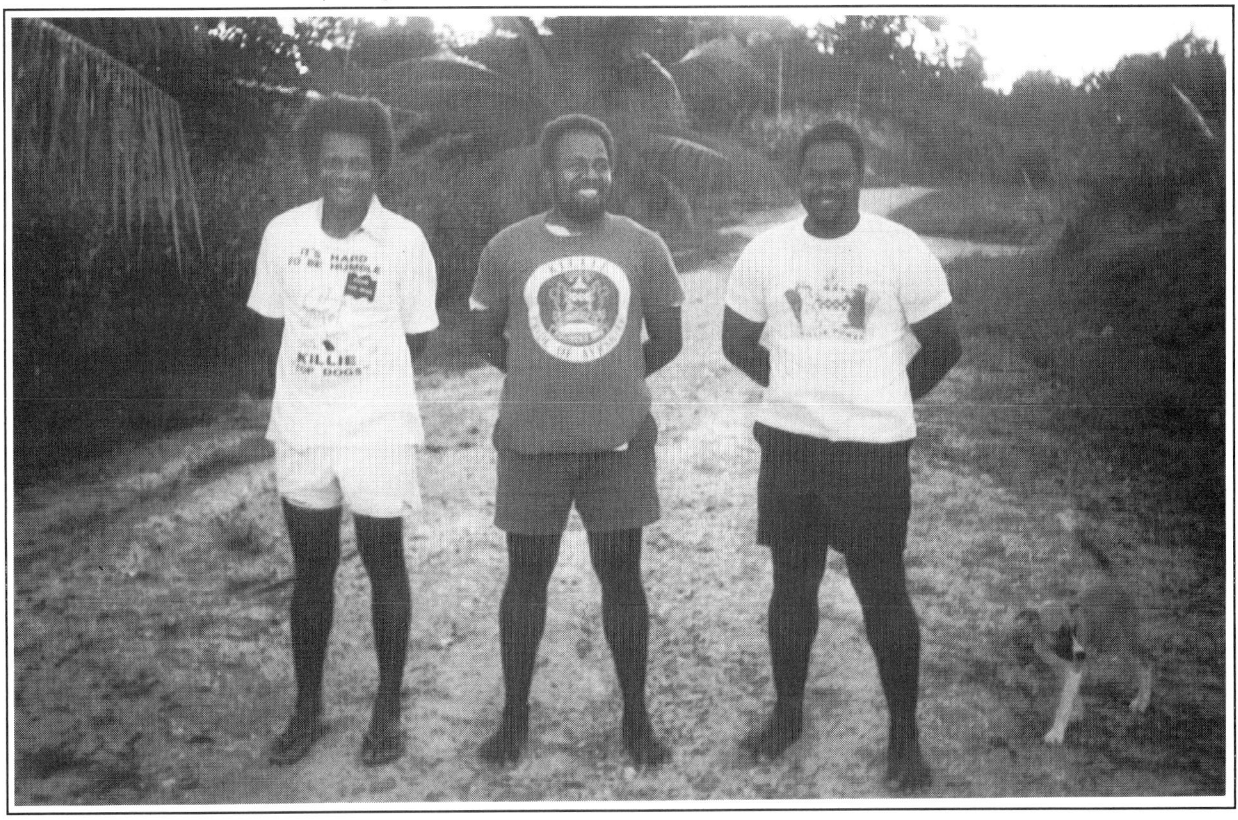

KILMARNOCK
FOOTBALL CLUB
CONFIDEMUS
KILMARNOCK F.C.
SCOTTISH LEAGUE
PREMIER DIVISION
KILMARNOCK
V
DUNDEE
Saturday
7th August
1993
KO 3.00pm
SEASON 1993/94
ISSUE No. 1
MATCH SPONSORS
THE
KILMARNOCK
STANDARD
MAYS
OFFICIAL MATCHDAY PROGRAMME OF KILMARNOCK F.C.
PRICE £1.00

Back in the Premier Division again - the first league match.

A dramatic change to the structure of the Scottish League format was agreed before the start of the season. At the end of 1993-94 the League would be re-organised into four divisions each containing 10 clubs. In order to achieve this, **three** teams would be relegated from the Premier Division. The decision had been approved by a solitary vote at the League AGM with the Raith Rovers representative defying the instructions of his Board by voting **for** the controversial scheme. So to did Dundee, like Raith one of the favourites for the drop. Drowning men have been known to clutch at straws - this was the first instance of a pair of non-swimmers tying lead weights to their feet and plunging head first into the river.

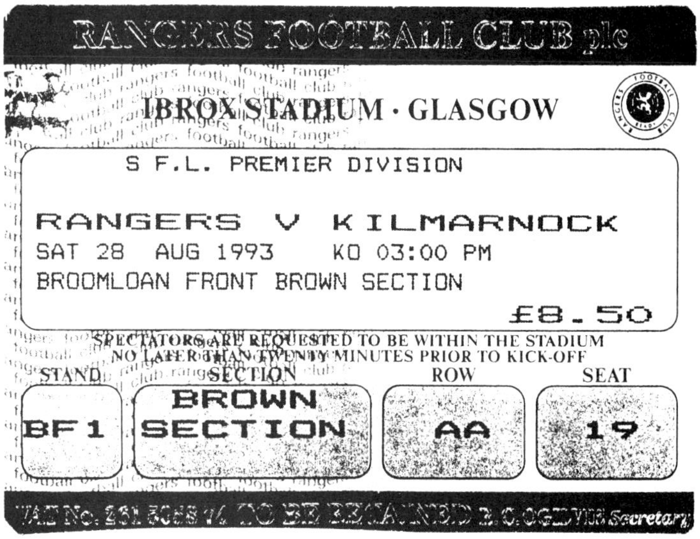

The first of six meetings during the season with Champions-elect Rangers. This match, resulted in an epic Killie victory.

For Kilmarnock it was a hard decision to accept. Club Chairman Robert Fleeting was on record as favouring a top flight of 16 clubs, as was manager Tommy Burns and the overwhelming bulk of the supporters. At least the task facing the club was clear. In a League which would lose 25% of its members, Kilmarnock had to finish 9th or better. In the four previous seasons when there had been a 44 game programme, no club had finished third bottom with more than 34 points. It was assumed, not unreasonably, that a total in excess of that figure would be enough for survival. But not by Tommy Burns. He asserted that teams that looked toward simple survival often failed to achieve their aim. Burns declared that he was aiming to finish 4th top rather than 4th bottom.

While this confident approach won plaudits from all, many supporters were deeply concerned about the club's chances. The close season had come and gone and the only new faces at Rugby Park were Tom Brown, a striker recruited from junior side Glenafton, and defender Andy Millen from Hamilton, whose value was eventually fixed at £75,000 by a transfer tribunal. But this unknown pair immediately demonstrated their ability when Kilmarnock stepped onto the Rugby Park pitch to face Dundee on August 7th 1993. And what a reception they got. Just 1,203 had watched Killie's last Premier game - against Motherwell in May 1983. Now a crowd of 8,162 basked in the sunshine as Killie ran the game from start to finish. When Dundee did mount a rare attack, it was the immaculate Millen who cleared any danger. And up front, the diminutive Brown gave many examples of his salmon-like ability in the air before turning in the crowded penalty area and, with a marvellous display of close control and composure, stabbed the ball home to mark Killie's return to the big time with a flourish. The 1-0 margin could have been five or six, such was the Ayrshire side's superiority. But the two points on offer were eagerly accepted by the home support.

Opening day joy was soon dissipated by a disturbing turn of events both off and on the pitch. Goal hero Tom Brown sustained a back injury and it was discovered that a four-game ban he picked up in his junior days would still have to be served. Ambitious bids for Celtic pair Charlie Nicholas and Peter Grant were knocked back and the new stadium proposals were rejected by the Regional Council who accepted an offer from a supermarket company worth three times the £2M Killie had bid for the Scott-Ellis playing fields. On the field came a hat-trick of reversals. Morton knocked Killie out of the League Cup at Rugby Park, then came defeats away to Aberdeen and home to Motherwell in the League. The Pittodrie loss was particularly hard to bear as Killie had outclassed the Dons and had been denied what looked a surefire penalty.

So, as Kilmarnock visited Ibrox at the end of August, voices were already raised questioning the ability of the Rugby Parkers to survive. The thought of Killie defenders Montgomerie and Millen trying to tame the gigantic pairing of the awesome Mark Hateley and £4M man Duncan Ferguson provoked condescending mirth from the Rangers legions. But tame them they did. In the first half, Killie gave as good as they got. In the second period they did even better. With 62 minutes gone, McSkimming sent over a cross which eluded the 'Gers defence and teenager Mark Roberts headed past Maxwell to put Killie in front. Every ticket allocated to Kilmarnock for this match had been snapped up and the 3,600 Killie fans right behind the goal went wild with delight. Killie continued to press but Rangers equalised through Pressley in 72 minutes. But the young defender changed from hero to villain in injury time. With the clock showing 94 minutes, Pressley was caught in possession by Porteous who fired in a shot which Maxwell, in the Rangers goal, blocked. But running in was Bobby Williamson who tapped the ball past the stricken 'keeper to pull off an amazing triumph. It was Rangers first home defeat since March 1992, Killie's first away Premier win since May 1981 and their first victory at Ibrox since November 1960! 3,600 pairs of lungs yelled in unison *"Killie are back"*. Not a single Rangers player or supporter dared to contradict them.

Reports of the epic triumph spread across Britain and beyond. It was a national news item in the UK and made the headlines of the sporting press in France, Italy, Holland and Germany. The side that couldn't be beaten by European Champions Marseilles had been humbled by the pride of Ayrshire.

It was also the launch-pad for a nine-game unbeaten run. Draws with Hibs and St.Johnstone at home were followed by a victory at Tynecastle, courtesy of an incredible 30-yard drive from Mark Skilling. Then came an emphatic 3-1 home win over Partick Thistle. Killie couldn't quite repeat their Ibrox heroics against the other half of the 'Old Firm' but they took a useful point away from Parkhead in what proved to be Liam Brady's last home game in charge of that troubled club. Now the fear was that Celtic would come looking for Tommy Burns and Billy Stark to take over the ailing Glasgow giant. Relief was etched on the face of every Killie fan as it became clear that Lou Macari was the man the Celtic Board were after.

Further draws with Dundee United, Raith (after trailing 2-0 with less than 20 minutes to play), and Aberdeen kept Killie riding high in the table. Before the Aberdeen game the placings were:-

	P	W	D	L	F	A	Pts
1. Hibernian	11	6	3	2	17	9	15
2. Aberdeen	11	4	5	2	13	8	13
3. Kilmarnock	11	4	5	2	11	8	13
4. Motherwell	11	5	3	3	13	11	13
5. Rangers	11	4	4	3	14	13	12

The players and staff were recognised too. During the season, Mark Skilling made the Scottish under-21 team, Both Andy Millen and Shaun McSkimming were selected for the Scotland 'B' squad, and Bobby Geddes sat on the bench as substitute 'keeper during Scotland's World Cup match in Malta.

Inspirational player/manager
Tommy Burns in action

Tommy Burns and Jim Stewart also became part of Craig Brown's new Scotland set-up. But form took a slight dip. The unbeaten run came to an end at bottom club Dundee. During the 2-2 draw at Motherwell came another wonderful goal as Ian Porteous lobbed the ball over 'Well's Krivokapic and lobbed again, this time over 'keeper Dykstra for a superb finish. The home game with Rangers was a sell-out and the 19,162 who watched Killie lose 2-0 was a new record for Rugby Park in the Premier Division.

A last-minute midweek loss against Hibs took Killie to within two points of the relegation zone but the faith placed in the management duo was shown at the AGM where Burns and Stark signed contracts to keep them at Rugby Park until 1996. The loss for the year was £221,234 but this was entirely due to transfer fees and promotion bonuses. And the club's overdraft had risen by only £13,000. Turnover had increased by a massive 581% since the present Board took office. It was also announced that although the Scott-Ellis proposals would continue to be pursued to the end, contingency plans were being laid to turn Rugby Park into an all-seater ground.

A last-minute equaliser against Celtic at home set Killie up for another successful run. They didn't lose a single goal during their next five matches as they beat St. Johnstone and Partick Thistle away, drew at home to Hearts, away to Dundee United and beat Raith Rovers at home. Yet there was still a lack of firepower in attack. What would happen if the side's defensive consistency should break down? Efforts were made to secure a striker. Both Tommy Coyne (who trained at Rugby Park for a spell) and Owen Coyle were mentioned as targets. But both moves failed. Coyne, because Motherwell met the terms he was seeking, and Coyle as he embarked on a glory run in the F.A. Cup with giant-killing Bolton.

Killie entered the second half of the season in 6th place, just three points behind the leading trio of Rangers, Aberdeen and Motherwell, but a 3-1 defeat at Aberdeen brought an unhappy end to 1993 as Bobby Williamson was red-carded and Mark Skilling, scorer of the Killie goal, played his last match of the season. The midfield star underwent a double hernia operation and was expected to be out for two months, but two became three, four and then five. Eight different players would wear his number five shirt before the end of the campaign and the talented youngster's loss was sorely felt.

It didn't seem that way at first as 1994 was welcomed with three points from two home games. A 0-0 draw with Motherwell quickly being followed up by a 1-0 win over Dundee. With 27 points from 25 games, Europe seemed a likelier possibility than relegation. Then came a horrendous 10-game spell without a win. Two weeks running Killie conceded three second half goals in rapid collapses. In seven minutes at Ibrox and in four minutes at home to Hibs. Draws away to Hearts and home to St. Johnstone kept them in mid-table, then came a home defeat by Partick Thistle after Killie had led at the break and an 89th minute losing goal at Celtic Park. Killie still battled on. They came from behind to rescue a point against Dundee United, fought back for the second time this season from two goals down at Raith, but lost to a late strike from the Starks Park side. There was an unlucky defeat at home to Aberdeen in a game riddled with appalling refereeing decisions as Aberdeen were awarded a clearly offside goal, two stonewall penalties were denied to Killie, and a last minute equaliser prevented after the referee awarded Aberdeen a free kick for two Dons players falling over one another! But there were no such excuses for failure the following week as Killie put in their worst display of the season in losing 3-0 away to relegation certainties Dundee.

At last though, Killie had been successful on the transfer front. An audacious bid for Gerry Creaney was rejected when Celtic demanded over £600,000 for the player, but Craig Napier joined Stark, McCluskey and Millen as the latest recruit from Hamilton. And Alan McInally, son of 1960's hero Jackie, was signed from Bayern Munich until the end of the season. Doubts persisted though as to how well the big striker had recovered from a succession of bad injuries.

Despite the increasingly desperate League situation, Killie were a team transformed in the Scottish Cup. Ayr United were despatched a lot easier than the 2-1 scoreline suggests in front of nearly 13,000 at Rugby Park. Then came a sweet triumph at Cappielow as Killie avenged their earlier League Cup defeat, and a 1-0 win at home over Dundee sent Kilmarnock into the last four of the Scottish Cup for the first time in 22 years. Their semi-final opponents were Rangers, but two crucial League games had to be played before Killie strode the stage of the revamped Hampden Park.

On a night when defeat would have plunged them into the bottom three, Gus McPherson's 35 yard stinger beat St. Johnstone's 'keeper Rhodes for the only goal of the match. But Killie's joy was short-lived as Hearts won 1-0 at Rugby Park three days later and another transfer target - Aberdeen's Andy Roddie - declined the chance to join Kilmarnock. It was confirmed at last that Killie would stay at Rugby Park. At the end of the season work would start on constructing an 18,200 all-seater ground. News of backing from the Football Trust had been relayed to Bob Fleeting by the Trust's Scottish Vice-Chairman, Tom Wharton, just in time. The Board were able to place an order for the steel required, half an hour before the deadline for ordering expired. More than 30 years after he had denied them that last-minute League Cup Final equaliser, 'Tiny' Wharton had at last given a decision Kilmarnock's way.

Then, with Killie having a free day as they prepared to face Rangers on the Sunday, their rivals took full advantage. As Kilmarnock took the field for their Cup semi-final they knew that for the first time they had dropped into the bottom three:-

	P	W	D	L	F	A	Pts	GD
7. Hearts	38	9	17	12	33	40	35	-7
8. Partick Th.	37	10	14	13	41	50	34	-9
9. St.Johnstone	38	8	17	13	32	45	33	-13
10. Kilmarnock	37	9	14	14	30	42	32	-12
11. Raith Rovers	37	5	15	17	37	66	25	-29
12. Dundee	38	6	11	21	35	53	23	-18

Those stout advocates of three going down - Raith and Dundee - had no chance of survival. Killie had a game in hand, but that was away to fellow-strugglers Partick.

The last month of the season was going to be one of the most exciting - and nervous - that Scottish football had ever known.

But all that was far from the players minds as they faced - and bested - Rangers. Hateley was marked out of the game by Paterson and even with Durie, McCoist and Duncan Ferguson joining in the action, Killie remained the better side. Had Tom Brown's 64th minute cut-back found Ally Mitchell's right foot rather than his left then the game would have been won there and then. As it was, Kilmarnock - the team whose new ground was valued at less than the two Rangers substitutes - returned to Hampden the following Wednesday. And again they made Rangers look second best. Tom Black's 17th minute opener took Killie to a dressing room lead. At the start of the second half, it was almost 2-0 as Ally Mitchell's shot forced Maxwell into a scrambling save over the bar. But, a minute later, came the latest in the century-old line of controversial Rangers goals. Durrant crossed, Hateley headed, the ball bounced down off the bar and the referee awarded a goal. The official, Mr Mottram, was the only Scots referee to officiate in the 1994 World Cup; an inspired choice given that a World Cup was once won by such a 'goal' as this one. Some commentators even averred that Hateley was offside. The Killie players protested furiously that the ball had never crossed the line, but to no avail. Four minutes later, Hateley added a (legitimate) second goal and despite Killie's best efforts they were out - beaten by a team they had outclassed over 180 minutes.

Killie had to pick themselves up quickly - and they did. they beat Celtic 2-0 to record their first home League win in over three months but then folded again immediately. Another late goal saw them lose away to Partick and this was followed by a poor 0-0 draw against Raith, a result which left the table looking like this:-

	P	W	D	L	F	A	Pts	GD
7. Hearts	40	9	18	13	33	42	36	-9
8. Partick Thistle	40	11	14	15	42	53	36	-11
9. St. Johnstone	40	9	18	13	33	45	36	-12
10. Kilmarnock	40	10	15	14	32	43	35	-11
11. Raith Rovers	39	5	16	18	37	70	26	-33
12. Dundee	40	7	11	22	37	55	25	-18

Kilmarnock had gained the 35 points that looked a likely safety target at the start of the season, yet they found themselves in the relegation zone with four games left to play. Their only consolation was that some of their rivals still had to play each other, meaning that Killie's fate was still very much in their own hands. But their remaining games offered little hope. They had three games away from home against teams lying 2nd, 5th and 6th in the League, while their only home match was against the Champions, Rangers. When they took the field against Dundee United on April 26th, it was the weary Ayrshire outfit's 6th match in the last 16 days. Many suspected that, for Kilmarnock, it was almost all over. But the apostles of doom had forgotten that it was precisely when they were written off that this Kilmarnock team was at its most dangerous. After 12 minutes, United's McKinlay lost possession to Ally Mitchell who worked a one-two with Gus McPherson before floating the ball to the back post where Bobby Williamson joyfully slammed home his first League goal since November. In the 54th minute, McPherson's cross was met with exquisite timing by McSkimming and Killie were two up.

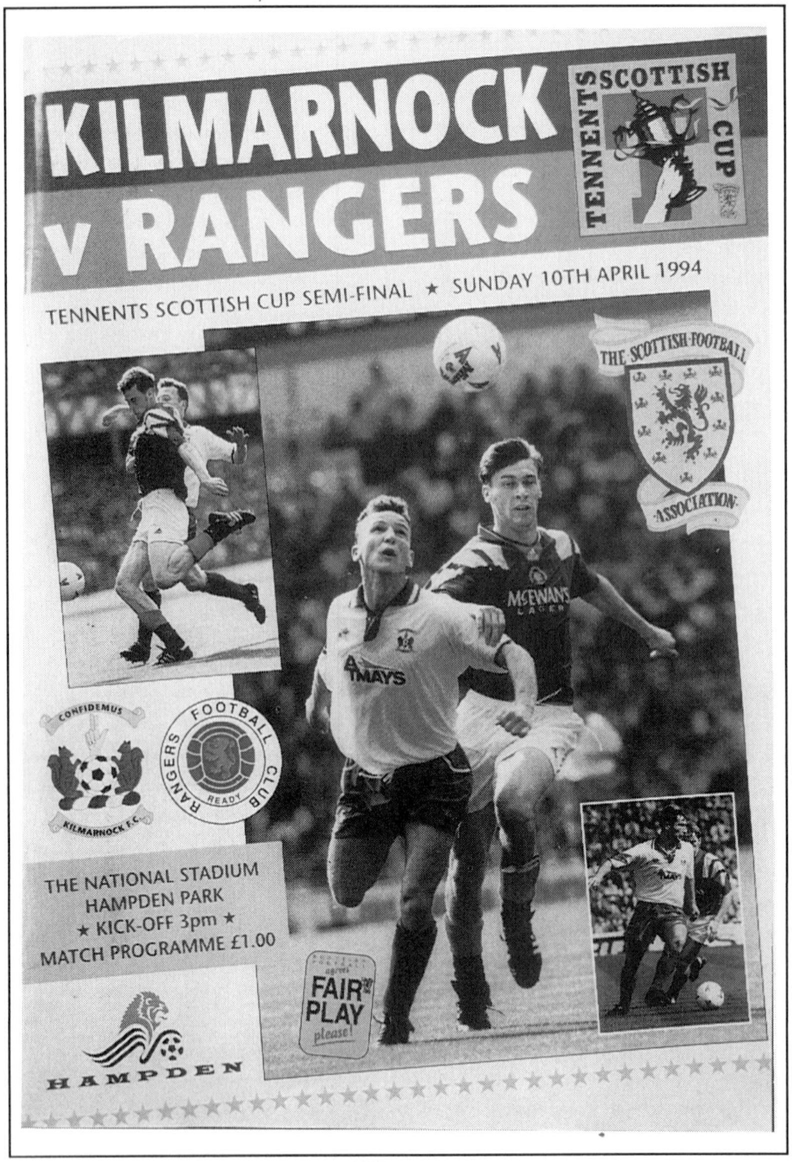

Relegation worries were cast aside with the excitement of a Scottish Cup semi-final appearance against Rangers - and Killie nearly produced another shock result.

Even when United pulled one back, Killie remained in command and Williamson completed a night of glory by scoring again two minutes from the end. Hailing a *"famous win"* which lifted Killie out of the bottom three, the *'Scotsman'* said *"No side in Scotland have played with greater energy or worked harder this season"*.

Four days later, it all seemed to have been in vain as one-time Killie target Tommy Coyne netted the only goal of the game at Motherwell with just eight minutes to play. With their rivals all picking up points, the situation looked desperate for Kilmarnock. But an upbeat comment came from Tommy Burns who said *"It could all change again next Saturday"*.

	P	W	D	L	F	A	Pts	GD
7. Partick Th.	42	12	15	15	45	55	39	-10
8. Hearts	42	9	20	13	34	43	38	-9
9. St.Johnstone	42	9	20	13	34	46	38	-12
10. Kilmarnock	42	11	15	16	35	45	37	-10
11. Raith Rovers	42	5	18	19	40	75	28	-35
12. Dundee	42	7	12	23	38	57	26	-19

There were over 18,000 inside Rugby Park for the visit of Rangers the following week. It was meant to be a gala occasion - the last time anyone would stand on the terraces. The bulldozers were due to move in the next day in the first phase of the rebuilding of the ground. But the high stakes of survival were vividly summed up by one reporter when he described the atmosphere as being one of *"festive dread"*.

Killie overcame their nerves to have the best of the first half but only a Burns header, well held by 'keeper Scott, troubled Rangers. With 74 minutes gone, Stark sent a lovely through ball to Millen, who broke away, and with only the 'keeper to beat sent the ball agonizingly wide. Still Killie refused to give up. Five minutes later they were awarded a free kick, 25 yards out. Tom Black struck a firm, low shot through a ruck of players which squeezed inside the goal. It was sweet revenge after the agony of the Cup defeat. The jubilant Killie fans anxiously awaited news of events elsewhere. A Partick draw and Hearts win meant that those sides were virtually safe but St. Johnstone had lost at home to Aberdeen. Killie moved a point ahead of the men from Perth. For the fifth time in the last seven seasons, Kilmarnock's fate would be decided in their very last match.

MATCH OF THE SEASON

May 14th 1994.
Hibernian 0 Kilmarnock 0

*Shannen Caldwell couldn't understand the nervous look on her father's face. At just six months old, she was far too young to realise how important this day was. She closed her eyes and went to sleep. A few miles from where Shannen's father stood nervously around the radio, there was a sedate game of bowls in progress. But 79 years old James Johnston found it difficult to concentrate on events on the rink as he tuned in his transistor. A season ticket holder at Rugby Park for the past **60 years**, he had first watched Killie in the cup-winning season of 1919-20. He new **exactly** how important an occasion it was.*

As did the players, management, staff and the supporters. Some 6,000 of them travelled to Edinburgh to see the game against Hibs. All the complications and permutations bandied around since August had boiled down to this: if Killie won they were safe, a draw would do unless St. Johnstone won by four goals away to Motherwell. Within five minutes it seemed Killie had gone ahead. On the left, Mitchell found McSkimming who crossed to McCluskey. He touched the ball on to Tom Brown who bundled it over the line. Killie's celebrations were muted by the sight of a linesman's flag indicating offside.

Killie continued to dominate - Black, Brown, McPherson and McCluskey all had first-half chances but no goals came. A wild shot from a well-placed Wright was Hibs only contribution. The second half was controlled by Kilmarnock as much as the first but worrying news arrived fifteen minutes from the end. St. Johnstone had taken the lead at Motherwell. One slip, one mistake and Killie would go down. From the bench Billy Stark relayed the news to Andy Millen, reckoning that the level-headed defender would know who to tell - and who not to! A cross from McSkimming found Brown and his header nearly made all the worrying superfluous but 'keeper Jim Leighton clasped the ball safely to his body right on the line. Killie still surged forward, seeking the goal which would end all doubt. As 6,000 pairs of eyes glanced back and forth from watch to pitch, Kilmarnock won a free kick just outside the penalty area. As the players lined up the final whistle blew and the ecstatic Ayrshire fans sang and danced on the Easter Road terraces.

The players celebrated too. Burns and Stark collapsed, crying, into each other's arms. The players applauded the supporters. Those unable to play in this match emerged to join their colleagues. Scarves were thrown to the players and shirts thrown back to the fans. Tommy Burns kissed the badge on his jersey and bowed in homage to the supporters. And in scenes echoing the previous year, celebrations started back in Ayrshire that the returning fans would join and continue until well into the night. The team that few thought had much chance of survival in August had triumphed. And their famous victories at Ibrox, Tynecastle and Tannadice had ensured that once more the name of Kilmarnock would echo throughout the land. More than 200,000 supporters had passed through the Rugby Park turnstiles and the average attendance of over 9,000 was the highest since 1965. As their supporters had proclaimed from the outset, Killie were back. To stay. The final table looked like this:-

	P	*W*	*D*	*L*	*F*	*A*	*Pts*
1. Rangers	*44*	*22*	*14*	*8*	*74*	*41*	*58*
2. Aberdeen	*44*	*17*	*21*	*6*	*58*	*36*	*55*
3. Motherwell	*44*	*20*	*14*	*10*	*58*	*43*	*54*
4. Celtic	*44*	*15*	*20*	*9*	*51*	*38*	*50*
5. Hibernian	*44*	*16*	*15*	*13*	*53*	*48*	*47*
6. Dundee Utd.	*44*	*11*	*20*	*13*	*47*	*48*	*42*
7. Hearts	*44*	*11*	*20*	*13*	*37*	*43*	*42*
8. Kilmarnock	*44*	*12*	*16*	*16*	*36*	*45*	*40*
9. Partick Thistle	*44*	*12*	*16*	*16*	*46*	*57*	*40*
10. St. Johnstone	*44*	*10*	*20*	*14*	*35*	*47*	*40*
11. Raith Rovers	*44*	*6*	*19*	*19*	*46*	*80*	*31*
12. Dundee	*44*	*8*	*13*	*23*	*42*	*57*	*29*

400 miles away, in London, Alex Ferguson was enjoying watching his Manchester United side complete the League and Cup 'Double'. A packed room of pressmen could scarcely believe their ears as he refused to answer questions until they could meet a request of his own. *"Tell me"*, inquired British football's most successful manager, *"How did Kilmarnock get on?"*.

One man who could have enlightened Alex was James Johnston. He switched off his transistor radio, thought happily ahead to his 76th season as a Kilmarnock supporter, and turned contentedly to watch the bowls. A couple of miles away, young Shannen's father switched his radio off and raised a celebratory glass to his lips. As he did so, his daughter opened her eyes .... and smiled.

The end of the road for Rugby Park - as was.
But at least the 1994/95 season at the 'new' Ground will continue
to host Premier Division football.

MEMORABLE PLAYERS

This book was always intended to be a history of Kilmarnock Football Club rather than individual players, and anyone interested in the detailed histories of the men who played for Killie should obtain a copy of the excellent *'WHO'S WHO OF KILMARNOCK FC'* by Bill Donnachie (Mainstream Publishing 1989). Nevertheless, it would be remiss of me not to mention a few of the more prominent figures of the past 125 years.

GOALKEEPERS

"Killie for keepers" is a phrase with a long history and in the 1960's and 70's no fewer then **four** Kilmarnock custodians were selected to play for Scotland. The distinguished quartet were: **Campbell Forsyth, Bobby Ferguson, Ally Hunter and Jim Stewart**. **Sandy McLaughlan** played for the Scottish League. Yet the two longest-serving 'keepers' come from just before and just after the illustrious period. **Jimmy Brown** who played for an SFA representative team while with Hearts, and **Alan McCulloch**, another who played for the Scottish League as well as the Under 21 team, notched up almost 850 first-team appearances between them. With McCulloch's successor, **Bobby Geddes**, an Under 21 internationalist while at Dundee, being called up into the full Scotland squad in 1993-94, it means that every recognised first choice Killie 'keeper' over the past **forty** years has also worn a Scotland jersey as well. A record unmatched by any other club.

DEFENDERS

James Orr was the first Killie full-back to play for Scotland. He was succeeded in that role by the famous pairing of **William Agnew** and **Jamie Mitchell** in the first decade of this century. Mitchell spent over 20 years at Rugby Park and although he lost almost two seasons through injury, his 410 League appearances was overtaken by only Mattha' Smith and Frank Beattie up until the mid-1980's. **Joe Nibloe** played a record 132 consecutive League matches for Killie as well as becoming the club's most-capped player with 11 appearances for Scotland. **Billy Dickson** used to have the fans singing *"Dickson is better than Gemmell"* in the early 70's as he won five Scottish caps. His defensive partner, **Andy King**, was unlucky not to win a cap. Overtaking Mitchell in the appearance stakes as defenders came **Alan Robertson** and **Stuart McLean** with 35 years experience between them in both good times and bad. These two models of consistency are, deservedly, Kilmarnock's record holders for League appearances. **Matt Watson**, another long-server, was 'Player of the Year' during the Championship season and **Ralph Collins** was the anchor of the side throughout the 1950's, while **Freddie Milloy**, a great full-back, saw his career interrupted by the War.

MIDFIELD AND CENTRAL DEFENCE

The modern, if clumsy, way to describe the old-fashioned half-back line. The centre-half was the spine of any good team and Killie have had their share. **Geordie Anderson** was the first Rugby Park pivot to don Scotland's colours and he was later joined by **Tom Smith, Willie Toner** and the man who displaced Toner in the first team, **Jackie McGrory**. Jackie rarely missed a match, playing alongside **Frank Beattie** for many seasons. Beattie, who returned from a long lay-off due to a broken leg, was nearly 38 when he played his last game for Killie, having been a fixture at Rugby Park for almost two decades.

Unfortunate not to be capped, Frank was in the fine tradition of Killie wing-halves. The **McPherson** brothers, **John** and **Davie**, both played for Scotland in Killie's pre-League days. As did that tigerish left-half, **Jocky Johnstone**. Between the wars, **Hugh Morton** and **George Robertson** also wore the national colours. In addition Morton shares with **Jock McEwan**, the record number of Scottish Cup appearances by Killie players. Morton and McEwan were the linch-pins of the famous Cup-fighting team, worthy successors to **Mattha' Shortt**, hero of the first cup triumph in 1920. **Bob Thyne**, a wartime cap, was the rock of the immediate post-war period. In more recent times, **Paul Clarke** and **Derek McDicken** brought both skill and tenacity to their task. And in the last few seasons, Kilmarnock supporters have been privileged to watch one of the modern greats, **Tommy Burns**, enjoy a long Indian Summer at Rugby Park. But it would be wrong to depart this section without mentioning **George Maxwell**. Not just a faithful servant, but a penalty-taker second to none. His lethal precision from the spot helps George into the list of top scorers, the only non-forward to appear there.

WINGERS

Considered a luxury in the modern era but the sight of a winger in full flight is still the sweetest move to watch in football; its rarity actually increasing its pleasure. Just under one hundred years ago, Kilmarnock had two truly great left-wingers, **Bob Findlay** and **Bob Templeton**. Both played for Scotland and both thrilled the Killie support at a time when, sadly, recording facilities were of a primitive nature. Fading pages of musty newsprint are all the memories that are left of these two heroes. After them came **Malcolm McPhail**, whose solitary cap came in a 'victory' international, unrecognised by the world at large. In turn, he was succeeded by **David Lyner**, a Belfast man, who became the only Kilmarnock player to achieve international recognition for a country other than Scotland, playing twice for Northern Ireland while at Rugby Park.

On the right wing in the 30's came **Willie Connell**, whose goal tally would have been the envy of many a front man. But not **Brian McIlroy**, that free-scoring left-winger of the 60's. His plundering of the opposition goalmouth making him third top scorer of all time at Rugby Park. But even those who admired McIlroy would concede that, on the other side of the pitch, was the greatest winger to ever wear the blue-and-white; **Tommy McLean**. From the night he tore Eintracht apart until the day he left for Ibrox, this wee magician was lionized by the supporters. A match for both Johnstone and Henderson, he forced both legendary 'Old Firm' stars aside as he took his place in the Scotland team.

THE STRIKERS

Two centre-forwards have worn the blue of Scotland. The legendary figures of **Sandy Higgins** and **James 'Bummer' Campbell**. Although he never played in the Scottish League, Higgins scored at least 86 goals for Killie and, in all probability, his true total was very much higher, as accurate records of those days are difficult to obtain. 'Bummer' Campbell scored at least 186 times for Killie in all matches - a total none can match - but like Higgins, his exact number will never be known.

Highest scorer in recognised first team games is **Willie Culley**. But even taking friendlies and charity games into account, Culley can 'only' claim another 20 goals, less than what can safely be accredited to the 'Bummer'. But Culley scored frequently at a time when **three** defenders had to be between attacker and goal in order to be onside. At the same time, **Mattha' Smith**, double-cup winner and a supreme inside-forward rather than an out-and-out goal-getter, scored over 100 in the League and, despite missing a season after suffering a leg-break, set an appearance record which would stand for 40 years.

There was **'Peerie' Cunningham** and his 34 League goals in a single season. **'Bud' Maxwell** was next, averaging nearly a goal a game. **Alan Collins** may have become Killie's greatest goalscorer had the war not intervened. **Andy Kerr** burst onto the scene with 90 goals in just 101 League matches, including a handful at centre-half! **Ronnie Hamilton**, scorer as a 16 year old on his debut, was leading marksman in the side that won the Championship. But that team also contained three of the club's all-time top five scorers; **Bertie Black** and **Jackie McInally** joining McIlroy in earning that distinction. The top post-war goalscorer didn't join up until after 1965. **Eddie Morrison**'s feats placing him second only to Culley in the all-time list.

There are so many more who could be mentioned; **Eric Murray**, that stylish performer of the 1960's, the tragic **Benny Thomson**, wonder winger of the 30's and the only Kilmarnock player to die during the Second World War when his Merchant Navy ship was sunk. The list could go on but a line has to be drawn somewhere. If the spirit of the past five years can be maintained then who knows? Maybe in 2019 when Killie celebrate their 150th anniversary, someone, somewhere will write the latest chapter in their history with the names of today's top players like **McSkimming, Reilly, Roberts, Skilling** and **Mitchell** entering the Hall of Fame alongside others as yet unheard of, or possibly even unborn.

STATISTICS SECTION

MOST OVERALL APPEARANCES

Dates given are period player was registered as a Kilmarnock player eg. 1964-74 = from 1964-65 - 1973-74. Substitutions are **included** in the totals but also marked in brackets. In addition to the Scottish League, Scottish Cup and Scottish League Cup, Other (1st Class) includes the following:- War Funds Cup, both Victory Cups, 'B' Division Supplementary Cup, the War Cup of 1940, Western League 1939-40, the five Scottish League matches played in 1939-40, the 1945-46 Scottish League season, Summer Cup, Spring Cup, B&Q Cup, Texaco/Anglo Scottish Cup, USA tournaments, Inter-Cities Fairs Cup and the European Cup. In addition to the player listed here, there have been another two players called Hugh Morton. Both played in the early 1900's and should not be confused with the player on this page.

SCOTTISH LEAGUE

1	Alan Robertson	481 (3)
2	Stuart McLean	478 (34)
3	Alan McCulloch	440
4	Frank Beattie	422 (1)
5	Mattha' Smith	415
6	Jamie Mitchell	410
7	Paul Clarke	362 (5)
8	Jock McEwan	353
9	Derrick McDicken	345 (24)
10	Hugh Morton	340
11	Jackie McGrory	336
12	Matt Watson	323 (2)
13	George Maxwell	309 (24)
14	Willie Culley	301
15	Eddie Morrison	268 (7)
16	Freddie Milloy	266
17	Mattha' Shortt (1910-16, 1918-22)	262
18	Joe Nibloe (1924-33)	248
19	Ralph Collins	246
20	Malcolm McPhail (1915-24)	245

SCOTTISH CUP

=1	Jock McEwan	42
=1	Hugh Morton	42
3	Frank Beattie	40
=4	George Anderson (1897-1905, 1906-09)	35
=4	Jackie McGrory	35
=4	Matt Watson	35
7	James Campbell (1888-1901)	33
8	Joe Nibloe	31
=9	Jocky Johnston (1889-1902)	30
=9	Stuart McLean	30
=11	Bertie Black	29
=11	Jimmy Brown	29
=11	Alan McCulloch	29

SCOTTISH LEAGUE CUP

1	Frank Beattie	80
2	Alan Robertson	76 (1)
3	Matt Watson	74
4	Derrick McDicken	67
=5	Bertie Black	59
=5	Jackie McGrory	59
7	Ralph Collins	58
8	Jimmy Brown	55
9	George Maxwell	54 (4)
=10	Andy King	51
=10	Brian McIlroy	51 (1)
=10	Bob Thyne (1946-55)	51

OVERALL APPEARANCES

ALL FIRST CLASS MATCHES, 300 APPEARANCES OR MORE

	Player	Service	League	Scottish Cup	League Cup	Other (1st Class)	Total
1	Alan Robertson	1972-89	481 (3)	28	76 (1)	22	607 (4)
2	Frank Beattie	1953-72	422 (1)	40	80	59 (1)	602 (2)
3	Stuart McLean	1973-91	478 (34)	30	50 (3)	14 (1)	572 (38)
4	Alan McCulloch	1972-91	440	29	47	7	523
5	Jackie McGrory	1960-73	336	35	59	46	476
6	Matt Watson	1954-68	323 (2)	35	74	42	474 (2)
7	Derrick McDicken	1972-85	345 (24)	25 (2)	67	17 (2)	454 (28)
8	Paul Clarke	1974-86	362 (5)	25 (1)	49 (1)	16 (1)	452 (8)
9	Mattha' Smith	1916-31	415	24	-	1	440
10	Jamie Mitchell	1900-04, 06-21	410	23	-	2	435
11	George Maxwell	1968-82	309 (24)	21	54 (4)	20 (1)	404 (29)
12	Jock McEwan	1923-35	353	42	-	-	395
13	Hugh Morton	1922-32, 33-37	340	42	-	-	382
14	Eddie Morrison	1966-76	268 (7)	21 (1)	45 (2)	18	352 (10)
=15	Bertie Black	1952-67	234	29	59	25	347
=15	Andy King	1960-72	224 (3)	24	51	48	347 (3)
17	Brian McIlroy	1960-70	218 (2)	24	51 (1)	39	332 (3)
18	Ralph Collins	1949-59	246	21	58	5	330
19	Jackie McInally	1959-68	212 (1)	24	48	44	328 (1)
20	Freddie Milloy	1932-40, 45-48	266	22	4	30	322
21	Jimmy Brown	1953-61	231	29	55	6	321
22	Willie Culley	1911-23	301	13	-	3	317
23	Tommy McLean	1962-71	216	22	34	41 (1)	313 (1)

Of those who took part in the 1993-94 campaign, the player with most appearances was:

	Player	Service	League	Scottish Cup	League Cup	Other (1st Class)	Total
	Ray Montgomerie	1988-94	217 (9)	15	9 (1)	7	248 (10)

TOP GOALSCORERS

SCOTTISH LEAGUE

1	Willie Culley	149
2	Eddie Morrison	121
3	Mattha' Smith	109
4	Brian McIlroy	105
5	'Bud' Maxwell	103
6	'Peerie' Cunningham	102
7	Andy Kerr	90
8	Jackie McInally	86
9	Bertie Black	85
10	Gerry Mays	79
11	Andy Cunningham	75
12	Alan Collins	60
13	Malcolm McPhail	55
14	Jimmy Robertson	54
15	George Maxwell	53
16	Ian Fleming	51
17	Willie Connell	49
=18	Tommy McLean	48
=18	Jimmy Williamson	48
=18	'Bumper' Campbell	48

SCOTTISH CUP

1	* 'Bummer' Campbell	20
2	'Bud Maxwell	19
3	Jackie McInally	15
4	Davie Maitland (1897-1902)	14
5	Willie Connell	13
6	Benny Thomson	12
=7	John Aitken (1928-34)	10
=7	Bertie Black	10
=7	Jimmy Ramsay	10
=10	* Sandy Higgins (1882-88, 1894-95)	9
=10	Gerry Mays	9
=10	Eddie Morrison	9
=10	Vernon Wentzel	9

* Campbell and Higgins' figures represent the minimum number of goals each scored. Regrettably it has not proved possible to identify all 19th century goalscorers.

SCOTTISH LEAGUE CUP

1	Gerry Mays	23
2	Brian McIlroy	22
3	Bertie Black	21
4	Jackie McInally	20
=5	Andy Kerr	19
=5	Eddie Morrison	19
7	Willie Harvey	15
8	Ian Fleming	14
9	Tommy McLean	12
10	Joe McBride (1956-60)	10

OVERALL GOALSCORING

ALL FIRST CLASS MATCHES, 50 GOALS OR MORE

Player		Service	League	Scottish Cup	League Cup	Other (1st class)	Total
1	Willie Culley	1911-23	149	8	-	2	159
2	Eddie Morrison	1966-76	121	9	19	5	154
3	Brian McIlroy	1960-70	105	8	22	17	152
4	Jackie McInally	1959-68	86	15	20	16	137
5	Bertie Black	1952-67	85	10	21	13	129
6	'Bud' Maxwell	1929-34, 39-40	103	19	-	2	124
7	Andy Kerr	1959-63	90	4	19	6	119
8	Mattha' Smith	1916-31	109	6	-	-	115
9	Gerry Mays	1952-59	79	9	23	-	111
10	'Peerie' Cunningham	1925-31	102	8	-	-	110
11	Alan Collins	1936-40, 45-48	60	4	5	22	91
12	Andy Cunningham	1909-15	75	6	-	-	81
13	Tommy McLean	1962-71	48	5	12	8	73
14	'Bummer' Campbell	1888-1901	48	20	-	-	68
15	George Maxwell	1968-82	53	4	8	2	67
=16	Ian Fleming	1970-76	51	-	14	-	65
=16	Willie Harvey	1951-58	42	7	15	1	65
18	Willie Connell	1927-34	49	13	-	-	62
=19	John Bourke	1978-83, 87-89	44	6	7	2	59
=19	Ross Mathie	1969-73	41	6	7	5	59
=19	Malcolm McPhail	1915-24	55	2	-	2	59
22	Jimmy Robertson	1934-38	54	4	-	-	58
23	Ronnie Hamilton	1961-66	38	1	4	13	56
24	Jimmy Ramsay	1920-24, 26-33	44	10	-	-	54
25	Benny Thomson	1934-40	39	12	-	2	53
26	Davie Curlett	1949-58	40	3	9	-	52
27	Jimmy Williamson	1927-37	48	3	-	-	51

Of those who took part in the 1993/94 campaign, the top goalscorer was:

	Bobby Williamson	1991-94	36	4	1	-	41

BASIC SEASONAL STATISTICS

Season	Av Home Lg Att	League Scorer	Most League Appearances
1895-96	2,200	Fisher 9	*McPherson, *Johnstone 19
1896-97	1,333	Campbell 12	*McLean 18
1897-88	2,000	Campbell 11	*Busby 18
1898-99	2,643	Campbell, Reid 12	*Findlay 18
1899-00	4,688	Howie 6	*Craig, *Anderson 18
1900-01	4,200	A.Reid 7	*Craig, *Muir, *A.Reid 20
1901-02	4,611	Graham, Morton 5	*Craig,*Busby,*Agnew,*McPherson,*Anderson,*Mitchell all 18
1902-03	3,727	R.Findlay 5	*Anderson 22
1903-04	3,440	Blair 5	*Gunzeon 26
1904-05	4,545	Blair 8	*Aitken, *Blair 26
1905-06	3,692	J.Young 12	Aitken 30/31 (possible)
1906-07	3,911	Maxwell, Agnew, Skillen 5	Mitchell 27/34
1907-08	5,894	Templeton 7	Mitchell, Howie 33/34
1908-09	5,747	Douglas 12	*D.Armour
1909-10	4,882	Cunningham 18	Mitchell 32/34
1910-11	5,575	Cunningham 14	*Kirkwood 34
1911-12	4,453	Cunningham 14	Templeton 30/34
1912-13	5,191	Cunningham 11	Blair, Cunningham 31/34
1913-14	5,263	Neil 12	Cunningham 37/38
1914-15	4,294	Neil 20	Mackie 37/38
1915-16	4,333	Culley 23	Blair, Mackie 37/38
1916-17	3,474	Culley 16	*McPhail 38
1917-18	5,000	Culley 16	Blair 33/34
1918-19	5,438	Culley 20	*McPhail 34
1919-20	5,857	Culley 14	*Gibson 42
1920-21	7,143	J.R.Smith 24	*Gibson 42
1921-22	6,952	Culley 20	Gibson, Culley 40/42
1922-23	7,763	Jackson 15	*Jackson 38
1923-24	7,316	Gray 19	*J.Morton, Gibson, *Borland 38
1924-25	6,632	M.Smith 14	*Hood 38
1925-26	7,158	Weir 26	Hood 37/38
1926-27	6,632	H.Cunningham 19	*Nibloe 38
1927-28	6,763	H.Cunningham 34	*Nibloe, *Ramsay 38
1928-29	7,516	H.Cunningham 23	Connell 37/38
1929-30	6,895	McGowan 18	McEwan, M.Smith 37/38
1930-31	6,895	Maxwell 18	*Clemie 38
1931-32	7,053	Maxwell 20	Connell 37/38
1932-33	6,316	Maxwell 32	*McEwan 38
1933-34	7,552	Maxwell 33	*Milloy 38
1934-35	6,158	J.Robertson 23	* Kelvin 38
1935-36	6,618	Beattie 19	*Leslie, *Beattie 38
1936-37	6,294	J.Robertson 12	*Thomson 38
1937-38	8,447	Collins 14	*Ross 38
1938-39	8,361	Reid 17	*Hunter, *Reid 38
1939-40#	2,962	Collins 20	*Gallacher 30

Season	Av Home Lg Att	League Scorer	Most League Appearances
1945-46	11,267	Walsh 21	Walsh 29/30
1946-47	13,755	Collins 9	Downie 28/30
1947-48	7,214	Collins 24	*Collins 30
1948-49	8,501	McLaren 21	McLaren 29/30
1949-50	9,900	Johnston 13	Thyne 29/30
1950-51	8,013	Jones 10	Benson 29/30
1951-52	10,533	Mathie 16	*Niven 30
1952-53	9,547	Mays 20	*Niven 30
1953-54	11,560	Harvey 17	*Brown, *Russell, *Henaughan 30
1954-55	15,948	Jack 8	*Brown 30
1955-56	12,600	Curlett 12	Brown 33/34
1956-57	12,593	Mays 18	Brown, Harvey 31/34
1957-58	11,636	Mays 15	*Toner 34
1958-59	10,330	Black, Wentzel 13	*Watson, *Black 34
1959-60	13,138	McInally 16	*Watson 34
1960-61	12,451	Kerr 34	*Richmond, *Kerr 34
1961-62	10,478	Kerr 23	*Richmond 34
1962-63	8,777	Kerr 25	*Watson, *McGrory, *Beattie 34
1963-64	8,891	McIlroy 24	*Forsyth, *McGrory, *McIlroy 34
1964-65	10,476	Hamilton 15	*Murray 34
1965-66	8,706	McIlroy 20	*Ferguson 34
1966-67	8,439	McIlroy 16	*McGrory 34
1967-68	5,694	Queen, Morrison 14	*McGrory, *T.McLean 34
1968-69	8,294	Morrison, McIlroy 13	*McLaughlan, *McGrory 34
1969-70	6,724	Mathie 21	*McLaughlan,*Mathie,*Morrison*,Cook+all 34
1970-71	5,933	T.McLean 10	*Dickson 34
1971-72	5,717	Mathie 15	*Hunter, *Maxwell *Cook 34
1972-73	4,489	Morrison 16	*Smith, *Morrison 34
1973-74	3,639	Fleming 33	*Rodman, *Sheed 36
1974-75	7,022	Fleming, Morrison 11	*Rodman 34
1975-76	4,239	Fallis 10	*Stewart, *Robertson, *Fallis 26
1976-77	5,849	Fallis 10	*Robertson 36
1977-78	2,834	McDowell 13	*Stewart 39
1978-79	3,033	Bourke 21	*McCulloch 39
1979-80	6,990	Street 9	*McCulloch 36
1980-81	4,507	Bourke 5	McLean+ 34/36
1981-82	2,643	Bourke 14	*McCulloch,*Armstrong,*Robertson+ 39
1982-83	3,463	Gallacher 9	*J.Clark 36
1983-84	1,360	Gallacher, R.Clark 11	*McCulloch 39
1984-85	1,351	B.Millar 12	*P.Clarke+ 39
1985-86	1,949	Bryson 14	McCulloch, P.Clarke+, Bryson+ 38/39
1986-87	1,899	Bryson 10	*McGuire+ 44
1987-88	1,846	Harkness 15	*McLean 44
1988-89	2,488	Watters 12	*McCulloch 39
1989-90	3,254	Watters 23	Tait+, Watters+ 38/39
1990-91	4,939	Williamson 14	Geddes 38/39
1991-92	4,388	Campbell, Mitchell 10	McPherson+ 43/44
1992-93	4,686	McCluskey 11	*Geddes 44
1993-94	9,161	Williamson 7	*Geddes, *Black, *Millen 44

Western League, * Ever present, + including appearances as substitute

FULL STATISTICAL SECTION

Total seasonal record:	1873-95
Scottish Cup match-by-match:	1873-95
Kilmarnock season-by-season:	1895-1994 All League, Scottish Cup, Scottish League Cup, European, American & other first class fixtures. Dates, results, half-time, attendances, scorers & line-ups.

EXPLANATION OF ABBREVIATIONS IN THIS SECTION

P = games Played, W = Won, D = Drawn, L = Lost, F = Goals scored for, A = Goals against, Pts = Points won. H-T = Half-Time, Res = Result. Att = Attendance. AET = After Extra Time, W/O = Walk-Over, Scr = Scratched, NK = Not Known, P/O = Play-Off, QF = Quarter Final, SF = Semi Final, F = Final, Pos = Position. " = replaced by substitute no. 12. * = replaced by substitute no.14. G = Goal Average, GD = Goal Difference. 'Home' matches in capitals, 'Away' matches in lower case.

Home attendances until November 1956 are based on newspaper reports, as are away figures until August 1961. From those respective dates onwards the figures are taken from the records of Kilmarnock Football Club (Home), the Scottish Football League (League, and League competitions, Away) and the press and TV (other).

Although the Scottish League has had different names for its divisions at various times, for the convenience of the reader I have referred to Division One and Division Two until the major re-organisation of 1975 and to the Premier, First and Second Divisions since that time. Where a division is known by other names (eg. 'B' division) this has been mentioned in the text wherever relevant.

Acknowledgements of assistance with this section are listed elsewhere and any errors must be attributed solely to myself.

Scottish Cup: 1873 - 1895

Season	Rd	Date	Opposition	H.	Res	Att.	Goalscorers	1	2	3	4	5	6	7	8	9	10	11	Notes
1873-74	1	18 Oct	Renton	0-0	0-2			R. Rankin	J.W. Railton	R. Lipscomb	J.B. Wilson	W. Drennan	J. Wallace	C. Cowie	D. Sturrock	G. Blair	G. Paxton		1
1874-75	1	17 Oct	VALE OF LEVEN ROV		4-0		Brown, Wallace, Sturrock, NK	"	G.H. Lipscomb	T. Ferguson	G. Paxton	W. Mitchell	D. Sturrock	J.B. Wilson	F. Reid	P. Brown	D. Brown	J. Wallace	
	2	21 Nov	Eastern (Glasgow)		0-3			"	"	"	W. Thomson	J. Paxton	"	"	"	"	"	"	
1875-76	1	9 Oct	AYR EGLINTON	3-0	8-0		A.Ferguson, NK 7 goals	"	"	"	G. Paxton	W. Thomson	D. Brown	P. Brown	J. Wallace	J.B. Wilson	D. Sturrock	A. Ferguson	
	2	6 Nov	Clydesdale	0-2	0-6			"	"	"	"	"	J. Paxton	"		"	"	"	2
1876-77	1		BYE																
	2	21 Oct	MAUCHLINE	0-1	1-2		Thomson	"	W. Thomson	G.H. Lipscomb	T. Ferguson	G. Paxton	J.B. Wilson	A. Ferguson	R. Hamilton	J. Ferguson	D. Brown	P. Brown	3
1877-78	1	29 Sep	HURLFORD		5-1		NK												
	2	20 Oct	Ayr Academical	0-0	0-1														
1878-79	1	28 Sep	KILBIRNIE		0-2														
1879-80	1	20 Sep	AYR ACADEMICAL		W/O														
	2	11 Oct	Mauchline		2-6		NK												
1880-81	1	11 Sep	STEWARTON		W/O														
	2	9 Oct	AYR F.C.	4-1	6-3		NK	Cumming	Bone	McLean	Cunningham	Wallace	Hamilton	Andrews	W. Miller	R. Miller	Barclay	Black	
	3	6 Nov	Mauchline		3-3		NK	"	"	"	Whiteside	Cuthbertson	"	Plumtree	Wallace	"	"	"	4
	3r	13	MAUCHLINE		0-3			"	"	"	"	"	"	"	"	"	"	"	
1881-82	1	10 Sep	LARGS ATHLETIC		6-0		Hay(2), NK 4 goals	"	Whiteside	Walker	Young	Burnett	Morton	Wallace	Hay	Kirkland	Robertson	"	
	2	8 Oct	AUCHINLECK BOSWELL	1-1	7-1		Burnett,Robertson,Hamilton,Morton,NK 3	"	Walker	Whiteside	"	"	"	"	"	Hamilton	"	"	
	3	22	KILBIRNIE	1-0	2-0		Wallace, Hay	"	"	"	"	"	"	"	"	"	"	"	5
	4	19 Nov	OUR BOYS DUNDEE	1-2	9-2		NK	"	"	"	"	"	"	"	"	"	"	"	
	5	10 Dec	Arthurlie	0-0	1-4	2000	Hamilton	"	"	"	"	"	"	"	"	"	"	"	
1882-83	1	16 Sep	MAUCHLINE	1-0	2-0		McSkimming, Hay	"	Cunningham	Lucas	Burnett	Black	McCartney	Wark	Hamilton	Hay	Howat	McSkimming	
	2	30	HURLFORD	1-1	2-6		Hamilton, NK	"	Lucas	Walker	Young	McCartney	Burnett	"	"	McSkimming	Hay	Black	
1883-84	1	8 Sep	KILBIRNIE		W/O														
	2	29	HURLFORD	1-0	3-0	1000	Grier, McLaughland, Wark	McCall	Lucas	Young	Grier	Burnett	Wark	Wallace	Ramsay	Higgins	G. Black	McLaughland	
	3	3 Nov	Thornliebank	0-1	1-2		Higgins	"	"	"	Burnett	Grier	A. Black	G. Black	Wark	Walker	Higgins	Wallace	6
1884-85	1	27 Sep	Hurlford		1-3		NK	Cumming	Young	Ramsay	Grier	Jas McPherson	Burnett	Cox	Wallace	"	"	Black	7
	2	4 Oct	Annbank		1-4		NK												
1885-86	1	12 Sep	ANNBANK	3-0	7-1		NK												
	2	17 Oct	HURLFORD	1-1	1-1	2000	Higgins												8
	2r	7 Nov	Hurlford	0-1	2-2	2000	Smith, NK												
	2r	14	HURLFORD	0-3	1-5		Smith												
1886-87	1	11 Sep	CUMNOCK		W/O														
	2	2 Oct	LANEMARK	6-1	10-2		NK												
	3	23	LUGAR BOSWELL	2-1	7-2		Walker(2), Higgins, NK 4 goals												
	4		BYE																
	5	4 Dec	DUNBLANE	2-0	6-0		NK												
	QF	25	QUEENS PARK	0-4	0-5	2500		Richmond	Miller	Porteous	Sawers	Dunn	Mitchell	Smith	Higgins	Walker	McGuinness	John McPherson	9
1887-88	1	3 Sep	AYR THISTLE	5-0	8-2		McPherson(2), Taylor(2), NK 4 goals	"	Porteous	West	Stewart	A. Young	Jas McPherson	Lyle	Smith	Taylor	"	"	
	2		BYE																
	3	15 Oct	Dykebar	1-2	2-2	3000	McGuinness, Smith	Richmond	Porteous	A. Young	Mason	Dunn	Mitchell	Taylor	Smith	Higgins	McGuinness	John McPherson	
	3r	22	DYKEBAR	6-0	9-1	3000	Higgins(3),Taylor(2),McGuinness(2),NK 2 goals	"	"	"	Dunn	Mitchell	W. Young	"	"	"	"	"	
	4	5 Nov	Partick Thistle	1-1	2-2	4000	McPherson(2)	"	"	"	"	"	"	"	"	"	"	"	
	4r	12	PARTICK THISTLE	0-1	1-4	5000	McGuiness	"	"	"	"	"	"	"	"	"	"	"	
1888-89	1	1 Sep	Lugar Boswell	1-0	5-0		Forbes(2), Russell, J.Campbell, Lyle	Gray	Porteous	Stevenson	Mitchell	Dunn	A. Campbell	Gardiner	Lyle	Forbes	Russell	J. Campbell	
	2	22	KILBIRNIE	1-2	1-3	5000	Brodie	"	"	"	"	Russell	"	"	"	Brodie	J. Campbell	Taylor	
1889-90	1	7 Sep	ANNBANK	0-1	2-3	4000	J.Campbell, NK	"	Stevenson	Smith	Paterson	A. Campbell	J. Campbell	Tannahill	"	"	Reid	"	
1890-91	1	6 Sep	ANNBANK	3-2	4-4		Porter(2), Kelvin, Cunningham	"	Paterson	Orr	Porter	J. Campbell	Johnstone	"	Brodie	A. Campbell	Cunningham	Kelvin	
	1r	13	Annbank	1-4	2-6		Kelvin(2)	"	Porter	"	Paterson	"	"	"	"	Reid	"	"	
1891-92	1	28 Nov	East Stirling	4-0	6-1	3000	Tannahill(2), McAvoy, Campbell, O.G., NK	Henderon	Hunter	"	"	"	"	"	D. McPherson	Brodie	McAvoy	"	
	2	19 Dec	Rangers	0-0	0-0	2000		"	"	"	"	"	"	"	"	"	"	"	
	2r	26	RANGERS	1-0	1-1	3000	Brodie	"	"	"	"	"	"	"	"	"	"	"	
	2r	23 Jan	Rangers	2-1	2-3	4000	McPherson, Kelvin	"	"	"	"	"	"	"	"	"	"	"	10
1892-93	1	26 Nov	Albion Rovers	0-1	2-1		Todd(2)	Cochrane	"	R. Brown	Broadhurst	"	"	"	Cook	Trodder	Todd	McAvoy	
	2	28 Jan	QUEENS PARK	0-1	0-8			"	Watson	"	"	"	"	"	Richardson	Cook	McAvoy	Todd	
1893-94	1	25 Nov	ST. BERNARDS	1-3	1-3	3000	Brodie	McMillan	Hunter	"	Ghee	"	"	Loudon	D. McPherson	Brodie	"	Kelvin	11
1894-95	1	24 Nov	EAST STIRLING	2-1	5-1		Higgins(3), Campbell, McLean	Cochrane	Busby	"	D. McPherson	Miller	"	Brodie	Higgins	J. Campbell	"	McLean	12
	2	15 Dec	St. Bernards	0-1	1-3	2000	Campbell	"	"	"	"	"	"	"	"	"	"	"	

NOTES:

1. Played at Crosshill (Queens Park F.C. Ground) - Kilmarnock fielded only 10 men. **2.** Kilmarnock fielded only 10 men. **3.** Mauchline's second goal (84 mins.) disputed by Killie - game ended at that time. SFA adjudicated in Mauchline's favour.
4. Originally played 23/10/80. Mauchline won 2-1, Killie successfully protested that full 90 minutes not played. **5.** Kilbirnie walked off after Killie's second goal, with 20 minutes left to play. Result stood. **6.** Originally played 20/10/83 - Also 2-1 to Thornliebank, but Kilmarnock protest successful. **7.** Originally played 20/9/84 - Killie won 6-1. Hurlford successful protest (breach of registration rules) - Kilmarnock made similar protest prior to kick-off on 27/9/84. Hurlford disqualified, Kilmarnock reinstated to competition.
8. Originally played 3/10/85. Kilmarnock 3 Hurlford 4. Killie protested successfully re. breach of registration. Kilmarnock failed to appear for scheduled replay on 24/10/85. On 31/10/85, replay at Ayr was abandoned after 80 mins., score 1-1. 7/11/85, 2-2 AET.
9. 'Kilmarnock Herald' lists no.2, Watson not Millar. **10.** At Westmarch (St. Mirren F.C. Ground). **11.** Kilmarnock played in qualifying competition: 2/9 Kilmarnock 5 Morton 3. 23/9 Kilmarnock 1 Newmilns 0. 14/10 Kilmarnock 3 Motherwell 3. 21/10 Motherwell 1 Kilmarnock 3. **12.** Kilmarnock played in qualifying competition: Away to Pollokshaws - W/O. 22/9 Carfin 4 Kilmarnock 4. 29/9 Kilmarnock 4 Carfin 2. 13/10 Dykehead 1 Kilmarnock 3.

Victory in the Scottish Qualifying Cup in 1897 was the first trophy won in a competition contested by teams from outside Ayrshire.
Back: J.Q.McPherson(Trainer),T.Busby,A.Alexander(Treas.),J.Ralston,J.Taylor(Sec.),R.Brown,R.Thomson(Vice-Pres.)
Middle:D.Watson,C.Smith(Match Sec.),J.Campbell,J.W.Somerville (Vice-Pres.),A.Richmond,A.McLean,R.Gibson
Front: D.McPherson,A.Paterson,J.Johnstone
(Smith didn't play in the Final but took the place of R.McAvoy, who was unavailable for the photo)

Division Two Champions, Kilmarnock reached their first Scottish Cup Final in 1898, losing 2-0 to Rangers.
Back: J.Q.McPherson(Trainer), D.McPherson, T.Busby, J.McAllan, R.Brown, J.Johnstone
Front: R.Muir, D.Maitland, J.Campbell, G.Anderson, W.Reid, R.Findlay

SEASON 1895-96 Division Two

No.	Date	Opposition	H.T.	Res.l	Att.	Goalscorers	Gordon	Busby	Maxwell	McPherson	J.Brown	Johnstone	Watson	Fisher	Campbell	McAvoy	Cox	R.Brown	McLean	Harrow	Sawers	Ralston	Smith	"Richards"
1	17 Aug	Leith Athletic	1-1	1-3	1500	McAvoy	1	2	3	4	5	6	7	8	9	10	11							
2	24	MOTHERWELL	2-1	7-1	2000	Watson,McAvoy,Cox(3),McPherson,Fisher	1		2	6	5	4	7	8	9	10	11	3						
3	31	MORTON	2-0	5-1	2000	Cox(2), Fisher, Campbell, McAvoy	1		3	6	5	4	11	10	9	8	7	2						
4	7 Sep	Partick Thistle	2-1	2-2	2000	J.Brown, McAvoy	1	2	3	4	5	6	7	8	9	10	11							
5	14	RENTON	3-2	4-2	2000	Fisher(2), Watson, Cox	1	3	2	6	5	4	10	8	9		11		7					
6	28	Port Glasgow Athletic	0-3	1-6		Fisher	1	3	2	4	5	6		8	9	10	7		11					
7	19 Oct	Renton	0-1	0-3			1			2	4	6	7	9	5	8	10	3	11					
8	26	Morton	1-1	3-2	1500	McAvoy, McLean, McPherson	1	2		4	5	6	7	8	9	10		3	11					
9	9 Nov	Airdrieonians	2-2	3-5		Harrow(2), Campbell	1	2		4	5	6	7	8	9	10		3		11				
10	16	Motherwell	1-2	4-2*		Campbell(2), McLean, Not known	1	3		6	5	4	8		9		7	2	11					
11	21 Dec	Linthouse	0-0	3-1		Campbell, McLean, Watson	1	2		4		6	8	10	5	9		3	11					7
12	1 Feb	LINTHOUSE	0-2	3-2	2000	Fisher(2), McLean	1	2		4	5	6	8	10		9	7	3	11					
13	22	AIRDRIEONIANS	4-2	6-4		McAvoy(2), McLean(2), Watson, Fisher	1	3		6	5	4	10	9		8	11	2	7					
14	7 Mar	ABERCORN	0-3	2-4		Watson, McAvoy	1	3		6	5	4	11		9	8		2	7		10			
15	14	PORT GLASGOW ATH.	1-0	2-1		Fisher, Campbell		3		6	5	4		9	7	10	11	2			8	1		
16	21	LEITH ATHLETIC	0-0	1-0	3000	McLean		3		6	5	4		9		10	11	2	7		8	1		
17	11 Apr	PARTICK THISTLE	2-1	2-3		Not known(2)		3		6	5	4		9		10	11	2	7		8	1		
18	18	Abercorn	0-2	2-3		Campbell(2)		3		6	5	4		10	9	8	7	2		11		1		
19	20 May	Renton+	1-2	1-2		McLean		3		6	5	4	11		9	8		2	7			1	10	
						Apps.	14	16	6	19	18	19	14	17	15	17	14	15	12	2	4	5	1	1
						Goals				2	1		5	9	8	8	6		7	2				

* Abandoned after 73 minutes. Result allowed to stand, Kilmarnock fielded only 10 men.
+ Play-off for 3rd/4th place at Cathkin Park.

Pos	P.	W.	D.	L.	F.	A.	Pts.
4th	18	10	1	7	51	45	21

Scottish Cup

No.	Date	Opposition	H.T.	Res.	Att.	Goalscorers	Gordon	Busby	Maxwell	McPherson	J.Brown	Johnstone	Watson	Fisher	Campbell	McAvoy	Cox	R.Brown	McLean	Harrow	Sawers	Ralston	Smith	"Richards"
1	18 Jan	Annbank	1-3	2-3		Campbell, McLean	1	2		4		6	7	5	9	10	8	3	11					

SEASON 1896-97 Division Two

No.	Date	Opposition	H.T.	Res.	Att.	Goalscorers	Ralston	H.Smith	Busby	Johnstone	J.Brown	McPherson	McLean	Richmond	Campbell	McAvoy	Watson	R.Brown	Fulton	Baillie	Muir	Paterson	McArthur	Cochran	Dowdles	Revie	Anderson	Edgar	Findlay	McLatchie	Reid	Scott	Miller
1	15 Aug	RENTON	1-1	5-1	3000	Campbell(3), Richmond, McAvoy	1	2	3	4	5	6	7	8	9	10	11																
2	22	Leith Athletic	0-1	1-4	2000	Campbell	1	3	2		5	4	11	10	9	7	8		6														
3	5 Sep	DUMBARTON	3-0	5-1	1000	Campbell,J.Brown,McLean,Watson,Fulton	1		2		5	4	11	10	9	8	7	3	6														
4	10 Oct	Morton	1-2	2-3		R.Brown, Campbell	1		2	6		4	11	10	9	8	7	3	5														
5	17	LEITH ATHLETIC	1-0	1-0	2000	Watson	1		2		5	4	11	10	9	8	7	3	6														
6	2 Jan	Airdrieonians	2-3	5-4		McLean,Richmond,Campbell,N.K.,McPherson			2	6		4	11	10	9	8	7	3	5	1													
7	6 Mar	Renton	1-0	2-1		McArthur(2)		3	2				11				8		6		1	10	9	4	7		5						
8	20	Port Glasgow Athletic	1-3	2-5		Richmond, Campbell			2	4		6	7	8	9		11	3	5		1	10											
9	27	PARTICK THISTLE	1-1	1-3	2500	McLean			2	5		4	11	10	9		8	3	6		1		7										
10	10 Apr	Dumbarton	1-0	6-0		Revie(2),McArthur,Campbell,Dowdles,McLean			2	4		6	7		5			3			1		9	8	10	11							
11	17	Partick Thistle	0-1	0-2	5000				2	6		4	11		5	8		3			1		9	10		7							
12	27	Linthouse	1-0	1-1	1000	Findlay		2				4	7		9	8		3	6		1			10				5	11				
13	1 May	Motherwell	0-1	2-1	3000	McLean, Campbell			2			6	11		9	8		3	4		1					10	5		7				
14	6	MOTHERWELL	0-0	4-0	500	McLean(2), Campbell(2)			2	6		4	7		9	8		3			1			10			5		11				
15	8	LINTHOUSE	0-0	0-3	500			2				4	7		9	8		3	6		1			10			5			11			
16	11	PORT GLASGOW ATH.	2-0	3-0	1000	Reid(2), McLean			2	6		4	7		5	8		3			1			9					11		10		
17	13	AIRDRIEONIANS	1-1	1-2	500	Cochran			2			4	7		5	8		3			1			9			6		11		10		
18	15	MORTON	2-1	3-2	1000	McLean(2), Findlay			2	6		4	7			8		3			1			9			5		11		10		
						Apps.	5	5	16	10	4	17	18	8	16	14	9	15	11	1	12	2	4	9	2	3	6	1	6	1	3		
						Goals					1	1	10	3	12	1	2	1	1				3	1	1	2			2		2		

Pos	P.	W.	D.	L.	F.	A.	Pts.
3rd	18	10	1	7	44	33	21

Scottish Cup

No.	Date	Opposition	H.T.	Res.	Att.	Goalscorers	Ralston	H.Smith	Busby	Johnstone	J.Brown	McPherson	McLean	Richmond	Campbell	McAvoy	Watson	R.Brown	Fulton	Baillie	Muir	Paterson	McArthur	Cochran	Dowdles	Revie	Anderson	Edgar	Findlay	McLatchie	Reid	Scott	Miller
1	9 Jan	Motherwell	3-2	3-3	1000	Campbell, McAvoy, Richmond	1		2	6		4	11	10	9	8	7	3	5														
1R	16	MOTHERWELL	2-1	5-2	2000	McLean(2), Campbell, McAvoy, Watson			2	4		6	7	8	9	10	11	3	5		1												
2	6 Feb*	FALKIRK	6-2	7-3	3000	Campbell(3),Richmond(2),McAvoy,McPherson			2	4		6	7	8	9	10	11	3			1	5											
QF	13	THIRD LANARK	1-1	3-1	7000	Campbell, Richmond, Scott			2	6		4	11	10	9	8		3			1											7	5
SF	13 Mar	Dumbarton	1-1	3-4	6000	Campbell(3)			2	6		4	11	10	9	8	7	3			1												5

* Originally played 23 January. Kilmarnock 3 - Falkirk 1 (Scorers: McLean, Richmond, Watson), Falkirk Successfully appealed over pitch markings.

Kilmarnock played in the Qualifying Competition this season, results as follows:

	Date	Opposition		Res.		Goalscorers
	29 Aug	Lugar Boswell		6-2		Campbell(3), J.Brown, Not known(2)
	12 Sep	SALTCOATS VICTORIA		13-2		Campbell(8),McAvoy,McLean,Richmond,N.K.(2)
	26	AYR		7-1		Campbell(3),McAvoy,Richmond,Watson,McLean
	24 Oct	HURLFORD		4-2		Campbell(2), J.Brown, Watson
	7 Nov	Partick Thistle		5-2		McAvoy,McLean,Campbell,Richmond,McPherson
	21	DUNBLANE		2-0		Watson(2)
	5 Dec	MOTHERWELL*		4-1		Richmond, Campbell, McAvoy, McPherson

* Played at Hampden Park

SEASON 1897-98 Division Two

No.	Date	Opposition	H.T.	Res.	Att.	Goalscorers	McCowan	Busby	Brown	McPherson	Anderson	Johnstone	McLean	McAvoy	Campbell	Reid	Findlay	McAllan	Maitland	Muir	Watson	Baillie	Cochran	Doig	Gordon
1	4 Sep	Motherwell	0-1	2-1	2000	Campbell(2)	1	2	3	4	5	6	11	8	9	10				7					
2	11	ABERCORN	4-1	7-1		Campbell(2),McAvoy(3),McPherson,Findlay	1	2	3	4	5	6	7	8	9	10	11								
3	25	Morton	2-2	4-3	3000	Campbell(2), McPherson, Findlay		2	3	4	5	6	7	8	9	10	11					1			
4	9 Oct	LEITH ATHLETIC	2-1	3-1	3000	McAvoy, Reid, Maitland		2	3	4		6	7	8	5	10	11	1	9						
5	16	AYR	4-1	5-2		Findlay(2), Maitland(2), McPherson		2	3	6		4	7	8		10	11	1	9	5					
6	23	MORTON	5-0	5-2	1500	Reid(3), Campbell, McLean		3	2	6	5		11	10	9	8	7	1					4		
7	30	Abercorn	0-2	1-4	2500	Findlay		2	3	4	5	6	11		9	8	7	1		10					
8	6 Nov	Hamilton Acas.	1-0	3-2	1200	Findlay, Maitland, Watson		2	3	4	5	6			8	10	11	1	9		7				
9	13	LINTHOUSE	4-0	5-0		Maitland(3),Findlay,Watson		2	3	4	5	6			8	10	11	1	9		7				
10	20	Leith Athletic	1-1	2-2		McAvoy, McLean		2	3	4	5	6	7	8	9	10	11	1							
11	27	AIRDRIEONIANS	4-1	5-2	1000	Anderson,Johnstone,McLean,Reid,Maitland		2		4	5	6	7	8		10	11	1	9					3	
12	18 Dec	MOTHERWELL	4-0	6-2	2500	Anderson(2),Muir(2),Campbell,Maitland		3	2	6	5	4			9	8	7	1	11	10					
13	12 Feb	Airdrieonians	1-2	1-2		Anderson		2	3	4	5			9		10	11	1	8	7			6		
14	5 Mar	HAMILTON ACAS.	2-0	5-0		McPherson,McLean,McAvoy,Muir,Campbell		2	3	6	5	4	7	8	9				10	11					1
15	12	Ayr	1-0	3-0	2500	McPherson, McAvoy, Muir		2	3	6	5	4		10	9		7			11			8		1
16	19	Linthouse	1-0	3-0	2000	Anderson, Campbell, Maitland		2	3	4	5	6	11		9	10			8	7					1
17	2 Apr	PORT GLASGOW ATH.	0-0	2-1	2000	McPherson, Muir		2	3	4	5	6		10	9		11	1	8	7					
18	9	Port Glasgow	1-1	2-4		Findlay, Campbell		2	3		5	6		10	9		11	1	8	7			4		
						Apps.	2	18	17	17	16	16	11	13	15	14	15	12	11	10	2	1	4	1	3
						Goals				6	5	1	4	7	11	5	8		10	5	2				

Pos	P.	W.	D.	L.	F.	A.	Pts.
1st	18	14	1	3	64	29	29

Scottish Cup

1	6 Jan	6th GRV	2-1	5-1		Muir(2), Campbell, Maitland, Reid		2	3	4	5	6			9	10	11	1	7	8					
2	22	LEITH ATHLETIC	4-1	9-2	3500	Muir(2),Andrsn(2),Reid(2),McPhrsn,Mtlnd,Cpbll		2	3	4	5	6			9	10	11	1	8	7					
QF	5 Feb	Ayr Parkhouse	5-2	7-2	6000	Reid(2),Findlay(2),Campbell,Muir,Maitland		2	3	6	5	4			9	8	7	1	10	11					
SF	19	DUNDEE	1-2	3-2	11000	Reid, Findlay, Maitland		2	3	4	5	6			9	10	11	1	8	7					
F	26 Mar	Rangers*	0-0	0-2	1300			2	3	6	5	4			9	8	7	1	10	11					

* Played at Hampden Park

SEASON 1898-99 Division Two

No.	Date	Opposition	H.T.	Res.	Att.	Goalscorers	Paterson	Busby	Brown	McPherson	Anderson	Carr	Muir	Howie	Campbell	Reid	Findlay	Johnstone	Maitland	Craig	Young	McAvoy	Hewitt	Aitken
1	27 Aug	AIRDRIEONIANS	2-0	5-0	4000	Reid(2), McPherson, Howie, Findlay	1	2	3	4	5	6	7	8	9	10	11							
2	3 Sep	Abercorn	1-1	2-1	1500	Findlay, Maitland	1	2	3	4	5		7		9	10	11	6	8					
3	10	PORT GLASGOW ATH.	2-1	4-1	4000	Muir(2), McPherson, Findlay	1	2	3	4	5		7		9	10	11	6	8					
4	24	Morton	2-1	2-1	3000	Reid, Maitland		2	3	4			7	8	5	10	11	6	9	1				
5	8 Oct	LEITH ATHLETIC	3-2	5-3	4000	Reid(3), Findlay, Maitland		2	3	4		5	7		9	10	11	6	8	1				
6	15	MORTON	1-0	2-0	2000	Reid, Young		2	3	4	5		7	8		10	11	6		1	9			
7	22	Airdrieonians	2-3	4-4		Campbell(2), Anderson, Reid		3	2	4	5		8		9	10	11	6		1		7		
8	5 Nov	LINTHOUSE	5-0	8-0	1500	Howie(4),Maitland(2),Campbell,Findlay		2	3		5	4		8	9	10	11	6	7	1				
9	19	Ayr	1-0	1-1		Reid		2	3	4	5		7		9	10	11	6	8	1				
10	26	ABERCORN	2-0	3-0	1500	Muir, Howie, N.K.		2	3	4	5	6	7	9		10	11		8	1				
11	3 Dec	Hamilton Acas	1-1	7-1		Campbell(2),Findly(2),Andrsn,Jhnstne,Mtlnd		2	3		5	4	7		9	10	11	6	8	1				
12	10	HAMILTON ACAS	2-1	7-1		Campbell(3),Maitland(2),Muir,Findlay		2			5	4	7		9	10	11	6	8	1			3	
13	17	Port Glasgow Athletic	2-0	5-4		Howie(3), Findlay, Maitland		3	2	4	5		7	10		9	11	6	8	1				
14	7 Jan	AYR	2-1	5-1		McPherson,Muir,Reid,Findlay,Maitland		2	3	4	5		7	10		9	11	6	8	1				
15	18 Mar	Motherwell	2-0	3-3	2000	Muir, Campbell, Maitland			3	4	5		7	10	9		11	6	8	1			2	
16	8 Apr	Linthouse	1-0	2-0		Howie, O.G.		2	3	4	5		7	10	9		11	6	8	1				
17	15	Leith Athletic	2-2	3-3		Campbell(2), Findlay		2	3	4	5		7	10	9	8	11	6		1				
18	22	MOTHERWELL	4-0	5-0	1500	Reid(2), McPherson, Howie, Campbell		2	3	4	5			8	9	10	11	6	7	1				
						Apps.	3	17	17	15	16	6	16	11	14	16	18	16	14	15	1	1	2	
						Goals				4	2		6	11	12	12	11	1	11		1			

Pos	P.	W.	D.	L.	F.	A.	Pts.
1st	18	14	4	0	73	24	32

Scottish Cup

1	14 Jan	Orion	2-0	2-0	5000	Findlay(2)		2	3	4	5		7		9	10	11	6	8	1				
2	11 Feb	East Stirling	0-0	1-1	6500	Reid		2	3		5		7	10	4	9	11	6	8	1				
2R	18	EAST STIRLING	0-0	0-0	8000			2	3		5		7	10	4	9	11	6	8	1				
2R	25	East Stirling*	3-1	4-2	8000	Muir(3), Campbell		2	3		5		7		9	10	11	6	8	1				4
QF	11 Mar	ST. MIRREN	0-2	1-2	11129	McPherson			3	4	5		8		9	10	11	6	7	1				2

* Played at Cathkin Park

SEASON 1899-1900 Division One

No.	Date	Opposition	H.T.	Res.	Att.	Goalscorers	Craig	Busby	Brown	McPherson	Anderson	McCrone	Muir	Howie	Campbell	Reid	Findlay	Johnstone	Maitland	Morton	Terras	Duncanson	Ferguson	Hewitt	Young
1	19 Aug	St. Mirren	1-0	1-0	5000	Findlay	1	2	3	4	5	6	7	8	9	10	11								
2	26	CELTIC	0-2	2-2	11000	Howie(2)	1	2	3		5	4	7	8	9	10	11	6							
3	2 Sep	Hibernian	0-2	1-3	7500	Howie	1	2	3		5	4	7	8	9		11	6	10						
4	9	RANGERS	2-1	2-4	10000	Howie, Johnstone	1	2	3	4	5		7	8		10	11	6	9						
5	16	ST. BERNARD'S	1-1	2-1	3500	Anderson, Howie	1	2	3	4	5		7	10	9		11	6	8						
6	23	Hearts	0-0	0-1	5000		1	2	3	4	5		7	10	9			6	8	11					
7	30	THIRD LANARK	1-0	1-1	2700	Morton	1	2	3	4	5			8	9	10		6	7	11					
8	7 Oct	CLYDE	1-0	3-1	3000	Campbell(2), Maitland	1	2	3	4	5			10	9				8	11	6	7			
9	14	HIBERNIAN	0-1	0-3	4500		1	2	3	4	5		7	8	9	10	11	6							
10	21	DUNDEE	1-0	2-1	3000	Campbell(2)	1	2	3	4	5		7		9	10		6	8				11		
11	4 Nov	St. Bernard's	1-0	1-1	600	Ferguson	1	2	3	4	5		7	8		10		6		11			9		
12	11	ST. MIRREN	1-1	2-2	1500	McPherson, Findlay	1	2	3	4	5		7			10	11	6	8				9		
13	25	Third Lanark	1-1	1-2	3000	Findlay	1	2	3	4	5		7	10			11	6	8				9		
14	9 Dec	Rangers	1-2	1-6	5000	Findlay	1		3	4	5		7	10	9		11	6	8					2	
15	16	Celtic	1-1	3-3	2000	Howie, Maitland, Reid	1	2	3	4	5		7	10		9	11	6	8						
16	30	Clyde	3-1	3-2		Young(3)	1	2		4	5		7	8			11	6	9					3	10
17	6 Jan	Dundee	3-1	3-3	4000	Ferguson, Muir, Reid	1	2		4	5		7		9	10		6	8				11	3	
18	17 Mar	HEARTS	1-1	2-1	3000	Reid, Muir	1	2	3	4	5		7			10	11	6	9				8		
						Apps.	18	17	16	16	18	3	16	14	11	11	12	16	14	4	1	1	6	3	1
						Goals				1	1		2	6	4	3	4	1	2	1			2		3

Pos	P.	W.	D.	L.	F.	A.	Pts.
5th	18	6	6	6	30	37	18

Scottish Cup

No.	Date	Opposition	H.T.	Res.	Att.	Goalscorers	Craig	Busby	Brown	McPherson	Anderson	McCrone	Muir	Howie	Campbell	Reid	Findlay	Johnstone	Maitland	Morton	Terras	Duncanson	Ferguson	Hewitt	Young
1	13 Jan	EAST STIRLING	0-0	2-0	1000	Howie, Maitland	1	2		4	5		7	10	9			6	8	11				3	
2	27	ORION	4-0	10-0	3000	Maitland(5),Howie(2),Campbell,Mortn,Terrs	1	2	3		5		7	10	9			6	8	11	4				
QF	17 Feb	Celtic	0-2	0-4	8000		1		3		5		7	10	9			6	8	11	4			2	

SEASON 1900-01 Division One

No.	Date	Opposition	H.T.	Res.	Att.	Goalscorers	Craig	Busby	Muir	McPherson	Anderson	Johnstone	A.Reid	Howie	Campbell	W.Reid	Ferguson	Maitland	Crerar	Brown	Jas Wyllie	Graham	Hewitt	Morton	Woodburn	Agnew	Mitchell	Robertson
1	18 Aug	Partick Thistle	0-0	2-1	5000	A.Reid, Campbell	1	2	3	4	5	6	7	8	9	10	11											
2	22	Third Lanark	0-2	2-3	2000	Anderson, Crerar	1	2	3	4	5	6	7	8		10	11		9									
3	25	DUNDEE	1-0	2-0	3500	McPherson, Maitland	1	2	3	4	5	6	7	10	9		11	8										
4	1 Sep	Rangers	1-5	1-5	9500	Crerar	1	2	3	4	5		7	8	6	10	11		9									
5	8	HIBERNIAN	2-2	2-2	4000	McPherson, Ferguson	1	2	8	4	5		7			10	11		9	3	6							
6	15	Dundee	0-1	0-3	10000		1		2	4	5		7	8			11		10	3	6	9						
7	22	PARTICK THISTLE	2-1	2-1	3500	Muir(2)	1	2	7	4	5	6	11			10			8	3		9						
8	6 Oct	QUEENS PARK	0-1	2-1	2000	Busby, A.Reid	1	2	8	4	5		11			10					6	9	3	7				
9	13	St. Mirren	0-2	1-3	3000	W.Reid	1		8	4	5	6	11			10				2		9	3	7				
10	20	MORTON	1-1	4-1	4000	Crerar(2), Graham, A.Reid	1	2	7	4	5		11			10			8	3	6	9						
11	27	Celtic	0-1	0-1	5000		1	2	7	4	5		11			10		8			6	9	3					
12	3 Nov	CELTIC	1-0	2-1	6500	Graham, A.Reid	1	2	7	4	5		11			10		8			6	9	3					
13	10	HEARTS	1-1	1-3	2500	Graham	1	2	7	4	5	6	11			10		8				9	3					
14	24	Hibernian	2-2	2-2	3000	Busby, Maitland	1	2	7		5		11			10		8			6	9	3		4			
15	1 Dec	RANGERS	1-0	1-2	10000	Graham	1	2	7	4	5		11			10					6	9	3	8				
16	8	Hearts	0-5	0-7	3000		1		2		5		11			10		8				9		7	6	3	4	
17	15	Queens Park	5-0	5-5	4500	Graham(2), A.Reid(2), Maitland	1	2	7	4			11	10				8			5	9			6	3		
18	22	ST. MIRREN	1-2	2-2	2500	Howie, A.Reid	1	2	7	4			11	10	5			8				9			6	3		
19	29	Morton	0-2	2-3	4000	Busby, Muir	1	2	7	4			11	10								9	3	8	6		5	
20	1 Jan	THIRD LANARK	2-1	2-1	3500	Howie(2)	1		7	4			11	10				8				9			6	3	5	2
						Apps.	20	16	20	18	16	6	20	9	4	14	6	9	6	5	9	15	8	5	6	4	3	1
						Goals		3	3	2	1		7	3	1	1	1	3	4			6						

Pos	P.	W.	D.	L.	F.	A.	Pts.
5th	20	7	4	9	35	47	18

Scottish Cup

No.	Date	Opposition	H.T.	Res.	Att.	Goalscorers	Craig	Busby	Muir	McPherson	Anderson	Johnstone	A.Reid	Howie	Campbell	W.Reid	Ferguson	Maitland	Crerar	Brown	Jas Wyllie	Graham	Hewitt	Morton	Woodburn	Agnew	Mitchell	Robertson
1	12 Jan	AIRDRIEONIANS	3-1	3-2	3000	Maitland(3)	1	2	7	4	5		11	10				8				9			6	3		
2	9 Feb*	Celtic	0-3	0-6	12000		1	2	7	4	5		11	10				8				9				3	6	

* Match was scheduled for 26/1/01 but the referee failed to appear. The clubs played a friendly instead, Celtic winning 2-1; Kilmarnock team was exactly the same as appeared in the cup-tie, Muir scored for Killie.

The opening of the new Rugby Park in August 1899 was an auspicious occasion. The Division Two flag was unfurled, Cup holders Celtic were the visitors, and it was Killie's first home game in Division One.

SEASON 1901-02 Division One

No.	Date	Opposition	H.T.	Res.	Att.	Goalscorers	Craig	Busby	Agnew	McPherson	Anderson	Mitchell	A.Reid	John Wyllie	Graham	Howie	Norwood	Maitland	Morton	T.Findlay	R.Findlay	Brown	Chapman
1	17 Aug	RANGERS	3-1	4-2	6000	Graham(2), Howie, Norwood	1	2	3	4	5	6	7	8	9	10	11						
2	24	Dundee	0-0	0-0	10000		1	2	3	4	5	6	7	8	9	10	11						
3	31	HIBERNIAN	0-0	0-0	5500		1	2	3	4	5	6	7	8	9	10	11						
4	7 Sep	Rangers	0-2	2-3	16000	Howie(2)	1	2	3	4	5	6		9	8	10		7	11				
5	14	MORTON	0-0	2-0	5000	Anderson, Morton	1	2	3	4	5	6		9	8	10		7	11				
6	21	Hearts	0-1	0-3	7000		1	2	3	4	5	6	7		9	10		8	11				
7	28	CELTIC	0-0	0-1	8000		1	2	3	4	5	6		9	8	10		7	11				
8	5 Oct	Morton	0-1	1-1		Wyllie	1	2	3	4	5	6		9	8	10		7	11				
9	12	ST. MIRREN	1-0	1-2	3000	Wyllie	1	2	3	4	5	6		9	8	10		7	11				
10	19	HEARTS	1-0	1-0	4000	Morton	1	2	3	4	5	6		9	7	8			11	10			
11	2 Nov	Third Lanark	0-0	0-0	4500		1	2	3	4	5	6			9	8			7	10	11		
12	9	DUNDEE	3-0	4-0	3500	Graham(2), Howie, Morton	1	2	3	4	5	6			9	8			11	10		7	
13	16	Hibernian	0-3	0-5			1	2	3	4	5	6		8	9				11	10		7	
14	7 Dec	THIRD LANARK	0-2	1-2	2000	T.Findlay	1	2	3	4	5	6		9		8			11	10		7	
15	21	St. Mirren	0-1	1-1		Morton	1	2	3	4	5	6			9	8			7	10			11
16	28	Celtic	1-2	2-4	3000	Graham, Morton	1	2	3	4	5	6			9	8			7	10			11
17	18 Jan	QUEENS PARK	0-0	1-1	4500	McPherson	1	2	3	4	5	6			9	10		8	7				11
18	15 Mar	Queens Park	0-0	1-0	4000	McPherson	1	2	3	4	5	6		9	8	10			11			7	
						Apps.	18	18	18	18	18	18	4	12	17	17	3	7	15	7	1	4	3
						Goals				2	1			2	5	4	1		5	1			

Pos	P.	W.	D.	L.	F.	A.	Pts.
7th	18	5	6	7	21	25	16

Scottish Cup

							Craig	Busby	Agnew	McPherson	Anderson	Mitchell	A.Reid	John Wyllie	Graham	Howie	Norwood	Maitland	Morton	T.Findlay	R.Findlay	Brown	Chapman
1	11 Jan	PARTICK THISTLE	2-0	4-0	4000	Graham(2), Chapman, Maitland	1	2	3	4	5	6			9	10		8	7				11
2	25	DUNDEE	1-0	2-0	6200	Howie, Mitchell	1	2	3	4	5	6			9	8		7	11	10			
QF	22 Feb*	Rangers	0-0	0-2	11600		1	2	3	4	5	6			9	8		7	11	10			

* The match was scheduled for February 8th, because of bad weather conditions, the game played on this day was classed as a friendly. Rangers won 3-0.

ESTABLISHED 1790.

R. B. RUSSELL,

CUTLER & HAIRDRESSER,

63 and 67 Portland Street

(Directly Opposite George Hotel).

AN EFFICIENT STAFF IN CONSTANT ATTENDANCE.

Ornamental Hair of Every Description.

Ladies' Combings carefully made up.

Perfumes and Toilet Requisites.

ALSO, FIRST CLASS CUTLERY IN GREAT VARIETY.

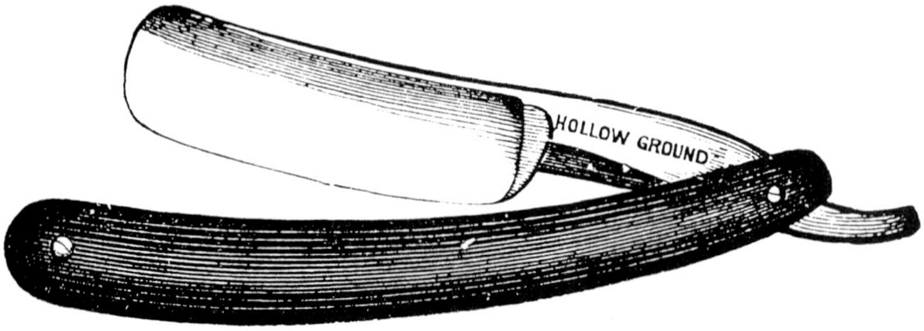

THE FAMED "AULD KILLIE" RAZOR,

Practically Tested before being sent out. Price 3/6, 4/- & 4/6.

'The Cutler', R.B.Russell, was a long-serving Kilmarnock official who was also a well-known local trader. The fearsome-looking "Auld Killie" razor makes the modern supporter give thanks that we live in the age of the disposable blade!

SEASON 1902-03 Division One

No.	Date	Opposition	H.T.	Res.	Att.	Goalscorers
1	16 Aug	Partick Thistle	1-0	1-2	4500	G.Young
2	23	MORTON	0-2	4-2	3000	Muir, T.Findlay, R.Findlay, Morton(7)
3	30	Dundee	0-1	0-2	8500	
4	6 Sep	HIBERNIAN	1-2	1-4	4000	T.Findlay
5	13	Morton	0-0	1-0	5500	R.Findlay
6	20	CELTIC	0-2	1-3	7000	Wyllie
7	27	St. Mirren	0-3	0-4	4000	
8	4 Oct	PORT GLASGOW ATH.	1-0	1-0	2500	Wilson
9	11	QUEENS PARK	0-0	1-1	4500	Crichton
10	18	Third Lanark	0-1	0-2	4000	
11	25	PARTICK THISTLE	1-0	2-0	3000	G.Young, R.Findlay
12	1 Nov	Celtic	0-2	1-3	4000	Gibson
13	8	THIRD LANARK	2-1	2-2	3500	G.Young, T.Findlay
14	15	Hibernian	1-1	1-2	5000	G.Young
15	22	HEARTS	1-3	1-3	3000	O.G.
16	29	Rangers	0-4	0-5	4500	
17	6 Dec	Hearts	1-0	1-1		McPherson
18	13	DUNDEE	0-1	0-2	4000	
19	20	RANGERS	0-0	0-0	4000	
20	27	ST. MIRREN	0-3	2-3	2500	McKay, Wilson
21	31 Jan	Queens Park	2-1	3-2		R.Findlay(2), Gibson
22	14 Feb	Port Glasgow Athletic	0-0	1-0	2000	T.Findlay

No.	Craig	Busby	Morton	McPherson	Anderson	Mitchell	Morton	G.Young	Mair	T.Findlay	R.Findlay	Wyllie	Wilson	McConnell	Crichton	Gibson	McKay	R.Young
1	1	2	3	4	5	6	7	8	9	10	11							
2	1	2	3	4	5		7	8	9	10	11	6						
3	1	2	3	4	5	6	7	8	9	10	11							
4	1	2	3	4	5	6			9	10	11	7	8					
5	1	2	3	4	5	6	7			10	11	9	8					
6	1	2	3	4	5	6	7			10	11	9	8					
7	1	2	3	4	5	6	7		8	10	11	9						
8	1		3	4	5	7	11			10		9	8	2	6			
9	1		2	4	5	6	11	9		10			8	3	7			
10	1		2	4	5	6	7	9		10	11		8	3				
11	1	2		4	5	6	7	9			11		10	3		8		
12	1		2	4	5		7	9			11		10	3	6	8		
13	1		2	4	5	6	7	9		10	11			3		8		
14	1	2			5	6	7	9			11			3	4	8	10	
15	1		2		5	6	7	9			11			3	4	8	10	
16	1	2	3	4	5	6	7			10	11					8	9	
17	1		3	4	5	6	11	7		10		2				8	9	
18	1		3	4	5	6		7		10	11	2				8	9	
19	1		2	4	5		11					7	10	3	6	8	9	
20			2	4	5	6	11						10	3	7	8	9	1
21	1		2		5	6	7			10	11	9		3	4	8		
22	1		2		5	6	7			10	11	9		3	4	8		
Apps.	21	10	20	18	22	19	20	12	5	16	17	11	10	12	9	12	7	1
Goals				1			1	4	1	4	5	1	2		1	2	1	

Pos	P.	W.	D.	L.	F.	A.	Pts.
9th	22	6	4	12	24	43	16

Scottish Cup

No.	Date	Opposition	H.T.	Res.	Att.	Goalscorers
1	17 Jan	Arbroath	3-0	3-1	3000	McKay(2), T.Findlay
2	24	Rangers	0-1	0-4	7500	

No.	Craig	Busby	Morton	McPherson	Anderson	Mitchell	Morton	G.Young	Mair	T.Findlay	R.Findlay	Wyllie	Wilson	McConnell	Crichton	Gibson	McKay	R.Young
1	1		2	4		6	11			10		7		3	5	8	9	
2	1		2	4	5	6	11			10		7		3		8	9	

SEASON 1903-04 Division One

No.	Date	Opposition	H.T.	Res.	Att.	Goalscorers
1	15 Aug	QUEENS PARK	0-1	2-1	3500	Blair, O.G.
2	22	Morton	2-2	2-4	4000	Graham, Blair
3	29	PARTICK THISTLE	0-2	1-3	4000	McLeod
4	5 Sep	Dundee	0-1	0-4	6000	
5	12	HIBERNIAN	0-0	0-0	3000	
6	19	MORTON	1-0	1-1	3000	McPherson
7	26	Hearts	1-1	1-2	6000	Blair
8	3 Oct	PORT GLASGOW ATH.	0-0	0-4	3500	
9	10	Airdrieonians	1-1	2-1	4000	Banks, R.Findlay
10	17	ST. MIRREN	0-0	2-0	3000	McPherson, R.Findlay
11	24	Motherwell	0-2	0-2	3000	
12	31	THIRD LANARK	0-0	1-2	4300	R.Findlay
13	7 Nov	DUNDEE	0-1	0-1	3800	
14	14	CELTIC	1-4	1-6	4500	McPherson
15	21	Partick Thistle	0-1	0-4	2000	
16	28	AIRDRIEONIANS	0-0	0-2		
17	5 Dec	RANGERS	1-1	2-2		Banks, Gibson
18	12	Port Glasgow Athletic	0-1	1-4	3000	Banks
19	19	St. Mirren	0-2	0-3	1800	
20	26	Queens Park	1-0	1-1	3000	Blair
21	9 Jan	MOTHERWELL	2-0	2-1	1800	Blair, Morton(No.11)
22	16	Rangers	0-1	0-3	4000	
23	5 Mar	HEARTS	1-3	2-3		Gibson, Morton(No.11)
24	12	Hibernian	2-2	2-2		Morton(No.11), Wyllie
25	26	Third Lanark	2-1	2-3	4500	Gibson(2)
26	23 Apr	Celtic	1-1	1-6		Banks

No.	Craig	Morton	Gunzeon	McPherson	Anderson	Wyllie	Graham	Gibson	Blair	McKay	McGimpsey	Morton	Crichton	McLeod	Banks	R.Findlay	Young	Fairgray	T.Findlay	Mitchell	W.McDonald	J.McDonald	Davidson
1	1	2	3	4	5	6	7	8	9	10	11												
2	1	2	3	4	5	6	7	8	9		10	11											
3	1	2	3	4		5	7		9	11	10		6	8									
4	1	2	3	4		5	7	8	9			11	6		10								
5	1	2	3	4		5	7		10		8	11		6	9								
6	1	2	3	4		5	7		10		8	11	6		9								
7	1	2	3		5	4	7		9			11	6	8					10				
8	1		3	4	5	2	7		10			11	6		9				8				
9	1	2	3	4	5	7		8	10				6		9	11							
10	1	2	3	4	5	7		8	10				6		9	11							
11	1	2	3	4	5	7		8	10				6		9	11							
12		2	3		5			8	10			7	6		9	11	1			4			
13	1	2	3	4	5				10			7	6	8	9			11					
14		2	3	4	5			8	10		7		6		9		1		11				
15		2	3		5				10		8	7	4		9	11	1			6			
16	1	2	3		5				9	10	8		6		7	11				4			
17	1	2	3	4	5	7		8		10			6		9	11							
18	1	2	3	4	5	7		8		10			6		9	11							
19	1		3	4	5	2			10	8		7			9	11				6			
20	1		3	4	5	2		8	10	9		11			7					6			
21	1		3	4		2		8	10	9		11	5		7					6			
22	1	2	3			5		8	10	9		11	6		7					4			
23	1	2	3		5	4		8	10			11			9						6	7	
24	1	2	3		5	4		7	10	8		11			9					6			
25	1		3		5	2		8	10	9		11								6	4	7	
26	1		3	4	5	2		8	10			11			9					6		7	
Apps.	23	20	26	18	20	21	8	17	24	11	8	17	17	4	21	9	3	1	3	10	2	3	
Goals				3			2	4	5			3		1	4	3							

Pos	P.	W.	D.	L.	F.	A.	Pts.
14th	26	4	5	17	26	65	13

Scottish Cup

No.	Date	Opposition	H.T.	Res.	Att.	Goalscorers
1	23 Jan	Nithsdale Wands	2-1	2-2	900	Blair(2)
1R	30	NITHSDALE WANDS	1-1	1-1	2500	McKay
1R	6 Feb	NITHSDALE WANDS	1-1	2-1*	4000	Davidson, Gibson
2	13	ALBION ROVERS	2-1	2-2	4000	R.Findlay, Gibson
2R	20	Albion Rovers	0-0	1-0	4000	Blair
QF	27	Third Lanark	0-2	0-3	12000	

No.	Craig	Morton	Gunzeon	McPherson	Anderson	Wyllie	Graham	Gibson	Blair	McKay	McGimpsey	Morton	Crichton	McLeod	Banks	R.Findlay	Young	Fairgray	T.Findlay	Mitchell	W.McDonald	J.McDonald	Davidson
1	1		3		5	2		8	10	9		11	6		7					4			
1R	1		3	4	5	2			10	8			6		7	11							9
1R	1	2	3	4	5	7		8	10				6			11							9
2	1	2	3	4	5	7		8	10				6			11							9
2R	1	2	3	4	5	7		8	10				6			11							9
QF	1	2	3	4	5	7		8	10			11	6										9

* After extra time.

Davie McPherson.

His two bothers played for Killie. His father was John Q., who was Killie Trainer (and later became Trainer to both Scotland and England). 1903/04 was Davie's last season. He was the last survivor of the team which played Kilmarnock's first League match.

SEASON 1904-05 Division One

No.	Date	Opposition	H.T.	Res.	Att.	Goalscorers	Young	Battles	Aitken	Johnstone	Crichton	W.McDonald	Currie	Gibson	Banks	Blair	Morton	W.Monteith	J.McDonald	Anderson	Fairfoul	McQueen	Wyllie	Hendron	Maxwell	Graham
1	20 Aug	HEARTS	1-0	3-2	4500	Banks, Blair, Gibson	1	2	3	4	5	6	7	8	9	10	11									
2	27	MOTHERWELL	0-2	0-2	4000			2	3	4	5	6	7	8	9	10	11	1								
3	3 Sep	PORT GLASGOW ATH.	0-0	1-1	3000	W.McDonald		2	3	4	5	6	7		9	10	11	1	8							
4	10	Morton	1-1	1-2	4000	Morton		2	3	4	5	6	7		9	10	11	1	8							
5	17	THIRD LANARK	0-0	0-0	4000			2	3	4	5	6		7	9	10	11	1	8							
6	24	Dundee	0-2	0-3	5000			2	3	4	8	6	7		9	10	11	1		5						
7	1 Oct	HIBERNIAN	1-0	2-1	4000	Blair(2)		2	3	4		6	7			10	11	1		5	8	9				
8	8	QUEENS PARK	2-1	2-1	4500	Banks, Blair		2	3	4		6	7		11	10		1		5	8	9				
9	15	Port Glasgow Athletic	1-1	1-1		Blair		2	3	4	6		7		11	10		1		5	8	9				
10	22	Airdrieonians	1-0	1-1		Currie		2	3		6	4	7		11	10		1		5	8	9				
11	29	ST. MIRREN	1-0	1-0		Banks		2	3		4	6	7	8	11	10		1		5		9				
12	5 Nov	CELTIC	0-3	0-3	8000			2	3	8	4	6	7		11	10		1		5		9				
13	12	Third Lanark	1-0	1-3	4500	Wyllie		2	3	4	5	6	7		11	10		1				9	8			
14	19	Motherwell	0-1	1-2	3500	Wyllie		2	3	4	6	7			11	10		1		5			9	8		
15	26	Hibernian	1-0	1-2	2500	Blair		2	3	4	6		7		8	10	11	1		5	9					
16	3 Dec	RANGERS	0-1	0-4	6500			2	3	4	5	6	7		8	10	11	1			9					
17	10	Partick Thistle	0-2	0-2	5000				3	2		6			4	10	11	1		5	8			9	7	
18	17	Queens Park	0-1	1-1	2000	Maxwell		2	3		4	6			9	10	11	1		5	8				7	
19	24	MORTON	0-0	1-0	2000	Fairfoul	1	2	3		4	6			9	10	11			5	8				7	
20	31	Celtic	0-2	1-3	4000	Maxwell	1	2	3	4	6				11	10				5	8			9	7	
21	2 Jan	PARTICK THISTLE	0-2	3-2	5000	Banks(3)	1	2	3	4		6			9	10	11			5	8				7	
22	7	Hearts	2-1	3-1	4000	Graham(3)	1	2	3			6			4	10	11			5	8				7	9
23	14	AIRDRIEONIANS	1-0	1-0	4500	Maxwell		2	3		5	6			4	10	11	1			8				7	9
24	21	Rangers	2-4	2-6		Maxwell(2)		2	3			6			4	10	11	1		5	8				7	9
25	11 Feb	DUNDEE	1-0	2-1		Blair(2)			3		4	6			2	10	11	1		5	8				7	9
26	18	St. Mirren	0-1	0-1					3	4	5	6			2	10	11	1			7			8		9
						Apps.	5	23	26	18	20	23	14	4	25	26	18	21	3	17	16	7	2	4	9	5
						Goals						1	1	1	6	8	1				1		2		5	3

Pos	P.	W.	D.	L.	F.	A.	Pts.
9th	26	9	5	12	29	45	23

Scottish Cup

No.	Date	Opposition	H.T.	Res.	Att.	Goalscorers	Young	Battles	Aitken	Johnstone	Crichton	W.McDonald	Currie	Gibson	Banks	Blair	Morton	W.Monteith	J.McDonald	Anderson	Fairfoul	McQueen	Wyllie	Hendron	Maxwell	Graham
1	28 Jan	BEITH	1-2	2-2		Morton(2)			3	2	4	6				10	11	1		5	8				7	9
1R	4 Feb	Beith	1-1	1-3	4000	Maxwell	1		3		3	6			4	10	11			5	8				7	9

Bob Findlay

Foolishly let go this year, International winger Findlay returned to haunt Kilmarnock. Time and again he scored vital goals against his old Rugby Park team-mates.

SEASON 1905-06 Division One

No.	Date	Opposition	H.T.	Res.	Att.	Goalscorers
1	19 Aug	Rangers	1-2	2-3	10000	Fairfoul, A.Graham
2	26	CELTIC	2-3	2-4	8500	Banks, Maxwell
3	2 Sep	Aberdeen	0-1	0-2	8000	
4	9	MORTON	1-1	3-1	3000	Banks, A.Graham, J.Young
5	16	Hearts	0-1	0-3	7000	
6	30	MOTHERWELL	0-0	1-0	3000	J.Young
7	7 Oct	Dundee	0-2	1-2	4000	A.Graham
8	14	ST. MIRREN	3-3	5-3	3000	A.Graham(2), J.Young(2), McDonald
9	21	PARTICK THISTLE	1-2	1-2	3000	Brown
10	28	Airdrieonians	1-1	1-1		A.Graham
11	4 Nov	FALKIRK	0-1	2-1	3500	Cameron, W.Shaw
12	11	QUEENS PARK	4-0	7-0	3500	J.Young(3), Galloway(3), Banks
13	18	HEARTS	1-0	1-1	5000	Fairfoul
14	25	Port Glasgow Athletic	1-0	2-3	1700	Morton, Brown
15	2 Dec	Third Lanark	0-2	0-5	4000	
16	9	HIBERNIAN	0-1	0-2	3500	
17	16	DUNDEE	1-2	2-2	3000	A.Graham, J.Young
18	23	Queens Park	0-1	1-4	4000	Fairfoul
19	30	ABERDEEN	1-0	2-1	3000	A.Graham, Maxwell
20	2 Jan	Celtic	0-0	0-2	6500	
21	6	RANGERS	1-2	1-3	6000	Fairfoul
22	13	Partick Thistle	0-1	1-2	2800	J.Young
23	20	THIRD LANARK	1-0	2-0		A.Graham, W.Shaw
24	3 Feb	AIRDRIEONIANS	0-0	0-0	4000	
25	10 Mar	Motherwell	0-0	1-5	3000	Fairfoul
26	17	Falkirk	1-2	3-7	3000	Brown, Fairfoul, J.Young
27	31	Hibernian	0-1	1-2	2500	J.Young
28	7 Apr	Morton	0-2	0-3	2000	
29	28	PORT GLASGOW ATH.	2-0	3-2	3000	Brown, J.Young, Maxwell
30	12 May	St. Mirren	1-0	1-2		Wishart
31	15	Port Glasgow Athletic*	0-1	0-6		

* Cathkin Park Play-off for 3rd last place.

No.	W.Monteith	Duncan	Aitken	Banks	W.Shaw	McDonald	Maxwell	Fairfoul	A.Graham	J.Young	Morton	Crichton	R.Young	Grant	Galloway	Brown	Watson	Cameron	Bridges	Fullarton	Wishart	McLounie	McQueen	Black	Gibson	McKeown	NcCallum	Moffat	Drain	S.Graham	H.C.Shaw	H.Monteith
1	1	2	3	4	5	6	7	8	9	10	11																					
2	1	2	3	10	5	6	7	8	9		11	4																				
3	1	2	3	4	5	6	7	8	9	10	11																					
4	1	2	3	4	5		7	8	9	10	11	6																				
5		2	3	4		6	7	8	9	10	11	5	1																			
6			3	9	5	6			7	10	11	4	1	2	8																	
7			3	4		6	7	8	9	10		5	1	2		11																
8			3	4		6	7	8	9	10		5	1	2		11																
9	1		3	4		6	7	8	9	10		5				11	2															
10	1		3	4	5	6	7	8	9	10						11	2															
11	1		3	4	5		7	8		10		6				11	2	9														
12	1		3	4	5	6		8		9	7				10	11	2															
13	1		3	4	5	6		8		9	7				10	11	2															
14	1		3		5	6		8		9	7	4			10	11	2															
15	1		3	4	5	6		8	9	10	7					11	2															
16	1	3		4	5			8		9	7	6			10		2		11													
17	1	2	3		5	6		8	9	10	7	4				11																
18	1		3		5	6		8	9	10	7	4				11	2															
19	1	2	3		5	6	7	8	9	10						11				4												
20	1	2	3		5		7	8	9			6			10	11				4												
21	1	2	3		5			8		9	7	6			10	11				4												
22	1		3			6		5	9	10		4				11	2			7	8											
23			3		5	6		8	9	10		4	1				2			7		11										
24	1	2	3		5	6		4	9						10					7	8	11										
25			3		5	6	7	8	9	10			1			11	2			4												
26			3		5		7	10	9	6			1			11	2			4	8											
27		2	3		5		7			10		6	1			11				4	8		9									
28		2	3				7	4	9			5	1			11					8			6	10							
29			3		5		7			9			1			11				4	8			6	10	2						
30			3							9						11				4	8			6			2	5	10	7		1
31			3																	4	8	11	7	6			2	5	9	10		1
Apps.	19	13	30	15	23	20	17	26	21	26	14	18	10	3	8	21	13	1	1	12	8	3	2	4	2	1	2	2	2	2		2
Goals				3	2	1	3	6	9	12	1				3	4		1			1											

Pos	P.	W.	D.	L.	F.	A.	Pts.
15th	30	8	4	18	46	68	20

Scottish Cup

Rd	Date	Opposition	H.T.	Res.	Att.	Goalscorers
1	27 Jan	CLYDE	2-0	2-1	6000	Crichton, Fairfoul
2	10 Feb	PORT GLASGOW ATH.	1-2	2-2	4000	J.Young(2)
2R	17	Port Glasgow Athletic	0-0	0-0	5000	
2R	24	Port Glasgow Athletic* +	0-0	0-0	6000	
2R	3 Mar	Port Glasgow Athletic*	0-1	0-1	5000	

Rd	W.Monteith	Duncan	Aitken	Banks	W.Shaw	McDonald	Maxwell	Fairfoul	A.Graham	J.Young	Morton	Crichton	R.Young	Grant	Galloway	Brown	Watson	Cameron	Bridges	Fullarton	Wishart	McLounie	McQueen	Black	Gibson	McKeown	NcCallum	Moffat	Drain	S.Graham	H.C.Shaw	H.Monteith
1	1		3		5	6		8	9	10		4					2			7		11										
2	1		3		5	6		8	9	10		4					2			7		11										
2R			3		5	6	7	8	9	10		4	1				2					11										
2R			3		5	6	7	8	9	10		4	1				2					11										
2R			3		5	6		8	9	10	11	4	1				2														7	

* Played at Cathkin Park + After Extra Time

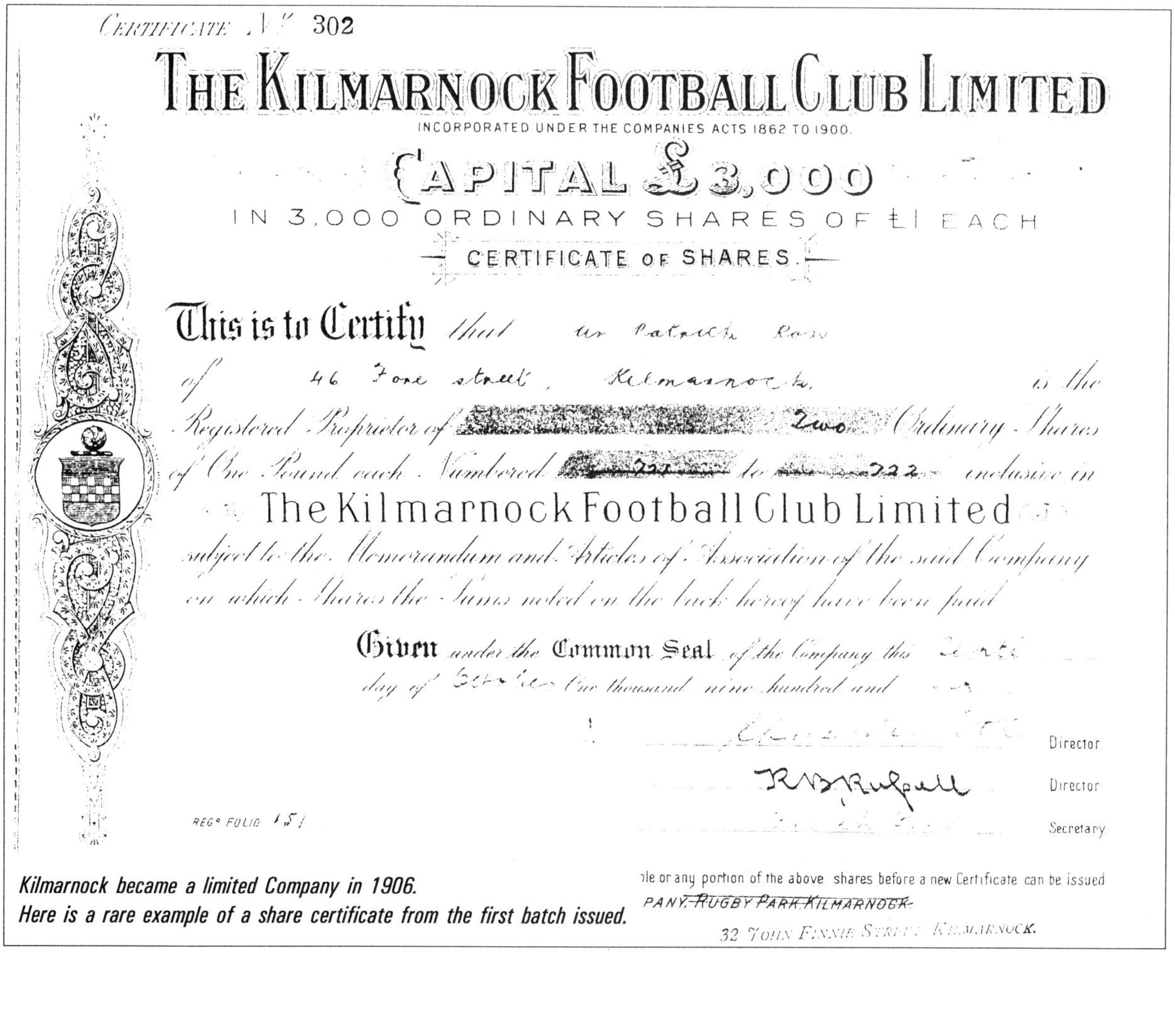
CERTIFICATE No. 302

THE KILMARNOCK FOOTBALL CLUB LIMITED

INCORPORATED UNDER THE COMPANIES ACTS 1862 TO 1900.

CAPITAL £3,000

IN 3,000 ORDINARY SHARES OF £1 EACH

CERTIFICATE OF SHARES.

This is to Certify that Mr Patrick Ross of 46 Fore street, Kilmarnock. is the Registered Proprietor of Two Ordinary Shares of One Pound each Numbered 221 to 222 inclusive in

The Kilmarnock Football Club Limited

subject to the Memorandum and Articles of Association of the said Company on which Shares the Sums noted on the back hereof have been paid

Given under the Common Seal of the Company this day of One thousand nine hundred and

Director

R. B. Russell Director

Secretary

REGd FOLIO 151

...ble or any portion of the above shares before a new Certificate can be issued

...PANY, RUGBY PARK, KILMARNOCK.

32 JOHN FINNIE STREET KILMARNOCK.

Kilmarnock became a limited Company in 1906.
Here is a rare example of a share certificate from the first batch issued.

SEASON 1906-07 Division One

No.	Date	Opposition	H.T.	Res.	Att.	Goalscorers
1	18 Aug	AIRDRIEONIANS	0-1	0-1	6000	
2	25	Celtic	0-3	0-5	14000	
3	1 Sep	PARTICK THISTLE	2-1	3-1	4000	Maxwell, Graham, Drain
4	8	CLYDE	0-2	1-2	3000	Shaw
5	15	Hibernian	0-1	0-1	5000	
6	22	HAMILTON A.	0-0	1-0	3500	Moffat
7	29	St. Mirren	0-0	0-3	4500	
8	6 Oct	Queens Park	0-0	1-1	3000	Maxwell
9	13	RANGERS	0-3	1-5	7000	Moffat
10	20	Port Glasgow Athletic	1-1	2-3	1500	Howie, Wishart
11	27	ABERDEEN	0-1	1-3	2500	Linward
12	3 Nov	Dundee	2-1	2-4	5000	Brown, Skillen
13	10	Motherwell	0-2	0-3	2500	
14	17	HEARTS	0-1	2-2	3000	Skillen(2)
15	24	FALKIRK	0-2	1-4	3000	Agnew
16	1 Dec	HIBERNIAN	1-2	1-3	4000	Linward
17	8	Third Lanark	0-1	1-2	1500	Barton
18	15	Morton	2-0	2-2	2500	Maxwell, Morton
19	22	Airdrieonians	0-1	0-1	1000	
20	29	CELTIC	0-2	2-2	5000	Drain, Maxwell
21	1 Jan	ST. MIRREN	1-0	1-0	6000	O.G.
22	5	Partick Thistle	0-2	0-3	3000	
23	12	THIRD LANARK	2-3	3-3	3000	Agnew(2), Drain
24	19	Aberdeen	0-0	0-3	4000	
25	9 Feb	Clyde	0-2	0-2	5000	
26	2 Mar	QUEENS PARK	2-0	3-1	3000	Barton, Howie, Livingstone
27	9	DUNDEE	1-2	1-3	4000	Maxwell
28	16	Hearts	0-1	0-1	2000	
29	23	MOTHERWELL	3-0	3-2	3000	Barton, Graham, Howie
30	30	Hamilton A.	2-0	2-0	2500	Graham, Howie
31	6 Apr	MORTON	1-0	3-0	2500	Agnew, Barton, Skillen
32	13	Falkirk	1-1	1-2	3000	Agnew
33	20	Rangers	0-1	0-3	2000	
34	27	PORT GLASGOW ATH.	0-0	2-1	4000	Morton, Skillen

No.	Monteith	McCallum	McKeown	Fullarton	Moffat	Black	Maxwell	Wishart	T.Brown	Graham	Linward	Williams	Crichton	Drain	Shaw	Agnew	Morton	Howie	Mitchell	W.Johnstone	Skillen	Anderson	R.Barton	Young	Neill	Livingstone	H.Wilson	A.Brown
1	1	2	3	4	5	6	7	8	9	10	11																	
2		2	3		5	6	7	8		10	11	1	4	9														
3	1	2	3	4	6		7	8		10	11			9	5													
4	1	3	2	4	6		7	8		10	11			9	5													
5	1	2		4	6		7	8		10	11				5	3	9											
6	1	2			9	6	7	8		10	11		4		5	3												
7	1	2		4		6	7			10	11			9	5	3		8										
8	1	2			5	6	7	8		9	11							10	3	4								
9	1	2			5	6	7	8		9	11							10	3	4								
10	1	2		4			7	8			11				5	3		10	6		9							
11	1	2					7			8	11		4		5	3		10	6		9							
12					5			8				1	6		4	3	7	10	2		9	5						11
13							7	8				1	6	10	4	3			2		9	5						11
14						6		8				1			4	3		10	2		9	5	7					11
15						6		8				1			4	3		10	2		9	5	7					11
16							8				11	1	6		4	3		10	2		9	5	7					
17		2					8				11	1	4			3	9	10	6			5	7					
18		2					8				11	1	4			3	9	10	6			5	7					
19		2					8				11		4	10		3	9		6			5	7	1				
20		2					8				11		4	10		3	9		6			5	7	1				
21		2					8				11		4	10		3	9		6			5	7	1				
22		2					9	8			11		4	10		3	7		6			5		1				
23							8			9				10	4	3	11		6			5	7	1	2			
24							8			9			6	10	4	3	7		2			5		1				11
25		2				6	7			8	11			10		3			4			5		1		9		
26		2				6								10	4		11	8	3			5	7	1		9		
27						6	8								4	3	11	10	2			5	7	1		9		
28							8						4				11	10	3			5	7	1	2	9		6
29		2								8					4	3	11	10	6			5	7	1		9		
30						6				9			4	10		3	11	8	2			5	7	1				
31						6				10					5	3	11	8	2	4	9		7	1				
32						6				10					4	3	11	8	2		9	5	7	1				
33						6								10	4	3	11	8	2		9	5	7	1				
34													6		4	3	11	8	2		9	5	7	1			10	
Apps.	10	20	4	6	9	15	24	14	1	17	19	8	16	15	21	26	19	20	27	3	11	22	18	16	2	5	1	6
Goals					2		5	1		3	2			3	1	5	2	4			5					1		1

Pos	P.	W.	D.	L.	F.	A.	Pts.
17th	34	8	5	21	40	72	21

Scottish Cup

No.	Date	Opposition	H.T.	Res.	Att.	Goalscorers
1	2 Feb*	CLACHNACUDDIN	3-0	4-0	3000	Drain, Graham, Maxwell, Morton
2	16	HEARTS	0-0	0-0	8000	
2R	23	Hearts	0-1	1-2	15000	Agnew

No.	Monteith	McCallum	McKeown	Fullarton	Moffat	Black	Maxwell	Wishart	T.Brown	Graham	Linward	Williams	Crichton	Drain	Shaw	Agnew	Morton	Howie	Mitchell	W.Johnstone	Skillen	Anderson	R.Barton	Young	Neill	Livingstone	H.Wilson	A.Brown
1		2				6	8			9	11			10		3	7			4		5		1				
2						6	7	8					4	10		3	11		2			5		1		9		
2R						6	7	8					4	10		3	11		2			5		1		9		

* Originally scheduled for 26/1. Ground declaired unsafe but a friendly took place, Kilmarnock winning 1-0. Scorer: Linward.

The Kilmarnock team which faced St. Mirren away on September 29th 1906.
Back: G.Fullarton, W.Shaw, F.Frew(Secretary), D.McCallum, W.Agnew
Middle: J.Maxwell, D.Howie, H.Monteith, S.Graham, W.Linward
Front: T.Drain, H.Black
In a transitional season, not a single player who lined up for the first League match also played in the last.

SEASON 1907-08 Division One

No.	Date	Opposition	H.T.	Res.	Att.	Goalscorers
1	17 Aug	Hearts	0-1	0-1	9000	
2	24	THIRD LANARK	1-1	2-2	5500	Howie, Skillen
3	31	Partick Thistle	0-2	2-2	3000	Morton, Skillen
4	7 Sep	Rangers	0-0	0-1	14000	
5	14	CELTIC	0-0	0-0	15000	
6	21	Queens Park	1-1	1-1	8000	H.Wilson
7	28	CLYDE	0-1	2-2	5000	Livingstone(2)
8	5 Oct	Aberdeen	0-1	0-1	7000	
9	12	MORTON	1-1	1-2	4500	Howie
10	19	Hibernian	0-2	1-3	3500	Agnew
11	26	FALKIRK	0-3	1-6	7000	Agnew
12	2 Nov	Motherwell	0-0	2-1	4500	A.Armour, Barton
13	9	PORT GLASGOW ATH.	1-0	1-1	4200	H.Wilson
14	16	AIRDRIEONIANS	0-0	0-1	4000	
15	23	Dundee	0-2	0-4		
16	30	Clyde	0-0	0-0	2800	
17	7 Dec	HAMILTON A.	1-0	2-0	3500	Howie, Templeton
18	14	HIBERNIAN	2-0	3-0	4500	H.Wilson, Templeton(2)
19	21	Celtic	1-1	1-4	9000	A.Armour
20	28	MOTHERWELL	0-0	2-0	3500	A.Armour, Templeton
21	1 Jan	ST. MIRREN	1-2	2-2	6500	Agnew, Templeton
22	2	Falkirk	0-3	0-5	7500	
23	4*	Port Glasgow Athletic	1-2	1-4		Howie
24	11	PARTICK THISTLE	0-0	0-1	6000	
25	18	St. Mirren	0-0	0-0	5000	
26	1 Feb	HEARTS	0-0	2-0	5000	Barton, Walker
27	15	QUEENS PARK	1-1	2-2	6000	Agnew, Templeton
28	29	ABERDEEN	0-0	1-0	6500	Templeton
29	7 Mar	RANGERS	0-1	0-2	8000	
30	14	Airdrieonians	0-0	0-1	3000	
31	21	DUNDEE	0-1	1-1	5500	Hunter
32	4 Apr	Hamilton A.	3-2	3-3	3000	A.Armour, Crichton, T.Findlay
33	22	Morton	0-0	2-2	2000	Agnew, Barton
34	25	Third Lanark	2-4	3-6	3000	Hunter(3)

No.	R.Young	Mitchell	Agnew	A.Wilson	Anderson	Shaw	Barton	Howie	Skillen	H.Wilson	Morton	Walker	Nisbet	Livingstone	Strachan	McAllister	Allison	Templeton	A.Armour	McCallum	Halley	Doolan	J.Young	Crichton	Hunter	T.Findlay	Neilson	Johnstone	Murray
1	1	2	3	4	5	6	7	8	9	10	11																		
2	1	2	3	4	5	6	7	8	9	10	11																		
3	1	2	3	4	5		7	8	9	10	11	6																	
4	1	2	3	4	5	6	7	8		10	9		11																
5	1	2	3	4	5	6	7	8	9	10	11																		
6	1	2	3	4	5	6	7	8	9	10	11																		
7	1	2	3		5	6	7	8		10	11	4		9															
8	1	2	3	4	5	6	7	8	9	10	11																		
9	1	2	3	4	5	6	7	8		10	11	9																	
10		2	3	4	5	6		9		10					1	7	8	11											
11		2	3	4		5		8		10	9		7		1			11									6		
12		2	3	4		6	7	8		10		5			1			11	9										
13		2	3			6	7	4		10	11	5			1		8		9										
14		4	3	6			7	8		10	11	5			1				9	2									
15		2	3	4		6	7	8		10	9	5			1			11											
16		2	3	4		6		8		10	11	5		9	1						7								
17		2	3	4		6		8		10		5			1			11	9		7								
18		6	3	4				8		10		5			1			11	9	2	7								
19		2	3	4		6		8		10		5			1			11	9		7								
20		2	3	4		6		8		10		5			1			11	9		7								
21		2	3	4		6		8		10		5			1			11	9		7								
22		2	3	4	5	6	10	8							1			11	9		7								
23		2		10	5	6*	7"	8				4																	
24	1	6	2	4	5		10	8						9				11			7	3							
25	1	2	3	10	5	6	7	8				4						11	9										
26	1	2	3		5	6	10	8				4				7		11			9								
27	1	2	3	4	5		10	8				6				7		11	9										
28	1	2		8	5							6				7		11	9			3	10					4	
29	1	2		4	5			8				6				7		11	10	3			9						
30	1			4	5	6	7	8											10		11		9	3					2
31	1	2	3	4	5	6		8								7			10		11				9				
32	1	2	3		5			8				6						11	7					4	9	10			
33	1	2	3		5	6	8	4								7		11							9	10			
34	1	2	3		5	6	8	4										11	7						9	10			
Apps.	20	33	30	28	23	26	22	33	6	21	14	20	2	3	13	7	2	19	17	3	11	2	3	2	4	3	1	1	1
Goals			5				3	4	2	3	1	1		2				7	4					1	4	1			

* Kilmarnock fielded only seven players.

Pos	P.	W.	D.	L.	F.	A.	Pts.
15th	34	6	13	15	38	61	25

* No.1 for first 45 minutes

" No.1 for second 45 minutes

Scottish Cup

1	23 Jan	HAMILTON A.	1-1	2-1	4000	A.Wilson, Shaw
2	8 Feb	DUNBLANE	3-0	3-0	4000	A.Wilson, Templeton, Walker
QF	22	Hibernian	1-0	1-0	11000	McAllister
SF	28 Mar	ST. MIRREN	0-0	0-0	15000	
SFR	11 Apr	St. Mirren	0-1	0-2	20000	

Round	R.Young	Mitchell	Agnew	A.Wilson	Anderson	Shaw	Barton	Howie	Skillen	H.Wilson	Morton	Walker	Nisbet	Livingstone	Strachan	McAllister	Allison	Templeton	A.Armour	McCallum	Halley	Doolan	J.Young	Crichton	Hunter	T.Findlay	Neilson	Johnstone	Murray
1	1	2	3	10	5	6	7	8				4						11	9										
2	1	2	3	10	5	6	9	8				4				7		11											
QF	1	2	3	4	5			8				6				7		11	10				9						
SF	1	2	3		5	6		8				4				7		11							9	10			
SFR	1	2	3	4	5			8				6						11	7						9	10			

Geordie Anderson

Nearing the end of his magnificent career, Geordie was awarded a benefit match in 1908.

SEASON 1908-09 Division One

No.	Date	Opposition	H.T.	Res.	Att.	Goalscorers
1	15 Aug	PARTICK THISTLE	1-0	4-1	5000	D.Armour, Barton, Boyd, Templeton
2	19	Clyde	2-2	2-5	5000	D.Armour, Barton
3	22	Celtic	0-4	1-5	11000	D.Armour
4	29	AIRDRIEONIANS	0-1	0-1	4000	
5	5 Sep	Hamilton A.	0-0	0-0	2500	
6	12	RANGERS	0-2	0-5	9000	
7	19	MOTHERWELL	1-0	4-1	3500	Mitchell(2), Halley, Young
8	26	Aberdeen	0-1	0-2	7000	
9	3 Oct	St. Mirren	0-3	0-3		
10	10	Hearts	0-0	0-0	7500	
11	17	FALKIRK	2-0	3-1	4800	Douglas(2), Howie
12	24	QUEENS PARK	1-0	1-1	6300	Douglas
13	31	PORT GLASGOW ATH.	0-0	1-0	3800	A.Ramsay
14	7 Nov	CLYDE	2-0	2-1	5800	Douglas, A.Ramsay
15	14	Dundee	0-2	0-5	8000	
16	21	HIBERNIAN	0-0	0-1	3500	
17	28	THIRD LANARK	3-1	4-2	3800	Howie, Mitchell, D.Armour, Douglas
18	12 Dec	MORTON	0-0	2-1	3500	Douglas, A.Ramsay
19	19	Rangers	1-1	1-1	8000	A.Ramsay
20	26	DUNDEE	2-0	2-0	5500	Howie, Templeton
21	1 Jan	ST. MIRREN	1-0	1-1	8500	A.Ramsay
22	2	CELTIC	1-0	3-1	13000	Douglas, Howie, Mitchell
23	4	Third Lanark	0-1	0-4	11500	
24	9	Hibernian	1-1	1-2	5500	O.G.
25	6 Feb	Morton	0-0	1-1	3000	Bulloch
26	13	Airdrieonians	0-0	1-1	4000	McDermott
27	20	HEARTS	1-3	2-5	5500	Douglas, McDermott
28	27	Partick Thistle*	0-0	1-0	2900	Halley
29	6 Mar	Queens Park	2-0	2-0	2500	Douglas, Barrie
30	13	ABERDEEN	3-2	3-2	4000	Douglas, Howie, Templeton
31	20	HAMILTON A.	1-1	3-1	3300	Douglas(2), A.Ramsay
32	27	Motherwell	0-0	1-2		Bulloch
33	3 Apr	Falkirk	1-2	1-3		Glass
34	17	Port Glasgow Athletic	0-0	0-2		

No.	Aitken	D.Armour	Mitchell	Howie	Barrie	Shaw	A.Armour	A.Ramsay	Barton	Boyd	Templeton	Halley	Black	Douglas	Young	Gray	Crichton	Glass	McAllister	Kirkcaldy	Anderson	Stevenson	Bulloch	McDermott
1	1	2	3	4	5	6	7	8	9	10	11													
2	1	2	3	4	5	6	7	8	9	10	11													
3	1	2	3	8	5	6	7		9	10	11	4												
4	1	2	3	4	5			8	7	10	11		6	9										
5	1	2	3	10	5	6	8		7		11	4		9										
6	1	2	3	8	5	6	9				7	4			10	11								
7	1	2	3	10	5	6	7				11	4		9	8									
8	1	2	3	10	5		7			6	11	4		9	8									
9	1	2		10	5	6	7	8			11	4		9			3							
10	1	2	3	10	5		7	8			11	4		9				6						
11	1	3		10	5		7	8			11	4		9			2	6						
12	1	2	3	10	5		7	8				4		9		11		6						
13	1	2	3	10	5		7	8				4		9		11		6						
14	1	2	3	10	5		7	8			11	4		9				6						
15	1	3	2	10	5			8			11	4		9				6	7					
16	1	2	3	10	5		7	8			11	4		9				6						
17	1	2	3	10	5		7	8			11			9				6		4				
18	1	2	3	10	5		7	8			11			9				4		6				
19	1	2	3	10	5		7	8			11			9			4	6						
20	1	2	3	10	5		7	8			11	4		9				6						
21	1	2	3	10	5		7	8			11	4		9				6						
22	1	2	3	10	5		7	8				4		9		11		6						
23	1	2		10				8				4		9		11	3	6	7		5			
24	1	2	3	10	5		7	8				4		9		11		6						
25		2	3		5		7	8			11	4						6				1	9	10
26	1	2	3	5			7	8			11	4						6					9	10
27	1	2	3	5			7	8			11	4		9				6						10
28	1	2		10	5		8				11	4		9			3	6	7					
29	1	2	3	10	5		7	8			11	4		9				6						
30	1	2	3	10	5		7	8			11	4		9				6						
31	1	2	3	10	5		7	8			11	4		9				6						
32	1	2	3	10	5		8				11	4						6	7				9	
33	1	2	3	10	5	4	7				11	9						8					6	
34	1	2	3		5	6		8			11	4						10	7				9	
Apps.	33	34	30	32	31	9	30	26	5	5	29	28	1	25	3	6	5	25	5	2	1	1	5	3
Goals			4	5	1		4	6	2	1	3	2		12	1			1					2	2

* Played at Rugby Park

Pos	P.	W.	D.	L.	F.	A.	Pts.
10th	34	13	7	14	47	61	33

Scottish Cup

No.	Date	Opposition	H.T.	Res.	Att.	Goalscorers
1	23 Jan	Hearts	0-1	1-2	18000	Howie

No.	Aitken	D.Armour	Mitchell	Howie	Barrie	Shaw	A.Armour	A.Ramsay	Barton	Boyd	Templeton	Halley	Black	Douglas	Young	Gray	Crichton	Glass	McAllister	Kirkcaldy	Anderson	Stevenson	Bulloch	McDermott
1	1	2	3	10	5		7	8			11	4		9									6	

The team that played Airdrieonians at Rugby Park on August 29th 1908.
Back: P.Carrick (Trainer), W.B.Grieve (Secretary), A.Douglas, R.Barton, A.Armour, R.Aitken, R.Ramsay, J.Boyd, J.McDonald (Treasurer)
Front: D.Howie, J.Mitchell, A.Barrie (Captain), W.Black, R.Templeton

SEASON 1909-10 Division One

No.	Date	Opposition	H.T.	Res.	Att.	Goalscorers
1	16 Aug	Rangers	0-1	0-3	12000	
2	21	St. Mirren	0-2	1-2	6000	Barrie
3	28	AIRDRIEONIANS	2-1	3-3	5000	Cunningham(2), Chalmers
4	4 Sep	Third Lanark	0-5	0-7	6000	
5	11	QUEENS PARK	2-1	6-1	5000	Ramsay(3),A.Armour,Cunningham,Hastie
6	18	Hibernian	0-2	1-2	4000	Hastie
7	25	HAMILTON A.	1-0	1-0	4000	Douglas
8	2 Oct	Hearts	0-2	0-3	5000	
9	9	MOTHERWELL	2-0	2-1	4000	Cunningham(2)
10	16	Dundee	0-1	2-2	7500	Cunningham(2)
11	23	RANGERS	0-0	0-2	9500	
12	30	Port Glasgow Athletic	0-1	1-1	3000	A.Armour
13	6 Nov	CLYDE	2-1	6-3	4000	Cunningham(2),Halley(2),Barrie,Anderson
14	13	Falkirk	0-2	0-4	7000	
15	20	HIBERNIAN	1-0	4-0	5000	A.Armour, Cunningham, Howie, Ramsay
16	27	Airdrieonians	1-0	2-2		Halley, Ramsay
17	4 Dec	Celtic	1-1	1-2	6000	Howie
18	11	MORTON	0-0	2-0	2000	A.Armour, Howie
19	25	CELTIC	0-1	0-1	10000	
20	1 Jan	ST. MIRREN	1-0	2-1	10500	Cunningham, Howie
21	3	Motherwell	1-2	1-3	6000	Cunningham
22	8	Partick Thistle	0-1	0-3	5000	
23	15	THIRD LANARK	0-0	0-0	3000	
24	12 Feb	Hamilton A.	3-1	7-1	3000	Cunningham(3), Howie(2), McAllister(2)
25	19	PARTICK THISTLE	1-1	2-1	4000	Anderson, Cunningham
26	26	ABERDEEN	0-1	0-2	4000	
27	5 Mar	Morton	0-2	0-4	4000	
28	12	PORT GLASGOW A.	1-0	4-0	3000	Howie(2), Hastie, McAllister
29	19	FALKIRK	0-1	0-2	3000	
30	26	Aberdeen	1-0	1-0	6000	Howie
31	2 Apr	Clyde	0-0	0-0	2000	
32	9	Queens Park	1-0	1-1	3000	Howie
33	26	DUNDEE	1-1	2-1	3000	Howie, Cunningham
34	30	HEARTS	0-1	1-1	4000	Cunningham

No.	Aitken	D.Armour	Mitchell	Glass	Barrie	R.Anderson	A.Armour	Ramsay	Douglas	Cunningham	Gray	Howie	Templeton	Halley	Chalmers	Stevenson	Kirkwood	Hastie	Glover	McNeill	"Mack"	Ewing	Doolan	McAllister	Allan	Neilson
1	1	2	3	4	5	6	7	8	9	10	11															
2	1	2	3	4	5	6	7	8	9			10	11													
3	1	2	3		5	6	7			10		8	11	4	9											
4	1	2	3		5	6	7			10		8	11	4	9											
5			3	6	5		7	8		9			11	4		1	2	10								
6			3	6	5		7	8	9				11	4		1	2	10								
7			3	6	5		7	8	9				11	4		1	2	10								
8			3		5	6	7	8				9	11	4		1	2	10								
9			3	6			7	8		9		5	11	4		1	2	10								
10	1		3	6	5		7			9		8	11	4			2	10								
11	1		3		5	6	7			9		8	11	4			2	10								
12	1		3		5	6	7					10	11	4	9		2	8								
13	1	2	3		5	6	7	8		9		10	11	4												
14	1		3		5	6	7	8				9	11	4			2	10								
15	1		3		5	6	7	8		9		10	11	4			2									
16	1		3		5	6	7	8				4	11	9			2	10								
17	1		3		5	6	7			9		8	11	4			2	10								
18	1		3		5	6	7			9		8	11	4			2	10								
19	1		3		5	6	7	8		9		10		4	11		2									
20			3		5	6	7			9		10		4	11		2	8	1							
21			3		5	6	7	8		9		10		4	11	1	2									
22	1		3		5	6		8						4	11		2	10		9	7					
23	1	2	3		5	6				9		10		4	11						8	7				
24			2		5	6				9		8		4				10	1		11		3	7		
25			2		5	6				9		8	11	4				10	1				3	7		
26		2	3	4	5	6	7			9		8						10	1					11		
27		2		4	5	6				9		8	11					10	1				3	7		
28		2	3		5	6				9		8	11					10	1			4		7		
29		2				6		8		9		5		4	11		3	10	1					7		
30			3		5	6						10	11	4	8		2		1					7	9	
31			3		5	6	9					10		4	8		2		1					7		11
32			3		5	6	7			9		8	11	4			2	10	1							
33			3		5	6				9		8	11	4	7		2	10	1							
34			3			6				9		8	11	4	5		2	10	1					7		
Apps.	16	10	32	9	31	29	24	15	4	24	1	29	24	29	13	6	23	23	12	1	3	2	3	9	1	1
Goals					2	2	4	5	1	18		11		3	1			3						3		

Pos	P.	W.	D.	L.	F.	A.	Pts.
11th	34	12	8	14	53	59	32

Scottish Cup

No.	Date	Opposition	H.T.	Res.	Att.	Goalscorers
1	22 Jan	THIRD LANARK	0-0	0-0	8500	
1R	5 Feb*	Third Lanark	0-1	0-2	6000	

No.	Aitken	D.Armour	Mitchell	Glass	Barrie	R.Anderson	A.Armour	Ramsay	Douglas	Cunningham	Gray	Howie	Templeton	Halley	Chalmers	Stevenson	Kirkwood	Hastie	Glover	McNeill	"Mack"	Ewing	Doolan	McAllister	Allan	Neilson
1	1		3		5	6	7	8		9		10		4			2							11		
1R			3		5	6	7			9		8		4			2	10	1		11					

* Scheduled for 29/1. Owing to poor weather, the game was played as a friendly. Thirds won 6-1, Hastie scored for Killie.

The players line up in positional order for this home match with Hamilton on September 25th 1909.
C.Thomas (Trainer), Stevenson, Kirkwood, Mitchell, Halley, Barrie, Glass, Armour, Ramsay, Douglas, Hastie, Templeton

SEASON 1910-11 Division One

No.	Date	Opposition	H.T.	Res.	Att.	Goalscorers	Rennie	Kirkwood	Mitchell	Allan	Barrie	Anderson	A.Armour	Gilchrist	Cunningham	Howie	Templeton	Chalmers	Johnstone	Glover	Halley	Cameron	Train	Gray	Shortt	Dunlop	Doolan	Burnett
1	15 Aug	Clyde	0-0	0-0	10000		1	2	3	4	5	6	7	8	9	10	11											
2	20	AIRDRIEONIANS	0-1	0-1	6000		1	2	3	4	5	6	7	8	9		11	10										
3	27	St. Mirren	0-0	1-1	6500	Mitchell	1	2	3	9	5	6	7	8	10		11		4									
4	3 Sep	CELTIC	1-0	1-0	8500	Gilchrist	1	2	3		5	6	7	9	10	8	11		4									
5	10	Morton	0-0	0-0	6000		1	2	3		5	6	7	9	10	8	11		4									
6	17	HEARTS	2-0	3-1	7500	Allan(2), Cunningham	1	2	3	9	5	6	7		10	8	11		4									
7	24	Partick Thistle	0-0	0-1	5500		1	2	3	9	5	6	7		10	8	11		4									
8	1 Oct	THIRD LANARK	1-2	1-5		Gilchrist	1	2	3		5	6	7	9	10	8	11		4									
9	8	Dundee	1-1	1-2		Gilchrist		2	3		5	6	7	9	10	8	11			1	4							
10	15	ABERDEEN	0-1	0-1	7000		1	2	3		5	6	7	9		8	11	10			4							
11	22	MOTHERWELL	1-0	1-0	3000	Cunningham	1	2	3		5	6	7	8	9	10	11				4							
12	29	Falkirk	0-1	2-2		Howie, Mitchell	1	2	3		5	6	7	8	9	10	11				4							
13	5 Nov	HAMILTON A.	1-0	3-0	4000	Cunningham(2), Howie	1	2	3		5	6	7	8	9	10	11				4							
14	12	Rangers	0-1	0-3	6000		1	2	3		5	6	7		9	10	11				4	8						
15	19	CLYDE	1-0	5-2	6000	Howie(3), Anderson, Cunningham	1	2	3		5	6	7	8	9	10	11				4							
16	26	Hibernian	0-0	1-0	4000	Gilchrist	1	2	3			6	7	8	9	10	11				4		5					
17	3 Dec	DUNDEE	1-0	2-0	7000	Allan, Cunningham	1	2	3	9	5	6	7	8	10		11				4							
18	10	Raith Rovers	1-0	1-1	5000	Allan	1	2	3	9	5	6	7	8			11				4			10				
19	17	Celtic	0-2	0-2	6000		1	2	3		5	6	7	8	9	10	11				4							
20	24	QUEENS PARK	1-1	2-1	2000	Cunningham, Gray	1	2	3			6	7	8	9	10					4		5	11				
21	31	RANGERS	0-2	0-2	12000		1	2	3		5	6	7	8	9	10	11				4							
22	2 Jan	ST. MIRREN	2-0	2-2	9000	Barrie, Cunningham	1	2	3	9	5	6			10		11	7			4	8						
23	7	Airdrieonians	1-1	1-3		Shortt	1	2	3	9	5	6				10	11	7			4				8			
24	14	HIBERNIAN	2-1	3-1	3200	Cunningham, Gilchrist, Halley	1	2	3		5	6		7	9	10	11				4				8			
25	21	Third Lanark	1-0	2-0		Cunningham, Howie	1	2	3		5	6	7	8	9	10	11				4							
26	4 Feb	MORTON	1-1	2-3	4000	Cunningham, Dunlop	1	2	3		5	6	7		10		11				4				8	9		
27	11	Hearts	0-1	0-5	6000			2	3		5		7	10			11				4		6		8	9		1
28	18	Aberdeen	1-0	1-1	10000	Cunningham	1	2	3		5		7	8	9	10	11				4		6					
29	25	Queens Park	0-1	1-1	4000	Cunningham	1	2	3		5	6	7	8	9	10	11						4					
30	4 Mar	PARTICK THISTLE	0-0	1-1	3000	Barrie	1	2	3		5	6	7	8	9	10	11						4					
31	25	RAITH ROVERS	0-0	1-0	3000	Howie	1	2			5	6	7	8	9	10	11				4						3	
32	1 Apr	Motherwell	0-1	0-1			1	2	3		5	6	7	8		10	11				4				9			
33	8	FALKIRK	1-1	2-2	4000	Barrie, Cunningham	1	2	3		5	6			9	10	11				7		4		8			
34	10	Hamilton A.	1-0	2-0	2000	Allan, Howie	1	2	3	9	5	6			10	8	11				7		4					
						Apps.	32	34	33	10	32	32	29	26	29	27	33	4	6	1	24	2	8	2	6	2	1	1
						Goals			2	5	3	1		5	14	8					1			1	1	1		

Pos	P.	W.	D.	L.	F.	A.	Pts.
10th	34	12	10	12	42	45	34

Scottish Cup

No.	Date	Opposition	H.T.	Res.	Att.	Goalscorers	Rennie	Kirkwood	Mitchell	Allan	Barrie	Anderson	A.Armour	Gilchrist	Cunningham	Howie	Templeton	Chalmers	Johnstone	Glover	Halley	Cameron	Train	Gray	Shortt	Dunlop	Doolan	Burnett
1	28 Jan	Rangers	0-1	1-2	40000	A.Armour	1	2	3		5	6	7	8	9	10	11				4							

The famous Mattha' Short who made his debut at Airdrie in January 1911.

SEASON 1911-12 Division One

No.	Date	Opposition	H.T.	Res.	Att.	Goalscorers	Smart	Kirkwood	Mitchell	Steel	Barrie	Anderson	Armour	J.Cunningham	Mackay	A.Cunningham	Templeton	Thomson	Shortt	Train	Clark	Orr	Allan	Carson	Johnstone	Hannigan	Hastie	Lynch	Wilkinson	Davidson	Burnett	W.Cunningham	Dunlop	Wilson	Logan	Ballantyne	Buchan	Gray	Culley	Blair	Watson	McBean
1	16 Aug	Clyde	0-1	1-3	6000	J.Cunningham	1	2	3	4	5	6	7	8	9	10	11																									
2	19	Airdrieonians	0-1	0-1	3500		1		3	4	5	6		8	9	10	11	2	7																							
3	26	St. Mirren	0-0	4-2	7000	J+A Cunningham, Clark(2)	1		3		5	6		8		9	11	2	10	4	7																					
4	2 Sep	Third Lanark	0-1	0-2	6000		1		3		5	6		8		9	11	2	10	4	7																					
5	9	HAMILTON A.	1-2	2-3	5500	A.Cunningham, Templeton	1	2			5	6	7	8		9	11	3	10	4																						
6	16	Hearts	0-0	1-1	10000	A.Cunningham	1	2	3		5		7	8		9	11		10			4	6																			
7	23	CELTIC	0-1	0-2	6000		1	2	3		5		7	8		9	11		10			4	6																			
8	30	Aberdeen	1-0	2-1	4000	J.Cunningham, Carson		2	3		5		7	8			11		1		10	4	6	9																		
9	7 Oct	RAITH ROVERS	2-1	3-1	4000	Armour, J.Cunningham(2)	1	2	3		5		7	8		10	11					4	6	9																		
10	14	Morton	0-1	0-2	7000		1	2	3		5		7	8		10	11					6	4	9																		
11	21	QUEENS PARK	1-0	1-2	3200	A.Cunningham	1	2	3		5		7	8		9	11		10			4	6																			
12	28	Motherwell	0-0	1-0		A.Cunningham	1	2	3		5		7	10		9	11		8				6		4																	
13	4 Nov	PARTICK THISTLE	0-1	0-1	4000		1	2	3		5			10		9	11		8		7		6		4																	
14	11	Raith Rovers	0-2	2-3	5200	Kirkwood, Hannigan	1	2	3		5	6		8			11		10				4	9		7																
15	18	HEARTS	0-1	1-3	4500	A.Cunningham	1	2	3	5		6	7	8		10	11						4	9																		
16	25	DUNDEE	1-0	1-0	4500	A.Cunningham	1	2	3				7			10	11					4	6	9	5		8															
17	2 Dec	Hibernian	0-0	1-0	4500	J.Cunningham	1	2	3				7	9		10	11					4	6		5		8															
18	9	THIRD LANARK	0-0	0-0	3000		1	2	3		4		7	9		10	11						6		5		8															
19	16	FALKIRK	0-0	1-0	5000	A.Cunningham	1	2	3		4			9		10	11								5		8	6	7													
20	23	CLYDE	0-1	1-3	4500	A.Cunningham	1	2	3		4			9		10	11								5		8	6	7													
21	30	Rangers	1-5	1-6		A.Cunningham	1	2			5	6		8		10	11					4		9					7	3												
22	1 Jan	ST. MIRREN	1-1	1-1	9000	Wilkinson		3			5	6		9		10	11		8			4							7		1	2										
23	6	AIRDRIEONIANS	1-0	2-1	4000	A.Cunningham, Clark		3			5	6		11		10					9	4					8		7		1	2										
24	13	Hamilton A.	0-0	0-4	4000			3			5	6		11							9						8	4	7		1	2	10									
25	20	HIBERNIAN	0-2	1-2	4000	A.Cunningham					5	6		8		10	11						4						7		1	2		2	9							
26	3 Feb	Queens Park	0-1	0-1			1		3		5	6		11		10	7				9				4							2			8							
27	2 Mar	Partick Thistle	1-1	1-3	8000	A.Cunningham	1	2	3		5	6				9	11		4					10											8	7						
28	9	MOTHERWELL	1-0	1-1	3500	A.Cunningham	1	2	3		5	6				9	11		4					10											8	7						
29	16	MORTON	0-0	1-0	3000	Ballantyne		2	3							10			4		9		6				8				1					7	5	11				
30	23	Dundee	1-5	2-5		Logan(2)		2	3			6							4								8				1		10		9	7	5	11				
31	30	RANGERS	2-1	3-2	4000	Logan, Shortt, O.G.		2	3			6					11		4								8				1				10	7	5		9			
32	6 Apr	Falkirk	0-1	0-2	6000			2	3							6	11		4								8		7		1				10		5		9			
33	13	Celtic	0-1	0-2	2500				3		5	6				10	11		4													2			8	7			9	1		
34	27	ABERDEEN	2-0	3-0	4000	Logan(2), Shortt		2	3		5					10	11		4																8		6		9	1	7	
						Apps.	23	28	28	3	27	18	13	25	2	29	30	4	20	3	8	11	15	9	8	1	11	3	8	1	8	6	2	1	9	6	5	2	4	2	1	
						Goals		1					1	6		14	1		2		3			1		1			1						5	1						

Pos	P.	W.	D.	L.	F.	A.	Pts.
16th	34	11	4	19	38	60	26

Scottish Cup

No.	Date	Opposition	H.T.	Res.	Att.	Goalscorers	Smart	Kirkwood	Mitchell	Steel	Barrie	Anderson	Armour	J.Cunningham	Mackay	A.Cunningham	Templeton	Thomson	Shortt	Train	Clark	Orr	Allan	Carson	Johnstone	Hannigan	Hastie	Lynch	Wilkinson	Davidson	Burnett	W.Cunningham	Dunlop	Wilson	Logan	Ballantyne	Buchan	Gray	Culley	Blair	Watson	McBean
1	27 Jan	HAMILTON A.	1-0	1-0	10000	A.Cunningham		2			5	6		11		10	7				9				4						1				8							3
2	10 Feb	Leith Athletic	1-0	2-0	6000	A.Cunningham(2)		2	3			6				10	11			5	9				4				7		1				8							
QF	24	CLYDE	0-2	1-6	19564	Logan		2	3			6		9		10	11			5					4						1				8	7						

Robert B. Russell

In the 'Portrait Gallery' of players and officials produced by the 'Kilmarnock Standard' this year, it was stated that "For the past thirty years there has been no better-known football enthusiast in Kilmarnock and district than The Cutler". The legendary veteran would continue to be associated with Killie for nearly another thirty years!

SEASON 1912-13 Division One

No.	Date	Opposition	H.T.	Res.	Att.	Goalscorers
1	17 Aug	PARTICK THISTLE	2-0	2-1	6000	Culley(2)
2	24	St. Mirren	0-2	0-4	10000	
3	31	CELTIC	0-1	0-2	9000	
4	7 Sep	Hamilton A.	1-1	1-3	4000	Watson
5	14	MORTON	1-1	1-1	6000	Armstrong
6	21	THIRD LANARK	0-0	2-0	5000	Armstrong, Kirsop
7	28	Raith Rovers	0-0	0-0	4000	
8	30	Rangers	0-2	0-3	14000	
9	5 Oct	DUNDEE	0-0	2-0	4000	A.Cunningham, Duff
10	12	Clyde	0-0	0-0	4000	
11	19	AIRDRIEONIANS	0-0	0-1	4050	
12	26	Hearts	0-3	0-5	10000	
13	2 Nov	QUEENS PARK	0-0	2-1	4000	Culley, Watson
14	9	Aberdeen	0-0	0-0	7000	
15	16	HIBERNIAN	0-1	0-1		
16	23	Falkirk	0-0	0-0	3000	
17	30	Partick Thistle	0-2	1-4	5000	Logan
18	7 Dec	Airdrieonians	0-3	2-3		A.Cunningham, Duff
19	14	MOTHERWELL	0-0	0-1	6000	
20	21	Third Lanark	0-0	0-0	2000	
21	28	HEARTS	0-0	2-2	4000	A.Cunningham, Duff
22	1 Jan	ST. MIRREN	1-1	2-1	10000	A.Cunningham, Dickie
23	4	Morton	2-1	3-1	7000	Culley, Dickie(2)
24	11	CLYDE	1-1	3-2	4000	A.Cunningham, Dickie
25	18	HAMILTON A.	1-1	1-1	5000	Duff
26	1 Feb	Dundee	0-0	0-0	5000	
27	1 Mar	RANGERS	1-2	2-3	6000	A.Cunningham, Maxwell
28	8	ABERDEEN	2-0	3-1	3000	Culley, A.Cunningham, Templeton
29	15	RAITH ROVERS	1-3	4-3	4000	Dickie(2), Culley, A.Cunningham
30	22	Queens Park	1-1	1-1	6000	Duff
31	29	Celtic	1-1	1-4	8000	A.Cunningham
32	12 Apr	Motherwell	0-0	1-0	4000	A.Cunningham
33	19	Hibernian	0-1	0-4	4000	
34	30	FALKIRK	1-1	1-1	3000	O.G.

No.	Blair	Mitchell	Trialist	Brown	Aitken	Duff	Buchan	Kirsop	Logan	Culley	A.Cunningham	Templeton	Kirkwood	Watson	Shortt	W.Cunningham	Law	Dickie	Armstrong	Goodwin	Bond	Clark	Steel	Maxwell	Murray	McKay	Burnett	Neil	Trialist
1	1	2		3	4	5	6	7	8	9	10	11																	
2	1	3			4	5	6		8	9	10	11	2	7															
3	1	3			5		6		8	9	10	11	2	7	4														
4	1	3			5		6		8	9	10			7	4	2	11												
5	1	3					6	7		9	10				4	2	11	5	8										
6	1	3					5	7		9	10	11			4	2		6	8										
7	1	3					5	7	8	9	10	11			4	2		6											
8	1	3					5	7	8	9	10	11			4	2		6											
9	1	3				5			8	9	10	11		7	4	2		6											
10	1	3				5			8	9	10	11		7	4	2		6											
11	1	3				5			8	9	10	11		7	4	2		6											
12	1	3					5		8	9	10	11		7	4	2		6											
13	1	3				5	6			9	10	11		7	4	2				8									
14	1	3				5	6			10	9	11	2		4					8	7								
15	1					5	6	7		10	9	11	3		4	2				8									
16	1	3			4	5	10	7	9			11	2					6		8									
17	1	3			4	5		7	9		10	11	2					6		8									
18	1	3				5		7	9		10	11	2		4			6		8									
19	1	3				5				9	10	11	2	7	4					8		6							
20	1	3			4	5			9		10	11	2		7			6		8									
21	1	3				6					9	11	2		4			10		8			5	7					
22	1	3			6	5					9	11			4	2		10		8				7					
23	1	3				5				9		11			4	2		10		8			6	7					
24	1			3		5				8	9	11			4	2		10		7			6						
25	1	3				5				8	9	11			4	2		10		7			6						
26	1						5			9		11			4	2				8			6	7	3	10			
27	1			3		5				9	8	11			4			10					6	7	2				
28	1					2	5			9	8	11			4			10		7			6		3				
29	1					5				9	8	11			4	2		10		7			6		3				
30	1					5				9	8	11	2		4			10		7			6		3				
31	1		5			2				11	8				4			10		7			6		3				9
32		3				5				11	8				4			10		7			6		2		1	9	
33		3				5				11	8				4	2				7		6			9	10	1		
34		3				5					8	11			4			10		7			6		2		1	9	
Apps.	31	26	1	3	8	26	15	9	14	27	31	29	11	9	30	18	2	24	2	21	1	2	12	5	9	2	3	2	1
Goals						5		1	1	6	11	1		2				6	2					1					

Pos	P.	W.	D.	L.	F.	A.	Pts.
11th	34	10	11	13	37	54	31

Scottish Cup

No.	Date	Opposition	H.T.	Res.	Att.	Goalscorers
1	25 Jan	NITHSDALE W.	1-0	3-0	6000	A.Cunningham, Maxwell, Steel
2	8 Feb	ABERCORN	1-1	5-1	8000	Dickie(3), A.Cunningham, Maxwell
QF	22	HEARTS	0-1	0-2	16000	

No.	Blair	Mitchell	Trialist	Brown	Aitken	Duff	Buchan	Kirsop	Logan	Culley	A.Cunningham	Templeton	Kirkwood	Watson	Shortt	W.Cunningham	Law	Dickie	Armstrong	Goodwin	Bond	Clark	Steel	Maxwell	Murray	McKay	Burnett	Neil	Trialist
1	1					5				8	9	11	3		4	2		10					6	7					
2	1					5				8	9	11			4	2		10					6	7	3				
QF	1	3				5					9	11			4	2		10		8			6	7					

Later called "The Stanley Matthews of his day", BOB TEMPLETON was already a big star when he joined Killie; having played for Aston Villa, Newcastle, Arsenal & Celtic. 1912-13 was his last season at Rugby Park. He played for Fulham for a couple of seasons before returning to Kilmarnock as landlord of the Royal Hotel.

SEASON 1913-14 Division One

No.	Date	Opposition	H.T.	Res.	Att.	Goalscorers
1	16 Aug	RANGERS	0-2	1-6	9000	Goodwin
2	23	Dunbarton	1-1	1-1	7000	Culley
3	30	CLYDE	1-0	2-2	6000	A.Cunningham(2)
4	6 Sep	Queens Park	0-3	1-3	9000	Duff
5	13	AYR UNITED	0-1	0-1	6000	
6	20	Airdrieonians	0-1	1-3	4000	Neil
7	27	HIBERNIAN	0-1	0-3	4000	
8	4 Oct	Third Lanark	1-0	1-1	5000	Culley
9	11	RAITH ROVERS	1-1	3-1	5000	Dickie, Neil, Waddell
10	18	Morton	0-1	0-2	7000	
11	25	HAMILTON A.	3-2	5-2	4000	A.Cunningham(2), McCurdie(2), Goodwin
12	1 Nov	Celtic	0-1	0-4	12000	
13	8	Motherwell	0-1	0-4	6000	
14	15	FALKIRK	0-3	2-3	4000	Culley, Neil
15	22	Partick Thistle	2-2	2-4	12000	Culley, A.Cunningham
16	29	DUNDEE	0-0	0-0	5000	
17	6 Dec	Aberdeen	1-1	2-1	7000	Culley, Neil
18	13	HEARTS	0-2	0-3	6000	
19	20	Hamilton A.	0-3	0-6	3000	
20	27	PARTICK THISTLE	1-0	2-0	3000	Neil, Whittle
21	1 Jan	ST. MIRREN	1-0	3-1	9000	Whittle(2), A.Cunningham
22	3	Clyde	0-0	0-0	6000	
23	6	St. Mirren	0-1	1-1	4000	A.Cunningham
24	10	THIRD LANARK	1-0	1-1	4000	A.Cunningham
25	17	Hibernian	1-0	1-0	7000	Whittle
26	24	DUMBARTON	3-0	6-0	5000	Neil(3), Whittle(3)
27	31	Falkirk	1-2	1-4	3000	Whittle
28	14 Feb	Raith Rovers	1-1	1-1	5000	Neil
29	28	AIRDRIEONIANS	2-1	3-2	4000	A.Cunningham, Neil, Watson
30	7 Mar	Hearts	1-0	1-0	8000	Goldie
31	14	Ayr United	0-0	0-0	6000	
32	21	Rangers	0-1	0-1	12000	
33	28	QUEENS PARK	3-0	3-0	5000	Whittle(3)
34	8 Apr	CELTIC	0-1	0-1	5000	
35	11	Dundee	1-1	1-3	7000	Neil
36	18	MORTON*	0-1	0-1	8000	
37	22	ABERDEEN	1-2	1-2	4000	Culley
38	25	MOTHERWELL	0-0	2-0	4000	Culley, Neil

* Played away owing to agricultural show at Rugby Park

No.	Blair	Murray	Mitchell	Shortt	Duff	Steel	Goodwin	A.Cunningham	Whittle	Dickie	Neil	Burnett	Culley	Grant	Mackie	W.Cunningham	Clark	Fulton	McCurdie	Smith	Waddell	Hamilton	Watson	G.Goldie	Vickers
1	1	2	3	4	5	6	7	8	9	10	11														
2		2	3	4	5	6		8	9	10	7	1	11												
3		2	3	4	5			8	9	10	7		11	1	6										
4			3	4	5		7	8	9	10			11	1	6	2									
5		2	3	4	5	6		10	9		8		11	1			7								
6		3		4	2	6		10		5	7		11	1				8	9						
7		2		4				10			7		11	1	6		9	8		3	5				
8		2	3				7	8		10	11		9	1	6			4			5				
9		2	3				7	8		10	11		9	1	6			4			5				
10		2	3				7	8		10	11		9	1	6			4			5				
11		2	3				7	8		10	11			1	6			4	9		5				
12		2	3	6			7	8		10			11	1				4	9		5				
13		2	3				7	8		10			11	1	6			4	9		5				
14		3					7	10		11	8		9	1	6	2		4			5				
15		2					7	10		11	8		9	1	6			4			5	3			
16		2	3	7				10			8		9	1	6		11	4			5				
17		2	3				7	10			8		9	1	6		11	4			5				
18		2	3					10	11		8		9	1	6		7	4			5				
19		2	3					10			8			1	6		7	4	9		5		11		
20		2	3					10	9		8			1	6			4			5		11	7	
21		2	3	4				10	9		8			1	6						5		11	7	
22		2	3	4				10	9		8			1	6						5		11	7	
23		2	3	4				10	9		8			1	6						5		11	7	
24		2	3	4				10	9		8			1	6						5		11	7	
25			3	4				10	9		8			1	6	2					5		11	7	
26			3	4				10	9		8			1	6	2					5			7	11
27			3	4					9		8		10	1	6	2					5			7	11
28			3	4				10	9		8			1		2		6			5			7	11
29		2	3	4				10	9		8			1				6			5		11	7	
30	1		3	6				10	9	5	8					2		4						7	11
31	1		3	6				10	9		8					2		4			5			7	11
32	1	2	3	6				10	9		8							4			5		11	7	
33		2	3	6				10	9				8	1				4			5		11	7	
34	1	2	3	6				10	9		8							4			5		11	7	
35	1	2	3	6				10	9		8							4			5		11	7	
36	1		3	6				10	9				8			2		4			5			7	11
37	1		3	6				10	9				8			2		4			5			7	11
38	1		3	4				10		5	8		9		6	2							11	7	
Apps.	9	28	34	27	6	4	11	37	24	15	32	1	21	28	23	11	6	25	5	1	30	1	13	19	7
Goals					1		2	9	11	1	12		7						2		1		1	1	

Pos	P.	W.	D.	L.	F.	A.	Pts.
12th	39	11	9	18	48	68	31

Scottish Cup

1		Bye				
2	7 Feb	HAMILTON A.	1-1	3-1	11000	A.Cunningham, Goldie, Neil
3	21	PARTICK THISTLE	1-3	1-4	12000	Whittle

No.	Blair	Murray	Mitchell	Shortt	Duff	Steel	Goodwin	A.Cunningham	Whittle	Dickie	Neil	Burnett	Culley	Grant	Mackie	W.Cunningham	Clark	Fulton	McCurdie	Smith	Waddell	Hamilton	Watson	G.Goldie	Vickers
1																									
2			3	4				10	9		8			1		2		6			5		11	7	
3			3	4				10	9		8			1		2		6			5		11	7	

The last peacetime season. No fewer than 21 Kilmarnock players and 3 Directors served in the armed forces during the First World War. Seven players failed to return, having made the supreme sacrifice :-
David Slimmon, Alex McCurdie, Charles Vickers, John Rollo, Alexander Barrie, James Maxwell and Daniel McKellar.

SEASON 1914-15 Division One

No.	Date	Opposition	H.T.	Res.	Att.	Goalscorers
1	15 Aug	Morton	0-1	1-3	7000	Culley
2	22	CLYDE	0-2	0-3	5000	
3	29	Rangers	0-2	1-2	15000	Neil
4	5 Sep	HEARTS	0-1	0-2	4000	
5	12	Motherwell	0-3	2-3	5000	Campbell(2)
6	19	AYR UNITED	1-2	1-2	8500	Campbell
7	26	Airdrieonians	1-0	2-0	3000	Armour, Vickers
8	3 Oct	FALKIRK	0-0	1-0	5000	Armour
9	10	Third Lanark	0-2	2-3	6000	Armour, Culley
10	17	Partick Thistle	0-0	0-0	10000	
11	24	HIBERNIAN	2-1	5-1	6000	Culley(2), Neil(2), Hamilton
12	31	Dundee	1-0	1-0	4000	Neil
13	7 Nov	CELTIC	0-2	1-3	6200	Hamilton
14	14	Raith Rovers	0-1	0-3	3000	
15	21	St. Mirren	1-1	3-2	3000	Neil(2), A.Cunningham
16	28	ABERDEEN	4-0	5-2	2000	Neil(2), Armour, Culley, A.Cunningham
17	5 Dec	Queens Park	0-0	0-1	4000	
18	12	RANGERS	0-0	0-1	3000	
19	19	Aberdeen	0-1	0-3	4000	
20	26	AIRDRIEONIANS	2-0	2-1	3000	Goldie, Neil
21	1 Jan	ST. MIRREN	0-0	2-1	5000	Culley, A.Cunningham
22	2	Hibernian	0-1	1-3	3000	A.Cunningham
23	4	Celtic	0-1	0-2	8000	
24	9	RAITH ROVERS	3-0	3-1	2000	Culley(2), Neil
25	16	DUMBARTON	3-0	4-0		Neil(4)
26	23	Clyde	0-0	0-1	1800	
27	30	HAMILTON A.	0-0	1-0	4000	A.Cunningham
28	6 Feb	Hearts	0-2	1-3	8000	Neil
29	13	PARTICK THISTLE	0-0	2-0		A.Cunningham, Neil
30	20	Ayr United	0-1	0-2	10000	
31	27	QUEENS PARK	0-0	3-0	4000	Armour, Culley, A.Cunningham
32	6 Mar	MOTHERWELL	1-2	2-2	4000	Culley, Neil
33	13	Hamilton A.	0-0	0-0	4000	
34	20	DUNDEE	2-2	3-2	4000	A.Cunningham(2), McKellar
35	27	THIRD LANARK	1-1	2-1		Culley, Neil
36	3 Apr	Dumbarton	0-0	0-1	2000	
37	10	Falkirk	1-2	2-3		Culley, Neil
38	24	MORTON	1-1	2-2	3000	Howie, Neil

No.	Blair	W.Cunningham	Mitchell	Shortt	Campbell	Mackie	G.Goldie	Neil	Culley	A.Cunningham	McKellar	McCurdie	Millar	Morton	Hamilton	Armour	Vickers	Fulton	Slimmon	Dickie	Armstrong	Goodwin	Howie
1	1	2	3	4	5	6	7	8	9	10	11												
2	1	2	3	4	5	6	7	8		10	11	9											
3		2	3	4		6	7	8		5	11	9	1	10									
4		2	3	4		6	7	8		5	11	9	1	10									
5			3	4	9	6	7	8		5	11		1	10	2								
6			3	4	9	6	11	8		5			1	10	2	7							
7		2	3	4		6	7		10	8			1		5	9	11						
8		2	3	4		6	7		10	8			1		5	9	11						
9		2	3			6	7		10	8			1		5	9	11	4					
10		2	3	4		6		9	10	8	11		1		5	7							
11		2		4		6		9	10	8	11		1		5	7			3				
12		2		4		6		9	10	8	11		1		5	7			3				
13		2		4		6		9	10	8	11		1		5	7			3				
14		2		4		6	7	9	10	8	11		1		5				3				
15		2		4		6	7	9	10	8	11		1		5				3				
16		2		4		6		9	10	8			1		5	7	11		3				
17		2		4		6		9	10	8			1		5	7	11		3				
18		2	11	4		6	7	8		10		9	1		5				3				
19	1	2	11	4		6				8		9			5	7			3	10			
20	1	2		4		6	7	8	10		11	9			5				3				
21	1	2		4		6	7	9	10	8	11				5				3				
22	1	2			4	6		9	10	8	11		1		5	7			3				
23	1	2		4	9	6		8	10		11		1		5	7			3				
24	1	2		4		6		9	10	8			1		5	7	11		3				
25	1	2		4		6		9	10	8			1		5	7	11		3				
26	1	2		4		6		9	10	8			1		5	7	11		3				
27	1	2	3	4		6		9	10	8	11				5	7							
28	1	2	3	6				9	10	8	11				5	7		4					
29	1	2	3	4		6		9	10	8	11				5	7							
30	1	2	3	4		6		9	10	8					5	7	11						
31	1	2	3	4		6		9	10	8	11				5	7							
32	1	2	3	4		6		9	10	8					5	7				11			
33		2	3	4		6		9	10	8	11		1			7				5			
34		2	3	4		6		9	10	8	11		1			7				5			
35	1	2	3	4		6		9	10	8	11					7				5			
36	1	2	3	4		10			9	8	11				6	7				5			
37	1	2	3	4		6		9	10		11					7				5	8		
38	1	2	3	4		6		11	10						5						7	8	9
Apps.	20	36	24	36	6	37	14	33	31	34	24	6	18	4	30	27	9	2	16	7	2	1	1
Goals					3		1	20	12	9	1				2	5	1						1

Pos	P.	W.	D.	L.	F.	A.	Pts.
12th	38	15	4	19	55	59	34

Andy Cunningham

His six seasons at Rugby Park established him as one of the greatest players of the times. He was transferred to Rangers in 1915.

SEASON 1915-16 Division One

No.	Date	Opposition	H.T.	Res.	Att.	Goalscorers	Blair	Hamilton	Mitchell	Shortt	Dickie	Mackie	G.Goldie	Fulton	Culley	Armstrong	McKellar	Murray	Armour	Goodwin	Anderson	Burnett	McAlpine	Slimmon	McPhail	Neil	McKnight	J.Goldie
1	21 Aug	ABERDEEN	3-0	5-0	3000	Culley(3), Armstrong, G.Goldie	1	2	3	4	5	6	7	8	9	10	11											
2	28	Falkirk	0-0	0-0			1	2	3	4	5	6	7	8	9	10	11											
3	4 Sep	RANGERS	0-2	0-3	8000		1	5	3	4		6	7	8	9	10	11	2										
4	11	Hearts	0-0	1-0	5000	Culley	1	2	3	4	5	6	7	8	9	10	11											
5	18	MOTHERWELL	0-0	1-0	4000	Culley	1	2	3	4	5	6		8	9	10	11		7									
6	25	DUMBARTON	3-1	5-1	4000	Culley(2), Armour, Murray, Shortt	1	2	3	4	5	6	8		9		11	10	7									
7	2 Oct	Hamilton A.	1-4	2-5	5000	Culley, G.Goldie	1	2	3	4	5	6	7	8	9		11			10								
8	9	HIBERNIAN	0-0	0-0	3000		1	2	3	4	5	6		8	9	10	11		7									
9	16	Airdrieonians	0-0	0-0	4000		1	2	3	4	5	6		8	9	11				7	10							
10	23	AYR UNITED	0-1	0-1	6000		1	2	3	4	5	6		8	9	10	11		7									
11	30	PARTICK THISTLE	1-0	1-1	4000	Dickie	1	2	3	4	5	6		8	9	10	11		7									
12	6 Nov	Raith Rovers	0-1	1-1	3000	Culley		2	3	4	5	6		8	9	7	11	10				1						
13	13	DUNDEE	2-0	2-0	3000	Armstrong, Fulton	1	2	3	4	5	6		8	9	10	11		7									
14	20	Celtic	0-1	0-2	4000		1	2	3	4		6		5	9	10	11		7		8							
15	27	QUEENS PARK	3-0	4-0	3000	Culley(3), Armour	1	5	3	4		6		8	9	11		2	7		10							
16	4 Dec	St. Mirren	0-0	0-3	3000		1	5	3	4		6		8	9	11		2	7		10							
17	11	Morton	0-0	0-2	4000		1	5	3	4		6	7	8	9	11		2			10							
18	18	THIRD LANARK	1-1	1-1	4000	Culley	1	2	3	4	5	6		8	9	10			7						11			
19	25	Ayr United	0-1	0-2	5000		1		3		5	10		4	9	8		2	7				6		11			
20	1 Jan	ST. MIRREN	0-1	1-1	5000	Dickie	1	2		4	5				8				7				6	3	11	9	10	
21	3	RAITH ROVERS	1-0	2-0	4000	Culley, McKnight	1	2	3	4	5	6		8	9				7						11		10	
22	8	Aberdeen	0-0	0-2	4000		1	2	3	4	5	6	7	8											11	9	10	
23	15	CLYDE	0-0	0-1	3000		1	2	3	4		6			10	8			7				5		11	9		
24	22	Rangers	1-0	1-3	4000	McKnight	1	2	3		5	6	7		9										11	8	10	4
25	29	HAMILTON A.	1-0	3-0	3000	Anderson, Culley, McPhail	1	2	3		5	6	7	8	9						10				11			4
26	5 Feb	Queens Park	1-1	2-1	3000	Culley, Dickie	1	2	3		5	6	7	8	9			10							11			4
27	12	Partick Thistle	0-3	0-4	5000		1	2	3		5	6		8	9						10				11	7		4
28	19	AIRDRIEONIANS	1-0	4-0		Culley(3), Fulton	1	2	3		5	6	7	8	9						10				11			4
29	26	Hibernian	0-0	0-1	3000		1	2	3		5	6	7	8	9						10				11			4
30	4 Mar	CELTIC	0-2	0-3	10000		1	2	3			5	7	8	9	6					10				11			4
31	11	Motherwell	1-1	1-1	3500	Dickie	1		3		5	6	7	8	9	10		2							11			4
32	18	MORTON	0-1	1-1	5000	Armstrong	1	2	3		5	6	7	8	9	10									11			4
33	1 Apr	FALKIRK	1-2	1-3	3000	Culley	1	2	3		5	6	7	8	9	10									11			4
34	8	Dundee	0-2	0-2	5000		1	9	3	4		6	7	8				2			10				11			5
35	15	HEARTS*	1-1	3-1	3000	Culley(2), G.Goldie	1	2	3	4		6	7	8	9	10									11			5
36	18	Clyde	1-0	1-1	1000	McPhail	1	2		4		6	7	8	9	10		3							11			5
37	22	Third Lanark	1-1	2-1	3000	Armstrong, Culley	1	2		4		6	7	8	9	10		3							11			5
38	29	Dumbarton	1-0	1-1	3000	G.Goldie	1	2	3	4		6	7	8	9	10									11			5
						Apps.	37	36	35	27	26	37	22	34	36	26	13	12	14	2	11	1	3	1	21	5	4	15
						Goals				1	4		4	2	23	4		1	2		1				2		2	

* Played at Ayr, owing to agricultural show at Rugby Park.

Pos	P.	W.	D.	L.	F.	A.	Pts.
10th	38	12	11	15	46	49	35

With Cunningham gone, WILLIE CULLEY stepped out of the shadows, going on to become Kilmarnock's highest-ever total scorer in recognised first-class fixtures. 23 League goals made 1915-16 his most productive season

SEASON 1916-17 Division One

No.	Date	Opposition	H.T.	Res.	Att.	Goalscorers	Blair	T.Hamilton	Patrick	Henderson	J.Goldie	Johnstone	G.Goldie	Smith	Culley	Rutherford	McPhail	Mitchell	Armstrong	Fulton	Mackie	"Burnett"	"Brown"	Dorbie	Lock	R.Hamilton	Hempsey	Sinclair	Harris	Gordon	"Goldie"
1	19 Aug	Falkirk	0-0	0-1	3000		1	2	3	4	5	6	7	8	9	10	11														
2	26	MORTON	3-1	3-2	4000	G.Goldie, McPhail, Smith	1	2	3	4	5	6	7	8	9	10	11														
3	2 Sep	Clyde	1-0	1-1	6000	Culley	1	2	3	4	5	6	7	8	9	10	11														
4	9	AYR UNITED	1-2	1-2	6500	Culley	1	2		4	5		7	8	9	10	11	3			6										
5	16	Rangers	0-3	0-3	10000		1	2		4	5	6			9	10	11	3	7	8											
6	23	HIBERNIAN	0-1	1-3	4000	T.Hamilton	1	2	3	4	5	6		8	9	10	11		7												
7	30	Motherwell	0-0	1-0	5000	McPhail	1	2	3	4	5	6	7	8	9	10	11														
8	7 Oct	Partick Thistle	0-1	1-1	8000	Armstrong	1	2	3	4	5	6	7	8		10	11		9												
9	14	HEARTS	1-0	3-0	1000	McPhail, Patrick, Rutherford	1	2	9	4	5			8		10	11	3		7	6										
10	21	Aberdeen	1-0	1-1	4000	Rutherford			3	4	5			8	9	10	11	2		7	6	1									
11	28	DUNDEE	2-0	3-0	4000	Culley(2), Henderson		2		4	5			8	9	10	11	3		7	6	1									
12	4 Nov	Raith Rovers	2-0	4-0	2000	Armstrong(2), Fulton(2)		2		4	5			8		10	11	3	9	7	6	1									
13	11	THIRD LANARK	1-1	2-1	3000	McPhail, Rutherford	1	2		4	5			8	9	10	11	3		7	6										
14	18	AIRDRIEONIANS	1-1	1-3	3500	Culley	1	2		4	5			8	9	10	11	3		7	6										
15	25	Dumbarton	1-0	1-1	3000	McPhail	1	2	3	4	5			8		10	11		9	7	6										
16	2 Dec	Queens Park	0-0	1-0	2000	McPhail	1	2	3	4	5			8		10	11		9	7	6										
17	9	HAMILTON A.	2-0	4-0	2000	Culley(3), T.Hamilton	1	2	3		5			8	9	10	11			7	6		4								
18	16	Ayr United	1-0	2-0	4000	Fulton, Smith	1	2	3	4	5			8	9	10	11			7	6										
19	23	RAITH ROVERS	1-0	3-0	2000	Culley(2), McPhail		2	3	4	5			8	9	10	11			7	6	1									
20	30	Dundee	0-0	2-0	4000	Mitchell, Smith		2	3	4	5			8		10	11	9		7	6			1							
21	1 Jan	ST. MIRREN	1-1	1-4	6000	Rutherford	1	2	3	4	5			8	9	10	11			7	6										
22	2	Morton	0-2	1-2	2000	Fulton	1		3	4			7	8	9	10	11	2		5	6										
23	6	PARTICK THISTLE	0-0	0-1	3000		1	2		4	5			8	9	10	11	3		7	6										
24	13	St. Mirren	1-2	1-2	5000	Smith	1	2		7	4			8	9	10	11	3		5	6										
25	20	Hibernian	0-2	1-2	4000	Fulton	1		3	4	5			8		10	11	2	9	7	6										
26	27	ABERDEEN	4-0	7-0	2000	McPhail(2),Armstrng,Cully,Fltn,J.Gldie,Smth	1	2		4	5	6		8	9		11	3	10	7											
27	3 Feb	Hamilton A.	0-1	0-3	4000		1	2	3	4	5	6		8		10	11		9	7											
28	10	QUEENS PARK	2-0	4-2	3500	Smith(2), McPhail(2)		2			5		9	8		10	11	3		4	6				1	7					
29	17	Airdrieonians	1-0	2-3	2500	Armstrong, T.Hamilton		2		4	5			8		10	11	3	9	7	6						1				
30	24	CELTIC	1-1	2-2	6000	Fulton, T.Hamilton		2	3	4	5			8	9	10	11			7	6							1			
31	3 Mar	CLYDE	0-0	2-0	2000	Smith, McPhail		2	3	4	5			8	9	10	11			7	6							1			
32	10	MOTHERWELL	1-0	3-0	2500	Culley, Rutherford, Smith		2		4	5			8	9	10	11	3			6							1			7
33	17	Third Lanark	0-0	0-3	5000		1	2	3	4	5		7			10	11		9	8	6										
34	24	DUMBARTON	0-0	0-0	3000		1	2	3		5	4		8		10	11		9		6										7
35	31	RANGERS	2-0	4-1	5000	Rutherford(3), McPhail	1	2		4	5			8	9	10	11	3		7	6										
36	7 Apr	Hearts	0-0	0-0	3000		1	2	8	4	5						11	3		7	6								9	10	
37	14	FALKIRK	3-1	4-1	3000	Culley(3), Smith	1		3	4	5	6		8	9	10	11	2		7											
38	21	Celtic	2-0	2-0	18000	Culley, Smith	1		3	4	5			8	9	10	11	2		7	6										
						Apps.	28	33	25	35	37	11	9	35	25	36	38	21	12	29	28	4	1	1	1	1	1	3	1	1	2
						Goals		4	1	1	1		1	11	16	8	13	1	5	7											

Pos	P.	W.	D.	L.	F.	A.	Pts.
6th	38	18	7	13	69	45	43

Malcolm McPhail

The free-scoring left-winger who played a big part in Killie's rise to the forefront of the Scottish game. His younger brother Bob played for Airdrie, Rangers and Scotland. Malcolm wore the dark blue in an 'unofficial' Victory International.

SEASON 1917-18 Division One

No.	Date	Opposition	H.T.	Res.	Att.	Goalscorers	Blair	T.Hamilton	Mitchell	Henderson	J.Goldie	Mackie	Fulton	Smith	Culley	Rutherford	McPhail	G.Hamiton	A.Goldie	Johnstone	Miller	Patrick	M.Thom	Hopecroft	A.Thom	Young	Neave	Dickie	Farrell	Thomson	Lees
1	18 Aug	RANGERS	0-0	0-1	10000		1	2	3	4	5	6	7	8	9	10	11														
2	25	Hibernian	1-0	3-0	7000	Culley, A.Goldie, Rutherford	1	2	3	4	5	6			9	10	11	7	8												
3	1 Sep	AYR UNITED	2-0	2-0	5000	Culley, Smith	1	2	3	4	5	6		8	9		11	7	10												
4	8	Falkirk	0-1	0-1	3000		1	2	3	4	5	6		8	9	10	11	7													
5	15	ST. MIRREN	3-0	5-1	5000	A.Goldie(2), Culley, McPhail, Smith	1	2	3	4	5	6	7	8	9		11		10												
6	22	Motherwell	1-1	1-1	5000	Fulton	1	2	3	4	5		7	8	9		11		10	6											
7	29	MORTON	2-0	4-0		Culley(2), A.Goldie, T.Hamilton	1	2	3		5	6	7	8	9		11		10	4											
8	6 Oct	HEARTS	1-0	4-3	4000	McPhail(2), Fulton, Rutherford		2			5	6	7		9	10	11		8	4	1	3									
9	13	Celtic	2-1	3-2	18000	McPhail(2), Smith	1	2	3	4	5	6	7	8	9	10	11														
10	20	THIRD LANARK	2-0	3-1		Culley(2), Smith	1	2	3	4	5	6	7	8	9	10	11														
11	27	Dumbarton	2-1	4-1	3000	Culley(2), A.Goldie, T.Hamilton	1	2	3	4	5				9	10	11	7	8	6											
12	3 Nov	PARTICK THISTLE	0-0	0-0	5000		1	2	3	4	5	6	7	8	9	10	11														
13	10	Airdrieonians	0-0	1-0	5000	Culley	1	2	3	4	5	6	7	8	9		11		10												
14	17	MOTHERWELL	2-0	4-0	4000	Fulton(2), J.Goldie, Smith	1	2	3	4	5	6	9	8			11	7	10												
15	24	Ayr United	1-0	3-0	5000	Fulton, G.Hamilton, McPhail	1	2	3	4	5	6	9	8		10	11	7													
16	1 Dec	HAMILTON A.	1-2	2-3	4000	Rutherford(2)	1	2		4	5	6	7	8	9	10	11					3									
17	8	Hearts	0-2	0-3	6000		1	2	3			6	5	8	9	10	11	7		4											
18	15	Clyde	2-0	2-1	4000	McPhail, Smith	1	2	3	4		6	9	8			11	7	10	5											
19	22	CLYDEBANK	2-0	4-2	4000	Fulton(3), A.Goldie	1		2		5	6	9	8			11	7	10	4			3								
20	29	Queens Park	0-1	0-3	8000		1	2	3	4		6	9	8			11	7	10	5											
21	1 Jan	St. Mirren	0-0	0-2	12000		1		2	4		6		8		10			9	5			3	7	11						
22	5	HIBERNIAN	1-1	3-1	4000	Culley(2), Young	1	2	3	4		6		8	9	10		7		5						11					
23	12	Morton	1-0	2-2	3000	A.Goldie(2)	1	2	3	4		6		8	9	5	11		10							7					
24	26	Partick Thistle	2-0	3-0	10000	Culley(2), Smith	1	2	3	4		6	7	8	9	5	11		10												
25	2 Feb	DUMBARTON	0-0	0-0	5000		1	2	3	4		6	7	8	9	5	11		10												
26	9	FALKIRK	1-0	3-0	4000	T.Hamilton, McPhail, Smith	1	2		4			7	8	9		11		10	6			3				5				
27	16	Third Lanark	1-1	1-1	6000	Smith	1	2	3	4			9	8			11		10	6			7				5				
28	23	CLYDE	2-0	4-0	5000	Smith(3), Culley	1	2		4				8	9		11	7	10	6			3				5				
29	2 Mar	Rangers	0-2	0-3	20000		1	2	3	4		6	7	8	9		11		10								5				
30	16	QUEENS PARK	2-0	3-1	5000	G.Hamilton, McPhail, Smith	1	2	3	4				8	9		11	7		6							10	5			
31	23	Clydebank	0-0	0-1	9000		1	2	3	4				8	9		11	7	10	6							5				
32	30	CELTIC	0-2	1-3	8000	McPhail	1	2	3	4					9		11	7	10	6							5		8		
33	6 Apr	Hamilton A.	0-0	1-4	5000	Culley	1	2	3	4		6	9	8	10		11	7									5				
34	13	AIRDRIEONIANS	2-0	3-0	3000	Fulton, A.Goldie, McPhail	1	2	3	4		6	8		9		11	7	10								5				
						Apps.	33	32	30	30	17	26	23	29	27	16	32	17	23	16	1	2	5	1	1	2	9	1	1		
						Goals		3			1		9	13	16	4	11	2	9							1					

Pos	P.	W.	D.	L.	F.	A.	Pts.
3rd	34	19	5	10	69	41	43

Scottish War Funds Cup

							Blair	T.Hamilton	Mitchell	Henderson	J.Goldie	Mackie	Fulton	Smith	Culley	Rutherford	McPhail	G.Hamiton	A.Goldie	Johnstone	Miller	Patrick	M.Thom	Hopecroft	A.Thom	Young	Neave	Dickie	Farrell	Thomson	Lees
1	9 Mar	St. Mirren	2-1	3-2*		Culley(2), McPhail	1		2	4			9	8	10		11	7		6			3								5
2	20 Apr	Morton	0-2	1-7	5000	McPhail	1	2	3			6	9				11	7		8			10				5			4	

* after extra time

John Wallace

The club's founder died in Australia in November 1917.

SEASON 1918-19 Division One

No.	Date	Opposition	H.T.	Res.	Att.	Goalscorers	Hamilton	Shortt	Neave	Mackie	A.Goldie	Culley	Howie	McPhail	Blair	Turner	Gray	Dickie	McHallum	J.Goldie	Johnstone	Lock	Potts	Murray	Mitchell	Fulton	Shankland	Guthrie	McAllister	Riddell	Rundell	Landells	Stevenson	McGregor	Neil	Burnett
1	17 Aug	Motherwell	0-0	2-1		Culley, A.Goldie	2	4	5	6	8	9	10	11											3				7							1
2	24	QUEENS PARK	1-0	1-0	5000	Culley	2	4	5	6	8	9	10	11	1	7									3											
3	31	Clydebank	0-1	1-3	5000	Culley	2	4	5	6	8	9	10	11	1										3				7							
4	7 Sep	HIBERNIAN	3-1	7-1	5000	Culley(4), A.Goldie(2), Guthrie	2	4	5		10	9		11	1	7					6				3			8								
5	14	Morton	1-0	2-2	7000	Culley, Shortt		4	5	6	10	9	8	11	1						3				2											
6	21	AIRDRIEONIANS	2-1	3-1	3000	A.Goldie(2), Fulton	2	4	5	6	10	9	8	11	1											7										
7	28	DUMBARTON	0-0	0-0	3000		2	4	5	6	10	9	8	11	1						3					7										
8	5 Oct	St. Mirren	1-1	5-1	6000	Culley(2), McPhail(2), A.Goldie	2	4	3	6	10	9	8	11								1				7				5						
9	12	CELTIC	1-0	1-1	10000	Culley	2	4	3	6	10	9	8	11		7						1								5						
10	19	Third Lanark	0-1	4-3	4000	Culley(2), A.Goldie, Howie	2	5	3	6	10	9	8	11			7					1				4										
11	26	PARTICK THISTLE	0-1	0-3	5000		2	5	3	6	10		8	11			9					1	4			7										
12	2 Nov	Hearts	0-0	4-1	6000	Turner(2), Gray, McPhail	2	5	3	6			8	11		9	7					1	4					10								
13	9	Falkirk	1-0	1-0	4000	"Fulton"	2	5	3	6			8	11			7					1	4					10								
14	16	AYR UNITED	0-2	2-3	6000	Fulton, Turner	2	4	6					11		9	7	5				1			3	8		10								
15	23	Clyde	0-0	1-1	6000	Turner	2	5	3	6				11	1	10	7				4		8													
16	30	MOTHERWELL	0-0	0-2	6000		2	4		6				11	1	9	7						8					10		5		3				
17	7 Dec	HAMILTON A.	3-0	5-0	4000	McPhail(3), Mackie, Turner	2	5		10				11	1	9	7				6		8										4			
18	14	Ayr United	1-2	1-3	7000	Dickie	2	5	3			9		11	1	8	7	10			6												4			
19	21	Rangers	0-4	0-8	10000			5		10		9	8	11	1		7	3			6		4									2				
20	28	FALKIRK	0-0	0-0	3000		2	4		6		9		11	1		7		10															3		
21	1 Jan	ST. MIRREN	0-2	1-3	8000	Howie	2	4		6		9	8	11	1		7	5	10															3		
22	4	Hibernian	3-0	4-1	5000	Culley(3), McHallum	2	8	3	6		9		11	1		7	5	10				4													
23	11	RANGERS	0-0	1-0	10000	McPhail	2	4		6		9		11	1		7	8	10	5				3												
24	18	Airdrieonians	0-1	2-2	4000	Dickie, Mackie	2	4		10				11	1		7	9	8	5	6			3												
25	25	CLYDE	3-0	5-3	4000	McPhail, Culley, Dickie(2), Gray			2	6		9		11	1		7	8	10	5				3							4					
26	1 Feb	Celtic	1-1	1-2	25000	Culley	2	4	7	6		9		11	1			8	10	5				3												
27	8	THIRD LANARK	0-1	0-1	6000		2	4	6			9		11	1		7	8	10	5				3												
28	15	Partick Thistle	0-1	0-4	6000		2	4		6		9		11	1			8		5				3			10				7					
29	22	HEARTS	2-0	2-2	5000	Fulton, McHallum	2	4		6				11	1		7	8	10	5				3		9										
30	8 Mar	Dumbarton	0-0	1-0	3000	Culley	2		3	6		9		11	1		7		10	5							8				4					
31	15	CLYDEBANK	1-1	2-3		McPhail, Shankland	2		3	6		9		11	1				10	5							8				4				7	
32	22	MORTON	0-1	0-1	4000		2		3	6		9		11	1		7	10		5							8									
33	29	Queens Park	1-1	2-1	8000	Culley, Gray	2			6		10		11	1		7			5							8				4				9	
34	5 Apr	Hamilton A.	0-1	0-2	4000			4	2	10				11	1		7	5	3								8								9	
						Apps.	30	29	24	30	11	24	14	34	26	9	22	14	12	11	8	7	8	7	6	7	6	5	2	3	5	2	2	2	3	1
						Goals		1		2	7	20	2	9		5	3	4	2							3	1	1								

Pos	P.	W.	D.	L.	F.	A.	Pts.
9th	34	14	7	13	61	59	35

Victory Cup

No.	Date	Opposition	H.T.	Res.	Att.	Goalscorers	Hamilton	Shortt	Neave	Mackie	A.Goldie	Culley	Howie	McPhail	Blair	Turner	Gray	Dickie	McHallum	J.Goldie	Johnstone	Lock	Potts	Murray	Mitchell	Fulton	Shankland	Guthrie	McAllister	Riddell	Rundell	Landells	Stevenson	McGregor	Neil	Burnett
1	1 Mar	Albion Rovers	0-0	1-1*		Hamilton	2	4	8	6		9			1		7	10		5				3											11	
1R	5	ALBION ROVERS	0-0	0-1			2	8	3	6		9		11	1				10	5											4				7	

* A.E.T.

The following players made one appearance each (match number/position):
Ford (6/3), Hart (15/9), McQueen (17/3), McLean (20/5), McNeill (20/8), Henderson (32/4), Lees (33/3), Campbell (34/6), "Fulton" (13/9), "McAllister (5/7)

Long-serving official Charles Smith became Chairman during Killie's jubilee season and wrote the first history of the club "by an old player" as he modestly described himself.

SEASON 1919-20 **Division One**

No.	Date	Opposition	H.T.	Res.	Att.	Goalscorers	Blair	Hamilton	Murray	Shortt	Gibson	Mackie	McNaught	Shankland	McLean	Higgins	McPhail	Neave	Donnelly	McHallum	Clark	Mitchell	Bagan	Maitland	M.Smith	Culley	Playfair	Elliott	J.R.Smith	Cherry	Lambie	Garrity	Houston	Bolland
1	16 Aug	CLYDE	0-1	2-1	5000	McLean, McPhail	1	2	3	4	5	6	7	8	9	10	11																	
2	23	Raith Rovers	0-1	1-5	7000	McLean	1	2	3	4	5	6	7	8	9	10	11																	
3	27	Celtic	0-0	0-1	10000		1	2		4	5	6			9	8	11	3	7	10														
4	30	ALBION ROVERS	0-0	1-0	5000	Donnelly	1	2	3	4	5	6			9	8	11		7	10														
5	1 Sep	Dumbarton	0-1	2-2	4000	Clark, Higgins	1	2	3	4	5	6	7			8	11			10	9													
6	6	Hamilton A.	0-1	2-5	4000	Higgins, Mackie	1	2	3	4	5	6	7			8	11			10	9													
7	9	Partick Thistle	0-0	0-1	7000		1	2		7	6	10				8	11	5		9		3	4											
8	13	DUMBARTON	2-1	3-1	5000	Clark(2), McHallum	1	2			3		7			8	11	5		10	9		4	6										
9	15	RANGERS	0-3	1-7	15000	McHallum	1	2			3		7			8	11	5		10	9		4	6										
10	20	Ayr United	0-2	0-5	8000		1	2		4	3	6			9	8	11	5		10			7											
11	4 Oct	Rangers	0-2	0-5	6000		1	2			5	6			9	10	11	3	7				4		8									
12	11	MORTON	0-1	0-1	4000		1	2		5	3	6	7				11			10			4		8	9								
13	18	FALKIRK	0-0	3-0	4000	Culley(2), McLean	1	2		5	3		7		10		11						4	6	8	9								
14	25	Motherwell	1-1	1-1	6000	Culley	1	2		5	3		7		10		11						4	6	8	9								
15	1 Nov	ST. MIRREN	2-1	3-2	5000	McNaught, McPhail, M.Smith	1	2		5	3		7			10	11						4	6	8	9								
16	8	Airdrieonians	0-0	0-0	4000		1	2		5	3		7			10	11						4	6	8	9								
17	15	Aberdeen	0-0	0-1	10000		1	2		5	3		7			10	11	4						6	8	9								
18	22	HEARTS	1-1	2-1	6000	McNaught, McPhail	1	2		5	3		7			10	11						4	6	8	9								
19	29	CLYDEBANK	0-0	2-4	5000	Higgins, McPhail	1	2		5	3		7		9	10	11						4	6	8									
20	6 Dec	Third Lanark	1-0	1-0	5000	Culley	1	2		5	3	6			10	7	11								8	9	4							
21	13	Hibernian	0-3	1-4	11000	McPhail		2		5	3				10	7	11							6	8	9	4	1						
22	20	PARTICK THISTLE	1-0	2-0	6000	M.Smith(2)	1	2		5	3	6	7				11						4		8	10			9					
23	27	Queens Park	1-1	3-1	8000	McPhail(2), Culley	1	2		5	3	6	7				11						4		8	10			9					
24	1 Jan	St. Mirren	0-0	2-1	7000	J.R. Smith, M.Smith	1		2	5	3	6	7			10	11						4		8				9					
25	3	AYR UNITED	1-1	2-1	13000	Culley, J.R. Smith	1	2		5	3	6	7				11						4		8	10			9					
26	5	Falkirk	0-0	0-1	4000		1	2		5	3	6	7				11						4		8	10			9					
27	10	Dundee	1-2	2-3	11000	M.Smith, J.R. Smith	1	2		5	3	6				7	11						4		8	10			9					
28	17	CELTIC	0-2	2-3	10000	Gibson, McPhail	1	2		5	3	6				7	11						4		8	10			9					
29	24	RAITH ROVERS	0-0	2-0	5000	Culley, J.R. Smith	1	2		5	3	6	7			8	11						4			10			9					
30	31	AIRDRIEONIANS	3-0	3-2	6000	Culley(2), J.R. Smith	1	5			3	6	7			8	11						2			10	4		9					
31	14 Feb	THIRD LANARK	1-0	1-0	6000	Culley	1	2		5	3		7			9	11						4		8	10				6				
32	28	HIBERNIAN	3-0	4-1	5000	J.R. Smith(2), Culley, M.Smith	1	2		5	3		7				11	6					4		8	10			9					
33	13 Mar	DUNDEE	1-2	4-2	7000	McPhail(2), Culley, O.G.		2		5	3		7				11	6					4		8	10		1	9					
34	20	HAMILTON A.	2-1	2-1	7000	Culley, McPhail	1	2		5	3		7				11	6					4		8	10			9					
35	3 Apr	Clyde	0-1	1-2	8000	J.R. Smith	1	2			3		7				11	6					4		8	10			9		5			
36	7	QUEENS PARK	1-0	1-0	5000	Higgins	1	2		5	3		7			9	11								8	10	4			6				
37	10	Clydebank	0-0	0-1	6000		1	2		5	3		7				11	6					4		8	10						9		
38	19	MOTHERWELL	0-0	0-1	5000		1	2		5	3		7				11	6					4		8	10			9					
39	21	ABERDEEN	0-1	0-3	3000		1	2		5	3					7							4		8				9	6		10	11	
40	26	Morton*	0-0	0-4	5000		1	2		5	3		7				11	6					4		8									10
41	28	Hearts	1-0	1-0	11000	McLean	1	2		5	3		7		9		11	6					4		8									10
42	1 May	Albion Rovers	1-0	2-0	6500	Culley, McLean	1	2		5	3		7		9			6					4		8	10							11	
						Apps.	40	41	6	37	42	20	32	2	13	26	40	16	3	9	4	1	32	10	30	26	4	2	15	3	1	2	2	2
						Goals					1	1	2		5	4	11		1	2	3				6	14			8					

* Kilmarnock fielded only 10 players

Pos	P.	W.	D.	L.	F.	A.	Pts.
9th	42	20	3	19	59	74	43

Scottish Cup

Rd	Date	Opposition	H.T.	Res.	Att.	Goalscorers	Blair	Hamilton	Murray	Shortt	Gibson	Mackie	McNaught	Shankland	McLean	Higgins	McPhail	Neave	Donnelly	McHallum	Clark	Mitchell	Bagan	Maitland	M.Smith	Culley	Playfair	Elliott	J.R.Smith	Cherry	Lambie	Garrity	Houston	Bolland
1		Bye																																
2	7 Feb	Alloa Athletic	1-0	2-0	10000	Culley, Higgins	1	2		5	3	6	7			8	11						4			10			9					
3	21	QUEENS PARK	1-1	4-1	20000	J.R.Smith(2), Hamilton, McPhail	1	2		5	3		7				11	6					4		8	9			10					
QF	6 Mar	Armadale	2-0	2-1	8000	Culley, J.R.Smith	1	2		5	3		7				11	6					4		8	10			9					
SF	27	Morton*	1-2	3-2	50000	J.R.Smith(2), McPhail	1	2		5	3		7				11	6					4		8	10			9					
F	17 Apr	Albion Rovers*	1-1	3-2	95000	Culley, Shortt, J.R.Smith	1	2		5	3		7				11	6					4		8	10			9					

* Played at Hampden

The first Kilmarnock team to win the Scottish Cup.
Back: P.Carrick, T.Hamilton, T.Blair, D.Gibson, J.McWhinnie, H.Spence Middle: J.McNaught, M.Smith, J.R. Smith, W.Culley, M.McPhail. Front: J.Bagan, M.Shortt, R.Neave.
Later, another picture would be taken, allowing not only all the club officials to get in the picture, but also Archie Mackie who was injured earlier in the campaign. A fitting gesture.

SEASON 1920-21 Division One

No.	Date	Opposition	H.T.	Res.	Att.	Goalscorers
1	18 Aug	Third Lanark	3-2	4-4	8000	J.R.Smith(2), McNaught, M.Smith
2	21	Morton	1-6	2-9	10000	J.R.Smith, McPhail
3	25	RAITH ROVERS	1-0	1-0	5000	McPhail
4	28	RANGERS	1-0	1-2	15000	O.G.
5	1 Sep	Clydebank	1-1	2-2	6000	J.R.Smith(2)
6	4	Hibernian	0-0	0-0	10000	
7	7	St. Mirren	0-0	2-1	4000	Goldie, J.R.Smith
8	11	QUEENS PARK	1-1	1-1	5000	M.Smith
9	18	Raith Rovers	0-2	0-2	10000	
10	22	MORTON	1-1	3-1	4000	Ramsay, J.R.Smith, M.Smith
11	25	CLYDEBANK	1-1	2-2	7000	Hamilton, McConnell
12	2 Oct	Ayr United	0-0	0-0	8000	
13	9	HAMILTON A.	1-0	5-0	7000	J.R.Smith(3), M.Smith(2)
14	16	Albion Rovers	0-1	0-2	9000	
15	23	MOTHERWELL	0-2	0-3	10000	
16	30	Dundee	0-0	1-3	15000	J.R.Smith
17	6 Nov	PARTICK THISTLE	0-0	0-1	6000	
18	13	Celtic	0-0	0-2	8000	
19	20	THIRD LANARK	3-2	3-2	7000	Hamilton(2), Ramsay
20	27	Hearts	1-2	1-4	17000	Ramsay
21	4 Dec	Clyde	0-1	2-1	8000	J.R.Smith(2)
22	11	ABERDEEN	1-0	1-0	7000	J.R.Smith
23	18	Dumbarton	0-1	0-1	3000	
24	25	FALKIRK	2-0	2-0	7000	Ramsay(2)
25	1 Jan	ST. MIRREN	2-0	3-2	10000	J.R.Smith(2), Goldie
26	3	Airdrieonians	0-2	0-3	7000	
27	8	Rangers	0-1	0-2	15000	
28	15	HEARTS	0-1	1-2	7000	Culley
29	9 Feb	ALBION ROVERS	2-0	3-1	5000	J.R.Smith(2), Jackson
30	12	Hamilton A.	0-0	0-2	10000	
31	16	Falkirk	0-2	0-2	4500	
32	19	AIRDRIEONIANS	1-0	2-0	3000	Ramsay, M.Smith
33	23	DUMBARTON	0-0	4-1	2000	Murray, Culley, M.Smith, McPhail
34	26	Partick Thistle	1-0	1-1	10000	J.R.Smith
35	5 Mar	AYR UNITED	2-1	2-1	10000	Culley, J.R.Smith
36	12	Aberdeen	0-0	1-1	10000	M.Smith
37	19	DUNDEE	3-0	5-0	6000	Culley,McNaught,Murray,J.R.Smith,M.Smith
38	26	CELTIC	0-1	3-2	12000	Culley, McNaught, M.Smith
39	2 Apr	HIBERNIAN	0-1	1-3	8000	Murray
40	9	CLYDE	0-0	0-1	7000	
41	16	Queens Park	0-0	2-1	12000	J.R.Smith(2)
42	30	Motherwell	0-0	1-0	8000	J.R.Smith

No.	Cree	Hamilton	Gibson	Bagan	J.Goldie	Neave	McNaught	M.Smith	J.R.Smith	Culley	McPhail	Hillcoat	Shortt	Ramsay	Fullarton	Robertson	Playfair	Garrity	Wilson	Houston	McHallum	McConnell	Cherry	Jackson	Bolland	Walker	Pollock	Frew	Lorimer	Murray
1		2	3	4		6	7	8	9	10	11	1	5																	
2	1	2	3	4	5	6	7	8	9	10	11																			
3			3	4	5	6	7		9		11	1		10	2	8														
4		2	3	4		6	7	8	9		11	1	5	10																
5		2	3		4	6	7		9	10	11	1	5	8																
6		2	3	4		6	7	8	9		11	1	5	10																
7			3		5	2	7	8	9			1		10			4	6	11											
8		2	3	4	5	6	7	8	9	10		1								11										
9		2	3	4		6	7	8	9	10		1							11		5									
10		2	3		5	6	7	8	9	11		1		10				4												
11		2	3		5	6	7	8		11		1		10				4				9								
12		2	3			6	7	8	9	10	11	1	5					4												
13		2	3			6	7	8	9	11		1	5	10				4												
14		2	3			6	7	8	9	11		1	5	10				4												
15		2	3			6	7	8	9	10	11	1	5					4												
16		2	3		5		7	8	9	10	11	1						4					6							
17		2	3	4	5	6	7	8	9	10	11	1																		
18		2	3	4	5	6	7	8	9	10	11	1																		
19		2	3	4	5	6		8	9		11	1		10										7						
20		2	3	4				8	9		11	1	5	10						7			6							
21		2	3					8	9		11	1	5	10			4			7			6							
22		2	3					8	9		11	1	5	10			4			7			6							
23		2	3						9		11	1	5	10			4			7			6		8					
24		2	3		4	6		8	9			1		10		11								7		5				
25		2	3		4		7	8	9		11	1		10		6										5				
26		2	3		4		7	8	9		11	1		10		6										5				
27		2	3		4	6		8	9			1		10		11				7						5				
28		2	3		4	6	7			9	11	1		10		8										5				
29		2	3		4	6		8	9		11	1	5	10										7						
30			3		4	6		8	9		11	1		10				7										5		2
31		2	3		4	6	7	8	9		11	1	5	10																
32		2	3		4	6	7	8	9		11	1	5	10																
33			3			6	7	8	9	10	11		5														4		1	2
34			3		4	6	7	8	9	10	11	1	5																	2
35			3		4	6	7	8	9	10	11	1	5																	2
36			3		4	6	7	8	9	10	11	1	5																	2
37			3		4	6	7	8	9	10	11	1	5																	2
38			3		4	6	7	8		9	11	1	5	10																2
39			3		4	6	7	8	9	10	11	1	5																	2
40	1		3		4	6	7	8		9			5	10						11										2
41	1		3		4	6	7	8	9	10			5							11										2
42	1		3		4		7	8	9		11		5	10													6			2
Apps.	4	29	42	11	29	34	33	38	38	24	31	37	25	26	1	6	4	9	2	8	1	1	5	3	1	5	2	1	1	11
Goals		3			2		3	10	24	5	3			6								1		1						3

Pos	P.	W.	D.	L.	F.	A.	Pts.
12th	42	17	8	17	62	68	42

Scottish Cup

No.	Date	Opposition	H.T.	Res.	Att.	Goalscorers
1	22 Jan	Arbroath	1-0	4-2	5000	J.R.Smith(2), Culley, Ramsay
2	5 Feb	ABERDEEN	1-1	1-2	12000	Hamilton

No.	Cree	Hamilton	Gibson	Bagan	J.Goldie	Neave	McNaught	M.Smith	J.R.Smith	Culley	McPhail	Hillcoat	Shortt	Ramsay	Fullarton	Robertson	Playfair	Garrity	Wilson	Houston	McHallum	McConnell	Cherry	Jackson	Bolland	Walker	Pollock	Frew	Lorimer	Murray
1		2	3		4	6	7		9	10	11	1		8												5				
2		2	3		4	6			9	10	11	1		8										7		5				

Walter Jackson

The younger brother of the famous Alex Jackson was originally an outside-right who later converted successfully to centre-forward.

SEASON 1921-22 Division One

No.	Date	Opposition	H.T.	Res.	Att.	Goalscorers	Neil	Murray	Gibson	Gray	Goldie	Pollock	McNaught	M.Smith	Skinner	Ramsay	McPhail	Shortt	Neave	Culley	Gunn	Watson	Garrity	Jackson	Frew	Robertson	Scott	Herron	Hood	Cherry	Good	Howat	Bailey	Cree	Logue
1	15 Aug	Albion Rovers	0-1	0-4			1	2	3	4	5	6	7	8	9	10	11																		
2	20	DUMBARTON	1-0	1-0	10000	Culley,	1	2	3		4		7	8		9		5	6	10	11														
3	23	MORTON	1-0	2-1	9000	Culley, Watson	1	2	3		4		7			10		5	6	9	11	8													
4	27	Clyde	0-0	0-3	8000		1	2	3	7	4					10		5	6	9	11	8													
5	3 Sep	ALBION ROVERS	1-0	1-1	12000	Pollock	1	2	3		4	8			9			5		10	11		6	7											
6	10	Rangers	0-1	0-1	20000		1	2	3		4		7		9		11	5		10		8	6												
7	17	ABERDEEN	1-3	2-3	7000	Skinner, Watson	1	2	3		4		7		9		11	5		10		8	6												
8	21	ST. MIRREN	0-0	1-1	5000	Frew	1	2	3		5		7		9		11			10		8	6		4										
9	24	Raith Rovers	0-1	0-4	15000		1	2	3		5		7			10	11			9		8			4					6					
10	1 Oct	AYR UNITED	0-1	2-2	12000	McPhail, Watson	1	2	3		5			8			11			9		10		7	4					6					
11	8	Hamilton A.	1-4	1-7	9000	Watson	1	2	3		5			8			11			10		9	6	7	4										
12	15	THIRD LANARK	1-0	3-0	4000	Culley(3)	1	2	3		6		7	8			11	5		9		10			4										
13	22	Dundee	0-3	0-5	10000		1	2	3		6		7	8			11	5		9		10			4										
14	29	HIBERNIAN	1-1	1-1	5000	Culley	1		3		6			8			11	5		9		10		7	4	2									
15	5 Nov	Partick Thistle	0-0	0-2	12000		1		3					8		6	11			9		10		7	5	2	4								
16	12	CELTIC	3-1	4-3	10000	Jackson, McNaught, Shortt, Watson	1		3		6		7	8				5		11		10		9	4	2									
17	19	MOTHERWELL	0-0	4-0	8000	Jackson(2), Watson, O.G.	1		3	7	6			8				5		11		10		9	4	2									
18	26	Airdrieonians	0-0	0-2	5000		1		3	7	6			8				5		11		10		9	4	2									
19	3 Dec	QUEENS PARK	1-0	2-0	5000	Jackson(2)	1		3		6		7	8				5		11		10		9	4	2									
20	10	Morton	1-1	1-5	8000	Culley	1		3				7	8		6		5		11		10		9	4	2									
21	17	RAITH ROVERS	0-1	2-2	4000	Gibson, Watson			3				7	8		6		5		11		10		9	4	2								1	
22	24	Clydebank	0-1	1-1	3000	Smith	1		3		4		7	8		6	11	5		10				9		2									
23	26	Hearts	0-1	0-1	10000		1		3				7	8		6	11	5		10				9		2	4								
24	31	HEARTS	2-0	3-0	7000	Smith(2), McPhail	1		3	7				8		6	11	5		10				9		2	4								
25	2 Jan	St. Mirren	1-1	1-1	14000	Gray	1		3	7				8		6	11	5		10				9		2	4								
26	3	AIRDRIEONIANS	1-1	2-1	7000	Culley, Smith	1		3	7				8		6		5		11		10		9		2	4								
27	7	Dumbarton	0-3	3-5	4000	Culley, Gray, Smith	1		3	7				8		6		5		11		10		9		2	4								
28	14	Falkirk	1-1	1-2	5000	Bailey	1	3						8				5	6	11		10		7		2	4						9		
29	21	CLYDEBANK	1-1	3-2	6000	Culley(2), Smith	1				5			8		6	11			10				7		2	4		3				9		
30	4 Feb	Hibernian	0-2	0-3	8000		1		3		5					10	11					8		7		2	4				6				9
31	15	DUNDEE	3-0	5-3	3000	Culley(3), Jackson(2)			3	7	5			8		6	11			10				9			4	1	2						
32	18	Ayr United	2-3	2-4	6000	Culley, Jackson			3	7				8		6	11			10				9	5		4	1	2						
33	25	FALKIRK	0-1	1-2	5000	Smith			3		5		7	8			11			10				9	4			1	2		6				
34	1 Mar	Motherwell	0-0	0-3					3		5			8			11			9		10		7	4			1			6	2			
35	4	PARTICK THISTLE	2-0	2-1	8000	Culley, Jackson			3		5		7	8		6	11			10				9	4			1				2			
36	11	Celtic	0-1	0-1	6000				3		5		7	8	9	6	11			10						2	4	1							
37	18	CLYDE	1-0	1-0	5000	Skinner			3		5		7	8	9	6	11			10			4			2		1							
38	25	Queens Park	1-0	1-1	10000	Culley			3		5		7	8		6	11	4		10		9						1	2						
39	1 Apr	HAMILTON A.	0-1	1-1	2000	Culley			3	9	5		7	8		10		4		11								1	2		6				
40	8	Aberdeen	0-0	1-0	10000	Culley			3		5		7	8		6	11	4		9		10						1	2						
41	24	RANGERS	0-1	1-2	12000	Culley			3		5			8		6	11			9		10		7				1	2	4					
42	29	Third Lanark	0-1	0-2	5000				3		5			8		6	11			9		10		7				1	2	4					
						Apps.	29	14	40	11	32	2	22	34	7	26	28	25	4	40	4	27	6	27	18	19	12	12	9	4	4	2	2	1	1
						Goals			1	2		1	1	7	2		2	1		20		7		9	1								1		

Pos	P.	W.	D.	L.	F.	A.	Pts.
17th	42	13	9	20	56	83	35

Scottish Cup

							Neil	Murray	Gibson	Gray	Goldie	Pollock	McNaught	M.Smith	Skinner	Ramsay	McPhail	Shortt	Neave	Culley	Gunn	Watson	Garrity	Jackson	Frew	Robertson	Scott	Herron	Hood	Cherry	Good	Howat	Bailey	Cree	Logue
1	28 Jan	Caledonian	2-0	5-1	1000	Culley(2), Gray, Scott, Watson	1		3	7	5					6	11			10		8		9		2	4								
2	11 Feb	ST. MIRREN	0-2	1-4	15000	Culley			3	7				8		6	11	5		10				9		2	4	1							

Killie hadn't stopped nursing local talent. Dreghorn lad BOBBY HOWAT made his debut this season.

SEASON 1922-23 Division One

No.	Date	Opposition	H.T.	Res.	Att.	Goalscorers
1	16 Aug	ABERDEEN	1-0	1-0	9000	Culley
2	19	Albion Rovers	0-0	1-1	7000	Jackson
3	26	AYR UNITED	1-0	2-0	12000	Jackson, Ramsay
4	2 Sep	Dundee	0-2	0-2	15000	
5	9	CLYDE	2-0	4-1	10000	Culley(2), Smith(2)
6	16	Hamilton A.	3-2	3-3	6000	Brown(2), Ramsay
7	23	RAITH ROVERS	1-1	1-2	7000	Brown
8	30	Hibernian	0-0	1-1	18000	Brown
9	7 Oct	ALLOA ATHLETIC	1-1	2-2	8000	Culley(2)
10	14	Morton	2-0	4-1		Culley(3), Smith
11	21	HEARTS	1-0	1-2	5000	Culley
12	28	St. Mirren	0-2	0-2	11000	
13	4 Nov	MOTHERWELL	0-2	0-6	6000	
14	11	AIRDRIEONIANS	0-1	0-1	7000	
15	18	Aberdeen	0-0	0-5	10000	
16	25	FALKIRK	0-0	1-0	6000	Culley
17	2 Dec	Third Lanark	0-0	2-1	7000	McPhail, Morton
18	16	PARTICK THISTLE	0-1	1-3	6000	Lyner
19	23	Celtic	0-0	2-1	8000	Jackson, Lyner
20	27	Alloa Athletic	0-1	3-3		Dunlop, Goldie, McPhail
21	30	HIBERNIAN	0-0	1-0	5000	Ramsay
22	1 Jan	ST. MIRREN	1-2	1-2	14000	McPhail
23	2	Ayr United	1-1	1-2	11000	Jackson
24	6	DUNDEE	0-0	2-0	8000	Jackson, Ramsay
25	20	RANGERS	1-2	1-2	15000	Jackson
26	3 Feb	CELTIC	2-2	4-3	7500	Jackson, McCulloch, Rattray, Smith
27	7	Raith Rovers	0-1	0-1		
28	10	Hearts	0-4	0-5	13000	
29	17	HAMILTON A.	3-0	3-0	6000	Lyner, McCulloch, Smith
30	3 Mar	Airdrieonians	1-2	1-4	4000	Jackson
31	10	Clyde	0-1	0-2	5000	
32	17	ALBION ROVERS	4-0	7-0	6000	Jackson(4), Lyner, McCulloch, Rattray
33	21	THIRD LANARK	1-0	2-0	4000	Jackson, Dunlop
34	24	Partick Thistle	0-0	1-1	10000	Jackson
35	31	MORTON	2-1	3-2	7000	Jackson, Lyner, Rattray
36	7 Apr	Motherwell	0-1	1-4	3000	Dunlop
37	21	Rangers	0-1	0-1	10000	
38	28	Falkirk	0-0	0-0	5000	

No.	Herron	Hood	Gibson	Turnbull	Goldie	Ramsay	Jackson	Smith	Brown	McLeavy	Culley	McPhail	H.Morton	Harvey	Watson	McCulloch	Morris	J.Morton	Dunlop	Lyner	Murray	Skillen	Marshall	Rattray
1	1	2	3	4	5	6	7	8	9	10	11													
2	1	2	3	4	5	6	7	8	9	10	11													
3	1	2	3	4	5	6	7	8	9		10	11												
4	1	2	3	4	5	6	7	8	9		10	11												
5	1	2	3	4	5	6	7	8	9		10		11											
6	1	2	3	4	5	6	7	8	9		10		11											
7	1	2	3	4	5	6	7	8	9		10		11											
8	1	2	3	4		6	7	8	9		10		11	5										
9	1	2	3	4		6	7	8	9		10		11	5										
10	1		3		4	6	7	8	9		10	11	2	5										
11	1		3		4	6	7	8	9		10	11	2	5										
12	1		3	4	2	6	7	8	9		10	11		5										
13	1		3	4	6		7	8	9				2	5	10	11								
14	1	2	3	4	5	6	7	8	9		10					11								
15	1	2	3	6	5		9	8			10	11				7	4							
16		2	3	5	4	6	7	8	10		9	11						1						
17		2	3	5	4	6	9	8	10			11	7					1						
18		2	3	4		6	9	8								11		1	5	7	10			
19		2	3	6	4	10	9	8				11						1	5	7				
20		2	3	6	4	10	9	8				11				7		1	5					
21		2	3	4		10	9	8				11	6					1	5	7				
22		2	3	4		10	7	8	9			11	6					1	5					
23		2	3		4		7		9		8	11	6					1	5			10		
24		2	3		4	10	9	8				11	6					1	5	7				
25		2			4	10	9	8				11	6					1	5	7			3	
26		2		3	4		9	8					6			11		1	5	7				10
27		2		3	4		9	8					6			11		1	5	7				10
28		3	2		4		9	8					6			11		1	5	7				10
29		2	3		4		9	8					6			11		1	5	7				10
30		2	3		4		9	8					6			11		1	5	7				10
31		2	3			6	9	8					4			11		1	5	7				10
32		2	3		4	6	9	8								11		1	5	7				10
33		2	3		4	6	9	8								11		1	5	7				10
34		2	3		4	6	9	8					11					1	5	7				10
35		2	3		4	6	9	8								11		1	5	7				10
36		2	3	6			9	8				11					4	1	5	7				10
37		2	3		4	6	9	8				11						1	5	7				10
38		2	3		4	6	9		8			11						1	5	7				10
Apps.	15	34	35	23	31	29	38	36	19	2	16	18	21	6	1	14	2	23	21	18	1	1	1	13
Goals					1	4	15	5	4		10	3	1			3			3	5				3

Pos	P.	W.	D.	L.	F.	A.	Pts.
15th	38	14	7	17	57	66	35

Scottish Cup

Rd	Date	Opposition	H.T.	Res.	Att.	Goalscorers
1	13 Jan	BROXBURN	1-0	5-0	7000	Jackson(4), Smith
2	27	EAST FIFE	0-0	1-1	8000	Culley
2R	31	East Fife	0-1	0-1	6000	

Rd	Herron	Hood	Gibson	Turnbull	Goldie	Ramsay	Jackson	Smith	Brown	McLeavy	Culley	McPhail	H.Morton	Harvey	Watson	McCulloch	Morris	J.Morton	Dunlop	Lyner	Murray	Skillen	Marshall	Rattray
1		2			6	10	9	8				11	4					1	5	7			3	
2		2			4	10	9	8			11		6					1	5	7			3	
2R		2		5	4	6	9	8			10		11					1		7			3	

The 1922-23 first team 'pool' (although the word wasn't used then)
Back: P.Carrick, M.Smith, D.Brown, W.Culley, A.Herron, J.Turnbull, J.Ramsay, J.McWhinnie
Front: J.Goldie, R.Howart, W.Jackson, J.Hood, J.Harvey, D.Corbett, M.McLeavy, D.Gibson, M.McPhail.
Note: Trainers, Carrick & McWhinnie included, but Spence (Manager) omitted from the portrait.

SEASON 1923-24 Division One

No.	Date	Opposition	H.T.	Res.	Att.	Goalscorers	J.Morton	Hood	Gibson	Willis	Dunlop	Ramsay	Lyner	Davidson	Gossman	Rattray	Borland	Skillen	Gray	Smith	Howat	H.Morton	McEwan	Brown	Greig	McPhail	Allison	Adams	Campbell
1	18 Aug	QUEENS PARK	0-1	1-4	17000	Dunlop	1	2	3	4	5	6	7	8	9	10	11												
2	25	Ayr United	0-0	0-0	8000		1	2	3	4	5	6	7		9	8	11	10											
3	1 Sep	HIBERNIAN	0-1	2-1	10000	Ramsay, Skillen	1	2	3	4	5	6	7		9	8	11	10											
4	8	Clyde	1-1	1-1	3000	Borland	1	2	3	4	5	6	7		9	8	11	10											
5	15	HAMILTON A.	0-0	1-0	7000	Gray	1	2	3	4	5	6	7		8		11	10	9										
6	22	Clydebank	1-1	2-1	3000	Gray, Ramsay	1	2	3	4	5	6	7		8		11		9	10									
7	29	DUNDEE	0-1	1-3	6000	Ramsay	1	2	3	4	5	6	7		8		11		9	10									
8	6 Oct	Morton	1-0	2-0	4000	Gray(2)	1	2	3	4	5	6	7				11	10	9	8									
9	13	FALKIRK	2-0	2-1	8000	Gray(2)	1	2	3	4		6	7				11	10	9	8	5								
10	20	Motherwell	0-3	0-4	6000		1	2	3	4		6	7				11	10	9	8	5								
11	27	ST. MIRREN	1-0	2-0	10000	Gray, Skillen	1	2	3	4		6	7				11	10	9	8	5								
12	3 Nov	ABERDEEN	1-0	2-1	5000	Lyner, Willis	1	2	3	4		6	7				11	10	9	8	5								
13	10	Hearts	0-2	1-4		Skillen	1	2	3	4		6	7				11	10	9	8		5							
14	17	RAITH ROVERS	1-1	1-2	5000	Smith	1	2	3	4		6	7				11	10	9	8		5							
15	24	Third Lanark	0-0	1-2	5000	Ramsay	1	2	3	5		10	7				11		9	8		4	6						
16	1 Dec	Airdrieonians	1-1	2-2	7000	Gray, Ramsay	1	2	3	5		10					11		9	8		7	6	4					
17	8	CELTIC	0-0	1-1	12000	Gray	1	2	3	5		10					11		9	8		7	6	4					
18	15	Partick Thistle	0-2	2-2	10000	Gray(2)	1	2	3	5		10	7				11		9	8			6	4					
19	22	HEARTS	1-0	2-1	10000	Gray, Smith	1	2	3	5		10	7				11		9	8			6	4					
20	29	THIRD LANARK	0-0	0-0	5000		1	2	3	5		10	7				11		9	8			6	4					
21	1 Jan	St. Mirren	0-0	1-0	13000	Gray	1	2	3	5		10	7				11		9	8			6	4					
22	2	AYR UNITED	0-1	1-1	12000	Borland	1	2	3	5		10	7				11		9	8			6	4					
23	5	Queens Park	0-2	1-3	12000	Gray	1	2	3	5		10	7				11		9	8			6	4					
24	12	CLYDEBANK	1-1	2-3	5000	Gossman, Willis	1	2	3	5		10			7	8	11		9				6	4					
25	19	Dundee	1-1	2-4	14000	McPhail, Smith	1		3	5							7	10	9	8		4	6		2	11			
26	2 Feb	PARTICK THISTLE	0-1	3-1	5000	Gray(2), Ramsay	1		3	5		10					7		9	8		4	6	2		11			
27	13	MORTON	1-2	1-3	1000	Gray	1		3	5		6					7		9	8		4		2		11	10		
28	19	Rangers	0-1	0-2	10000		1		3	5		10	7				11		9	8		4	6	2					
29	27	Hibernian	0-2	1-3	4000	Smith	1		3	5		10	7				11		9	8		4	6	2					
30	5 Mar	RANGERS	0-1	1-1	10000	Willis	1		3	9			7				11	10		8		4	6	2				5	
31	8	Celtic	0-2	1-2	16000	Skillen	1		3	9			7				11	10		8		4	6	2				5	
32	15	CLYDE	1-0	3-0	3000	Borland, Smith, Adams	1		3	4			7				11	10		8		2		6				5	9
33	29	Hamilton A.	1-2	1-2	6000	Campbell	1		3	4			7				11	10		8		2		6				5	9
34	2 Apr	AIRDRIEONIANS	0-2	1-2	4000	Gray	1		3	5							11	10	7	8		2	6	4					9
35	5	Raith Rovers	1-2	1-4	5000	Gray	1		3	4						7	11		9	8		2		6				5	10
36	12	Falkirk	1-1	1-2	4000	Smith	1	2	3								11	10	9	8		4		6				5	7
37	19	Aberdeen	0-2	0-2	10000		1		3						7	10	11		9	8		4	6	2				5	
38	26	MOTHERWELL	1-0	1-0	4000	Brown	1	2	3								11	10	9	8		4	6	7				5	
						Apps.	38	26	38	35	8	28	27	1	9	7	38	19	30	32	4	19	19	22	1	3	1	8	5
						Goals				3	1	6	1		1		3	4	19	6				1		1		1	1

Pos	P.	W.	D.	L.	F.	A.	Pts.
16th	38	12	8	18	48	65	32

Scottish Cup

No.	Date	Opposition	H.T.	Res.	Att.	Goalscorers	J.Morton	Hood	Gibson	Willis	Dunlop	Ramsay	Lyner	Davidson	Gossman	Rattray	Borland	Skillen	Gray	Smith	Howat	H.Morton	McEwan	Brown	Greig	McPhail	Allison	Adams	Campbell
1	26 Jan	CELTIC	1-0	2-0	17200	Gray, Ramsay	1		3	5		10					7		9	8		4	6	2		11			
2	9 Feb	Ayr United	0-0	0-1	16562		1		3	5		10					7		9	8		4	6	2		11			

Killie's influential midfielder BOBBY BROWN attacks Hearts in December 1923 with JOE WILLIS in support

SEASON 1924-25 Division One

No.	Date	Opposition	H.T.	Res.	Att.	Goalscorers	Gould	Hood	Gibson	H.Morton	Clark	Brown	Walker	Smith	Gray	Bird	Borland	McEwan	Wilson	Nibloe	Weir	J.Morton	Willis	Adams	Lindsay	Rock	Dunlop
1	16 Aug	Morton	1-0	2-2	6000	Borland(2)	1	2	3	4	5	6	7	8	9	10	11										
2	20	Queens Park	1-1	2-1	8000	Gray, Borland	1	2	3	6	5	4	7	8	9	10	11										
3	23	HIBERNIAN	0-1	0-1	8000		1	2	3	6	5	4	7	8	9	10	11										
4	30	Rangers	0-1	1-1	18000	Clark	1	2	3	4	5		7	8	9		11	6	10								
5	6 Sep	AIRDRIEONIANS	2-1	2-3	8000	Brown, Smith	1	2	3	4	5	7		8	9		11	6	10								
6	13	Dundee	0-0	1-3	12000	Wilson	1	2		4	5		7	8			11	6	10	3	9						
7	20	HAMILTON A.	1-2	1-3	8000	Smith		2		4	5		7	8			11	6	10	3	9	1					
8	27	Falkirk	0-0	0-0	7000		1	2		4	5		7	8	9	10	11	6		3							
9	4 Oct	THIRD LANARK	1-2	2-2	7000	Gray, Borland	1	2		4	5		7	8	9	10	11	6		3							
10	11	QUEENS PARK	1-1	3-1	7000	Borland, Gray, Walker	1	2			5	4	7	8	9		11	6	10	3							
11	18	Ayr United	1-0	1-0	8000	Gray	1	2	3		5	4	7	8	9		11	6	10								
12	25	Cowdenbeath	0-3	2-5	7000	Smith(2)	1	2		4	5		7	8	9		11	6	10	3							
13	1 Nov	ST. MIRREN	3-1	3-2	7000	Bird, Gray, Smith	1	2	3		5	4	7	8	9	10	11	6									
14	8	Celtic	0-1	0-6	8000		1	2	3	9	5	4	7	8		10	11	6									
15	15	Raith Rovers	0-2	1-3	7000	Brown	1	2	3			4	7	8			11	6	10		9		5				
16	22	HEARTS	1-0	2-1	3000	Brown, McEwan	1	2	3		5	8	7		9	10		6						4	11		
17	29	Aberdeen	0-0	0-0	12000		1	2	3		5	8	7		9	10		6						4	11		
18	6 Dec	MOTHERWELL	0-1	0-2	6000		1	2	3	11	5		7	8		10		6					4			9	
19	13	St. Johnstone	2-4	2-4	6000	Bird, Smith	1	2	3		5	7		8		10		6						4	11	9	
20	20	RAITH ROVERS	1-0	3-0	7000	Lindsay(2), Smith	1	2	3	4		10	7	8	9			6							11		5
21	27	PARTICK THISTLE	0-0	1-1	5000	Walker	1	2	3	4		10	7	8	9			6							11		5
22	1 Jan	AYR UNITED	2-0	4-1	12000	Gray(2), Brown, Dunlop	1	2	3	4		10	7	8	9			6							11		5
23	3	Hibernian	0-0	0-2	13000		1	2	3	4	5	10	7	8	9			6							11		
24	5	St. Mirren	0-1	0-3	5000		1	2	3	4		10	7	8	9			6							11		5
25	10	DUNDEE	1-1	4-1	6000	Smith(2), Hood, McEwan	1	2	3			10	7	8	9			6					4		11		5
26	17	Third Lanark	0-1	0-2	6000		1	2	3			10	7	8	9			6					4		11		5
27	31	ABERDEEN	0-0	0-1	6000		1	2		3		10	7	8	9			6					4		11		5
28	11 Feb	Airdrieonians	2-2	2-4	5000	McEwan, Rock	1	2		3			7	8		10		6					4		11	9	5
29	14	Partick Thistle	1-2	1-2	5000	Hood	1	2		3			7	8		10		6					4		11	9	5
30	25	MORTON	2-0	3-1	3000	Smith(2), Dunlop	1	2	3	6		10	7	8									4		11	9	5
31	28	FALKIRK	0-0	1-0	10000	Rock	1	2	3			10	7	8				6					4		11	9	5
32	11 Mar	Hamilton A.	1-2	1-2	5000	Smith	1	2	3	4			7	8	10			6							11	9	5
33	14	Hearts	1-1	1-1	20000	Dunlop	1	2	3	4			7	8	10			6							11	9	5
34	21	COWDENBEATH	0-0	0-0	5000		1	2	3	4			7	8	10	9		6							11		5
35	28	RANGERS	0-0	0-0	12000		1	2	3	4		7	9	8	10			6							11		5
36	4 Apr	Motherwell	0-1	1-2		Walker	1	2	3	4		7	9	8	10			6							11		5
37	15	CELTIC	1-1	2-1	4000	Rock, Smith	1	2	3	4			7	8	10			6							11	9	5
38	22	ST. JOHNSTONE	2-0	4-0	2000	Rock, Gray, Walker, Smith	1	2	3	4			7	8	10			6							11	9	5
						Apps.	37	38	29	28	19	24	36	36	28	14	15	34	8	6	3	1	9	3	22	10	18
						Goals		2			1	4	4	14	8	2	5	3	1						2	4	3

Pos	P.	W.	D.	L.	F.	A.	Pts.
12th	38	12	9	17	53	64	33

Scottish Cup

Rd	Date	Opposition	H.T.	Res.	Att.	Goalscorers	Gould	Hood	Gibson	H.Morton	Clark	Brown	Walker	Smith	Gray	Bird	Borland	McEwan	Wilson	Nibloe	Weir	J.Morton	Willis	Adams	Lindsay	Rock	Dunlop
1	24 Jan	ARBROATH ATHLETIC	2-0	3-0	6000	Bird, Rock, Smith	1	2		6				8		10				3	7		4		11	9	5
2	7 Feb	HEARTS	2-0	2-1	14000	Lindsay, Rock	1	2		3		7		8					10				4	6	11	9	5
3	21	DYKEHEAD	0-0	5-0	6100	Lindsay(2), Bird, Rock, Weir	1	2		3		7				10		6			8		4		11	9	5
QF	7 Mar	RANGERS	1-0	1-2	31502	Bird	1	2		3		7		8				6	10				4		11	9	5

Alex Gibson

His term as Chairman was interrupted by war, he returned to the head of club affairs in 1924.

SEASON 1925-26 Division One

No.	Date	Opposition	H.T.	Res.	Att.	Goalscorers	Gould	Hood	Gibson	Morton	B.Brown	McEwan	Walker	Smith	Rock	Gray	Crump	Marshall	Lindsay	Reilly	Cunningham	Nibloe	Weir	Dunlop	A.Brown	McCall	Clemie	Mathieson	Ritchie	Wishart
1	15 Aug	QUEENS PARK	2-0	2-1	10000	Gray, Walker	1	2	3	4	5	6	7	8	9	10	11													
2	22	Hibernian	0-2	0-8	17000		1	2	3	4	5	6	7	8	9	10	11													
3	29	CLYDEBANK	1-1	2-2	5000	Gray, Rock	1	2	3	4		6	7	8	9	10		5	11											
4	5 Sep	Falkirk	1-2	1-6	8000	Rock	1	2	3	4		6	7	8	9	10		5	11											
5	12	MORTON	2-0	2-0	7000	Gray, Cunningham	1	2	7	4	3			6	9	10			11	5	8									
6	19	Hamilton A.	2-2	2-2	6000	Lindsay, Weir	1	2	5	4				8		10			11	6	7	3	9							
7	26	COWDENBEATH	0-1	1-1	5000	Lindsay	1	2	5					4	9	10			11	6	7	3	8							
8	3 Oct	Rangers	0-2	0-3	20000		1	2	5	4				8	9	10			11	6	7	3								
9	10	AIRDRIEONIANS	2-1	3-2	10000	Lindsay(2), O.G.	1	2	3	4				8		10			11	6	7		9	5						
10	17	ST. MIRREN	0-1	2-3	12000	Gray, Weir	1	2	3	4			7	8		10			11	6			9	5						
11	24	Dundee United	0-0	1-3	8000	Weir	1	2		4				7		10			11	6		3	9	5	8					
12	31	Aberdeen	1-2	2-3	12000	Hood, Lindsay	1	2		4		10	7	8					11	6		3	9	5						
13	7 Nov	ST. JOHNSTONE	1-1	3-2	6000	Weir(2), Lindsay	1	2		4		6	7	8		10			11			3	9	5						
14	14	Partick Thistle	2-1	4-2	8000	Weir(2), Smith, Walker	1	2		4		6	7	8					11			3	9	5		10				
15	21	RAITH ROVERS	2-0	3-0	3000	Weir(2), Smith	1	2		4		6	7	8					11			3	9	5		10				
16	28	Hearts	0-1	0-1	16000		1	2		4		6	7	8					11			3	9	5		10				
17	5 Dec	RANGERS	1-2	2-2	10000	Hood, Smith	1	2		4		6	7	8					11			3	9	5		10				
18	12	Dundee	0-1	0-1	9000		1	2		4		6	7	8					11			3	9	5		10				
19	19	FALKIRK	1-1	2-3	5000	McCall, Weir	1	2		4		6	7	8					11			3	9	5		10				
20	26	Raith Rovers	3-3	5-4	3000	Weir(2), Dunlop, Smith, Walker	1	2		4		6	7	8					11		10	3	9	5						
21	1 Jan	St. Mirren	3-1	4-1	12000	Weir(2), Cunningham, Walker	1	2		4		6	7	8					11		10	3	9	5						
22	2	DUNDEE UNITED	1-1	2-3	10000	Weir, Morton	1	2		4		6	7	8					11		10	3	9	5						
23	4	HAMILTON A.	4-1	4-1	7000	Crump(2), Rock, Smith		2		4		6	7	8	9	10	11					3					1	5		
24	9	Morton	1-1	2-1	4000	Cunningham(2)	1	2		4		6	7	8			11				10	3	9					5		
25	16	DUNDEE	2-1	5-2	7000	Smith(2), Lindsay, Cunningham, Weir	1	2		4		6	7	8					11		10	3	9	5						
26	30	St. Johnstone	0-0	2-0	8000	Cunningham, Lindsay	1	2		4		6	7	8					11		10	3	9	5						
27	10 Feb	CELTIC	1-0	2-1	8000	Cunningham, Weir	1	2		4		6	7	8					11		10	3	9	5						
28	13	PARTICK THISTLE	2-0	3-3	8000	Weir(2), McCall	1	2		4		6		8					11		7	3	9			10		5		
29	20	Clydebank	1-2	1-5	4000	Dunlop	1			2		6	7	8					11		10	3	9	5					4	
30	27	Motherwell	1-1	2-1	6000	McCall, Morton	1	2		4		6		8			11				7	3	9	5		10				
31	13 Mar	Cowdenbeath	0-0	0-1	5000			2		4		6		8		9	11				7	3		5		10	1			
32	17	ABERDEEN	1-0	3-0	4000	Weir(3)		2		4		6					11				8	3	9	5		10	1			7
33	20	HEARTS	3-1	5-1	8000	Weir(2), Wishart(2), McCall		2		4		6					11				8	3	9			10	1	5		7
34	27	Queens Park	1-1	2-2	10000	Cunningham, Weir		2		4		6					11				8	3	9	5		10	1			7
35	3 Apr	Celtic	0-0	0-0	12000			2		4		6		8			11				10	3	9	5			1			7
36	10	MOTHERWELL	0-0	1-2	6000	Dunlop		2		4		6		8			11					3	9	5		10	1			7
37	17	Airdrieonians	1-3	2-3	4500	Crump, Weir		2				6		8			11			4	10	3	9	5			1			7
38	24	HIBERNIAN	0-1	2-1	5000	Cunningham, Smith		2		4		6		8			11				10	3	9	5			1			7
						Apps.	29	37	10	36	3	31	22	35	8	14	13	2	25	9	22	31	30	26	1	13	9	4	1	7
						Goals		2		2			4	8	3	4	3		8		9		26	3		4				2

Pos	P.	W.	D.	L.	F.	A.	Pts.
9th	38	17	7	14	79	77	41

Scottish Cup

No.	Date	Opposition	H.T.	Res.	Att.	Goalscorers	Gould	Hood	Gibson	Morton	B.Brown	McEwan	Walker	Smith	Rock	Gray	Crump	Marshall	Lindsay	Reilly	Cunningham	Nibloe	Weir	Dunlop	A.Brown	McCall	Clemie	Mathieson	Ritchie	Wishart
1	23 Jan	CELTIC	0-1	0-5	24174		1	2		4		6	7	8					11		10	3	9	5						

MATTHA' SMITH, who played in both Cup-winning sides in the 20's, was at his peak in 1925-26. The following year he would sustain a broken leg. His League appearance record stood for nearly forty years. Even today, he is still Kilmarnock's third top all-time League scorer.

SEASON 1926-27 Division One

No.	Date	Opposition	H.T.	Res.	Att.	Goalscorers
1	14 Aug	CELTIC	1-2	2-3	20000	Cunningham, McEwan
2	21	Motherwell	0-1	0-1	6000	
3	28	DUNFERMLINE	1-2	2-3	10000	Cunningham, R.Walker
4	4 Sep	Dundee United	0-1	2-1	10000	R.Walker, Weir
5	11	ST. JOHNSTONE	1-0	2-0	4000	Weir(2)
6	18	Partick Thistle	0-3	0-5	20000	
7	25	HEARTS	1-2	1-4	6000	McCall
8	27	Aberdeen	0-4	1-5	15000	Crump
9	2 Oct	Airdrieonians	0-1	0-2	3000	
10	9	ABERDEEN	0-0	0-0	4000	
11	16	MORTON	2-0	2-0	3000	Cunningham, D.Walker
12	23	Queens Park	0-1	0-1	10000	
13	30	St. Mirren	0-0	0-1	9000	
14	6 Nov	FALKIRK	1-1	1-1	5000	Cunningham
15	13	DUNDEE	3-0	3-2	5000	Wishart(2), Leitch
16	20	Clyde	0-0	1-1	5000	Brown
17	27	HAMILTON A.	0-0	0-1	5000	
18	4 Dec	Hibernian	1-1	1-5	8000	McCall
19	11	Cowdenbeath	1-0	1-3	4000	Cunningham
20	18	RANGERS	0-0	0-0	12000	
21	25	Celtic	0-1	0-4	12000	
22	1 Jan	ST. MIRREN	1-2	2-2	15000	Mathieson, Murphy
23	3	Dunfermline	3-1	3-2	4000	Cunningham, Leitch, Thomson
24	8	DUNDEE UNITED	2-0	3-0	4000	Cunningham(2), Murphy
25	15	St. Johnstone	2-0	3-3	8000	Cunningham(3)
26	29	PARTICK THISTLE	0-0	2-0	4000	Cunningham, Ramsay
27	12 Feb	AIRDRIEONIANS	2-1	4-2	6000	Cunningham(2), Morton, Reilly
28	19	Hearts	1-0	1-1	10000	Cunningham
29	26	Morton	1-3	2-3	5000	Cunningham, Ramsay
30	5 Mar	QUEENS PARK	1-0	2-2	6000	Murphy, Ramsay
31	12	MOTHERWELL	1-2	1-4	6000	Cunningham
32	19	Falkirk	1-0	1-0	6000	Weir
33	26	Dundee	2-0	2-1	6000	Cunningham, Thomson
34	2 Apr	CLYDE	1-1	4-1	4000	Weir(3), Cunningham
35	9	Hamilton A.	0-1	0-2	4000	
36	20	HIBERNIAN	2-0	4-0	2000	Weir(2), Murphy, Ramsay
37	23	COWDENBEATH	1-1	1-4	5000	Ramsay
38	30	Rangers	0-1	0-1	8000	

No.	Clemie	Hood	Nibloe	Morton	Dunlop	McEwan	Smith	Mathieson	Cunningham	Weir	Crump	Wishart	R.Walker	D.Walker	McCall	McLeod	Marshall	Reilly	Leitch	Brown	Gould	Scott	Thomson	Murphy	Ramsay	Paton	Leslie
1	1	2	3	4	5	6	7	8	10	9	11																
2	1	2	3	4		6		5	8		11	7	9		10												
3	1	2	3	4		6			8	9	11		7		10	5											
4	1	2	3			6			8	9			7		10	5	4	11									
5	1	2	3	4		6			8	9		7			10	5		11									
6	1	2	3			6			8	9		7			10	5	4	11									
7	1	2	3			6			10	9			7		11	5		4	8								
8	1	2	3			6				9	11		7		10	5		4		8							
9	1	2	3			6				9	11		7		10	5		4		8							
10		2	3	10	5	6			8		11	7		9		4					1						
11		2	3	10	5	6			8		11	7		9		4					1						
12		2	3	10	5	6			8	7	11			9		4					1						
13		2	3	11		6			8	9		7			10	5		4			1						
14		2	3	4		6			8	9		7				5			11		1	10					
15		2	3	4		6			8	9		7				5			11	10	1						
16		2	3	4		6			8	9		7				5			11	10	1						
17		2	3	4		6			8	9		7				5			11	10	1						
18		2	3	4					9		11				10	5		6	7	8	1						
19		2	3	4					9	10	11					5		6	7	8	1						
20		2	3	4		6		5	10	9		7						11		8	1						
21		2	3	4		6		5		8			9						7	10	1		11				
22		2	3	4		6		5		9									7		1		11	8	10		
23		2	3	4		6			9							5			7		1		11	8	10		
24		2	3	4		6			9							5			7		1		11	8	10		
25		2	3	4		6			9							5			7		1		11	8	10		
26		2	3	4		6			9							5			7		1		11	8	10		
27		2	3	4					9	8						5		6	7		1		11		10		
28	1	2	3	4					9							5		6	7				11	8	10		
29	1	2	3	4					9							5		6	7				11	8	10		
30	1	2	3	4					9							5		6	7				11	8	10		
31	1		3	2		6			9		11					5		4	7					8	10		
32	1		3	4					8	9						5		6					11	7	10	2	
33	1		3	4					8	9						5		6					11	7	10	2	
34	1		3	4					8	9						5		6					11	7	10	2	
35	1		3	4					8	9						5		6					11	7	10	2	
36	1		3	4		6			8	9						5							11	7	10		2
37	1		3	4		6			8	9						5							11	7	10		2
38	1		3	4		6			8	9						5							11	7	10	2	
Apps.	20	30	38	33	4	28	1	5	34	26	11	11	7	3	10	33	2	19	18	9	18	1	17	16	17	5	2
Goals				1		1		1	19	9	1	2	2	1	2			1	2	1			2	4	5		

Pos	P.	W.	D.	L.	F.	A.	Pts.
16th	38	12	8	18	54	71	32

Scottish Cup

No.	Date	Opposition	H.T.	Res.	Att.	Goalscorers
1	22 Jan	PEEBLES ROVERS	1-0	3-1	4000	Cunningham(2), Ramsay
2	5 Feb	DUNDEE	0-1	1-1	13000	Ramsay
2R	9	Dundee	1-2	1-5	12000	Murphy

No.	Clemie	Hood	Nibloe	Morton	Dunlop	McEwan	Smith	Mathieson	Cunningham	Weir	Crump	Wishart	R.Walker	D.Walker	McCall	McLeod	Marshall	Reilly	Leitch	Brown	Gould	Scott	Thomson	Murphy	Ramsay	Paton	Leslie
1		2	3	4		6		5	9										7		1		11	8	10		
2		2	3	4		6			9							5			7		1		11	8	10		
2R		2	3	4		6			9							5			7		1		11	8	10		

Signed in May 1927, JIMMY WILLIAMSON played for Killie for ten years, including the 1929 Cup Final in which he scored. He was also Assistant Manager at Rugby Park after the Second World War.

SEASON 1927-28 Division One

No.	Date	Opposition	H.T.	Res.	Att.	Goalscorers	Clemie	Hood	Nibloe	Morton	McLeod	Reilly	Murphy	Cunningham	Weir	Ramsay	Thomson	Williamson	Millar	McEwan	Paton	Pirrie	Smith	Mathieson	Cunningham(Celtic)	Robertson	Connell	Hogg	Leslie	R.Walker
1	13 Aug	Hearts	1-0	1-0	22000	Weir	1	2	3	4	5	6	7	8	9	10	11													
2	16	Celtic	1-2	1-6	15000	Ramsay	1		3	4	5	6	7	8	9	10	11				2									
3	20	PARTICK THISTLE	2-2	2-3	10000	Cunningham(2)	1	2	3	4	5	6	7	9		10		8	11											
4	27	Aberdeen	2-0	2-1	12000	Murphy, Weir	1	2	3	4	5		7	9	8	10			11	6										
5	3 Sep	BO'NESS	1-1	3-1	6000	Cunningham(3)	1	2	3	4	5		7	9	8	10			11	6										
6	10	Cowdenbeath	0-0	1-1		Cunningham	1	2	3	4	5		7	9	8	10			11	6										
7	17	MOTHERWELL	1-1	1-3	8000	Millar	1	2	3	4	5		7	9	8	10			11	6										
8	24	St. Johnstone	0-0	1-1	7000	Cunningham		2	3	4	5		7	9	8	10			11	6		1								
9	1 Oct	AIRDRIEONIANS	1-2	2-2	7000	Cunningham, Smith		2	3	4			7	9		10	11			6		1	8	5						
10	8	Bo'ness	1-0	1-2	4000	Cunningham		2	3	4			8	9		10	11			6		1	7	5						
11	15	ST. MIRREN	2-1	6-2	7000	Cunningham(2),Mortn,Mrphy,Rmsy,Thomsn		2	3	4	5		7	9		10	11			6		1	8							
12	22	QUEENS PARK	1-1	1-1	6000	Ramsay		2	3	4	5		7	9		10	11			6		1	8							
13	29	Raith Rovers	0-0	3-1	5000	Thomson, Ramsay, Weir		2	3	4			7		9	10	11			6		1	8	5						
14	5 Nov	Falkirk	0-2	0-6	7000			2	3	4			7		9	10	11			6		1	8	5						
15	12	Dundee	0-1	0-7	7000			2	3	4			7	9		10	11			6		1	8		5					
16	19	CLYDE	1-0	3-0	5000	Cunningham (No.9(2), Cunningham(No.5)	1		3	4		6	7	9		10	11						8		5	2				
17	26	Hamilton A.	1-2	1-3	3000	Cunningham	1		3	4		6	7	9		10	11						8		5	2				
18	3 Dec	HIBERNIAN	0-1	2-1	5000	Cunningham(2)	1		3	4	5	6		9		10	11						8		7	2				
19	10	DUNFERMLINE	2-0	2-1	5000	Cunningham, Ramsay	1		3	4		6	7	9		10	11	8						5		2				
20	17	RANGERS	1-1	1-1	14440	Cunningham	1		3	4	5	6	7	9		10	11						8			2				
21	24	HEARTS	3-0	5-0	6000	Cunningham,Murphy,Morton,Ramsay,Smith	1		3	4	5	6	7	9		10	11						8			2				
22	2 Jan	St. Mirren	1-1	1-1	20000	Morton	1		3	4	5	6	7	9		10	11						8			2				
23	3	COWDENBEATH	0-0	2-1	7500	Thomson, Weir	1		3	4	5		7	9	8	10	11			6						2				
24	7	ABERDEEN	2-0	2-1	3000	Cunningham(2)	1		3	4	5			9	8	10	11			6						2	7			
25	14	Motherwell	2-1	3-3	5000	Murphy(2), Cunningham	1		3	4	5		8	9		10	11			6						2	7			
26	28	CELTIC	1-1	2-2	18000	Cunningham, Murphy	1		3	4	5		11	9		10				6			8			2	7			
27	8 Feb	Airdrieonians	1-0	2-0		Cunningham(2)	1		3	4	5		11	9		10				6			8			2	7			
28	11	ST. JOHNSTONE	0-1	1-7	8000	Cunningham	1		3	4	5	6	11	9		10							8			2	7			
29	25	Queens Park	2-2	3-5	15000	Cunningham(2), Ramsay	1		3	4				9		10	11			6			8			2	7	5		
30	29	RAITH ROVERS	0-0	1-0	3000	Cunningham	1		3	4				9		10	11			6			8				7	5	2	
31	7 Mar	Partick Thistle	0-2	0-2	3000		1		3	4				9		10	11			6			8				7	5	2	
32	10	FALKIRK	1-1	1-1	3000	Ramsay	1		2		5		11	9		10				6			8			3	7	4		
33	17	DUNDEE	1-2	1-2	3000	Ramsay	1		3	4	5		11	9		10				6			8				7		2	
34	24	Clyde	1-0	1-1	4000	McEwan	1		3	4	5		11			10				6			8			2	7			9
35	31	HAMILTON A.	1-1	3-1	3000	Connell, Cunningham, Smith	1		3	4	5			9		10	11			6			8				7		2	
36	7 Apr	Hibernian	0-0	1-3		Millar	1		3	4	5			9		10			11	6			8			2	7			
37	14	Dunfermline	3-0	4-0	1000	Cunningham(3), Ramsay	1		3		5			9		10			11	6			8	2			7	4		
38	21	Rangers	0-3	1-5	28000	Cunningham	1		3		5			9		10			11	6			8			2	7	4		
						Apps.	30	14	38	35	27	11	29	35	11	38	23	2	9	27	1	8	26	6	4	18	15	6	4	1
						Goals				3			6	34	4	10	3		2	1			3		1		1			

Pos	P.	W.	D.	L.	F.	A.	Pts.
8th	38	15	10	13	68	78	40

Scottish Cup

No.	Date	Opposition	H.T.	Res.	Att.	Goalscorers	Clemie	Hood	Nibloe	Morton	McLeod	Reilly	Murphy	Cunningham	Weir	Ramsay	Thomson	Williamson	Millar	McEwan	Paton	Pirrie	Smith	Mathieson	Cunningham(Celtic)	Robertson	Connell	Hogg	Leslie	R.Walker
1	21 Jan	Leith Athletic +	2-1	3-2	7000	Connell, Ramsay, Thomson	1		3	4	5		8	9		10	11			6						2	7			
2	4 Feb	Forfar Athletic	1-1	2-1	3000	Cunningham, Murphy	1		3	4	5		11	9		10				6			8			2	7			
3	18	QUEENS PARK	3-2	4-4	21267	Smith(2), Cunningham, Morton	1		3	4	5			9		10	11			6			8			2	7			
3R	22	Queens Park	0-0	0-1	36000		1		3	4	5		11	9		10				6			8			2	7			

+ Played at Easter Road

Joining Killie from a Cumnock juvenile team in December 1927, TOM SMITH went on to play for Scotland as well as for Kilmarnock in the 1932 Cup Final. He won an English FA Cup Winner's medal with Preston North End and returned to Kilmarnock as Manager in 1945.

SEASON 1928-29 Division One

No.	Date	Opposition	H.T.	Res.	Att.	Goalscorers	Clemie	Robertson	Nibloe	Morton	Hogg	McEwan	Connell	Williamson	Cunningham	Ramsay	Clark	M.Smith	Weir	Dunlop	Paterson	Leslie	Bernard	Aitken	Mathieson	Stewart	T.Smith	McLaren
1	11 Aug	Rangers	0-3	2-4	20000	Cunningham, Ramsay	1	2	3	4	5	6	7	8	9	10	11											
2	18	HIBERNIAN	1-0	1-0	8000	Williamson	1	2	3	4	5	6	7	8	9	10	11											
3	25	Airdrieonians	0-1	1-2	4000	Ramsay	1	2	3	4	5	6	7	8	9	10	11											
4	1 Sep	DUNDEE	2-0	3-1	6000	Cunningham, Morton, Smith	1	2	3	4	5	6	7		9	10		8	11									
5	8	Celtic	0-1	0-3	18000		1	2	3	4	5	6	7		9	10		8	11									
6	15	ABERDEEN	0-1	0-1	6000		1	2	3	4	5	6	7	10	9			8	11									
7	22	THIRD LANARK	2-0	3-0	8000	Cunningham, Paterson, Ramsay	1	2	3	4			7		9	10	6	8		5	11							
8	24	Aberdeen	1-1	1-2	13000	Smith	1		3	4			7		9	10	6	8		5	11	2						
9	29	Clyde	1-1	1-1	7000	Connell	1	2	3	4			7		9	10	6	8		5	11							
10	6 Oct	St. Johnstone	0-1	0-1	6000			2	3	4			7		9	10	6	8		5	11		1					
11	13	PARTICK THISTLE	2-0	2-2	6000	Connell(2)		2	3	4			7		9	10	6	8		5	11		1					
12	20	St. Mirren	2-2	4-5	7000	Connell, Cunningham, Morton, Smith		2	3	4		6	7		9	10		8		5	11		1					
13	27	COWDENBEATH	2-1	4-2	5000	Cunningham(3), Dunlop		2	3		4	6	7		9			8	10	5	11		1					
14	3 Nov	Motherwell	0-0	3-2	8000	Cunningham(2), Smith	1	2	3	4		6	7		9	10		8		5	11							
15	10	QUEENS PARK	5-0	7-4	5000	Smith(4), Cunningham(2), Ramsay	1	2	3	4		6	7		9	10		8		5	11							
16	17	Ayr United	1-2	4-2	14000	Morton, Ramsay, Paterson, Smith	1	2	3	4		6	7		9	10		8		5	11							
17	24	HEARTS	1-0	3-2	10000	Connell(2), Cunningham	1	2	3	4		6	7		9	10		8		5	11							
18	1 Dec	Falkirk	1-1	2-2	5000	Cunningham, Morton	1	2	3	4		6	7		9	10		8		5	11							
19	8	RAITH ROVERS	3-0	7-1	5500	Cunningham(4), Connell(2), Morton	1	2	3	4		6	7		9	10		8		5	11							
20	15	Hamilton A.	1-0	2-0	4000	Cunningham, Paterson	1	2	3	4		6	7		9	10		8		5	11							
21	22	Hibernian	1-0	1-1	2000	Ramsay	1	2	3	4		6	7		9	10		8		5	11							
22	29	RANGERS	1-2	1-3	30000	Dunlop	1	2	3	4		6	7		9	10		8		5	11							
23	1 Jan	ST. MIRREN	0-2	2-4	15000	Cunningham, Smith	1		3	4		6	7		9	10		8		5		2		11				
24	2	Cowdenbeath	0-2	0-2			1	2	3	4		6	7	8	9					5	11				10			
25	5	AIRDRIEONIANS	0-1	0-2	4000		1	2	3	4		6	7		9	10			8	5				11				
26	12	Dundee	1-1	3-1	8000	Connell, Cunningham, Paterson	1	2	3	4		6	7		9	10		8		5	11							
27	26	HAMILTON A.	0-0	0-0	5000		1	2	3	4		6	7		9	10		8		5	11							
28	9 Feb	Third Lanark	1-2	3-2	6000	Cunningham, Dunlop, Smith	1	2	3	4		6	7		9	10		8		5	11							
29	23	ST. JOHNSTONE	0-1	1-1	4000	Ramsay	1	2		4		6	7		9	10		8		5	11	3						
30	9 Mar	MOTHERWELL	3-1	4-2	5000	Paterson(2), Smith, Weir	1	2	3	4		6	7	10				8	9	5	11							
31	12	Partick Thistle	1-1	1-2	900	Connell	1	2	3	4		6	7	10				8	9	5	11							
32	20	Queens Park	0-1	0-2	4000				3		4	6			9	10					7		1	11	8	5	2	
33	30	Hearts	1-1	3-3	15000	Connel(2), Aitken	1	2	3	4		6	7	10				8	9					11		5		
34	1 Apr	CLYDE	2-0	3-1	4000	Aitken, Cunningham, Ramsay		2			4	6	7		9	10							1	11	8	5	3	
35	9	FALKIRK	0-0	1-1	4000	Smith	1	2		4		6	7	10	9			8						11		5	3	
36	20	Raith Rovers	3-0	3-5	500	Williamson(2), Cunningham	1	2	3	4	5	6	7	10	9			8						11				
37	24	AYR UNITED	0-2	1-2	6000	McEwan	1	2	3	4		6	7	10	9			8						11		5		
38	27	CELTIC	1-1	2-3	6300	Aitken, Williamson	1	2	3	4		6	7	10	9			8						11		5		
						Apps.	32	35	35	35	10	33	37	12	35	28	8	31	8	25	24	3	6	9	3	6	3	
						Goals				5		1	12	4	23	8		13	1	3	6			3				

Pos	P.	W.	D.	L.	F.	A.	Pts.
10th	38	14	8	16	79	74	36

Scottish Cup

No.	Date	Opposition	H.T.	Res.	Att.	Goalscorers	Clemie	Robertson	Nibloe	Morton	Hogg	McEwan	Connell	Williamson	Cunningham	Ramsay	Clark	M.Smith	Weir	Dunlop	Paterson	Leslie	Bernard	Aitken	Mathieson	Stewart	T.Smith	McLaren
1	19 Jan	GLASGOW UNIVERSITY	4-0	8-1	3500	Rmsy(3),Cnnll,Cnninghm,McEwn,Ptrsn,Smth		2	3	4		6	7		9	10		8		5	11		1					
2	2 Feb	BO'NESS	2-1	3-2	4000	Connell, Cunningham, Ramsay	1		3	4		6	7		9	10		8		5	11				2			
3	16	Albion Rovers	0-0	1-0	7000	Connell	1	2	3	4		6	7		9	10	11	8		5								
QF	2 Mar	Raith Rovers	3-1	3-2	11500	Cunningham, Paterson, Smith	1	2	3	4		6	7		9	10		8		5	11							
SF	23	Celtic*	1-0	1-0	40000	Weir	1	2	3	4		6	7	10				8	9		11							5
F	6 Apr	Rangers#	0-0	2-0	114708	Aitken, Williamson	1	2	3	4		6	7	10	9			8						11				5

* Ibrox # Hampden

The Scottish Cup comes to Kilmarnock for the second time, after an epic victory over the favourites, Rangers.
Back: H.Spence(Secretary), G.Neil, R.H.Thomson, H.Alexander, T.Robertson, S.Clemie, J.Nibloe, R.Thomson, T.Wylie, J.L.Morison, J.Walker
Middle: Douglas Dick, W.Connell, H.Cunningham, J.Weir, M.Smith, J.Ramsay, J.Williamson, J.Aitken, A.S. McCulloch (Chairman)
Front: T.Wallace (Assistant Trainer), H.Morton, H.McLaren, J.Dunlop, J.McEwan, J.McWhinnie (Trainer)

SEASON 1929-30 Division One

No.	Date	Opposition	H.T.	Res.	Att.	Goalscorers
1	10 Aug	HAMILTON A.	3-0	3-0	7000	Cunningham, Williamson(2)
2	17	Hearts	0-1	1-1	20000	Williamson
3	24	CLYDE	1-0	2-1	8000	Cunningham, M.Smith
4	31	Queens Park	1-1	4-1	18000	Connell(3), Paterson
5	7 Sep	AYR UNITED	1-0	2-0	14000	Cunningham(2)
6	14	Morton	2-2	2-4	10000	Cunningham(2)
7	21	RANGERS	1-0	1-0	23000	Paterson
8	28	Dundee	0-1	2-2	10000	Connell, M.Smith
9	5 Oct	Partick Thistle	1-2	2-3	20000	McGowan, M.Smith
10	12	ST. JOHNSTONE	1-1	3-1	7000	McEwan, M.Smith, Wllliamson
11	19	Cowdenbeath	0-1	3-2	3000	McEwan, Morton, Williamson
12	26	ST. MIRREN	1-3	2-3	6000	Connell, McGowan
13	2 Nov	ABERDEEN	2-1	4-2	10000	Paterson(2), McGowan, M.Smith
14	9	Airdrieonians	0-1	2-2	3000	McGowan, Paterson
15	16	DUNDEE UNITED	0-2	0-2	5000	
16	23	FALKIRK	2-1	3-2	5500	Connell, Cunningham, Williamson
17	30	Hibernian	0-0	0-0	3500	
18	7 Dec	Motherwell	0-1	0-2	2000	
19	14	CELTIC	1-1	1-1	7000	Williamson
20	21	Hamilton A.	0-1	1-1	3000	Weir
21	28	HEARTS	0-1	2-1	4000	Aitken, O.G.
22	1 Jan	St. Mirren	1-1	1-3	5000	Cunningham
23	2	COWDENBEATH	3-1	3-2	7000	Cunningham(2), Clark
24	4	Clyde	0-0	1-1	7000	Cunningham
25	11	QUEENS PARK	1-4	1-5	4000	Cunningham
26	25	Ayr United	1-1	1-1	11000	M.Smith
27	8 Feb	Rangers	0-3	0-4	25000	
28	15	MORTON	3-0	7-2	3000	McGowan(5), Ramsay, O.G.
29	22	PARTICK THISTLE	0-0	1-1	5000	McEwan
30	1 Mar	St. Johnstone	1-1	3-1	2000	McGowan(2), M.Smith
31	8	Aberdeen	0-2	3-4	12000	Wales(2), M.Smith
32	15	AIRDRIEONIANS	5-0	7-1	5000	McGowan(4),Cunningham,Paterson,M.Smith
33	22	Dundee United	4-2	4-6	5000	McGowan, Ramsay, M.Smith, Wales
34	29	Falkirk	0-0	0-1	2000	
35	5 Apr	HIBERNIAN	0-0	3-1	4500	Morton, McEwan, McGowan
36	12	MOTHERWELL	1-1	2-3	3000	Cunningham, McGowan
37	19	Celtic	0-2	0-4	4000	
38	21	DUNDEE	0-2	0-2	3000	

No.	Clemie	Robertson	Nibloe	Morton	Dunlop	McEwan	Connell	M.Smith	Cunningham	Williamson	Paterson	Ramsay	McGowan	T.Smith	Leslie	Hogg	Aitken	Weir	Stewart	Clark	G.B.Wilson	Irvine	McLeod	Wales
1	1	2	3	4	5	6	7	8	9	10	11													
2	1	2	3	4	5	6	7	8	9	10	11													
3	1	2	3	4	5	6	7	8	9	10	11													
4	1	2	3	4	5	6	7	8	9	10	11													
5	1	2	3	4	5	6	7	8	9	10	11													
6	1	2	3	4	5	6	7	8	9		11	10												
7	1	2	3	4	5	6	7	8	9		11	10												
8	1	2	3	4	5	6	7	8	9		11	10												
9	1	2	3	4	5	6	7	8			11	10	9											
10	1		3	4	5	6	7	8		10	11		9	2										
11	1	2	3	4	5	6	7	8		10	11		9											
12	1	2		4	5	6	7	8		10	11		9		3									
13	1	3		4	5	6	7	8		10	11		9	2										
14	1	2	3	4	5	6	7	8		10	11		9											
15	1	2	3	4	5	6	7	8		10	11		9											
16	1	4	3		5	6	7	8	9	10	11			2										
17	1		3		5	6	7	8	9	10				2		4	11							
18	1		3	4	5	6	7	8	9	10				2			11							
19	1		3	4	5	6	7	8		10				2			11	9						
20	1		3	4	5	6	7	8		10				2			11	9						
21	1		3	4		6	7	8		10				2			11	9	5					
22	1		3	4		6	7	8	9			10		2			11		5					
23	1	2	3	4					9	8	7	10					11		5	6				
24			3			6	7	10	9		11			2		4					1	5	8	
25			3		5	6		8	9		7	10		2			11				1		4	
26	1	2	3	4	5	6		8	9		7	10					11							
27	1	2	3		5	6		8	9	7		10				4	11							
28	1	2	3			6		8	7		11	10	9			4			5					
29	1	2	3	4		6		8	7		11	10	9						5					
30	1	2	3	4		6		8				10	9				11		5					7
31	1	2	3	4		6		8	9		11	10				5								7
32	1	2	3			6		8	7		11	10	9						5			4		
33	1	2	3			6		8				10	9				11		5			4		7
34	1	2	3	4		6		8	9		11	10				5								7
35	1	2	3	4		6		8				10	9			5	11							7
36	1	2	3	4		6		8	11			10	9			5								7
37	1	2	3	4		6		8	9		11	10				5								7
38	1		3			6		8				10	9	2		5	11					4		7
Apps.	36	28	36	29	23	37	23	37	24	19	26	20	15	12	1	10	14	3	8	1	2	4	2	8
Goals				2		4	6	10	14	7	6	2	18				1	1		1				3

Pos	P.	W.	D.	L.	F.	A.	Pts.
8th	38	15	9	14	77	73	39

Scottish Cup

No.	Date	Opposition	H.T.	Res.	Att.	Goalscorers
1	18 Jan	PAISLEY ACAS.	7-0	11-1	3000	Weir(6),Aitken(2),Connell,Ramsay,Wlliamsn
2	1 Feb	Hamilton A.	0-1	2-4	12000	Cunningham, McEwan

No.	Clemie	Robertson	Nibloe	Morton	Dunlop	McEwan	Connell	M.Smith	Cunningham	Williamson	Paterson	Ramsay	McGowan	T.Smith	Leslie	Hogg	Aitken	Weir	Stewart	Clark	G.B.Wilson	Irvine	McLeod	Wales
1	1	2	3	4		6	7			8		10					11	9	5					
2	1	2	3	4	5	6		8	9	10	7						11							

Bobby Muir (1898 Cup Final) arranged Killie's 1st overseas tour in 1930. Glasgow Central Station is the starting point for the journey to North America. On engine: McKenzie(Dir), Dick(Dir), Spence(Sec), Robertson,McEwan,Clark,Wales,Williamson,Walters,Smith,Leslie,Clemie. Standing on Platform: McCulloch(Pres), Graham (Sec SFA), Alexander(Dir), McWhinnie (in cap, Trainer), Wylie (behind McWhinnie, Dir), McGowan, Smith, Maxwell, Nibloe, Cunningham, Stewart, Aitken, Ramsay. Kneeling in front: Baillie Muirhead (SFA & Motherwell F.C.), Morison (Dir), Abbott (Ship.Agent), Fleming (Pres.SFA), Abbott (Ayrshire FA), Irvine (sitting on buffer).

SEASON 1930-31 Division One

No.	Date	Opposition	H.T.	Res.	Att.	Goalscorers
1	9 Aug	Celtic	1-2	1-3	20000	Ramsay
2	16	PARTICK THISTLE	1-0	2-0	8000	Cunningham, M.Smith
3	23	Airdrieonians	1-3	3-4	4000	Connell, Nicol, M.Smith
4	30	HEARTS	0-1	0-1	9500	
5	6 Sep	Motherwell	1-0	1-1	5000	Connell
6	13	AYR UNITED	1-1	2-1	8000	Ramsay, M.Smith
7	20	St. Mirren	0-2	2-4	10000	Duncan, Maxwell
8	27	COWDENBEATH	0-1	0-1	7000	
9	4 Oct	Leith Athletic	1-0	1-0	7000	Connell
10	11	DUNDEE	0-1	1-2	6000	Aitken
11	18	RANGERS	1-0	1-0	15000	Connell
12	25	Falkirk	2-1	2-4	5000	Maxwell(2)
13	1 Nov	HAMILTON A.	2-1	3-1	4000	Wales(2), Morton
14	8	Aberdeen	0-1	0-2	13000	
15	15	EAST FIFE	3-0	5-1	4000	Wales(4), Connell
16	22	Hibernian	1-3	2-3	1000	Connell, T.Smith
17	29	QUEENS PARK	1-1	2-1	5000	Aitken, Maxwell
18	6 Dec	Morton	1-1	2-2	3000	Maxwell(2)
19	13	CLYDE	1-0	2-1	4000	Aitken, Maxwell
20	20	CELTIC	0-1	0-3	16000	
21	27	Partick Thistle	1-1	1-3	8000	Irvine
22	1 Jan	ST. MIRREN	1-1	2-3	15000	Maxwell(2)
23	3	AIRDRIEONIANS	1-0	1-0	5000	Aitken
24	5	Cowdenbeath	0-1	1-3	1000	Maxwell
25	10	Hearts	2-0	4-1	15000	Connell, Maxwell, Morton, Ramsay
26	24	MOTHERWELL	0-2	1-4	5000	McEwan
27	7 Feb	LEITH ATHLETIC	1-0	2-1	5000	Aitken(2)
28	21	Rangers	0-0	0-1	8000	
29	7 Mar	Hamilton A.	0-0	0-0	1500	
30	11	FALKIRK	1-0	1-1	4000	Napier
31	18	ABERDEEN	0-0	1-1	4000	Duncan
32	21	East Fife	0-3	1-4	3000	Aitken
33	28	Dundee	1-0	2-0	4000	Maxwell, Muir
34	4 Apr	HIBERNIAN	1-0	4-0	4000	Maxwell(3), Aitken
35	18	MORTON	2-0	3-0	2500	Maxwell, Aitken
36	21	Queens Park	0-2	0-2		
37	25	Clyde	2-0	3-0	1500	Connell, Maxwell, McEwan
38	29	Ayr United	0-0	0-1	12000	

No.	Clemie	Leslie	Nibloe	Morton	Stewart	Clark	Connell	M.Smith	Cunningham	Ramsay	Aitken	Robertson	McEwan	Nicol	Young	T.Smith	Duncan	Maxwell	Kenmuir	Wales	Napier	Irvine	Muir	Parry	Falconer
1	1	2	3	4	5	6	7	8	9	10	11														
2	1		3	4	5		7	8	9			2	6	10	11										
3	1		3	4	5		7	8	9			2	6	10	11										
4	1		3	4			7	8	9		11	2	6			5	10								
5	1		3	4			7	8		10	11	2	6			5		9							
6	1		3	4			7	8		10	11	2	6			5		9							
7	1		3	4			7	8		10		2	6			5	9	11							
8	1		3	4			7	8		10		2	6			5		11	9						
9	1		3	4			7	8	9		11	2	6			5	10								
10	1		3	4			7	8	9		11	2	6			5	10								
11	1		3	4			7	8			11	2	6			5	10	9							
12	1		3	4			7	8			11	2	6			5	10	9							
13	1		3	4			7				11	2	6			5	10	9		8					
14	1		3	4			7	8			11	2	6			5	10	9							
15	1		3	4			7	8			11	2	6			5	10			9					
16	1		3	4			7				11	2	6			5	10			9	8				
17	1		3	4			7				11	2	6			5	10	9			8				
18	1		3	4			7				11	2	6			5	10	9			8				
19	1		3	4							11	2	6			5	10	9		7	8				
20	1		3	4			7			10	11	2	6			5		9			8				
21	1		3	4			7			10	11	2	6			5					8	9			
22	1		3	4			7				11	2	6			5	10	9		8					
23	1	3		4			7				11	2	6			5	10	9			8				
24	1	3					7				11	2	6			5		9		8	10	4			
25	1		3	4			7			10	11	2	6			5		9					8		
26	1		3	4			7			10	11	2	6			5		9					8		
27	1		3	4			7	8		10	11	2	6			5		9							
28	1	3		2			7			10	11		6			5		9				4	8		
29	1	2	3										6			5	11	9			10	4	8	7	
30	1	2	3		5		7			11				6			9				10	4	8		
31	1	3		2	5		7				11						9	10			6	4	8		
32	1		3	2	5		7			6	11						9				10	4	8		
33	1	3		4			7				11						10	9			6	5	8		2
34	1	2	3	4			7				11						10	9			6	5	8		
35	1	2	3	4			7				11		6					9			10	5	8		
36	1		3	4			7				11		6			2		9			10	5	8		
37	1	2	3	4			7				11		6			5		9			10		8		
38	1	2	3	4			7				11		6			5		9			10		8		
Apps.	38	12	33	35	6	1	36	15	6	13	32	26	32	3	2	29	21	27	1	6	18	11	13	1	1
Goals				2			8	3	1	3	9		2	1		1	2	18		6	1	1	1		

Pos	P.	W.	D.	L.	F.	A.	Pts.
11th	38	15	5	18	59	60	35

Scottish Cup

1	17 Jan	Inv'ness Citadel	2-0	7-0	3000	Maxwell(3), Muir(2), Aitken, Connell
2	31	HEARTS	2-2	3-2	14000	Maxwell, Connell, Ramsay
3	14 Feb	Montrose	1-0	3-0	3000	Aitken, Connell, McEwan
QF	28	Bo'ness	0-1	1-1	6258	Aitken
QFR	4 Mar	BO'NESS	2-0	5-0	8300	Connell(3), Maxwell(2)
SF	14	Celtic*	0-1	0-3	53973	

Round	Clemie	Leslie	Nibloe	Morton	Stewart	Clark	Connell	M.Smith	Cunningham	Ramsay	Aitken	Robertson	McEwan	Nicol	Young	T.Smith	Duncan	Maxwell	Kenmuir	Wales	Napier	Irvine	Muir	Parry	Falconer
1	1		3	4			7			10	11	2	6			5		9					8		
2	1		3	4			7			10	11	2	6			5		9					8		
3	1		3	4			7			10	11	2	6			5		9					8		
QF	1	2	3	4			7			10	11		6			5		9					8		
QFR	1	2	3	4			7			10	11		6			5		9					8		
SF	1	2	3	4			7			10	11		6			5	9						8		

* Hampden

The lethal 'Bud' Maxwell, goalscoring hero of the Rugby Park fans in the early 30's (including a future Archbishop of Canterbury). He was transferred to Preston becoming one of three former Killie players who helped that team win the F.A. Cup in 1938.

SEASON 1931-32 Division One

No.	Date	Opposition	H.T.	Res.	Att.	Goalscorers	Clemie	Leslie	Nibloe	Morton	T.Smith	McEwan	Connell	Muir	Maxwell	Napier	Aitken	Falconer	McLeod	Nicholson	Duncan	Sneddon	McDougall	Bell	Gilmour	Irvine	Kelvin	Williamson	Robertson	Nicol
1	8 Aug	AIRDRIEONIANS	3-1	4-2	7000	Connell, Maxwell, Muir, Napier	1	2	3	4	5	6	7	8	9	10	11													
2	15	Hearts	0-3	0-3	25000		1	3		4	5	6	7	8	9	10	11	2												
3	19	Hamilton A.	1-0	3-1	7000	Aitken, Connell, Napier	1	3		4	5	6	7	8	9	10	11	2												
4	22	MOTHERWELL	1-0	1-0	12000	Maxwell	1	2	3	4	5	6	7	8	9	10	11													
5	26	QUEENS PARK	1-1	4-1	7000	Connell(2), Maxwell, McEwan	1	3		4	5	6	7		9	10	11	2	8											
6	29	Third Lanark	1-1	3-1	16000	Maxwell(3)	1	3		4	5	6	7		9		11	2	8		10									
7	2 Sep	MORTON	0-0	1-0	5000	Aitken	1		3	4	5	6			9		11	2	8	7	10									
8	5	ST. MIRREN	1-0	3-0	9000	McEwan(2), Aitken	1	2	3	4	5	6	7	8	9		11				10									
9	9	Dundee United	0-0	0-0	8000		1	2	3	4	5	6	7		9		11		8		10									
10	12	Ayr United	1-1	1-1	10000	McEwan	1	2	3	4	5	6	7		9	8	11				10									
11	19	COWDENBEATH	1-0	3-2	5000	Connell, Maxwell, McEwan	1	2	3	4	5	6	7		9		11				10	8								
12	26	Partick Thistle	2-1	2-4	15000	Connell, McEwan	1	2	3	4		6	7		9	10	11					8	5							
13	3 Oct	CELTIC	2-2	2-3	20000	Duncan, McEwan	1	2	3	4		6	7		9		11				10	8	5							
14	10	Dundee	1-1	1-1	10000	Maxwell	1	2	3	4	5	6	7		9		11				10	8								
15	17	Clyde	0-0	0-0	8000		1	2	3	4	5	6	7		9		11				10	8								
16	24	FALKIRK	2-1	2-1	4000	Connell, Maxwell	1	2	3	4	5	6	7	8	9		11				10									
17	31	Leith Athletic	0-1	1-3	3000	McEwan	1	2	3	4	5	6	7	8	9		11				10									
18	14 Nov	Aberdeen	1-0	1-1	9000	Maxwell		2	3	4	5	6	7		9		11		8		10			1						
19	21	HAMILTON A.	0-1	1-1	4000	Maxwell		2	3	4	5	6	7		9		11		8		10			1						
20	28	Queens Park	0-2	0-2	6000				3	4	5	6	7		9		11	2	8		10			1						
21	5 Dec	Morton	1-2	1-3	4000	Connell		2	3	4	5	6	7		9		11		8		10			1						
22	12	DUNDEE UNITED	4-0	8-0	5000	Aitken(5), Maxwell(2), Connell		2	3	4	5	6	7		9		11		8		10			1						
23	19	Airdrieonians	0-0	2-0	2000	Duncan, Gilmour		2	3	4		6	7	8			11				10		5	1	9					
24	26	HEARTS	0-1	2-1	4000	Aitken(2)		2	3	4	5	6	7				11		8		10			1	9					
25	1 Jan	St. Mirren	0-2	0-2	10000			2	3	4		6	7				11		8		10		5	1	9					
26	2	AYR UNITED	2-1	5-1	10000	Maxwell(3), Connell, Duncan		2	3	4	5	6	7		9		11		8		10			1						
27	9	Motherwell	0-2	0-4	6000			3		4	5	6	7		9		11	2	8		10			1						
28	23	THIRD LANARK	1-0	2-1	8000	Aitken, Connell		2	3		5	6	7		9		11		8					1		4	10			
29	6 Feb	PARTICK THISTLE	2-2	3-4	7000	Connell, Maxwell, Nibloe		2	3	4	5	6	7		9		11		8					1				10		
30	20	DUNDEE	0-0	0-0	6000			2	3		5	6	7		9	8								1	11	4	10			
31	27	CLYDE	0-0	1-0	6000	Gilmour		2	3	4	5		7			6			8		11			1	9		10			
32	12 Mar	LEITH ATHLETIC	1-3	6-3	3000	Aitken(2), Connell(2), Maxwell(2)		2	3	4	5	6	7		9		11		8		10			1						
33	19	Rangers	0-1	0-3	16000			2	3	4	5	6	7		9		11		8		10			1						
34	2 Apr	Falkirk	1-2	1-4	5000	Maxwell		2	3		5	6	7	8	9						10			1	11	4				
35	6	ABERDEEN	0-1	0-2	2000			3			5	6	7	8	9		11				10			1		4			2	
36	9	Cowdenbeath	1-1	1-7	1000	Gilmour	1	3		4			7			6	11		8		10		5		9				2	
37	23	Celtic	0-3	1-4	7000	Duncan		2	3		5	6	7				11				9			1	8		10			4
38	30	RANGERS	2-4	2-4	10000	Aitken, Leslie		2	3	4		6	7			5	11				10			1	9			8		
						Apps.	18	36	31	33	32	36	37	10	31	11	35	7	19	1	29	5	5	20	9	4	4	2	2	1
						Goals		1	1			8	14	1	20	2	14				4				3					

Pos	P.	W.	D.	L.	F.	A.	Pts.
9th	38	16	7	15	68	70	39

Scottish Cup

No.	Date	Opposition	H.T.	Res.	Att.	Goalscorers	Clemie	Leslie	Nibloe	Morton	T.Smith	McEwan	Connell	Muir	Maxwell	Napier	Aitken	Falconer	McLeod	Nicholson	Duncan	Sneddon	McDougall	Bell	Gilmour	Irvine	Kelvin	Williamson	Robertson	Nicol
1	16 Jan	EAST FIFE	2-1	4-1	5700	Aitken, Connell, Duncan, McLeod		2	3	4	5	6	7		9		11		8		10			1						
2	30	ALBION ROVERS	1-0	2-0	7593	Connell, McLeod		2	3	4	5	6	7		9		11		8		10			1						
3	13 Feb	Dundee United	0-1	1-1	12969	Maxwell		2	3	4	5	6	7		9		11		8		10			1						
3R	17	DUNDEE UNITED	2-0	3-0	9410	Aitken, Duncan, Maxwell		2	3	4	5	6	7		9		11		8		10			1						
QF	5 Mar	Dunfermline	1-1	3-1	10000	Maxwell(2), Duncan		2	3	4	5	6	7		9		11		8		10			1						
SF	26	Airdrieonians*	2-0	3-2	28138	Aitken, Maxwell, McEwan		2	3	4	5	6	7	8	9		11				10			1						
F	16 Apr	Rangers#	1-0	1-1	111982	Maxwell		2	3	4	5	6	7	8	9		11				10			1						
FR	20	Rangers#	0-1	0-3	105695			2	3	4	5	6	7	8	9		11				10			1						

* Firhill # Hampden

So near to more Scottish Cup Final glory, Killie lost to Rangers in a replay. Of the 12 players listed, 10 played in all 8 cup ties, Muir & McLeod being the odd men out. Back: J.McKenzie, G.Neil, H.Brown, J.Leslie, W.Bell, J.Nibloe, H.Alexander, T.Wylie. Middle: J.Walker, R.Thomson, J.McLeod, J.Muir, D.Dick (Chairman), J.Duncan, J.Aitken, J.Morison, H.Spence(Sec) Front: J.McWhinnie (Trainer), T.Smith, J,McEwan, T.Wallace (Asst Trainer). (players not in photo' W.Connell, J.Maxwell, H.Horton).

SEASON 1932-33 Division One

No.	Date	Opposition	H.T.	Res.	Att.	Goalscorers
1	13 Aug	Motherwell	2-2	3-3	11000	Maxwell(3)
2	20	THIRD LANARK	3-0	6-0	9000	Maxwell(3), Kelvin, McEwan, Sneddon
3	24	Aberdeen	0-5	1-7	12000	McEwan
4	27	Cowdenbeath	0-1	1-4		Maxwell
5	3 Sep	PARTICK THISTLE	2-0	3-0	7000	Maxwell(2), Connell
6	10	St. Mirren	2-1	2-3	7000	Maxwell, Williamson
7	14	HAMILTON A.	1-1	3-2	4000	Aitken, Maxwell, McEwan
8	17	AYR UNITED	3-4	3-5	10000	Maxwell(2), Connell
9	24	Celtic	0-0	0-0	6000	
10	1 Oct	EAST STIRLING	1-1	2-1	5000	Connell(2)
11	8	Airdrieonians	1-1	1-2	2000	Maxwell
12	15	DUNDEE	1-2	2-2	5000	Aitken, McEwan
13	22	ST. JOHNSTONE	2-2	5-4	5000	Maxwell(2), Williamson, McEwan, Muir
14	29	Rangers	0-2	0-2	6000	
15	5 Nov	ABERDEEN	1-1	4-3	8000	Connell(2), Aitken, McEwan
16	12	Hamilton A.	0-0	0-0		
17	19	QUEENS PARK	0-0	3-1	10000	Maxwell(2), Sneddon
18	26	MORTON	0-1	1-1	6000	Maxwell
19	3 Dec	Hearts	0-1	0-1	10000	
20	10	CLYDE	1-1	1-2	4000	Sneddon
21	17	Falkirk	0-1	2-2	4000	McEwan, Sneddon
22	24	MOTHERWELL	1-1	1-3	9000	McEwan
23	31	Third Lanark	1-3	2-3	6000	Maxwell(2)
24	2 Jan	ST. MIRREN	0-1	0-1	7000	
25	3	Ayr United	1-1	3-2	10000	Maxwell(2), Napier
26	7	COWDENBEATH	3-1	4-1	4000	Maxwell(2), Aitken, McEwan
27	14	Partick Thistle	2-0	3-1	9000	Maxwell(2), Gilmour
28	28	CELTIC	0-2	2-2	12000	Liddell, Sneddon
29	11 Feb	East Stirling	1-1	3-2	4000	Maxwell(2), Sneddon
30	25	AIRDRIEONIANS	2-0	2-4	3000	Maxwell, Sneddon
31	11 Mar	St. Johnstone	0-4	1-6	6000	Muir
32	18	RANGERS	1-3	2-6	7000	Liddell, O.G.
33	29	Dundee	0-3	0-3	1000	
34	8 Apr	Morton	2-4	2-5	1500	Duncan, Gilmour
35	12	HEARTS	0-0	0-0	2000	
36	22	Clyde	1-0	1-0	4000	McEwan
37	26	Queens Park	1-0	2-1		Gilmour, Maxwell
38	29	FALKIRK	0-1	1-1	3000	Maxwell

No.	Milliken	Leslie	Milloy	Glass	Smith	McEwan	Connell	Sneddon	Maxwell	Kelvin	Aitken	Williamson	Duncan	Bell	Muir	MacDougall	Napier	A.D.Turner	Taylor	Kenmuir	"Newman"	Falconer	Liddell	Gilmour	Landsborough	Beattie	McDonald
1		2	3	4	5	6	7	8	9		11	10		1													
2		2	3	4	5	6	7	8	9	10	11			1													
3		2	3	4	5	6	7	8		10	11			1										9			
4		2	3	4	5	6	7	8	9	10	11										1						
5	1	2	3	4	5	6	7	8	9		11	10															
6	1	2	3	4	5	6	7	8	9		11	10															
7	1	2	3	4	5	6	7	8	9		11	10															
8	1	2	3	4	5	6	7	8	9		11		10														
9	1	2	3	4	5	6	7	8	9		11	10															
10	1	2	3	4	5	6	7	8	9		11	10															
11		2	3	4	5	6	7		9		11	10		1	8												
12		2	3	4		6	7		9		11	10		1	8	5											
13		2	3	4		6	7		9		11	10		1	8		5										
14	1	2	3	4		6	7		9		11	10			8		5										
15	1	2	3	4	5	6	7	8	9		11	10															
16	1	2	3	4	5	6		8	9		11	10								7							
17	1	2	3	4	5	6		8	9		11	10						7									
18	1	2	3	4	5	6		8	9		11	10						7									
19	1	2	3	4	5	6		8	9		11	10						7									
20	1	2	3		5	6		8	9		11	10						7	4								
21	1	2	3		5	6		8	9		11				10				4	7							
22	1		3	4	5	6		10	9		11	8								7		2					
23	1	2	3	4	5	6		8	9		11						10						7				
24	1	2	3	4	5	6			9		11				8								7	10			
25	1	2	3	4		6		8	10	11							5						7	9			
26	1	2	3	4	5	6		8	9		11												7	10			
27		2	3	4	5	6		8	9		11			1									7	10			
28	1	2	3	4		6		8	9		11												7	10	5		
29	1	2	3	4	5	6		8	9		11												7	10			
30	1	2	3	4	5	6		8	9		11												7	10			
31	1	2	3	4		6					11	10			8		5						7	9			
32	1	2	3	4		6		8			11		9										7	10	5		
33		2		4	5	6		8			11		9	1						10			7				3
34		2	3	4		6		8			11		9	1			5						7	10			
35	1	2	3	4	5	6		8	9	11													7			10	
36	1	2	3	4	5	6		8	9		11												7	10			
37	1	2	3	4	5	6			9		11				8								7	10			
38	1	2	3	4	5	6			9		11				8								7			10	
Apps.	28	37	37	36	30	38	15	30	33	5	36	18	4	9	9	1	6	4	2	4	1	1	16	13	2	2	1
Goals						10	6	7	32	1	4	2	1		2		1						2				

Pos	P.	W.	D.	L.	F.	A.	Pts.
14th	38	13	9	16	72	86	35

Scottish Cup

Rd	Date	Opposition	H.T.	Res.	Att.	Goalscorers
1	21 Jan	LOCHGELLY	3-0	3-1	3615	Maxwell(2), Gilmour
2	4 Feb	St. Mirren	1-0	1-0	12000	Aitken
3	16	RANGERS	1-0	1-0	32745	Liddell
QF	4 Mar	MOTHERWELL	1-2	3-3	20658	Maxwell(2), McEwan
QFR	8	Motherwell	0-3	3-8	23000	Glass(2), Maxwell

Rd	Milliken	Leslie	Milloy	Glass	Smith	McEwan	Connell	Sneddon	Maxwell	Kelvin	Aitken	Williamson	Duncan	Bell	Muir	MacDougall	Napier	A.D.Turner	Taylor	Kenmuir	"Newman"	Falconer	Liddell	Gilmour	Landsborough	Beattie	McDonald
1	1	2	3	4	5	6		8	9		11												7	10			
2	1	2	3	4	5	6		8	9		11												7	10			
3	1	2	3	4	5	6		8	9		11												7	10			
QF	1	2	3	4	5	6		8	9		11												7	10			
QFR	1	2	3	4	5	6		8	9		11												7	10			

WILLIAM LIDDELL who scored the goal which gave Killie another sensational Cup win over Rangers. It was the only tie the Ibrox side lost between 1931-1937.

SEASON 1933-34 Division One

No.	Date	Opposition	H.T.	Res.	Att.	Goalscorers	Miller	Leslie	Milloy	Glass	Smith	McEwan	Liddell	Williamson	Maxwell	Beattie	Keane	Kennedy	Morton	Landsborough	Kelvin	MacDonald	Connell	Kenmuir	Ross	Anderson	Gilmour	Bradley
1	12 Aug	COWDENBEATH	2-0	4-1	7000	Keane, Liddell, Maxwell, Williamson	1	2	3	4	5	6	7	8	9	10	11											
2	16	THIRD LANARK	1-1	1-2	8000	Maxwell	1	2	3	4	5	6	7	8	9		11	10										
3	19	Partick Thistle	2-1	3-2	10000	Liddell(2), Maxwell	1		3	4	5	6	7	8	9		11	10	2									
4	23	ABERDEEN	1-0	2-0	7000	Keane, Maxwell	1		3	4	5	6	7	8	9		11	10		2								
5	26	CELTIC	3-2	4-3	14000	Liddell(2), Maxwell, Williamson	1		3		5	6	7	8	9		11	10	4	2								
6	2 Sep	Hibernian	1-1	1-4	15000	Maxwell	1		3	4	5	6	7	8	9		11	10	2									
7	9	ST. MIRREN	2-0	3-0	6000	Maxwell(2), Liddell	1		3		5	6	7	8	9		11	10	2		4							
8	13	Hamilton A.	1-1	2-2	3000	Kelvin, Maxwell	1		3		5	6	7	8	9		11		4	2	10							
9	16	Third Lanark	0-0	1-1	6000	Glass	1		3	4	5	6	7	8	9		11				10	2						
10	23	AIRDRIEONIANS	2-1	7-1	5000	Maxwell(3), Keane(2), Connell, McEwan	1		3	4	5	6		8	9		11		2		10		7					
11	30	Ayr United	1-1	1-1	12000	Keane	1		3	4	5	6	7	8			11		2		10		9					
12	7 Oct	MOTHERWELL	1-1	1-3	15000	Keane	1		3	4	5	6	7	8	9		11		2		10							
13	14	Dundee	2-0	2-0	10000	Connell, Maxwell	1		3		5	6	7	10	9		11		2		4		8					
14	21	St. Johnstone	2-0	3-0	4000	Maxwell(3)	1		3		5	6	7	10	9		11		2		4		8					
15	28	RANGERS	0-2	1-3	16000	Maxwell	1		3		5	6	7	10	9		11		2		4		8					
16	4 Nov	Aberdeen	0-1	0-2	12000		1		3	4	5	6	7	8	9		11	10	2									
17	11	HAMILTON A.	1-0	1-1	6000	Maxwell	1		3	4		6	7	10	9		11	8	2	5								
18	18	Queens Park	2-0	4-3	6000	Keane, Kennedy, Maxwell, O.G.	1		3	4		6		8	9		11	10	2	5			7					
19	25	Queen of the South	1-1	1-4	9000	Keane	1	2	3	4	5	6		8	9		11	10					7					
20	2 Dec	HEARTS	0-2	2-5	8000	Maxwell, Williamson	1		3	4	5	6	7	8	9		11	10	2									
21	9	Clyde	0-0	1-0	4000	Maxwell	1		3	4	5	6	7		9		11	10	2	8								
22	16	FALKIRK	0-0	1-1	6000	McEwan	1		3	4	5	6	7	10	9		11		2	8								
23	23	Cowdenbeath	1-0	1-0	1500	Maxwell	1		3		5		7	10	9		11		4	8		2		6				
24	30	PARTICK THISTLE	0-0	2-0	7000	Maxwell, Williamson	1		3		5		7	10	9		11			8		2		6	4			
25	1 Jan	St. Mirren	0-3	1-3	15000	Kennedy	1		3	4		6		10	9		11	8	2		5		7					
26	2	AYR UNITED	3-1	4-2	12000	Maxwell(2), Keane, Kennedy	1		3		5	6			9		11	10	4	8			7			2		
27	6	Celtic	0-2	1-4	4000	Landsborough	1		3		5	6			9		11	10	4	8			7			2		
28	13	HIBERNIAN	0-0	2-0	5000	Landsborough, Maxwell	1		3		5	6			9		11	10	2	8	4		7					
29	27	Airdrieonians	1-1	1-3		Williamson	1		3	4		6		10			11			8	5		7			2	9	
30	17 Feb	CLYDE	2-2	2-2	5000	Maxwell(2)	1		3		5	6		10	9	11					4		7		8	2		
31	24	Motherwell	0-2	0-2	5000		1		3	4	5	6		8			11	10					7			2	9	
32	3 Mar	DUNDEE	0-2	1-3	4000	Maxwell			3		5	6		10	9		11				4		7		8	2		1
33	10	ST. JOHNSTONE	1-0	1-0	2500	Liddell	1		3		5	6	7	10	9		11	8			4					2		
34	17	Rangers	0-1	2-2	6000	Keane, Williamson	1		3		5	6	7	10	9		11	8			4					2		
35	31	QUEEN OF THE SOUTH	0-0	3-0	7000	Keane(2), Maxwell	1		3		5	6	7	10	9		11	8			4					2		
36	7 Apr	Hearts	1-0	1-1	3500	Keane	1		3		5	6	7	10	9		11	8			4					2		
37	18	QUEENS PARK	0-1	3-1	3000	Kennedy, Maxwell, Williamson	1		3		5	6	7	10	9		11	8			4					2		
38	28	Falkirk	1-1	2-2	2000	Maxwell(2)	1		3		5	6	7	10	9		11	8			4					2		
						Apps.	37	3	38	19	34	36	27	34	35	2	37	23	22	13	20	3	15	2	3	12	2	1
						Goals				1		2	7	7	33		13	4		2	1		2					

Pos	P.	W.	D.	L.	F.	A.	Pts.
7th	38	17	9	12	73	64	43

Scottish Cup

Round	Date	Opposition	H.T.	Res.	Att.	Goalscorers	Miller	Leslie	Milloy	Glass	Smith	McEwan	Liddell	Williamson	Maxwell	Beattie	Keane	Kennedy	Morton	Landsborough	Kelvin	MacDonald	Connell	Kenmuir	Ross	Anderson	Gilmour	Bradley
1	20 Jan	Airdrieonians	0-1	1-1	7245	Keane	1		3		5	6	7		9		11	10	2	8	4							
1R	24	AIRDRIEONIANS	3-1	3-2	6969	Landsborough, Maxwell, McEwan	1		3		5	6		10	9		11		2	8	4		7					
2	3 Feb	Albion Rovers	0-0	1-2	11665	Williamson	1		3		5	6		10	9		11		2	8	4		7					

These eleven players were a potent combination as Killie finished 7th in the League, their best position since 1918.
Back: Glass, Smith, Morton, Miller, Milloy, McEwan. Front: Liddell, Williamson, Maxwell, Kennedy, Keane

SEASON 1934-35 Division One

No.	Date	Opposition	H.T.	Res.	Att.	Goalscorers	Miller	Anderson	Milloy	Morton	Kelvin	McEwan	Lidell	A.Robertson	J.Robertson	Beattie	Keane	Ross	Kennedy	McCarthy	Glass	Brown	Smith	Williamson	Black	Gilmour	Leslie	Kenmuir	Landsborough	Fyfe	Thomson	Cook	Meechan
1	11 Aug	Celtic	1-1	1-4	15000	O.G.	1	2	3	4	5	6	7	8	9	10	11																
2	18	HIBERNIAN	0-1	0-1	5000		1	2	3	4	5		7			10	11	6	8	9													
3	22	St. Johnstone	1-0	1-2		J.Robertson	1	2	3		5		7		9	10	11	6	8		4												
4	25	Airdrieonians	1-2	2-3		Williamson(2)		2	3		4	6	7		10							1	5	8	9	11							
5	1 Sep	AYR UNITED	3-2	6-3	8000	Keane(2),J.Robertson(2),Beattie,Williamson	1	2	3		4				9	10	11	6					5	8	7								
6	4	RANGERS	0-1	1-3	13000	J.Robertson	1	2	3		4				9	10	11	6					5	8	7								
7	8	St. Mirren	2-0	2-0	5000	Beattie, J.Robertson	1		3		4				9	10	11	6					5	8	7		2						
8	15	FALKIRK	2-0	4-1	5000	J.Robertson(3), Black	1		3		4				9	10	11	6					5	8	7		2						
9	22	Motherwell	1-2	2-3	1500	J.Robertson, Williamson	1		3		4				9	10	11	6					5	8	7		2						
10	24	Aberdeen	1-0	3-1	9000	Keane(2), Black	1		3		4				9	10	11	6					5	8	7		2						
11	29	PARTICK THISTLE	1-0	2-0	6000	Keane, J.Robertson	1		3		4				9	10	11	6					5	8	7		2						
12	6 Oct	Dunfermline	2-1	2-2	3000	Black(2)	1		3		4				9	10	11	6					5	8	7		2						
13	13	DUNDEE	0-0	2-0	5000	Beattie, J.Robertson	1		3		4				9	10	11	6					5	8	7		2						
14	20	ABERDEEN	1-1	1-3	6000	Beattie	1		3		4				9	10	11	6					5	8	7		2						
15	27	Hamilton A.	0-3	2-4	5000	Beattie, Keane	1		3		4				9	10	11	6					5	8	7		2						
16	3 Nov	QUEENS PARK	2-0	5-0	6000	Beattie(3), J.Robertson, Williamson	1		3		4				9	10	11	6					5	8	7		2						
17	10	QUEEN OF THE SOUTH	1-0	3-1	6000	Black, Keane, O.G.	1		3		4				9		11	6	10				5	8	7		2						
18	17	Hearts	2-0	2-2	18000	J.Robertson(2)	1		3		4				9	10	11						5	8	7		2	6					
19	24	CLYDE	0-0	2-0	7000	Black, Keane	1		3		4				9	10	11	6					5	8	7		2						
20	1 Dec	Albion Rovers	0-0	0-1			1		3		4				9	10	11	6					5	8	7		2						
21	8	ST. JOHNSTONE	0-0	1-0	4000	Williamson	1		3		4				9	10	11						5	8	7		2	6					
22	15	Rangers	2-1	3-2	12000	Black, Keane, Williamson	1		3		4				9	10	11						5	8	7		2	6					
23	22	CELTIC	1-2	2-3	15000	Beattie, J.Robertson	1		3		4				9	10	11						5	8	7		2	6					
24	29	Hibernian	0-0	0-1	9000		1		3		4		7		9		11						5	10			2	6	8				
25	1 Jan	ST. MIRREN	1-2	1-4	4000	Kenmuir	1			5	4				9		11	6	8						7		2	10		3			
26	2	Ayr United	1-1	1-2	12000	Landsborough	1	2	3		4				9	10	11	6					5		7				8				
27	5	AIRDRIEONIANS	0-0	0-0	5000		1	2	3		4				9		11	6					5						8		7	10	
28	12	Falkirk	1-3	2-5	6000	Beattie, J.Robertson	1	2	3		4				9	10	11	6					5					8			7		
29	19	MOTHERWELL	1-1	3-3	8000	Keane(2), J.Robertson	1		3		4				9	10	11	6					5	8	7		2						
30	2 Feb	Partick Thistle	1-2	2-4	8000	Keane, J.Robertson	1	2	3		4				9	10	11	6					5	8							7		
31	16	DUNFERMLINE	0-3	1-3	3000	J.Robertson	1		3		4		7		10		11	6					5	8			2						9
32	23	Queens Park	2-0	4-1	4000	Beattie(2), Williamson(2)	1		3		4					10	11	6					5	8	9		2				7		
33	2 Mar	Dundee	1-0	2-0	4000	Leslie, O.G.	1		3		4					10	11						5	8	9		2	6			7		
34	9	Clyde	1-0	1-1	4000	Beattie	1		3		4				9	10	11						5	8			2	6			7		
35	16	HAMILTON A.	3-0	4-1	5000	J.Robertson(2), Williamson, Beattie	1	2	3		4				9	10	11	6					5	8							7		
36	30	Queen of the South	0-0	1-0		Williamson	1	2	3		4				9	10	11	6					5	8							7		
37	13 Apr	HEARTS	1-2	3-3	4000	J.Robertson(2), Beattie	1	2	3		4				9	10	11	6					5	8							7		
38	27	ALBION ROVERS	2-1	2-1	2000	Beattie, Williamson		2	3		4					10	11	6				1	5	8	9						7		
						Apps.	36	14	37	3	38	2	6	1	34	32	37	29	4	1	1	2	34	31	26	1	24	9	3	1	10	1	1
						Goals									23	16	12							12	7		1	1	1				

Pos	P.	W.	D.	L.	F.	A.	Pts.
9th	38	16	6	16	76	68	38

Scottish Cup

No.	Date	Opposition	H.T.	Res.	Att.	Goalscorers	Miller	Anderson	Milloy	Morton	Kelvin	McEwan	Lidell	A.Robertson	J.Robertson	Beattie	Keane	Ross	Kennedy	McCarthy	Glass	Brown	Smith	Williamson	Black	Gilmour	Leslie	Kenmuir	Landsborough	Fyfe	Thomson	Cook	Meechan
1	26 Jan	Galston	0-0	1-0	4211	Black	1		3		4				9	10	11	6					5	8	7		2						
2	9 Feb	Hearts	0-1	0-2	36863		1		3		4				9	10	11	6					5	8	7		2						

JOHN KEANE, who scored the decisive third goal as Kilmarnock won at Ibrox for the first time ever in December 1934.

SEASON 1935-36 Division One

No.	Date	Opposition	H.T.	Res.	Att.	Goalscorers	Miller	Leslie	Milloy	Morton	Smith	Kenmuir	Thomson	Williamson	Robertson	Beattie	Keane	Brown	Ross	Clark	Milliken	Black	McClure	Roberts	Alexander	"Russell"	Fyfe	Gallacher
1	10 Aug	MOTHERWELL	2-0	2-3	9000	Robertson, Williamson	1	2	3	4	5	6	7	8	9	10	11											
2	17	Third Lanark	0-0	2-3	8000	Robertson, Thomson		2	3		5	4	7	8	9	10	11	1	6									
3	24	AIRDRIEONIANS	0-0	2-2	6000	Robertson, Williamson	1	2	3		5	4	7	8	9	10	11		6									
4	28	Queen of the South	1-2	1-2	9500	Beattie	1	2	3	4	5		7	8	9	10	11		6									
5	31	Ayr United	1-1	3-1	17500	Clark, Robertson, Thomson	1	2	3	4	5		7	8	11	10			6	9								
6	7 Sep	DUNFERMLINE	0-1	1-2	6000	Thomson	1	2	3	4	5		7	8	10	11			6	9								
7	14	Partick Thistle	0-1	0-2	7000		1	2	3	4	5		7		8	10	11		6	9								
8	18	ST. JOHNSTONE	2-1	4-1		Beattie, Keane, Ross, Williamson	1	2	3		5		7	8	9	10	11		6		4							
9	21	ARBROATH	3-0	5-0	5000	Beattie(3), Milloy, Williamson	1	2	3		5		7	8	9	10	11		6		4							
10	28	Hibernian	0-1	1-3	5000	Beattie	1	2	3		5		7	8	9	10	11		6		4							
11	5 Oct	CELTIC	0-0	1-1	15000	Robertson	1	2	3		5		7	8	9	10	11		6		4							
12	12	Dundee	0-0	0-0	5500		1	2	3	11	5			8	9	10			6		4	7						
13	19	Hamilton A.	1-0	2-3	3000	Milloy, Williamson	1	2	3				7	8	9	10			6	11	4		5					
14	26	ABERDEEN	1-4	2-5	6000	Beattie, Robertson	1	2	3				7	8	9	10			6		4		5	11				
15	2 Nov	Albion Rovers	1-1	3-2	4000	Beattie, Robertson, Ross	1	2	3		5		7		9	10			6		4			11	8			
16	9	HEARTS	0-0	2-0	6000	Robertson, Thomson	1	2	3		5		7	8	9	10			6		4			11				
17	16	QUEENS PARK	1-1	1-1	7000	Robertson		2	3		5		7	8	9	10			6		4			11		1		
18	23	Clyde	0-0	0-1	5000		1	2	3		5		7	8	9	10			6		4			11				
19	30	Rangers	1-0	1-2	8000	Thomson	1	2	3		5		7	8	9	10			6		4			11				
20	7 Dec	QUEEN OF THE SOUTH	2-1	4-2	5000	Beattie(2), Robertson(2)	1	2	3		5		7	8	9	10			6		4			11				
21	14	St. Johnstone	0-0	0-0	3500		1	2	3		5		7	8	9	10			6		4			11				
22	28	THIRD LANARK	1-0	1-0	5000	Thomson	1	2	3		5		7	8	9	10			6		4			11				
23	1 Jan	Arbroath	0-0	0-0			1	2	3		5		7	8	9	10			6		4			11				
24	2	AYR UNITED	3-0	7-2	17500	Robertson(4), Beattie, Roberts, Williamson	1	2			5		7	8	9	10			6		4			11			3	
25	4	Airdrieonians	2-1	4-1		Beattie(2), Roberts(2)	1	2			5			8	9	10			6		4	7		11			3	
26	11	Dunfermline	0-0	1-0	4000	Robertson	1	2			5		7	8	9	10			6		4			11			3	
27	15 Feb	Celtic	0-1	0-4	6000		1	2	3				7	8	9	10			6				5	11	4			
28	22	PARTICK THISTLE	1-1	2-1	4000	Beattie, Thomson	1	2	3				7	8	9	10			6		4		5	11				
29	29	DUNDEE	1-1	4-1	3000	Robertson, Beattie, Williamson, Roberts	1	2	3	4			7	8	9	10			6				5	11				
30	7 Mar	HAMILTON A.	3-2	4-3	3000	Beattie(2), Roberts, Williamson	1	2	3	4			7	8	9	10			6				5	11				
31	14	Aberdeen	1-2	1-2	8000	Robertson	1	2	3	4			7	8	9	10			6				5	11				
32	21	ALBION ROVERS	2-0	2-2	4000	Roberts, Thomson	1	2	3		4		7	8		10			6	9			5	11				
33	1 Apr	Hearts	1-1	2-4		Beattie(2)	1	2		4	5		7	8	9	10			6					11			3	
34	4	Motherwell	1-1	2-3	3000	Roberts, Williamson	1	2	3		5		7	8	9	10			6				4	11				1
35	8	HIBERNIAN	0-1	0-1	4000		1	2			5		7	8	9	10			6		4			11			3	
36	11	Queens Park	0-1	0-1	5000			2			6		7		9	10		1			4		5	11			3	8
37	25	RANGERS	0-2	0-3	7000			2	3		4		7		9	10		1	6				5	11				8
38	29	CLYDE	2-0	2-0		Kenmuir, Williamson		2	3		5	9	7	8		10		1	6		4			11				
						Apps.	33	38	32	10	31	4	36	34	36	38	9	4	36	5	23	2	11	25	2	1	6	2
						Goals			2			1	8	10	18	19	1		2	1				7				

Pos	P.	W.	D.	L.	F.	A.	Pts.
8th	38	14	7	17	69	64	35

Scottish Cup

							Miller	Leslie	Milloy	Morton	Smith	Kenmuir	Thomson	Williamson	Robertson	Beattie	Keane	Brown	Ross	Clark	Milliken	Black	McClure	Roberts	Alexander	"Russell"	Fyfe	Gallacher
1	29 Jan	East Stirling	2-1	5-2	4000	Robertson(3), Thomson(2)	1	2	3		5		7	8	9	10			6		4			11				
2	8 Feb	Falkirk	0-1	1-1	20000	Robertson	1	2	3		5		7	8	9	10			6		4			11				
2R	12	FALKIRK	0-0	1-3*	15000	Thomson	1	2	3				7	8	9	10			6		4		5	11				

* A.E.T.

Kilmarnock line-up for their first away League game of 1935-36 at Third Lanark's Cathkin Park.
Back: T.Smith (captain), M.Kenmuir, J.Leslie, W.Brown, F.Milloy, S.Ross
Front: B.Thomson, J.Williamson, J.Robertson, R.Beattie, J.Keane

SEASON 1936-37 Division One

No.	Date	Opposition	H.T.	Res.	Att.	Goalscorers	Miller	Leslie	Milloy	Milliken	Smith	Ross	Thomson	Williamson	Clarkson	Beattie	Roberts	J.Robertson	Alexander	G.Robertson	McClure	McAvoy	Anderson	Fyfe	Henry	Gallacher	Collins	Morton	Gillespie	Brown	Brownlie
1	8 Aug	Third Lanark	0-1	1-2	10000	Clarkson	1	2	3	4	5	6	7	8	9	10	11														
2	15	DUNDEE	1-0	1-1		Beattie	1	2	3	4	5	6	7		9	10	11	8													
3	19	THIRD LANARK	0-2	0-3	4500		1	2	3	4	5	6	7	8	9	10	11														
4	22	Dunfermline	3-0	5-0	5500	Clarkson(2), Thomson(2), Williamson	1	2	3		5		7	8	9	10	11		4	6											
5	29	PARTICK THISTLE	1-0	1-0	6000	Clarkson	1	2	3		5	6	7	8	9	10	11			4											
6	5 Sep	Celtic	0-0	4-2	8000	Beattie, J.Robertson, Thomson, Williamson	1	2	3		5	6	7	8		10	11	9		4											
7	9	Dundee	1-2	2-2		Roberts(2)	1	2	3			6	7	8		10	11	9		4	5										
8	12	HIBERNIAN	3-1	3-2	5000	Thomson(2), Beattie	1	2	3			6	7		9	10	11	8		4	5										
9	19	St. Mirren	0-1	2-3	8000	Clarkson, J.Robertson	1	2	3			6	7		9	10	11	8		4	5										
10	26	ARBROATH	2-0	2-0	5000	Beattie, Clarkson	1	2	3			6	7	8	9	10	11			4	5										
11	3 Oct	Motherwell	0-1	1-2		Williamson	1	2	3			6	7	8	9	10	11			4	5										
12	10	FALKIRK	2-1	3-2	6000	Beattie, Roberts, Williamson	1	2	3		5	6	7	8	9	10	11			4											
13	17	ALBION ROVERS	2-1	3-1	4000	Roberts(2), Ross	1	2	3		5	6	7	8	9	10	11			4											
14	24	Hearts	0-2	0-5	9000		1	2	3		5	6	7	8	9	10				4		11									
15	31	Queens Park	1-1	1-2	5000	Thomson	1	3			5	6	7	8	9	10		11		4			2								
16	7 Nov	CLYDE	2-1	3-1	4000	Williamson(2), Roberts	1	3				6	7	8		10	11	9		4	5		2								
17	14	RANGERS	1-2	1-2	15000	J.Robertson	1	3				6	7	8		10	11	9		4	5		2								
18	21	Queen of the South	0-1	0-1	5000		1	3			5	6	7	8		10	11	9		4			2								
19	28	ST. JOHNSTONE	2-1	4-2	4000	J.Robertson(3), Beattie	1				5	6	7	8		10	11	9		4			2	3							
20	5 Dec	HAMILTON A.	2-1	2-2	3000	Beattie, Thomson	1				5	6	7			10	11	9		4			2	3	8						
21	12	Aberdeen	0-2	0-2	14000		1	3				6	7	8		10	11	9		4	5		2								
22	19	DUNFERMLINE	2-0	3-3	3000	Henry(2), J. Robertson	1	3				6	7			10	11	9		4	5		2		8						
23	26	Partick Thistle	0-3	0-4	8000		1	3					7			10	11	9		6	5		2		8	4					
24	1 Jan	ST. MIRREN	1-1	2-1	15000	Ross, O.G.	1	3				4	7	8		10	11	9		6	5		2								
25	2	Falkirk	0-2	0-5	10000		1	3				4	7			10	11	9		6	5		2				8				
26	9	CELTIC	2-1	3-3	12000	Beattie, Collins, J.Robertson	1	3				4	7			10	11	9		6	5		2				8				
27	16	Hibernian	0-0	0-0	5000		1	3				4	7			10	11	9		6	5		2				8				
28	23	MOTHERWELL	0-0	0-1	7000		1	3				4	7			10	11			6	5						8	2	9		
29	6 Feb	Arbroath	0-0	0-0	2000		1	2				4	7	8	9	10	11		3	6	5										
30	20	Albion Rovers	3-0	3-1	3000	Roberts, J.Robertson, Thomson	1		3			6	7	8		10	11	9	2	4	5										
31	27	Rangers	0-3	0-8			1		3			4	7	8		10	11	9	2	6	5										
32	6 Mar	HEARTS	1-0	3-0	8000	J.Robertson, Ross, Thomson			3			6	7			10		9	2	4	5						8			1	11
33	20	Clyde	0-2	0-2	5000				3			6	7			10		9			5		2			4	8			1	11
34	3 Apr	QUEEN OF THE SOUTH	1-0	1-0	3500	Thomson			3			6	7			10	11	9		4	5		2				8			1	
35	10	St. Johnstone	0-1	3-1	3000	Collins, Roberts, J.Robertson			3			6	7			10	11	9			5		2			4	8			1	
36	16	Hamilton A.	1-0	2-2		Thomson, J.Robertson			3			6	7			10	11	9			5		2			4	8			1	
37	23	QUEENS PARK	0-0	0-0	2000				3			6	7				11	10		4	5		2				8		9	1	
38	29	ABERDEEN	1-1	1-2	3000	Collins		2	3				7			10	11			4	5					6	8		9	1	
						Apps.	31	28	23	3	13	35	38	21	14	37	34	26	5	32	25	1	18	2	3	5	11	1	3	7	2
						Goals						3	11	6	6	8	8	12							2		3				

Pos	P.	W.	D.	L.	F.	A.	Pts.
11th	38	14	9	15	60	70	37

Scottish Cup

No.	Date	Opposition	H.T.	Res.	Att.	Goalscorers	Miller	Leslie	Milloy	Milliken	Smith	Ross	Thomson	Williamson	Clarkson	Beattie	Roberts	J.Robertson	Alexander	G.Robertson	McClure	McAvoy	Anderson	Fyfe	Henry	Gallacher	Collins	Morton	Gillespie	Brown	Brownlie
1	30 Jan	BRECHIN CITY	0-2	1-2	2727	Roberts	1	3				4	7	8	9	10	11			6	5		2								

Bobby Beattie

A brilliant schemer who completed the ex-Killie triumvirate which won F.A. Cup Winners medals at Preston in 1938.

SEASON 1937-38 Division One

No.	Date	Opposition	H.T.	Res.	Att.	Goalscorers
1	14 Aug	AYR UNITED	2-1	2-1	10000	Collins, McGowan
2	21	Partick Thistle	0-2	0-3	10000	
3	25	Ayr United	1-4	2-4	12000	McGowan, J.Robertson
4	28	CELTIC	0-0	2-1	19000	McGowan, Leslie
5	4 Sep	Hibernian	0-0	1-1	12000	McGowan
6	11	ST. MIRREN	0-1	0-3	10000	
7	15	PARTICK THISTLE	0-1	1-3	3500	McGowan
8	18	St. Johnstone	1-4	2-6	4000	Collins, Thomson
9	25	MOTHERWELL	0-1	0-2	4000	
10	2 Oct	Dundee	2-0	2-1	6000	McGowan, Ross
11	9	TTHIRD LANARK	2-2	4-2	4000	McGowan(2), Collins, Gallacher
12	16	Falkirk	2-2	2-2	7500	Collins, Ross
13	23	QUEENS PARK	0-1	1-3	4000	Ross
14	30	Clyde	1-1	2-2		Thomson(2)
15	6 Nov	Rangers	0-3	1-4		Henry
16	13	QUEEN OF THE SOUTH	1-0	1-1	5000	Ross
17	20	Arbroath	0-1	1-2	3500	Roberts
18	27	Hamilton A.	1-3	2-4	3500	Gillespie, Thomson
19	4 Dec	ABERDEEN	3-0	3-3	6000	Collins, McAvoy, Thomson
20	11	Morton	1-2	2-4	3000	Gillespie, Collins
21	25	Celtic	0-6	0-8		
22	29	HIBERNIAN	0-1	0-3	5000	
23	1 Jan	St. Mirren	0-0	2-0		Collins(2)
24	3	FALKIRK	1-1	2-2	10000	Collins, McAvoy
25	8	ST. JOHNSTONE	1-1	2-2	10000	Thomson, McAvoy
26	15	Motherwell	1-2	3-4		Collins, McGrogan, Thomson
27	29	DUNDEE	1-0	3-1	4000	McGrogan, Ross, Thomson
28	5 Feb	Third Lanark	2-0	4-2		Thomson(2), Collins, G.Robertson
29	12	HEARTS	1-1	3-1	12000	Collins, McAvoy, Reid
30	19	Queens Park	0-0	1-1	10000	Reid
31	26	CLYDE	1-0	2-1	10000	Reid, McGrogan
32	12 Mar	RANGERS	0-1	2-1	21000	McGrogan, Thomson
33	26	ARBROATH	1-0	2-1	7000	Collins, McGrogan
34	9 Apr	Aberdeen	1-2	1-2	10000	Thomson
35	13	HAMILTON A.	1-1	2-2	8000	McAvoy, McGrogan
36	16	Queen of the South	0-2	1-3	8500	Collins
37	29	MORTON	1-0	3-0	8000	Gallacher, Henry, Gillespie
38	30	Hearts	1-2	1-5	14000	Gillespie

No.	Brown	Leslie	Milloy	G.Robertson	McClure	Ross	Thomson	Collins	McGowan	Beattie	Howie	Stewart	J.Robertson	McAvoy	Anderson	Fyfe	Gallacher	Roberts	Hunter	Henry	Gillespie	Marsh	Milliken	Turnbull	Reid	McGrogan	Borthwick	Gillan	McIntyre
1	1	2	3	4	5	6	7	8	9	10	11																		
2	1	2	3	4	5	6	7	8	9	10	11																		
3	1	2	3	4		6	7	8	9	10		5	11																
4	1	2	3	4	5	6	7	8	9	10			11																
5	1	2	3	4	5	6	7	8	9	10			11																
6	1	2	3	4	5	6	7	8	9	10			11																
7	1	2	3	4	5	6	7	10	9	8				11															
8	1			4	5	6	7	10	9	8				11	2	3													
9	1		3	4	5	6	7	10		8			9	11	2														
10	1	2	3	4	5	8	7	10	9					11			6												
11	1	2	3	4	5	8	7	10	9					11			6												
12	1	2	3	4	5	8	7	10	9					11			6												
13	1	2	3	4	5	8	7	10	9					11			6												
14	1	2	3	4	5	8	7	10					9				6	11											
15		2	3	4	5	8	7						9				6	11	1	10									
16			3	4	5	8	7					6	9		2			11	1	10									
17			2	8	5	6	7	10					9			3	4	11	1										
18			2	4		6	7	8				5		10		3		11	1		9								
19			2	4	5	6	7	8						10		3		11	1		9								
20			2	4		6	7	8					5	10		3		11	1		9								
21			3	4		6	7	8					5	10				11			9	1	2						
22			3	4	5	6	7	8						10	2			11				1		9					
23			3	4	5	6	7	9						10		2		11				1			8				
24			3	4	5	6	7	9						10		2		11				1			8				
25			3	4	5	6	7	9						10		2		11				1			8				
26			3		5	6	7	9						10		2						1	4		8	11			
27			3	4	5	6	7	9						10		2						1			8	11			
28			3	4		6	7	9				5		10		2			1						8	11			
29			3	4		6	7	9				5		10		2			1						8	11			
30			3	4		6	7	9				5		10		2			1						8	11			
31			3	4		6	7	9				5		10		2			1						8	11			
32			3	4		6	7	9				5		10		2			1						8	11			
33			3	4		6	7	9				5		10		2			1						8	11			
34		3		4		6	7	9				5		10		2			1						8	11			
35			3	4	5	6	7	9						10		2			1						8	11			
36			3		5	6	7	9						10		2	4		1						8	11			
37			3	4		6						5				2	8			10	9					7	11		1
38			3	4		6										2	7			10	9			5			11	8	1
Apps.	14	14	36	36	25	38	36	34	12	9	2	11	11	26	4	21	10	12	15	4	6	7	2	2	14	12	2	1	2
Goals		1		1		5	12	14	8				1	5			2	1		2	4				3	6			

Pos	P.	W.	D.	L.	F.	A.	Pts.
18th	38	12	9	17	65	91	33

Scottish Cup

No.	Date	Opposition	H.T.	Res.	Att.	Goalscorers
1	22 Jan	DUMBARTON	2-0	6-0	9000	McAvoy, Reid(2), Fyfe, Thomson(2)
2	12 Feb	BYE				
3	5 Mar	Celtic	2-0	2-1	39839	Collins, McGrogan
QF	19	AYR UNITED	1-0	1-1	27442	Thomson
QFR	23	Ayr United	1-0	5-0	23785	Thomson(2), Collins, McAvoy, McGrogan
SF	2 Apr	Rangers*	1-1	4-3	70833	Collins(2), Thomson(2)
F	23	East Fife*	1-1	1-1	80091	McAvoy
FR	27	East Fife*	2-1	2-4#	92716	McGrogan, Thomson

No.	Brown	Leslie	Milloy	G.Robertson	McClure	Ross	Thomson	Collins	McGowan	Beattie	Howie	Stewart	J.Robertson	McAvoy	Anderson	Fyfe	Gallacher	Roberts	Hunter	Henry	Gillespie	Marsh	Milliken	Turnbull	Reid	McGrogan	Borthwick	Gillan	McIntyre
1			3	4	5	6	7	9						10		2						1			8	11			
2																													
3			3	4		6	7	9				5		10		2			1						8	11			
QF			3	4		6	7	9				5		10		2			1						8	11			
QFR			3	4		6	7	9				5		10		2			1						8	11			
SF			3	4		6	7	9				5		10		2			1						8	11			
F			3	4		6	7	9				5		10		2			1						8	11			
FR			3	4		6	7	9				5		10		2			1						8	11			

* Hampden # After Extra Time

* GIANT KILLERS OF 1938 *

The caption says it all. Kilmarnock knocked both Celtic and Rangers out of the Scottish Cup on their way to the Final. Back: Stewart, Fyfe, Hunter, Leslie, G.Robertson Front: Thomson, Reid, Collins, Ross, McAvoy, McGrogan. Inset: Milloy

SEASON 1938-39 Division One

No.	Date	Opposition	H.T.	Res.	Att.	Goalscorers	Hunter	Fyfe	Milloy	G.Robertson	Stewart	Ross	Thomson	Reid	Collins	McAvoy	Borthwick	Drysdale	Turnbull	McGrogan	Harvey	Gallacher	Henry	Davidson	Wyllie	Cahill
1	13 Aug	Celtic	1-3	1-9	15000	McAvoy	1	2	3	4	5	6	7	8	9	10	11									
2	20	HIBERNIAN	0-0	0-1	8000		1	3		4	5	6	7	8	9	10	11	2								
3	24	CELTIC	0-0	0-0	20000		1	2	3		5	6	7	8		10		4	9	11						
4	27	Motherwell	1-2	2-5		Turnbull(2)	1	2	3		5	6	7	8		10	11	4	9							
5	3 Sep	ST. JOHNSTONE	1-0	1-0	8000	McGrogan	1	2	3			6	7	8		10		5	9	11	4					
6	10	St. Mirren	0-0	1-0	7000	Turnbull	1	2	3		5			8	10			6	9	11	4	7				
7	14	Hibernian	1-0	1-0	8000	Reid	1		3		5	6		8	9	10		2		11	4	7				
8	17	ARBROATH	0-0	1-1	3000	McAvoy	1		3		5	6		8	9	10		2		11	4	7				
9	24	Third Lanark	3-1	3-3	7000	Harvey, Henry, Reid	1	2	3		5			8	7			4	9	11	6		10			
10	1 Oct	PARTICK THISTLE	2-1	4-2	7000	Borthwick, Drysdale, Henry, McGrogan	1		3		5			8	9		11	4		7	6		10	2		
11	8	Ayr United	1-1	2-2	12000	Collins, Drysdale	1	2	3		5		7	8	9			4		11	6		10			
12	15	FALKIRK	1-0	1-1	7000	Henry	1	2	3		5			8	9		11	4		7	6		10			
13	22	RANGERS	1-0	3-1	18000	McGrogan, Reid, Thomson	1	2	3		5		7	8		10		4		11	6				9	
14	29	Queen of the South	0-2	0-2	7700		1	2	3		5		7	8	9	10		4		11	6					
15	5 Nov	RAITH ROVERS	3-2	4-2	5000	Collins, McAvoy, Reid, Thomson	1	2	3		5		7	8	9	10		4		11	6					
16	12	HAMILTON A.	2-0	2-2	5500	Ross, Thomson	1	2	3		5	9	7	8		10		4		11	6					
17	19	Aberdeen	1-0	2-1	12000	McGrogan, Thomson	1		3		5	9	7	8		10		4	2	11	6					
18	26	ALBION ROVERS	1-1	4-2	6000	Ross(2), McAvoy, Reid	1		3		5	9	7	8		10		4	2	11	6					
19	3 Dec	Hearts	1-1	1-2	16000	Thomson	1		3		5	9	7	8		10		4	2	11	6					
20	10	Queens Park	2-0	5-1	8000	Ross(3), Thomson(2)	1		3		5	9	7	8		10		4	2	11	6					
21	17	CLYDE	1-2	1-4	5000	Reid	1		3		5	9	7	8		10		4	2	11	6					
22	28	MOTHERWELL	0-1	1-3	3000	McAvoy	1	3				9	7	8		10		4	2	11	6				5	
23	31	St. Johnstone	1-1	3-1	4000	McAvoy(2), Borthwick	1	3			5	9		8		10	11	4	2		6				7	
24	2 Jan	ST. MIRREN	2-1	3-2	18000	Reid(3)	1	3			5	9	7	8		10	11	4	2		6					
25	3	Falkirk	0-1	0-4	12000		1	3			5	9	7	8	10			4	2	11	6					
26	7	THIRD LANARK	2-1	5-2	8000	Borthwick(2), Thomson, Milloy, Reid	1		3		5	9	7	8		10	11	4	2		6					
27	28	AYR UNITED	2-0	2-2	14500	Reid(2)	1		3	4		9		8		10	11	5	2		6				7	
28	11 Feb	Arbroath	1-1	1-4	3500	Reid	1		3	4			7	8	9	10		5	2	11	6					
29	18	Partick Thistle	0-2	3-4	6000	Ross(2), Drysdale	1		3			9	7	8		10		4	2	11	6				5	
30	25	Rangers	2-0	2-2	10000	McGrogan(2), Ross	1		3			9		8		10		4	2	11	6				5	7
31	8 Mar	QUEEN OF THE SOUTH	1-1	1-1	2500	Ross	1		3			9	7	8		10		4	2	11	6				5	
32	11	Raith Rovers	2-1	3-2	5000	McGrogan(2), Ross	1		3			9		8		10		4	2	11	6				5	7
33	18	Hamilton A.	1-2	1-3		Reid	1		3			9	7	8		10		4	2	11	6				5	
34	1 Apr	Albion Rovers	1-3	1-6		Reid	1		3			9	7	8		10		4	2	11	6				5	
35	5	ABERDEEN	0-1	0-3	4000		1	2	3		5			8		11				7	6		10		9	4
36	8	HEARTS	3-0	4-1	6000	Collins(3), Reid	1		3		5		7	8	9	10		4	2	11	6					
37	22	QUEENS PARK	2-0	3-0	5000	McGrogan(2), Harvey	1		3		5		7	8	9	10		4	2	11	6					
38	29	Clyde	0-3	1-5		Collins	1		3		5		7	8	9	10		4	2	11	6					
						Apps.	38	18	33	4	28	25	27	38	16	32	9	36	26	31	34	3	5	1	11	3
						Goals			1			10	8	17	6	7	4	3	3	9	2		3			

Pos	P.	W.	D.	L.	F.	A.	Pts.
10th	38	15	9	14	73	86	39

Scottish Cup

No.	Date	Opposition	H.T.	Res.	Att.	Goalscorers	Hunter	Fyfe	Milloy	G.Robertson	Stewart	Ross	Thomson	Reid	Collins	McAvoy	Borthwick	Drysdale	Turnbull	McGrogan	Harvey	Gallacher	Henry	Davidson	Wyllie	Cahill
1	21 Jan	BERWICK RANGERS	2-0	6-1	6439	Barthwick(2), Ross(2), McAvoy, Thomson	1		3	4		9	7	8		10	11	5	2		6					
2	4 Feb	Hibernian	1-0	1-3	32394	Ross	1		3	6		9	7	8		10	11	5	2		4					

George Robertson

Killie's inspirational international right-half.

SEASON 1939-40 Division One

No.	Date	Opposition	H.T.	Res.	Att.	Goalscorers	Hunter	Turnbull	Milloy	Drysdale	Stewart	Harvey	Thomson	Reid	Collins	McAvoy	McGrogan	McClure	Bell	Dornan	Wyllie	Rodman	Gallacher
1	12 Aug	MOTHERWELL	2-0	3-3	14000	Collins(2), McAvoy	1	2	3	4	5	6	7	8	9	10	11						
2	19	St. Johnstone	2-0	3-0	3500	Collins, McAvoy, McGrogan	1	2	3	4		6	7	8	9	10	11	5					
3	23	Motherwell	2-2	2-4		McGrogan, Reid	1	2	3	4		6	7	8	9	10	11	5					
4	26	THIRD LANARK	0-0	0-1	8000		1	2	3	4		6	7	8	9	10	11	5					
5	2 Sep	Arbroath	0-1	2-1	4000	Collins, Reid		2		4		6		8	9		11		1	3	5	7	10
						Apps.	4	5	4	5	1	5	4	5	5	4	5	3	1	1	1	1	1
						Goals								2	4	2	2						

Fixtures abandoned - 2nd World War

Western League

No.	Date	Opposition	H.T.	Res.	Att.	Goalscorers	Hunter	Turnbull	Milloy	Drysdale	Stewart	Harvey	Thomson	Reid	Collins	McAvoy	McGrogan	Bell	Dornan	Rodman	Moulds	Henry	Gallacher	Mennie	Maxwell	Neil	Kirkpatrick	Bothwick	Gardiner	"Newman"	Gillespie	Brawley	Stevenson	MacDonald	"Junior"
1	21 Oct	Third Lanark	1-0	2-3		Gallacher, McGrogan	1		3	4		6		8	9		11		2		5	7	10												
2	28	DUMBARTON	2-0	5-0	3000	Collins(4), Thomson			3	4		6	7	8	9		11	1	2		5		10												
3	4 Nov	Airdrieonians	0-2	0-3			1	11	3	4		6		8	9				2		5		10	7											
4	11	MOTHERWELL	1-0	1-1	3000	McGrogan		7	3	4	5	6		8	9		11	1	2				10												
5	18	Celtic	0-0	1-1	3000	Turnbull		7	3	4	5	6		8	9		11	1	2				10												
6	25	PARTICK THISTLE	1-1	5-2	2000	Collins(2), Reid, Gallacher(2)		7	3	4	5	6		8	9			1	2				10		11										
7	2 Dec	Rangers	0-0	1-4	5500	Collins			3	4	5	6		8	9		7	1	2				10		11										
8	9	MORTON	3-1	4-2	1000	Collins(3), Maxwell		7	3	4	5	6		8	9			1	2				10		11										
9	16	Queen of the South	1-4	2-4		Collins, Turnbull		11	3	4	5	6		8	9			1	2				10			7									
10	23	QUEENS PARK	0-0	2-1	3000	McAvoy(2)			3		5	6		8	9	10	7	1	2				4		11										
11	30	Albion Rovers	2-1	3-2		Collins, McGrogan, Reid	1	7	3	4	5	6		8	9		11		2				10												
12	1 Jan	St. Mirren	1-0	3-3		Collins(2), Turnbull	1	7	3	4		6			9	10	11		2		5		8												
13	2	AYR UNITED	1-0	3-1	5000	Collins(2), Gallacher		7	3	4	5				9		11	1					6	2	10		8								
14	6	HAMILTON A.	1-3	1-4	3000	Collins		7		4	5			8	9		11	1	3				6	2	10										
15	13	CLYDE	1-2	1-2		Collins		2	3	4	5			8	9	10	7	1					6		11										
16	10 Feb	Motherwell	1-0	1-2	3000	Reid	1		3	4	5	6		8	9		7						2		10			11							
17	17	CELTIC	2-1	3-2	5500	Collins(2), Kirkpatrick	1		3	4	5	6			9	10	7						2		11		8								
18	16 Mar	QUEEN OF THE SOUTH	0-2	1-3	4000	Maxwell	1		3	4	5			8			11		2				10		9		7		6						
19	30	ALBION ROVERS	2-0	6-2	3000	Rodman(2), 'Newman'(2), Gallacher, Reid	1		3	4	5	6		8			11		2	9			10							7					
20	2 Apr	THIRD LANARK	0-1	1-2	2000	Gillespie	1		3	4							7		2	8	5		10						6	11	9				
21	6	ST. MIRREN	0-1	3-1	2000	Gallacher, McGrogan, Rodman	1			4	5	6		8			11		2	9			10	3						7					
22	10	Dumbarton	1-2	2-2		Gallacher, 'Newman'	1					6					7		2		5		10				8			11	9	3			4
23	13	Ayr United	1-1	3-2	2500	Rodman(2), Gardiner	1		3	4	5	6		8					2	10			7						11		9				
24	20	Hamilton A.	0-0	0-0	2500		1			4	5	6		8			11		2	10			7								9	3			
25	24	Partick Thistle	0-4	2-5		Gillespie, 'Newman'	1				5		7						2		4		10				11		6	8	9	3			
26	27	Clyde	0-1	2-1	3000	McGrogan, Rodman				4	5	6		8			11	1	2	9									10			3	7		
27	11 May	Morton	0-0	0-2			1		3	4	5			8					2	9			7				11		10			6			
28	15	RANGERS	1-1	3-1		Gillespie(2), Gallacher	1				5						7		2	8			10						6		9	3		4	11
29	18	Queens Park	1-0	1-0		Reid	1			4	5			8			7		2	10			6								9	3			11
30	25	AIRDRIEONIANS	0-5	1-5	2000	McGrogan	1			4	5			8			11		2	9			10						6			3	7		
						Apps.	18	11	22	26	24	20	2	23	17	4	23	12	26	10	7	1	29	4	10	1	6	1	8	5	7	7	2	1	3
						Goals		3					1	5	20	2	6			16			8		2		1		1	4	4				

Pos	P.	W.	D.	L.	F.	A.	Pts.
8th	30	13	5	12	63	63	31

War Cup

No.	Date	Opposition	H.T.	Res.	Att.	Goalscorers	Hunter	Turnbull	Milloy	Drysdale	Stewart	Harvey	Thomson	Reid	Collins	McAvoy	McGrogan	Bell	Dornan	Rodman	Moulds	Henry	Gallacher	Mennie	Maxwell	Neil	Kirkpatrick	Bothwick	Gardiner	"Newman"	Gillespie	Brawley	Stevenson	MacDonald	"Junior"
1	24 Feb	AYR UNITED	0-0	1-0	8631	Gallacher	1		3	4	5	6	7		9		11						8	2	10										
1	2 Mar	Ayr United (Agg: 3-2)	0-1	2-2	9941	Collins, Thomson	1		3	4	5	6	7		9		11		2				8		10										
2	9	ALBION ROVERS	1-0	2-1	7586	Collins, McGrogan	1		3	4	5	6	7	8	9		11		2						10										
QF	23	Dundee United	0-2	0-3	10000		1		3	4	5	6	7	8	9		11		2				10												

Nephew of 1890's player, Richie McAvoy, DOUGLAS McAVOY toured North America with the SFA in 1939. He returned to Rugby Park after the war but was transferred to Liverpool in 1947.

SEASON 1945-46 Division One

No.	Date	Opposition	H.T.	Res.	Att.	Goalscorers
1	11 Aug	Queens Park	2-0	3-2	5000	Turnbull(2), McLaren
2	18	ABERDEEN	0-3	1-4	12000	O.G.
3	25	Morton	0-4	1-6	9000	Scott
4	1 Sep	RANGERS	0-5	0-7	17000	
5	8	Queen of the South	0-1	1-2	8000	Ballantyne
6	15	CLYDE	0-0	0-0	5000	
7	22	Hamilton A.	2-3	4-4	4000	Walsh(2), Harrison, McLaren
8	29	HEARTS	2-0	2-2	12000	Walsh, Redmond
9	6 Oct	MOTHERWELL	2-3	2-5	12000	Harrison, Walsh
10	13	HIBERNIAN	1-2	3-4	10000	McAvoy, McLaren, Walsh
11	20	Falkirk	1-1	4-3	9000	Walsh(2), Harrison, Turnbull
12	27	Partick Thistle	2-2	3-5	4000	Henry, Horton, Walsh
13	3 Nov	ST. MIRREN	5-2	6-4	15000	McIntyre(2),Ballant'e,Bradford,Turnbull,Walsh
14	10	Third Lanark	0-1	1-4	3000	McLaren
15	17	CELTIC	2-0	2-1	20000	Walsh(2)
16	24	QUEENS PARK	1-0	2-2	15000	McAvoy, McLaren
17	1 Dec	Aberdeen	0-1	0-2	14000	
18	8	MORTON	1-1	1-1	6000	Harrison
19	15	Rangers	0-3	1-5		Walsh
20	22	Clyde	0-1	0-3	6000	
21	29	HAMILTON A.	0-1	0-2	7000	
22	1 Jan	QUEEN OF THE SOUTH	1-0	1-1	10000	Walsh
23	2	Hearts	0-1	4-1	15000	Walsh(3), McLaren
24	5	Motherwell	2-1	2-2	8000	Walsh(2)
25	12	Hibernian	1-0	1-4	11000	McLaren
26	26	PARTICK THISTLE*	1-0	2-1	11000	McLaren, Walsh
27	2 Feb	St. Mirren	0-2	1-4	7000	Walsh
28	9	THIRD LANARK	0-1	1-3	9000	Davie
29	16	Celtic	1-1	1-1	20000	Walsh
30	6 Apr	FALKIRK	2-1	6-2	8000	Devlin(2), Davie, Sinclair, J.Taylor Turnbull

No.	Walsh	Turnbull	Bradford	Milloy	M.McDonald	Jenkins	Geddes	M.McLaren	Ballantyne	Johnstone	Horton	Harrison	Dornan	Harvey	McIntyre	Drury	McAvoy	King	Wilson	Davie	Cavin	Downie	J.Taylor	A.Taylor	Whyte	Burns	Shufflebottom	Sinclair	Scott	McClure	Hood	Mitchell	Stevenson	Devlin	D.McDonald	Dougan
1	9	8					4	10		2	6		3			11			1								5	7								
2	9	6					4	10		2			3			11			1		8						5									
3	9	5		3			4	10		2									1				6						7							
4	9	8	2				4		11		6		3				10	7	1											5						
5	9	8	5				4		11	2							10	7	1				6													
6	9	2	5	3			4		11			10						8							6	1										
7	9	2	5	3			4	10	11			8						7							6	1										
8	9	2	5	3			4		11		6	8					10																			
9	9	2	5	3			4		11			8					10	7														6				
10	9	2	5	3		1	4	10				8					11															6	7			
11	9	8	5	3		1	4		11			10									7				6						2					
12	9		5	3	6	1			11		4										8										2					
13	9	8	5	3	6	1		10	11	2	4				7																					
14	9	8	5	3	6	1		10	11	2	4				7																					
15	9	8	5	3		1	4	10	11	2	6							7																		
16	9	8	5	3	6	1		10		2	4				7		11																			
17	9	8	5		6	1		10	11	3	4				7																					
18	9	8	5	3	6	1			11	2	4	10			7																					
19	9	8	5	3	6	1	4			2		10			7									11												
20	9	8	5	3	6	1	4			2				10	7									11												
21	9		5	3	10	1							2	4	7		11				8															
22	9	8	5	3	6	1		10			7		2	4			11																			
23	9	8	5	3	6	1	4	10			7			2		11																				
24	9	8	5	3	6	1	4	10				7		2		11																				
25	9	2	5		6	1	4	10				8		3	7	11																				
26	9	4	5	3	6	1		10				7	2			11				8																
27	9	4	5	3	6	1		10					2			11				8									7							
28	9	3	5		6			10					2	4		11				8		1											7			
29	9	8	5	3	6								2	4						10		1		11												7
30		2		3	10		4							6						8		1	11					7		5				9		
Apps.	29	28	26	23	18	18	18	17	13	12	12	11	9	9	9	8	8	6	5	5	4	3	3	3	3	2	2	2	2	2	2	2	2	1		1
Goals	21	5	1					8	2		1	4			2		2			2			1					1	1					2		

* Played at Somerset Park

Pos	P.	W.	D.	L.	F.	A.	Pts.
15th	30	7	8	15	56	87	22

The following players made one League appearance each, their position ('P') in the corresponding match ('M') was as follows:
Bell (P1 M9): Cox (P6 M21): Henry (P10 M12, 1 goal): Hunter (P1 M8): Jessop (P11 M3): Loneskie (P3 M5): Marshallsay (P7 M2):
Melia (P7 M6): Pattison (P7 M12): Quinn (P2 M17): Also Redmond made 2 appearances (P8 M3 & P7 M8). A total of 47 players used in League matches.

Southern League Cup

No.	Date	Opposition	H.T.	Res.	Att.	Goalscorers
1	23 Feb	ABERDEEN	0-1	1-1	16000	Turnbull
2	2 Mar	Partick Thistle	0-1	0-3	15000	
3	9	HIBERNIAN	1-0	1-0	12000	Devlin
4	16	Aberdeen	0-0	0-1	15000	
5	23	PARTICK THISTLE	1-1	2-2	12000	D.McDonald, J.Taylor
6	30	Hibernian	0-2	0-4	20000	

No.	Walsh	Turnbull	Bradford	Milloy	M.McDonald	Jenkins	Geddes	M.McLaren	Ballantyne	Johnstone	Horton	Harrison	Dornan	Harvey	McIntyre	Drury	McAvoy	King	Wilson	Davie	Cavin	Downie	J.Taylor	A.Taylor	Whyte	Burns	Shufflebottom	Sinclair	Scott	McClure	Hood	Mitchell	Stevenson	Devlin	D.McDonald	Dougan
1		8	5	3	6								2	4						10		1		11											9	7
2		9	5	3	6			8					2	4		11						1												10		7
3		4	5	3	8								2	6								1		11										10	9	7
4		4			8								2	6								1		11						5	3			10	9	7
5		4		3	8								2	6						7		1	11							5				10	9	
6		4	3				8						2	6						7		1		11						5				10	9	

Pos	P.	W.	D.	L.	F.	A.	Pts.
4th	6	1	2	3	4	11	4

Victory Cup

No.	Date	Opposition	H.T.	Res.	Att.	Goalscorers
1	20 Apr	East Fife	0-1	0-2	9000	
1	27	EAST FIFE	1-0	3-0*	9000	Devlin(2), Walsh
2	4 May	Aberdeen	1-1	1-1	15000	Walsh
2	13	ABERDEEN (Agg: 1-4)*	0-0	0-3	20000	

No.	Walsh	Turnbull	Bradford	Milloy	M.McDonald	Jenkins	Geddes	M.McLaren	Ballantyne	Johnstone	Horton	Harrison	Dornan	Harvey	McIntyre	Drury	McAvoy	King	Wilson	Davie	Cavin	Downie	J.Taylor	A.Taylor	Whyte	Burns	Shufflebottom	Sinclair	Scott	McClure	Hood	Mitchell	Stevenson	Devlin	D.McDonald	Dougan
1	7	2	5	3	10		4							6						8		1	11											9		
1	9	4	2	3	6															8		1	11					7		5				10		
2	9	4	2	3	10									6		11						1						7		5				8		
2	9	4	2	3	10									6		11						1						†		5				8		

* After extra time, Agg: 3-2 † Player 7 was A.Collins

The Germans never bombed Rugby Park. This is what it looked like after five years in the hands of the British Army. The first continental visitors to the ground were the prisoners-of-war who helped get the pitch ready for the resumption of football in 1945.

SEASON 1946-47 Division One

No.	Date	Opposition	H.T.	Res.	Att.	Goalscorers	Downie	Hood	Landsborough	Turnbull	McClure	McDonald	Sinclair	Reid	Walsh	Devlin	Kirkpatrick	Davie	Cavin	McAvoy	Milloy	McLeish	Collins	Bradford	Drury	Hunter	Geddes	Thyne	Stevenson	Dornan	Henry	McCulloch	Cox	Harkness
1	10 Aug	QUEENS PARK	0-1	2-2	14000	Devlin, Turnbull	1	2	3	4	5	6	7	8	9	10	11																	
2	14	Aberdeen	0-0	0-1	18000		1	2	3	4	5		7	8	9	10		6		11														
3	17	Rangers	2-1	2-3	25000	Devlin, Walsh	1	2	3	4	5	10			9	8		6	7	11														
4	21	HAMILTON A.	0-1	1-1	14000	McLeish	1	2		4	5	10			9	8	11	6			3	7												
5	24	MORTON	1-1	2-3	15000	Devlin, Turnbull	1	2		4	5	11		8		10		6			3	7	9											
6	28	Clyde	1-0	3-3	6000	Turnbull(3)	1	2	3	8		4				10		6				7	9	5	11									
7	31	FALKIRK	0-1	2-1	12000	Collins, Devlin	1	2	3	8		4				10		6				7	9	5	11									
8	4 Sep	Hibernian	0-2	0-6	20000		1	2	3	8		4				9		6				7		5	11						10			
9	7	QUEEN OF THE SOUTH	0-0	1-3	10000	Turnbull		2	3	8		4					11	6		10		7	9	5		1								
10	14	Hearts	0-0	0-2	25000		1	2	3	8							11	6		10		7	9	5			4							
11	2 Nov	PARTICK THISTLE	3-0	3-1	15000	McAvoy(2), O.G.	1	2	3	6				8	9	4	11			10								5	7					
12	9	St. Mirren	0-0	1-3	10000	McAvoy	1		2	6				8	9	4	11			10	3							5	7					
13	16	Motherwell	1-0	1-2	8000	Collins	1	2	3					8		4	11	6		10			9					5	7					
14	23	THIRD LANARK	0-0	0-2	8000		1		3					8		4	11	6		10			9					5	7	2				
15	30	Celtic	0-3	2-4	15000	Collins(2)	1		3	8						4	11	6		10			9					5	7	2				
16	7 Dec	Queens Park	0-0	1-0	8000	Kirkpatrick	1		3	4					9	10	11	6					8					5	7	2				
17	14	ABERDEEN	1-0	2-1	10000	Stevenson(2)	1		3	4					9	8		6		11								5	7	2	10			
18	21	Hamilton	1-1	2-2	3500	Stevenson, Walsh	1		3	4					9		11	6		10							2	5	7		8			
19	28	CLYDE	1-1	2-2	15000	Henry(2)	1	2	3	4					9	10	11	6										5	7		8			
20	1 Jan	Queen of the South	1-1	1-1	14500	Walsh	1	2		3				8	9	4		6		11			10					5	7					
21	2	RANGERS	0-2	0-2	32325		1	2		3				8	9	4		6					10		11			5	7					
22	4	HEARTS	0-0	0-0	10000		1	2	3					8	9	4		6					10					5	7			11		
23	18	HIBERNIAN	1-1	3-5	15000	Henry(2), Collins	1		3	2				8		4		6					9					5	7		10			11
24	1 Feb	Falkirk	1-2	3-3	9000	Collins(2), McLeish	1		3	2				8		4		6				7	9					5			10			11
25	8	Morton	0-0	0-0	5000		1		3	2				8		4		6				7	9					5			10		11	
26	15 Mar	Third Lanark*	1-1	4-1	12000	Collins(2), Drury, Reid	1	3		2				8		6		4		10		7	9		11			5						
27	22	MOTHERWELL	1-0	2-0	16000	Drury, McAvoy	1	3		2				8		6		4		10		7	9		11			5						
28	29	CELTIC	0-2	1-2	12000	McLeish	1	3	2	4				8		6				10		7	9		11			5						
29	5 Apr	ST. MIRREN	1-2	1-5	8000	Devlin	1	2	3	4				8		6				10			9		11			5	7					
30	12	Partick Thistle	2-1	2-5	15000	Turnbull, McAvoy		3		2						9		4		10					11	1	6	5	7		8			
						Apps.	28	21	23	27	5	8	2	17	13	27	12	25	1	17	3	12	19	5	9	2	3	20	15	4	8	1	1	2
						Goals				7				1	3	5	1			5		3	9		2				3		4			
						21																												

* at Hampden

Pos	P.	W.	D.	L.	F.	A.	Pts.
15th	30	6	9	15	44	66	

Pos	P.	W.	D.	L.	F.	A.	Pts.
3rd	6	3	0	3	12	11	6

League Cup Section AA

No.	Date	Opposition	H.T.	Res.	Att.	Goalscorers	Downie	Hood	Landsborough	Turnbull	McClure	McDonald	Sinclair	Reid	Walsh	Devlin	Kirkpatrick	Davie	Cavin	McAvoy	Milloy	McLeish	Collins	Bradford	Drury	Hunter	Geddes	Thyne	Stevenson	Dornan	Henry	McCulloch	Cox	Harkness
1	21 Sep	PARTICK THISTLE	3-1	3-2	12000	Collins, Kirkpatrick, McAvoy	1	2	3	7				8		4	11	6		10			9	5										
2	28	Hearts	1-1	1-3	25757	McAvoy	1	2	3	7				8		4	11	6		10			9	5										
3	5 Oct	Clyde	0-1	2-3	12000	Walsh, O.G.	1	2	3	7	5			8	9	4	11	6		10														
4	12	Partick Thistle	0-0	3-1	15000	McAvoy(3)	1	2	3	7				8		4	11	6		10			9					5						
5	19	HEARTS	1-0	2-0	20000	Collins, Reid	1	2	3	7				8		4	11	6		10			9					5						
6	26	CLYDE	1-1	1-2	20000	McAvoy	1	2	3	7				8		4	11	6		10			9					5						

Scottish Cup

No.	Date	Opposition	H.T.	Res.	Att.	Goalscorers	Downie	Hood	Landsborough	Turnbull	McClure	McDonald	Sinclair	Reid	Walsh	Devlin	Kirkpatrick	Davie	Cavin	McAvoy	Milloy	McLeish	Collins	Bradford	Drury	Hunter	Geddes	Thyne	Stevenson	Dornan	Henry	McCulloch	Cox	Harkness
1	25 Jan	Falkirk	0-1	0-2	12522		1		3	2						4		6		10			9					5	7		8			11

'Swig' Turnbull

One of the few experienced pre-war players available to Killie in a disastrous season.

SEASON 1947-48

Division Two

No.	Date	Opposition	H.T.	Res.	Att.	Goalscorers	Hunter	Turnbull	Hood	Devlin	Thyne	Davie	McLeish	Collins	Walsh	Cavin	Drury	Mennie	Morrison	McAvoy	Freckleton	Stevenson	McLaren	Archibald	Henderson	Cox	J.Lamont	Maxwell	Pattison	Murdoch	W.Lamont	Healy	McCulloch	White	Geddes
1	13 Aug	St. Johnstone	1-1	2-2	6000	Collins, Cox	1	2	3	6	5	4		9			11			10		7				8									
2	27	RAITH ROVERS	3-0	7-1	9700	Collins(3), Walsh(3), Turnbull	1	2	3	4	5	6	7	8	9		11			10															
3	20 Sep	Ayr United	3-2	3-2	12000	Drury(2), Turnbull	1	2	3	4	5	6	7	8	9	10	11																		
4	27	DUNDEE UNITED	1-1	5-2	8000	Collins(3), Walsh(2)	1	2	3	4	5	6	7	8	9	10	11																		
5	4 Oct	Stenhousemuir	0-1	0-1	2300		1	2	3	4	5	6	7	8	9	10	11																		
6	11	HAMILTON A.	2-0	3-0	10000	Collins(2), McAvoy	1	5	3	4		6	7	8		10	11	2		9															
7	18	Leith Athletic	1-1	1-3	4000	Drury	1	5	3	4		6	7	8		10	11	2		9															
8	25	DUNFERMLINE	3-0	3-0	12000	Devlin(2), Drury	1	6	3	9	5		7	8			11	2	4	10															
9	1 Nov	Cowdenbeath	0-0	0-1	7000		1	5	3	9		6	7	8			11	2	4	10															
10	8	EAST FIFE	0-0	0-2	8000		1	4	3	9	5	6	7	8			11	2		10															
11	15	ARBROATH	1-0	2-1	6000	Collins(2)	1	4	3	6	5		7	8			11	2		9	10														
12	22	Albion Rovers	1-1	1-2	6000	Collins	1	4	3	6	5		8	9			11	2			10	7													
13	29	ALLOA ATHLETIC	2-1	5-1	6000	Collins(2), McAvoy, Stevenson, Turnbull	1	4	3	6	5		8	9			11	2		10		7													
14	6 Dec	DUMBARTON	1-0	2-2	6000	Collins, McAvoy	1	4	3		5	6	8	9			11	2		10		7													
15	13	Stirling Albion	0-1	1-2	6000	Turnbull	1	4	3		5	6	8	9			10	2				7	11												
16	20	ST. JOHNSTONE	1-0	1-0	8000	Turnbull	1	4	3		5	6		8		7		2			10		11	9											
17	27	Raith Rovers	1-0	3-4	4500	Cavin(2), Turnbull	1	4	3		5	6		9		7		2			10		11		8										
18	1 Jan	AYR UNITED	3-2	4-4	6000	Collins, Drury, Mennie, Pattison		4	3		5			9		8	11	2					10				1	6	7						
19	3	Dundee United	1-2	3-2	11000	Cavin, Collins, McLaren		4	3		5			9		8	11	2					10				1	6	7						
20	10	STENHOUSEMUIR	2-1	7-2	5506	Turnbull(3), McLaren(2), Collins, Drury	1	8	3		5	4	7	9			11	2					10					6							
21	17	Hamilton A.	1-2	1-3	3500	Drury	1	8	3		5	4		9		7	11	2					10					6							
22	31	LEITH ATHLETIC	3-1	6-2	5000	Collins(2), Cavin, Drury, McLaren, Turnbull	1	4	3		5	8		9		7	11	2					10					6							
23	14 Feb	Dunfermline	1-2	1-3	3000	Cavin	1	4	3		5	8		9		7	11	2					10					6							
24	21	COWDENBEATH	0-2	1-3	5000	Turnbull		2	3		5	8		9		7	11	4					10					6		1					
25	28	East Fife	1-0	3-1	8000	Collins, Drury(2)		4	3		5	8		9		7	11	2					10					6		1					
26	6 Mar	Arbroath	0-3	1-5	3000	Collins			3		5	8		9		7	11	2	4				10					6		1					
27	13	ALBION ROVERS	1-2	1-4	9000	Collins			3		5	8		9				2	4		10		11					6	7	1					
28	20	Alloa Athletic	0-3	1-4	5000	Collins	1				5	4		9		8	11	3			10							6	7		2				
29	26	Dumbarton	0-1	2-1		Henderson, Stevenson	1	4	3		5	6		10			9	2				7	11		8										
30	3 Apr	STIRLING ALBION	1-1	2-2	4000	Davie, Drury	1		3		5	4		8			11	2					10					6	7			9			
						Apps.	24	26	29	13	27	24	15	30	4	16	27	25	4	10	6	6	15	1	2	1	2	12	5	4	1	1			
						Goals		11		2		1		24	5	5	11	1		3		2	4		1	1			1						

Pos	P.	W.	D.	L.	F.	A.	Pts.
6th	30	13	4	13	72	62	30

League Cup Section BD

Pos	P.	W.	D.	L.	F.	A.	Pts.
3rd	6	2	2	2	12	12	6

No.	Date	Opposition	H.T.	Res.	Att.	Goalscorers	Hunter	Turnbull	Hood	Devlin	Thyne	Davie	McLeish	Collins	Walsh	Cavin	Drury	Mennie	Morrison	McAvoy	Freckleton	Stevenson	McLaren	Archibald	Henderson	Cox	J.Lamont	Maxwell	Pattison	Murdoch	W.Lamont	Healy	McCulloch	White	Geddes
1	9 Aug	Ayr United*	1-2	2-2	13500	Stevenson, Turnbull	1	2	3	6	5		4	9			11			10		7												8	
2	16	EAST FIFE	0-0	0-0	13000		1	2	3	6	5	4		9						10		7	11		8										
3	23	Stirling Albion	3-2	3-5	5535	Collins(2), McLaren	1	8	3	4	5	6	7	9				2		10			11												
4	30	AYR UNITED	1-0	1-2	14000	Turnbull	1	2	3	4	5	6	7		9		11			10															8
5	6 Sep	East Fife	2-1	3-1	7000	Cavin, Collins, Drury	1	2	3	4	5	6	7	8	9	10	11																		
6	13	STIRLING ALBION	2-1	3-2	10000	Walsh(2), Drury	1	2	3	4	5	6	7	8	9		11			10															

* Kilmarnock were numbered for the first time.

Scottish Cup

No.	Date	Opposition	H.T.	Res.	Att.	Goalscorers	Hunter	Turnbull	Hood	Devlin	Thyne	Davie	McLeish	Collins	Walsh	Cavin	Drury	Mennie	Morrison	McAvoy	Freckleton	Stevenson	McLaren	Archibald	Henderson	Cox	J.Lamont	Maxwell	Pattison	Murdoch	W.Lamont	Healy	McCulloch	White	Geddes
1	24 Jan	East Fife	0-1	0-2	12000		1	8	3		5	4		9		7	11	2					10					6							

B Division Supplementary Cup

No.	Date	Opposition	H.T.	Res.	Att.	Goalscorers	Hunter	Turnbull	Hood	Devlin	Thyne	Davie	McLeish	Collins	Walsh	Cavin	Drury	Mennie	Morrison	McAvoy	Freckleton	Stevenson	McLaren	Archibald	Henderson	Cox	J.Lamont	Maxwell	Pattison	Murdoch	W.Lamont	Healy	McCulloch	White	Geddes
1	5 Jan	STIRLING ALBION	0-2	1-2	5000	McLaren		4	3		5			8		9	11	2					10				1	6					7		

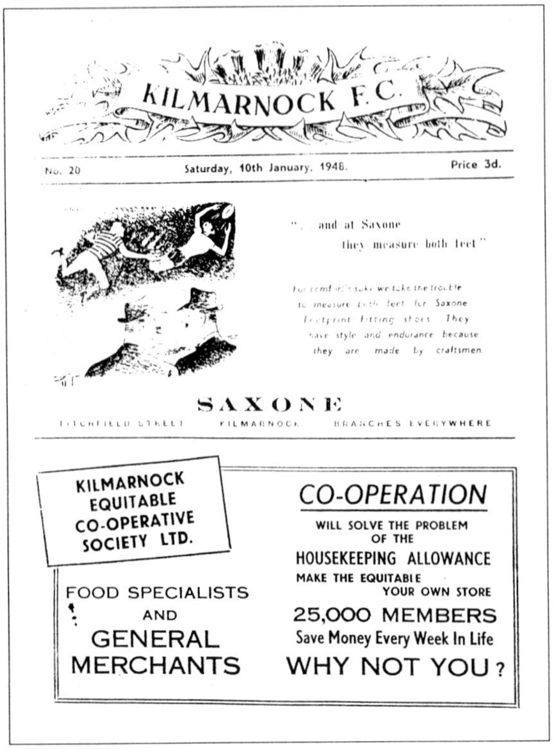

The lower League proved tougher than Kilmarnock supporters anticipated but occasionally the team still gave glimpses of their former glory. This programme is for the home game against Stenhousemuir which Killie won 7-2.

SEASON 1948-49 Division Two

No.	Date	Opposition	H.T.	Res.	Att.	Goalscorers	Purdie	Mennie	Hood	Gordon	Thyne	Miller	Hunter	Hamill	Clive	Brown	McLaren	Bowman	McCulloch	Drury	Murdoch	Lamont	Smith	McMahon	Anderson	Maxwell	McLeish	Sinclair	Lambie	Aitken	McFarlane	Hamilton	Fitzsimmons	Saddington	Sherry	Boyd	Black	Archibald
1	14 Aug	EAST STIRLING	3-1	3-2	12000	Brown, Clive, McLaren	1	2	3	4	5	6	7	8	9	10	11																					
2	18	Queens Park	1-1	3-2	10000	McLaren(2), Clive	1	2	3		5		7	4	9	8	10			11						6												
3	21	AYR UNITED	0-2	1-2	13000	Drury	1		3		5		7	4	9	8	10			11						6						2						
4	28	Arbroath	0-0	1-1	5000	Drury	1		3		5	6		4	9	8	10	2	7	11																		
5	1 Sep	HAMILTON A.	3-1	3-1	10000	Bowman, Clive, Hamill	1	2	3		5			8	9		10	4	7	11			6															
6	4	Dundee United	0-3	1-4	8000	Hamill	1	2	3		5	6		8	9		10	4	7	11																		
7	23 Oct	Stirling Albion	0-2	1-3	4574	McLaren		2			5		7		10		11	4			1	3	6	8	9													
8	30	DUNFERMLINE	1-0	1-2	6000	Clive	1	2	3		5	6	7	4	9		11						10	8														
9	6 Nov	Cowdenbeath	0-1	0-1	3500		1	2	3		5		7		9		10			11			6			4												
10	13	STENHOUSEMUIR	0-0	1-0	5377	McLaren	1		2		5				10		8			11		3	6			4		7	9									
11	20	Airdrieonians	0-1	0-5	6000		1		2		5	8			9		10			11		3	6			4		7										
12	27	DUMBARTON	1-1	4-2	7263	McLaren(2), Clive, Smith			2	4	5	11			9		10					3	6				7			8	1							
13	4 Dec	ST. JOHNSTONE	2-1	3-1	9219	McLaren(3)			3	4	5	11			9		10	2					6				7			8	1							
14	11	Raith Rovers	2-1	2-3	8000	McLaren, Aitken			3	4	5	11			9		10	2					6				7			8	1							
15	18	ALLOA ATHLETIC	4-0	6-0	9000	Clive(3), Bowman, McLaren, McLeish			3	4	5	11			9		10	2					6				7			8	1							
16	25	QUEENS PARK	1-0	1-1	12522	McLaren			3	4	5	11			9		10	2					6				7			8	1							
17	1 Jan	Ayr United	1-1	1-1	13422	Clive			2	4	5	7			9		10					3	6							8	1		11					
18	3	ARBROATH	3-0	8-0	13000	McLaren(3), Sinclair(3), Clive(2)			2	4	5				9		10					3	6					7		8	1		11					
19	8	East Stirling	0-1	0-3	2500				2	4	5				9		10					3	6					7		8	1		11					
20	15	DUNDEE UNITED	2-0	3-3	6300	Hunter(2), McLaren			2	6		3	7		9		10													8	1		11	4	5			
21	29	Hamilton A.	0-3	1-3	4000	Gordon			3	4			7		6	8	10		9												1		11		5	2		
22	5 Feb	STIRLING ALBION	0-2	0-2	6000				3	6	5		4			8	10		9								7				1		11			2		
23	12	Dunfermline	0-2	2-3	5000	Clive, McCulloch			3	4					7	8			9		1		6							10			11		5	2		
24	19	COWDENBEATH	0-0	2-2	6832	Fitzsimmons, McCulloch			3	4		11				8	10		9		1		6										7		5	2		
25	26	Stenhousemuir	1-4	2-6	1500	Aitken, McCulloch				6	5	11	7				10		9		1									8		3		4		2		
26	5 Mar	AIRDRIEONIANS	1-2	3-3	5000	Brown, Hunter, McLaren			3	6			7			10	11											9	5	8	1	2		4				
27	12	Dumbarton	2-1	2-2	2500	Hunter, McLaren			3	6			7			8	10											9	5			2	11	4			1	
28	19	St. Johnstone	0-0	0-1	4000				3	7			9			10	11						6							8	1	2			5			4
29	26	RAITH ROVERS	2-0	3-1	6000	McLaren(2), Smith			3		5	6					11						10					7	9	8	1	2						4
30	2 Apr	Alloa Athletic	0-1	0-1	4000				3		5	6					11						10						9	8		2		4			1	
						Apps.	10	7	28	18	23	16	13	7	22	11	29	8	8	8	4	7	19	2	1	5	6	7	5	15	14	7	9	5	5	5	2	2
						Goals				1			4	2	12	2	21	2	3	2			2				1	3		2			1					

Pos	P.	W.	D.	L.	F.	A.	Pts.
11th	30	9	7	14	58	61	25

Additional League appearances: McSkimming (Position 7, Game 30) and Dalziel (Position 8, Game 9).

League Cup Section BB

Pos	P.	W.	D.	L.	F.	A.	Pts.
3rd	6	2	2	2	14	13	6

No.	Date	Opposition	H.T.	Res.	Att.	Goalscorers	Purdie	Mennie	Hood	Gordon	Thyne	Miller	Hunter	Hamill	Clive	Brown	McLaren	Bowman	McCulloch	Drury	Murdoch	Lamont	Smith	McMahon	Anderson	Maxwell	McLeish	Sinclair	Lambie	Aitken	McFarlane	Hamilton	Fitzsimmons	Saddington	Sherry	Boyd	Black	Archibald
1	11 Sep	East Stirling	1-1	1-2	4000	Bowman	1	2		8	4	3			9		10	5		11			6				7											
2	18	QUEENS PARK	1-3	3-3	10000	Clive, Lambie, McLaren	1	2	3		4	6	7		10		11	5									8		9									
3	25	ALLOA ATHLETIC	2-1	4-3	8000	Bowman, Lambie, McLaren, Miller	1	2	3		4	6	7		10		11	5					8						9									
4	2 Oct	EAST STIRLING	2-1	4-1	8000	Bowman, Hunter, Lambie, McLaren		2	3		4	6	7		10		11	5					8						9		1							
5	9	Queens Park	1-0	2-2	15000	Clive, McLaren		2				6		4	8		10	5		11		3			7				9		1							
6	16	Alloa Athletic	0-2	0-2	6000			2			5	6			8		10	4	11			3			7				9		1							

Scottish Cup

No.	Date	Opposition	H.T.	Res.	Att.	Goalscorers	Purdie	Mennie	Hood	Gordon	Thyne	Miller	Hunter	Hamill	Clive	Brown	McLaren	Bowman	McCulloch	Drury	Murdoch	Lamont	Smith	McMahon	Anderson	Maxwell	McLeish	Sinclair	Lambie	Aitken	McFarlane	Hamilton	Fitzsimmons	Saddington	Sherry	Boyd	Black	Archibald
1	22 Jan	Dumbarton	1-2	2-5	10090	Hunter, McLaren			2	4	5		7		9		10					3	6							8	1		11					

B Division Supplementary Cup

No.	Date	Opposition	H.T.	Res.	Att.	Goalscorers	Purdie	Mennie	Hood	Gordon	Thyne	Miller	Hunter	Hamill	Clive	Brown	McLaren	Bowman	McCulloch	Drury	Murdoch	Lamont	Smith	McMahon	Anderson	Maxwell	McLeish	Sinclair	Lambie	Aitken	McFarlane	Hamilton	Fitzsimmons	Saddington	Sherry	Boyd	Black	Archibald
1	25 Aug	Queens Park	1-1	2-1	7500	McLaren(2)	1		3		5	6	7	4	9	8	10	2		11																		
QF	25 Apr	ALLOA ATHLETIC	4-0	5-1	3000	McLaren(2), Lambie(2), Aitken			2		5		7			8	11					3	6						9	10	1			4				
SF	4 May	Raith Rovers	0-1	1-5		McLaren			2		5		7			8	11					3	6						9	10	1			4				

Jimmy Hood jnr.

Like his father before him, Jimmy was a stalwart Killie defender.

SEASON 1949-50 Division Two

No.	Date	Opposition	H.T.	Res.	Att.	Goalscorers	J.Brown	Hood	Lamont	Doig	Thyne	Middlemass	Hardy	Cowan	Reid	Paton	McLaren	Black	J.McGhee	J.W.McGhee	McSkimming	Finlay	Norwood	G.Brown	Boyd	Clive	Benson	McKay	Collins	McKenzie	McGill	Donaldson	Aitken	Rae	McDowell	Johnston	Davidson	Hamilton
1	10 Sep	Albion Rovers	0-1	1-3	4000	Hardy	1	2	3	4	5	6	7	8	9	10	11																					
2	17	ARBROATH	2-0	2-2	8000	McSkimming(2)			3	4	2	6	7	8			10	1	5		9	11																
3	24	Ayr United	1-0	1-2	16000	McLaren		2	3	4		6	7			10	11		5		9		1	8														
4	1 Oct	DUNDEE UNITED	0-1	2-3	6000	Hardy, Paton			3	4	5		7	6		8	11				9		1		2	10												
5	8	Morton	1-1	1-3	10000	McKay			3	4	5		6		9	8	11		2							10	1	7										
6	15	QUEENS PARK	2-2	3-3	6000	Clive, McGill, Paton			3	4	5		11			8										9	1	7	2	6	10							
7	22	FORFAR ATHLETIC	1-1	3-1	6000	Clive, McKay, McGill			3	4	5					8										9	1	7	2	6	10	11						
8	5 Nov	COWDENBEATH	1-0	2-0	6000	Donaldson, Reid		3		4	5	6	8		9												1	7	2		10	11						
9	12	Stenhousemuir	2-0	2-0	2000	Reid(2)			3	4	5	6			9												1	7	2		10	11	8					
10	19	AIRDRIEONIANS	0-1	1-1	10500	O.G.			3	4	5	6			8												1	7	2		10	11		9				
11	26	Dumbarton	1-0	1-0	2000	Donaldson		3		4	5	6				8											1	7	2		10	11		9				
12	3 Dec	St. Johnstone	0-2	0-2	6000			3		4	5	6														9	1	7	2		10	11			8			
13	10	HAMILTON A.	1-0	2-0	9000	Johnston(2)		3		4	5	6															1	7	2		8	11			10	9		
14	17	Alloa Athletic	0-2	3-2	1200	Johnston(2), Donaldson		3		4	5	6				8											1	7	2		10	11				9		
15	24	ALBION ROVERS	1-0	2-1	8000	Johnston, Donaldson		3		4	5	6		10		8											1	7	2			11				9		
16	31	Arbroath	1-0	2-1	3500	Johnston(2)		3		4	5	6		10		8											1	7	2			11				9		
17	2 Jan	AYR UNITED	3-0	4-0	23000	Cowan(2), Johnston, Paton		3		4	5	6		10		8											1	7	2			11				9		
18	3	Dundee United	0-1	0-3	8000			3		4	5	6		10		8											1	7	2			11				9		
19	7	MORTON	0-0	2-0	19000	Cowan, Donaldson		3		4	5	6		10		8											1	7	2			11				9		
20	14	Queens Park	1-0	3-1	27205	Cowan, Donaldson, Johnston		3		4	5	6		10		8											1	7	2			11				9		
21	21	Forfar Athletic	0-1	0-1	3600			3		4	5	6		10		8											1	7	2			11				9		
22	4 Feb	DUNFERMLINE	2-0	3-2	12000	Johnston(2), Middlemass		3	2	4	5	6				8										10	1	7				11				9		
23	18	STENHOUSEMUIR	3-2	3-2	10000	Donaldson, Johnston, Paton		3		4	5	6				8										10	1	7	2			11				9		
24	25	Airdrieonians	0-1	0-2	16000			3		4	5	6				8											1	7	2			11				9	10	
25	4 Mar	DUMBARTON	1-0	1-1	9000	Johnston				4	5																1	7	2			11			8	9	10	3
26	11	ST. JOHNSTONE	1-1	1-1	9000	McDowell		3		4	5		6														1	7	2			11			8	9	10	
27	18	Hamilton A.	0-1	0-1	3000			3			5	6	4	10												9	1	7	2			11			8			
28	25	ALLOA ATHLETIC	1-0	3-0	7000	J.W.McGhee(2), Cowan					5	6	4	10						9						3	1	7	2			11			8			
29	1 Apr	Cowdenbeath	2-2	2-3	4000	Davidson, Donaldson				4	5	6		7						9						3	1		2		10	11					8	
30	29	Dunfermline	0-1	0-2	5000					2	5	6				8				11						3	1				10	7	4			9		
						Apps.	1	19	10	28	29	24	10	13	5	19	5	1	2	3	3	1	2	1	1	11	26	24	23	2	11	24	2	2	6	15	4	1
						Goals						1	2	5	3	4	1			2	2					2		2			2	8			1	13	1	

Pos	P.	W.	D.	L.	F.	A.	Pts.
8th	30	14	5	11	50	43	33

Additional League appearance: Wyllie (Position 6, Match 25).

League Cup Section BD

Pos	P.	W.	D.	L.	F.	A.	Pts.
4th	6	2	0	4	10	15	4

No.	Date	Opposition	H.T.	Res.	Att.	Goalscorers	J.Brown	Hood	Lamont	Doig	Thyne	Middlemass	Hardy	Cowan	Reid	Paton	McLaren	Black	J.McGhee	J.W.McGhee	McSkimming	Finlay	Norwood	G.Brown	Boyd	Clive	Benson	McKay	Collins	McKenzie	McGill	Donaldson	Aitken	Rae	McDowell	Johnston	Davidson	Hamilton
1	13 Aug	St. Johnstone	2-2	2-3	7000	Clive, Middlemass	1	3		4	5	6	10				11					7			2	9							8					
2	17	QUEENS PARK	2-0	2-0	12000	Aitken, Clive	1	2	3	4	5	6	10				11									9							8					
3	20	Dunfermline	0-2	1-5	8000	Middlemass	1	3	2	4	5	6	10		7		11									9							8					
4	27	ST. JOHNSTONE	2-0	2-0	10000	McLaren, Reid		2	3	4	5	6	7		9	8	10									11												
5	31	Queens Park	1-0	1-3	8000	Paton		2	3	4	5	6	7		9	8	10									11												
6	3 Sep	DUNFERMLINE	1-1	2-4	7000	Middlemass, Paton		2	3	4	5	6	7		9	8	11																10					

Additional League Cup appearances: Calder (Position 1, Matches 4,5 & 6), Feeney (Position 7, Match 2).

Scottish Cup

No.	Date	Opposition	H.T.	Res.	Att.	Goalscorers	J.Brown	Hood	Lamont	Doig	Thyne	Middlemass	Hardy	Cowan	Reid	Paton	McLaren	Black	J.McGhee	J.W.McGhee	McSkimming	Finlay	Norwood	G.Brown	Boyd	Clive	Benson	McKay	Collins	McKenzie	McGill	Donaldson	Aitken	Rae	McDowell	Johnston	Davidson	Hamilton
1	28	STIRLING ALBION	1-1	1-1	22000	Johnston		3		4	5	6		10		8											1	7	2			11				9		
1R	1 Feb	Stirling Albion	0-2	1-3	9400	Donaldson		3		4	5	6				8										10	1	7	2			11				9		

B Division Supplementary Cup

No.	Date	Opposition	H.T.	Res.	Att.	Goalscorers	J.Brown	Hood	Lamont	Doig	Thyne	Middlemass	Hardy	Cowan	Reid	Paton	McLaren	Black	J.McGhee	J.W.McGhee	McSkimming	Finlay	Norwood	G.Brown	Boyd	Clive	Benson	McKay	Collins	McKenzie	McGill	Donaldson	Aitken	Rae	McDowell	Johnston	Davidson	Hamilton
1	12 Sep	DUNDEE UNITED	2-0	4-3	6000	McLaren(3), Finlay			3	4		6	7	8			10		5		9	11	1															2
QF	25 Apr	AIRDRIEONIANS	2-0	2-1	4000	Middlemass, Paton		3		4	5	6		7		8										2	1				10	11				9		
SF	10 May	St. Johnstone	0-2	2-2	5000	Davidson, Johnston	1	3		4	5	6																7	2		10	11				9	8	
SFR	23/8/50	ST. JOHNSTONE *	1-1	2-1+	9000	J.W.McGhee, Donaldson #		3			5	6								9						10	1	7	2			11						

\+ After extra time # Russell played at No.4 and Wilson played at No.8. * Played in season 1950-51. Final never played. Competition abandoned for 1950-51.

This team were watched by record crowds for the 'B' Division but faded badly near the end of the season. 22,000 attended the drawn cup tie with Stirling Albion, where this photo was taken.
Back: J.Brown (Trainer), Hood, Collins, Benson, Thyne, Doig, Middlemass (Capt)
Front: McKay, Paton, Johnston, Cowan, Donaldson

SEASON 1950-51 Division Two

No.	Date	Opposition	H.T.	Res.	Att.	Goalscorers	Benson	Collins	Hood	Russell	Thyne	Middlemass	McKay	Clive	Menzies	Irving	Donaldson	Kelly	Johnston	Doig	Jones	Davidson	Bootland	McGill	Paton	Borland	Anderson	Caldwell	Cowan	Aitken	McGhee	Wilson	McDonald	Neil	Apsley	Bruce
1	9 Sep	QUEEN OF THE SOUTH	0-1	0-1	11500		1	2	3	4	5	6	7	8	9	10	11																			
2	16	Arbroath	0-0	2-0	3000	Johnston, McKay	1	2		4	5	6	7	8		10	11	3	9																	
3	23	AYR UNITED	0-1	0-1	13000		1	2		6	5	10	7			8	11	3		4	9															
4	30	Dundee United	1-3	2-5	5000	Jones(2), McKay	1	2		4	5	6	7			8		3			9	10	11													
5	7 Oct	ALBION ROVERS	2-2	3-2	8000	Jones(2), McKay	1	2		4	5	6	7			8		3			9	10		11												
6	14	Queens Park	1-1	1-2	13000	Irving	1			4	5	6	7	2		8		3			9			11	10											
7	21	Forfar Athletic	0-0	0-0	2400		1	2		4	5	6	7			8		3			9			11	10											
8	28	DUNFERMLINE	0-1	1-1	10500	Jones	1	2		4	5	6	7			8		3			9			10		11										
9	4 Nov	Cowdenbeath	0-3	0-3	4000		1	2		6	5		7					3		4	9				10	11	8									
10	11	ALLOA ATHLETIC	2-2	2-2	7000	Hood, Johnston	1	2	3	4			7			8			9					10		11		5	6							
11	18	Hamilton A.	2-0	3-2	5000	Aitken, McGhee, Menzies	1	2	3	4					9	10										7		5	6	8	11					
12	25	DUMBARTON	0-1	1-3	7000	McGhee	1	2	3	4					9	10										7		5	6	8	11					
13	2 Dec	ST. JOHNSTONE	0-2	2-2	8000	McKay, Menzies	1	2		4	5		7		9			3		6						11			10	8						
14	9	Stirling Albion	0-0	0-1	9000		1	2		4	5		7		9			3		6			11						10	8						
15	16	STENHOUSEMUIR	0-2	1-2	5000	Bootland	1	2		4	5		7		9			3		6			11		10							8				
16	23	Queen of the South	1-0	1-0	6500	Menzies	1	2		4	5		7		9			3		6			11		10							8				
17	30	ARBROATH	1-1	1-1	5500	Menzies	1	2		4	5		7		9			3		6			11		10							8				
18	1 Jan	Ayr United	0-0	0-1	14000		1	2			5	4			9		7	3		6			11						10			8				
19	2	DUNDEE UNITED	1-0	2-0	10000	Bootland, Thyne	1	2			5	4			9	10		3		6			11			7							8			
20	13	QUEENS PARK	0-1	3-4	9000	Bootland, Johnston, McDonald		2		4	5	6				10		3	9				11			7							8	1		
21	20	FORFAR ATHLETIC	1-0	1-1	6000	Menzies	1	2		4	5	6			9	10		3								7					11	8				
22	3 Feb	Dunfermline	1-3	2-4	4000	Hood, Johnston	1	2	3	6	5		7				11		9	4						8			10							
23	10	COWDENBEATH	1-0	4-0	5000	Hood(2), Jones, Donaldson	1	5	3			6	7	2			11			8	9					10				4						
24	17	Alloa Athletic	0-1	4-1	3000	Borland(2), Donaldson, Hood	1	5	3			6	7	2			11			8	9					10				4						
25	24	HAMILTON A.	1-1	1-1	9000	Doig	1	5	3			6	7	2			11			8	9					10				4						
26	3 Mar	Dumbarton	1-1	1-2	3000	Jones	1	5	3	4	10	6		2						8	9		11			7										
27	10	St. Johnstone	0-1	0-1	6000		1	2	3	4	5	6	7							8	9		11			10										
28	17	STIRLING ALBION	0-0	1-1	5700	Jones	1	2	3	6	5		7	4						8	9		11			10										
29	24	Stenhousemuir	0-2	1-4		Doig	1		3	4	5	6		2		10				8	9		11												7	
30	7 Apr	Albion Rovers	1-1	3-1	4000	Jones(2), O.G.	1	2	3	4	5	6				10	8				9		11			7										
						Apps.	29	28	13	25	24	19	21	9	11	16	9	17	4	17	15	2	13	5	6	17	1	3	7	7	3	5	2	1	1	
						Goals			5		1		4		5	1	2		4	2	10		3			2				1	2		1			

Pos	P.	W.	D.	L.	F.	A.	Pts.
12th	30	8	8	14	44	49	24

League Cup Section BA

Pos	P.	W.	D.	L.	F.	A.	Pts.
3rd	6	1	2	3	9	10	4

No.	Date	Opposition	H.T.	Res.	Att.	Goalscorers	Benson	Collins	Hood	Russell	Thyne	Middlemass	McKay	Clive	Menzies	Irving	Donaldson	Kelly	Johnston	Doig	Jones	Davidson	Bootland	McGill	Paton	Borland	Anderson	Caldwell	Cowan	Aitken	McGhee	Wilson	McDonald	Neil	Apsley	Bruce
1	12 Aug	DUNFERMLINE	2-1	3-1	12000	Donaldson, Johnston, McGill	1	2	3	6	5		7				11		9	4		10		8												
2	16	Ayr United	2-2	2-2	16000	Donaldson, Thyne	1	2	3	6	5		7				11		9	4				8					10							
3	19	Dumbarton	0-1	0-1	5500		1	2	3	6	5		7				11		9	4				8					10							
4	26	Dunfermline	4-2	4-5	7000	Clive(2), Donaldson, McKay	1	2	3	6	5	10	7	8			11			4											9					
5	30	AYR UNITED	0-1	0-1	18000		1	2	3	6	5	10	7	8			11			4											9					
6	2 Sep	DUMBARTON	0-0	0-0	8000					6	5		7	2			11	3		4				10							9	8				1

Scottish Cup

No.	Date	Opposition	H.T.	Res.	Att.	Goalscorers	Benson	Collins	Hood	Russell	Thyne	Middlemass	McKay	Clive	Menzies	Irving	Donaldson	Kelly	Johnston	Doig	Jones	Davidson	Bootland	McGill	Paton	Borland	Anderson	Caldwell	Cowan	Aitken	McGhee	Wilson	McDonald	Neil	Apsley	Bruce
1	27 Jan	East Stirling	0-1	1-2	2500	McKay	1	2		6	5		7	8		10	11	3	9	4																

Malky McDonald took over as manager this season. Player shortages forced him out of retirement. He played twice, scoring one goal.

SEASON 1951-52 Division Two

No.	Date	Opposition	H.T.	Res.	Att.	Goalscorers	Niven	Collins	Hood	Stewart	Thyne	Middlemass	Donaldson	Henaughan	Mathie	Harvey	Clark	Bunten	Doig	Russell	McKay	Caldwell	Borland	Anderson	Clive	Jack	Cowan	Grant	Henderson	McLachlan	Kelly	Boyd
1	8 Sep	Clyde	2-1	3-1	12000	Donaldson(2), Harvey	1	2	3		5		7	8	9	10	11		4	6												
2	15	DUMBARTON	1-0	2-1	12000	Donaldson, Russell	1	2	3		5		7	8	9	10	11		4	6												
3	22	Ayr United	1-1	2-3	18000	Hood, Harvey	1	2	3		5		7	8	9	10	11		4	6												
4	29	ALBION ROVERS	0-0	3-1	12000	Donaldson(2), Henaughan	1	2	3		5	6	11	8	9	10			4		7											
5	6 Oct	Dunfermline	1-2	2-5	7000	O.G., Mathie	1	2	3		5	6	11	8	9	10			4		7											
6	13	STENHOUSEMUIR	0-1	0-2	9000		1	2	3	4		6	11	8	9	10					7	5										
7	20	Forfar Athletic	0-1	0-1	2500		1	2	3		5	6	11	8	9	10				4	7											
8	27	ST. JOHNSTONE	1-0	3-0	8000	Mathie(2), Borland	1	2	3		5	6	11	8	9	10				4			7									
9	3 Nov	ARBROATH	1-0	4-0	8000	Mathie(2), Henaughan, Thyne	1	2	3		5	6		8	9	10	11			4			7									
10	10	Dundee United	0-1	0-1	2200		1	2	3		5	6	11	8	9	10				4			7									
11	17	ALLOA ATHLETIC	0-0	1-0	8000	Harvey	1	2	3		5	6	11	8	9	10				4			7									
12	24	Cowdenbeath	0-3	1-3	3000	Thyne	1	2	3		5	6	11	8	9					4				7	10							
13	1 Dec	Queens Park	0-1	0-1	7000		1	2	3		5	6	11	10					8	4				7	9							
14	8	HAMILTON A.	2-1	3-2	7000	Mathie(2), Donaldson	1	2	3		5	6	11	8	9	10				4				7								
15	15	Falkirk	2-1	3-3	9000	Mathie(2), Henaughan	1	2	3		5	6	11	8	9	10				4				7								
16	22	CLYDE	0-0	1-2	20000	Donaldson	1	2	3		5	6	11	8	9	10				4				7								
17	29	Dumbarton	1-2	2-4	4000	Anderson, Harvey	1	2	3		5	6	11		9	8				4				7		10						
18	1 Jan	AYR UNITED	3-0	4-0	14000	Donaldson(2), Anderson, Harvey	1	2	3		5	6	11		9	8				4				7		10						
19	5	DUNFERMLINE	3-0	5-3	9000	Mathie(2), Clark, Harvey, Middlemass	1	2	3		5	6			9	8	11			4				7		10						
20	9	Albion Rovers	0-0	0-0	400		1		3		5	6			9	8	11			4				7	2	10						
21	12	Stenhousemuir	1-1	2-1	1500	Harvey, Thyne	1		3		5	6	11			8				4				7	2	9	10					
22	19	FORFAR ATHLETIC	1-0	3-0	10000	Cowan, Jack, Harvey	1	2	3		5	6	11			8				4				7		9	10					
23	13 Feb	Arbroath	0-1	1-2	1000	Mathie	1	2	3		5		11		9			6		4			8	7			10					
24	16	DUNDEE UNITED	2-2	2-6	11000	Henderson, Mathie	1	2	3		5	6	11		9					4				7				8	10			
25	20	St. Johnstone	1-0	2-0	1500	Anderson, Cowan	1	2	3			6	11		9								8	7			10	4				5
26	23	Alloa Athletic	1-1	2-1	3500	Cowan, Mathie	1	2	3	6			11		9				4			5		7			10			8		
27	1 Mar	COWDENBEATH	3-0	5-1	8000	Jack(2), Middlemass(2), Mathie	1	2	3		5	6	11		9					4				7		8	10					
28	8	QUEENS PARK	2-0	3-1	10000	Jack, Mathie, O.G.	1	2	3		5	6	11		9					4				7		10	8					
29	15	Hamilton A.	0-1	1-2	3000	Clark	1	2	3		5	6			9		11			4				7		10	8					
30	22	FALKIRK	1-1	2-1	12000	Anderson, Cowan	1	2			5	6	11		9	8				4				7			10				3	
						Apps.	30	28	29	2	27	25	26	16	27	21	7	1	7	25	4	2	6	19	4	9	9	2	1	1	1	1
						Goals			1		3	3	9	3	16	8	2			1			1	4		4	4		1			

Pos	P.	W.	D.	L.	F.	A.	Pts.
5th	30	16	2	12	62	48	34

League Cup Section BB

Pos	P.	W.	D.	L.	F.	A.	Pts.
2nd	6	4	0	2	9	4	8

No.	Date	Opposition	H.T.	Res.	Att.	Goalscorers	Niven	Collins	Hood	Stewart	Thyne	Middlemass	Donaldson	Henaughan	Mathie	Harvey	Clark	Bunten	Doig	Russell	McKay	Caldwell	Borland	Anderson	Clive	Jack	Cowan	Grant	Henderson	McLachlan	Kelly	Boyd
1	11 Aug	AYR UNITED	0-0	3-0	16000	Mathie(3)	1	2	3	4	5	6	7	8	9	10	11															
2	15	Forfar Athletic	0-1	1-2	3000	Clark	1	2	3	4	5	6	7	8	9	10	11															
3	18	Dumbarton	0-1	0-1	5000		1	2	3	4	5		7	8	9	10	11	6														
4	25	Ayr United	0-1	2-1	8500	Hood, Mathie	1	2	3		5		7	8	9	10	11		4	6												
5	29	FORFAR ATHLETIC	1-0	1-0	12000	Harvey	1	2	3		5		7	8	9	10	11		4	6												
6	1 Sep	DUMBARTON	0-0	2-0	14000	Harvey, Mathie	1	2	3		5		7	8	9	10	11		4	6												

Scottish Cup

No.	Date	Opposition	H.T.	Res.	Att.	Goalscorers	Niven	Collins	Hood	Stewart	Thyne	Middlemass	Donaldson	Henaughan	Mathie	Harvey	Clark	Bunten	Doig	Russell	McKay	Caldwell	Borland	Anderson	Clive	Jack	Cowan	Grant	Henderson	McLachlan	Kelly	Boyd
1	26 Jan	STENHOUSEMUIR	2-0	2-0	12000	Harvey, Jack	1	2	3		5	6	11			8				4				7		9	10					
2	9 Feb	Aberdeen	1-1	1-2	19000	Harvey	1	2	3		5	6	11			8				4				7		9	10					

B Division Supplementary Cup

No.	Date	Opposition	H.T.	Res.	Att.	Goalscorers	Niven	Collins	Hood	Stewart	Thyne	Middlemass	Donaldson	Henaughan	Mathie	Harvey	Clark	Bunten	Doig	Russell	McKay	Caldwell	Borland	Anderson	Clive	Jack	Cowan	Grant	Henderson	McLachlan	Kelly	Boyd
1	29 Mar	FALKIRK	0-0	1-0	9000	Harvey	1	2			5	6	11	10		8				4				7		9					3	
QF	12 Apr	Hamilton A.	0-0	1-0	5000	Jack	1	2	3		5	6	11	10		8				4				7		9						
SF	19	CLYDE	0-2	1-3	12000	Middlemass	1	2	3		5	6	11	10		8				4				7		9						

JIMMY MIDDLEMASS was 29 before he turned senior with Kilmarnock -- his only professional club. He was an inspiration in the fight for promotion.

SEASON 1952-53 Division Two

No.	Date	Opposition	H.T.	Res.	Att.	Goalscorers	Niven	Collins	Hood	Russell	Thyne	Middlemass	Anderson	Harvey	Mays	Jack	Murray	Clive	Kelly	Donaldson	Mathie	Henaughan	McDonald	Imrie	Stewart	Milloy	McCorkindale	Lee	Mackay	Curlett
1	6 Sep	ALLOA ATHLETIC	0-0	1-2	10800	Middlemass	1	2		4	5	6	7	8	9	10	11		3											
2	20	AYR UNITED	0-1	0-1	15000		1	2		4	5	6	7	8	9	10			3	11										
3	27	Queens Park	0-2	3-2	10000	Henaughan, Mathie, Middlemass	1	2	3	4	5	6		8	7	10					9	11								
4	11 Oct	Dunfermline	0-0	1-2	5000	Harvey	1	2	3	4	5	6		8	9	10	11					7								
5	18	MORTON	1-1	3-2	12000	Henaughan(2), Middlemass	1	2	3	4	5	6		8	9	10	11					7								
6	1 Nov	Stirling Albion	0-2	1-3	8000	Mays	1	2	3	4	5	6	11	8	9		10					7								
7	8	DUMBARTON	1-0	2-1	10000	Mays, O.G.	1	2	3	4	5	6		10	7		11					8	9							
8	15	ST. JOHNSTONE	1-1	2-3	11500	Middlemass, Thyne	1	2	3	4	5	6		10	7		11					8	9							
9	22	Hamilton A.	0-0	2-2	6000	Thyne, Mays	1	2	3		5	6		8	9	10	11					7			4					
10	29	STENHOUSEMUIR	2-0	4-1	7000	Jack(2), Mathie, Murray	1	2	3	6	5				7	10	11				9	8			4					
11	6 Dec	COWDENBEATH	0-0	2-0	8000	Murray, Stewart	1	2	3	6	5				7	10	11				9	8			4					
12	13	Arbroath	1-1	2-2	3200	Murray(2)	1	2	3	6	5				7	10	11				9	8			4					
13	20	Alloa Athletic	2-0	2-1	2500	Jack, Mathie	1	2	3	6	5				7	10	11				9	8			4					
14	27	DUNDEE UNITED	0-0	1-0	9000	Mathie	1	2	3	6	5				7	10	11				9	8			4					
15	1 Jan	Ayr United	0-0	2-0	18500	Mays(2)	1	2	3	6	5			8	9	10	11					7			4					
16	3	QUEENS PARK	0-1	0-1	14000		1	2	3	6	5			8	9	10	11					7			4					
17	10	Albion Rovers	1-0	1-2	1500	Mays	1	2	3	6	5			8	9	10	11					7			4					
18	17	DUNFERMLINE	2-0	2-3	8000	Mays, Thyne	1	2	3	4	5	6			7		11				9	10		8						
19	31	Morton	1-0	4-1	5000	Jack(2), Murray, Thyne	1	2	3	4	5	6		8	9	10	11					7								
20	21 Feb	STIRLING ALBION	3-0	6-0	8000	Henaughan(2), Mays(2), Middlemass(2)	1		3	4	5	6		8	9	10	11	2				7								
21	28	Dumbarton	2-3	2-4	1800	Harvey, Mays	1		3	4	5	6		8	9	10	11	2				7								
22	7 Mar	St. Johnstone	0-0	2-1	3200	Jack(2)	1	2	3	4		6		8	9	10	11					7						5		
23	14	HAMILTON A.	1-0	6-1	11000	Mays(2),Harvey,Henaughan,Jack,Murray	1	2		4	5	6		8	9	10	11					7				3				
24	21	Stenhousemuir	1-0	4-0	2000	Harvey, Jack(2), Murray	1	2		4	5	6		8	9	10	11					7				3				
25	28	Cowdenbeath	1-2	3-2	1500	Mays(3)	1	2		4	5	6		8	9	10	11					7				3				
26	4 Apr	ARBROATH	2-0	4-0	9000	Jack(2), Mays, Middlemass	1	2		4	5	6		8	9	10	11					7				3				
27	11	ALBION ROVERS	3-0	4-0	5400	Jack, Mays, Middlemass, Murray	1	2		4	5	6		8	9	10	11					7				3				
28	18	Dundee United	2-1	4-5	2000	Mays(3), Russell	1	2		4	5	6		8	9	10	11					7				3				
29	22	Forfar Athletic	0-4	0-6	1400		1	2	3	4	5		7	8	9											11			6	10
30	25	FORFAR ATHLETIC	2-0	4-0	4500	Harvey(2), Jack, McCorkindale	1	2	3	4	5	6		8		10						7	9				11			
						Apps.	30	28	22	29	29	21	4	24	29	25	26	2	2	1	7	27	3	1	9	7	1	1	1	1
						Goals				1	4	8		6	20	14	8				4	6			1		1			

Pos	P.	W.	D.	L.	F.	A.	Pts.
4th	30	17	2	11	74	48	36

League Cup Section BA

Pos	P.	W.	D.	L.	F.	A.	Pts.
1st	6	5	0	1	15	8	10

No.	Date	Opposition	H.T.	Res.	Att.	Goalscorers	Niven	Collins	Hood	Russell	Thyne	Middlemass	Anderson	Harvey	Mays	Jack	Murray	Clive	Kelly	Donaldson	Mathie	Henaughan	McDonald	Imrie	Stewart	Milloy	McCorkindale	Lee	Mackay	Curlett
1	9 Aug	ALLOA ATHLETIC	3-1	3-1	8500	Anderson, Harvey, Mays	1	2	3	4	5	6	7	8	9	10	11													
2	13	Dunfermline	2-1	4-3	7500	Anderson, Jack, Murray, O.G.	1	2	3	4	5	6	7	8	9	10	11													
3	16	Arbroath	0-1	0-2	3100		1	2	3	4	5	6	7	8	9	10	11													
4	23	Alloa Athletic	0-0	1-0	3000	Mays	1		3	4	5	6	7	8	9	10	11	2												
5	27	DUNFERMLINE	2-2	3-2	12500	Jack, Mays, Middlemass	1		3	4	5	6	7	8	9	10	11	2												
6	30	ARBROATH	2-0	4-0	10000	Mays(2), Harvey, Jack	1	2	3	4	5	6	7	8	9	10	11													
QF	13 Sep	St. Johnstone	3-1	3-1	8600	Donaldson(2), Mays	1	2		4	5	6		8	9	10	11		3	7										
QF	17	ST. JOHNSTONE (Agg 7-2)	1-1	4-1	12000	Jack(2), Harvey, Mays	1	2		4	5	6	7	8	9	10			3	11										
SF	4 Oct	Rangers*	0-0	1-0	45715	Jack	1	2	3	4	5	6		8	9	10	11					7								
F	25	Dundee*	0-0	0-2	51830		1	2	3	4	5	6		8	9	10	11					7								

* Played at Hampden Park

Scottish Cup

No.	Date	Opposition	H.T.	Res.	Att.	Goalscorers	Niven	Collins	Hood	Russell	Thyne	Middlemass	Anderson	Harvey	Mays	Jack	Murray	Clive	Kelly	Donaldson	Mathie	Henaughan	McDonald	Imrie	Stewart	Milloy	McCorkindale	Lee	Mackay	Curlett
1	24 Jan	Stranraer	2-0	4-0	4100	Murray, Henaughan, Jack, Mays	1	2	3	4	5	6		8	9	10	11					7								
2	7 Feb	Hamilton A.	1-1	2-2	19210	Middlemass, Murray	1	2	3	4	5	6		8	9	10	11					7								
2R	11	HAMILTON A.	0-2	0-2	13000		1	2	3	4	5	6		8	9	10	11					7								

This team shocked Scottish soccer by beating Rangers & reaching the League Cup Final as a 'B' Division side. Back: J.Brown(Trainer), J.Middlemass, R.Thyne, J.Russell, J.Niven, R.Collins, J.Hood, D.Mathie (Reserve). Front: T.Henaughan, W.Harvey, G.Mays, W.Jack, M.Murray

SEASON 1953-54 Division Two

No.	Date	Opposition	H.T.	Res.	Att.	Goalscorers	Brown	McLachlan	Hood	Russell	Thyne	Middlemass	Henaughan	Harvey	Mays	Curlett	McCorkindale	Stewart	Murray	Collins	Jack	Milloy	Black	McFarlane	Baillie
1	5 Sep	Dunfermline	0-1	0-1	7500		1		3	4	5	6	7	8		10			11	2	9				
2	19	Ayr United	0-1	0-1	15000		1	6	3	4	5		7	8	9	10			11	2					
3	26	ALBION ROVERS	0-2	0-3	10000		1	6		4	5		11	8	9	10				2		3	7		
4	3 Oct	Morton	4-1	6-4	8000	Harvey(2), Mays(2), Curlett, Henaughan	1	6		4	5		11	8	9	10				2		3	7		
5	10	DUNDEE UNITED	0-2	3-2	9000	Henaughan, Mays, McLachlan	1	6		4	5		11	8	9	10				2		3	7		
6	17	Alloa Athletic	0-0	0-1	3500		1	6	3	4	5		11	8	9	10				2			7		
7	24	FORFAR ATHLETIC	3-0	6-0	8000	Harvey(3), Curlett, Henaughan, Jack	1	6	3	4	5		11	8		10			7	2	9				
8	31	ARBROATH	1-0	4-0	7500	Harvey(2), Curlett, Jack	1	6	3	4	5		11	8		10			7	2	9				
9	7 Nov	Third Lanark	0-0	0-2	7000		1	6	3	4	5		11	8		10				2	9			7	
10	14	Dumbarton	2-1	5-2	2500	Harvey(2), Jack(2), Hood	1	6	3	4	5		11	8		10			7	2	9				
11	21	COWDENBEATH	0-0	1-0	9000	Jack	1		3	4	5	6	11	8		10			7	2	9				
12	28	St. Johnstone	4-0	4-1	7500	Curlett(2), Harvey, Henaughan	1		3	4	5	6	11	8		10			7	2	9				
13	5 Dec	Motherwell	0-0	2-0	14500	Harvey(2)	1		3	4	5	6	11	8		10			7	2	9				
14	12	STENHOUSEMUIR	0-1	6-2	10300	Henaughan(3),Curlett,Middlemass,Murray	1		3	4	5	6	11	8		10			7	2	9				
15	19	DUNFERMLINE	1-1	2-2	12000	Curlett, Jack	1		3	4	5	6	11	8		10			7	2	9				
16	26	Queens Park	1-0	1-1	7143	Harvey	1		3	4	5	6	11	8		10			7	2	9				
17	1 Jan	AYR UNITED	0-2	0-3	20000		1		3	4	5	6	11		9	8			7	2	10				
18	2	Albion Rovers	1-0	1-1	9000	Harvey	1	5	3	4		6	11	8	9				7	2	10				
19	9	MORTON	2-0	2-0	11000	Henaughan, Jack	1	5	3	4		6	11	8	7	10				2	9				
20	16	Dundee United	0-0	2-0	6500	Curlett, Harvey	1	5	3	4		6	11	8	7	10				2	9				
21	23	ALLOA ATHLETIC	2-0	2-0	10000	Jack, Russell	1		3	4	5	6	11	8	7	10				2	9				
22	30	Cowdenbeath	0-1	0-6	2500		1	6	3	4	5		11	8	7	10				2	9				
23	6 Feb	Forfar Athletic	2-1	3-2	2500	Curlett, Harvey, Middlemass	1		3	4	5	6	11	8	7	10				2	9				
24	20	Arbroath	0-0	1-0	3450	Henaughan	1	2		4	5	6	11	8	7	10					9	3			
25	6 Mar	DUMBARTON	2-1	7-2	8000	Curlett(2),Mddlemss(2),Hnaughn,Jack,Mays	1			4	5	6	11	8	7	10				2	9	3			
26	20	ST. JOHNSTONE	3-0	5-0	10000	Mays(2), Harvey, Henaughan, Jack	1			4	5	6	11	8	7	10				2	9	3			
27	31	MOTHERWELL	2-1	4-2	15000	Henaughan(2), Curlett, Mays	1	3		4	5	6	11	8	7	10				2	9				
28	3 Apr	Stenhousemuir	0-0	1-0	2500	Middlemass	1	3		4	5	6	11	8	7	10				2	9				
29	17	THIRD LANARK	0-0	1-1	21600	Mays	1	3		4	5	6	11	8	7	10				2	9				
30	24	QUEENS PARK	1-0	2-0	12000	Curlett, Jack	1	3		4	5	6	11	8	7	10					9				2
						Apps.	30	18	20	30	27	20	30	29	19	29			13	28	25	6	4	1	1
						Goals		1	1	1		5	13	17	8	13			1		11				

Pos	P.	W.	D.	L.	F.	A.	Pts.
2nd	30	19	4	7	71	39	42

League Cup Section BC

Pos	P.	W.	D.	L.	F.	A.	Pts.
1st	6	5	0	1	14	5	10

No.	Date	Opposition	H.T.	Res.	Att.	Goalscorers	Brown	McLachlan	Hood	Russell	Thyne	Middlemass	Henaughan	Harvey	Mays	Curlett	McCorkindale	Stewart	Murray	Collins	Jack	Milloy	Black	McFarlane	Baillie
1	8 Aug	Motherwell	0-2	0-3	13400		1	2	3	4	5		7	8	9	10	11	6							
2	12	MORTON	0-0	1-0	12000	Harvey	1	2	3	4	5	6	7	8	9	10			11						
3	15	DUNDEE UNITED	3-0	4-1	14000	Curlett, Harvey, Mays, Russell	1	2	3	4	5	6	7	8	9	10			11						
4	22	MOTHERWELL	2-0	4-1	18000	Curlett(2), Mays(2)	1		3	4	5	6	7	8	9	10			11	2					
5	26	Morton	2-0	2-0	7000	Jack, Mays	1	5	3	4		6	7		9	8			11	2	10				
6	29	Dundee United	2-0	3-0	8000	Curlett, Middlemass, Murray	1	5	3	4		6	7	8		10			11	2	9				
QF	12 Sep	PARTICK THISTLE	1-3	4-3	20244	Mays(2), Harvey, Middlemass	1		3	4	5	6	7	8	9	10			11	2					
QF	16	Partick Thistle (Agg: 4-7)	0-2	0-4	21688		1	6	3	4	5		7	8	9				11	2	10				

Scottish Cup

No.	Date	Opposition	H.T.	Res.	Att.	Goalscorers	Brown	McLachlan	Hood	Russell	Thyne	Middlemass	Henaughan	Harvey	Mays	Curlett	McCorkindale	Stewart	Murray	Collins	Jack	Milloy	Black	McFarlane	Baillie
1		1 Bye																							
2	13 Feb	Rangers	1-0	2-2	40000	Henaughan, Murray	1		3	4	5	6	11	8		10			7	2	9				
2R	17	RANGERS	0-2	1-3	33545	Jack	1			4	5	6	11	8		10			7	2	9	3			

10 years at Rugby Park regular, BOB THYNE later became club Chairman. Promotion in 1954 was especially sweet for Bob. Only he and Jimmy Hood remained from the team relegated in 1947.

SEASON 1954-55 Division One

No.	Date	Opposition	H.T.	Res.	Att.	Goalscorers	Brown	Collins	Rollo	Russell	Thyne	Middlemass	Murray	Harvey	Mays	Curlett	Henaughan	McLachlan	Black	Beattie	Hood	Imrie	Newbiggin	Toner	Jack	Dougan	Mackay	Flavell	Baillie	Watson	Clark
1	11 Sep	EAST FIFE	0-0	0-0	15000		1	2		4	5	6	7	8	9	10	11				3										
2	18	St. Mirren	0-0	0-2	20000		1	2		4	5	6	7	8	9	10	11				3										
3	25	DUNDEE	0-2	0-2	15000		1	2		4	5	6	10	8	9		11		7		3										
4	2 Oct	Celtic	1-3	3-6	30000	Curlett, Mays, Henaughan	1	2	3	4	5	6	8		7	10	11					9									
5	9	PARTICK THISTLE	1-0	1-2	12000	Beattie	1	2		4	5	6	7		9	10	11			8	3										
6	16	Stirling Albion	1-0	2-1	7000	Curlett(2)	1	2		4	5		11	8	7	9				10	3		6								
7	30	Hibernian	1-0	2-3	27500	Mays, Hood	1	2	6	4	5		11	8	7	9				10	3										
8	6 Nov	Rangers	0-3	0-6	40000		1	2	6	4	5		11	8	7	10					3			9							
9	20	Falkirk	2-4	3-5	12000	Toner(2), Hood	1	2	6		5		11	8	7					10	3		4	9							
10	24	HEARTS	0-2	1-3	7500	Beattie	1	2	3		5	6	7	8			11			10			4	9							
11	27	Clyde	1-0	1-1	10000	Toner	1	2	3		5	6	7			4	11			8				9	10						
12	4 Dec	ABERDEEN	0-2	0-4	13500		1		3		5	6	7			4	11			8	2			9	10						
13	11	QUEEN OF THE SOUTH	4-1	4-1	12500	Harvey, Jack, Mackay, Murray	1	2	3				7	8		4	11							9	10	5	6				
14	18	Raith Rovers	0-0	0-0	6000		1	2	3				7	8	9	4	11								10	5	6				
15	25	East Fife	1-1	5-1	5000	Jack(2), Henaughan, Imrie, Mays	1	2	3					8	7	4	11					9			10	5	6				
16	1 Jan	ST. MIRREN	1-1	1-1	28000	Henaughan	1	2	3				7	8		4	11								10	5	6	9			
17	3	Dundee	3-1	5-2	17000	Jack(2), Harvey, Henaughan, Murray	1	2	3				7	8		4	11								10	5	6	9			
18	8	CELTIC	0-0	1-2	24518	Murray	1	2	3				7	8		4	11								10	5	6	9			
19	29	Motherwell	1-0	1-0	12000	Henaughan	1	2	3	4			7	8			11								10	5	6	9			
20	12 Feb	HIBERNIAN	0-2	0-3	18000		1		3				7	8		4	11								10	5	6	9	2		
21	26	RANGERS	1-0	1-0	24000	Flavell	1		3				7			4	11			10				8		5	6	9	2		
22	5 Mar	Queen of the South	0-0	0-1	10000		1		3				7			4	11			10				8		5	6	9		2	
23	12	FALKIRK	0-0	2-0	18000	Flavell, Toner	1		3				7			4	11			10				8		5	6	9		2	
24	19	CLYDE	0-1	2-1	20000	Beattie, Murray	1		3				7			4	11			10				8		5	6	9		2	
25	30	Aberdeen	0-3	1-4	17000	Mackay	1		3				7			4	11			10				8		5	6	9		2	
26	6 Apr	Hearts	2-0	2-2		Murray, O.G.	1		3				7			4	8			10						5	6	9		2	11
27	9	RAITH ROVERS	2-0	2-2	12000	Clark, Flavell	1	2	3				7			4	8			10						5	6	9			11
28	13	MOTHERWELL	1-1	1-2	12000	Mays	1	2	3					8	7	4				10						5	6	9			11
29	16	Partick Thistle	2-0	3-0	18000	Harvey, Jack, Mays	1	2	3	4				8	7	6									10	5		9			11
30	30	STIRLING ALBION	1-0	2-1	7200	Jack(2)	1	2	3	4					7	6								8	10	5		9			11
						Apps.	30	22	25	11	12	8	26	18	14	26	23		1	15	9	2	3	12	12	18	16	15	2	5	5
						Goals							5	3	5	3	5			3	2	1		4	8		2	3			1

Pos	P.	W.	D.	L.	F.	A.	Pts.
10th	30	10	6	14	46	58	26

League Cup Section AA

Pos	P.	W.	D.	L.	F.	A.	Pts.
3rd	6	2	1	3	8	11	5

No.	Date	Opposition	H.T.	Res.	Att.	Goalscorers	Brown	Collins	Rollo	Russell	Thyne	Middlemass	Murray	Harvey	Mays	Curlett	Henaughan	McLachlan	Black	Beattie	Hood	Imrie	Newbiggin	Toner	Jack	Dougan	Mackay	Flavell	Baillie	Watson	Clark
1	14 Aug	RAITH ROVERS	1-0	3-2	18000	Curlett, Harvey, Middlemass	1	2	3	4	5	6	7	8	9	10	11														
2	18	Motherwell	0-2	0-3	17000		1	2	3	4	5	6	7	8	9	10	11														
3	21	ST. MIRREN	2-0	2-2	19700	Harvey, Mays	1	2	3	4		6	11	8	9	10		5	7												
4	28	Raith Rovers	1-0	1-0	12000	Mays	1	2	3	4		6	7	8	9	10	11	5													
5	1 Sep	MOTHERWELL	0-1	0-1	22000		1	2	3	4		6	7	8	9	10	11	5													
6	4	St. Mirren	1-0	2-3	15000	Beattie, Curlett	1	2	3	4	5		11		9	10		6	7	8											

Scottish Cup

No.	Date	Opposition	H.T.	Res.	Att.	Goalscorers	Brown	Collins	Rollo	Russell	Thyne	Middlemass	Murray	Harvey	Mays	Curlett	Henaughan	McLachlan	Black	Beattie	Hood	Imrie	Newbiggin	Toner	Jack	Dougan	Mackay	Flavell	Baillie	Watson	Clark
5	5 Feb	East Fife	2-0	2-1	11000	Flavell, Harvey	1	2	3				7	8		4	11								10	5	6	9			
6	19	CELTIC	0-1	1-1	31000	Henaughan	1	2	3				7	8		4	11								10	5	6	9			
6R	23	Celtic	0-0	0-1	41000		1		3				7	8		4	11								10	5	6	9	2		

Gerry Mays was signed on a free transfer from Dunfermline three months before his 31st birthday, and was considered to be a stop-gap. He amazed everyone by playing for a further seven years and scoring over 100 goals. However 1954/55 (his third with Killie) was a relatively lean season for him, for both appearances and goals scored.

SEASON 1955-56 Division One

No.	Date	Opposition	H.T.	Res.	Att.	Goalscorers	Brown	Collins	Rollo	Curlett	Dougan	Newbiggin	Mays	Murray	Flavell	Jack	Henaughan	Toner	Russell	Black	Taggart	Catterson	Lawlor	Clark	Harvey	Beattie	Bowie	Watson	Mackay	Fletcher	Stewart	Bunten
1	10 Sep	AIRDRIEONIANS	1-0	2-1	12500	Catterson, Lawlor	1	2	3	4								5		7	6	9	10	11	8							
2	17	East Fife	1-0	1-2	5800	Catterson	1	2	3	4								5		7	6	9	10	11		8						
3	24	ST. MIRREN	1-0	1-1	10000	Lawlor		5	3	4										7	6	9	10	11	8		1	2				
4	1 Oct	Hibernian	1-1	1-2	20000	Catterson	1	5	3	4										7	6	9	10	11	8			2				
5	8	PARTICK THISTLE	0-0	0-1	12000		1	5	3	4					11					7	6	9			8	10		2				
6	15	Stirling Albion	2-1	2-1	7000	Flavell, Harvey	1	5	3	4				11	9					7	6				8	10		2				
7	22	DUNDEE	0-0	0-0	12000		1	5	3	4				11	9					7	6				8	10		2				
8	29	Motherwell	0-0	1-2	12000	Curlett	1		3	9			7	11				5			4				8	10		2	6			
9	5 Nov	QUEEN OF THE SOUTH	1-1	2-2	15000	Flavell(2)	1		3	4			7	11	9			5							8	10		2	6			
10	12	Raith Rovers	1-1	1-2	8000	Mackay	1		3	9			7		11			5			4				8	10		2	6			
11	19	RANGERS	0-1	1-2	25600	Beattie	1		3	4			7		9		11				6				8	10		2	5			
12	26	Clyde	1-0	3-1	9000	Beattie, Harvey, Mays	1		3	9			7		11				4		6				8	10		2	5			
13	3 Dec	FALKIRK	3-1	4-4	10500	Beattie(2), Flavell, Mays	1		3	9			7		11				4		6				8	10		2	5			
14	10	Celtic	2-0	2-0	15000	Curlett(2)	1		3	9			7					5			4				8	10		2	6	11		
15	17	ABERDEEN	0-0	1-0	14000	Curlett	1		3	9			7					5			4		8			10		2	6	11		
16	24	HEARTS	0-2	2-4	17000	Mays(2)	1		3	9			7				8	5			4					10		2	6	11		
17	31	Dunfermline	1-0	3-0	7000	Beattie, Curlett, Mays	1		3	9			7		11			5			4					10		2	6	8		
18	2 Jan	St. Mirren	2-1	2-2	20000	Beattie, Mays	1		3		5		7		9		11	4								10		2	6	8		
19	7	EAST FIFE	2-0	3-0	10000	Beattie(2), Fletcher	1	5	3	9			7		11			4								10		2	6	8		
20	14	Airdrieonians	1-2	2-3	8000	Curlett(2)	1	5	3	9			7		11											10		2	6	8	4	
21	21	HIBERNIAN	0-0	0-1	14000		1	5	3	9			7		11											10		2	6	8	4	
22	28	Partick Thistle	0-1	1-1	12000	Mays	1	5	3	9			7		11										8	10		2	6		4	
23	11 Feb	STIRLING ALBION	1-1	3-2	10000	Flavell(3)	1	5	3	9			7		11										8			2		10	4	6
24	25	Dundee	1-0	1-1	11000	Flavell	1	5	3	9			7		11										8	10		2	6		4	
25	3 Mar	MOTHERWELL	2-0	2-1	10600	Flavell, Mays	1	5	3	9			7		11						6				8	10		2			4	
26	10	Queen of the South	0-0	0-2	7000		1	2			5			11	9					7					8	10		3	6		4	
27	17	RAITH ROVERS	1-1	1-1	10000	Beattie	1	2		9	5			7	11										8	10		3	6		4	
28	24	Rangers	1-2	2-3	30000	Curlett, Fletcher	1	2		9	5		7	11												10		3	6	8	4	
29	31	CLYDE	1-0	1-0	10000	Murray	1	2		9	5		7	11												10		3	6	8	4	
30	7 Apr	Falkirk	0-0	0-0	7000		1	2		9	5		7	11											8	10		3	6		4	
31	13	CELTIC	0-0	0-0	13000		1	2		9			7		11			5					10					3	6	8	4	
32	21	Aberdeen	1-1	2-3	15000	Beattie, Flavell	1	2		9			7		11			5								10		3	6	8	4	
33	25	Hearts	2-0	2-0	13000	Curlett(2)	1	2		9			7		11			5								10		3	6	8	4	
34	28	DUNFERMLINE	0-0	3-0	8000	Curlett(2), Mays	1	2		9			7		11			5								10		3	6	8	4	
						Apps.	33	23	25	32	6		25	9	23		3	15	2	8	17	5	6	4	20	29	1	32	25	15	15	1
						Goals				12			9	1	10							3	2		2	10			1	2		

Pos	P.	W.	D.	L.	F.	A.	Pts.
8th	34	12	10	12	52	45	34

League Cup Section AA

Pos	P.	W.	D.	L.	F.	A.	Pts.
2nd	6	2	3	1	7	7	7

No.	Date	Opposition	H.T.	Res.	Att.	Goalscorers	Brown	Collins	Rollo	Curlett	Dougan	Newbiggin	Mays	Murray	Flavell	Jack	Henaughan	Toner	Russell	Black	Taggart	Catterson	Lawlor	Clark	Harvey	Beattie	Bowie	Watson	Mackay	Fletcher	Stewart	Bunten
1	13 Aug	ST. MIRREN	0-0	0-0	20000		1	2	3	4	5	6	7	8	9	10	11															
2	17	Dundee	2-0	2-1	16000	Jack, Murray	1	2	3	4	5	6	7	8	9	10	11															
3	20	AIRDRIEONIANS	1-0	2-0	18000	Murray, Rollo	1	2	3	4		6	7	8	9	10	11	5														
4	27	St. Mirren	0-1	0-3	15000		1	2	3	4		6	7	8	9	10	11	5														
5	31	DUNDEE	0-0	0-0	16000		1	2	3	8		6						5	4	7		9	10	11								
6	3 Sep	Airdrieonians	1-2	3-3	8000	Catterson, Clark, Harvey	1	2	3	4								5		7	6	9	10	11	8							

Scottish Cup

No.	Date	Opposition	H.T.	Res.	Att.	Goalscorers	Brown	Collins	Rollo	Curlett	Dougan	Newbiggin	Mays	Murray	Flavell	Jack	Henaughan	Toner	Russell	Black	Taggart	Catterson	Lawlor	Clark	Harvey	Beattie	Bowie	Watson	Mackay	Fletcher	Stewart	Bunten
5	4 Feb	Falkirk	1-0	3-0	10808	Beattie(2), Curlett	1	5	3	9			7		11										8	10		2	6		4	
6	18	QUEEN OF THE SOUTH	2-2	2-2	24300	Harvey, Flavell	1	5	3	9			7		11										8	10		2	6		4	
6R	22	Queen of the South	0-1	0-2	14000		1	5	3	9			7		11										8	10		2	6		4	

This aerial shot was included in Kilmarnock's greetings card this season, reflecting the new optimism at Rugby Park.

SEASON 1956-57 Division One

No.	Date	Opposition	H.T.	Res.	Att.	Goalscorers	Brown	Collins	J.Stewart	R.Stewart	Toner	Mackay	Muir	W.Harvey	Curlett	Beattie	Burns	T.Harvey	Baillie	Dougan	Mays	Taggart	Fletcher	Lawlor	Watson	Black	Campbell	Falls	Malloy	Catterson	Caven	Neil	Milloy	Hill	McBain
1	8 Sep	Dundee	0-0	1-1	14000	Curlett	1	2	3	4	5	6	7	8	9	10	11																	
2	15	Rangers	1-0	1-0	30000	Curlett	1	2	3	4		6	7	8	9	10	11			5															
3	22	St. Mirren	0-1	0-2	10000		1	2	3	4		6	7	8	9	10	11			5															
4	29	EAST FIFE	0-1	1-1	10000	Curlett	1	2	3	4		6	7	8	9	10	11			5															
5	6 Oct	Dunfermline	1-1	1-2	7000	Muir	1	2	3			6	7	8	4		11			5	9			10											
6	13	AYR UNITED	3-0	4-1	18000	Burns, W.Harvey, Mays, Muir	1	2		4	5	6	7	8			11				9		10		3										
7	20	Partick Thistle	1-1	1-2	12000	Collins	1	2		4	5	6	11	8							9		10		3	7									
8	27	Hibernian	0-0	0-0	14000		1	2		4	5	6	7	8		10					9				3	11									
9	3 Nov	FALKIRK	0-0	1-1	10500	Beattie	1	2			5	6	7	8		10	11				9				3		4								
10	10	Aberdeen	0-1	3-1	11000	Fletcher, Beattie, Mays	1	2			5		7	8		10					9		11		3		6	4							
11	17	Hearts	1-2	2-3	14000	Black, Mays	1	2			5	6		8		10	11				9				3	7	4								
12	24	RAITH ROVERS	2-0	3-0	9246	Beattie(2), Mays	1	2			5	6	7	8		10					9				3	11	4								
13	1 Dec	MOTHERWELL	2-0	2-2	14873	Black, Beattie	1	2			5	6	7	8		10					9				3	11	4								
14	8	Queen of the South	0-0	3-0	6500	Black(2), Mays		2			5	6	7	8		10					9				3	11	4		1						
15	15	AIRDRIEONIANS	0-2	3-4	8037	Beattie, Mays, Muir		2			5	6	7	8		10					9				3	11	4		1						
16	22	RANGERS	1-0	3-2	22436	Mays(2), W.Harvey	1	2		4	5	6	7	8		10					9				3	11									
17	29	Queens Park	0-0	2-1	9000	Black, Muir	1	2		4	5	6	7	8		10					9				3	11									
18	1 Jan	ST. MIRREN	1-1	3-2	18055	Burns, Mays, Muir	1	2		4	5	6	7	8			11				9				3	10									
19	2	Celtic	0-1	1-1	14000	Mays	1	2		4	5	6	7	8			11				9				3	10									
20	5	DUNDEE	2-0	4-0	13788	Mays(2), Beattie, Mackay	1	2		4	5	6		8		10	11				9				3	7									
21	12	East Fife	0-0	0-0	6000		1	2		4	5	6		8		10	11				9				3	7									
22	19	DUNFERMLINE	0-0	0-0	11160		1		3	4	5	6		8		10	11				9				2	7									
23	26	Ayr United	1-0	2-0	18000	Black, W.Harvey	1		3	4	5	6	7	8		10					9				2	11									
24	9 Feb	PARTICK THISTLE	0-1	1-1	13776	Mays	1		3		5	6	7	8		10					9				2	11	4								
25	23	HIBERNIAN	1-1	2-1	9297	Caven, Muir	1		3	4	5	6	7	8			11								2	10					9				
26	6 Mar	Falkirk	0-1	0-2	15000		1		3	4	5	6	7	8			11								2	10					9				
27	9	ABERDEEN	2-0	2-1	13859	Curlett, Mays	1	2	3	4	5	6	7		8		11				9					10									
28	16	HEARTS	1-0	4-1	18598	Mays(2), Curlett, W.Harvey	1	2	3	4	5	6		8	9		11				7					10									
29	30	Motherwell	0-0	2-0	10000	Black, Curlett	1	2	3	4		6	7	8	9		11			5						10									
30	3 Apr	QUEEN OF THE SOUTH	0-0	1-3	9159	Black	1	2	3	4		6	11			10				5	7					8					9				
31	13	Airdrieonians	1-0	1-0	8000	W.Harvey	1	2	3	4	5	6	7	8			11				9					10									
32	15	Raith Rovers	0-2	2-4	6000	Mays(2)							11			10					9	6	8				2	4				1	3	5	7
33	26	CELTIC	0-0	0-0	6917		1	2	3	4	5		11	8	9						7	6				10									
34	27	QUEENS PARK	0-0	1-0	6388	Curlett	1	2	3	4	5		11	8	9						7	6				10									
						Apps.	31	28	17	24	27	30	29	31	10	21	19			6	27	3	4	1	21	25	9	2	2		3	1	1	1	1
						Goals		1				1	6	5	7	7	2				18		1			8					1				

Pos	P.	W.	D.	L.	F.	A.	Pts.
3rd	34	16	10	8	57	39	42

League Cup Section 3

Pos	P.	W.	D.	L.	F.	A.	Pts.
4th	6	1	2	3	8	14	4

No.	Date	Opposition	H.T.	Res.	Att.	Goalscorers	Brown	Collins	J.Stewart	R.Stewart	Toner	Mackay	Muir	W.Harvey	Curlett	Beattie	Burns	T.Harvey	Baillie	Dougan	Mays	Taggart	Fletcher	Lawlor	Watson	Black	Campbell	Falls	Malloy	Catterson	Caven	Neil	Milloy	Hill	McBain
1	11 Aug	DUNFERMLINE	0-0	0-0	12000		1	2			5	6		8	9	10	11				7	4			3											
2	15	St. Mirren	0-1	2-2	10000	Curlett, Mays	1	2				6		8	9	10	11			5	7	4			3											
3	18	QUEEN OF THE SOUTH	0-2	2-3	10000	W.Harvey, Mays	1	2				6		8	9	10	11			5	7	4			3											
4	25	Dunfermline	0-1	1-5	7000	Mays		2		4		6		8	9	10	11	1	3	5	7															
5	29	ST. MIRREN	1-3	1-4	12000	Catterson		2		4	6		7		10		11	1	3	5			8						9					
6	1 Sep	Queen of the South	1-0	2-0	7000	Curlett, W.Harvey		2		4	5		7	8	9		11		3			6	10		3											

Scottish Cup

No.	Date	Opposition	H.T.	Res.	Att.	Goalscorers	Brown	Collins	J.Stewart	R.Stewart	Toner	Mackay	Muir	W.Harvey	Curlett	Beattie	Burns	T.Harvey	Baillie	Dougan	Mays	Taggart	Fletcher	Lawlor	Watson	Black	Campbell	Falls	Malloy	Catterson	Caven	Neil	Milloy	Hill	McBain
5	2 Feb	AYR UNITED	0-0	1-0	22192	Beattie	1		3	4	5	6	7	8		10					9				2	11									
6	16	East Fife	0-0	0-0	8716		1		3	4	5	6	7	8		10					9				2	11									
6R	20	EAST FIFE	0-0	2-0	18656	Black, Mays	1		3	4	5	6	7	8			11				9				2	10									
QF	2 Mar	AIRDRIEONIANS	2-0	3-1	23509	Mays(2), W.Harvey	1		3	4	5	6	7	8			11				9				2	10									
SF	23	Celtic *	1-0	1-1	109145	Mays	1	2	3	4		6		8	9		11			5	7					10									
SFR	27	Celtic *	2-1	3-1	76963	Mays(2), Black	1	2	3	4	5	6		8	9		11				7					10									
F	20 Apr	Falkirk *	1-1	1-1	81375	Curlett	1	2	3	4	5	6		8	9		11				7					10									
FR	24	Falkirk *	0-1	1-2#	79960	Curlett	1	2	3	4	5	6		8	9		11				7					10									

* Played at Hampden Park # After extra time, at 90 minutes 1-1

Gerry Mays (No.7) puts Killie ahead in the first of their two Scottish Cup Semi-Finals against an unusually-garbed Celtic, which saw Killie reach their first post-war Scottish Cup Final. The terraces were packed. Over 186,000 saw the two matches with Celtic and in excess of another 160,000 took in the Final and replay against Falkirk.

SEASON 1957-58 Division One

No.	Date	Opposition	H.T.	Res.	Att.	Goalscorers	Brown	Collins	J.Stewart	R.Stewart	Toner	Mackay	Curlett	Beattie	Mays	Black	Burns	Taggart	Muir	Harvey	Neil	Henaughan	Jamieson	Kennedy	Hill	McBride	Milloy	Lawlor	Falls	Wentzel	Watson	Chalmers	Ross
1	7 Sep	AIRDRIEONIANS	1-0	3-1	10740	Beattie, Burns, Mays	1	2	3	4	5	6	7	8	9	10	11																
2	21	ST. MIRREN	3-0	4-2	11954	Mays(2), Burns, R.Stewart	1	2	3	4	5	6			9	10	11		7			8											
3	5 Oct	THIRD LANARK	0-2	2-4	8414	Mays(2)	1		3		5	6	7	8	9				11			10	2	4									
4	12	East Fife	1-1	2-1	5000	Henaughan, Mays	1			4	5	3		8	9	10			7			11		6	2								
5	19	CLYDE	1-1	3-2	13937	Beattie, Burns, Mays	1		2	4	5	3		8	9	10	11		7					6									
6	26	QUEENS PARK	1-0	3-1	11821	Black, Beattie, Mays	1		2	4	5	3		8	9	10	11		7					6									
7	2 Nov	Celtic	0-2	0-4	33915		1		2	4	5	3		8	9	10	11		7					6									
8	9	Rangers	3-1	4-3	45000	Beattie(2), Curlett, Mays	1	2	3	4	5		8	10	9	11			7					6									
9	16	MOTHERWELL	0-0	0-1	13748		1	2	3	4	5		8	10	9	11			7					6									
10	23	Aberdeen	0-1	2-1	15000	Curlett(2)	1	2	3	4	5		8		9	11			7			10		6									
11	30	PARTICK THISTLE	2-0	4-1	12590	Mays(2), Black, Curlett	1	2	3	4	5		8		9	11			7			10		6									
12	7 Dec	Falkirk	1-1	1-1	10000	Mays	1	2	3	4	5		8	10	9				7			11		6									
13	14	Hearts	0-2	1-2	25000	Mays	1	2	3	4	5		8	10	9	11						7		6									
14	21	HIBERNIAN	0-3	1-4	12562	Mays	1	2	3	4	5		8	10	9				7			11		6									
15	25	Dundee	0-1	0-2	9000		1	2	3	4	5		7	8			11					10		6		9							
16	28	Raith Rovers	0-0	1-1	8000	McBride	1	2	3	4	5		7	8	11							10		6		9							
17	1 Jan	St. Mirren	1-2	1-2	10000	Beattie	1	2	3	6	5		4	8	11				7			10				9							
18	2	QUEEN OF THE SOUTH	2-0	2-0	12040	Beattie, O.G.	1	2		4	5		7	10	9					8				6			3	11					
19	4	Airdrieonians	0-1	1-2	8500	Harvey	1	2		4	5		7	10	9					8				6			3	11					
20	11	DUNDEE	1-0	1-1	10312	Curlett	1	2		4	5		7	10	9	11				8				6			3						
21	18	Third Lanark	0-0	1-2	12000	McBride	1	2			5		7		9	11				8				6		10	3		4				
22	1 Feb	Queen of the South	1-0	2-1	6500	Mays, Muir	1	2	3		5				9	11			7	8				6		10			4				
23	22	CELTIC	0-1	1-1	21897	McBride	1	2	3		5					11			7	8				6		10			4	9			
24	8 Mar	Motherwell	1-1	2-2	10000	Burns, Chalmers	1	2	3	4	5					10	11		7					6		8						9	
25	10	RANGERS	2-1	3-3	15335	McBride(2), Burns	1	2	3		5					10	11					7		6		8			4			9	
26	15	EAST FIFE	3-0	4-0	7844	Black(3), Chalmers	1		3		5					10	11					7		6		8			4		2	9	
27	19	ABERDEEN	1-0	2-0	7809	Black(2)	1		3		5					10	11					7		6		8			4		2	9	
28	22	Partick Thistle	0-0	0-2	10000		1		3		5					10	11					7		6		8			4		2	9	
29	29	FALKIRK	1-1	1-1	6457	McBride			3		5					10	11					7		6		8			4		2	9	1
30	5 Apr	HEARTS	0-1	1-1	15865	O.G.	1		3		5	6			9	10	11					7		4		8					2		
31	12	Hibernian	1-0	2-1	18000	Black, McBride	1	2			5	6				10	11			8		7		4		9					3		
32	16	Clyde	1-0	2-3		Black, McBride	1	2			5	6		8		10	11					7		4		9					3		
33	26	RAITH ROVERS	1-0	1-1	4478	Black		2			5	6		8		10	11		7					4						9	3		1
34	30	Queens Park	1-1	2-1	500	Beattie, Wentzel		2		4	5	6		8		10	11		7											9	3		1
						Apps.	31	24	25	21	34	12	16	20	22	26	17		18	7		19	1	30	1	15	4	2	8	3	9	6	3
						Goals				1			5	8	15	10	5		1	1		1				8				1		2	

Pos	P.	W.	D.	L.	F.	A.	Pts.
5th	34	14	9	11	60	55	37

League Cup Section 4

Pos	P.	W.	D.	L.	F.	A.	Pts.
1st	6	3	3	0	12	6	9

No.	Date	Opposition	H.T.	Res.	Att.	Goalscorers	Brown	Collins	J.Stewart	R.Stewart	Toner	Mackay	Curlett	Beattie	Mays	Black	Burns	Taggart	Muir	Harvey	Neil	Henaughan	Jamieson	Kennedy	Hill	McBride	Milloy	Lawlor	Falls	Wentzel	Watson	Chalmers	Ross
1	10 Aug	HEARTS	1-0	2-1	19806	Harvey, Mays	1	2	3	4	5				9	10	11	6	7	8													
2	14	Dundee	0-0	3-0	15000	Beattie, Burns, Mays		2	3	4	5			10	9		11	6	7	8	1												
3	17	QUEENS PARK	1-1	3-1	13587	Beattie, Harvey, Taggart		2	3	4	5			10	9		11	6	7	8	1												
4	24	Hearts	0-1	1-1	25000	Mays	1	2	3	4	5		7	8	9	10	11	6															
5	28	DUNDEE	0-0	1-1	13535	Mays	1	2	3	4	5		7	8	9	10	11	6															
6	31	Queens Park	1-1	2-2	5500	Curlett, Mays	1	2	3	4	5		7	8	9	10	11	6															
QF	11 Sep	RANGERS	1-0	2-1	26803	Muir, O.G.	1	2	3	4	5	6		8	9	10	11		7														
QF	14	Rangers (Agg: 3-4)	1-1	1-3	66000	Black	1	2	3	4	5	6		8	9	10	11		7														

Scottish Cup

No.	Date	Opposition	H.T.	Res.	Att.	Goalscorers	Brown	Collins	J.Stewart	R.Stewart	Toner	Mackay	Curlett	Beattie	Mays	Black	Burns	Taggart	Muir	Harvey	Neil	Henaughan	Jamieson	Kennedy	Hill	McBride	Milloy	Lawlor	Falls	Wentzel	Watson	Chalmers	Ross
2	15 Feb	VALE OF LEITHEN	4-0	7-0	9795	McBride(3), Harvey(2), Wentzel(2)	1	2	3		5					11			7	8				6		10			4	9			
3	1 Mar	QUEEN OF THE SOUTH	0-1	2-2	20477	Black, McBride	1		3		5					7			11	8				6		10			4	9	2		
3R	5	Queen of the South	0-0	0-3	11000		1	2	3	4	5				9	7			11	8				6		10							

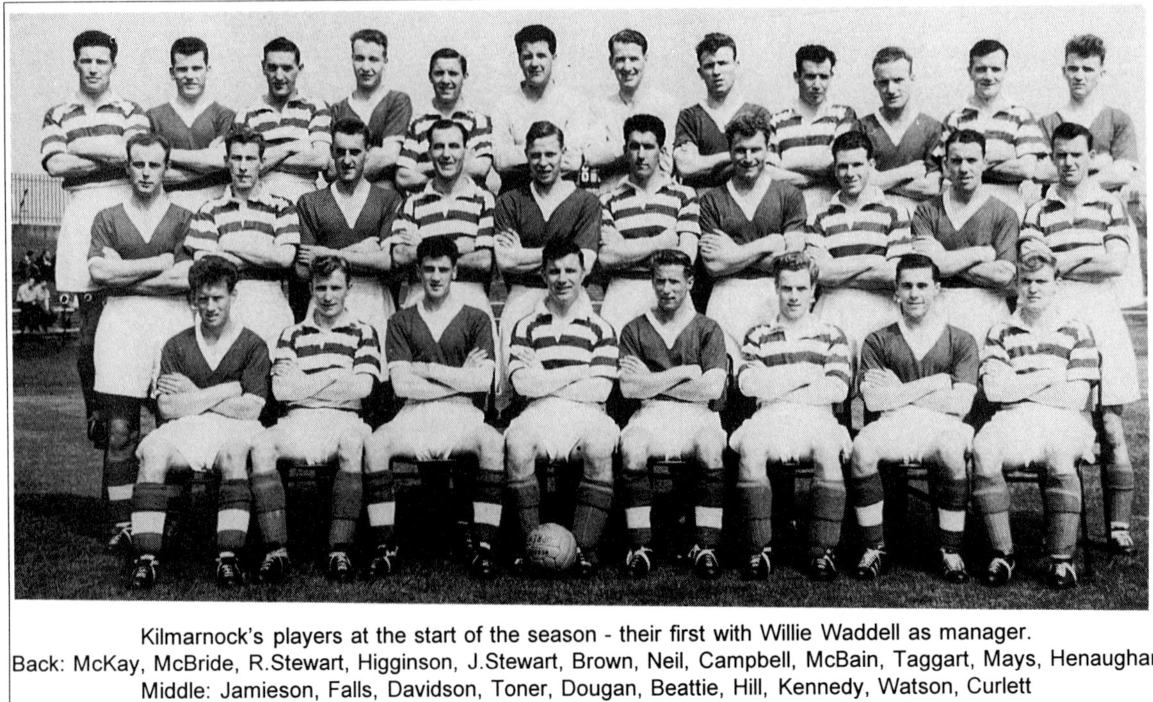

Kilmarnock's players at the start of the season - their first with Willie Waddell as manager.
Back: McKay, McBride, R.Stewart, Higginson, J.Stewart, Brown, Neil, Campbell, McBain, Taggart, Mays, Henaughan
Middle: Jamieson, Falls, Davidson, Toner, Dougan, Beattie, Hill, Kennedy, Watson, Curlett
Front: Cowan, Harvey, McPike, Collins, Muir, Black, Horn, Burns

SEASON 1958-59 Division One

No.	Date	Opposition	H.T.	Res.	Att.	Goalscorers	J.Brown	Watson	J.Stewart	R.Stewart	Toner	Mackay	H.Brown	Henaughan	McBride	Black	Burns	Collins	Kennedy	Chalmers	Muir	Beattie	O'Connor	Ross	Dougan	Mays	Wentzel	Grant	McPike	T.Brown
1	20 Aug	HIBERNIAN	1-0	1-1	9955	Black	1	2	3	4	5	6	7	8	9	10	11													
2	6 Sep	St. Mirren	2-0	2-0	11000	Black, Henaughan	1	3			5	6	7	8	9	10	11	2	4											
3	13	CELTIC	1-2	1-4	22286	McBride	1	3			5	6	7	8	9	10		2	4		11									
4	20	Dundee	0-1	0-1	12000		1	2	3		5	6	7		9	10			4		11	8								
5	27	STIRLING ALBION	1-1	3-3	9974	Henaughan(2), H.Brown	1	3			5	6	7	8	9	10		2	4		11									
6	4 Oct	Airdrieonians	0-0	0-3	7500		1	3		4	5	6	7		9	10		2			11		8							
7	11	DUNFERMLINE	0-0	1-1	8391	O.G.		3		4		6	7		9	10		2			11		8	1	5					
8	18	QUEEN OF THE SOUTH	3-0	5-0	7770	R.Stewart(3), McBride, Muir	1	3		8		6	7		9	10		2			11	4			5					
9	25	Raith Rovers	0-0	0-1	8000		1	3		8	5	6	7		9	10		2			11	4								
10	29	Partick Thistle	1-1	1-1	10000	Black	1	3		8		6			9	10		2		7	11	4			5					
11	1 Nov	ABERDEEN	2-0	2-0	6791	Black, McBride	1	3		8		6			9	10		2		7	11	4			5					
12	8	Falkirk	0-0	0-0	10000		1	3		8		6	7		9	10		2			11	4			5					
13	15	Motherwell	1-0	1-1	13000	Black	1	3				6	7	8	9	10		2			11	4			5					
14	22	RANGERS	0-1	0-3	25672		1	3				6	7	8	9	10		2			11	4			5					
15	29	HEARTS	2-1	3-2	15269	Wentzel(2), Black	1	3			2	6			8	10					11	4			5	7	9			
16	13 Dec	RAITH ROVERS	0-0	2-0	6743	McBride(2)	1	3			2	6			8	10					11	4			5	7	9			
17	20	Clyde	3-1	4-2	10000	Black(2), Mays, McBride	1	3		6	2				8	10					11	4			5	7	9			
18	27	Hibernian	1-1	3-4	12000	Wentzel(2), R.Stewart	1	3		6	2				8	10					11	4			5	7	9			
19	1 Jan	ST. MIRREN	0-0	1-0	10869	Mays	1	3		6	2				8	10						4			5	7	9	11		
20	10	DUNDEE	0-0	1-0	8726	Wentzel	1	3		6	2				8	10						4			5	7	9	11		
21	17	Stirling Albion	1-0	1-3	4000	Wentzel	1	3		6	2				8	10						4			5	7	9	11		
22	21	Celtic	0-0	0-2	8000		1	3		6	2				8	10						4			5	7	9	11		
23	24	AIRDRIEONIANS	1-1	4-2	9594	Wentzel(4)	1	3		6	2				8	10						4			5	7	9	11		
24	7 Feb	Dunfermline	3-0	3-0	6000	Black, McBride, R.Stewart	1	3		6	2				8	10	11					4			5	7	9			
25	18	Queen of the South	1-1	2-2	6500	Mays, McBride	1	3		6	2				8	10	11					4			5	7	9			
26	21	PARTICK THISTLE	1-2	1-2	8897	Wentzel	1	3		6	2				8	10	11					4			5	7	9			
27	4 Mar	Aberdeen	2-1	2-2	5000	Black, Burns	1	2		6		3		8		10	11				7	4			5		9			
28	7	FALKIRK	1-1	4-1	7491	Muir(2), Black, Wentzel	1	2		6		3		8		10	11				7		4		5		9			
29	18	MOTHERWELL	1-2	1-3	7298	Wentzel	1	2		6		3			8	10	11					4			5	7	9			
30	21	Rangers	0-1	0-1	30000		1	3		6				8		10	11	2			7	4			5		9			
31	24	Third Lanark	0-0	0-2	2500		1	3		6				10		11		2			7	4			5		9			8
32	28	Hearts	1-0	1-3	18000	Black	1	2		6		3		8		10	11					4			5	7	9			
33	18 Apr	CLYDE	3-0	4-1	5799	Black, Mays, McBride, McPike	1	2		6		3			8	10	11					4			5	7			9	
34	21	THIRD LANARK	1-0	4-0	4086	Black, Burns, McPike, O.G.	1	2		6		3			8	10	11					4			5	7			9	
						Apps.	33	34	2	26	19	22	12	11	29	34	12	14	4	2	20	27	3	1	27	16	18	5	2	1
						Goals				5			1	3	10	13	2				3					4	13		2	

Pos	P.	W.	D.	L.	F.	A.	Pts.
8th	34	13	8	13	58	51	34

League Cup Section 4

Pos	P.	W.	D.	L.	F.	A.	Pts.
1st	6	4	0	2	12	6	8

No.	Date	Opposition	H.T.	Res.	Att.	Goalscorers	J.Brown	Watson	J.Stewart	R.Stewart	Toner	Mackay	H.Brown	Henaughan	McBride	Black	Burns	Collins	Kennedy	Chalmers	Muir	Beattie	O'Connor	Ross	Dougan	Mays	Wentzel	Grant	McPike	T.Brown
1	9 Aug	ABERDEEN	0-1	1-2	8758	Kennedy	1	3			5	6	7		8	10	11	2	4	9										
2	13	Falkirk	1-0	3-1		McBride(2), R.Stewart	1	3		4	5	6	7	8	9	10	11	2												
3	16	Hibernian	1-0	3-0	17000	Black, Henaughan, McBride	1	3		4	5	6	7	8	9	10	11	2												
4	23	Aberdeen	2-0	2-0	14000	McBride(2)	1	3		4	5	6	7	8	9	10	11	2												
5	27	FALKIRK	1-1	1-2	10463	Black	1	3		4	5	6	7	8	9	10	11	2												
6	30	HIBERNIAN	2-0	2-1	15700	Burns, McBride	1	3			5	6	7	8	9	10	11	2	4											
QF	10 Sep	DUNFERMLINE	2-0	4-1	14275	Black, H.Brown, Kennedy, McBride	1	3			5	6	7	8	9	10	11	2	4											
QF	16	Dunfermline (Agg: 7-4)	2-2	3-3		H.Brown, Henaughan, McBride	1	2	3		5	6	7	8	9	10			4		11									
SF	1 Oct	Hearts*	0-1	0-3	41527		1	3		4	5	6	7	8	9	10		2												

* Played at Easter Road

Scottish Cup

No.	Date	Opposition	H.T.	Res.	Att.	Goalscorers	J.Brown	Watson	J.Stewart	R.Stewart	Toner	Mackay	H.Brown	Henaughan	McBride	Black	Burns	Collins	Kennedy	Chalmers	Muir	Beattie	O'Connor	Ross	Dougan	Mays	Wentzel	Grant	McPike	T.Brown
1		Bye																												
2	14 Feb	Dumbarton	4-1	8-2	8804	McBride(3), Wentzel(3), Burns, Mays	1	3		6	2				8	10	11					4			5	7	9			
3	28	Hamilton A.	0-0	5-0	10391	Black(2), Wentzel(2), Burns	1	2		6		3	8			10	11					4			5	7	9			
QF	14 Mar	Aberdeen	1-2	1-3	19000	Mays	1	2		6		3			8	10	11					4			5	7	9			

HEARTS — **KILMARNOCK**

HEARTS		KILMARNOCK
MARSHALL, GLIDDEN, BAULD, McBRIDE, TONER, J. BROWN		

CRAWFORD — H. BROWN

CUMMING — KENNEDY

YOUNG — HENAUGHAN

THOMSON — COLLINS

MARSHALL — GLIDDEN — BAULD — McBRIDE — TONER — J. BROWN

KIRK — WATSON

MURRAY — BLACK

MacKAY — McKAY

HAMILTON — MUIR

Referee—
J. P. Barclay, Kirkcaldy

Linesmen—
J. S. Jack, Glasgow
R. A. Neave, Glasgow

JIMMY BROWN
Kilmarnock

WILLIE BAULD
Hearts

Kilmarnock were now a respected force in the League and both Cups. They lost this Semi-Final to Hearts at a supposedly 'neutral' Easter Road. But Killie were on the brink of their most successful era ever.

SEASON 1959-60 Division One

No.	Date	Opposition	H.T.	Res.	Att.	Goalscorers	J.Brown	Watson	Cook	Stewart	Toner	Kennedy	Copeland	McInally	McBride	Black	McPike	Baillie	Dougan	MacKay	Wentzel	O'Connor	Henaughan	Muir	Burns	Beattie	Horn	H.Brown	Anton	T.Brown	Richmond	Kerr	Bryceland
1	19 Aug	Celtic	0-1	0-2			1	2	3	4	5	6	7	8	9	10	11															
2	5 Sep	ST. MIRREN	0-2	0-5	12276		1	2	3				7	8	9				5			6	10		11	4							
3	12	Airdrieonians	2-1	3-1	5000	Wentzel, Black(2)	1	2	3				7		8	10			5		9	6	11			4							
4	19	STIRLING ALBION	2-0	2-0	7672	Black, Wentzel	1	2	3						8	10			5		9	6	7			4	11						
5	26	Hibernian	1-3	2-4	20000	McBride, Wentzel	1	2	3				7		10	8			5		9	6				4	11						
6	3 Oct	DUNDEE	1-1	2-2	8206	McBride, McInally	1	2	3				7	8	9	10				5		6				4	11						
7	10	Partick Thistle	2-2	2-3	15000	McBride, Watson	1	2	3				7	8	9	10				5		6				4	11						
8	17	ABERDEEN	1-0	2-0	7149	Black(2)	1	2			5				9	10				3		6	8			4	11	7					
9	24	Arbroath	2-0	3-0	4000	McBride, Wentzel	1	2			5				9	10				3	7	6	8			4	11						
10	31	MOTHERWELL	1-0	2-0	11478	Beattie, Muir	1	2			5			8	9	10				3	7	6		11		4							
11	7 Nov	THIRD LANARK	0-1	3-2	9927	Black, O'Connor, Wentzel		2			5			8	9	10				3	7	6		11		4			1				
12	14	Hearts	0-2	1-3	18000	McInally	1	2			5			8	9	10				3	7	6		11		4							
13	21	AYR UNITED	0-0	2-0	19355	McBride, Wentzel	1	2			5			8	9	10				3	7	6		11		4							
14	28	DUNFERMLINE	1-2	3-2	9047	Black, T.Brown, Muir	1	2			5			8		10				3	7	6		11		4				9			
15	5 Dec	Rangers	0-2	0-5	20000		1	2			5			8		10				3	7	6		11		4				9			
16	12	RAITH ROVERS	0-0	1-0	8897	McInally	1	3			5	6		8		10					7			11		4				9	2		
17	19	Clyde	0-1	2-1	8000	McInally(2)	1	3	9		5	6		8		10					7			11		4					2		
18	26	CELTIC	1-1	2-1	15948	Black, Kerr	1	3			5	6		8		10					7			11		4					2	9	
19	1 Jan	St. Mirren	3-0	3-0	18000	Kerr, Muir, Wentzel	1	3			5	6		8		10					7			11		4					2	9	
20	2	AIRDRIEONIANS	1-0	1-0	13971	Kerr	1	3		2	5	6		8		10					7			11		4						9	
21	9	Stirling Albion	1-0	1-0	5316	Kerr	1	3		2	5	6		8		10					7			11		4						9	
22	16	HIBERNIAN	0-0	3-1	17448	Kerr, McInally, Muir	1	3			5	6		8		10					7			11		4					2	9	
23	23	Dundee	1-0	4-0	15000	Muir(2), Black, McInally	1	3			5	6		8		10					7			11		4					2	9	
24	6 Feb	PARTICK THISTLE	3-0	5-1	13132	McInally(3), Muir, Wentzel	1	3			5	6		8		10					7			11		4					2	9	
25	1 Mar	ARBROATH	2-0	3-2	8337	McInally(2), Kerr	1	3		7	5	6		8		10								11		4					2	9	
26	5	Motherwell	1-0	2-1	16000	Black, McInally	1	3		7	5	6		8		10								11		4					2	9	
27	14	Third Lanark	0-2	4-3	10000	Muir(2), McInally, Stewart	1	3		7	5	6		8		10								11		4					2	9	
28	19	HEARTS	0-0	2-1	26584	McInally, Muir	1	3		7	5	6		8		10								11		4					2	9	
29	22	Aberdeen	0-0	1-0	13000	Black	1	3		7	5	6		8		10					11					4					2	9	
30	26	Ayr United	2-0	3-1	19000	Kerr(2), McInally	1	3		7	5	6		8		10								11		4					2	9	
31	4 Apr	Dunfermline	0-0	0-1	14000		1	3		7	5	6		8		10								11		4					2	9	
32	16	RANGERS	1-1	1-1	26925	Black	1	3		7	5	6		8		10								11		4					2	9	
33	27	Raith Rovers	1-0	2-0	6000	Black, Wentzel	1	3		2		6		8		10					7			11		4					5	9	
34	30	CLYDE	0-1	0-2	6986		1	3		2		6		8		10					7			11		4					5	9	
						Apps.	33	34	8	13	26	20	6	29	13	33	1		4	10	22	14	5	24	1	33	6	1	1	3	17	17	
						Goals		1		1				16	6	13					9	1		10		1				1		8	

Pos	P.	W.	D.	L.	F.	A.	Pts.
2nd	34	24	2	8	67	45	50

League Cup Section 3

Pos	P.	W.	D.	L.	F.	A.	Pts.
3rd	6	2	1	3	13	13	5

No.	Date	Opposition	H.T.	Res.	Att.	Goalscorers	J.Brown	Watson	Cook	Stewart	Toner	Kennedy	Copeland	McInally	McBride	Black	McPike	Baillie	Dougan	MacKay	Wentzel	O'Connor	Henaughan	Muir	Burns	Beattie	Horn	H.Brown	Anton	T.Brown	Richmond	Kerr	Bryceland
1	8 Aug	HEARTS	0-0	0-4	16378		1	3		8		4	7			10	11	2	5	6	9													
2	12	Stirling Albion	1-0	2-2	4500	Wentzel(2)	1	2	3	4			7	8		10	11		5	6	9													
3	15	ABERDEEN	2-1	2-3	10427	McInally, Wentzel	1	2	3	4		6	7	8		10	11		5		9													
4	22	Hearts	0-1	0-2	30000		1	2	3	4			7	8	9	11			5			6	10										
5	26	STIRLING ALBION	3-0	5-0	6118	McInally(2) Copeland, McBride, O'Connor	1	2	3	4			7	8	9				5			6	10	11									
6	29	Aberdeen	2-0	4-2	8000	Burns, Henaughan, McBride, McInally	1	2	3	4			7	8	9				5			6	10		11								

Scottish Cup

No.	Date	Opposition	H.T.	Res.	Att.	Goalscorers	J.Brown	Watson	Cook	Stewart	Toner	Kennedy	Copeland	McInally	McBride	Black	McPike	Baillie	Dougan	MacKay	Wentzel	O'Connor	Henaughan	Muir	Burns	Beattie	Horn	H.Brown	Anton	T.Brown	Richmond	Kerr	Bryceland
1	30 Jan	STRANRAER	2-0	5-0	8506	Wentzel(2), Black, McInally, Muir	1	3			5	6		8		10					7			11		4					2	9	
2	22 Feb	Hearts	0-1	1-1	33869	Muir	1	3		7	5	6		8		10								11		4					2	9	
2r	24	HEARTS	1-0	2-1	24359	Muir, Stewart	1	3		7	5	6		8		10								11		4					2	9	
3	27	MOTHERWELL	0-0	2-0	29412	McInally(2)	1	3		7	5	6		8		10								11		4					2	9	
QF	12 Mar	Eyemouth United	2-1	2-1	2900	Black, McInally	1	3		7	5	6		8		10								11		4					2	9	
SF	2 Apr	Clyde*	2-0	2-0	43900	Kerr, Muir	1	3		7	5	6		8		10								11		4					2	9	
F	23	Rangers+	0-1	0-2	108017		1	3		7	5	6		8		10								11		4					2	9	

* Played at Ibrox + Played at Hampden

New York Int. Tourn.

Pos	P.	W.	D.	L.	F.	A.	Pts.
1st	5	4	1	0	11	2	9

No.	Date	Opposition	H.T.	Res.	Att.	Goalscorers	J.Brown	Watson	Cook	Stewart	Toner	Kennedy	Copeland	McInally	McBride	Black	McPike	Baillie	Dougan	MacKay	Wentzel	O'Connor	Henaughan	Muir	Burns	Beattie	Horn	H.Brown	Anton	T.Brown	Richmond	Kerr	Bryceland
1	25 May	Bayern Munich	0-1	3-1	10444	Bryceland, Kerr, McInally	1	3			5	6		8							7			11		4					2	9	10
2	30	Glenavon	0-0	2-0	6000	Muir, Watson	1	3			5	6		8							7			11		4					2	9	10
3	1 Jun	Burnley	1-0	2-0	13000	Kerr, Wentzel	1	3			5	6		8							7			11		4					2	9	10
4	8	Nice	0-0	1-1	12861	McInally	1	3			5	6		8							7			11		4					2	9	10
5	18	New York Americans	1-0	3-1	11704	McInally, Muir, O.G.	1			3	5	6		8							7			11		4					2	9	10
F	6 Aug	Bangu	0-1	0-2	25044		1	3			5	6		8		10					9			11		4		7			2		

Glenavon and New York Americans matches played at Roosevelt Stadium, Jersey City. All other games played at Polo Grounds, New York

Killie play Hearts, their opening League Cup tie. 50 weeks & 53 games later the season ends with Killie in runners-up spots in the League, Scottish Cup & the New York Tournament, the best year to date.

Back: Baillie, Watson, Brown, Kennedy, Dougan, Mackay.
Front: Copeland, Stewart, Wentzel, Black, McPike

SEASON 1960-61 Division One

No.	Date	Opposition	H.T.	Res.	Att.	Goalscorers	J.Brown	Richmond	Watson	Beattie	Toner	Kennedy	Muir	McInally	Kerr	Black	McIlroy	Wentzel	H.Brown	Stewart	O'Connor	Davidson	McGrory	McLaughlan	Cook	King
1	24 Aug	CELTIC	0-1	2-2	23745	McInally(2)	1	2	3	4	5	6	7	8	9	10	11									
2	10 Sep	St. Mirren	0-0	1-0	15000	Muir	1	2	3	4	5	6	7	8	9	10	11									
3	17	HIBERNIAN	1-0	3-2	11995	Black, Kerr, Wentzel	1	2	3	4	5	6		8	9	10	11	7								
4	24	Ayr United	1-2	2-2	17500	Kerr, Richmond	1	2	3	4	5	6		8	9	10	11		7							
5	1 Oct	Raith Rovers	1-0	1-1	6000	McIlroy	1	2	3		5	6		8	9	10	11		7	4						
6	8	CLYDE	0-0	1-0	11657	Kerr	1	5	3	4		6		8	9	10	11		7	2						
7	15	Dundee	0-0	0-1	16000		1	2	3	4	5				9	10	11		7	8	6					
8	22	ST. JOHNSTONE	2-1	2-2	9409	Black, Kerr	1	2	3	4	5	6		8	9	10	11		7							
9	2 Nov	THIRD LANARK	1-0	3-1	4361	H.Brown, Kerr, Muir	1	2	3		5	6	11		9	10	7		8			4				
10	5	Airdrieonians	0-0	1-1	8000	McIlroy	1	2	3	6			11		9	10	7		8			4	5			
11	12	HEARTS	1-1	2-1	13393	Kerr(2)		2	3	6	5		11		9	10	7		8			4		1		
12	19	Dundee United	1-0	4-2	12000	Kerr(3), McIlroy		2	3	6	5	10	11		9		7		8			4		1		
13	26	Rangers	2-2	3-2	55000	H.Brown, Kerr, McInally		2	3		5	6	11	10	9	7			8			4		1		
14	3 Dec	MOTHERWELL	3-2	5-3	11533	Kerr(4), McInally		2	3		5	6	11	10	9	7			8			4		1		
15	10	Aberdeen	1-2	2-3	14000	Kerr, McInally		2	3		5	6	11	10	9	7			8			4		1		
16	17	DUNFERMLINE	0-1	1-1	8783	Kerr		2	3		5	6	11	10	9	7			8			4		1		
17	24	Partick Thistle	1-2	3-2	20000	Kerr(3)		2	3	6	5	10	11	8	9				7			4		1		
18	31	Celtic	1-0	2-3	26000	H.Brown, Kennedy		2	3	6	5	10	11	8	9				7			4		1		
19	2 Jan	ST. MIRREN	1-1	1-2	18240	Kerr		2	3	6	5	4	11	8	9	10			7					1		
20	7	Hibernian	0-0	0-4	18000			2		4	5	6	11	8	9		10		7					1	3	
21	14	AYR UNITED	2-0	5-1	14907	McInally(2), Davidson, Kerr, Muir		2	3	4	5	6	11	10	9				7			8		1		
22	21	RAITH ROVERS	3-0	6-0	9841	Kerr(3), H.Brown, Davidson, McInally		2	3	4	5	6	11	10	9				7			8		1		
23	4 Feb	Clyde	1-1	3-1	8000	Black, Kerr, McInally		2	3	4	5	6	11	10	9	8			7					1		
24	18	DUNDEE	1-0	2-1	10191	Davidson, McInally		2	3	4	5	6	11	10	9				7			8		1		
25	25	St. Johnstone	0-1	1-1	8800	Kerr		2	3	4	5	6	11		9	10			7			8		1		
26	4 Mar	Third Lanark	1-0	1-0	8500	Kerr		2	3	4		6	11	10	9				7			8	5	1		
27	11	ABERDEEN	1-0	4-1	8360	McInally(2), Davidson, Kerr		2		4	5	6	11	10	9				7			8		1	3	
28	15	AIRDRIEONIANS	1-0	1-0	7841	Kerr		2	3	4	5	6	11	10	9				7			8		1		
29	18	Hearts	1-0	1-0	22000	Kerr		2	3	4	5	6	11	10	9		7		8					1		
30	25	DUNDEE UNITED	0-0	1-1	8012	Muir		2	3	4	5	6	11	10	9	8			7					1		
31	1 Apr	RANGERS	2-0	2-0	29528	Kerr, Muir		2	3	4	5	6	11	10	9	8			7					1		
32	8	Motherwell	3-0	3-1	17000	Black(2), Kerr		2	3	4	5	6	11	10	9	8			7					1		
33	29	PARTICK THISTLE	4-1	4-1	9865	H.Brown(2), Black, Kerr		2	3	4	5	6	11	10	9	8			7					1		
34	1 May	Dunfermline	1-1	4-2	10917	Black(2), McInally(2)		2	3	4	5	6	11	10	9	8			7					1		
						Apps.	10	34	32	28	31	31	28	28	34	23	14	1	31	3	1	17	2	24	2	
						Goals		1				1	5	14	34	8	3	1	6			4				

Pos	P.	W.	D.	L.	F.	A.	Pts.
2nd	34	21	8	5	77	45	50

League Cup Section 3

Pos	P.	W.	D.	L.	F.	A.	Pts.
1st	6	4	1	1	12	7	9

No.	Date	Opposition	H.T.	Res.	Att.	Goalscorers	J.Brown	Richmond	Watson	Beattie	Toner	Kennedy	Muir	McInally	Kerr	Black	McIlroy	Wentzel	H.Brown	Stewart	O'Connor	Davidson	McGrory	McLaughlan	Cook	King
1	13 Aug	HIBERNIAN	1-1	4-2	15451	Black(3), Kerr	1	2	3	4	5	6	11	8	9	10		7								
2	17	Airdrieonians	1-0	2-0	7000	Beattie, Kerr	1	2	3	4	5	6	11	8	9	10		7								
3	20	DUNFERMLINE	2-1	2-1	13251	Kerr, Muir	1	2	3	4	5	6	11	8	9	10		7								
4	27	Hibernian	1-2	2-2	23000	Black, O.G.	1	2	3	4	5	6	7	8	9	10	11									
5	31	AIRDRIEONIANS	2-0	2-0	11661	Black, Muir	1	2	3	4	5	6	7	8	9	10	11									
6	3 Sep	Dunfermline	0-1	0-2	6919		1	2	3	4	5	6		8	9	10	11		7							
QF	14	Clyde	0-0	2-1	18000	Kerr, Wentzel	1	2	3	4	5	6		8	9	10	11	7								
QF	21	CLYDE (Aggregate: 5-2)	2-0	3-1	15990	McIlroy(2), Kerr	1	2	3	4	5	6		8	9	10	11		7							
SF	12 Oct	Hamilton A.*	1-0	5-1	15000	Black(2), Kerr(2), McInally	1	2	3	4	5	6		8	9	10	11		7							
F	29	Rangers+	0-1	0-2	82063		1	2	3	4	5	6	11	8	9	10			7							

* Played at Ibrox + Played at Hampden

Scottish Cup

No.	Date	Opposition	H.T.	Res.	Att.	Goalscorers	J.Brown	Richmond	Watson	Beattie	Toner	Kennedy	Muir	McInally	Kerr	Black	McIlroy	Wentzel	H.Brown	Stewart	O'Connor	Davidson	McGrory	McLaughlan	Cook	King
1		Bye																								
2	11 Feb	HEARTS	0-2	1-2	18383	Davidson		2	3	4	5	6	11	10	9				7			8		1		

New York Tournament

Pos	P.	W.	D.	L.	F.	A.	Pts.
5th	7	2	2	3	12	13	6

No.	Date	Opposition	H.T.	Res.	Att.	Goalscorers	J.Brown	Richmond	Watson	Beattie	Toner	Kennedy	Muir	McInally	Kerr	Black	McIlroy	Wentzel	H.Brown	Stewart	O'Connor	Davidson	McGrory	McLaughlan	Cook	King
1	25 May	Everton	0-2	1-2	5000	Kerr		2	3	4	5	6	11	10	9	8			7					1		
2	30	Karlsruhe	1-1	2-3	10000	Kennedy, Muir		2	3	4	5	6	11	10	9	8			7					1		
3	1 Jun	New York Americans	2-0	4-0	7000	Black, H.Brown, Kerr, Watson		2	3	4	5	6	11		9	8			7			10		1		
4	6	Montreal Concordia	1-1	4-2	4000	Kerr(2), Black, McInally		2	3	4	5	6	11	10	9	8			7					1		
5	10	Besiktas	0-1	1-1	2000	Muir		2	3	4	5	6	11	10	9	8			7					1		
6	14	Dynamo Bucharest	0-0	0-0	3000				3	4	5	6	11	10	9	8			7					1		2
7	18	Bangu	0-2	0-5	4000			2	3		5	6	11	10	9	8			7			4		1		

Karlsruhe, Dynamo Bucharest and Bangu matches played in New York. All other games played in Montreal.

More near misses, Killie finish second in both the League and League Cup. Back: J.Richmond, M.Watson, A.McLaughlan, F.Beattie, R.Kennedy, A.Kerr
Front: H.Brown, R.Black, W.Toner, J.McInally, W.Muir

SEASON 1961-62 Division One

No.	Date	Opposition	H.T.	Res.	Att.	Goalscorers	McLaughlan	Richmond	Watson	Davidson	Toner	Beattie	McIlroy	Mason	Black	McInally	Muir	Brown	Hamilton	McGrory	Kerr	Yard	Sneddon	Forsyth	Murray	King	O'Connor
1	23 Aug	CELTIC	2-1	3-2	19215	Black, McInally, Muir	1	2	3	4	5	6	7	8	9	10	11										
2	9 Sep	Airdrieonians	1-0	2-0	4029	McIlroy(2)	1	2	3	4	5	6	7	8	9	10		11									
3	16	ST. MIRREN	3-0	4-3	11492	Hamilton(2), Davidson, McIlroy	1	2	3	4	5	6	7	8	10		11		9								
4	23	Hibernian	1-1	2-3	13181	McInally, Mason	1	2	3	4	5	6	7	8	11	10			9								
5	30	ST. JOHNSTONE	1-0	2-0	11848	Mason, Muir	1	2	3	4		6	7	8	9	10	11			5							
6	7 Oct	Dundee	2-2	3-5	12677	Black, McIlroy, McInally	1	2	3	4		6	7	8	9	10	11			5							
7	14	THIRD LANARK	2-1	2-2	12681	Black, Hamilton	1	2	3	4		6		8	9	10	11		7		5						
8	21	Dundee United	0-1	2-1	8975	Black, Yard	1	2	3	4		6			9	10	11	7			5	8					
9	28	FALKIRK	1-0	2-0	9630	Richmond, Yard	1	2	3	4		6			9	10	11	7			5	8					
10	4 Nov	Partick Thistle	3-2	4-2	11614	McInally(2), Yard(2)	1	2	3	4		6			9	10	11	7			5	8					
11	11	RAITH ROVERS	2-0	2-3	8252	Black, McInally	1	2	3	4		6			9	10	11	7			5	8					
12	18	Stirling Albion	0-1	2-2	4231	Black, Kerr	1	2	3	4	5	6			8		11	7			9		10				
13	25	DUNFERMLINE	0-0	2-2	9391	McInally, Watson	1	2	3	4	5	6			7	8	11				9		10				
14	2 Dec	ABERDEEN	3-1	4-2	6885	Kerr, Muir, Sneddon, Yard	1	2	3	6	5	4			7		11				9	8	10				
15	16	Hearts	1-1	3-3	11225	Black, Richmond, Yard	1	2	3	6	5	4			7		11				9	8	10				
16	23	MOTHERWELL	0-1	1-2	11525	Beattie	1	2	3	6	5	4			7		11				9	8	10				
17	30	RANGERS	0-1	0-1	21992		1	2	3	6	5	4	11		9	10	7					8					
18	6 Jan	Celtic	1-1	2-2	33940	Kerr, McIlroy		2	3	4	5	6	11			7					9	8	10	1			
19	10	AIRDRIEONIANS	2-1	4-2	5488	Kerr(2), Sneddon, Yard		2	3	4		6	11			7				5	9	8	10	1			
20	13	HIBERNIAN	1-1	4-2	8599	Kerr(2), McIlroy, Yard		2	3	4		6	11			7				5	9	8	10	1			
21	17	St. Mirren	0-1	1-2	5547	McIlroy		2	3	4		6	11			7				5	9	8	10	1			
22	20	St. Johnstone	2-0	2-0	7133	Mason, O.G.	1	2	3	4	5	6	11	10		7			9			8					
23	3 Feb	DUNDEE	0-0	1-1	14314	Kerr	1	2	3	4	5	6	11	10				7			9	8					
24	10	Third Lanark	1-2	1-3	8760	Yard	1	2	3	4	5	6		10			11	7			9	8					
25	21	DUNDEE UNITED	2-0	5-3	5584	Kerr(4), McIlroy	1	2	3	4	5	6	11	8				7			9		10				
26	24	Falkirk	1-0	1-0	4910	Kerr	1	2	3		5	6	11	8				7			9		10		4		
27	3 Mar	PARTICK THISTLE	1-0	1-1	9805	Kerr	1	2	3		5	6	11	8				7			9		10		4		
28	14	Raith Rovers	0-1	2-2	2021	Kerr(2)	1	2	3	4	5		11		8			7			9		10		6		
29	17	STIRLING ALBION	0-1	2-1	4671	Kerr, McIlroy	1	2	3	4	5	6	11		8			7			9		10				
30	24	Dunfermline	0-1	0-2	7528		1	2	3	4	5	6	11		8			7			9		10				
31	31	Aberdeen	1-2	3-3	3269	Kerr(2), McInally	1	4	3		5	6				8	11	7			9		10			2	
32	7 Apr	HEARTS	0-0	2-0	6750	Kerr(2)	1	3			5					8	11	7			9		10		4	2	6
33	21	Motherwell	0-0	2-0	4236	Black, Kerr	1	5	3						11	8		7			9		10		4	2	6
34	28	Rangers	0-0	1-1	39848	Kerr	1	3							11	8		7		5	9		10		4	2	6
						Apps.	30	34	32	28	22	30	19	13	22	21	18	18	4	6	26	15	19	4	6	4	3
						Goals		2	1	1		1	9	3	8	8	3		3		23	9	2				

Pos	P.	W.	D.	L.	F.	A.	Pts.
5th	34	16	10	8	74	58	42

League Cup Section 4

Pos	P.	W.	D.	L.	F.	A.	Pts.
2nd	6	3	0	3	18	8	6

No.	Date	Opposition	H.T.	Res.	Att.	Goalscorers	McLaughlan	Richmond	Watson	Davidson	Toner	Beattie	McIlroy	Mason	Black	McInally	Muir	Brown	Hamilton	McGrory	Kerr	Yard	Sneddon	Forsyth	Murray	King	O'Connor
1	12 Aug	St. Mirren	0-0	0-1	16149		1	2	3	4	5	6			8	10	11	7			9						
2	16	HEARTS	1-0	1-2	13841	Beattie	1	2	3	4	5	6			8	10	11	7							9		
3	19	Raith Rovers	3-0	7-1	3837	McIlroy(3), Kerr(2), McInally, O.G.	1	2	3	4	5	6	7	8		10	11				9						
4	26	ST. MIRREN	1-1	6-1	15838	Black(2), McIlroy(2), Beattie, Mason	1	2	3	4	5	6	7	8	9	10	11										
5	30	Hearts	0-0	0-2	17035		1	2	3	4		6	7	8	9	10				5	11						
6	2 Sep	RAITH ROVERS	2-0	4-1	7359	McInally(2), McIlroy, O.G.	1	2	3	4	5	6	7	8	9	10		11									

Scottish Cup

No.	Date	Opposition	H.T.	Res.	Att.	Goalscorers	McLaughlan	Richmond	Watson	Davidson	Toner	Beattie	McIlroy	Mason	Black	McInally	Muir	Brown	Hamilton	McGrory	Kerr	Yard	Sneddon	Forsyth	Murray	King	O'Connor
1		Bye																									
2	27 Jan	Brechin City	4-1	6-1	1834	Yard(4), Kerr, O.G.	1	2	3	4	5	6	11	10				7			9	8					
3	17 Feb	ROSS COUNTY	2-0	7-0	8568	Masson(3), Kerr, McIlroy, Richmond, Yard	1	2	3	4	5	6	11	10				7			9	8					
QF	10 Mar	RANGERS	1-1	2-4	35995*	Black, Kerr	1	2	3	4	5	6	11		8			7			9		10				

* Record attendance for Rugby Park, 36,500 tickets sold.

Work is underway to turn Rugby Park into a first class ground for their first class team. The new stand is being built on top of the old one.

SEASON 1962-63 Division One

No.	Date	Opposition	H.T.	Res.	Att.	Goalscorers	McLaughlan	Richmond	Watson	Davidson	McGrory	Beattie	Brown	Yard	Kerr	Sneddon	Muir	O'Connor	Black	McIlroy	King	McInally	Forsyth	Mason	Hamilton	Murray	Toner	McFadzean
1	22 Aug	PARTICK THISTLE	1-2	1-2	9522	Muir	1	2	3	4	5	6	7	8	9	10	11											
2	8 Sep	St. Mirren	4-1	4-2	11342	Black, Brown, O'Connor, Sneddon	1	2	3		5	6	7		9	10		4	8	11								
3	15	THIRD LANARK	1-1	2-2	8448	Kerr, O.G.	1	2	3		5	6	7		9	10		4	8	11								
4	22	Queen of the South	0-1	1-1	7600	Kerr	1		3		5	6	7		9	10		4	8	11	2							
5	29	AIRDRIEONIANS	5-0	8-0	7317	Kerr(5), O'Connor(2), Sneddon	1	2	3		5	6	7		9	10		4	8	11								
6	6 Oct	Celtic	0-0	1-1	36407	Kerr	1	2	3		5	6	7		9	10		4	8	11								
7	13	HEARTS	2-1	2-2	19057	Black, Sneddon	1		3		5	6	7		9	10		4	8	11	2							
8	20	Dundee	0-1	0-1	14863		1		3		5	6			9	10		4	7	11	2	8						
9	31	MOTHERWELL	2-1	7-1	5951	Blck, Brwn, Kerr, McIlry, Msn, O'Cnnr, Rchmnd		2	3		5	6	7		9			4	10	11			1	8				
10	3 Nov	Clyde	4-0	5-0	4559	Mason(3), Hamilton, Kerr		2	3		5	6	7		9			4	11				1	8	10			
11	10	RAITH ROVERS	1-1	3-1	7522	Beattie, Brown, Kerr	1	2	3		5	6	7		9			4	11					8	10			
12	17	Hibernian	0-0	2-0	3867	Kerr, Mason	1	2	3		5	6	7		9			4	11					8	10			
13	24	Dundee United	1-1	3-3	10934	Kerr(3)	1	2	3		5	6	7		9			4	11					8	10			
14	1 Dec	DUNFERMLINE	2-0	3-0	9055	Hamilton(2), Kerr	1	2	3		5	6	7		9			4	11					8	10			
15	8	Rangers	1-4	1-6	40319	Black	1	2	3		5	6	7		9	8		4	11						10			
16	15	FALKIRK	3-0	3-1	5707	Mason(2), McIlroy	1	2	3		5	6	7		9				10	11				8		4		
17	22	Aberdeen	0-0	0-1	11945		1	2	3		5	6	7		9				10	11				8		4		
18	29	Partick Thistle	1-2	2-3	12481	Black, O.G.	1	2	3		5	6	7					11	9					8	10	4		
19	1 Jan	ST. MIRREN	2-1	2-1	7980	Hamilton, Mason	1	2	3		5	6			9			4	11	7				8	10			
20	2	Third Lanark	0-0	1-0	7493	Black	1	2	3		5	6			9			4	11	7				8	10			
21	5	QUEEN OF THE SOUTH	5-0	7-0	7718	Hamilton(2), Kerr(2), Black, McIlroy, Mason	1	2	3		5	6			9			4	11	7				8	10			
22	9 Mar	CLYDE	0-1	3-2	7350	Black, Mason, Sneddon	1	2	3		5	6	7			10		4	9	11				8				
23	16	Raith Rovers	1-0	4-1	1851	Kerr(3), O'Connor	1	2	3		5	6	7		9	10		4	11			8						
24	18	Hearts	2-1	3-2	13591	Kerr(2), O.G.	1	2	3		5	6	7		9	10			11			8				4		
25	23	HIBERNIAN	1-0	2-0	7692	Black, Mason	1	2	3		5	6	7		9	10		4	11					8				
26	27	CELTIC	2-0	6-0	16002	Black(2), Kerr(2), Mason, Sneddon		2	3		5	6	7		9	10			11				1	8		4		
27	6 Apr	Dunfermline	0-1	1-1	5336	Mason			3		5	6	7	9		10		4	11		2		1	8				
28	13	Motherwell	0-2	1-2	4553	Black		2	3		5	6	7	9		10		4	11				1	8				
29	20	Falkirk	3-0	5-0	4492	McIlroy(2), Yard(2), Black		2	3		5	6	7	9		10		4	8	11			1					
30	24	Aidrieonians	0-0	3-0	2600	Yard(2), Black		2	3		5	6	7	9		10			8	11			1			4		
31	27	ABERDEEN	1-1	2-2	6436	Yard(2)		2	3		5	6	7	9		10		4	8	11			1					
32	1 May	DUNDEE UNITED	1-0	2-2	4505	McIlroy, O.G.		2	3		5	6	7	9		10			8	11			1			4		
33	11	DUNDEE	1-0	1-0	6147	McInally		2	3		5	6		9					7	11		8	1		10	4		
34	13	RANGERS	0-0	1-0	12801	Yard		2	3		5	6	7	9					10	11		8	1			4		
						Apps.	23	30	34	1	34	34	29	9	24	20	1	25	33	20	4	5	11	17	11	9		
						Goals		1				1	3	7	25	5	1	5	14	6		1		13	6			

Pos	P.	W.	D.	L.	F.	A.	Pts.
2nd	34	20	8	6	92	40	48

League Cup Section 3

Pos	P.	W.	D.	L.	F.	A.	Pts.
1st	6	5	1	0	20	8	11

No.	Date	Opposition	H.T.	Res.	Att.	Goalscorers	McLaughlan	Richmond	Watson	Davidson	McGrory	Beattie	Brown	Yard	Kerr	Sneddon	Muir	O'Connor	Black	McIlroy	King	McInally	Forsyth	Mason	Hamilton	Murray	Toner	McFadzean
1	11 Aug	AIRDRIEONIANS	1-0	4-0	9797	Kerr(2), Davidson, McInally	1	2	3	4		6	7		9	10	11					8					5	
2	15	Dunfermline	0-2	3-3	7404	Brown(2), Beattie	1	2	3	4	5	6	7		9	10	11					8						
3	18	Raith Rovers	1-2	3-2	4870	Brown, Kerr, Sneddon	1	2	3	4	5	6	7	8	9	10				11								
4	25	Airdrieonians	2-0	4-0	3721	Kerr(2), Black, Brown	1	2	3	4	5	6	7		9	10			8	11								
5	29	DUNFERMLINE	2-2	3-2	10901	Black, Kerr, McIlroy	1	2	3		5	6	7		9	10		4	8	11								
6	1 Sep	RAITH ROVERS	2-1	3-1	6540	Kerr, McIlroy, O.G.	1	2	3		5	6	7		9	10		4	8	11								
QF	12	Partick Thistle	1-0	2-1	21404	Brown, McIlroy	1	2	3		5	6	7		9	10		4	8	11								
QF	19	PARTICK THIS. (Agg. 5-2)	1-0	3-1	14920	Kerr(2), Black	1	2	3		5	6	7		9	10		4	8	11								
SF	10 Oct	Rangers*	2-2	3-2	76043	Black, Kerr, McIlroy	1	2	3		5	6	7		9	10		4	8	11								
F	27	Hearts*	0-1	0-1	51280		1	2	3		5	6	7		9			4	8	11		10						

* Hampden

Scottish Cup

No.	Date	Opposition	H.T.	Res.	Att.	Goalscorers	McLaughlan	Richmond	Watson	Davidson	McGrory	Beattie	Brown	Yard	Kerr	Sneddon	Muir	O'Connor	Black	McIlroy	King	McInally	Forsyth	Mason	Hamilton	Murray	Toner	McFadzean
1		Bye																										
2	26 Jan	QUEEN OF THE SOUTH	0-0	0-0	10812		1	2	3		5	6			9			4	11	7				8	10			
3	11 Mar	Queen of the South	0-0	0-1	10370		1	2	3		5	6	7		9	10			11			8				4		

U.S. Tournament

Pos	P.	W.	D.	L.	F.	A.	Pts.
3rd	6	2	3	1	17	13	7

No.	Date	Opposition	H.T.	Res.	Att.	Goalscorers	McLaughlan	Richmond	Watson	Davidson	McGrory	Beattie	Brown	Yard	Kerr	Sneddon	Muir	O'Connor	Black	McIlroy	King	McInally	Forsyth	Mason	Hamilton	Murray	Toner	McFadzean
1	30 May	West Ham United	1-1	3-3	14532	Black, Richmond, Yard		2	3		5	6		9		10			11	7		8	1			4		
2	2 Jun	Preussen Munster*	2-1	5-2	6000	Black(2), McFadzean, McInally, Murray		2	3		5	6	7	9					11			8	1			4		10
3	5	Oro (Mexico)	0-1	3-3	7138	McFadzean(2), Black		2	3		5	6	7	9					11			8	1			4		10
4	12	Valenciennes+	0-0	1-2	7000	Yard		2	3		5	6	7	9					11			8	1			4		10
5	19	Mantova	2-0	2-2	7473	Black, McFadzean			3		5	6	7	9					11		2	8	1			4		10
6	23	Recife	1-0	3-1	5826	Black, Murray, O'Connor			3			5		9		11		6	7		2	8	1			4		10

* Played at Chicopee, Massachussetts + Played at Chicago All other games - New York

To quote F.D.Roosevelt: "A day that will live in infamy". The programme for the notorious League Cup Final when referee 'Tiny' Wharton disallowed what looked a perfectly good goal from Killie's Frank Beattie, allowing Hearts to win the trophy.

SEASON 1963-64 Division One

No.	Date	Opposition	H.T.	Res.	Att.	Goalscorers	Forsyth	King	Richmond	Murray	McGrory	O'Connor	Brown	McFadzean	Yard	Black	McIlroy	Watson	Beattie	Mason	Sneddon	McInally	Layburn	Hamilton	McLaughlan	Dickson	McLean
1	21 Aug	East Stirling	0-0	2-0	4656	Brown, McIlroy	1	2	3	4	5	6	7	8	9	10	11										
2	7 Sep	ST. MIRREN	0-0	2-0	7247	Black(2)	1	2		4	5		7			9	11	3	6	8	10						
3	14	Airdrieonians	3-1	5-4	3607	McIlroy(2), Murray, O'Connor, Sneddon	1	2		4	5	7	8			9	11	3	6		10						
4	21	DUNFERMLINE	0-0	0-3	8285		1	2		4	5	7				9	11	3	6		10	8					
5	28	Hibernian	0-0	2-0	11030	Murray(2)	1	2		9	5	4	7				11	3	6		10	8					
6	5 Oct	PARTICK THISTLE	3-0	3-0	6470	King, McIlroy, McInally	1	2		9	5	4	7				11	3	6		10	8					
7	12	Falkirk	0-1	1-1	4843	McIlroy	1	2		9	5	4	7				11	3	6		10	8					
8	19	ABERDEEN	1-0	2-0	5685	McIlroy, Murray	1	2		9	5	4	7				11	3	6		10	8					
9	26	HEARTS	2-1	3-1	8469	McInally(2), McIlroy	1	2		9	5	4	7				11		6		10	8	3				
10	2 Nov	Queen of the South	1-0	4-0	5089	McIlroy(2), Murray, Brown	1	2		9	5	4	7				11	3	6		10	8					
11	9	DUNDEE UNITED	1-0	2-0	7214	McIlroy, Sneddon	1	2		9	5	4	7				11	3	6		10	8					
12	16	RANGERS	0-0	1-1	27624	McIlroy	1	2			5	4		9		7	11	3	6		10	8					
13	23	Celtic	0-2	0-5	27548		1	2			5	4	7	9			11	3	6		10	8					
14	30	MOTHERWELL	3-0	5-2	6679	Murray(2), McIlroy, McInally, Sneddon	1	2		9	5	4	7				11	3	6		10	8					
15	7 Dec	DUNDEE	1-1	1-1	10166	Murray	1	2		9	5	4	7				11	3	6		10	8					
16	14	St. Johnstone	1-0	2-0	6126	Brown, Murray	1	2		9	5	4	7				11	3	6		10	8					
17	21	Third Lanark	0-1	2-1	2909	McInally(2)	1	2		9	5	4	7				11	3	6		10	8					
18	28	EAST STIRLING	2-0	4-1	7566	Brown, McIlroy, McInally, Mason	1	2		9	5	4	7				11	3	6	10		8					
19	1 Jan	St. Mirren	1-0	3-1	10225	McIlroy, Mason, Murray	1	2		9	5	4	7				11	3	6	10		8					
20	2	AIRDRIEONIANS	3-1	4-1	10642	McInally(2), Murray, Sneddon	1	2		9	5	4	7				11	3	6		10	8					
21	4	Dunfermline	1-2	3-2	7663	McIlroy(3)	1	2		9	5	4	7				11	3	6		10	8					
22	18	HIBERNIAN	1-1	2-1	9554	King, Murray	1	2		9	5	4	7				11	3	6		10	8					
23	1 Feb	Partick Thistle	0-2	0-2	18165		1	2		9	5	4	7				11	3	6		10	8					
24	8	FALKIRK	6-0	9-2	7758	McIlroy(4), McInally,(3), Beattie, Brown	1			9	5		7	4			11	3	6		10	8	2				
25	19	Aberdeen	0-0	0-0	6165		1	2		9	5	4	7	8			11	3	6		10						
26	22	Hearts	0-0	1-1	13639	King	1	2		9	5		7	4			11	3	6		10			8			
27	29	QUEEN OF THE SOUTH	2-1	2-1	8340	McIlroy(2)	1	2		9	5		7	4			11	3	6		10			8			
28	11 Mar	Dundee United	1-2	1-2	7916	McIlroy	1	2		9	5		7	4			11	3	6		10	8					
29	14	Rangers	0-2	0-2	45870		1	2			5		7	4		9	11	3	6		10	8					
30	21	CELTIC	1-0	4-0	11459	McInally(2), Murray(2)	1	2		9	5			4		7	11	3	6		10	8					
31	1 Apr	Motherwell	0-0	0-2	3663		1	2		9	5		7	4			11		6		10	8	3				
32	4	Dundee	1-1	1-2	11796	McInally	1	2		9	5		7	4			11		6		10	8	3				
33	18	ST. JOHNSTONE	2-0	4-1	4321	Hamilton(3), McInally	1				5		7	4			11	3	6		10	8	2	9			
34	25	THIRD LANARK	1-0	2-0	3672	Hamilton(2)	1	2			5		7	4			11	3	6	8	10			9			
						Apps.	34	32	1	29	34	23	31	14	1	7	34	30	33	4	31	27	5	4			
						Goals		3		14		1	5			2	24		1	2	4	16		5			

Pos	P.	W.	D.	L.	F.	A.	Pts.
2nd	34	22	5	7	77	40	49

League Cup Section 3

Pos	P.	W.	D.	L.	F.	A.	Pts.
2nd	6	2	2	2	9	9	6

No.	Date	Opposition	H.T.	Res.	Att.	Goalscorers	Forsyth	King	Richmond	Murray	McGrory	O'Connor	Brown	McFadzean	Yard	Black	McIlroy	Watson	Beattie	Mason	Sneddon	McInally	Layburn	Hamilton	McLaughlan	Dickson	McLean
1	10 Aug	Queen of the South	0-0	4-1	7787	McInally(3), Hamilton	1	2		4	5	6	7		9	11		3				8		10			
2	14	CELTIC	0-0	0-0	20246		1	2		4	5	6	7		9	11		3				8		10			
3	17	RANGERS	1-1	1-4	34246	McInally	1	2	3	4	5	6	7	10		11						8		9			
4	24	QUEEN OF THE SOUTH	1-0	2-0	6851	Sneddon(2)	1	2	3	4	5		7		9	10	11		6		8						
5	28	Celtic	0-1	0-2	11104		1	2	3	4	5		7	10	9	11			6		8						
6	31	Rangers	0-1	2-2	34570	Beattie, Brown	1	2	3	4	5		7	9		11			6	8	10						

Scottish Cup

No.	Date	Opposition	H.T.	Res.	Att.	Goalscorers	Forsyth	King	Richmond	Murray	McGrory	O'Connor	Brown	McFadzean	Yard	Black	McIlroy	Watson	Beattie	Mason	Sneddon	McInally	Layburn	Hamilton	McLaughlan	Dickson	McLean
1	11 Jan	GALA FAIRYDEAN	1-0	2-1	8717	McInally, Murray	1	2		9	5	4	7				11	3	6		10	8					
2	25	Hamilton A.	1-1	3-1	9378	McIlroy(2), O.G.	1	2		9	5	4	7				11	3	6		10	8					
3	15 Feb	ALBION ROVERS	1-0	2-0	10238	Beattie, Murray	1	2		9	5		7	4			11	3	6		10	8					
QF	7 Mar	Falkirk	1-1	2-1	14000	McIlroy(2)	1	2		9	5		7	4			11	3	6		10	8	3				
SF	28	Dundee*	0-1	0-4	32664		1	2		9	5			4		7	11		6		10	8					

* Ibrox

Summer Cup

Pos	P.	W.	D.	L.	F.	A.	Pts.
1st	6	5	1	0	19	5	11

No.	Date	Opposition	H.T.	Res.	Att.	Goalscorers	Forsyth	King	Richmond	Murray	McGrory	O'Connor	Brown	McFadzean	Yard	Black	McIlroy	Watson	Beattie	Mason	Sneddon	McInally	Layburn	Hamilton	McLaughlan	Dickson	McLean
1	2 May	MOTHERWELL	1-1	2-2	4519	Hamilton, Sneddon	1	2			5		7	4			11	3	6	8	10			9			
2	6	Queen of the South	0-1	3-1	2466	McIlroy(2), Hamilton		2			5		7	4			11	3	6		10	8		9	1		
3	9	AIRDRIEONIANS	1-0	4-0	4120	McIlroy(2), Hamilton, McFadzean		2			5		7	4			11	3	6		10	8		9	1		
4	13	Motherwell	2-1	4-1	3811	Hamilton(3), Sneddon		2			5		7	4			11	3	6		10	8		9	1		
5	15	QUEEN OF THE SOUTH	1-0	4-0	4310	Hamilton(2), McIlroy, Sneddon		2			5		7	4			11	3	6		10	8		9	1		
6	20	Airdrieonians	2-0	2-1	1034	Mason(2)				4			7	5			11	3	6	9	10	8			1	2	
SF	27	HIBERNIAN	3-3	4-3	8716	Hamilton, McIlroy, McInally, O.G.		2			5			4			11	3	6		10	8		9	1		7
SF	30	Hibernian (Agg. 4-6)	0-2	0-3	17273			2		4	5						11	3	6		10	8		9	1		7

More Cup heartbreak. Kilmarnock were favourites to win this Scottish Cup Semi-Final clash with Dundee but turned in a disappointing performance in a 4-0 defeat.

SEASON 1964-65 Division One

No.	Date	Opposition	H.T.	Res.	Att.	Goalscorers	Forsyth	King	Watson	O'Connor	McGrory	Beattie	Murray	McInally	Hamilton	Sneddon	McIlroy	McFadzean	McLean	Ferguson	Brown	Malone	Mason	Dickson	Black	McDonald	Shepherd
1	19 Aug	THIRD LANARK	0-0	3-1	5197	Watson, O'Connor, Hamilton		2	3	4	5	6	7	8	9	10	11										
2	5 Sep	St. Mirren	0-0	2-0	4636	McIlroy, Hamilton	1	2	3		5	6	4	8	9	11	7	10									
3	12	AIRDRIEONIANS	1-0	2-0	5299	Hamilton, McInally	1	2	3		5	6	4	8	9	11	7	10									
4	19	St. Johnstone	0-0	1-0	4829	McInally	1	2	3		5	6	4	8	9	11	7	10									
5	26	DUNFERMLINE	0-0	1-0	10755	Hamilton	1	2			5	6	4	8	9	10	11	3	7								
6	3 Oct	Hibernian	1-0	2-1	15471	Hamilton(2)		2	3		5	6	4	8	9	11	7	10		1							
7	10	PARTICK THISTLE	0-0	0-0	8379		1		3		5	6	4	8	9	10	11	2	7								
8	17	Dundee	0-1	3-1	13171	Murray, Sneddon, McInally	1	2	3		5	6	4	8	9	11	7	10									
9	28	CELTIC	3-0	5-2	19122	McInally(2), McFadzean(2), Hamilton	1	2	3		5	6	4	8	9	11	7	10									
10	31	Dundee United	0-0	1-0	8567	McInally	1	2	3		5	6	4	8	9	11	7	10									
11	7 Nov	MOTHERWELL	1-0	1-1	9698	Hamilton	1	2	3		5	6	4	8	9	11	7	10									
12	14	RANGERS	0-0	1-1	32021	Beattie	1	2	3		5	6	4	8	9	11		10	7								
13	21	Aberdeen	0-1	1-1	9101	McInally	1	2	3		5	6	4	8	9	11		10	7								
14	28	Clyde	2-0	2-1	4863	McFadzean, McInally	1	2	3		5	6	4	8	9	11	7	10									
15	5 Dec	FALKIRK	2-0	2-0	5535	McInally, Sneddon	1	2	3			6	4	8	9	10	11	5	7								
16	12	Morton	0-2	1-5	10306	Hamilton	1	2	3			6	4	8	9	10	11	5			7						
17	19	HEARTS	2-1	3-1	18285	McIlroy, Sneddon, Hamilton	1	2	3		5	6	4		9	10	11	8	7								
18	26	Third Lanark	2-0	4-0	2549	McLean(2), McInally, McIlroy	1	2	3		5		4	8	9	10	11	6	7								
19	1 Jan	ST. MIRREN	2-0	4-0	12039	Hamilton(2), Sneddon, Murray	1	2	3		5	6	4	8	9	10	11		7								
20	2	Airdrieonians	0-0	1-2	7808	Hamilton	1	2	3		5	6	4	8	9	10		11	7								
21	9	ST. JOHNSTONE	0-0	0-0	6694		1	2	3		5	6	4	8	9	11			7			10					
22	16	Dunfermline	0-0	0-1	9766		1	2	3		5	6	4	8	9	10	11		7								
23	30	Partick Thistle	0-1	0-1	6560		1	2	3		5	6	4	7		10	11	8					9				
24	13 Feb	DUNDEE	1-1	1-4	7158	Hamilton	1	2	3		5	6	4	8	9	10	11		7								
25	16	HIBERNIAN	1-1	4-3	10535	Black(2), Murray, King	1	2			5	6	4	8	9	10			7					3	11		
26	27	Celtic	0-1	0-2	21875		1	2	3		5	6	4	8	9	11	7	10									
27	10 Mar	DUNDEE UNITED	1-1	4-2	5756	Black(2), McIlroy, McLean	1	2	3		5		4	8			11	6	7			10			9		
28	13	Motherwell	0-0	2-0	4096	McIlroy, Mason		2			5		4	8			11	6	7	1			10	3	9		
29	20	Rangers	0-0	1-1	30574	Mason		2			5	6	4	8			11	3	7	1			10		9		
30	27	ABERDEEN	2-0	2-1	5193	Murray, McIlroy		2			5	6	4		10		11	3	7	1			8		9		
31	3 Apr	CLYDE	2-0	2-1	5816	McInally, Hamilton		2	3		5	6	4	7	10		11	8		1					9		
32	7	Falkirk	1-0	1-0	2569	McIlroy		2	3		5	6	4	7	10		11	8		1					9		
33	17	MORTON	0-0	3-0	10605	Black(2), McIlroy		2	3		5	6	4	8		10	11		7	1					9		
34	24	Hearts	2-0	2-0	36346	Sneddon, McIlroy		2	3		5	6	4	8		10	11		7	1					9		
						Apps.	26	33	29	1	32	31	34	32	28	28	29	26	19	8	1	2	4	2	9		
						Goals		1	1	1		1	4	11	15	5	9	3	3				2		6		

Pos	P.	W.	D.	L.	F.	A.	Pts.
1st	34	22	6	6	62	33	50

League Cup Section 3

Pos	P.	W.	D.	L.	F.	A.	Pts.
2nd	6	3	2	1	9	5	8

No.	Date	Opposition	H.T.	Res.	Att.	Goalscorers	Forsyth	King	Watson	O'Connor	McGrory	Beattie	Murray	McInally	Hamilton	Sneddon	McIlroy	McFadzean	McLean	Ferguson	Brown	Malone	Mason	Dickson	Black	McDonald	Shepherd
1	8 Aug	HEARTS	0-0	1-1	8832	McIlroy	1	2	3	4	5	6	7	8	9	10	11										
2	12	Partick Thistle	0-0	0-0	7767		1	2	3	4	5	6	7	9		10	11				8						
3	15	Celtic	0-1	1-4	22017	Watson	1	2	3	4	5	6	7	9		10	11				8						
4	22	Hearts	0-0	1-0	10391	McInally	1	2	3	4	5	6	7	8	9	10	11										
5	26	PARTICK THISTLE	2-0	4-0	6344	Hamilton(2), Murray, McInally	1	2	3	4	5	6	7	8	9	10	11										
6	29	CELTIC	0-0	2-0	10834	Hamilton, McIlroy	1	2	3	4	5	6	7	8	9	10	11										

Scottish Cup

No.	Date	Opposition	H.T.	Res.	Att.	Goalscorers	Forsyth	King	Watson	O'Connor	McGrory	Beattie	Murray	McInally	Hamilton	Sneddon	McIlroy	McFadzean	McLean	Ferguson	Brown	Malone	Mason	Dickson	Black	McDonald	Shepherd
1	6 Feb	COWDENBEATH	1-0	5-0	6276	McInally(3), McLean(2)	1	2	3		5	6	4	8	9	10	11		7								
2	20	East Fife	0-0	0-0	9003		1	2			5	6	4	8	9	10			7					3	11		
2R	24	EAST FIFE	1-0	3-0	10201	McInally(2), Hamilton	1	2			5	6	4	8	9	10	11		7					3			
QF	6 Mar	Celtic	0-1	2-3	47000	McInally(2)	1	2	3		5	6	4	8	9		11	10			7						

Inter-Cities Fairs Cup

No.	Date	Opposition	H.T.	Res.	Att.	Goalscorers	Forsyth	King	Watson	O'Connor	McGrory	Beattie	Murray	McInally	Hamilton	Sneddon	McIlroy	McFadzean	McLean	Ferguson	Brown	Malone	Mason	Dickson	Black	McDonald	Shepherd
1	2 Sep	Eintracht F.	0-0	0-3	35000		1	2	3		5	6	7	8		10	11	4							9		
1	22	EINTRACHT F. (Agg. 5-4)	2-1	5-1	14930	Hamilton(2), McIlroy, McFadzean, McInally	1	2			5	6	4	8	9	10	11	3	7								
2	11 Nov	EVERTON	0-0	0-2	23561		1	2	3		5	6	4		9	11	7	10							8		
2	23	Everton (Agg. 1-6)	1-2	1-4	30730	McIlroy	1	2	3	6	5		4	8	9	11	7	10									

Summer Cup

Pos	P.	W.	D.	L.	F.	A.	Pts.
2nd	6	4	1	1	17	9	9

No.	Date	Opposition	H.T.	Res.	Att.	Goalscorers	Forsyth	King	Watson	O'Connor	McGrory	Beattie	Murray	McInally	Hamilton	Sneddon	McIlroy	McFadzean	McLean	Ferguson	Brown	Malone	Mason	Dickson	Black	McDonald	Shepherd
1	1 Mar	AIRDRIEONIANS	2-0	3-1	3904	Sneddon, McInally, Murray		2	3		5	6	4	8		10	11		7	1					9		
2	5	Third Lanark	0-0	3-0	667	Black(2), McIlroy		2	3		5	6	4	8		10	11		7	1					9		
3	8	MOTHERWELL	0-0	1-1	5061	McInally		2	3		5	6	4	8		10	11		7	1					9		
4	12	Airdrieonians	0-0	4-2	861	McIlroy, McIlroy, Sneddon, Murray		2	3		5		4	8		10	11	6	7	1			9				
5	15	THIRD LANARK	3-1	6-2	3718	McIlroy(2), Murray(2), Black, McInally		2	3		5		4	8		10	11	6	7	1					9		
6	19	Motherwell	0-1	0-3	6519			2			5	6	4	8		10	11	3	7	1			9				

New York Int. Tourn.

Pos	P.	W.	D.	L.	F.	A.	Pts.
4th	6	1	1	4	5	11	3

No.	Date	Opposition	H.T.	Res.	Att.	Goalscorers	Forsyth	King	Watson	O'Connor	McGrory	Beattie	Murray	McInally	Hamilton	Sneddon	McIlroy	McFadzean	McLean	Ferguson	Brown	Malone	Mason	Dickson	Black	McDonald	Shepherd
1	4 Jul	Ferencvaros	1-0	1-2	6000	O.G.		2	3			5	4		9	10	11	6	7	1					8		
2	7	West Bromwich Albion	1-0	2-0	5000	Black, Hamilton		2				5	4		9	10	11	6	7	1				3	8		
3	11	Polonia Bytom	1-1	1-1	5000	Sneddon		2				5	4		9	11		6	7	1			10	3	8		
4	18	West Bromwich Albion	0-2	0-2	4000			2	3	6		5	4		9	10	11	8	7	1							
5	21	Polonia Bytom	0-1	0-2	4000			2	3	6		5	4		9	10	11	8	7	1							
6	25	Ferencvaros	1-1	1-4	5000	McIlroy		2		10		5					11	8	7	1		9		3		4	6

All the years of second prizes pale into insignificance as Kilmarnock finally land the big one - the Scottish Leauge Championship comes to Ayrshire after a stunning 2-0 win over erstwhile leaders Hearts. The reserves look happy too, also on display the Reserve League Cup.

Back: Smillie, Shepherd, Malone, Forsyth, T.Brown, McDonald, O'Connor.
Middle: McNeill (2nd XI Manager), H.Brown, Bitten, Murray, McGrory, Ferguson, McFadzean, McInally, Dickson, Layburn, Murdoch (Assistant Trainer)
Front: Waddell (Manager), McLean, Mason, Black, Watson, Beattie (Capt), King, Sneddon, Hamilton, McIlroy, McCrae (Trainer)

SEASON 1965-66 Division One

No.	Date	Opposition	H.T.	Res.	Att.	Goalscorers	Ferguson	King	Watson	Murray	Beattie	McFadzean	McLean	Hamilton	Black	Sneddon	McIlroy	McInally	McGrory	O'Connor	Malone	Dickson	Mason	Brown	Queen	Layburn	Bertelsen
1	25 Aug	PARTICK THISTLE	0-0	2-1	7806	McIlroy(2)	1	2	3	4	5	6	7	8	9	10	11										
2	11 Sep	Hibernian	2-0	3-3	13385	McIlroy(3)	1	2	3	4	5	6	7		9	10	11	8									
3	18	ST. MIRREN	2-0	3-1	6538	McFadzean, McLean, Hamilton	1	2	3	4	6	10	7	9			11	8	5								
4	25	Dunfermline	0-0	0-1	7104		1	2	3		6		7	9		10	11	8	5	4							
5	2 Oct	HAMILTON A.	2-1	3-1	5155	McIlroy, McLean, King	1	2	3		6		7	10	9		11		5	4	8						
6	9	Stirling Albion	1-1	3-2	3985	Hamilton(2), McIlroy	1	2		4	6	10	7	9			11	8	5			3					
7	16	DUNDEE	2-2	5-3	7829	Hamilton(2), McFadzean(2), McLean	1	2		4	6	10	7	9			11	8	5			3					
8	23	Morton	2-0	4-1	8458	McIlroy(3), Hamilton	1	2		4	6	10	7	9			11	8	5			3					
9	30	CLYDE	0-0	1-2	6362	Hamilton	1	2		4	6	10	7	9			11	8	5			3					
10	6 Nov	Aberdeen	0-0	0-1	8907		1	2	3	4	6		7	9	8	10	11		5								
11	13	MOTHERWELL	1-0	5-0	6689	McIlroy(2), McInally, Murray, Hamilton	1	2	3	4		6	7	9		10	11	8	5								
12	20	Rangers	0-3	0-5	33225		1	2		4			7	9		10	11	8	5	6		3					
13	27	Celtic	0-0	1-2	21131	McIlroy	1	2	3	4		6	7	9			11	8	5	10							
14	11 Dec	Falkirk	1-1	2-3	2617	McLean, McFadzean	1	2		4		6	7				11	8	5	10		3	9				
15	18	Dundee United	0-0	0-0	7170		1	2		4	6	10					11	8	5			3	9	7			
16	25	ST. JOHNSTONE	2-0	3-1	4493	McLean, McIlroy, Hamilton	1	2			6	4	7	9			11	8	5			3	10				
17	1 Jan	St. Mirren	5-1	7-4	3906	McIlroy(2),McInally(2),Mason,McLean,Murry	1		3	4	6	10	7				11	8	5			2	9				
18	3	HIBERNIAN	1-0	1-0	11298	Mason	1	2		4	6		7			10	11	8	5			3	9				
19	8	Partick Thistle	0-1	0-1	6310		1	2	3	4	6	10	7				11	8	5				9				
20	15	DUNFERMLINE	0-0	1-0	8526	McInally	1	2	3	4	6		7			10	11	8	5				9				
21	22	Hamilton A.	2-0	4-1	2573	Queen(2), Mason, McInally	1	2	3	4	6		7				11	8	5				9		10		
22	29	STIRLING ALBION	1-0	2-1	5651	Queen, O.G.	1	2	3	4	6		7				11	8	5				9		10		
23	12 Feb	Dundee	2-0	2-0	8782	Black(2)	1	2	3	4	6		7		9		11	8	5						10		
24	26	Clyde	1-1	4-1	5137	Queen, Murray, Black, McLean	1	2	3	4	6		7		9		11	8	5						10		
25	28	MORTON	2-0	4-0	7148	McInally(2), Queen, Murray	1	2		4	6		7		9	11		8	5						10	3	
26	9 Mar	ABERDEEN	0-0	1-3	5592	McLean	1	2		4	6	3	7		11			8	5						10		9
27	12	Motherwell	2-0	3-0	4383	McInally(2), McIlroy	1	2		4	6	3	7				11	8	5						10		9
28	19	RANGERS	0-0	1-1	25372	McLean	1	2		4	5	3	7				11	8		6					10		9
29	29	CELTIC	0-2	0-2	25035		1	2		4	5	3	7		9		11	8		6					10		
30	4 Apr	HEARTS	0-2	2-2	5026	McInally, Bertelsen	1	2		4	6	3	7				11	8	5						10		9
31	9	Hearts	1-2	3-2	6209	McIlroy(2), Bertelsen	1	2	3	4	6		7				11	8	5						10		9
32	16	FALKIRK	1-0	1-0	3773	McIlroy	1	2	3	4	6		7				11	8	5						10		9
33	23	DUNDEE UNITED	0-0	1-0	5711	Queen	1	2	3	4	6		7				11	8	5						10		9
34	30	St. Johnstone	0-0	1-1	2441	Bertelsen	1	2	3	4	6		7				11	8	5						10		9
						Apps.	34	33	19	31	30	19	33	13	9	9	32	31	30	7	1	10	9	1	14	1	8
						Goals		1		4		4	9	9	3		20	10					3		6		3

Pos	P.	W.	D.	L.	F.	A.	Pts.
3rd	34	20	5	9	73	46	45

League Cup Section 3

Pos	P.	W.	D.	L.	F.	A.	Pts.
1st	6	5	0	1	11	3	10

No.	Date	Opposition	H.T.	Res.	Att.	Goalscorers	Ferguson	King	Watson	Murray	Beattie	McFadzean	McLean	Hamilton	Black	Sneddon	McIlroy	McInally	McGrory	O'Connor	Malone	Dickson	Mason	Brown	Queen	Layburn	Bertelsen
1	14 Aug	St. Johnstone	1-0	1-0	5810	McIlroy	1	2	3	4	5	6	7		9	10	11	8									
2	18	PARTICK THISTLE	1-0	2-0	9756	McIroy, Black	1	2	3	4	5	6	7		9	10	11	8									
3	21	Dunfermline	0-1	3-1	9073	McLean, Sneddon, McIlroy	1	2	3	4	5	6	7		9	10	11	8									
4	28	ST. JOHNSTONE	0-0	3-0	7309	Black(2), Sneddon	1	2	3	4	5	6	7		9	10	11	8									
5	1 Sep	Partick Thistle	1-1	2-1	3926	McIlroy, McInally	1	2	3	4	5	6			9	10	11	8						7			
6	4	DUNFERMLINE	0-0	0-1	6858		1	2	3	4	5	6			9	10	11	8						7			
QF	15	AYR UNITED	0-0	2-0	10728	McIlroy, Black	1	2	3	4	6	8	7		9	10	11		5								
QF	22	Ayr United (Agg: 4-2)	1-2	2-2	8495	Murray, McIlroy	1	2	3	4	6	8	7	9		10	11		5								
SF	6 Oct	Rangers *	1-3	4-6	54702	McLean(3), McInally	1	2	3	4	6		7	10	9		11	8	5								

* Hampden

Scottish Cup

No.	Date	Opposition	H.T.	Res.	Att.	Goalscorers	Ferguson	King	Watson	Murray	Beattie	McFadzean	McLean	Hamilton	Black	Sneddon	McIlroy	McInally	McGrory	O'Connor	Malone	Dickson	Mason	Brown	Queen	Layburn	Bertelsen
1	5 Feb	Morton	0-1	1-1	9735	Queen	1	2	3	4	6		7				11	8	5				9		10		
1R	9	MORTON	2-0	3-0	11109	Beattie, Black, Queen	1	2	3	4	6		7		9		11	8	5						10		
2	21	MOTHERWELL	2-0	5-0	13209	McIlroy, Queen, Black, McInally, O.G.	1	2	3	4	6		7		9		11	8	5						10		
QR	5 Mar	Dunfermline	1-0	1-2	19363	McInally	1	2		4	6	3	7		9	11		8	5						10		

European Champions Cup

No.	Date	Opposition	H.T.	Res.	Att.	Goalscorers	Ferguson	King	Watson	Murray	Beattie	McFadzean	McLean	Hamilton	Black	Sneddon	McIlroy	McInally	McGrory	O'Connor	Malone	Dickson	Mason	Brown	Queen	Layburn	Bertelsen
1	8 Sep	17 Nentori	0-0	0-0	30000		1	2	3	4	5	6	7		9	10	11	8									
1	29	17 NENTORI (Agg: 1-0)	0-0	1-0	15717	Black	1	2	3		5	6	7	10	9		11	8		4							
2	17 Nov	REAL MADRID	1-1	2-2	24325	McLean, McInally	1	2	3	5		6	7	9		10	11	8		4							
2	1 Dec	Real Madrid (Agg: 3-7)	1-3	1-5	35000	McIlroy	1	2	3	5		6	7	9		10	11	8		4							

Kilmarnock and Ayr United prior to the second leg of the Ayrshire Cup Final in 1966 which Killie won 3-0 to regain the trophy from their county rivals who had just won promotion to Division One. Killie players are in the plain jerseys. Back: Watson, Ferguson (lighter jersey), Beattie. Middle: Murray, McInally, McGrory, Queen. Front: King, McLean, McIlroy, Mason.

SEASON 1966-67 Division One

No.	Date	Opposition	H.T.	Res.	Att.	Goalscorers	Dick	King	M.Watson	O'Connor	McGrory	Beattie	C.Watson	McFadzean	Bertelsen	Queen	McIlroy	Dickson	McInally	Ferguson	Murray	McLean	Sneddon	Brown	Rodman	Morrison
1	10 Sep	St. Mirren	0-1	2-3	3769	Bertelsen, McFadzean	1	2	3	4	5	6	7	8	9	10	11									
2	17	AYR UNITED	1-0	1-0	9094	C.Watson	1	2		4	5	6	7		9	10	11	3	8							
3	24	Clyde	2-1	3-1	2823	McIlroy, McInally, C.Watson		2		4	5	6	7	12		10"	11	3	8	1	9					
4	1 Oct	STIRLING ALBION	0-0	2-1	3689	McInally (2)		2		4	5	6"	10	12			11	3	8	1	9	7				
5	8	Dundee	1-0	1-1	9082	C. Watson		2		4	5	6	9	3		10	11		8	1		7				
6	15	HIBERNIAN	1-0	2-1	8341	Bertelsen, C.Watson		2		4	5	6	11	3	9	10			8	1		7				
7	29	AIRDRIEONIANS	0-0	1-0	5881	Bertelsen		2		4	5	6	11"	3	9	10		12	8	1		7				
8	5 Nov	PARTICK THISTLE	0-0	0-0	5132			2		4	5	6	11		9			3	8	1		7	10			
9	9	Rangers	0-1	0-3	28839			2	3	4	5		12		9	10"		6	8	1		7		11		
10	12	Dundee United	1-1	1-1	6278	O'Connor		2		4	5	6	10	3	9				8	1		7		11		
11	19	FALKIRK	1-0	3-0	4601	McInally, McLean, Bertelsen		2		4	5	6	10	3	9"			12	8	1		7		11		
12	26	St. Johnstone	3-0	3-1	3849	Murray(2), McIlroy		2		4	5	6	10	3			11	12	8	1	9	7"				
13	3 Dec	CELTIC	0-0	0-0	27136			2		4	5	6	10	3			11		8	1	9	7				
14	10	DUNFERMLINE	1-0	1-1	6921	McIlroy		2		4	5	6	10	3			11		8	1	9	7				
15	17	Motherwell	0-1	0-2	2601			2		4	5	6	10	3			11		8	1	9	7				
16	24	HEARTS	1-1	1-2	5039	McIlroy		2		4	5	6		3	9	10	11		8	1		7				
17	31	Aberdeen	0-0	0-4	12673			2		4	5	6		3	9	10	11		8	1		7				
18	2 Jan	ST. MIRREN	1-0	3-0	6626	Beattie, Queen, McInally		2		4	5	6	10	3		9			8	1		7	11			
19	3	Ayr United	2-1	3-2	7899	C.Watson(3)		2		4	5	6	10	3		9			8	1		7	11			
20	7	CLYDE	1-2	1-3	5885	McLean		2		4	5	6	10	8		9		3		1		7	11"	12		
21	14	Stirling Albion	0-0	4-1	3077	McIlroy, McInally, McLean, Queen		2		4	5	6	10	3		9	11		8	1		7				
22	21	DUNDEE	2-2	4-4	4685	McIlroy(2), C.Watson, McInally		2		4	5	6	10	3		9	11		8	1		7				
23	4 Feb	Hibernian	1-2	1-3	10862	Morrison	1	2			5		10	4			11	3	8			7			6	9
24	11	RANGERS	0-0	1-2	31551	McIlroy		2			5	6	10	3		9	11		8	1	4	7				
25	25	Airdrieonians	0-0	4-1	2595	Bertelsen(3), McIlroy		2		4	5	6	10	3	9		11		8	1		7				
26	4 Mar	Partick Thistle	1-0	2-1	4196	Queen, McLean		2	12	4	5	6	10"	3		9	11		8	1		7				
27	18	Falkirk	0-0	1-0	3041	McLean		2		4	5	6		3		9	11		8	1	10	7				
28	20	DUNDEE UNITED	1-0	4-0	4719	McIlroy(2), McInally, Bertelsen		2		4	5			3	9		11		8	1	6	7	10			
29	25	ST. JOHNSTONE	3-0	5-3	3948	McIlroy(3), McLean, Bertelsen		2		4"	5	6		3	9		11		8	1	10	7	12			
30	8 Apr	Dunfermline	1-0	1-1	4812	McIlroy		2			5	6	10	3		9	11		8	1	4	7				
31	12	MOTHERWELL	1-0	3-0	4994	McIlroy, Bertelsen, McLean			3		5	6	12	2	9	10	11"		8	1	4	7				
32	22	Hearts	0-1	0-1	5809					6	5			3	9	10	11	2	8	1	4	7				
33	1 May	ABERDEEN	0-0	1-1	5229	McLean		2		6	5		11	3	9	10			8	1	4	7				
34	15	Celtic	0-1	0-2	19077			2			5	6	11	3	9	10			8	1	4	7				
						Apps.	3	32	3	29	34	29	26	29	17	22	23	8	32	31	15	31	5	3	1	1
						Subs			1				2	2				3					1	1		
						Goals				1		1	8	1	10	3	16		8		2	8				1

Pos	P.	W.	D.	L.	F.	A.	Pts.
7th	34	16	8	10	59	46	40

League Cup Section 2

Pos	P.	W.	D.	L.	F.	A.	Pts.
3rd	6	2	2	2	6	3	6

1	13 Aug	STIRLING ALBION	2-0	2-0	5292	Bertelsen, Queen	1	2	3		5	6	8		9	10	11				4	7				
2	17	Hibernian	1-0	1-2	11159	Queen		2	3		5	6			9	10	11			1	4	7	8			
3	20	Rangers	0-0	0-0	51765			2	3	4	5	6		8	9	10	11			1		7				
4	27	Stirling Albion	0-0	0-0	3375		1	2	3	4	5	6		8	9	10	11					7				
5	31	HIBERNIAN	2-0	3-0	12285	McIlroy(2), Queen	1	2	3	4	5	6		8	9	10	11					7				
6	3 Sep	RANGERS	0-0	0-1	29743		1	2	3	4	5	6		8	9	10	11					7				

Scottish Cup

1	28 Jan	DUNFERMLINE	0-2	2-2	12847	McInally, King		2		4	5	6	10	3		9	11		8	1		7				
1R	1 Feb	Dunfermline	0-1	0-1	19000			2		4	5	6		3	10	9	11		8	1		7				

Inter-Cities Fairs Cup

1		Bye																								
2	25 Oct	Royal Antwerp	1-0	1-0	10000	McInally		2		4	5	6	11	3	9	10			8	1		7				
2	2 Nov	ROYAL ANTWERP (Agg: 8-2)	3-0	7-2	11963	McInally(2),McLean(2),Queen(2),C.Watson		2		4	5	6	11	3	9	10			8	1		7				
3	14 Dec	LA GANTOISE	1-0	1-0	8612	Murray		2		4	5	6	10	3		8	11			1	9	7				
3	21	La Gantoise (Agg: 3-1)	0-0	2-1*	9500	McInally, McLean		2		4	5	6		3	9	10	11		8	1		7				
QF	19 Apr	Lokomotiv Leipzig	0-1	0-1	30000				3		5	6			9	10	11	2	8	1	4	7				
QF	26	LOKOMOTIV LEIP. (Agg: 2-1)	1-0	2-0	15595	Murray, McIlroy		2			5	6	10	3	9		11		8	1	4	7				
SF	19 May	Leeds United	2-4	2-4	43189	McIlroy(2)		2		8	5	6	7	3	9	10	11			1	4					
SF	24	LEEDS UNITED (Agg: 2-4)	0-0	0-0	24831			2			5	6		3	9	10	11		8	1	4	7				

* After Extra Time. 90 minutes 0-1.

Kilmarnock travelled to the then East Germany to face Lokomotiv Leipzig in the Quarter-Finals of the Fairs (UEFA) Cup. They lost 1-0 but a 2-0 triumph in the return leg set them up for an enthralling Semi-Final with Leeds United which the English club won 4-2 on aggregate.

SEASON 1967-68 Division One

No.	Date	Opposition	H.T.	Res.	Att.	Goalscorers
1	9 Sep	MORTON	2-0	3-1	7508	Murray(2), McInally
2	16	Stirling Albion	0-0	0-0	2636	
3	23	AIRDRIEONIANS	1-2	2-2	4452	Cameron(2)
4	30	Dunfermline	1-0	2-1	3987	McInally, McIlroy
5	7 Oct	DUNDEE	0-0	0-0	4640	
6	14	Falkirk	1-1	1-1	3227	McIlroy
7	21	RAITH ROVERS	1-1	1-2	3286	Cameron
8	28	Clyde	0-0	1-2	1663	McIlroy
9	11 Nov	PARTICK THISTLE	0-1	0-3	2719	
10	15	Celtic	0-1	0-3	26727	
11	18	Motherwell	0-1	2-1	2270	Cameron, Morrison
12	25	Dundee United	0-1	2-3	5144	Morrison, McLean
13	2 Dec	HEARTS	2-2	3-2	5558	Morrison(2), Queen
14	9	ABERDEEN	1-0	3-0	4834	Morrison(2), Queen
15	16	St. Johnstone	1-0	1-0	2439	Cameron
16	23	Rangers	0-3	1-4	33239	Cameron
17	30	HIBERNIAN	0-0	1-0	6460	McLean
18	1 Jan	Morton	0-1	2-3	3762	Queen, Morrison
19	2	STIRLING ALBION	2-0	5-2	4743	Morrison(2), Queen, McIlroy, O.G.
20	20	Dundee	2-2	5-6	6310	Morrison(2), Cameron(2), McIlroy
21	3 Feb	FALKIRK	1-0	3-0	2400	Morrison, Queen, Cameron
22	6	DUNFERMLINE	0-0	1-1	3056	Queen
23	10	Raith Rovers	0-0	2-1	2836	Queen, Cameron
24	21	Airdrieonians	1-0	2-3	2322	Queen, Gilmour
25	28	CLYDE	1-0	5-1	2968	Queen(2), McLean, Cameron, Gilmour
26	2 Mar	CELTIC	0-3	0-6	18591	
27	13	Partick Thistle	0-0	0-1	1700	
28	16	MOTHERWELL	1-0	1-1	2333	Queen
29	6 Apr	Aberdeen	1-1	1-1	5465	Morrison
30	10	Hearts	0-0	0-1	6000	
31	13	ST. JOHNSTONE	1-0	1-0	2939	Morrison
32	17	DUNDEE UNITED	1-0	4-0	3020	Queen(2), McFadzean, Dickson
33	20	RANGERS	1-1	1-2	17286	McFadzean
34	27	Hibernian	1-1	3-3	4688	McLean, Queen, McFadzean

No.	McLaughlan	King	M.Watson	Murray	McGrory	Beattie	McLean	McInally	Cameron	Queen	McIlroy	C.Watson	McFadzean	Dickson	Gilmour	Coghill	Arthur	Morrison	Sinclair	Brown	Rodman	Dick	Sneddon
1	1	2	3	4	5	6	7	8	9	10	11												
2	1	2	3	4	5	6	7	8	9	10		11											
3	1	2"	12	4	5	6	7	8	9	10		11	3										
4	1		2	4	5	6	7	8	9"	10	11		3	12									
5	1		2	4	5	6	7		9	10	11			3	8								
6	1	2		4	5	6	7		9	10	11		3		8								
7	1	2		4	5	6	7		9	10	11		3		8								
8	1	2		4	5	6	7	8	9		11		3			10							
9	1	2		4"	5	6	7	8	9	12	11		3			10							
10	1				5	6	7		8	10	11		3	4			2	9					
11	1				5	6	7		8				3	4	10	11	2	9					
12	1			4	5	6	7		8				3				2	9	10	11			
13	1			4	5	6	7	12	11	8			3				2	9	10"				
14	1			4	5	6	7		11	8			3				2	9	10				
15	1			4	5	6"	7		11	8	12		3				2	9	10				
16	1			4	5	6	7		11	8			3				2	9	10				
17	1				5	6	7		9	8	11		3		4		2		10				
18	1				5	6	7		11"	8	12		3		4		2	9	10				
19	1				5		7			8	11		3	4	10		2	9			6		
20	1			4	5	6"	7		10	8	11		3		12		2	9					
21	1		3		5		7		11	8					4	10	2	9			6		
22	1	12	3		5		7		11	8			6		10		2	9"			4		
23	1		3		5		7		11	8			6		10		2	9			4		
24	1				5	6	7		11	8			3		10		2	9			4		
25	1				5	6	7		11	8			3		10		2	9			4		
26	1				5	6	7		11	8			3		10		2	9			4		
27	1				5	6	7		11	8			3		10		2	9			4		
28		3			5	6	7		11	8			4		10		2	9				1	
29	1	3		4	5	6	7			8	11		10				2	9					
30	1	3		4	5		7		12	8	11		10	6			2	9"					
31	1	3		4	5		7			8	11		10	6			2	9					
32	1	3		4	5		7			8	11		10	6			2	9					
33		3		4	5		7			8	11		10	6			2	9				1	
34		3		4	5"		7			8	11		10	6			2	9			12	1	
Apps.	31	14	7	21	34	25	34	6	27	30	17	2	30	9	15	4	25	24	7	1	8	3	
Subs		1	1					1	1	1	2			1	1						1		
Goals				2			4	2	11	14	5		3	1	2			14					

Pos	P.	W.	D.	L.	F.	A.	Pts.
7th	34	13	8	13	59	57	34

League Cup Section 1

Pos	P.	W.	D.	L.	F.	A.	Pts.
1st	6	3	2	1	11	5	8

No.	Date	Opposition	H.T.	Res.	Att.	Goalscorers
1	12 Aug	DUNFERMLINE	1-1	2-2	7269	Cameron, McInally
2	16	Airdrieonians	1-1	2-1	2596	Cameron, McInally
3	19	PARTICK THISTLE	2-0	4-0	5892	Cameron(3), McLean
4	26	Dunfermline	2-0	3-1	8155	Cameron(3)
5	30	AIRDRIEONIANS	0-0	0-0	5687	
6	2 Sep	Partick Thistle	0-0	0-1	3432	
QF	13	Morton	2-2	2-3	8777	Queen, McLean
QF	27	MORTON (Agg: 3-5)	0-0	1-2	14344	McInally

No.	McLaughlan	King	M.Watson	Murray	McGrory	Beattie	McLean	McInally	Cameron	Queen	McIlroy	C.Watson	McFadzean	Dickson	Gilmour	Coghill	Arthur	Morrison	Sinclair	Brown	Rodman	Dick	Sneddon
1	1	2		4	5	6		8	9	10	11	7	3"										12
2	1	2	3	4	5	6		8	9	10	11	7											
3	1	2	3	4	5	6"	7	8	9	10	11	12											
4	1	2	3	4	5		7	8	9	10	11			6									
5	1	2	3	4	5		7	8	9	10	11			6									
6	1	2	3	4	5	6	7	8	9	10	11												
QF	1	2	3	4	5	6	7	8	9	10	11												
QF	1		2	4	5	6	7	8	9	10	11		3										

Scottish Cup

No.	Date	Opposition	H.T.	Res.	Att.	Goalscorers
1	27 Jan	Partick Thistle	0-0	0-0	9800	
1R	31	PARTICK THISTLE	0-2	1-2	9191	Morrison

No.	McLaughlan	King	M.Watson	Murray	McGrory	Beattie	McLean	McInally	Cameron	Queen	McIlroy	C.Watson	McFadzean	Dickson	Gilmour	Coghill	Arthur	Morrison	Sinclair	Brown	Rodman	Dick	Sneddon
1	1		3	4	5		7		10	8	11		6				2	9					
1R	1		3	4	5		7		10	8	11		6				2	9					

One of the mainstays of the great team of the 1960's was international centre-half JACKIE McGRORY. An ever-present in the League this season, it was the fourth out of five times he would claim such a notable feat.

SEASON 1968-69 Division One

No.	Date	Opposition	H.T.	Res.	Att.	Goalscorers	McLaughlan	King	Dickson	Gilmour	McGrory	Beattie	T. McLean	Queen	Morrison	J. McLean	Cook	McIlroy	Arthur	Rodman	McFadzean	Evans	Sinclair	McKellar	Miller	Dick	Waddell
1	7 Sep	St. Mirren	1-1	1-1	5204	Queen	1	2	3	4	5	6	7	8	9	10	11										
2	14	MORTON	0-0	1-0	5812	Morrison	1	2	3	4	5	6	7	8	9	10		11									
3	21	Rangers	1-0	3-3	39407	Morrison(2), Queen	1	2	3	4	5		7	8	9	10	11		6								
4	28	DUNFERMLINE	0-1	0-1	6507		1	2	3	4	5		7	8	9	10	11		6								
5	5 Oct	Arbroath	1-1	2-1	3015	J.McLean(2)	1	2	3	4	5		7	8	9	10		11	6								
6	12	DUNDEE UNITED	3-0	3-0	5151	Morrison, T.McLean, J.McLean	1		3	4"	5	6	7	8	9	10	11		2	12							
7	19	Hibernian	0-0	0-1	8653		1	2	3	4	5		7	8	9	10	11		6								
8	26	RAITH ROVERS	0-4	4-4	4565	T.McLean(2), Morrison, McIlroy	1	2	3	4	5	12	7		9	10	8	11	6"								
9	2 Nov	Hearts	0-0	1-0	6943	T.McLean	1	2	3	4	5	6	7	8	9	10		11									
10	9	FALKIRK	1-1	5-1	4340	McIlroy(3), J.McLean, Morrison	1	2	3	4	5	6	7	8	9	10		11									
11	16	Partick Thistle	0-0	2-0	4400	McIlroy, Queen	1	2	3	4	5	6	7	8	9	10		11									
12	23	DUNDEE	1-0	1-0	6594	Morrison	1	2	3	4	5	6	7	8	9	10		11									
13	30	Clyde	1-0	1-2	3824	Morrison	1	2	3	4	5	6	7		9	10		11	12		8"						
14	7 Dec	Airdrieonians	0-0	2-0	2759	Morrsion, McIlroy	1	2	3	4	5	6"	7	8	9	10		11					12				
15	14	ST. JOHNSTONE	1-0	2-0	5154	Morrsion, J.McLean	1	2	3	4	5	6	7	8	9	10		11									
16	21	Celtic	0-1	1-1	37321	McIlroy	1	2	3	4	5	6	7	8	9	10		11									
17	28	ABERDEEN	1-0	2-1	7128	McIlroy, Morrison	1	2	3	4	5	6	7	8	9	10		11									
18	1 Jan	ST. MIRREN	0-0	0-0	12082		1	2	3	4	5	6	7	8	9"	10		11			12						
19	2	Morton	1-0	2-3	7300	McIlroy(2)	1	2	3	4	5		7	8	9	10"		11			6	12					
20	4	RANGERS	2-2	3-3	32893	Dickson, T.McLean, McIlroy	1	2	3	4	5	6	7	8	9	10		11									
21	11	Dunfermline	1-0	1-1	8662	O.G.	1	2	3	4	5	6	7		9	8		11			10						
22	18	ARBROATH	0-0	1-0	5544	J.McLean	1	2	3	4	5	6	7	9		8		11			10						
23	1 Feb	Dundee United	1-0	2-2	5076	Queen, Morrison	1	2		4	5	6"	7	8	9			11			3	10	12				
24	19	HIBERNIAN	1-0	2-1	5673	McIlroy, Queen	1	2	3	4	5	6	7	8	9			11				10					
25	22	HEARTS	0-0	1-0	7025	McIlroy	1	2	3	4	5	6	7		9			11					10				
26	26	Raith Rovers	0-0	0-0	2246		1	2	3	4"	5	6	7	8	9	10		11				12					
27	8 Mar	PARTICK THISTLE	0-1	1-1	4541	McFadzean	1	2	3	4	5		7		9	10		11			6	8					
28	12	Falkirk	1-1	1-1	2838	Dickson	1	2	3	4	5	6	7		9	10		11			12	8"					
29	15	Dundee	0-0	0-0	4345		1	2	3	4	5	6	7	8	9	10		11									
30	22	CLYDE	0-0	0-0	5042		1	2	3	4	5	6	7	8	9	10		11									
31	29	AIRDRIEONIANS	1-0	2-1	4069	Gilmour, McKellar	1	2	3	4	5	6	7	8	9"	10		11						12			
32	5 Apr	St. Johnstone	0-0	0-1	3748		1	2	3	4	5	6	7	8	10	11"						12		9			
33	19	Aberdeen	1-0	1-0	7502	Cook	1	2	3		5	6		4	9	8	7	11				10					
34	21	CELTIC	2-0	2-2	18873	Morrison, Queen	1	2	3		5	6	7	8	9	10		11				4					
						Apps.	34	33	33	32	34	27	33	28	33	31	7	28	6		6	7	1	1			
						Subs						1							1	1	2	3	2	1			
						Goals			2	1			5	6	13	6	1	13			1			1			

Pos	P.	W.	D.	L.	F.	A.	Pts.
4th	34	15	14	5	50	32	44

League Cup Section 2

Pos	P.	W.	D.	L.	F.	A.	Pts.
4th	6	0	3	3	5	14	3

No.	Date	Opposition	H.T.	Res.	Att.	Goalscorers	McLaughlan	King	Dickson	Gilmour	McGrory	Beattie	T. McLean	Queen	Morrison	J. McLean	Cook	McIlroy	Arthur	Rodman	McFadzean	Evans	Sinclair	McKellar	Miller	Dick	Waddell
1	10 Aug	Dundee	0-4	0-4	7648		1	3	4		5		7	8				11	2	6	10				9		
2	14	AIRDRIEONIANS	0-2	0-3	5446		1	3	4		5		7		9		11		6	2	10				8		
3	17	HEARTS	3-1	3-3	7213	Queen(2), Cook	1	2	6	4	5		7	8	9	10	11"			12	3						
4	24	DUNDEE	0-0	2-2	5435	T.McLean, Morrison	1	2	6	4	5		7		9	10	8	11			3						
5	28	Airdrieonians	0-1	0-2	3692		1	2	6	4		5	7	8	9	10	11				3						
6	31	Hearts	0-0	0-0	6283		1	2	6	4		5	7	8	9"	10	11	12			3						

Scottish Cup

No.	Date	Opposition	H.T.	Res.	Att.	Goalscorers	McLaughlan	King	Dickson	Gilmour	McGrory	Beattie	T. McLean	Queen	Morrison	J. McLean	Cook	McIlroy	Arthur	Rodman	McFadzean	Evans	Sinclair	McKellar	Miller	Dick	Waddell
1	25 Jan	GLASGOW UNIVERSITY	2-0	6-0	7771	Queen(3), McIlroy(2), O.G.	1	2	3	4	5	6	7	9		8"		11			10	12					
2	8 Feb	Montrose	0-1	1-1	2600	Morrison	1	2		4	5	6	7	8	9			11			3	10					
2R	12	MONTROSE	3-0	4-1	7385	T.McLean(3), Morrison	1	2	3	4	5	6	7	8	9			11				10					
QF	1 Mar	Aberdeen	0-0	0-0	22601		1	2	3	4	5	6	7		9	10		11				8					
QFR	5	ABERDEEN	0-1	0-3	18128		1	2	3	4	5		7	8	9	10		11			6						

USA Tournament (Representing St. Louis)

Pos	P.	W.	D.	L.	F.	A.	Pts.
5th	8	2	1	5	11	18	26

No.	Date	Opposition	H.T.	Res.	Att.	Goalscorers	McLaughlan	King	Dickson	Gilmour	McGrory	Beattie	T. McLean	Queen	Morrison	J. McLean	Cook	McIlroy	Arthur	Rodman	McFadzean	Evans	Sinclair	McKellar	Miller	Dick	Waddell
1	3 May	Aston Villa	1-0	1-2	8171	J.McLean	1	2	3		5	6		8	9	7		11		12		10					4"
2	9	West Ham United	1-1	2-1	7764	Queen, Morrison	1	2	3	4	5	6	7	8	9	10		11									
3	11	Wolves	1-2	2-3	3000	Morrison, T.McLean	1	2	3	4	5	6	7	8	9	10		11									
4	14	Dundee United	1-0	3-3	1200	Queen(2), T.McLean			2	4	5		12	9		10		7	3	6		8				1	11"
5	16	Wolves	0-2	0-3	5000		1"	2	3	4	5	6	7	8	9	10										12	11
6	23	Dundee United	0-0	0-1	5000		1	2"	3	4	5	6	7	8	9	11			12			10					
7	25	Aston Villa	2-0	2-1	5000	J.McLean, Queen	1		3	4	5	6"	7	8	9	11			2	12		10					
8	30	West Ham United	0-2	1-4	3008	Morrison	1		3	4	5		7		9	10		11	2	6		8					

Venues in order: Atlanta, Seattle, Kansas City, Dallas, St.Louis, St.Louis, St. Louis Baltimore

Centenary Match

No.	Date	Opposition	H.T.	Res.	Att.	Goalscorers	McLaughlan	King	Dickson	Gilmour	McGrory	Beattie	T. McLean	Queen	Morrison	J. McLean	Cook	McIlroy	Arthur	Rodman	McFadzean	Evans	Sinclair	McKellar	Miller	Dick	Waddell
1	12 Apr	EINTRACHT FRANKFURT	1-0	1-1	10513	Queen	1	2	3	4	5	6	7	8	9*	10"		11				12		14			

Players & officials assemble for special photo at Centenary match with Eintracht Frankfurt.

Back:
Rodman, Gold, Miller, Nicol, McFadzean, Beattie, McGrory, Gilmour, Anderson, Arthur

Middle:
King, R.Waddell, McKellar, McLaughlan, Dick, Queen, Maxwell, Morrison.

Front Standing:
Murdoch(Trainer), T.McLean, McIlroy, Neil, Sinclair, W.Waddell, Evans, J.McLean, Dickson, Rodman, Laws, Cook, Allan(Train).

Front:
McCrae(Manager), Robertson, Ralston (Doctor), Thyne, McIvor (Chairman), McCulloch,Kerr ,Lauchlan, Richmond, McNeil.

SEASON 1969-70 Division One

No.	Date	Opposition	H.T.	Res.	Att.	Goalscorers	McLaughlan	King	Dickson	Gilmour	McGrory	Beattie	T.McLean	Mathie	Morrison	J.McLean	W.Waddell	Cook	Strachan	Rodman	Maxwell	Arthur	Sheed	MacDonald	R.Waddell
1	30 Aug	Motherwell	0-0	0-1	6762		1	2	3	4	5	6	7	8	9	10	11"	12							
2	3 Sep	CELTIC	1-2	2-4	23821	Mathie, Morrison	1	2	3			6	7	8	9	10	4	11	5						
3	6	RAITH ROVERS	0-0	1-0	3978	Mathie	1	2	3	4		6	7	8	9		10	11	5						
4	13	Hearts	1-0	1-4	8227	Morrison	1	2	3	4		5"	7	8	9	10	12	11	6						
5	20	AYR UNITED	2-1	4-1	10087	Cook(2), T.McLean, Mathie	1	2	3	4	5		7	9	8	10		11	6						
6	27	St. Mirren	1-0	2-0	5342	Mathie, Morrison	1	2	3	4	5		7	9	8	10		11	6						
7	4 Oct	Partick Thistle	1-0	2-2	4025	Gilmour, Strachan	1	2	3	4	5		7	9	8	10		11	6						
8	11	DUNDEE	2-0	3-0	4895	Morrison, Mathie	1	2	3	4	5		7	9	8	10		11	6						
9	18	Dunfermline	0-1	1-2	7974	O.G.	1	2	3	4	5		7	9	8	10		11	6						
10	25	HIBERNIAN	1-1	2-2	7608	Gilmour, Mathie	1	2	3	4	5		7	9	8	10		11	6						
11	1 Nov	Clyde	3-2	3-2	1944	Cook, Mathie, Morrison	1	2	3	4			7	9	8	10		11	6	5					
12	8	MORTON	1-0	5-2	4141	T.McLean(2), Mathie(2), Dickson	1	2	3	4	5	6	7	9	8"	10	12	11							
13	15	Rangers	1-2	3-5	35499	Morrison(2), Mathie	1	2	3	4"	5	6	7	8	9	10	12	11							
14	29	ABERDEEN	0-0	0-2	5396		1	2	3	4	5	6	7	9	8			11	10						
15	2 Dec	ST. JOHNSTONE	3-0	4-1	3795	Mathie(2), Gilmour, Morrison	1	2	3	4	5		7	9	8		10	11	6						
16	6	Dundee United	1-1	2-2	5639	Mathie, Morrison	1	2	3	4	5		7	9	8		10	11	6						
17	13	MOTHERWELL	1-1	2-2	5027	Cook, T.McLean	1	2	3	4	5		7	9	8		10	11	6						
18	20	Celtic	1-2	1-3	31459	Morrison	1	2	3	4	5	6"	7	9	8		10	11	12						
19	1 Jan	ST. MIRREN	0-0	1-1	7587	T.McLean	1	2"	3	4	5		7	9	8		10	11	6		12				
20	3	Ayr United	0-1	2-3	12722	Mathie(2)	1		3	4	5		7	9	8		10	11	6			2			
21	17	HEARTS	0-0	0-0	5593		1	2	3	12	5		7	9	4	10		11	6				8"		
22	31	Raith Rovers	0-2	3-2	1713	MacDonald, Mathie, Morrison	1	2	3		5		7	9	8	10		11	6					4	
23	11 Feb	DUNDEE UNITED	1-0	3-1	4647	Cook, Mathie, Morrison	1	2	3	4	5		7	9	8	10		11						6	
24	25	PARTICK THISTLE	2-0	4-2	5173	Morrison(3), Mathie	1	2	3	4	5		7	9	8	10		11						6	
25	28	Dundee	0-2	0-3	7666		1	2	3	4	5		7	9	8	10		11						6	
26	7 Mar	DUNFERMLINE	1-0	1-0	5391	Mathie	1	2	3	4	5		7	9	8	10		11						6	
27	21	CLYDE	1-0	2-1	3811	T.McLean, Morrison	1	2	3	4	5		7	9	8	10		11						6	
28	25	Hibernian	1-1	1-2	7100	T.McLean	1	2	3	4			7	9	8	10		11		5				6	
29	28	Morton	0-0	1-1	2680	Mathie	1	2	3		6		7	9	8	10		11		5				4	
30	1 Apr	Airdrieonians	0-0	0-1	1431		1	2	3	4	6		7	9	8	10		11		5					
31	4	RANGERS	0-1	2-2	11135	J.McLean, T.McLean	1	2	3	4	6		7	9	8	10		11		5					
32	6	Aberdeen	1-0	2-2	6155	Mathie, Morrison	1	2	3	4	6		7	9	8			11		5				10	
33	11	AIRDRIEONIANS	1-0	1-0	2223	T.McLean	1	2	3	4"	6		7	9	8	12		11		5				10	
34	18	St. Johnstone	1-1	1-1	1954	Morrison	1	2		12	6			9	8	10	11"	7		5	3			4	
						Apps.	34	33	33	29	29	8	33	34	34	24	10	33	18	8	1	1	1	11	
						Subs				2						1	3	1	1		1				
						Goals			1	3			9	21	19	1		5	1					1	

Pos	P.	W.	D.	L.	F.	A.	Pts.
6th	34	13	10	11	62	57	36

League Cup Section 3

Pos	P.	W.	D.	L.	F.	A.	Pts.
2nd	6	3	1	2	12	5	7

No.	Date	Opposition	H.T.	Res.	Att.	Goalscorers	McLaughlan	King	Dickson	Gilmour	McGrory	Beattie	T.McLean	Mathie	Morrison	J.McLean	W.Waddell	Cook	Strachan	Rodman	Maxwell	Arthur	Sheed	MacDonald	R.Waddell
1	9 Aug	Partick Thistle	1-0	2-0	4915	Gilmour, Morrison	1	2	3	8	5	6	7		9	10		11							4
2	13	ST. JOHNSTONE	1-2	2-3	5603	Gilmour, T.McLean	1	2	3	8	5	6	7		9	10		11							4
3	16	Dundee	0-0	0-0	9207		1	2	3	8	5		7		9	10	6	11							4
4	20	St. Johnstone	0-1	1-2	7313	J.McLean	1	2	3	4	5	6	7	8	9	10		11							
5	23	PARTICK THISTLE	3-0	6-0	3472	Mathie(2),W.Waddell(2),T.McLean,Morrison	1	2	3	4	5	6	7	8	9	10	11								
6	27	DUNDEE	1-0	1-0	3971	King	1	2	3	4	5	6	7	8	9	10	11								

Scottish Cup

No.	Date	Opposition	H.T.	Res.	Att.	Goalscorers	McLaughlan	King	Dickson	Gilmour	McGrory	Beattie	T.McLean	Mathie	Morrison	J.McLean	W.Waddell	Cook	Strachan	Rodman	Maxwell	Arthur	Sheed	MacDonald	R.Waddell
1	24 Jan	PARTICK THISTLE	2-0	3-0	7763	Cook, Mathie, Morrison	1	2	3	4	5		7	9	8	10		11	6						
2	7 Feb	HEARTS	1-0	2-0	14782	Cook, Mathie	1	2	3		5		7	9	8	10		11	6					4	
QF	21	Motherwell	0-0	1-0	16514	Mathie	1	2	3	4	5		7	9	8	10		11						6	
SF	14 Mar	Aberdeen *	0-1	0-1	25812		1	2	3	4	5		7	9	8	10		11						6	

* Muirton Park, Perth

Inter-Cities Fairs Cup

No.	Date	Opposition	H.T.	Res.	Att.	Goalscorers	McLaughlan	King	Dickson	Gilmour	McGrory	Beattie	T.McLean	Mathie	Morrison	J.McLean	W.Waddell	Cook	Strachan	Rodman	Maxwell	Arthur	Sheed	MacDonald	R.Waddell
1	16 Sep	Zurich	2-2	2-3	13500	J.McLean, Mathie	1	2	3	4	5	6	7	11	9	10			8						
1	30	ZURICH (Agg: 5-4)	1-0	3-1	9593	McGrory, T.McLean, Morrison	1	2	3	4	5	12	7	9	8	10"		11	6						
2	19 Nov	SLAVIA SOFIA	2-0	4-1	9535	Mathie(2), Cook, Gilmour	1	2	3	4	5	6	7	9	8	10"	12	11							
2	26	Slavia Sofia (Agg: 4-3)	0-2	0-2	12000		1	2	3	4	5	6	7	9	8			11	10						
3	17 Dec	DINAMO BACAU	0-0	1-1	7749	Mathie	1	2	3	4	5	6	11	9	8		10	7							
3	13 Jan	Dinamo Bacau (Agg: 1-3)	0-1	0-2	20000		1	2	3	4"	5		7	9	8	10			6		12		11		

Killie enjoyed good runs in Europe and the Scottish Cup this season.
Back: R.Mathie, J.Gilmour, A.McDonald, E.Morrison, J.McGrory, H.Strachan
Front: T.McLean, A.King, A.McLaughlan, W.Dickson, J.McLean, J.Cook

SEASON 1970-71 Division One

No.	Date	Opposition	H.T.	Res.	Att.	Goalscorers	Hunter	Swan	Dickson	Morrison	Rodman	MacDonald	T.McLean	Sheed	Mathie	Maxwell	Cook	J.McCulloch	King	Gilmour	McGrory	Arthur	Johnston	McSherry	Gillespie	Leckie	Wylie	I.Fleming	Cairns	Graham	W.Waddell	McLaughlan	Whyte
1	29 Aug	Motherwell	0-2	1-4	5661	Cook	1	2	3	4	5	6	7	8"	9	10	11	12															
2	5 Sep	ST. MIRREN	0-0	1-2	4256	Mathie	1		3	8					9	10	11		2	4	5	6	7										
3	12	Ayr United	1-1	1-1	8488	McLean	1		3	9"	6		7		12	10	11			4	5	2		8									
4	19	ABERDEEN	0-4	0-4	5056		1	3	2	8			7		9	4	11"	12			5	6		10									
5	26	Cowdenbeath	2-1	2-1	3148	Morrison, Gilmour	1		3	9		6	7		11	8				4	5	2		10									
6	3 Oct	HEARTS	2-0	3-0	5365	McLean, Cook, Dickson	1		3	8	10	6	7		9	2	11			4	5												
7	10	Falkirk	0-1	0-3	4018		1		3	8"		6	7		9	2	11			4	5			12	10								
8	17	DUNDEE UNITED	1-1	2-1	3644	McCulloch, Mathie	1		3				7		9	6	11	8		2	5			10		4"	12						
9	24	MORTON	0-1	2-2	3743	Mathie, Cook	1		3		6		7		9	10	11		2	4	5			8									
10	31	Dundee	0-1	0-3	3578		1		3		6	8	7		9"	10	11		2	4	5			12									
11	7 Nov	ST. JOHNSTONE	1-2	2-4	3910	McLean, Mathie	1		3	8	6	10	7		12	2	11			4	5							9"					
12	14	Celtic	0-2	0-3	24410		1		3	9	2	6	7		12	8"	11			4	5								10				
13	21	Hibernian	0-1	0-1	6364		1		3	8	2	6	7		9"	12	11			4	5								10				
14	28	AIRDRIEONIANS	2-2	2-3	3912	Graham, McLean	1		3	9	2	6	7			12	11			4	5								10	8"			
15	5 Dec	Dunfermline	0-0	1-0	4164	Gilmour	1		3	9	8	6	7			2	11			4	5								10				
16	12	CLYDE	1-0	1-1	3805	Morrison	1		3	9	8	6	7			2	11			4	5								10				
17	19	Rangers	0-1	2-4	19450	McLean, Maxwell	1		3	9		6	7			8	11			4	5								10				2
18	26	MOTHERWELL	0-0	0-0	5323		1		3	9		6	7			8	11			4	5								10				2
19	1 Jan	St. Mirren	1-0	3-2	5934	McLean(2), Maxwell	1		3	9		6	7		8		11			4	5								10				2
20	2	AYR UNITED	1-0	1-1	15240	McLean	1		3	9		6	7		8		11			4	5								10				2
21	9	Aberdeen	0-1	0-3	19032		1		3	9		6	7		8		11			4	5								10				2
22	16	COWDENBEATH	1-1	2-1	4015	Gilmour, Waddell	1		3	12		6"	7		9					4	5								10	8	11		2
23	30	Hearts	0-1	0-2	8823				3	12		6	7		9		11			4	5								8"		10	1	2
24	6 Feb	FALKIRK	2-2	3-2	4712	McCulloch, Morrison, O.G.			3	8		6	7				11	9		4	5										10	1	2
25	20	Dundee United	1-1	2-3	3852	McCulloch, Cook			3	8			7			2	11	9		4	5										10	1	6
26	27	Morton	0-2	0-3	2324				3	8			7				11	9		4	5				6				12		10"	1	2
27	9 Mar	DUNDEE	0-1	1-1	3003	McLean	1		3	12		6	7		8		11	9		4	5								10"				2
28	13	St. Johnstone	1-2	3-2	8513	McCulloch, Morrison, O.G.	1		3	8		6	7		12		11	9		4"	5										10		2
29	20	CELTIC	1-0	1-4	17075	Morrison	1		3	8	12	6	7				11	9		4	5								10"				2
30	27	HIBERNIAN	3-0	4-1	4209	McCulloch, Gilmour, McLean, Cook	1		3	8		6	7				11	9		4	5								10"		12		2
31	10 Apr	DUNFERMLINE	0-0	0-0	5050		1		3	8"		6	7				11	9		4	5								10		12		2
32	14	Airdrieonians	1-1	1-1	2064	Cook	1		3	8		6	7				11	9		4	5										10		2
33	17	Clyde	0-0	1-0	1537	Waddell	1		3			6	7				11	9		4	5			8								10		2
34	24	RANGERS	1-1	1-4	8544	McCulloch	1		3	12		6	7				11	9		4	5			8								10"		2
						Apps.	30	2	34	26	11	27	33	1	16	17	32	12	3	32	33	4	1	7	2	1		1	16	2	9	4	18
						Subs			4	1				4	2		2						2			1		1		2		
						Goals			1	5			10		4	1	6	6		4										1	2		

Pos	P.	W.	D.	L.	F.	A.	Pts.
13th	34	10	8	16	43	67	28

League Cup Section 3

Pos	P.	W.	D.	L.	F.	A.	Pts.
2nd	6	4	1	1	8	4	9

No.	Date	Opposition	H.T.	Res.	Att.	Goalscorers	Hunter	Swan	Dickson	Morrison	Rodman	MacDonald	T.McLean	Sheed	Mathie	Maxwell	Cook	J.McCulloch	King	Gilmour	McGrory	Arthur	Johnston	McSherry	Gillespie	Leckie	Wylie	I.Fleming	Cairns	Graham	W.Waddell	McLaughlan	Whyte
1	8 Aug	AYR UNITED	0-0	1-0	7073	Mathie			3	8	6				9	10	11		2	4	5		7									1	
2	12	St. Mirren	2-0	3-1	4488	Gilmour, Cook, Mathie	1		3	8	6	12			9	10	11		2	4	5									7"		
3	15	Dundee	0-1	0-2	7644		1		3"	7	6	8			9	10	11	12	2	4	5											
4	19	ST. MIRREN	1-0	2-0	4931	McLean(2)		3		8	6		7		9	10	11		2	4	5											1	
5	22	Ayr United	0-0	0-0	7911			3		8"	5	6	7		9	10	11	12	2			4										1	
6	26	DUNDEE	2-0	2-1	3280	Mathie, McLean		2	3		5	6	7	8	9	10	11	12		4"												1	

Scottish Cup

No.	Date	Opposition	H.T.	Res.	Att.	Goalscorers	Hunter	Swan	Dickson	Morrison	Rodman	MacDonald	T.McLean	Sheed	Mathie	Maxwell	Cook	J.McCulloch	King	Gilmour	McGrory	Arthur	Johnston	McSherry	Gillespie	Leckie	Wylie	I.Fleming	Cairns	Graham	W.Waddell	McLaughlan	Whyte
3	23 Jan	Queens Park	1-0	1-0	5923	Waddell	1		3	12		6			9		7			4	5								10	8"	11		2
4	13 Feb	Morton	1-0	2-1	6840	McCulloch, Waddell			3	8		6	7				11	9		4	5										10	1	2
QF	6 Mar	AIRDRIEONIANS	0-3	2-3	11572	Dickson, Gilmour			3	8			7				11	9		4	5				6				10			1	2

European Fairs Cup

No.	Date	Opposition	H.T.	Res.	Att.	Goalscorers	Hunter	Swan	Dickson	Morrison	Rodman	MacDonald	T.McLean	Sheed	Mathie	Maxwell	Cook	J.McCulloch	King	Gilmour	McGrory	Arthur	Johnston	McSherry	Gillespie	Leckie	Wylie	I.Fleming	Cairns	Graham	W.Waddell	McLaughlan	Whyte
1	15 Sep	Coleraine	0-0	1-1	5000	Mathie	1		3	8	6		7		9	10	11			4	5	2											
1	29	COLERAINE (Agg: 3-4)	2-0	2-3	5911	McLean, Morrison	1	12	3	9		6	7		11*	8	14			4"	5	2		10									

Kilmarnock finished in the bottom half of the table for the first time in 16 years yet this team looked as strong as before. A perplexing time. Back: R.Mathie, A.McDonald, J.McGrory, B.Rodman, J.Gilmour, A.Hunter, W.Dickson. Front: T.McLean, G.Maxwell, E.Morrison, A.Cairns, J.Cook.

SEASON 1971-72 Division One

No.	Date	Opposition	H.T.	Res.	Att.	Goalscorers	Hunter	Whyte	Dickson	MacDonald	Rodman	McGrory	McSherry	Gilmour	J.McCulloch	Maxwell	Cook	J.Fleming	Beattie	Morrison	Cairns	I.Fleming	Mathie	King	Sheed	Lee	Stevenson
1	4 Sep	Falkirk	0-2	1-3	5897	Gilmour	1	2	3	4	5	6	7	8	9	10	11										
2	11	AYR UNITED	1-1	1-2	7774	Cook	1	2	3		5	6	7	8	9	4	11	10									
3	18	Motherwell	0-2	0-3	3774		1	2			5	6	7	8	9	3	11		4	10							
4	25	DUNDEE UNITED	1-0	2-0	3012	Cook, McSherry	1	2			5	6	10	8	9	4	11			7	3						
5	2 Oct	Partick Thistle	1-1	2-2	7491	Cook, Maxwell	1	2		5		6	10	8	9	4	11			7	3						
6	9	ABERDEEN	0-0	0-3	5963		1	2			5	6	10	8	9	4	11			7	3						
7	16	East Fife	0-1	0-2	3495		1	2			5	6	10	8	9"	4	11			12	3	7					
8	23	HEARTS	1-2	2-2	4536	Mathie, Morrison	1	2			5	6	7	8		4	11			10	3		9				
9	30	Rangers	1-1	1-3	25442	Mathie	1	2			5	6	7	8	10	4	11				3		9				
10	6 Nov	CLYDE	0-1	2-1	3714	Maxwell, Mathie	1	2			5	6	7	8		4	11			10	3		9				
11	13	Dunfermline	0-0	1-0	4344	Morrison	1	2			5	6	7	8		4	11			10	3		9				
12	20	AIRDRIEONIANS	1-0	5-2	3095	Mathie(2), Morrison, Cook, Maxwell	1	2			5	6	7	8		4	11			10	3		9				
13	27	Hibernian	2-1	2-3	7950	Mathie, Maxwell	1	2			5	6	7	8	12	4	11			10"	3		9				
14	4 Dec	Celtic	0-1	1-5	26824	Mathie	1	2			5	6	7	8		4	11			10	3		9				
15	11	ST. JOHNSTONE	1-0	2-0	3634	Cook, Maxwell	1	2"	12		5	6	7	8		4	11			10	3		9				
16	18	Dundee	0-0	0-2	4646		1		2		5	6	7	8"		4	11			10	3		9	12			
17	25	MORTON	2-1	4-2	4093	Cook(2), Gilmour, Mathie	1		2		5	6	7	8		4	11			10	3		9				
18	1 Jan	FALKIRK	0-0	2-0	5860	Cook, Mathie	1		2		5	6	7	8		4	11			10	3		9				
19	3	Ayr United	0-0	0-0	15265		1		2		5	6	7	8		4	11			10	3		9				
20	8	MOTHERWELL	0-0	1-0	5017	Mathie	1		2		5	6	7			4	11			10	3		9	12	8"		
21	15	Dundee United	1-1	2-1	3255	Morrison, Mathie	1		2		5	6	7	8		4	11			10	3		9				
22	22	PARTICK THISTLE	1-1	1-4	7056	Mathie	1	2	3		5	6	7	8		4	11					10	9				
23	29	Aberdeen	1-2	2-4	13823	I.Fleming, Cook	1	2	3		5	6	7	8		4	11					10	9				
24	12 Feb	EAST FIFE	2-2	2-3	3414	Maxwell	1	2	3		5	6		8		4	7			10	11		9				
25	19	Hearts	1-2	1-2	8503	Morrison	1		2		5	6	7	8		4	11			10	3		9				
26	4 Mar	RANGERS	0-0	1-2	14707	Mathie	1		2		5	6	7	8		4	11			10	3		9				
27	11	Clyde	2-0	3-0	1987	Morrison(2), Mathie	1		2		5	6	7	8		4	11			10	3		9				
28	21	DUNFERMLINE	0-0	0-0	3944		1		2		5	6	7	8		4	11			10	3		9				
29	25	Airdrieonians	2-0	4-0	4065	Morrison, Cook, Mathie, Gilmour	1	2	3		5	6	7	8		4	11			10			9				
30	3 Apr	HIBERNIAN	0-0	1-1	6118	O.G.	1	2	3		5	6	7	8		4	11			10			9				
31	8	CELTIC	0-1	1-3	12620	Morrison	1	2"	3		5	6	7	8		4	11			10	12		9				
32	15	St. Johnstone	0-2	1-5	2290	Maxwell	1		2		5	6	7	8		4	11			10	3	12	9"				
33	22	DUNDEE	0-1	0-3	2625		1		2		5	6	7	8		4	11			10	3		9				
34	29	Morton	1-1	1-1	2692	Morrison	1	2	3		5		7	8		4	11			9		10				6	
						Apps.	34	22	21	2	33	33	33	33	8	34	34	1	1	28	25	4	26		1	1	
						Subs			1						1					1	1	1		2			
						Goals							1	3		8	10			10		1	15				

Pos	P.	W.	D.	L.	F.	A.	Pts.
11th	34	11	6	17	49	64	28

League Cup Section 1

Pos	P.	W.	D.	L.	F.	A.	Pts.
2nd	6	2	1	3	7	9	5

No.	Date	Opposition	H.T.	Res.	Att.	Goalscorers	Hunter	Whyte	Dickson	MacDonald	Rodman	McGrory	McSherry	Gilmour	J.McCulloch	Maxwell	Cook	J.Fleming	Beattie	Morrison	Cairns	I.Fleming	Mathie	King	Sheed	Lee	Stevenson
1	14 Aug	Dundee United	0-0	0-1	6223		1	2	3	10		5			9	4	7	11	6	8							
2	18	MOTHERWELL	1-1	2-1	5138	Morrison, McCulloch	1	2	3	10"		5			9	4	11		6	8	12						7
3	21	Hibernian	0-1	1-3	12515	Beattie	1	2	3			5	10		9	4	11		6	8							7
4	25	Motherwell	0-0	0-2	3284		1	2	3		5	6	7	8	9	10	11"		4	12							
5	28	DUNDEE UNITED	2-1	4-2	3053	McSherry(2), McCulloch, Gilmour	1	2	3		5	6	7	8	9	10	11		4								
6	1 Sep	HIBERNIAN	0-0	0-0	4168		1	2	3		5	6	7	8	9	4	11			10							

Scottish Cup

No.	Date	Opposition	H.T.	Res.	Att.	Goalscorers	Hunter	Whyte	Dickson	MacDonald	Rodman	McGrory	McSherry	Gilmour	J.McCulloch	Maxwell	Cook	J.Fleming	Beattie	Morrison	Cairns	I.Fleming	Mathie	King	Sheed	Lee	Stevenson
3	5 Feb	ALLOA ATHLETIC	3-0	5-1	4415	Mathie(2), Maxwell, Morrison, Cook	1	2	3		5	6	7	8		4	11			10			9				
4	26	Elgin City	2-0	4-1	10506	Maxwell, Mathie, Cook, O.G.	1	12	2		5	6	7	8		4	11			10	3"		9				
QF	18 Mar	Raith Rovers	1-0	3-1	10815	Cook, Maxwell, Morrison	1		2		5	6	7	8		4	11			10	3		9				
SF	12 Apr	Celtic*	0-1	1-3	48398	Cook	1		2		5	6	7	8		4	11			10	3		9				

* Hampden

Once again Killie set off on a Cup run. With the exception of Whyte, all the players pictured here took part in a thrilling Scottish Cup Semi-Final which was won 3-1 by Celtic.
Back: J.Whyte, J.Gilmour, A.Hunter, G.Maxwell, J.McGrory, B.Rodman.
Front: A.Cairns, J.Cook, W.Dickson, J.McSherry, E.Morrison, R.Mathie

SEASON 1972-73 Division One

No.	Date	Opposition	H.T.	Res.	Att.	Goalscorers	Hunter	Whyte	Dickson	Gilmour	McGrory	Lee	Smith	Maxwell	Morrison	McSherry	Cook	I.Fleming	Cairns	Rodman	Cameron	J.McCulloch	Stewart	Robertson	Stevenson	McGovern	Sheed	Mathie
1	2 Sep	Celtic *	1-4	2-6	11661	Cook, Morrison	1	2	3	4	5"	6	7	8	9	10	11	12										
2	9	AYR UNITED	0-0	0-1	5425		1		2	4		6	7	5	9	10	11	8	3									
3	16	Motherwell	0-0	0-2	4451		1	2	3	8		4	11	6	9	7			10	5								
4	23	EAST FIFE	0-2	1-3	2542	Maxwell	1	2	3"	4		6	7	10	9			11		5	8	12						
5	30	RANGERS	1-1	2-1	10643	Morrison(2)		2		4			8	6	9	10	11			5			1	3	7			
6	7 Oct	Arbroath	2-2	3-3	2662	Cook(2), J.McCulloch		2		4			8	6	9	10	11			5		12	1	3	7"			
7	14	ST. JOHNSTONE	1-0	1-4	3061	Maxwell	1	2		8		4	7	6	9	10	11			5				3				
8	21	Dundee	0-1	0-1	5588		1	2		4		8	7	6	9	10	11			5				3				
9	28	AIRDRIEONIANS	1-1	3-1	2776	Morrison, Smith, Maxwell	1	2		4		8	7	6	9	10	11			5				3				
10	4 Nov	Hibernian	1-3	1-4	11172	Morrison	1	2		4		8	7	6	9	10	11			5				3				
11	11	DUMBARTON	0-0	2-2	3039	Morrison, Cook	1	2		4"		8	10	6	9	7	11			5	12			3				
12	18	Aberdeen	0-1	0-3	11054		1	2	8			6	10	4	9	7	11"		12	5				3				
13	25	Morton	0-2	1-2	3043	Morrison	1	2	6				8	4	9	7	11			5				3		10		
14	2 Dec	PARTICK THISTLE	2-0	2-3	3490	Morrison, O.G.	1	2	4				8	6	9		11			5	7"			3		10	12	
15	9	Hearts	0-0	0-0	6568			2	4				8	6	9		11			5	7		1	3		10		
16	16	DUNDEE UNITED	0-0	0-1	2536			2	4				8	6	9		11			5	7		1	3		10"	12	
17	23	Falkirk	0-1	2-3	3114	Smith, Maxwell		2	4				8	6	9		11			5	7		1	3		10		
18	1 Jan	Ayr United	1-0	1-1	8507	Morrison		2	4			12	8	6	9		11			5"	7		1	3		10		
19	6	MOTHERWELL	0-0	1-0	4083	Cameron		2	4			5"	8	6	9		11				7		1	3		10	12	
20	13	East Fife	0-1	0-3	3622			2	4			5	8		9	10	11						1	3		7	6	
21	20	Rangers	0-3	0-4	14515			2	4				8	5	9	10	11						1	3		7	6	
22	27	ARBROATH	1-0	2-0	2869	McSherry, Smith		2	4				8	6	9	7	11			5			1	3		10		
23	7 Feb	CELTIC	0-2	0-4	11185			2	4				8	6	9	7	11		3	5			1			10		
24	10	St. Johnstone	2-2	2-2	2124	McSherry, Smith		2	4				8	6	9	7	11		3	5			1			10"	12	
25	27	DUNDEE	0-1	1-2	2323	Fleming		2	4				10	6	8"	7	11	9		5			1	3			12	
26	3 Mar	Airdrieonians	0-0	1-0	4026	Morrison		2	4				10	6	8	7	11	9		5			1	3				
27	10	HIBERNIAN	0-0	2-2	6700	Morrison, Dickson		2	4				10	6	8	7	11	9		5			1	3				
28	17	Dumbarton	2-1	2-4	4141	Morrison, McSherry		2	4				10	6	8	7	11	9		5			1	3				
29	24	ABERDEEN	0-0	0-2	3908			2	4				10	6	8	7	11	9		5			1	3				
30	31	MORTON	1-0	2-1	2380	Morrison, Whyte		2	4				10	6	8	7	11	9		5			1	3				
31	7 Apr	Partick Thistle	0-0	1-1	5240	McSherry		2	4				10	6	8	7	11	9		5			1	3				
32	14	HEARTS	1-0	2-1	4036	Morrison, Rodman		2	4				10	6	8	7	11	9		5			1	3				
33	21	Dundee United	1-1	1-2	3634	Morrison		2	4				10	6	8	7		9		5			1	3			11	
34	28	FALKIRK	2-0	2-2	5314	Morrison, Sheed		2	3				10	6	8	7		9		5			1		11		4	
						Apps.	12	33	27	11	1	12	34	33	34	27	30	12	4	29	7		22	27	3	12	4	
						Subs						1						1	1		1	2					5	
						Goals		1	1				4	4	16	4	4	1		1	1	1					1	

* Played at Hampden Park

Pos	P.	W.	D.	L.	F.	A.	Pts.
17th	34	7	8	19	40	71	22

League Cup Section 4

Pos	P.	W.	D.	L.	F.	A.	Pts.
3rd	6	2	1	3	9	9	5

No.	Date	Opposition	H.T.	Res.	Att.	Goalscorers	Hunter	Whyte	Dickson	Gilmour	McGrory	Lee	Smith	Maxwell	Morrison	McSherry	Cook	I.Fleming	Cairns	Rodman	Cameron	J.McCulloch	Stewart	Robertson	Stevenson	McGovern	Sheed	Mathie
1	12 Aug	Stenhousemuir	0-0	1-1	1046	Mathie	1	2	10	4		6			8	7	11		3	5								9
2	16	DUNDEE UNITED	2-0	2-3	3548	Gilmour, Cook	1	2	10	4		6		12	8	7"	11		3	5								9
3	19	DUNFERMLINE	2-0	2-1	3066	Morrison, Mathie	1	2	10	4		6			8	7	11		3	5								9
4	23	Dundee United	1-1	1-2	4012	Morrison	1	2	10	4		6			8	7	11		3	5								9
5	26	STENHOUSEMUIR	1-0	3-1	2478	Morrison(3)	1	2	3	4		6	12		8	7"	11	9	10	5								
6	30	Dunfermline	0-0	0-1	2024		1	2		4		6	7		9	10	11	8	3	5								

Scottish Cup

No.	Date	Opposition	H.T.	Res.	Att.	Goalscorers	Hunter	Whyte	Dickson	Gilmour	McGrory	Lee	Smith	Maxwell	Morrison	McSherry	Cook	I.Fleming	Cairns	Rodman	Cameron	J.McCulloch	Stewart	Robertson	Stevenson	McGovern	Sheed	Mathie
3	3 Feb	QUEEN OF THE SOUTH	1-0	2-1	4378	McSherry, Morrison		2	4				8	6	9	7	11			5			1	3		10		
4	24	AIRDRIEONIANS	0-1	0-1	5828			2	4			6	8	10	9	7	11			5			1	3				

Texaco Cup

No.	Date	Opposition	H.T.	Res.	Att.	Goalscorers	Hunter	Whyte	Dickson	Gilmour	McGrory	Lee	Smith	Maxwell	Morrison	McSherry	Cook	I.Fleming	Cairns	Rodman	Cameron	J.McCulloch	Stewart	Robertson	Stevenson	McGovern	Sheed	Mathie
1	12 Sep	Wolves	1-0	1-5	8734	O.G.	1	12	2	4		6	10	8	9	7	11"		3	5								
1	26	WOLVES (Agg: 1-5)	0-0	0-0	3721			2		4			11	6	9	10				5		8	1	3	7			

Smiling faces at the start of the 1972-73 campaign but it ended in tears with Kilmarnock relegated after 19 years in the top flight. Back: Robertson, Cairns, Sheed, Stewart, Morrison, Maxwell, Whyte. Middle: Mathie, Smith, Gilmour, McDicken, Hunter, Lee, McGrory, McCulloch, Rodman. Front: Stevenson, Frye, Christie, Dickson, McSherry, Cook

SEASON 1973-74 Division Two

No.	Date	Opposition	H.T.	Res.	Att.	Goalscorers	Stewart	Whyte	Robertson	McDicken	Rodman	Gilmour	McSherry	Smith	Morrison	Sheed	Stevenson	Dickson	Maxwell	McGovern	Fleming	Cook	Ferguson	A.McCulloch	I.McCulloch	Cameron	Kerr	J.McCulloch
1	1 Sep	CLYDEBANK	2-2	3-2	2848	Stevenson(2), Morrison	1	2	3	4	5	6	7	8	9"	10	11	12										
2	5	Berwick Rangers	0-2	1-4	917	Morrison	1	2	3	4	5		7	8	9	10	11"		6	12								
3	8	St. Mirren	1-1	3-1	4768	Fleming(2), Cook	1	2	3		5		7	8	10	4			6		9	11						
4	15	MONTROSE	1-0	2-1	2607	Fleming, O.G.	1	2	3		5"		4	8	10	7			6		9	11	12					
5	19	Queen of the South	0-1	0-1	2463		1	2	3		5		4	8	10	7			6		9	11						
6	29	COWDENBEATH	2-2	4-3	2222	Morrison, Sheed, Maxwell, Smith	1	2			5	4	7"	10	9	8	12	3	6			11						
7	2 Oct	BERWICK RANGERS	1-2	2-3	2213	Gilmour, Morrison	1	2			5	4	7	10	9	8		3	6		12	11"						
8	6	Alloa Athletic	0-0	1-0	2004	Smith	1	2	3	6	5		7	11	9	10			4		8							
9	13	AIRDRIEONIANS	1-0	4-0	4281	Maxwell, Fleming, McSherry, Morrison	1	2	3		5		4	11	9	10			6		8	7						
10	20	Queens Park	0-0	2-0	1446	Fleming, Morrison	1	2	3		5	12	4	11"	9	10			6		8	7						
11	27	RAITH ROVERS	0-1	1-1	4181	Maxwell	1	2	3		5	12	4	11"	9	10			6		8	7						
12	10 Nov	Stranraer	1-1	2-2	1558	Fleming, Maxwell	1	2	3		5		7		9	10		6	4		8	11						
13	17	FORFAR ATHLETIC	2-0	5-1	2730	Fleming(2), Morrison(2), McSherry	1		3	5	2		4	11	9	10			6	12	8	7"						
14	21	Albion Rovers	3-0	4-3	295	Morrison(2), Smith(2)	1		3	5	2		4	7	9	10			6	11"	8	12						
15	1 Dec	BRECHIN CITY	1-1	3-1	2769	Fleming(2), Morrison		2	3		5		4	11	9	10			6		8	7		1				
16	22	Stirling Albion	0-0	1-1	1192	Cook	1	2	3		5		4	11	9	10			6		8	7						
17	29	Clydebank	0-0	2-1	1611	Fleming, Smith	1	2	3		5		4	11	9"	10			6		8	7				12		
18	1 Jan	ST. MIRREN	0-1	1-1	4599	Fleming	1	2	3		5		4		9	10	11		6		8	7"				12		
19	5	Montrose	2-0	2-0	914	Morrison, Sheed	1	2	3		5		4	11	9	10	7"		6		8				12			
20	12	HAMILTON	2-1	3-1	4927	Morrison, Smith, Fleming	1	2	3		5		4	11	9	10			6		8	7						
21	19	Cowdenbeath	3-0	4-2	788	Smith(2), Morrison, McSherry	1	2	3	12	5		4	11	9	10"			6		8	7						
22	2 Feb	ALLOA ATHLETIC	4-0	8-2	3515	I.McCllch(2),Flmng(2),Smth(2),Sheed,Mxwll	1	2	3	12	5			11	9*	10	14		6"		8	7			4			
23	9	Airdrieonians	0-0	0-0	7824		1	2	3		5		12	11	9	10			6		8	7			4"			
24	16	Stenhousemuir	0-0	1-0	978	Smith	1	2"	3	12	5		4	11	9	10			6		8	7						
25	2 Mar	Raith Rovers	1-2	1-3	2081	Cook	1		3		5		4	11	9	10"			6		8	7	2		12			
26	16	STRANRAER	3-1	4-1	3168	Morrison(3), Fleming	1		3		5		4"	11	9	10			6		8	7	2				12	
27	23	Forfar Athletic	3-3	5-3	697	Fleming(3), McDicken, Maxwell	1		3	14	5			11		10"			6		8	7	2		4	9	12*	
28	30	ALBION ROVERS	2-1	3-1	3067	Maxwell(2), Morrison	1		3	12	5			11	9	10			6		8	7	2"		4			
29	6 Apr	Brechin City	3-0	4-0	497	Fleming(2), Morrison(2)	1	2	3		5		4	11	9	10			6		8	7						
30	9	EAST STIRLING	1-0	4-0	3787	Fleming(2), Morrison, Robertson	1	2	3		5		4	11"	9	10			6		8	7			12			
31	13	STENHOUSEMUIR	2-0	3-1	3813	Fleming(2), Morrison	1	2	3		5		4	11	9	10			6		8	7						
32	16	QUEENS PARK	2-0	5-0	4225	Fleming(3), Morrison(2)	1	2	3		5		4	11	9	10			6		8	7						
33	20	East Stirling	1-1	3-1	1250	Maxwell, Cook, Fleming	1	2	3		5		4	11	9	10			6		8	7						
34	24	QUEEN OF THE SOUTH	0-0	1-0	4880	Fleming	1	2	3		5		4"	11	9	10			6		8	7			12			
35	27	STIRLING ALBION	0-1	2-1	5675	Fleming, Morrison	1	2	3		5		4"	11	9	10			6		8	7			12			
36	30	Hamilton	1-1	2-2	2852	Fleming(2)	1		3		5		4	11	9	10			6		8	7	2					
						Apps.	35	29	34	5	36	3	32	34	35	36	4	3	35	1	32	31	5	1	4	1		
						Subs				5		2	1				2	1		2	1	1	1		5	2	2	
						Goals			1	1		1	3	11	25	3	2		9		33	4			2			

Pos	P.	W.	D.	L.	F.	A.	Pts.
2nd	36	26	6	4	96	44	58

League Cup Section 5

Pos	P.	W.	D.	L.	F.	A.	Pts.
1st	6	3	2	1	13	4	8

No.	Date	Opposition	H.T.	Res.	Att.	Goalscorers	Stewart	Whyte	Robertson	McDicken	Rodman	Gilmour	McSherry	Smith	Morrison	Sheed	Stevenson	Dickson	Maxwell	McGovern	Fleming	Cook	Ferguson	A.McCulloch	I.McCulloch	Cameron	Kerr	J.McCulloch
1	11 Aug	East Stirling	1-1	2-3	1060	Smith, Cameron	1	2	3		5	4		8	9"	14	7	10*	6							12		11
2	15	HAMILTON	0-0	0-0	3169		1	2	3	4	5		7	8	9				6							10		11
3	18	QUEENS PARK	1-0	2-0	2591	Morrison, Smith	1	2	3	4	5		7	8	9	11			6							10"		12
4	22	Hamilton	3-0	4-0	2450	Smith, Morrison, McSherry, Stevenson	1	2	3	4	5		7	8	9	10	11		6									
5	25	Queens Park	1-0	1-1	1292	Sheed	1	2	3	4	5		7	8	9	10	11		6									
6	29	EAST STIRLING	1-0	4-0	2805	Morrison(2), Maxwell(2)	1	2	3	4	5	12	7*	8	9	10"	11		6	14								
2	12 Sep	St. Johnstone	0-0	0-1	3600		1	2	3		5		7	8	10	4			6		9	11						
2	10 Oct	ST. JOHNSTONE (Agg: 3-2)	2-0	3-1"	3478	Maxwell, Fleming, McSherry	1	2	3	6"	5		7	11	9	10		12	4		8							
QF	30	Albion Rovers	0-1	0-2	2821		1	2	3		5	4"	7		9	10			6		8	11				12		
QF	24 Nov	ALBION ROVERS (Agg 5-4)	4-1	5-2	5287	Robertson,Morrison,Cook, Fleming,Maxwell	1		3	5	2		4	7	9	10			6		8	11						
SF	5 Dec	Dundee *	0-0	0-1	4682		1	2	3		5		4	11	9	10			6		8	7						

" After Extra Time - 90 minutes 2-1. * Hampden.

Scottish Cup

No.	Date	Opposition	H.T.	Res.	Att.	Goalscorers	Stewart	Whyte	Robertson	McDicken	Rodman	Gilmour	McSherry	Smith	Morrison	Sheed	Stevenson	Dickson	Maxwell	McGovern	Fleming	Cook	Ferguson	A.McCulloch	I.McCulloch	Cameron	Kerr	J.McCulloch
3	26 Jan	Hibernian	2-3	2-5	14241	Morrison(2)	1	2	3	12	5		4	11	9				6		8	7			10"			

A record number of points & a highest-ever goals tally - thanks to the prolific pairing of Fleming & Morrison - put this outfit back into the big league after just 12 months absence.
Back: McCulloch, Maxwell, Robertson, Stewart, McDicken, Sheed, Whyte
Front: Cook, Morrison, Rodman, McSherry, Fleming, Smith

SEASON 1974-75 Division One

No.	Date	Opposition	H.T.	Res.	Att.	Goalscorers	Stewart	Maxwell	Robertson	I.McCulloch	Rodman	McDicken	Cook	Fleming	E.Morrison	Sheed	Smith	McSherry	Fallis	Kerr	Provan	McLean	A.McCulloch	Whyte	D.Morrison
1	31 Aug	Celtic	0-1	0-5	26482		1	2	3	4	5	6	7	8	9	10	11								
2	7 Sep	AYR UNITED	0-0	3-0	7279	Sheed(2), Fleming	1	2	3	4	5	6		8	9	10	11	7							
3	14	Hearts	1-1	1-1	7306	Fleming	1	2	3	4	5	6		8	9	10	11	7							
4	21	ABERDEEN	0-0	1-0	5727	McDicken	1	2	3	4	5	6		8	9	10	11	7							
5	28	RANGERS	0-2	0-6	19609		1	2	3	4	5	6		8	9"	10	11	7	12						
6	5 Oct	St. Johnstone	1-1	2-2	2579	E.Morrison, Sheed	1	2	3	4	5	6		8	9	10	11	7"	12						
7	12	DUNDEE	1-1	1-1	4951	Smith	1	2	3	4	5	6		8	9	10	11	7							
8	19	Motherwell	0-1	0-2	3628		1	2	3	4	5	6		8	9	10	11	7							
9	2 Nov	Partick Thistle	0-2	2-2	3676	E.Morrison, Sheed	1	2	3	4	5	6		8	9	10	7"	11		12					
10	9	Morton	2-0	3-2	2155	Sheed, McDicken, Smith	1	2	3	4	5	6		8	9	10	7	11							
11	13	HIBERNIAN	1-0	1-1	5240	McDicken	1	2	3	4	5	6		8	9	10	7	11							
12	16	DUNFERMLINE	2-1	2-4	5327	Fleming(2)	1	2	3	4	5	6		8	9	10		11			7				
13	23	Clyde	1-3	2-4	1605	E.Morrison(2)	1	2"	3	4	5	6		8*	9	10	7	11			14	12			
14	30	ARBROATH	0-2	2-2	3426	Sheed, E.Morrison	1			4	5	6		8	9	10	11				7	3		2	
15	14 Dec	AIRDRIEONIANS	2-2	3-3	3931	Maxwell(2), Fleming	1	6	3	8	4	5		11	9	10"	12				7	2			
16	21	Dundee United	2-0	4-3	4415	E.Morrison, Maxwell, Fleming, Sheed	1	11	3	4	5"	6		8	9	10	12				7	2			
17	28	CELTIC	0-1	0-1	17646		1	10	3	4	5	6		8	9		11				7	2			
18	1 Jan	Ayr United	2-2	2-3	9968	Smith, Fleming	1		3	4	5	6		8	9"	10	11		12		7	2			
19	4	HEARTS	1-0	1-1	7233	Fleming		11	3	4	5	6		8		10	9		12		7"	2	1		
20	11	Aberdeen	0-2	0-4	8462			6	3	4"	5				9*	10	8		11		7	2	1	12	14
21	1 Feb	ST. JOHNSTONE	1-1	1-1	3938	E.Morrison		12	3	4"	5	6		8	9*	10	11	14			7	2	1		
22	8	Dundee	1-2	1-4	4835	Sheed			3	4	5	6		8	9"	10	11			12	7	2	1		
23	15	Rangers	2-1	3-3	27157	McDicken, Provan, Fallis		12	3	4"	5	6		8	9*	10	11		14		7	2	1		
24	22	MOTHERWELL	2-0	3-1	6097	E.Morrison(2), Maxwell		2	3	12	5"	6			9	10	11		8		7	4	1		
25	26	Dumbarton	1-0	1-1	4069	Sheed		2	3		5	6			9	10	11		8		7	4	1		
26	1 Mar	Hibernian	1-0	2-0	7866	E.Morrison, Fallis		2	3		5	6			9	10	11		8		7	4	1		
27	8	PARTICK THISTLE	0-0	1-1	6676	Maxwell		2	3		5	6		12	9	10	11		8		7"	4	1		
28	15	MORTON	2-1	2-1	4155	Smith, Fleming		2	3		5	6		8	9"	10	11		12		7	4	1		
29	22	Dunfermline	1-1	1-1	2594	E.Morrison		2	3	12	5	6		8	9	10	11		7			4"	1		
30	29	CLYDE	0-0	2-0	5054	Smith, Maxwell		2	3	4	5	6		8	9	10	11				7		1		
31	5 Apr	Arbroath	0-0	0-0	1439			2	3	4	5	6			9		11		8		7	10	1		
32	12	DUMBARTON	0-2	1-2	5489	Fleming		2	3	4	5	6		12	9	10	11		8		7"		1		
33	19	Airdrieonians	2-1	2-2	3827	Fallis, McLean		2	3		5	6		8	9"	10	11		7		12	4	1		
34	26	DUNDEE UNITED	2-3	2-4	7589	Fallis, Fleming		2	3		5	6		8	12	10	11		9		7"	4	1		
						Apps.	18	29	33	26	34	33	1	27	32	32	31	12	10		20	19	16	1	
						Subs		2		2				2	1		2	1	6	2	2	1		1	1
						Goals		6				4		11	11	9	5		4		1	1			

Pos	P.	W.	D.	L.	F.	A.	Pts.
12th	34	8	15	11	52	68	31

League Cup Section 5

Pos	P.	W.	D.	L.	F.	A.	Pts.
1st	6	5	1	0	18	1	11

No.	Date	Opposition	H.T.	Res.	Att.	Goalscorers	Stewart	Maxwell	Robertson	I.McCulloch	Rodman	McDicken	Cook	Fleming	E.Morrison	Sheed	Smith	McSherry	Fallis	Kerr	Provan	McLean	A.McCulloch	Whyte	D.Morrison
1	10 Aug	MONTROSE	1-0	2-0	3264	I.McCulloch, Fleming	1	6	3	4		5	7	8		10	11		9					2	
2	14	Strenraer	1-0	5-0	1338	Fleming(3), Smith(2)	1	6	3	4		5	7	8		10	11		9					2	
3	17	Queens Park	2-0	2-0	1559	Fleming(2)	1	2	3	4	5	6	7	8		10"	11	12	9						
4	21	STRANRAER	2-0	2-0	3358	Maxwell, E.Morrison	1	2	3	4	5	6	7	8	9	10	11								
5	24	QUEENS PARK	3-0	6-0	3300	Fleming(2),E.Morrison,Cook,Smith,Rodman	1	2	3	4	5	6	7	8	9	10	11								
6	28	Montrose	1-0	1-1	1179	Fleming	1	2	3	4	5	6	7	8		10	11		9						
QF	11 Sep	HIBERNIAN	2-1	3-3	10022	Fleming(2), E.Morrison	1	2	3	4	5	6		8	9	10	11	7"	12						
QF	25	Hibernian (Agg: 4-7)	1-1	1-4	15694	E.Morrison	1	2	3	4	5	6		8	9	10	11	7							

Scottish Cup

No.	Date	Opposition	H.T.	Res.	Att.	Goalscorers	Stewart	Maxwell	Robertson	I.McCulloch	Rodman	McDicken	Cook	Fleming	E.Morrison	Sheed	Smith	McSherry	Fallis	Kerr	Provan	McLean	A.McCulloch	Whyte	D.Morrison
1	29 Jan	Hearts	0-0	0-2	21054				3	4	5	6		8	9	10	11				7	2	1		

Drybrough Cup

No.	Date	Opposition	H.T.	Res.	Att.	Goalscorers	Stewart	Maxwell	Robertson	I.McCulloch	Rodman	McDicken	Cook	Fleming	E.Morrison	Sheed	Smith	McSherry	Fallis	Kerr	Provan	McLean	A.McCulloch	Whyte	D.Morrison
QF	27 Jul	Hibernian	0-1	1-2	13272	Fallis	1	2	3	4	5	6	7	8	9"	10		12	11						

Kilmarnock still produced players of great individual talent in the 70's. GORDON SMITH, grandson of the legendary Mattha' Smith, was nicknamed 'Casper' on account of his ability to 'ghost' past defenders. His eventual transfer to Rangers split the board and antagonised the fans. Later, he became famous south of the border for missing an 'easy' shot at goal when playing for Brighton in the 1983 F.A. Cup Final.

SEASON 1975-76 First Division

No.	Date	Opposition	H.T.	Res.	Att.	Goalscorers
1	30 Aug	HAMILTON	4-2	4-2	3917	Smith, Fallis, Provan, E.Morrison
2	6 Sep	Airdrieonians	2-3	4-3	3683	E.Morrison(2), Fallis, Smith
3	13	PARTICK THISTLE	0-0	0-1	6375	
4	20	East Fife	2-2	4-2	2344	Smith(2), I.Fleming, Fallis
5	27	CLYDE	1-0	3-0	3610	I.Fleming(2), E.Morrison
6	4 Oct	ST. MIRREN	3-1	3-1	3577	E.Morrison(2), McLean
7	11	Montrose	0-1	0-2	1724	
8	18	ARBROATH	1-0	2-1	3801	Fallis, Smith
9	25	Morton	2-1	3-1	2137	I.Fleming(2), Smith
10	1 Nov	Falkirk	0-0	1-0	3862	Smith
11	8	QUEEN OF THE SOUTH	0-0	2-0	4345	Provan, Fallis
12	15	Dunfermline	0-0	0-1	2673	
13	22	DUMBARTON	1-0	1-0	4532	Fallis
14	29	Clyde	1-0	2-0	2662	McDicken, Fallis
15	6 Dec	St. Mirren	0-0	0-0	5800	
16	13	MONTROSE	0-0	1-1	3992	McLean
17	20	Arbroath	0-1	0-2	1838	
18	27	MORTON	3-0	3-2	4344	E.Morrison, Fallis, Smith
19	1 Jan	AIRDRIEONIANS	0-1	2-1	5010	Provan, Smith
20	3	Partick Thistle	0-1	0-2	11507	
21	10	DUNFERMLINE	3-0	4-0	3831	Fallis, Sheed, O.G 2
22	17	Dumbarton	0-1	0-3	2611	
23	31	EAST FIFE	1-1	2-1	4003	Clarke, McCulloch
24	7 Feb	Hamilton	0-0	1-1	3000	Rodman
25	21	FALKIRK	1-0	1-0	3773	Fallis
26	28	Queen of the South	0-2	1-2	4557	Rodman

No.	Stewart	McLean	Robertson	I.McCulloch	Rodman	McDicken	Provan	Fallis	E.Morrison	Sheed	Smith	Clarke	I.Fleming	Maxwell	Jenkins	Wilson	D.Morrison	Sharp	Murdoch	C.Fleming	Matthews	Ferguson	A.McCulloch
1	1	2	3	4	5	6"	7	8	9	10	11	12											
2	1	2	3	4	5	6"	7	8	9*	10	11	12	14										
3	1	2	3	4	5	14	7	8	9"	10*	11	6	12										
4	1	2	3	4	5	10	7	8"	9		11		12	6									
5	1	2	3	4	5	6	7	9	10		11		8										
6	1	2	3	4	5	6	7	9	10		11		8										
7	1	2	3	4	5	6	7"	9	10		11		8	12									
8	1	2	3	4	5	6	7"	9	10		11		8	12									
9	1	2	3	4	5	6"	12	10	11*		7		9	8	14								
10	1	2	3	4	5		7"	9			11	6	8	10								12	
11	1	2	3	4	5		7"	9	10		11	6	8			12							
12	1	2	3	4	5		7	9	10"		11	6	8			12							
13	1	2	3	4	5"	10	7	8		14	11	6	9*	12									
14	1	2	3	4		9	7	8		10	11"	5	12	6									
15	1	2	3	4		9	7	8		10	11	5		6									
16	1	2	3	4	12	9"	7	8		10	11	5		6									
17	1	2	3	4		9"	7	8		10	11	5		6			12						
18	1	2	3	4			7"	8	9	10	11	5		6			12						
19	1	2"	3	4	12		7	8	9	10	11	5		6									
20	1	12	3	4	6"		7	8	9	10	11	5		2									
21	1	12	3	4"	5		7	8		10	11	6		2				9					
22	1	2	3		5	4	7	8	12	10	11	6"						9					
23	1		3	7	5			8		10	11	6		2				9	4				
24	1		3	7	5			8		10	11	6		2				9	4				
25	1		3		5	9"	7	8		10	11	6		2			12		4				
26	1		3		5	9	7	8"		10		6		2				12	4	11			
Apps.	26	20	26	23	20	16	23	26	14	16	25	18	9	15				4	4	1			
Subs		2			2	1	1		1	1		2	4	3	1	2	3	1				1	
Goals		2		1	2	1	3	10	7	1	9	1	5										

Pos	P.	W.	D.	L.	F.	A.	Pts.
2nd	26	16	3	7	44	29	35

League Cup Section 4

Pos	P.	W.	D.	L.	F.	A.	Pts.
3rd	6	2	0	4	5	9	4

No.	Date	Opposition	H.T.	Res.	Att.	Goalscorers
1	9 Aug	PARTICK THISTLE	1-2	1-3	4724	Sheed
2	13	St. Johnstone	1-1	1-2	2293	I.Fleming
3	16	Dundee United	0-1	0-2	4050	
4	20	ST. JOHNSTONE	0-0	1-0	2383	McCulloch
5	23	DUNDEE UNITED	0-0	1-0	2795	Fallis
6	27	Partick Thistle	0-2	1-2	5211	E.Morrison

No.	Stewart	McLean	Robertson	I.McCulloch	Rodman	McDicken	Provan	Fallis	E.Morrison	Sheed	Smith	Clarke	I.Fleming	Maxwell	Jenkins	Wilson	D.Morrison	Sharp	Murdoch	C.Fleming	Matthews	Ferguson	A.McCulloch
1	1	4	3	7		6"		9		10*	11	5	8	2							12	14	
2	1	2	3	7		4		9		10	11	5	8	6									
3	1	2	3	11		4	7			10	9	5	8	6									
4	1	2	3	4		6	7	9	12		10"	5	8								11		
5	1	2"	3	4		6	7	11	9		10	5	8									12	
6	1	12	3	4	2	6	7	11	9		10	5	8"										

Scottish Cup

No.	Date	Opposition	H.T.	Res.	Att.	Goalscorers
3	24 Jan	Stenhousemuir	1-1	1-1	1870	Sheed
3R	28	STENHOUSEMUIR	0-0	1-0	4926	Smith
4	14 Feb	FALKIRK	1-0	3-1	6454	McDicken(2), O.G.
QF	6 Mar	Dumbarton	0-0	1-2	7796	Fallis

No.	Stewart	McLean	Robertson	I.McCulloch	Rodman	McDicken	Provan	Fallis	E.Morrison	Sheed	Smith	Clarke	I.Fleming	Maxwell	Jenkins	Wilson	D.Morrison	Sharp	Murdoch	C.Fleming	Matthews	Ferguson	A.McCulloch
3	1	2	3	4	5		7	8		10"	11	12		6				9					
3R	1		3	4	5		7	8		10	11	6		2				9					
4	1		3	4	5	9	7	8		10	11	6		2									
QF	1		3	4	5	9	7	8		10	11	6		2									

Spring Cup Section 2

Pos	P.	W.	D.	L.	F.	A.	Pts.
3rd	6	1	3	2	5	6	5

No.	Date	Opposition	H.T.	Res.	Att.	Goalscorers
1	10 Mar	Berwick Rangers	0-0	0-0	345	
2	13	ALLOA ATHLETIC	0-0	0-0	2568	
3	20	FALKIRK	0-0	0-1	2072	
4	27	Alloa Athletic	1-0	2-2	928	Maxwell, C.Fleming
5	3 Apr	BERWICK RANGERS	2-0	3-1	1445	Murdoch(2), Smith
6	10	Falkirk	0-2	0-2	2257	

No.	Stewart	McLean	Robertson	I.McCulloch	Rodman	McDicken	Provan	Fallis	E.Morrison	Sheed	Smith	Clarke	I.Fleming	Maxwell	Jenkins	Wilson	D.Morrison	Sharp	Murdoch	C.Fleming	Matthews	Ferguson	A.McCulloch
1	1		3	8	5	6	7			11	10			2				9	4				
2	1		3	8	5	6	7			11	10			2				9	4				
3	1		3	10	5	6	7				8			2				9	4	11			
4	1	14	3	10	5	6"				8	7	12		2				9	4	11*			
5			3	11	5			8		10	7	6		2				9	4	12			1
6	1	11	3	8"	5			9		10	7	6		2					4				

Flying winger DAVIE PROVAN was one of the heroes who put Killie into the Premier Division this term. He was later transferred to Celtic for a record fee between Scottish clubs.

SEASON 1976-77 Premier Division

No.	Date	Opposition	H.T.	Res.	Att.	Goalscorers	Stewart	S.McLean	Robertson	Murdoch	Clarke	Welsh	Provan	I.McCulloch	Fallis	Sheed	Smith	Sharp	Maxwell	Jardine	McDicken	A.McCulloch	Doherty	Ward	A.McLean	C.Fleming
1	4 Sep	MOTHERWELL	1-1	1-1	5163	Clarke	1	2	3	4	5	6	7	8	9"	10	11	12								
2	11	Rangers	0-0	0-0	24800		1	2	3	4	5	6	7	8	9	10	11									
3	18	Aberdeen	0-0	0-2	9566		1	2	3	4	5	6	7	8	9	10	11									
4	25	CELTIC	0-2	0-4	14615		1	2	3	4	5	6	7	8	9		11		10							
5	2 Oct	Hearts	2-1	2-2	9333	McCulloch, McDicken	1	2"	3	4	5	6		7	9	10	11		12		8					
6	23	Partick Thistle	0-1	1-2	4749	Fallis	1	2	3	4	5	6	7	8"	9	10			12		11*					
7	26	HIBERNIAN	1-0	1-1	4202	Smith	1	2	3	4	5	6	7		9	10	11				8					
8	30	AYR UNITED	4-0	6-1	6422	Fallis(3), Sheed, McDicken, Murdoch	1	2	3	4	5	6	7		9	10"	11		12		8					
9	3 Nov	Dundee United	0-2	0-3	4886		1	2	3	4	5	6	7		9	10	11	12			8"					
10	6	Motherwell	2-0	4-5	4754	Fallis(2), Maxwell, Smith	1	2	3	4*	5	6	7		9	10	11		12		8"				14	
11	13	RANGERS	0-3	0-4	14717			2*	3	4	5	6	7		9	10	11		12		8"	1			14	
12	20	ABERDEEN	1-0	1-2	4212	Smith	1	8	3	4	5	6	7		9	10	11		2							
13	27	Celtic	1-2	1-2	20337	McCulloch	1		3	4	5	6	7	8	9	10"	11		2		12					
14	18 Dec	DUNDEE UNITED	0-0	1-0	3529	Fallis	1		3	4	5	6	7	8	9		11"		2		10		12			
15	27	PARTICK THISTLE	0-0	0-0	5018		1	14	3	4	5	6	7	8	9"		11		2		10*		12			
16	1 Jan	Ayr United	1-1	1-3	7938	Smith	1		3	4	5	6	7	8	9		11		2		10					
17	3	MOTHERWELL	1-2	2-2	6309	Fallis, Maxwell	1		3	4	5	6	7	8	9		11		2		10					
18	8	Rangers	0-1	0-3	18189		1		3	4"	5	6	7	8	9	12	11		2		10					
19	22	CELTIC	1-1	1-3	14363	Fallis	1		3	4	5	6	7	8	9	12	11"		2		10					
20	5 Feb	Hearts	0-4	0-4	7226		1		3	4	5	6"	7	8	9	12	14		2		10		11*			
21	7	Aberdeen	0-0	0-2	8477		1		3	4	5		7	8	9	10			2		6				11	
22	12	HIBERNIAN	0-0	0-1	3397		1	2	3	4		5	8		9	10	7				6		12		11"	
23	15	HEARTS	1-1	2-1	3182	Robertson, McDicken	1		3	4	5	6	8		9	10	7		2		11					
24	19	Dundee United	0-3	0-4	5096		1	12	3	4	5	6"	8		9*	10	7		2		11		14			
25	5 Mar	Partick Thistle	1-2	1-3	3147	Smith	1	14	3	4"	5		8	10	11*		7		2	12	6		9			
26	9	Hibernian	0-2	0-2	3158		1		3	4		5	8	10			7		2	12	6		9			11"
27	12	AYR UNITED	0-0	0-1	4124		1		3	4	5		8	10			7	11	2	12	6		9"			
28	19	Motherwell	0-1	0-2	4080		1	12	3		5"		7	4		10	9	11*	2	8	6		14			
29	26	RANGERS	0-0	1-0	8037	Robertson	1		3	12	5		7	4	9	10"	11		2	8	6					
30	2 Apr	ABERDEEN	1-1	1-2	2330	McCulloch	1		3	10	5		7	4	9"		11	12	2	8	6					
31	9	Celtic	0-0	0-1	18759		1		3	10	5		7	4	9		11		2	8	6					
32	13	Ayr United	0-1	1-1	5046	Smith	1	12	3	10	5		7	4	9"		11		2	8	6					
33	16	HEARTS	2-0	2-2	2471	McDicken, Smith	1		3	10	5		7	4	9		11		2	8	6					
34	20	PARTICK THISTLE	1-1	1-3	1543	Provan	1	12	3	10	5		7	4	9*		11	14	2	8	6"					
35	23	Hibernian	0-0	0-0	3457		1	2	3	10	5		7"	4	14		12	11	6	8	9					
36	30	DUNDEE UNITED	1-1	1-2	1643	Fallis	1	2	3	10				4	9		7	11	6	8				5		
						Apps.	35	15	36	34	33	24	34	27	32	18	32	4	25	9	29	1	4	1	2	1
						Subs		6		1					1	3	2	4	5	3	1		5		2	
						Goals			2	1	1		1	3	10	1	7		2		4					

Pos	P.	W.	D.	L.	F.	A.	Pts.
10th	36	4	9	23	32	71	17

League Cup Section 2

Pos	P.	W.	D.	L.	F.	A.	Pts.
3rd	6	2	1	3	6	8	5

No.	Date	Opposition	H.T.	Res.	Att.	Goalscorers	Stewart	S.McLean	Robertson	Murdoch	Clarke	Welsh	Provan	I.McCulloch	Fallis	Sheed	Smith	Sharp	Maxwell	Jardine	McDicken	A.McCulloch	Doherty	Ward	A.McLean	C.Fleming
1	14 Aug	Aberdeen	0-2	0-2	11758		1	2	3	4	5	6	7	8		10	11	12			9"					
2	18	AYR UNITED	0-0	2-0	6408	Provan, Murdoch	1	2	3	4	5	6	7	8	9	10	11									
3	21	ST. MIRREN	0-0	1-1	4242	Fallis	1	2	3	4	5	6	7	8	9	10	11									
4	25	Ayr United	1-1	1-3	5173	McCulloch	1	2	3	4	5	6	7	8	9	10	11									
5	28	St. Mirren	0-0	0-1	3712		1	2	3	4	5	6	7	8	9	10	11									
6	1 Sep	ABERDEEN	1-0	2-1	2536	Smith, Welsh	1	2	3	4	5	6	7	8	9	10"	11		12							

Scottish Cup

No.	Date	Opposition	H.T.	Res.	Att.	Goalscorers	Stewart	S.McLean	Robertson	Murdoch	Clarke	Welsh	Provan	I.McCulloch	Fallis	Sheed	Smith	Sharp	Maxwell	Jardine	McDicken	A.McCulloch	Doherty	Ward	A.McLean	C.Fleming
3	29 Jan	Motherwell	0-3	0-3	8355		1		3	4	5	6	7	8	9		11"		2		10		12			

Anglo Scottish Cup

No.	Date	Opposition	H.T.	Res.	Att.	Goalscorers	Stewart	S.McLean	Robertson	Murdoch	Clarke	Welsh	Provan	I.McCulloch	Fallis	Sheed	Smith	Sharp	Maxwell	Jardine	McDicken	A.McCulloch	Doherty	Ward	A.McLean	C.Fleming
1	7 Aug	Motherwell	1-0	1-1	4706	Smith	1	2	3	4	5	6	7	8	9	10	11									
1	11	MOTHERWELL (Agg: 5-1)	2-0	4-0	5216	Fallis, P.Clarke, McDicken, O.G.	1	2	3	4"	5	6	7	8	9	10	11				12					
QF	14 Sep	Nottm Forest	0-0	1-2	8911	Smith	1	2	3	4	5	6	7	8	9	10	11									
QF	28	NOTTM FOREST (Agg: 3-4)	1-0	2-2*	4503	Fallis(2)	1	2	3	4	5"	6	7	8	9		11		10		12					

* After extra time. 90 mins. 2-1

The squad that gave Killie a taste of Premier action. Back: Wilson, A.McLean, Provan, I.McCulloch, S.McLean,Kelly, Murdoch, Hynds, Doherty. Middle:Allan(Physo), Fallis, Robertson,Sharp, A.McCulloch, McDicken, J.Stewart, Clarke, Welsh, Jenkins, R.Stewart(Train). Front: Fernie(Man), Fleming, Dixon, McQueen, Smith, Sheed, Gray, Rodman, Murray, Baird, Sneddon(Coach), Maxwell not in line-up.

SEASON 1977-78 First Division

No.	Date	Opposition	H.T.	Res.	Att.	Goalscorers	Stewart	Hynds	Robertson	Murdoch	Welsh	Maxwell	Provan	Jardine	Fallis	McLean	Smith	Doherty	Clarke	McGillivray	McDicken	McDowell	McCulloch	Arkison	Stein	Gray	Baird
1	13 Aug	MORTON	0-0	0-3	3462		1	2	3	4	5	6	7	8"	9	10	11	12									
2	20	Stirling Albion	1-0	1-2	2100	Murdoch	1		3	4	5	2"	7	8	9	12			6	11	10						
3	27	HEARTS	1-0	1-1	5003	Doherty	1		3	4"	2	10	8	12	7			9	5	11	6						
4	10 Sep	Queen of the South	0-0	0-1	2563		1		3	4	2		8		7"			12	5	11	6	10	9				
5	14	Hamilton	0-1	1-2	1748	Arkison	1		3		2	10	8	7"					5	11	6	9	4	12			
6	17	ARBROATH	1-0	3-0	2195	McDowell(2), McGillivray	1		3	10	2		8	12					5	11	6	9	4	7"			
7	24	AIRDRIEONIANS	0-0	0-0	2565		1		3	10	2		8"	7	12				5	11	6	9	4				
8	28	Montrose	0-0	0-0	989		1	12	3		2	6	7	10"					5	11	8	9	4				
9	1 Oct	Dundee	1-1	1-2	4719	McCulloch	1	10"	3	14	2	6	7		12				5	11*	8	9	4				
10	8	DUMBARTON	1-0	2-2	3186	Stein, McCulloch	1		3	10		2	7	11					5		6	9	4		8		
11	15	Alloa Athletic	0-1	2-1	1382	Murdoch, McCulloch	1		3	12		6	7	10		2				11"	5	8	4		9		
12	19	ST. JOHNSTONE	0-0	0-1	1905		1		3	11"			7	10		2			5	12	6	8	4		9		
13	22	Morton	1-0	2-0	4256	Maxwell, McDowell	1		3			10	7	4		2			5		6	8	11		9		
14	29	STIRLING ALBION	1-0	2-3	2896	Stein, Maxwell	1		3			10	7	4		2			5		6	8	11		9		
15	5 Nov	Hearts	0-1	2-1	7703	McDowell(2)	1		3			10	7	4		2			5		6	8	11		9		
16	12	QUEEN OF THE SOUTH	1-0	1-1	2494	Provan	1		3	12		10	7	4"		2			5		6	8	11		9		
17	19	Arbroath	1-1	2-2	1192	Maxwell, McDowell	1		3			10	7	4		2			5		6	8	11		9		
18	25	Airdrieonians	1-0	2-1	1636	Stein, Provan	1		3			10	7	4		2			5		6	8	11		9		
19	3 Dec	DUNDEE	1-0	1-0	3549	McDowell	1		3	12		10	7	4		2"			5		6	8	11		9		
20	10	Dumbarton	1-1	2-2	2174	McDowell, Maxwell	1				3	10	7	4		2			5		6	8	11		9		
21	17	ALLOA ATHLETIC	1-0	3-1	2795	Stein(2), McDowell	1				3	10	7	4		2			5		6	8	11		9		
22	24	East Fife	3-0	3-2	1391	Stein, Maxwell, Robertson	1		3		12	10	7	4"		2			5		6	8	11		9		
23	31	Hearts	0-2	0-3	13063		1		3			10	7	4		2			5		6	8	11		9		
24	2 Jan	QUEEN OF THE SOUTH	1-0	2-0	5154	Stein, Maxwell	1		3			10	7	4		2			5		6	8	11		9		
25	7	Stirling Albion	0-0	0-0	2137		1		3			10	7	4		2		12	5		6	8"	11		9		
26	14	HAMILTON	1-0	1-1	3548	McDowell	1		3	12	6	10	7	4		2"			5			8	11		9		
27	21	AIRDRIEONIANS	0-1	1-1	3370	Stein	1		3		6	10	7	4		2			5			8	11		9		
28	11 Feb	DUMBARTON	0-1	0-1	3649		1		3	11	2	10	7			4		12	5		6	8			9"		
29	25	ALLOA ATHLETIC	1-0	4-0	2005	Maxwell, Provan, Doherty, McDowell	1		3	11*	14	10	7	4		2		12	5		6	8"			9		
30	4 Mar	Morton	0-1	0-2	4036		1		3	11"	12	10	7	4		2		14	5		6	8			9*		
31	15	MONTROSE	1-1	5-1	1402	McCulloch(3), Jardine, McDowell	1			11	3	10		4		2		12	5		6	8*	7		9"	14	
32	18	St. Johnstone	0-1	0-2	1584		1			11	3	10		4		2		12	5		6	8*	7		9"	14	
33	22	Dundee	0-1	2-5	5295	McCulloch, Maxwell	1			11	3	10		4		2		9	5		6	8	7				
34	25	ST. JOHNSTONE	1-0	2-0	1997	McDowell, McCulloch	1				3	10	7	4		2		9	5		6	8	11				
35	1 Apr	Arbroath	0-0	0-1	921		1			11	3	10	7	4		2		9"	5		6	8			12		
36	8	East Fife	0-0	0-0	741		1			11	3	10	7	4		2			5		6	9		8			
37	15	MONTROSE	0-0	1-0	1337	Maxwell	1			11		10	7	4		2		9	5		6	8					3
38	22	Hamilton	1-0	3-1	1385	Doherty(2), Jardine	1			12		10	7	4		2		9	5"		6	8		11			3
39	29	EAST FIFE	0-0	0-0	1328		1			12		10	7	4		2		9	5		6	8"		11			3
						Apps.	39	2	28	17	20	35	36	34	4	30	1	7	37	9	36	36	28	4	23		3
						Subs		1		7	3			2	2	1		8		1				1	1	2	
						Goals		1	1	2		9	3	2				4		1		13	8	1	8		

Pos	P.	W.	D.	L.	F.	A.	Pts.
6th	39	14	12	13	52	46	40

League Cup

							Stewart	Hynds	Robertson	Murdoch	Welsh	Maxwell	Provan	Jardine	Fallis	McLean	Smith	Doherty	Clarke	McGillivray	McDicken	McDowell	McCulloch	Arkison	Stein	Gray	Baird
1		Bye																									
2	31 Aug	ST. MIRREN	0-0	0-0	5119		1		3	4	2	10	8	12	7			9"	5	11	6						
2	3 Sep	St. Mirren (Agg: 1-2)	0-0	1-2	9458	Fallis	1		3	4	2	10	8		7				5	11	6		9				

Scottish Cup

							Stewart	Hynds	Robertson	Murdoch	Welsh	Maxwell	Provan	Jardine	Fallis	McLean	Smith	Doherty	Clarke	McGillivray	McDicken	McDowell	McCulloch	Arkison	Stein	Gray	Baird
3	6 Feb	St. Mirren	1-1	2-1	10010	Maxwell, McDowell	1		3	11	12	10	7	4"		2			5		6	8			9		
4	27	Celtic	1-0	1-1	16000	McDowell	1		3	11		10	7	4		2		9	5		6	8					
4R	6 Mar	CELTIC	0-0	1-0	14137	McDicken	1		3			10	7	4		2		12	5		6	8"	11		9		
QF	11	Rangers	0-2	1-4	28000	McCulloch	1		3	14		10	7"	4		2		12	5		6	8*	11		9		

Davie Sneddon took over as manager but this was a year of consolidation for Kilmarnock.
Back: J.Doherty, J.Cockburn, R.Hamilton, D.McDowell, J.McNeill, H.Arkison, A.Ward, I.Baird.
Middle: H.Allan, E.Gray, J.McGillivray, D.McDicken, A.Robinson, J.Stewart, A.McCulloch, P.Clarke, K.Armstrong, G.Wilson, D.Hynds, W.Murray, R.Stewart. Front: D.Provan, F.Welsh, S.McLean, C.Stein, I.Jardine, D.Sneddon, A.Robertson, G.Maxwell, W.Murdoch, I.McCulloch.

SEASON 1978-79 First Division

No.	Date	Opposition	H.T.	Res.	Att.	Goalscorers	McCulloch	McLean	Robertson	Jardine	P.Clarke	McDicken	Provan	Maxwell	Cairney	J.Clark	Doherty	Welsh	McDowell	Street	Hughes	Baird	Bourke	Mauchlen	Gibson	Murdoch	Armstrong	Taylor
1	12 Aug	Clydebank	0-0	1-2	1854	Cairney	1	2	3	4	5	6	7	8	9	10	11											
2	19	AIRDRIEONIANS	0-0	2-0	2707	Cairney, Maxwell	1	3		4	5	6	7	8	9	10	11"	2	12									
3	26	Ayr United	0-0	0-0	4974		1	11	3	4	5	6		8	9	10		2	7"	12								
4	6 Sep	DUMBARTON	0-0	0-0	2420		1	2	3	4	5	6		10	9"	11			8	7	12							
5	9	DUNDEE	1-0	1-1	3113	Cairney	1	2	3	4	5	6	7	10	9	11	12		8"									
6	13	St. Johnstone	0-0	0-0	1292		1	2	3*	4	5	6		10	9	11	12	14	8"	7								
7	16	Stirling Albion	2-1	4-1	1325	McDicken, Provan, Doherty, Maxwell	1	3		4"	5	6	7	10	9	11	8	2				12						
8	23	MONTROSE	1-0	2-2	2447	Maxwell, Street	1	2	3	4	5	6		10	9	11	8			7								
9	26	Clyde	0-0	1-1	1301	McDowell	1	2	3	4"	5	6		10	9*	11	8	12	14	7								
10	30	Queen of the South	0-1	1-2	1423	Street	1	4	3	12	5	6		10	9	11	8	2	14	7*								
11	7 Oct	ABROATH	2-1	3-1	2556	McDowell, Maxwell, Jardine	1	2	3	4	5	6		10		11"	8	12	9	7*	14							
12	14	RAITH ROVERS	2-0	3-0	2621	Cairney, Hughes, Bourke	1	2	3	4	5	6		8	10		12				11"		9	7				
13	21	Hamilton	0-2	3-2	2601	Cairney, Maxwell, Bourke	1	2	3	4	5	6		8	10		12				11"		9	7				
14	28	Airdrieonians	0-3	1-4	2505	Bourke	1	2	3	4	5	6*		8	10		12				11"	14	9	7				
15	4 Nov	AYR UNITED	0-0	1-2	5946	Hughes	1	2	3	4*	5	6		11	8*		7	14			12		9	10				
16	11	Dundee	0-0	0-0	5620		1	8	3	4"	5	6		12				2			11		9	10	7			
17	18	STIRLING ALBION	1-0	5-0	2739	Bourke(2), Gibson, Doherty, Maxwell	1	4	3		5"	6		8	12		14	2*			11		9	10	7			
18	25	Montrose	3-0	4-0	874	Maxwell(2), Hughes, Jardine	1	2	3	4	5	6		8	9	10					11				7			
19	2 Dec	QUEEN OF THE SOUTH	0-0	0-0	2791		1		3	4*	5	6		2	12	10					11		9"	8	7	14		
20	9	Arbroath	0-2	2-3	880	Street, J.Clark	1	2	3			6		8	10*	11				14			9	4	7"	12	5	
21	16	Raith Rovers	1-1	3-1	1843	Bourke(2), Maxwell	1	2	3		5	6		8		4							9	10	7			11
22	23	HAMILTON	1-0	4-0	2850	Bourke(3), Gibson	1	2	3		5	6		8		4							9	10	7			11
23	20 Jan	MONTROSE	3-0	4-1	1906	Gibson(2), Bourke, P.Clarke	1	2	3		5	6		8		4				11			9	10	7			
24	3 Feb	ST. JOHNSTONE	3-0	3-2	3200	Bourke, J.Clark, O.G.	1	2	3		5	6		8	12	4				11			9"	10	7			
25	10	Arbroath	0-0	1-0	1284	Gibson	1	2	3		5	6		8	12	4				11			9"		7	10		
26	24	RAITH ROVERS	0-1	2-1	3267	Maxwell, Street	1	2	3	12	5"	6		8		4				11			9	10	7			
27	3 Mar	CLYDEBANK	0-0	0-0	3518		1	2	3	10	5	6		8	12	4					11"		9		7			
28	7	Ayr United	0-0	1-2	5693	J.Clark	1	2	3	10	5	6		8		4				11			9		7			
29	13	Dumbarton	1-0	3-0	1345	Bourke, Cairney, Maxwell	1	10	3	4"	5			8	11			2		12			9		7		6	
30	17	ST. JOHNSTONE	1-1	3-1	2315	Gibson(2), Cairney	1	2	3	10	5			8	11	4							9		7		6	
31	24	CLYDE	2-0	2-1	2517	Bourke(2)	1	2	3		5			8	11	4							9	10	7		6	
32	31	Clydebank	2-0	2-1	2519	Bourke, Gibson	1	2	3		5	6		8	11	4							9	10	7			
33	4 Apr	Stirling Albion	0-0	0-0	1252		1	2	3	12	5	6		8	11*	4				14			9	10"	7			
34	7	Clyde	1-0	1-0	2509	Bourke	1	2	3	8	5	6			11	4				12			9	10	7"			
35	11	AIRDRIEONIANS	1-0	1-0	2665	Bourke	1	2	3	8	5	6			11	4							9	10	7			
36	14	QUEEN OF THE SOUTH	2-1	3-1	2978	Bourke, Street, Cairney	1	10	3	8	5	6"			11	4		2		12			9		7			
37	21	Hamilton	0-0	0-1	2897		1	2	3	14	5	6		8*	12	4				11"			9	10	7			
38	25	DUNDEE	0-0	2-1	5072	Bourke, McDicken	1	2	3	8	5	6			11	4							9	10	7			
39	28	Dumbarton	1-0	3-1	2278	Bourke, Cairney, Gibson	1	2	3	8		6			11	4		5					9	10	7			
						Apps.	39	38	37	26	37	36	4	33	26	32	8	9	5	12	8		27	21	24	1	4	2
						Subs				4				1	6		6	4	3	6	3	2				2		
						Goals				2	1	2	1	11	9	3	2		2	5	3		21		9			

Pos	P.	W.	D.	L.	F.	A.	Pts.
2nd	39	22	10	7	72	35	54

League Cup

							McCulloch	McLean	Robertson	Jardine	P.Clarke	McDicken	Provan	Maxwell	Cairney	J.Clark	Doherty	Welsh	McDowell	Street	Hughes	Baird	Bourke	Mauchlen	Gibson	Murdoch	Armstrong	Taylor
1		Bye																										
2	30 Aug	ALLOA ATHLETIC	2-0	2-0	2080	McDowell, Street	1	11	3		5	6		8	9	10		2	7	4"	12							
2	2 Sep	Alloa Athletic (Agg: 3-1)	1-0	1-1	1301	Cairney	1	2	3	4	5	6		10	9	11			8	7								
3	4 Oct	MORTON	2-0	2-0	3967	Cairney, Maxwell	1	2	3	4	5	6		10	9"	11	8		7	12								
3	11	Morton (Agg: 4-5)	1-1	2-5*	5623	McDicken, Welsh	1	11"	3	4	5	6		10			7	2	8	14			9*				12	

* After Extra Time, 90 minutes 2-4.

Scottish Cup

							McCulloch	McLean	Robertson	Jardine	P.Clarke	McDicken	Provan	Maxwell	Cairney	J.Clark	Doherty	Welsh	McDowell	Street	Hughes	Baird	Bourke	Mauchlen	Gibson	Murdoch	Armstrong	Taylor
3	27 Jan	Clyde	1-0	5-1	2509	Bourke(2), Street, Gibson	1	2	3		5	6		8		4				11			9	10	7			
4	21 Feb	Rangers	0-1	1-1	17500	McDicken	1	2	3	14	5	6		8*	12	4				11"			9	10	7			
4R	26	RANGERS	0-1	0-1	19493		1	2	3	12	5	6		8		4				11			9	10"	7			

Sneddon's part-timers won promotion to the Premier in 1978-79. Back: Doherty, Cockburn, Clark, Hughes, McNeill, Welsh, Hynds, Black, Mauchlen, Arkison. Middle: Allan, Gibson, Maxwell, Clarke, Armstrong, McCulloch, Ward, Wilson, Gray, McBride, Stewart. Front: Sneddon, Cairney, Provan, McDowell, Jardine, McDicken, Robertson, McLean, Street, Baird (Murdoch & Robinson missing)

SEASON 1979-80 Premier Division

No.	Date	Opposition	H.T.	Res.	Att.	Goalscorers	McCulloch	McLean	Robertson	J.Clark	P.Clarke	McDicken	Doherty	Maxwell	Gibson	Mauchlen	Street	Bourke	Jardine	Hughes	Cairney	Houston	Cockburn	Welsh	Armstrong	Cramond
1	11 Aug	St. Mirren	0-1	2-2	7449	Doherty, P.Clarke	1	2	3	4	5	6	7	8	9	10	11									
2	18	DUNDEE UNITED	0-0	1-0	5882	Street	1	2	3	4	5	6	12	8	7	10	11"	9								
3	25	Celtic	0-3	0-5	24584		1	2	3	10	5	6	12	8	7		11	9"	4	14						
4	8 Sep	HIBERNIAN	0-0	1-0	4654	Jardine	1	2	3	4	5	6		10	8	11	7	9"	12							
5	15	Partick Thistle	0-0	0-0	5078		1	2	3	4	5	6		10	8	11"	12	9	7							
6	22	Morton	1-1	1-3	6618	Gibson	1	2	3	4	5	6		10"	8	7	14	9	12		11*					
7	29	RANGERS	1-0	2-1	15479	J.Clark, Cairney	1	2	3	4	5	6			8	10		9			11	7				
8	6 Oct	DUNDEE	2-1	3-1	4674	Maxwell(2), Bourke	1	2	3	4	5	6		10	8	11		9				7				
9	13	Aberdeen	1-2	1-3	12791	Houston	1	2	3	4	5	6		8	7	10"	12	9			14	11*				
10	20	ST. MIRREN	1-0	1-1	6377	Houston	1	2	3	4	5	6		8	11	10		9"			12	7				
11	27	Dundee United	0-2	0-4	6403		1	2	3	4	5	6	14	12	8	10		11			9"	7*				
12	3 Nov	CELTIC	1-0	2-0	16918	Street, Gibson	1	2	3	4	5	6		8	7	10	11	9								
13	10	Hibernian	0-1	1-1	5269	Maxwell	1	2	3	4	5	6		8	7	10	11	9								
14	17	PARTICK THISTLE	0-1	0-1	4951		1	2	3	4	5	6		8	7*	10	11"	9			14	12				
15	1 Dec	Rangers	1-1	1-2	16557	Houston	1		3	4	5	6		8	11	10	14	12			9"	7*	2			
16	15	Dundee	1-1	1-3	6016	O.G.	1		3	4	5		14	8	9*	10	12				11"	7		2	6	
17	29	DUNDEE UNITED	0-0	0-0	4515		1	3		4		6			8	10	11	9		12		7"		2	5	
18	5 Jan	HIBERNIAN	2-0	3-1	6092	Street(3)	1	3		4	5	6			8		11	9				7		2		10
19	12	Partick Thistle	0-0	1-1	4543	Street	1	3		4	5	6		8	9		11					7		2		10
20	19	Morton	0-0	2-1	5352	P.Clarke, Cramond	1	3		4	5			8	9	12	11"					7		2	6	10
21	9 Feb	DUNDEE	1-1	1-1	4432	Houston	1	3		4	5	6		8	11	10		9			12	7"		2		
22	23	Aberdeen	2-0	2-1	9567	Street, O.G.	1	3		4	5	6			9	8	11"				12	7		2		10
23	1 Mar	ST. MIRREN	0-0	1-1	6800	Mauchlen	1	3		4	5	6			9	8	11				12	7		2		10"
24	8	Dundee united	0-0	0-0	6497		1	3		4	5	6	12		9"	8	11					7		2		10
25	12	MORTON	0-0	1-1	4905	Mauchlen	1	3		4	5	6	14	12	9	8	11*					7		2		10"
26	15	CELTIC	1-0	1-1	14965	Street	1	3		4	5	6	12		9"	8	11					7		2		10
27	29	PARTICK THISTLE	0-0	0-1	3814		1	3			5	6	12	4	9	8	11					7"		2		10
28	1 Apr	ABERDEEN	0-1	0-4	5020		1	3			5	6	9	4	12	8	11					7		2		10"
29	5	MORTON	0-1	0-2	4309		1	2	3	4	5	6			7	8	11	9			12					10"
30	12	St. Mirren	1-0	1-3	6740	P.Clarke	1	8	3	4	5	6		14	7"		11	9			12			2		10*
31	16	Celtic	0-1	0-2	16695		1	10	3	4	5	6			12	8	11"	9			14	7*		2		
32	19	ABERDEEN	1-3	1-3	3533	Gibson	1	10	3	4	5	6			7	8	11	9						2		
33	21	Hibernian	1-0	2-1	2659	Houston(2)	1	2	3	4	5	6				8	11				9	7				10
34	23	RANGERS	1-0	1-0	8504	Street	1	2	3	4	5	6			10	8	11				9	7				
35	26	Dundee	0-0	2-0	4003	McDicken, Cairney	1	2	3	4	5	6				8*	11	12			9	7"		14		10
36	30	Rangers	0-1	0-1	7655		1	8	3	4	5	6					11"	12			9	7		2		10
						Apps.	36	34	24	34	35	34	2	19	31	30	26	30	2		9	24	1	17	3	15
						Subs							8	3	2	1	5	3	2	2	9	1		1		
						Goals				1	3	1	1	3	3	2	9	1	1		2	6				1

Pos	P.	W.	D.	L.	F.	A.	Pts.
8th	36	11	11	14	36	52	33

League Cup

							McCulloch	McLean	Robertson	J.Clark	P.Clarke	McDicken	Doherty	Maxwell	Gibson	Mauchlen	Street	Bourke	Jardine	Hughes	Cairney	Houston	Cockburn	Welsh	Armstrong	Cramond
1	15 Aug	ALLOA ATHLETIC	1-0	2-1	2491	Jardine, Doherty	1	2	3	8	5"	6	14	12	7	10			4	11	9*					
1	22	Alloa Athletic (Agg: 3-2)	0-0	1-1*	1696	Doherty	1	2	3	11	5	6	8		10		7"	9	4	12						
2	29	FORFAR ATHLETIC	0-0	2-0	2220	P.Clarke, Gibson	1	2	3	4	5	6	12	10	8	11	7"	9								
2	1 Sep	Forfar Athletic (Agg: 3-1)	1-0	1-1	1565	Maxwell	1	2	3	4	5	6		10	8	11	7	9								
3	26	Hibernian	1-0	2-1	4241	Cairney, Bourke	1	2	3	4	5	6		8	7"	10	12	9			11					
3	10 Oct	HIBERNIAN (Agg: 4-2)	2-1	2-1	5353	Maxwell, Bourke	1	2	3	4	5	6		8	7	10		9			11					
QF	31	Morton	1-1	2-3	6846	McLean, Street	1	2	3	4	5	6		8	7	10	11	9								
QF	24 Nov	MORTON (Agg: 5-5)#	0-0	3-2*	8407	P.Clarke, Gibson, Cairney	1	2	3	4	5*	6	14	8	7	10	11	9"			12					

* After extra time x 90 minutes 0-1

\# 90 mins - 1-0, Morton won on penalties 5-3

Scottish Cup

							McCulloch	McLean	Robertson	J.Clark	P.Clarke	McDicken	Doherty	Maxwell	Gibson	Mauchlen	Street	Bourke	Jardine	Hughes	Cairney	Houston	Cockburn	Welsh	Armstrong	Cramond
3	30 Jan	PARTICK THISTLE	0-0	0-1	7677		1	3		4	5	6		8	7			9			12	11"		2		10

Drybrough Cup

							McCulloch	McLean	Robertson	J.Clark	P.Clarke	McDicken	Doherty	Maxwell	Gibson	Mauchlen	Street	Bourke	Jardine	Hughes	Cairney	Houston	Cockburn	Welsh	Armstrong	Cramond
QF	28 Jul	ABERDEEN	0-0	1-0	4548	Street	1	2	3	4	5	6		8	7	10	11	9								
SF	1 Aug	RANGERS	0-0	0-2	10035		1	2	3	4	5	6		8	7	10	11	9								

Anglo-Scottish Cup

							McCulloch	McLean	Robertson	J.Clark	P.Clarke	McDicken	Doherty	Maxwell	Gibson	Mauchlen	Street	Bourke	Jardine	Hughes	Cairney	Houston	Cockburn	Welsh	Armstrong	Cramond
1	6 Aug	Dundee	1-0	1-1	3832	P.Clarke	1	10	3		5	6	12	8	7		11	9"	4					2		
1	8	DUNDEE (Agg: 4-4*)	2-1	3-3	3719	Street(2), Gibson	1	2	3	10	5	6	12	8	7"		11	9	4							

* (Agg: 4-4 Dundee won on away goals)

This Kilmarnock squad handled their premier opponents with ease this season.
Back: Kilpatrick,Gibson,McBride,Morrison,Brown,G.Wilson,McClurg,Black,Cockburn
Middle: Allan,Jardine,Bourke,McDicken,Clarke,McCulloch,Armstrong,Welsh,Robin,McLean,Stewart
Front: Sneddon,Doherty,Clark,Hughes,Maxwell,Robertson,Mauchlen,Street,McCready,Hamilton

SEASON 1980-81 Premier Division

No.	Date	Opposition	H.T.	Res.	Att.	Goalscorers	McCulloch	McLean	Robertson	A.Mauchlen	P.Clarke	McDicken	Houston	Gibson	Cairney	Cramond	Street	Doherty	Bourke	Maxwell	McBride	Morrison	Hughes	Cockburn	McCready	Armstrong	Brown	G.Wilson	A.Wilson	Black	McClurg	Bryce	J.Clark	Robin	Eadie	S.Mauchlen
1	9 Aug	Dundee United	0-1	2-2	5788	Street, A.Mauchlen	1	2	3	4	5	6	7	8	9	10	11"	12																		
2	16	CELTIC	0-3	0-3	13810		1	2	3	4	5	6		8	11"	10	7	12	9																	
3	23	Partick Thistle	0-0	1-0	3197	McBride	1	2	3	4	5	6		7			11			8	9	10														
4	6 Sep	HEARTS	0-0	0-1	3995		1	2	3	4	5"	6		11		10	7*			8	9		14	12												
5	13	Morton	0-1	0-2	3049		1"	2	3	8		6		7		10	11			12	9*				14	5							4			
6	20	RANGERS	0-3	1-8	15021	Bourke		2	3	8		6	7"	12		10*	11		9	14						5	1						4			
7	27	Airdrieonians	0-0	0-1	2736			2	3	4	5	6		7*		10	11*		9	8						14	1						12			
8	4 Oct	ST. MIRREN	0-4	1-6	3897	Cramond		2	3	4"	5	6	7	14		10	11*		9	8							1						12			
9	11	Aberdeen	0-0	0-2	11164				2	8	5	6	7	9"		10*	11	12						3			1	14					4			
10	18	DUNDEE UNITED	0-0	0-1	2719			14	2		5	6		11		10	7"	12	9	8*				3			1						4			
11	25	Celtic	1-2	1-4	16537	Cramond		12	2	8	5	6	7			10		11"			9			3			1						4			
12	1 Nov	PARTICK THISTLE	0-0	0-1	2417			10"	2	8	5	6	7			11					9		12	3			1						4			
13	8	AIRDRIEONIANS	1-0	1-1	2230	Houston		2	3	4	5	6	7			11"			10	8	9			12			1									
14	15	Rangers	0-1	0-2	15791			2	3	4	5	6	7			11"			10	8	9						1						12			
15	22	ABERDEEN	1-0	1-1	3319	Street		2	3	4	5	6	7			10	11			8	9								1							
16	29	St. Mirren	0-1	0-2	5300			2	3	4	5	6	7			10	11"		12		9								1				8			
17	6 Dec	Hearts	0-0	0-2	5183			2		8	5	6	12		11"				9	10	7			3					1	14			4*			
18	13	MORTON	2-1	3-3	2483	Armstrong, Bourke, Hughes		2		4	8	6	7						9		12		11"	3		5		10	1							
19	20	RANGERS	1-0	1-1	9172	Bourke		2			5		7	8*					9"	14	12		11	3		6		10	1		4					
20	1 Jan	CELTIC	1-2	1-2	7625	Hughes		2		12	5		7	8"					9				11	3		6		10	1		4					
21	3	Dundee United	0-2	0-7	6474			2		8	5		7						9"	14	12		11	3		6		10	1		4*					
22	10	ST. MIRREN	1-0	2-0	4385	A.Mauchlen, Doherty		2		10	8	6						7	9				11	3		5			1				4			
23	31	Morton	0-1	0-1	3497		1	2		10	8	6		12				7"	9				11	3		5							4			
24	21 Feb	Partick Thistle	1-0	1-1	1601	Bourke	1	8	2*			6			11				9	14	12		7"	3		5						10	4			
25	28	DUNDEE UNITED	0-0	0-1	2102		1	2		10	6	8			11"		7*		9		14			3		5						12	4			
26	7 Mar	St. Mirren	0-1	1-1	4203	Bourke	1	2*		10	6	8"							9	14	7		11	3		5						12	4			
27	11	Airdrieonians	0-3	0-3	2084		1			10	6*	8							9	14	7		11"	3		5						12	4	2		
28	14	ABERDEEN	0-0	1-0	2415	Doherty	1	8		10		6						11	9		7			3		5							4	2		
29	21	Rangers	0-1	0-2	8488		1	8		10		6						11*	9		7		14	3		5						12	4"	2		
30	24	HEARTS	1-0	2-0	1445	A.Mauchlen, McLean	1	8		10		6						11	9		7			3		5							4	2		
31	28	AIRDRIEONIANS	0-1	0-1	1849		1	8		10		6						11	9		7"		12	3		5							4	2		
32	4 Apr	Hearts	0-1	0-1	1866		1	8		10		6				12		7			9*			3		5						11	4	2"	14	
33	15	MORTON	0-0	0-0	973		1	2		8		6				11"		14	9					3	7*	5						12	4		10	
34	18	PARTICK THISTLE	0-1	0-1	1262		1	2		8		6				14			9					3*	7	5						11*	4	14	10	
35	25	Celtic	0-1	1-1	23050	Eadie	1	8	3			6							9					10	7	5							4	2	11	
36	2 May	Aberdeen	0-0	2-0	7002	McDicken, McCready	1	8	12	10		6							9					3	7	5							4	2"	11	
						Apps.	19	32	18	31	24	33	14	10	5	16	13	8	26	9	17	1	9	24	4	21	9	4	8		3	3	23	8	4	
						Subs		2	1	1			1	3		2		5	1	7	5		4	2	1	1		1		1		5	3	1	1	
						Goals		1		3		1	1			2	2	5	5		1		2		1	1									1	

Pos	P.	W.	D.	L.	F.	A.	Pts.
9th	36	5	9	22	23	65	19

League Cup

Rd	Date	Opposition	H.T.	Res.	Att.	Goalscorers	McCulloch	McLean	Robertson	A.Mauchlen	P.Clarke	McDicken	Houston	Gibson	Cairney	Cramond	Street	Doherty	Bourke	Maxwell	McBride	Morrison	Hughes	Cockburn	McCready	Armstrong	Brown	G.Wilson	A.Wilson	Black	McClurg	Bryce	J.Clark	Robin	Eadie	S.Mauchlen
1	13 Aug	AIRDRIEONIANS	1-0	1-0	2986	Cramond	1		2	4	5	6	11"	8	9	10		7	12					3												
1	20	Airdrieonians (Agg: 2-0)	0-0	1-0	2983	Cramond	1	2	3	4	5	6		7		10	11			8	9															
2	27	DUNFERMLINE	0-0	0-0	2273		1	2	3	4	5	6		11*			7"		12	8	9	10			14											
2	30	Dunfermline (Agg: 2-1)	1-0	2-1	3084	P.Clarke, McBride	1	2	3	10	5	6		8			12		9"	4	11*				7											
3	3 Sep	Dundee	0-0	0-0	4317		1	2	3	10	5	6		7			11		9	4	8															
3	24	DUNDEE	0-0	0-0*	2401		1	2	3	8		6	11	7"		10*	12		9	14						5	1						4			

* After extra time, Dundee won 5-3 on penalties.

Scottish Cup

Rd	Date	Opposition	H.T.	Res.	Att.	Goalscorers	McCulloch	McLean	Robertson	A.Mauchlen	P.Clarke	McDicken	Houston	Gibson	Cairney	Cramond	Street	Doherty	Bourke	Maxwell	McBride	Morrison	Hughes	Cockburn	McCready	Armstrong	Brown	G.Wilson	A.Wilson	Black	McClurg	Bryce	J.Clark	Robin	Eadie	S.Mauchlen
3	24 Jan	AYR UNITED	1-0	2-1	8185	McDicken, Hughes	1	2			8	6		4				7	9				11	3		5							10			
4	14 Feb	CLYDEBANK	0-0	0-0	3741		1	2				6		8"			11		9		7		12	3		5						10	4			
4R	18	Clydebank	0-0	1-1*	3400	Bourke	1	2	8			6			11				9		12		7"	3		5		14				10	4			
4R	23	Clydebank #	0-1	0-1	2340		1	2		8		6			12				9	7"	11			3		5		14				10	4			

* After extra time # At Love Street

Anglo-Scottish Cup

Rd	Date	Opposition	H.T.	Res.	Att.	Goalscorers	McCulloch	McLean	Robertson	A.Mauchlen	P.Clarke	McDicken	Houston	Gibson	Cairney	Cramond	Street	Doherty	Bourke	Maxwell	McBride	Morrison	Hughes	Cockburn	McCready	Armstrong	Brown	G.Wilson	A.Wilson	Black	McClurg	Bryce	J.Clark	Robin	Eadie	S.Mauchlen
1	30 Jul	EAST STIRLING	0-1	1-3	1563	A.Mauchlen	1	2	3	8	5"	6	11	7	9	10*									14	12							4			
1	6 Aug	East Stirling (Agg: 4-3)	0-0	3-0	1000	McDicken, Cairney, Houston	1	2	3	8	5	6	12	7	11	10			9														4"			
QF	9 Sep	Blackpool	0-0	1-2	4904	Cramond			3	4		6		7		10				8	9	2	11			5	1									
QF	14 Oct	BLACKPOOL (Agg: 5-4)	4-1	4-2	2656	Cramond(2), Bourke, Maxwell			2		5	6	7"	11		10		12	9	8				3			1						4			
SF	4 Nov	NOTTS COUNTY	1-2	1-2	2865	McBride		2	3	8	5	6	7			11			12		9						1						4			10"
SF	18	Notts County (Agg: 3-7)	0-2	2-5	4314	Street, McBride		2	3*	8	5	6				11	7			10	12			14			1						4			9"

Happy faces at the start of the campaign, but 80-81 was a grim season, as an injury-wracked outfit failed to maintain their Premier place. Back: Cockburn,Hughes,Bryce,McLean,Maxwell,A.Wilson, McClurg,McBride,Black,Cairney,Kilpatrick. Middle: Allan(Physio),G.Wilson,Houston,Bourke,Clarke, McCulloch,Armstrong,McDicken,Welsh,Morrison,Stewart(Asst.Train.). Front:Sneddon(Man),Doherty, Cramond Gibson,Robertson,Mauchlen,Street,Clark,McCready,Hamilton(Coach)

SEASON 1981-82 First Division

No.	Date	Opposition	H.T.	Res.	Att.	Goalscorers	McCulloch	McLean	Robertson	J.Clark	Armstrong	P.Clarke	Gallacher	Mauchlen	Bourke	Cockburn	McCready	McGivern	Eadie	McBride	McLeod	McDicken	Wilson	Bryce	Bryson	Robin	Cramond
1	29 Aug	MOTHERWELL	1-0	2-0	2694	Gallacher, O.G.	1	2	3	4	5	6	7	8	9	10	11"	12									
2	5 Sep	Hearts	1-0	1-0	4796	Robertson	1	2	3	4	5	6	7	8		10	11		9"	12							
3	8	Clydebank	0-0	0-0	1042		1	2	3	4	5	6		8		10	11	12	9	7"							
4	12	AYR UNITED	0-0	1-1	5477	Gallacher	1	2	12	4	5	6	7	8	9	3"	11				10						
5	16	Queen of the South	1-1	1-1	1722	P.Clarke	1	2	12	4	5	6	7	8	9*	3"	11		14		10						
6	19	QUEENS PARK	0-0	0-0	2337		1	2	3	4	5	6	7	8	9		11"	12			10						
7	23	St. Johnstone	2-0	2-0	1734	Bourke, J.Clark	1	2	3	4	5	6	7	8	9		11				10						
8	29	East Stirling	1-2	1-2	707	McCready	1	2	3	4	5	6	7	8	9		11"		12		10						
9	3 Oct	DUNFERMLINE	0-1	0-1	2137		1	2	3	4	5	6	7	8	9	12			14	11*	10"						
10	10	FALKIRK	1-0	2-2	1801	Eadie(2)	1		3	4"	5	6	7	8	9	2			11		10	12					
11	17	Hamilton	0-0	2-1	1247	Gallacher, Bourke	1		2	4"	5	6	7	12	14	3			9*	11	10	8					
12	24	Dumbarton	0-0	2-0	799	Mauchlen, J.Clark	1		2	4	5	6	7	12	9	3	11*		14		10"	8					
13	31	RAITH ROVERS	1-0	1-1	1859	Gallacher	1		2	4	5		7	8	9	3			11		10"	6	12				
14	7 Nov	HEARTS	0-0	0-0	3348		1		2	4	5		7	8	9	3		12	11"		10	6					
15	14	Motherwell	0-0	0-2	5068		1		2	4	5		7	8	9	3		12	11"		10	6					
16	21	QUEEN OF THE SOUTH	0-0	0-0	1591		1	14	2	4*	5		7"	8	9	3		12	11		10	6					
17	28	EAST STIRLING	1-0	2-0	1391	Eadie, Gallacher	1	8	2		5	6	7			3		11	9"	12	10	4*		14			
18	5 Dec	Dunfermline	2-1	2-1	1665	McBride, McDicken	1	8	2		5	6	7	14		3		11"		9	10*	4		12			
19	12	ST. JOHNSTONE	0-1	0-2	1811		1	8	2		5	6	7	12		3	11*	14		9	10"	4					
20	16 Jan	HAMILTON	2-2	2-2	1480	Mauchlen, Bryson	1	12	2		5	6	7	10	9	3					8	4"			11		
21	30	DUMBARTON	0-0	0-0	1346		1	12	2		5	6"	7	10	9	3		14			8	4			11*		
22	17 Feb	Falkirk	2-1	2-2	1115	Bourke(2)	1	14	2	4	5	6	7	10	9	3*		12			8				11"		
23	20	Queens Park	1-0	2-0	1253	P.Clarke, Gallacher	1	2	3		5	6	7	10	9			11"			8			4	12		
24	27	AYR UNITED	0-0	1-1	4687	McGivern	1	2	3	4	5	6	7	10	9			11			8"	12					
25	10 Mar	DUNFERMLINE	0-0	2-0	1356	Bryson, Bourke	1		2	4	5	6	7*	10	9	3"		11			8	12			14		
26	13	Raith Rovers	1-0	3-0	1220	Mauchlen, McDicken, Bourke	1	2	3	4	5	6		10"	9			11			7	8			12		
27	17	Ayr United	0-1	1-1	3663	McDicken	1	2	3	4"	5	6	7	10	9			11			8	12					
28	20	FALKIRK	1-1	4-1	1905	McLeod, Bourke, Armstrong, McDicken	1	2	3		5	6	7	10	9			11			8	4					
29	27	Motherwell	0-0	0-1	4816		1	2	3		5	6	7	10	9			11			8	4					
30	30	Queens Park	1-2	3-2	1197	Gallacher(2), McDicken	1	2	3	10	5	6	7		9			11"			8	4			12		
31	3 Apr	CLYDEBANK	0-0	0-0	2087		1	2	3	10	5	6	7	12	9			11*			8	4"			14		
32	6	Raith Rovers	2-3	3-3	1401	Bryson, P.Clarke, Bourke	1	2	3	10	5	6	7	12	9			14			8	4"			11*		
33	10	St. Johnstone	0-1	3-1	2209	Mauchlen, P.Clarke, Bourke	1	2	3	4	5	6	7	8	9			11			10						
34	17	HAMILTON	0-0	0-0	1878		1	2	3	4	5	6		10"	9			7*	14		8	12			11		
35	21	CLYDEBANK	1-0	2-0	1308	Bourke(2)	1	8	2	4"	5	6		10	9	3		7				12			11		
36	24	Dumbarton	0-0	2-0	715	McDicken(2)	1	4"	3		5	6	14	8	9			7				12		10*	11	2	
37	1 May	East Stirling	4-0	5-1	482	Bourke(2), McGivern, McLean, Robertson	1	8	3		5	6	7"	10	9			11				4			12	2	
38	8	HEARTS	0-0	0-0	9997		1	8	3		5	6	7	10	9			11			12	4"				2	
39	15	QUEEN OF THE SOUTH	5-0	6-0	2363	Gallacher(2),Armstrng,McDickn,Burke,O.G.	1	4	3	12	5	6	7	10"	9			11*			8	2			14		
						Apps.	39	28	37	27	39	35	34	31	33	20	10	18	9	5	32	20		2	7	3	
						Subs		4	2	1			1	6	1	1		10	5	2	1	7	1	2	7		
						Goals		1	2	2	2	4	10	4	4		1	2	3	1	1	8			3		

Pos	P.	W.	D.	L.	F.	A.	Pts.
2nd	39	17	17	5	60	29	51

League Cup Section 3

Pos	P.	W.	D.	L.	F.	A.	Pts.
2nd	6	2	2	2	5	8	6

No.	Date	Opposition	H.T.	Res.	Att.	Goalscorers	McCulloch	McLean	Robertson	J.Clark	Armstrong	P.Clarke	Gallacher	Mauchlen	Bourke	Cockburn	McCready	McGivern	Eadie	McBride	McLeod	McDicken	Wilson	Bryce	Bryson	Robin	Cramond
1	8 Aug	Aberdeen	0-2	0-3	8414		1	2		4"	5		7	8	9	3	11			12		6		10			
2	12	AIRDRIEONIANS	0-0	1-1	1901	Bourke	1	2		4	5		7	8	9	3	11			12		6		10"			
3	15	Hearts	0-1	1-1	7746	Wilson	1	2		4	5		7	8	9	3	12			11"		6	10				
4	19	Airdrieonians	1-0	1-0	1380	Bourke	1	2		4	5		7		9	3	11			12		6	10"				8
5	22	ABERDEEN	0-2	0-3	3118		1	2	12	4	5		7	8	9	3	11					6					10"
6	26	HEARTS	2-0	2-0	1388	J.Clark, McLean	1	2	3	4	5		7	8	9	10	11*	14				6"	12				

Scottish Cup

No.	Date	Opposition	H.T.	Res.	Att.	Goalscorers	McCulloch	McLean	Robertson	J.Clark	Armstrong	P.Clarke	Gallacher	Mauchlen	Bourke	Cockburn	McCready	McGivern	Eadie	McBride	McLeod	McDicken	Wilson	Bryce	Bryson	Robin	Cramond
3	6 Feb	MONTROSE	0-0	1-0	1418	Bourke	1	4	2		5		7	10*	9	3		11			8"	6		12	14		
4	13	ST. JOHNSTONE	1-0	3-1	2693	Bourke(2), McGiven	1		2	4	5	6	7"	10	9	3		12			8				11		
QF	6 Mar	Aberdeen	2-2	2-4	9000	McGiven, Gallacher	1	2	3	4	5"	6	7	10	9			11			8*	12			14		

In his first full season as manager, JIM CLUNIE assembled a promotion-winning team.
Back: Gallacher, McLaughlan, Eadie, McCulloch, A.Wilson, McClurg, McBride, Cockburn
Middle: D.Wilson(2ndXI Coach), Robin, G.Wilson, Strawhorn, Clarke, Bourke, Armstrong, McDicken, Morrison, Robertson, Stewart(2ndXI Train)
Front: Allan(Physio), McCready, McGeachie, Bryce, Maxwell, McGivern, Mauchlen, Clark, Crammond, Clunie(Manager)

SEASON 1982-83 Premier Division

No.	Date	Opposition	H.T.	Res.	Att.	Goalscorers	McCulloch	McDicken	Robertson	J.Clark	Armstrong	McClurg	Bryson	McLeod	Bourke	McLean	Gallacher	P.Clarke	Eadie	R.Clark	McKinna	McGivern	Cockburn	Mauchlen	Simpson	Clinging	Wilson	Cuthbertson	Muir
1	4 Sep	Morton	0-0	0-0	2349		1	2	3	4	5	6	7	8	9	10	11												
2	11	HIBERNIAN	0-1	1-1	2800	P.Clarke	1	2		4	5	3	7	8"			11	6	9	10	12								
3	18	Rangers	0-2	0-5	17350		1	2		4	5	3	12	8			11	6	9	10*		7"	14						
4	25	DUNDEE	0-0	0-0	2105		1	2		4	5		7	3		8	11	6	9"			12		10					
5	2 Oct	St. Mirren	2-2	2-3	3564	McLean, Mauchlen	1	2		4	5		7	3	9	8	11"	6				12		10					
6	9	DUNDEE UNITED	1-0	1-1	2446	Gallacher	1	2		4	5	10	14	3	12	8"	9	6		11*		7							
7	16	Celtic	0-0	1-2	11063	P.Clarke	1	2		4	5	10"	11	3	12	8	9	6				7							
8	23	ABERDEEN	0-1	0-2	3402		1	5	2	4		10	11	3	12	8"	9	6				7							
9	30	Motherwell	1-1	1-4	3016	McLean	1	5	2	4			12	10	9	8	11	6				7"	3						
10	6 Nov	MORTON	1-0	3-1	1854	J.Clark, Gallacher, Bourke	1	5"	2	4		12	11	10	14	8	9	6				7*	3						
11	13	Hibernian	1-1	2-2	4192	Bryson, McDicken	1	5	2	4			11	10"	12	8	9	6				7	3						
12	20	RANGERS	0-0	0-0	9194		1	5	2	4			11*	10	14	8	9	6"		12		7	3						
13	27	Dundee	0-3	2-5	4311	J.Clark, McLeod	1	5	2	4			11"	10	12	8	9	6				7	3						
14	4 Dec	ST. MIRREN	1-0	2-2	2209	P.Clarke(2)	1	5	2	4				10	9	8	11	6				7	3						
15	11	Dundee United	0-1	0-7	7259		1	5	2	4			12	10	9	8"	11	6				7	3						
16	18	CELTIC	0-1	0-4	9024		1	5	2	4		8"	11*	10			9	6		12	14	7	3						
17	27	Aberdeen	0-1	0-2	14411		1	5	3	4			12	8	9	2	11"	6				7	10						
18	1 Jan	MOTHERWELL	0-1	0-2	3314		1		3	4	5		14	8	9	2	11*	6				7	10"		12				
19	3	Morton	0-1	0-3	2015		1		3	4	5		11"	14	12	2	9*	8		6		7			10				
20	8	HIBERNIAN	0-2	0-2	2142		1			4	5		12	8		2"	9	6		3		7			10	11			
21	15	Rangers	0-0	1-1	11223	McGivern	1	2		4	5			8			9	6		3		7			10	11			
22	22	DUNDEE	1-0	2-0	1891	Gallacher, R.Clark	1	2		4	5		12	8			9	6		3		7			10	11"			
23	5 Feb	St. Mirren	0-1	0-2	3303		1	2		4	5		11	8	12		9	6		3		7"			10				
24	12	DUNDEE UNITED	0-2	0-5	1834			2		4	5	14		8			9	6		3	12	7"			10*		1		11
25	26	Celtic	0-1	0-4	10691		1	5		4		12		8	11		9	6		3		7"	2		10				
26	5 Mar	ABERDEEN	0-2	1-2	2436	Gallacher	1	5		4		2		8*	9	12	11			6		7"	3		10				14
27	12	Motherwell	0-2	1-3	2895	McGivern	1	5"		4			14	8*	9	12	11	6		3		7	2		10				
28	19	MORTON	2-0	4-0	1230	Gallacher(2), McGivern, P.Clarke	1			4	5		11"	8			9	6		3		7	2		10			12	
29	26	RANGERS	0-1	0-1	6648		1	12		4	5	8	11"	10			9	6		3		7	2						
30	2 Apr	Hibernian	1-2	1-8	4065	Gallacher	1	12		4	5	11"	14				9	6		3		7	2		10			8*	
31	9	Dundee	0-0	0-0	3376		1			4	5			8		2		6	9	3		7			10				11
32	23	Dundee United	0-4	0-4	7516		1	12		4	5"			8		2	14	6	9	3		7			10				11*
33	27	ST. MIRREN	0-2	2-2	1049	Gallacher(2)	1	5		4			12	8			11	6	9"	3		7	2		10				
34	30	CELTIC	0-2	0-5	7560		1	5		4			9	8			11	6		3		7"	2		10				12
35	4 May	Aberdeen	0-2	0-5	12002		1	5		4			9	8			11	6		3		7"	2		10				12
36	14	MOTHERWELL	1-1	1-1	1203	Simpson	1	12		4	5		9*	8				6"	14	3		7	2		10				11
						Apps.	35	27	13	36	20	10	18	34	10	19	33	34	6	21		32	20	2	17	3	1	1	4
						Subs		4				3	11	1	9	2	1		1	2	3	2	1		1			1	3
						Goals		1		2			1	1	1	2	9	5		1		3		1	1				

Pos	P.	W.	D.	L.	F.	A.	Pts.
10th	36	3	11	22	28	91	17

League Cup Section 8

Pos	P.	W.	D.	L.	F.	A.	Pts.
1st	6	4	1	1	13	3	9

No.	Date	Opposition	H.T.	Res.	Att.	Goalscorers	McCulloch	McDicken	Robertson	J.Clark	Armstrong	McClurg	Bryson	McLeod	Bourke	McLean	Gallacher	P.Clarke	Eadie	R.Clark	McKinna	McGivern	Cockburn	Mauchlen	Simpson	Clinging	Wilson	Cuthbertson	Muir
1	14 Aug	BERWICK RANGERS	2-0	4-0	1517	McLean, P.Clarke, Mauchlen, O.G.	1	2	3	4	5		14	12	9	8"	11	6				7*		10					
2	18	Hamilton	0-0	0-0	1472		1	2	3	4	5			10	9	8	11	6				7							
3	21	Queens Park	0-0	2-0	1005	McLean, McGivern	1	2	3	4	5		14	12	9	8"	11	6*				7		10					
4	25	HAMILTON	0-0	1-0	1582	Bourke	1	2	3	4		6	12	8"	9		11	5				7		10					
5	28	Berwick Rangers	0-1	1-2	672	McLean	1	2	3	4		5	14	8	9	12	11	6				7"		10*					
6	1 Sep	QUEENS PARK	1-0	5-1	1200	Bourke(2), McLean, Gallacher, Mauchlen	1	2	3	4		5	14	8	9	10*	11	6"				7		12					
PO	6	COWDENBEATH	1-0	1-0	1091	McLean	1	2	3	4	5	6	7*	8	9	10"	11		14					12					
PO	8	Cowdenbeath (Agg: 1-1)	0-1	0-1*	686		1	2	3	4	5	6	12	8	9	14	11*					7		10"					
QF	22	RANGERS	0-2	1-6	7903	McLean	1	6		4	5		7	8		2	11		9				3	10					
QF	6 Oct	Rangers (Agg: 1-12)	0-3	0-6	5342		1	6		4		8	12	3	9"	2	11	5				7		10					

* After extra time, Kilmarnock won 4-3 on penalties

Scottish Cup

No.	Date	Opposition	H.T.	Res.	Att.	Goalscorers	McCulloch	McDicken	Robertson	J.Clark	Armstrong	McClurg	Bryson	McLeod	Bourke	McLean	Gallacher	P.Clarke	Eadie	R.Clark	McKinna	McGivern	Cockburn	Mauchlen	Simpson	Clinging	Wilson	Cuthbertson	Muir
3	29 Jan	Partick Thistle	0-0	1-1	4398	Bryson	1	2		4	5		12	8			9	6		3		7			10	11"			
3R	2 Feb	PARTICK THISTLE	0-0	0-0*	3884		1	2		4	5	14	11"	8	12		9	6		3		7			10*				
3R	7	Partick Thistle	0-1	2-2*	4809	Gallacher, McGivern		2		4	5		11	8			9	6		3		7			10		1		
3R	9	PARTICK THISTLE	0-0	0-1	3745			2		4	5		11"	8	12		9	6		3		7			10		1		

* After extra time, 7/2/83 game: 1-1 after 90 mins.

Alan McCulloch

Kilmarnock's longest-serving 'keeper. With nine seasons behind him and another nine to go, it was thanks to McCulloch that Killie didn't lose 100 goals or more in this disastrous year.

SEASON 1983-84 First Division

No.	Date	Opposition	H.T.	Res.	Att.	Goalscorers	McCulloch	Robertson	Cockburn	McLeod	P.Clarke	R.Clark	McGivern	McDicken	Gallacher	Simpson	Bryson	J.Clark	McLean	Lowe	McKinna	Cuthbertson	McClurg	Walker	Brown	Holland
1	20 Aug	Ayr United	2-0	2-0	3129	Bryson, McDicken	1	2	3	4	5	6	7	8	9	10	11									
2	3 Sep	Partick Thistle	0-1	0-2	2252		1	2	3	8"	5	6	7	12	9	10	11	4								
3	10	FALKIRK	0-1	2-1	1485	R.Clark(2)	1	2	3	8"	5	6	7	4	9	10*	11	12	14							
4	14	MEADOWBANK	1-0	3-1	1028	McGivern, McLeod, Gallacher	1	2	3	10	5	6	7	4	9		11	8								
5	17	Hamilton	1-0	1-0	1407	R.Clark	1	2	3	10	5	6	7	4	9	12	11"	8								
6	24	ALLOA ATHLETIC	1-0	2-0	1415	McDicken, Gallacher	1	2"	3	10	5	6	7	4	9		11	8	12							
7	28	Clydebank	0-2	0-4	855		1		2	3	5	6	7	4	9	10"	11	8		12						
8	1 Oct	Clyde	1-0	1-0	791	R.Clark	1	2	3	10	5	6	7		9	8	11	4								
9	8	BRECHIN CITY	2-0	4-1	1420	McGivern(2), McKinna, McLeod	1	2	3	10	5	6	7			8"	11	4			9	12				
10	15	Airdrieonians	0-0	0-1	1317		1	2	3	10	5	6	7	12		8"	11	4			9					
11	22	DUMBARTON	0-0	2-2	1464	McDicken, Bryson	1	2	3	10	5	6	7"	8	9		11	4			12					
12	29	RAITH ROVERS	0-0	2-1	1397	R.Clark, P.Clarke	1	2	3	10	5	6	12	8	9		11"				7	4*	14			
13	5 Nov	Morton	1-0	2-2	1902	McKinna(2)	1	2	3	10	5	6		8"	9		11	4			7		12			
14	12	Meadowbank	1-1	1-2	836	Bryson	1	2"	3	10	5*	6	12	8	9		11	4			7		14			
15	19	HAMILTON	1-1	2-1	1257	Bryson, Gallacher	1	2	3	10	5	6	7"	8	9		11	4			12					
16	26	Brechin City	0-1	2-3	799	Gallacher, McKinna	1	2	3	10	5	6	7	8	9		11"	4			12					
17	3 Dec	CLYDE	0-1	0-1	1377		1	2	3	10	5	6	7	8	9"	14	11*	4			12					
18	10	Alloa Athletic	3-0	4-0	574	McGivern(2), McDicken, McKinna	1	2	3		5	6	7	8		10"	11	4	12		9					
19	17	CLYDEBANK	0-0	0-1	1149		1	2	3	12	5	6		8	7	10	11	4"			9					
20	26	Falkirk	0-0	3-1	3198	McDicken, Gallacher, O.G.	1	2	3	10	5	6	7	4	9	11			8							
21	31	PARTICK THISTLE	1-1	1-2	3111	R.Clark	1	2		3	5	6	7		9	10	11"		8			12	4			
22	3 Jan	AYR UNITED	0-0	1-0	2890	Cuthbertson	1	2	3	10	5	6	7		9	11			8			12	4"			
23	7	Dumbarton	1-3	3-4	907	McClurg(2), McGivern	1	2	3	10	5	6	7		9	11	12		8*			4"	14			
24	14	AIRDRIEONIANS	1-1	4-1	1310	McDicken(2), R.Clark(2)	1	3		8	5	6	7	4	9	10"	11		2			12				
25	4 Feb	MORTON	0-1	0-1	1313		1	3		8	5	6	7	4	9	10	11		2							
26	11	BRECHIN CITY	0-0	1-1	910	R.Clark	1	3		8	5	6	7	4	9	10	11		2							
27	25	Clydebank	0-0	0-3	766		1	3	12	8	5	6	7	4	9	10			2		11"					
28	29	Raith Rovers	0-0	1-2	768	Gallacher	1	3	12	8	5	6	7	4	9	10"			2		11					
29	3 Mar	Hamilton	1-0	1-1	874	McGivern	1	3	10	8	5		11	6	9"				2		12		4	7		
30	10	DUMBARTON	0-0	0-0	1140		1	3	12	8	5	6	11	4	9	10*			2		14			7"		
31	17	Airdrieonians	0-0	0-3	727		1	3		8		6	11"	4	12	10			2		9		5	7		
32	24	RAITH ROVERS	1-1	1-2	680	Brown	1	3				6	11	5		10			8	2	9			7	4	
33	31	Falkirk	0-2	0-2	1203		1	3		10			11	5	7				2"		9	4	6	12	8	
34	7 Apr	MEADOWBANK	1-0	1-1	539	Gallacher	1	3	10	8		12	11	5	7					2	9	4*	6"	14		
35	14	Partick Thistle	1-0	2-1	1854	Gallacher, O.G.	1	3	10			6	11	12	7	8			2		9		5"		4	
36	21	Clyde	0-2	1-2	633	R.Clark	1	3	10			6	11	12	7	8*			2		9	14	5"		4	
37	28	ALLOA ATHLETIC	1-0	2-0	460	R.Clark, McKinna	1	3	10			6	11	5	7				2		9	8			4	
38	5 May	AYR UNITED	0-0	3-0	1495	Gallacher(2), McKinna	1	3	10			6	11	5	7				2		9	8			4	
39	12	Morton	0-1	2-3	4547	Gallacher, McKinna	1	3	10"			6	11	5	7		12		2		9	8			4	
						Apps.	39	38	29	31	30	36	35	30	34	23	23	16	19	2	18	7	8	4	7	
						Subs			3	1		1	2	4	1	2	2	1	3	1	6	5	4	2		
						Goals				2	1	11	7	7	11		4				8	1	2		1	

Pos	P.	W.	D.	L.	F.	A.	Pts.
6th	39	16	6	17	57	53	38

League Cup Section 4

Round 3	Pos	P.	W.	D.	L.	F.	A.	Pts.
	2nd	6	3	1	2	9	6	7

							McCulloch	Robertson	Cockburn	McLeod	P.Clarke	R.Clark	McGivern	McDicken	Gallacher	Simpson	Bryson	J.Clark	McLean	Lowe	McKinna	Cuthbertson	McClurg	Walker	Brown	Holland
2	24 Aug	Queens Park	2-1	2-3	702	J.Clark(2)	1	2	3	8	5	6	7	10	9	12	11"	4								
2	27	QUEENS PARK (Agg: 5-4)	1-1	3-1	1506	McGivern(2), McDicken	1	2	3	8	5	6	7	10	9		11	4								
3	31	Hibernian	0-0	0-2	2681		1	2	3	8	5	6	7	10	9		11	4								
3	7 Sep	AIRDRIEONIANS	2-0	3-0	1046	Gallacher(3)	1	2	3	8	5	6	7	4	9	10	11	4								
3	5 Oct	Celtic	0-0	1-1	5435	Gallacher	1	2	3	10	5	6	7		9	8	11	4								
3	26	Airdrieonians	0-1	2-1	829	P.Clarke, Robertson		2	3	10	5	6	14	8"	9		11*	4			7		12			1
3	9 Nov	HIBERNIAN	2-0	3-1	2001	McDicken(2), P.Clarke	1	2	3	10	5	6	7"	8	9			4			11		12			
3	30	CELTIC	0-1	0-1	8793		1	2	3	10	5	6	7"	8	9	4	11				12					

Scottish Cup

							McCulloch	Robertson	Cockburn	McLeod	P.Clarke	R.Clark	McGivern	McDicken	Gallacher	Simpson	Bryson	J.Clark	McLean	Lowe	McKinna	Cuthbertson	McClurg	Walker	Brown	Holland
3	13 Feb	Aberdeen	0-0	1-1	15000	Gallacher	1	3	12	8	5	6	7	4*	9	10	11"		2		14					
3R	15	ABERDEEN	0-2	1-3	6106	McKinna	1	3	4	8	5	6	7		9	10			2		11					

There was to be no quick return to the top for Killie this year.
Back: Robertson, R.Clark, Clarke, Holland, McCulloch, McDicken, Brown, Bryson
Middle: McLeod, McGivern, Simpson, McLean, McKinna, McClurg, Gallacher, Johnstone, Cuthbertson
Front: Stewart, Cockburn, J.Clark, Clunie, Lowe, Johnstone, Allan. Missing from photo - Haswell, Kerr

SEASON 1984-85 First Division

No.	Date	Opposition	H.T.	Res.	Att.	Goalscorers	McCulloch	Cockburn	Robertson	Brown	McDicken	R.Clark	McGivern	McConville	McKinna	Bryson	McEachran	P.Clarke	Cuthbertson	McLean	Lowe	Cormack	Martin	Millar	McLeod	Melville	Pelosi	Sarwar	Cruickshanks	Houston
1	11 Aug	Motherwell	0-1	0-2	2384		1	2"	3	4	5	6	7	8	9	10*	11	12	14											
2	18	AYR UNITED	0-0	0-0	2013		1		3	4	5*	6	7	8	9		11"	12	10	2	14									
3	25	Clyde	0-0	1-4	749	Cuthbertson	1		3	8	4	6	7	10"	9*		11	5	12	2	14									
4	1 Sep	BRECHIN CITY	0-1	1-1	855	McGivern	1		3	8	4	6	7	10	12	11	9"	5		2										
5	8	FORFAR ATHLETIC	0-0	2-1	809	McEachran, McKinna	1		3	8"	4	6	7	10	12	11	9	5		2										
6	15	Clydebank	0-1	0-5	837		1	14	3	9	4	6"		10*	11	7	8	5		2	12									
7	22	HAMILTON	0-1	1-2	805	Bryson	1	9	3	8	6				11	7	10	5	12	4"	2									
8	29	AIRDRIEONIANS	0-3	0-5	1115		1	14	3		6		7		11	10*	9	5	4"	12	2	8								
9	6 Oct	Meadowbank	0-1	0-4	419		1	10	3		6*		7		12	11	9"	5	14	2	4	8								
10	13	FALKIRK	0-1	3-1	1210	Robertson, Bryson, McKinna	1	12	3	7	6			10	9	11"		5	4	2		8								
11	20	East Fife	0-0	1-0	1006	Cuthbertson	1		3	7	6		12	10	9"	11		5	4	2		8								
12	27	St. Johnstone	0-0	1-0	1513	P.Clarke	1		3	7	6		12	10	9	11		5	4	2		8"								
13	3 Nov	PARTICK THISTLE	0-0	0-0	1834		1	14	3	7	6		12	10	9"	11		5	4*	2		8								
14	10	Forfar Athletic	0-2	1-4	1060	McLean	1	10	3		6		4	8*	9	11"	12	5	7	2	14									
15	17	CLYDEBANK	0-0	1-1	1184	P.Clarke	1	14	3		6		7	4	9	10	11"	5	12	2		8*								
16	24	Hamilton	0-0	0-1	889			12	3"	10	6*		11	8	9		7	5	4	2	14					1				
17	1 Dec	Airdrieonians	0-1	1-2	1483	McGivern	1	3					7	11	9"	10	12	5		2	4	8	6							
18	8	MEADOWBANK	0-1	2-1	847	McLean, Millar	1	3					8	4"	9	11		6		2		7	5	10	12					
19	15	Brechin City	1-1	2-3	668	McGivern(2)	1	3					8		10	11		5	4	2		7"	6	9	12					
20	22	CLYDE	2-0	2-0	1303	Millar(2)	1	3					10	4	12	11		5	7"	2			6	9	8					
21	29	MOTHERWELL	0-0	0-0	2042		1	3					8	4	10	11		6		2			5	9	7					
22	2 Jan	Ayr United	0-0	0-1	4136		1	3					8	4	11*	10	14	6		2"	12		5	9	7					
23	5	EAST FIFE	0-0	1-1	1296	McKinna(2), Millar	1	3					8		10*	11	14	6		2	4	12	5	9	7"					
24	19	ST. JOHNSTONE	2-2	3-2	1451	McKinna(2), Millar	1	3					8		10	11		6		2	4		5	9	7					
25	2 Feb	Partick Thistle	0-0	0-1	1776		1	3			12		8		10	11		6"		2	4		5	9	7					
26	23	Motherwell	1-1	2-2	2288	Millar, McKinna	1		3		4"		7	8	10	11		6		2			5	9	12					
27	26	CLYDEBANK	0-0	0-0	1336		1		3				8	4"	10	11		6		2		12	5	9	7					
28	2 Mar	Brechin City	0-1	1-2	621	Millar	1		3				8		10	11		6"	4	2		12	5	9	7					
29	9	HAMILTON	1-0	1-1	1225	Millar	1	3	2		6		8*	4"	10	11		5			12	14		9	7					
30	13	Falkirk	0-2	2-3	1532	Cuthbertson, Millar	1	3	2		6		8		10	11		5	4					9	7					
31	16	Meadowbank	1-1	1-2	492	McGivern	1	3	2		6		8		10	11		5	4"	12		14		9	7*					
32	23	FORFAR ATHLETIC	0-0	1-0	1082	Millar	1	3	6				4	8"	10	11		12		2			5	9			7			
33	30	Ayr United	0-0	0-0	2404		1	3	2		8		12			11		6		4		7"	5	9			10			
34	6 Apr	FALKIRK	0-0	0-3	1632		1	3	2		5		8		12	11		6		4		10		9"			7*		14	
35	13	PARTICK THISTLE	2-0	2-0	1803	McKinna, Cuthbertson	1	3	2						10	11		6	8	4			5	9			7			
36	20	East Fife	2-0	2-0	875	Millar(2)	1	3	2		12				10*	11"		6	8	4			5	9	14		7			
37	27	St. Johnstone	3-2	4-2	781	Millar, Cormack, Cuthbertson, Pelosi	1	3	2							11		6	8	4		10	5	9	12		7"			
38	4 May	CLYDE	0-0	2-0	1692	Cuthbertson, P.Clarke	1	3	2						10	11		6	8	4			5	9			7			
39	11	AIRDRIEONIANS	1-2	1-4	1493	Bryson	1	3	2				10*			11		6	4	14			5"	9	12		7	8		
						Apps.	38	24	30	12	22	6	28	22	31	36	11	36	18	33	7	13	19	22	11	1	8	1		
						Subs		6			2		4		5		4	3	5	3	7	5			6				1	
						Goals			1				5		7	3	1	3	6	2		1		12			1			

Pos	P.	W.	D.	L.	F.	A.	Pts.
12th	39	12	10	17	42	61	34

League Cup

Rd	Date	Opposition	H.T.	Res.	Att.	Goalscorers	McCulloch	Cockburn	Robertson	Brown	McDicken	R.Clark	McGivern	McConville	McKinna	Bryson	McEachran	P.Clarke	Cuthbertson	McLean	Lowe	Cormack	Martin	Millar	McLeod	Melville	Pelosi	Sarwar	Cruickshanks	Houston
2	22 Aug	ALLOA ATHLETIC	1-0	1-1*	849	Cuthbertson	1		3*	4	5	6	7		9		11"	12	10	2	8									14
3	29	Dundee	1-0	1-1#	3367	McDicken	1		3	8*	4	6	7	11	9		12	5	10"	2	14									

* After extra time, Kilmarnock won 3-2 on penalties

After extra time, Dundee won 3-2 on penalties

Scottish Cup

Rd	Date	Opposition	H.T.	Res.	Att.	Goalscorers	McCulloch	Cockburn	Robertson	Brown	McDicken	R.Clark	McGivern	McConville	McKinna	Bryson	McEachran	P.Clarke	Cuthbertson	McLean	Lowe	Cormack	Martin	Millar	McLeod	Melville	Pelosi	Sarwar	Cruickshanks	Houston
3	9 Feb	Inverness Thistle	0-1	0-3	2500		1	6	3		4		9		11*	10	8			2	7"	12	5		14					

JIM CLUNIE's face tells its own story. Killie have just been hammered 5-0 at home by Airdrieonians and Clunie had resigned as Manager.

SEASON 1985-86 First Division

No.	Date	Opposition	H.T.	Res.	Att.	Goalscorers	Holland	Lowe	McLean	Robertson	Martin	P.Clarke	Cuthbertson	McCafferty	B.Millar	McGivern	Bryson	McCulloch	McNab	Cockburn	McKinna	Sarwar	McConville	G.Millar	Cook	McLeod	McGuire
1	10 Aug	ALLOA ATHLETIC	0-0	3-0	1439	McLean, B.Millar, McGivern	1	2	3	4	5	6	7	8	9	10	11										
2	17	Forfar Athletic	0-0	0-0	967			2	3	4	5	6	7	8	9	10	11	1									
3	24	HAMILTON	0-0	1-0	1754	B.Millar		2	3	4	5	6	7"	8	9	10	11	1	12								
4	31	Ayr United	0-1	0-3	2749			2"	3	4	5	6	7	8	9	10*	11	1	14	12							
5	7 Sep	PARTICK THISTLE	4-0	5-0	1944	Bryson, Cuthbertson, McLean, McGivern, Clarke			2	4	5	6	7"	8		10	11*	1	12	3	9	14					
6	14	Morton	0-0	0-3	1434				2	4	5	6	7"		9		11	1	14	3	10*	8	12				
7	21	CLYDE	1-0	1-1	2005	B.Millar			2	4	5	6			9	7	11	1	12	3	10"	8					
8	28	Brechin City	1-1	4-2	662	Bryson, Sarwar, McKinna, O.G.			2	4	5	6	7"		9*	10	11	1	12	3	14	8					
9	5 Oct	FALKIRK	1-0	1-0	1937	McLean			7	4	5	6			9	10	11	1		3		8		2			
10	12	MONTROSE	0-0	0-0	1498				2	4	5	6	7"		9	10	11*	1	14	3	12	8					
11	19	Dumbarton	0-1	0-1	1559				2	4	5	6	7*		9	10	11"	1	12	3	14	8					
12	26	Airdrieonians	0-0	2-1	1573	Clarke(2)			2	4	5	6	7		9	10		1		3	11	8					
13	2 Nov	EAST FIFE	1-1	2-2	1425	Cuthbertson(2)			3"	4	5	6	7		9*	10	12	1	14		11	8		2			
14	9	Partick Thistle	0-1	1-1	2441	Bryson				4	5	6	7		9	10	11	1		3		8		2			
15	16	MORTON	2-0	3-0	1837	Cockburn, Martin, Cuthbertson				4	5	6	7"		9	10	11	1	12	3		8		2			
16	23	Clyde	1-1	3-1	1102	McGivern(2), Clarke				4	5	6	7		9	10	11	1		3		8		2			
17	30	BRECHIN CITY	1-0	3-1	2787	Bryson, B.Millar, Cuthbertson				4	5	6	7		9	10	11	1		3		8		2			
18	7 Dec	Falkirk	0-0	1-0	2542	McGivern			12	4	5	6	7"		9*	10	11	1		3	14	8		2			
19	14	Montrose	0-1	1-4	616	McKinna				4	5	6	7"	14	9	10	11	1		3	12	8*		2			
20	21	DUMBARTON	1-2	1-4	2311	Bryson				4	5	6	7*	12		10	11	1	14	3	9	8		2"			
21	28	Hamilton	0-2	1-4	3271	Bryson				4	5	6	7	12		10	11	1		3	9	8"		2			
22	1 Jan	AYR UNITED	0-0	1-2	4119	Bryson			8*	4	5	6		7		10	11	1	12	3		14		2	9"		
23	4	FORFAR ATHLETIC	1-0	1-0	1679	B.Millar			3	4	5	6		7	9*	10	11	1		12	14	8		2"			
24	11	Alloa Athletic	1-0	4-1	682	B.Millar(2), McGivern, Cuthbertson			2	4	5	6	12	7"	9	10	11	1		3		8					
25	18	AIRDRIEONIANS	0-1	0-2	1711				2	4	5	6	7*	14	9	10	11"	1		3	12	8					
26	1 Feb	East Fife	1-2	2-2	940	Bryson(2)			2	4		5		6		8	10	1			9		7			3	11
27	8	MORTON	0-1	1-1	2252	Clarke			2	4		5		6		8	10	1			9		7			3	11
28	1 Mar	MONTROSE	3-0	3-0	1502	McNab, Bryson, McGuire			2	4		5	7	6		8	11	1	9	12						3	10
29	8	Hamilton	1-3	2-3	2345	McGivern(2)			2	4		5	12	6		8	11	1	9					7"		3	10
30	15	ALLOA ATHLETIC	1-0	2-0	1260	McCafferty, McNab			2	4		5	14	6		8	11	1	9	12				7*		3	10
31	22	Airdrieonians	0-1	0-1	1409				2	5			14	6		8	11	1	9	3*	12		7			4	10
32	25	Falkirk	1-0	1-1	2582	McNab			2	4"		5	12	6		8	11	1	9		14		7			3	10
33	29	BRECHIN CITY	1-0	1-2	1511	Bryson			2			5	14	6*		8	11	1	9	3	12		7			4	10
34	5 Apr	Clyde	1-0	3-1	820	McGivern(2), Bryson			2		5	6		4		8	11	1	9				7			3	10
35	9	EAST FIFE	1-0	2-0	1320	McGivern, McGuire			2		5	4		6		8	11	1	9"		12		7			3	10
36	12	Forfar Athletic	0-0	0-1	874				2		5	4		6		8	11	1	9"		12		7			3	10
37	19	DUMBARTON	1-0	3-0	2321	Bryson, Clarke, McGuire			2		5	4	14	6		8"	11	1	9	3	12		7*				10
38	26	Partick Thistle	0-0	0-2	2835				2		5	4		6			11	1	9	3	8		7			12	10
39	3 May	AYR UNITED	2-1	3-2	2369	McGuire(2), Bryson			8		5	4	7	6"			11	1		14	9	12		2*		3	10
						Apps.	1	4	31	32	31	38	22	22	21	36	37	38	11	23	11	19	10	15	1	12	14
						Subs			1				7	4			1		12	5	13	3	1			1	
						Goals			3		1	6	6	1	7	11	14		3	1	2	2					5

Pos	P.	W.	D.	L.	F.	A.	Pts.
3rd	39	18	8	13	62	49	44

League Cup

No.	Date	Opposition	H.T.	Res.	Att.	Goalscorers	Holland	Lowe	McLean	Robertson	Martin	P.Clarke	Cuthbertson	McCafferty	B.Millar	McGivern	Bryson	McCulloch	McNab	Cockburn	McKinna	Sarwar	McConville	G.Millar	Cook	McLeod	McGuire
2	20 Aug	St. Mirren	1-1	1-3	3435	B.Millar		2	3	4	5	6	7"	8	9	10	11	1	12								

Scottish Cup

No.	Date	Opposition	H.T.	Res.	Att.	Goalscorers	Holland	Lowe	McLean	Robertson	Martin	P.Clarke	Cuthbertson	McCafferty	B.Millar	McGivern	Bryson	McCulloch	McNab	Cockburn	McKinna	Sarwar	McConville	G.Millar	Cook	McLeod	McGuire
3	25 Jan	STIRLING ALBION	1-0	1-0	2199	McCafferty			2	4	5	6		7		10	11	1			9	8"	12			3	
4	15 Feb	Dundee United	0-0	1-1	6610	Bryson			2	4	5	6		7		10	11	1			9		8			3	
4R	19	DUNDEE UNITED	0-0	0-1	9054				2	4	5	6	12	7		10"	11	1	9				8			3	

The first full season in charge for EDDIE MORRISON as the former goalscoring hero attempts to restore his old club's fortunes.

SEASON 1986-87 First Division

No.	Date	Opposition	H.T.	Res.	Att.	Goalscorers	McCulloch	McLean	McLeod	Robertson	Martin	R.Clark	Cuthbertson	McCafferty	Cook	McGuire	Bryson	G.Millar	McGivern	Sarwar	J.Clark	Cockburn	McConville	B.Millar	McNab	Docherty	Lowe	Harkness	Holland	Houston	Marshall	McVeigh	Reid	Bell
1	9 Aug	East Fife	3-0	4-1	985	Bryson(2), Cook, McLeod	1	2	3	4	5	6	7"	8	9	10	11	12																
2	13	MORTON	2-1	2-2	2468	McGuire, Cook	1	2	3	4	5	6		8	9	10	11		7															
3	16	Forfar Athletic	1-1	1-3	863	Bryson	1	2	3	4	5	6"		8*	9	10	11	12	7	14														
4	23	MONTROSE	3-0	3-0	1447	Bryson, Martin, Cook	1	2	3	4	5	6		12	9	10	11*	14	7"		8													
5	30	Queen of the South	0-1	1-2	2588	Cook	1	2		4	5	6"		12	9	10	11		7		8	3												
6	6 Sep	DUNFERMLINE	1-1	1-2	2662	Cook	1	2	3	4	5	6		8"	9	12	11		7		10													
7	13	Airdrieonians	1-0	2-3	1577	Bryson(2)	1		3	4	5				9	10	11	2	12		6		7	8"										
8	16	DUMBARTON	1-1	2-1	1664	Bryson, O.G.	1	12	3	4"	5				9	10*	11	2	14		6		7		8									
9	20	Brechin City	1-1	2-2	572	Cook(2)	1	3		4	5				9	10	11	2	12		6		7"		8									
10	27	CLYDE	0-0	0-0	1761		1	3		4	5				9	10	11	2	12		6		7		8"									
11	30	Partick Thistle	0-0	0-1	1828		1	3	7	4	5				9	12	11	2	10		6			8"										
12	4 Oct	EAST FIFE	1-0	1-1	1306	Martin	1	6	3	4	5				9"	10	11	2	8		7		12											
13	8	Morton	0-1	0-2	1859		1	3	6	4	5					11		2	8		7*		14	9"		10	12							
14	11	Montrose	0-0	2-0	496	Harkness, McLean	1	7	6	3	5	4				11		2	8					12		10		9"						
15	18	FORFAR ATHLETIC	0-0	3-0	1440	Harkness, McGivern, Docherty	1	8	7"	3	5	4				11*		2	10		12			14		6		9						
16	25	AIRDRIEONIANS	1-0	2-0	1996	Harkness, McLeod	1	7	14	3	5	4				11"		2	8		10			12*		6		9						
17	29	Dumbarton	0-0	0-2	925			8	14	3	5	4				11"		2	10		7*		12			6		9	1					
18	1 Nov	Dunfermline	0-1	0-1	4179			8	12	3	5	4				11		2	10		7*		14			6"		9	1					
19	8	QUEEN OF THE SOUTH	1-1	3-2	2008	McGivern, McGuire, McLeod		8"	12	3	5	4				11*		2	10		7		14			6		9	1					
20	15	BRECHIN CITY	0-0	0-1	1600			8"	14	3	5	4	12			11		2	10		7					6*		9	1					
21	22	Clyde	0-0	0-0	939		1	8	12	3	5	4	7			11		2			10"					6		9						
22	29	PARTICK THISTLE	1-2	3-2	2502	Cuthbertson, R.Clark, McGuire	1	8	10	3	5	4	7			11		2					12			6"		9						
23	6 Dec	East Fife	1-0	1-2	1251	R.Clark	1	8	10	5"		4	7			11		2				3				6		9		12				
24	13	MORTON	1-0	2-0	1989	Harkness, McGuire	1					4	12		8	10	11	2			6	3	7"					9			5			
25	20	MONTROSE	1-0	1-0	1612	Harkness	1	12				4	7"		8	10	11	2			6	3						9				5		
26	27	Forfar Athletic	1-0	1-1	857	McGuire	1	12			5	4			8	10	11	2			7"	3						9				6		
27	1 Jan	Queen of the South	1-0	2-1	2009	Cook, McVeigh	1	7*			5	4	14		8	10	11	2				3						9"				6	12	
28	3	DUNFERMLINE	0-1	2-2	4855	McGuire, Reid	1	7			5	4	12		8*	10"	11	2				3						9				6	14	
29	24	AIRDRIEONIANS	0-0	0-0	1983		1	7		3"		4			8*	10	11	2			6		12					9				5	14	
30	27	DUMBARTON	1-2	1-2	2209	McVeigh	1	3			5	4	12		8*	10	11	2					7"					9				6	14	
31	7 Feb	CLYDE	1-0	1-1	1769	McLean	1	6			5	4			8*	10"	11	2				3	7			14		9					12	
32	17	Brechin City	0-1	0-1	513		1	6			5	4			8	10"	11	2				3	7					9					12	
33	28	EAST FIFE	3-0	3-1	1434	Reid(2), Harkness	1	8			5	4				10	11	2				3						9				6	7	
34	3 Mar	Partick Thistle	1-1	2-1	1383	Bryson, McGuire	1	2			5	4	7			10	11					3						9				6	8	
35	11	Morton	0-2	1-2	1971	Cuthbertson	1	2			5	4	7*			10	11	14				3	12					9				6	8"	
36	14	Montrose	0-1	1-1	417	Harkness	1	2			5	4	7			10*	11	14				3	12	8"				9				6		
37	21	FORFAR ATHLETIC	0-0	2-0	1059	Reid, Bryson	1	2			5	4				10	11					3				7"		9				6	8	12
38	28	QUEEN OF THE SOUTH	1-0	2-2	1675	Bryson, Reid	1	14			5					10	11"					3				12	2	9		6*		4	7	8
39	4 Apr	Dunfermline	1-0	1-0	3704	Harkness	1				5	4	14			10	11"	2				3				12		9*		7		6	8	
40	11	Dumbarton	2-1	2-3	1030	Reid(2)	1				5	4				10	11	2				3	12					9		7"		6	8	
41	18	Airdrieonians	0-0	3-4	1028	Cuthbertson, Reid, McVeigh	1				5	4	10			14	11*					3					2	9"		7		6	8	12
42	25	BRECHIN CITY	0-1	0-1	875		1				5	4	10"			12	11	2				3					14	9		7		6*	8	
43	2 May	Clyde	0-0	1-0	638	Reid	1	2		4	5		12			10	11					3						9		7"		6	8	
44	9	PARTICK THISTLE	0-0	1-0	1453	McVeigh	1	2		4	5		7"		12	11						3						9				6	8	10
						Apps.	40	34	14	26	40	34	11	4	21	40	32	30	15		20	21	8	4	3	12	2	31	4	6	1	18	11	2
						Subs		4	6				7	2	1	4		5	4	1	1		10	3		3	2			1			6	2
						Goals		2	3		2	2	3		8	7	10		2							1		8				4	9	

Pos	P.	W.	D.	L.	F.	A.	Pts.
6th	44	17	11	16	62	53	45

League Cup

No.	Date	Opposition	H.T.	Res.	Att.	Goalscorers	McCulloch	McLean	McLeod	Robertson	Martin	R.Clark	Cuthbertson	McCafferty	Cook	McGuire	Bryson	G.Millar	McGivern	Sarwar	J.Clark	Cockburn	McConville	B.Millar	McNab	Docherty	Lowe	Harkness	Holland	Houston	Marshall	McVeigh	Reid	Bell
2	20 Aug	AYR UNITED	0-0	1-2	3853	McCafferty	1	2	3	4	5	6		8	9	10	11		7															

Scottish Cup

No.	Date	Opposition	H.T.	Res.	Att.	Goalscorers	McCulloch	McLean	McLeod	Robertson	Martin	R.Clark	Cuthbertson	McCafferty	Cook	McGuire	Bryson	G.Millar	McGivern	Sarwar	J.Clark	Cockburn	McConville	B.Millar	McNab	Docherty	Lowe	Harkness	Holland	Houston	Marshall	McVeigh	Reid	Bell
3	31 Jan	Hearts	0-0	0-0	15227		1	3			5	4	7		8	10"	11	2										9				6	12	
3R	4 Feb	HEARTS	1-0	1-1*	14932	Bryson	1	3			5	4	7		8*	10	11	2					14					9"				6	12	
3R	9	HEARTS	0-1	1-3	14146	Martin	1	6			5	4	7*		8"	10	11	2				3	14					9					12	

* After extra time

Buoyed by their near miss in 85-86, this squad was hopeful of winning promotion but finished just above mid-table. Back: H.Houston, B.Millar, B.Holland, A.McCulloch, I.Bryson, R.McConville
Middle: J.McGuire, T.McCafferty, R.Sarwar, G.Millar, S.McLean, L.Lowe, E.McNab, S.McGivern
Front: R.Stewart, A.McAnespie, A.McLeod, A.Robertson, J.Cockburn, E.Morrison(Manager), H.Allan

SEASON 1987-88 First Division

No.	Date	Opposition	H.T.	Res.	Att.	Goalscorers
1	8 Aug	HAMILTON	0-2	0-2	2178	
2	12	East Fife	1-0	1-2	711	Reid
3	15	Dumbarton	0-1	3-1	824	Cuthbertson, Harknes, McInnes
4	22	FORFAR ATHLETIC	1-2	2-2	1235	Harkness, Reid
5	29	QUEEN OF THE SOUTH	0-0	0-2	1720	
6	5 Sep	Meadowbank	1-1	1-2	698	Cook
7	12	RAITH ROVERS	2-2	3-4	1436	Cuthbertson, Harkness, McInnes
8	15	Clydebank	0-2	0-2	857	
9	19	Airdrieonians	1-1	2-3	1513	Bryson, O.G.
10	26	CLYDE	2-0	2-0	1732	Harkness, Bryson
11	29	PARTICK THISTLE	1-0	1-1	2030	Harkness
12	3 Oct	Hamilton	1-1	1-1	3236	Harkness
13	6	EAST FIFE	1-0	2-0	1425	Harkness(2)
14	10	Forfar Athletic	0-0	0-2	896	
15	17	Raith Rovers	1-0	2-0	2276	Gilmour, Harkness
16	20	CLYDEBANK	0-2	1-3	1733	McGuire
17	24	DUMBARTON	0-0	1-0	1571	Gilmour
18	31	MEADOWBANK	1-2	2-4	1442	Harkness(2)
19	3 Nov	Partick Thistle	0-1	0-1	1434	
20	7	Queen of the South	0-0	4-1	1487	Reid(2), Bryson, McInnes
21	14	AIRDRIEONIANS	1-0	1-0	1978	Reid
22	21	Clyde	0-2	0-2	1242	
23	28	HAMILTON	0-0	1-0	1922	Harkness
24	5 Dec	East Fife	1-0	1-2	605	Bryson
25	12	RAITH ROVERS	0-0	1-1	1654	Reid
26	19	Clydebank	0-0	0-1	981	
27	26	Meadowbank	1-1	3-1	751	Harkness(2), McFarlane
28	2 Jan	QUEEN OF THE SOUTH	0-0	0-0	3230	
29	9	Airdrieonians	1-1	3-3	1588	McFarlane(2), Gilmour
30	16	CLYDE	2-1	3-1	1754	Cuthbertson, Harkness, Bryson
31	23	Dumbarton	0-1	0-1	1048	
32	6 Feb	FORFAR ATHLETIC	0-1	0-2	1281	
33	13	PARTICK THISTLE	0-0	0-1	2432	
34	27	Hamilton	0-0	0-1	2048	
35	5 Mar	Raith Rovers	0-1	2-2	1536	Davidson, Cuthbertson
36	12	CLYDEBANK	1-1	2-2	1549	Martin, Bourke
37	19	MEADOWBANK	0-0	0-0	1662	
38	26	Queen of the South	0-0	0-1	1578	
39	2 Apr	Forfar Athletic	0-0	1-1	713	Gilmour
40	9	DUMBARTON	0-0	3-1	2205	Gilmour, McGuire, Bryson
41	16	Clyde	0-0	0-0	1120	
42	23	AIRDRIEONIANS	1-0	4-1	1953	McGuire(2), Bourke, Gilmour
43	30	EAST FIFE	0-3	1-3	2488	Gilmour
44	7 May	Partick Thistle	0-0	1-0	3103	Gilmour

No.	Holland	G.Millar	Cockburn	Robertson	McVeigh	R.Clark	McConville	McLean	Harkness	Reid	Bryson	McGuire	McInnes	Lowe	Bell	Cook	Davidson	Cuthbertson	Martin	Wylde	Gilmour	Houston	McCulloch	McFarlane	Kearney	Candlish	Marshall	Bourke
1	1	2	3	4	5	6	7"	8*	9	10	11	12	14															
2	1			4	5			6	8	10"	11	9	7	2	3	12												
3	1			6	4			2	9	10	11		7		3		5	8										
4	1			6	4			2	9	12	10		7	14	3	11"		8*	5									
5	1		3	4	8"			2	9	10	11*		7		6	14		12	5									
6	1			4	6			2	9		10	12	7		3	11"			5	8								
7	1			4	6			2	10	12	11	14	7		3	9*		8"	5									
8				3	6	4		2	9"	10	11		7					12	5	8			1					
9				3	6	4		2	9*		11	12	7			14		8"	5	10			1					
10				3	14	4		2	9		11	12	7		6*			8"	5	10			1					
11				3		4		2	9		11		7		6			8	5	10			1					
12			6	3	4			2	9*		11"	12	7		14			8	5	10			1					
13				3	4		6"	2	9		11	12	7					8	5	10			1					
14				3		4		2	9		11	12	7		6"			8	5	10			1					
15				3		4	12	2	9		11"		7					8	5	6	10		1					
16				3		4	12	2	9		11	14	7					8"	5	6*	10		1					
17				3		4	12	2	9		11*	14	7					8"	5	6	10		1					
18				3		4		2	9		11	12	7					8"	5	6	10		1					
19		2					6	3		9		12	7		11"		4		5	8	10		1					
20		2					6	3		9	11		7				4	12	5	8"	10		1					
21		2						3		9	11"	12	7				4		5	8	10	6	1					
22		2						3		9	11"	12	7				4		5	8	10	6	1					
23		2						3	8	9"		12	7				4		5	10	11	6	1					
24		2						3	9	10"	11	12	7				4		5	6	8		1					
25		2					6	3	9	12	11	10*	7			14	4		5	8"			1					
26		2					10	3	9		12		7				4"		5	8	11		1	6				
27				3			10	2	9"		11					7	4		5	8	12		1	6				
28				3			10"	2	9		11		12			8	4		5	7			1	6				
29				3			10"	2	9		12					8	4		5	7	11		1	6				
30				3			6"	2	9		11					12	4	8	5	7	10		1					
31		7*		3			6	2	9		11"		12				4	8	5		10	14	1					
32							14	2	9		11"		7			12	4	8	5		10	6*	1		3			
33				3			8	2	9"		11		7				4			6	12		1			10	5	
34				3			8	2			11		7"				4	12	5	6	10		1			9		
35				3			8	2			11		7*				4	14		6	12		1			10"	5	9
36				3				2			11		12				4	8	5	7"	10		1				6	9
37		3						2	12		11		14				4	7"	5	8	10*		1				6	9
38		3					14	2	9"		11	12					4	7	5	8*	10		1				6	
39		3*						2	12		11	14					4	7"	5	8	10		1				6	9
40		3						2			11	7"	12				4		5	8	10		1				6	9
41		3						2			11	7					4		5	8	10		1				6"	9
42		3						2			11	7"	12				4	14	5	8	10		1				6	9*
43	1	3						2			11	7"	12				4	14	5	8	10						6*	9
44		3						2	12		11	7"					4		5	8	10		1				6	9
Apps.	8	18	3	27	11	10	14	44	30	11	40	7	29	1	10	6	27	20	39	36	25	4	36	4	1	3	11	9
Subs					1		5		3	3	2	18	8	1	1	6		7			3	1						
Goals									15	6	6	4	3			1	1	4	1		8			3				2

Pos	P.	W.	D.	L.	F.	A.	Pts.
10th	44	13	11	20	55	60	37

League Cup

No.	Date	Opposition	H.T.	Res.	Att.	Goalscorers	Holland	G.Millar	Cockburn	Robertson	McVeigh	R.Clark	McConville	McLean	Harkness	Reid	Bryson	McGuire	McInnes	Lowe	Bell	Cook	Davidson	Cuthbertson	Martin	Wylde	Gilmour	Houston	McCulloch	McFarlane	Kearney	Candlish	Marshall	Bourke
2	19 Aug	Hearts	1-2	1-6	9500	Bryson	1			6	4			2	9	10	11		7		3		5	8										

Scottish Cup

No.	Date	Opposition	H.T.	Res.	Att.	Goalscorers	Holland	G.Millar	Cockburn	Robertson	McVeigh	R.Clark	McConville	McLean	Harkness	Reid	Bryson	McGuire	McInnes	Lowe	Bell	Cook	Davidson	Cuthbertson	Martin	Wylde	Gilmour	Houston	McCulloch	McFarlane	Kearney	Candlish	Marshall	Bourke
3	30 Jan	Motherwell	0-0	0-0	6499					3			6	2	9		11		12				4	8	5		10	7"	1					
3R	3 Feb	MOTHERWELL	0-0	1-3	7591	Harkness				3			6	2	9		11		7				4	8	5		10		1					

A year of desperate struggle saw Killie take 2 points from the final game at Firhill, in order to stay in the 1st Div.
Back: H.Houston, S.Marshall, R.Clark, B.Holland, A.McCulloch, P.Martin, L.Lowe, F.Davidson.
Middle: L.Lindsay, R.McConville, D.Cook, J.McGuire, A.Bell, J.McVeigh, C.Harkness, I.McInnes.
Front: R.Stewart,A.McAnespie,S.Cuthbertson,I.Bryson, A.Robertson, S.McLean, J.Cockburn, E.Morrison, H.Allan

SEASON 1988-89 First Division

No.	Date	Opposition	H.T.	Res.	Att.	Goalscorers
1	13 Aug	Queen of the South	0-0	2-2	1694	McGuire, Gilmour
2	20	PARTICK THISTLE	0-0	0-1	2442	
3	27	AYR UNITED	1-0	2-0	5387	McGuire, Marshall
4	3 Sep	Clydebank	1-1	2-2	1307	McGuire, Cuthbertson
5	10	Airdrieonians	0-2	1-5	2016	Cook
6	17	CLYDE	1-1	1-2	1745	McDonald
7	24	Dunfermline	0-1	0-3	5379	
8	1 Oct	MORTON	1-3	3-4	1865	Cook, Martin, McInnes
9	8	Forfar Athletic	1-1	2-2	685	McGuire, Gilmour
10	15	Meadowbank	0-0	2-0	1185	Cook, Montgomerie
11	22	RAITH ROVERS	1-1	1-1	1965	Wylde
12	29	St. Johnstone	0-0	0-2	2308	
13	5 Nov	FALKIRK	0-1	0-2	2561	
14	12	AIRDRIEONIANS	0-1	0-3	1958	
15	19	Clyde	2-0	2-0	1028	McFarlane(2)
16	26	DUNFERMLINE	0-2	2-2	2761	Gilmour, Brannigan
17	3 Dec	Partick Thistle	1-0	1-0	2498	McFarlane
18	10	ST. JOHNSTONE	0-1	0-3	2501	
19	17	Raith Rovers	0-0	0-0	1514	
20	24	MEADOWBANK	1-0	1-0	2405	Watters
21	31	CLYDEBANK	1-0	1-0	2760	McLaughlin
22	3 Jan	Ayr United	0-2	1-4	8585	Faulds
23	7	Falkirk	0-2	0-2	3972	
24	14	QUEEN OF THE SOUTH	1-1	2-1	2264	Derek Walker, Watters
25	21	FORFAR ATHLETIC	1-1	2-1	1813	Watters(2)
26	18 Feb	CLYDE	0-0	0-0	1953	
27	25	St. Johnstone	0-1	2-2	2393	Watters, Reilly
28	1 Mar	Morton	0-1	2-2	1807	Watters, Harkness
29	4	AIRDRIEONIANS	0-1	1-1	2376	McLaughlin
30	11	Ayr United	1-1	1-2	5476	Montgomerie
31	18	FORFAR ATHLETIC	2-2	2-2	1584	Harkness, Faulds
32	25	Dunfermline	0-0	0-0	5906	
33	1 Apr	FALKIRK	0-0	0-0	3780	
34	8	Meadowbank	1-0	2-1	866	Harkness, Watters
35	15	RAITH ROVERS	1-0	1-2	2218	Harkness
36	22	Morton	0-1	0-3	1623	
37	29	PARTICK THISTLE	0-0	0-0	2932	
38	6 May	Clydebank	2-1	2-3	1643	Harkness, Stewart
39	13	Queen of the South	1-0	6-0	1570	Watters(5), Reilly

No.	McCulloch	Montgomerie	Robertson	Davidson	Martin	Marshall	McConville	Gilmour	Bourke	McDonald	McGuire	Cook	Harkness	McLean	Cuthbertson	Hughes	Wylde	McInnes	Brannigan	McFarlane	McQueen	Millar	McLaughlin	Reilly	Derek Walker	Flexney	Watters	David Walker	Lindsay	Spiers	Faulds	Stewart	Callaghan
1	1	2	3	4	5	6	7	8	9	10	11																						
2	1	2	3	4	5	6"	7	8	9	10	11	12																					
3	1	2	3	4	5	6	7	8		10*	11	12	9"	14																			
4	1		3	4	5	6	7	8		10	11"		9	2	12																		
5	1	2	3	4	5	6"	7	8		10	11	14	9*	12																			
6	1	2	3	4	5			8		10"	11	9	14	12		6	7*																
7	1	2	3	4	5	8*	14			10	11"		9	6			7	12															
8	1	2	4		5		14	8		11"		9	10	3		6*	7	12															
9	1	2	4		5		7	10			11	9	12	3		6	8"																
10	1	2	4		5	8"	12	11		10		9		3			7		6														
11	1	2	4		5			11		10		9"	12	3			7		6	8													
12	1	2	4			12	10"	8			11	9		3			7		5	6													
13	1	2		4		12		8		10"	11		9	3					5	6	7												
14	1			4				11		14		9	12	3			8		5	6*	7	2	10"										
15	1			4						12			9	3			8		5	6	7	2	10"	11									
16	1	3		4				14		10"	12		9	2			8		5	6	7*			11									
17	1	2		4				11			12	8	9	3			10"		6	5*		14		7									
18	1	2		4				14			11*	12	9"	3					6	5		10		8	7								
19	1	2				12							9	3					4	5		10"			8	6	7	11*	14				
20	1												9"	3					5	4*		2	11		7	6	8	14	12	10			
21	1			6									12	3					5	4		2	11		7		8"		14	10*	9		
22	1			6									12	3					5	4		2	11"		7		8		14	10*	9		
23	1			10									9						5	2*		3	11		4"	6	7	14	12		8		
24	1			4										3					5	12			11*	7	10	6"	8	14	2		9		
25	1	4		6										3						5			11"	7	10		8*	14	2	12	9		
26	1	2				5							14	3						12			11*	7	10"	6	8			4	9		
27	1	2				5							9	3						10"			12	7		6	8		14		11*		4
28	1	2				5							9	3"								12	10	7		6	8		14		11*		4
29	1	2				5							9							7"		3	10		12	6	8		14		11*		4
30	1	2		7		5*							9									3	10"		14	6	8	12			11		4
31	1	2		7*		5							9							14		3	10"		12	6	8				11		4
32	1	2		7		5							9	3									12	10		6	8				11"		4
33	1	2		7		5							9"	3									12	10	14	6	8					11*	4
34	1	2				5							9	3									11"	10	12	6	8					7	4
35	1	2				5							9	3*						12			14	10		6	8				11"	7	4
36	1	2		10		5							9*									3"	12	7	14	6	8					11	4
37	1	2		10		5							9	3						4				7		6					12	11	8*
38	1	2		7		5							9	3						4				10		6	8					11	
39	1	2		7		5							9"	3						4*			12	10	14	6	8					11	
Apps.	39	31	12	26	11	21	7	14	2	12	11	8	26	29		3	11		15	19	4	12	14	17	9	18	20	1	2	4	13	7	11
Subs						3	3	2		2	2	4	7	3	1			2		4		2	6		7			5	8	1	1		
Goals		2			1	1		3		1	4	3	5		1		1	1	1	3			2	2	1		12				2	1	

Pos	P.	W.	D.	L.	F.	A.	Pts.
13th	39	10	14	15	47	60	34

League Cup

Rd	Date	Opposition	H.T.	Res.	Att.	Goalscorers
2	17 Aug	FORFAR ATHLETIC	0-0	1-0	1523	Gilmour
3	23	Hibernian	0-1	0-1	8000	

Rd	McCulloch	Montgomerie	Robertson	Davidson	Martin	Marshall	McConville	Gilmour	Bourke	McDonald	McGuire	Cook	Harkness	McLean	Cuthbertson	Hughes	Wylde	McInnes	Brannigan	McFarlane	McQueen	Millar	McLaughlin	Reilly	Derek Walker	Flexney	Watters	David Walker	Lindsay	Spiers	Faulds	Stewart	Callaghan
2	1	2	3	4	5	6*	7"	8	9	10	11	14			12																		
3	1	2	3	4	5	6	7	8	9*	10	11"	14	12																				

Scottish Cup

Rd	Date	Opposition	H.T.	Res.	Att.	Goalscorers
3	28 Jan	Queen of the South	1-1	2-2	2941	Watters, Spiers
3R	1 Feb	QUEEN OF THE SOUTH	0-1	0-1	5623	

Rd	McCulloch	Montgomerie	Robertson	Davidson	Martin	Marshall	McConville	Gilmour	Bourke	McDonald	McGuire	Cook	Harkness	McLean	Cuthbertson	Hughes	Wylde	McInnes	Brannigan	McFarlane	McQueen	Millar	McLaughlin	Reilly	Derek Walker	Flexney	Watters	David Walker	Lindsay	Spiers	Faulds	Stewart	Callaghan
3	1	4		6*									12	3						5		2		7	10		8		14	11	9"		
3R	1	2		6		5							12	3						4				7	10*		8		14	11"	9		

By the season's end many players pictured here would not be part of the Rugby Park set-up, nor would Manager Eddie Morrison.
But the changes introduced failed to prevent relegation to the 2nd Divison despite some last day dramatics.
Back: Houston,Cook,Martin,McCulloch,Holland,Davidson,Marshall,McGuire.
Middle: Cuthbertson,David Walker,Hughes,Harkness,Lindsay,Kearney.
Front: Stewart,Clark,McConville,Robertson,McLean,Morrison(Manager),Allan.

SEASON 1989-90 Second Division

No.	Date	Opposition	H.T.	Res.	Att.	Goalscorers	McCulloch	Wilson	Davidson	Jenkins	Cody	Flexney	D.Thompson	Tait	M.Thompson	Reilly	Watters	Curran	Montgomerie	McLean	McFarlane	David Walker	McKinnon	McCabe	Geraghty	Callaghan	Marshall	Sludden	Burns	Spence	Wylde	McArthur	Quinn	Geddes	Porteous	McKellar
1	12 Aug	BRECHIN CITY	0-0	0-2	2342		1	2	3	4	5	6	7	8*	9"	10	11	12	14																	
2	19	Arbroath	1-0	1-1	1070	Curran	1	2		4	7	6		8		10	11	9		3	5															
3	26	Queens Park	0-0	0-1	1776		1	2	3*		4	6	7"	8		10	11	9	12	14	5															
4	2 Sep	EAST STIRLING	1-0	2-0	1767	Watters, Montgomerie	1	2	3"		14	5*	7	8		10	11	9	12	6	4															
5	9	COWDENBEATH	0-0	0-0	1804		1	2			12	5	7*	8"	14	10	11	9	3	6	4															
6	16	Stenhousemuir	0-0	3-0	954	M.Thompson(2), D.Thompson	1	14			10*	5	12	8	9	11		7"	2	6		3	4													
7	23	BERWICK RANGERS	1-0	2-0	1975	Curran, M.Thompson	1				10"	5	14	8	9	11	12	7*	2	6		3	4													
8	30	Stirling Albion	1-0	1-0	1818	Curran	1				14	5	7"	8	9	10*	12	11	2	6		3	4													
9	7 Oct	Montrose	0-0	1-0	810	Watters	1	10"				5	14	8	12	9	11	7*	2	6		3	4													
10	14	EAST FIFE	0-0	1-0	2456	Reilly	1				10*	5	12	8	14	9	11	7"	2	6		3	4													
11	21	Stranraer	0-0	0-1	2500		1				10	5	7	8		9	11		2	6		3	4													
12	28	DUMBARTON	0-0	3-0	2867	Watters(2), Tait	1			12		5	7"	8		10	11		2	6		3	4	9*	14											
13	4 Nov	QUEEN OF THE SOUTH	1-0	2-0	2988	Reilly, D.Thompson	1			10"		5	12	8		9	11		2	6		3	4	7												
14	11	East Stirling	0-0	1-2	1333	McCabe	1			14		5	12	8		9	11"		2	6		3	4	7		10*										
15	18	STIRLING ALBION	0-2	1-2	2473	Tait	1			5	10"			8		9	14	11		6		3	2	7*	12	4										
16	25	Berwick Rangers *	0-3	2-3	784	Curran, Marshall	1			12			14	8		9	11	7	2	6		3"	10			4*	5									
17	2 Dec	MONTROSE	0-0	1-1	2095	McFarlane	1				12		7*	5		10	9	11"		6	8	3	2		14	4										
18	23	ARBROATH	0-0	3-0	3336	Watters(3)	1					5		8			11	14	2	6	12		3		7*	4"		9	10							
19	26	Brechin City	1-1	1-3	1414	Burns	1				4"	5		8		7	11	12	2	6*	14		3					9	10							
20	2 Jan	QUEENS PARK	1-0	2-0	4843	Watters, Callaghan	1			12	4"	5		8			11	14	2				6		7	3		9*	10							
21	10	East Fife	1-1	2-4	1109	Watters, Burns	1			5	4"			8		7*	11		2	12		14	6			3		9	10							
22	13	Cowdenbeath	0-1	1-2	961	Reilly	1			5				8		12	11		2	3"		7	6		14	4		9*	10							
23	20	STENHOUSEMUIR	1-0	2-0	2777	Watters, Montgomerie	1				12	5					11*		2				6			8		9	10	3	4	7"	14			
24	27	STRANRAER	0-1	0-1	3550		1					5		12			11		2				6			8		9	10	3	4"	7*	14			
25	17 Feb	Arbroath	1-1	4-2	891	Callaghan, Tait, Sludden, Watters					12	5		8			9		2				4			7		10	6	3	11"			1		
26	24	Berwick Rangers	1-0	4-1	992	Watters(3), Sludden					11"	5		8			9		2				4			7		10	6	3	12			1		
27	3 Mar	EAST STIRLING	1-0	2-0	2747	Burns, Reilly						5		8		11	9		2				4			7		10	6	3				1		
28	6	STIRLING ALBION	1-0	1-0	3369	Watters						5		8		11"	9		2				4			7		10	6	3	12			1		
29	10	QUEENS PARK	2-0	3-0	3767	Watters(2), Montgomerie						5		8		11"	9		2				4			7		10	6*	3			14	1	12	
30	13	Queen of the South	0-2	1-2	2058	Flexney						5		8			9		2				4		12	7"		10	6	3				1	11	
31	17	Stenhousemuir	0-0	1-2	1730	Sludden						5		8			9			2			4		12	6"		10	11	3	14			1	7*	
32	24	Dumbarton	0-0	2-0	1609	Sludden, Tait				14		5		8		11*	9		2				4		12			10	6	3	7"					1
33	31	BRECHIN CITY	0-1	2-2	4767	Tait, Watters				4*		5		8		11	9		2						14	12		10	6	3	7"					1
34	3 Apr	Dumbarton	2-1	3-1	1475	Watters(2), Sludden				12		5		8		11	9		2				4		14	7"		10*	6	3						1
35	7	EAST FIFE	0-0	2-1	3266	Porteous, Tait					12*	5		8		11	9		2				4			7		10	6	3"					14	1
36	14	Stranraer	0-0	1-2	2410	Watters						5		8		11	9		2				4			7"		10	6	3	12					1
37	21	QUEEN OF THE SOUTH	2-0	4-1	3362	Watters, Sludden, McArthur, McKinnon						5		8		11"	9		2				4					10	6	3		12		1	7	
38	28	Montrose	1-0	3-1	1597	Sludden, Watters, O.G.						5		8		11"	9		2				4					10	6	3	12			1	7	
39	5 May	COWDENBEATH	1-0	2-1	8526	Flexney, McKinnon					14	5		8		11"	9		2				4					10*	6	3	12			1	7	
						Apps.	24	6	3	7	12	34	8	37	4	30	35	12	32	19	5	13	33	4	2	20	1	22	22	17	5	2		10	5	5
						Subs		1		6	8		7	1	3	1	3	4	3	2	2	1			9	1					6	1	3		2	
						Goals						2	2	6	3	4	23	4	3		1		2	1		2	1	7	3			1			1	

* Played at Tynecastle, owing to Berwick's ground being declared unfit

Pos	P.	W.	D.	L.	F.	A.	Pts.
2nd	39	22	4	13	67	39	48

League Cup

							McCulloch	Wilson	Davidson	Jenkins	Cody	Flexney	D.Thompson	Tait	M.Thompson	Reilly	Watters	Curran	Montgomerie	McLean	McFarlane	David Walker	McKinnon	McCabe	Geraghty	Callaghan	Marshall	Sludden	Burns	Spence	Wylde	McArthur	Quinn	Geddes	Porteous	McKellar
2	15 Aug	MOTHERWELL	0-2	1-4	3903	D.Thompson	1	2	3"	4	5	6	7		9*	10	11	14	12	8																

Scottish Cup

							McCulloch	Wilson	Davidson	Jenkins	Cody	Flexney	D.Thompson	Tait	M.Thompson	Reilly	Watters	Curran	Montgomerie	McLean	McFarlane	David Walker	McKinnon	McCabe	Geraghty	Callaghan	Marshall	Sludden	Burns	Spence	Wylde	McArthur	Quinn	Geddes	Porteous	McKellar
1		Bye																																		
2	30 Dec	Stranraer	0-1	1-1	3700	Watters	1			12	4	5		8	9"		11		2	3			6			7			10							
2R	6 Jan	STRANRAER	0-0	0-0*	5033		1			4*		5	12	8		9	11	14	2				6		7"	3			10							

* After extra time, Stranraer won 4-3 on penalties. This was the first time ever that penalty kicks decided the outcome of a Scottish Cup tie.

The management trio which guided Killie to promotion after just one season in the second Division.
Top: J.McSherry (Asst Man)
Middle: F.Coulston(Asst Man). Front: J.Fleeting(Man)

SEASON 1990-91 First Division

No.	Date	Opposition	H.T.	Res.	Att.	Goalscorers	Geddes	Montgomerie	Spence	McStay	Flexney	McKinnon	Stark	Tait	Watters	Callaghan	Shaw	Reilly	Sludden	Jenkins	Burns	Elliott	McKellar	Burgess	Curran	Wylde	Sloan	Williamson	McPherson	Smith	Agnew	Brayshaw	Campbell
1	25 Aug	Meadowbank	0-0	0-1	1767		1	2	3	4	5	6	7	8"	9	10	11*	12	14														
2	1 Sep	AIRDRIEONIANS	1-3	3-4	5287	Burns, Stark, Sludden	1	2	12		5	4	7	8*	9		14	11	10	3"	6												
3	8	Hamilton	1-1	1-3	2687	Tait	1	2	3	4"	5	6	7	8		12		9*	10		11	14											
4	15	FALKIRK	1-1	1-1	4629	Spence		2	3		5	4	7"	8		6		9	10		11	12	1										
5	18	Clydebank	3-1	3-1	2442	Burns, Reilly, Sludden	1	2	3		5	4	7	8	12	6		9	10"		11												
6	22	MORTON	1-0	3-1	4322	Stark, Watters, Sludden	1	2	3		5	4	7	8	12	6*		9"	10	14	11												
7	29	Dundee	0-0	1-1	4573	Callaghan	1	2	3*		5	4		8	12	6		9	10	7"	11			14									
8	6 Oct	Brechin city	1-0	2-0	1299	Callaghan, Sludden	1	2	3		5	4		8	9"	6		7	10		11*	12		14									
9	9	RAITH ROVERS	1-0	1-1	3953	Watters	1	2	3		5	4		8	9*	6		7"	10		11	12		14									
10	13	AYR UNITED	0-1	3-1	9802	Elliott, Callaghan, Burns	1	2	3		5	4		8	12	6		9"	10		11*	7		14									
11	20	Partick Thistle	0-0	0-2	4600		1	2	3		5	4	7	8		6		12	10"		11	9											
12	27	Forfar Athletic	2-0	2-2	1521	Sludden, Burns	1	2	3		5	4	7	8	9"	6		12	10		11												
13	3 Nov	CLYDE	0-0	2-1	3973	Sludden, Tait	1	2	3		5	4	7*	8		6		14	10		11	12			9"								
14	10	Airdrieonians	0-0	0-2	4400		1	2	3	7	5"	4	11	8		6		9	10							12							
15	17	MEADOWBANK	2-0	2-3	4198	Stark, Reilly	1	2"	3	5		4	11	8		12		6	10*		7						14	9					
16	24	Raith Rovers	1-1	1-1	2260	Burns	1	2	3	5		4	11	8		14		6*	10"		7						12	9					
17	1 Dec	BRECHIN CITY	1-1	2-1	3473	Williamson, Sloan	1	2	3		5	4	7"	8		6		12			11						10	9					
18	8	DUNDEE	2-0	2-1	4558	Williamson, Tait	1	2	3	14	5	4		8		6"		12			11	7					10*	9					
19	15	Morton	0-1	0-3	2724		1	2	3	14	5	4*	6	8				12			11	7"					10	9					
20	22	FORFAR ATHLETIC	0-0	1-0	3224	Williamson	1	2	3"		5			8		6		12	10		11	7		4				9					
21	2 Jan	Ayr United	2-0	2-1	9448	Burns, Sludden	1	2	3		5			8		6		12	10"		11	7		4				9					
22	5	PARTICK THISTLE	2-2	2-3	5588	Flexney, Callaghan	1	2	3		5			8		6			10		11	7		4				9					
23	12	HAMILTON	0-0	1-0	4767	Williamson	1	2	3*		5	14		8		6		12	10"		11	7		4				9					
24	19	Falkirk	1-0	1-1	6749	Sludden	1		3		5	2		8		6			10		11	7		4				9					
25	2 Feb	CLYDEBANK	2-0	3-0	4169	Williamson(3)	1	2	3		5			8				12	10"		11	7*		4			14	9	6				
26	16	PARTICK THISTLE	1-0	1-0	6073	Williamson	1	2	3		5			8				12	10"		11	7		4				9	6				
27	26	Clyde	1-0	1-1	1000	Silliamson	1	2		4	5			8		6					11	7						9	3"	10	12		
28	9 Mar	MORTON	1-0	1-1	4451	Williamson	1	2		4	5			8		6"			14		11	12						9	7	10*	3		
29	12	Forfar Athletic	1-0	1-1	977	Williamson	1	2		4	5			8		6"		12			11							9	7	10	3		
30	16	Airdrieonians	0-1	0-2	5000		1			8	5		7	12		6			14		11			4				9	2	10	3*		
31	23	FALKIRK	1-1	1-1	6664	Stark	1	12	3	4	5		6*	8		7		9	10		11								2"	14			
32	30	HAMILTON	0-0	1-0	4449	Flexney	1	2	3	4	5			8							11	7					12	9		10"		6	
33	6 Apr	Raith Rovers	1-0	2-1	1761	Williamson, Campbell	1	2	3	4	5		6	8							11							9		12		7"	10
34	10	Meadowbank	6-0	8-1	1107	Williamson(2),Campbell(2),Burns(2),Smith,Stark	1	2	3	4	5"		6*							8	11			12				9		7		14	10
35	13	BRECHIN CITY	1-0	2-2	4543	Stark, Campbell	1	2	3	4	5		6"			12				8	11			14				9		7*			10
36	20	Clydebank	0-0	0-0	2005		1	2	3"	4			6							8	11			5				9	7	12			10
37	27	Clyde	1-1	1-2	1700	Jenkins	1	14	3	4			6*	12						8	11	7"		5					2	9			10
38	4 May	DUNDEE	0-0	0-0	5712		1	2		4				5		6"				8	11	12						9	3	7			10
39	11	Ayr United	0-1	0-1	5894		1	2		4	5			7		6"				8	11							9	3	12			10
						Apps.	38	35	32	18	34	20	21	34	5	26	1	13	23	8	37	14	1	10	1		3	23	11	9	3	2	7
						Subs		2	1	2		1		2	4	4	1	13	3	1		7		6		1	4			4	1	1	
						Goals			1		2		6	3	2	4		2	8	1	8	1					1	14		1			4

Pos	P.	W.	D.	L.	F.	A.	Pts.
5th	39	15	13	11	58	48	43

League Cup

Rd	Date	Opposition	H.T.	Res.	Att.	Goalscorers	Geddes	Montgomerie	Spence	McStay	Flexney	McKinnon	Stark	Tait	Watters	Callaghan	Shaw	Reilly	Sludden	Jenkins	Burns	Elliott	McKellar	Burgess	Curran	Wylde	Sloan	Williamson	McPherson	Smith	Agnew	Brayshaw	Campbell
2	21 Aug	CLYDEBANK	1-2	3-2*	4777	Spence, Stark, Callaghan	1	2	3	4"		6	7	8	9	14	11*	12		5	10												
3	28	Rangers	0-0	0-1	32671		1	4	3"		5	6	7	8*	9	12	14	11		2	10												

* After extra time

Scottish Cup

Rd	Date	Opposition	H.T.	Res.	Att.	Goalscorers	Geddes	Montgomerie	Spence	McStay	Flexney	McKinnon	Stark	Tait	Watters	Callaghan	Shaw	Reilly	Sludden	Jenkins	Burns	Elliott	McKellar	Burgess	Curran	Wylde	Sloan	Williamson	McPherson	Smith	Agnew	Brayshaw	Campbell
3	26 Jan	ARBROATH	1-1	3-2	4991	Sludden(2), Burns	1		3		5	2		8		6"		12	10		11	7		4				9					
4	23 Feb	Dundee	0-2	0-2	7195		1	2	3		5			8		12		14	10		11	7		4"				9	6*				

B&Q Centenary Cup

Rd	Date	Opposition	H.T.	Res.	Att.	Goalscorers	Geddes	Montgomerie	Spence	McStay	Flexney	McKinnon	Stark	Tait	Watters	Callaghan	Shaw	Reilly	Sludden	Jenkins	Burns	Elliott	McKellar	Burgess	Curran	Wylde	Sloan	Williamson	McPherson	Smith	Agnew	Brayshaw	Campbell
1	2 Oct	STIRLING ALBION	1-0	4-1	2612	Sludden(3), Burns	1	2	3		5	4		8	7	6"		9	10		11*	12		14									
2	16	ARBROATH	2-0	3-1	3437	Sludden, Elliott, Stark	1	2	3		5	4	12	8	14	6"		9*	10		11	7											
QF	23	East Fife	1-0	2-1	2102	Sludden, Watters	1	2	3		5	4	7	8	9	12			10		11			6"									
SF	30	DUNDEE	0-1	0-2	7933		1	2	3		5	4	7	8		6		9"	10		11	12											

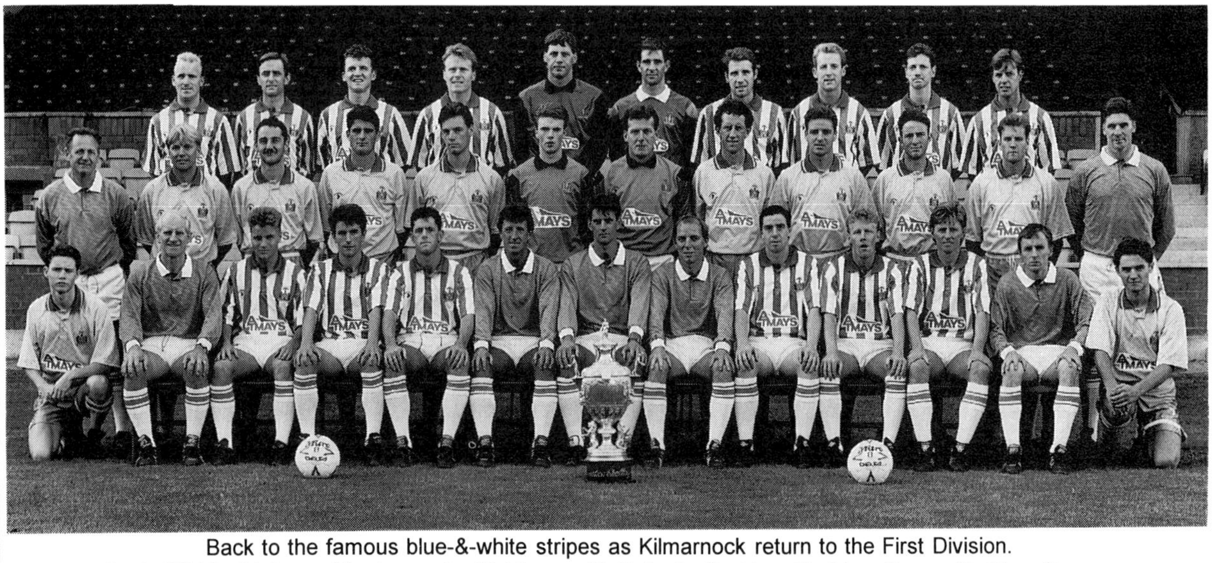

Back to the famous blue-&-white stripes as Kilmarnock return to the First Division.
Back: Wylde, McLean, Montgomerie, McKinnon, McCulloch, Geddes, Sludden, Burns, McStay, Spence
Middle: Hollas, Brown, McArthur, Davidson, Quinn, Osborne, McKellar, Stark, Flexney, Jenkins, Tait, Stewart.
Front: Geraghty, Allan, Elliott, Curran, Callaghan, Coulston, Fleeting, McSherry, Watters, Porteous, Reilly, Clark, Cody

SEASON 1991-92 First Division

No.	Date	Opposition	H.T.	Res.	Att.	Goalscorers
1	10 Aug	STIRLING ALBION	0-0	0-0	4416	
2	13	HAMILTON	1-2	1-2	4347	McSkimming
3	17	Partick Thistle	0-0	0-1	5537	
4	24	Meadowbank	1-2	3-2	1222	Williamson(2), Mitchell
5	31	AYR UNITED	0-0	1-1	8380	Montgomerie
6	7 Sep	Clydebank	1-0	1-1	2576	Campbell
7	14	MONTROSE	0-0	0-0	3478	
8	21	Dundee	1-1	1-2	3788	Williamson
9	28	RAITH ROVERS	1-0	1-0	3385	Campbell
10	5 Oct	Forfar Athletic	0-0	1-0	1019	Mitchell
11	8	MORTON	1-0	1-0	3677	Campbell
12	12	Stirling Albion	2-0	3-0	2065	Mitchell, McPherson, Williamson
13	19	PARTICK THISTLE	2-1	2-3	4962	Williamson, Campbell
14	26	CLYDEBANK	1-0	2-1	2231	T.Burns, Campbell
15	29	Montrose	1-2	2-2	1074	Jack, Mitchell
16	2 Nov	Ayr United	3-0	3-0	6064	T.Burns, Mitchell, Williamson
17	9	MEADOWBANK	0-0	1-0	3828	McPherson
18	16	FORFAR ATHLETIC	3-0	4-2	3560	Jack(2), Mitchell(2)
19	19	Morton	0-0	1-0	2637	Jack
20	23	DUNDEE	1-1	1-2	7137	Mitchell
21	30	Hamilton	1-0	2-2	3893	H.Burns, Williamson
22	3 Dec	Raith Rovers	0-1	1-1	2280	Williamson
23	7	STIRLING ALBION	0-0	2-0	3796	Williamson, H.Burns
24	14	Clydebank	2-0	3-0	2357	H.Burns, Mitchell, Campbell
25	28	Meadowbank	0-0	0-1	1505	
26	1 Jan	AYR UNITED	0-0	1-1	8211	Campbell
27	4	Forfar Athletic	0-0	0-0	1185	
28	7	MONTROSE	3-1	5-1	3183	Campbell(2), Jack, Black, O.G.
29	11	MORTON	0-0	0-1	4988	
30	18	HAMILTON	0-0	0-2	4662	
31	1 Feb	Partick Thistle	0-0	1-2	4483	Black
32	8	Dundee	1-0	1-1	5988	Jack
33	26	RAITH ROVERS	0-0	1-0	3657	McPherson
34	29	FORFAR ATHLETIC	0-0	2-0	3076	H.Burns, Campbell
35	14 Mar	MEADOWBANK	0-1	2-1	2884	Tait, Jack
36	21	Ayr United	0-0	2-0	5530	Tait, T.Burns
37	24	Morton	0-0	0-0	3015	
38	28	Stirling Albion	0-1	0-1	2083	
39	4 Apr	PARTICK THISTLE	0-2	1-3	5640	Black
40	7	CLYDEBANK	0-0	1-0	2094	Mitchell
41	11	Montrose	0-0	1-0	793	O.G.
42	18	DUNDEE	1-0	2-0	4933	Tait, O.G.
43	25	Hamilton	1-0	1-0	3449	Jack
44	2 May	Raith Rovers	0-1	1-1	1960	Porteous

No.	Geddes	McPherson	Reilly	Flexney	Burgess	Tait	Stark	Jack	Williamson	T.Burns	McSkimming	Porteous	Montgomerie	McStay	Mitchell	Campbell	McQuilter	Elliott	Callaghan	Brayshaw	Jenkins	H.Burns	Paterson	Black	Graham	Stephen	Clark	Reid	Roberts
1	1	2	3	4	5	6	7"	8	9	10	11*	12	14																
2	1	2	3	5		6		8	9	10	11			4	7														
3	1	12	3	5		6		8"	9	10	11		2	4	7														
4	1	2	3	5		6"		12	9	10	11		14	4	7	8*													
5	1	2	3	5		6			9	10	11	4"	12		7	8													
6	1	2	3	5		6"		14	9	10	11*	7	4			8	12												
7	1	2	3"	5				14	9	10	11	6	4		7*	8		12											
8	1	2		5				8	9	10	3	12	6		7	11"			4*	14									
9	1	2		5				8	9	10	3"	14	6		7	11*			4		12								
10	1	2		5				10"	9	6		8	3		7	11			12			4							
11	1	2	12	5					9	10	3		4		7	11			6"			8							
12	1	2	12	5		4			9	10	3	14			7	11*			6"			8							
13	1	2		5		4			9	10	3				7	11			6			8							
14	1	2	12	5		4		14	9	10	3				7	11*			6"			8							
15	1	2	12	4				10	9	6	3"				7	11						8	5						
16	1	2		4		12		10	9	6			3		7	11"						8	5						
17	1	2		4				10	9	6	12				7	11"						8	5	3					
18	1	2		4*		14		10	9"	6	12				7	11						8	5	3					
19	1	2						10	9	6			4		7	11						8	5	3					
20	1	2						10"	9	6	12		4		7	11						8	5	3					
21		2		4				10"	9	6*	12	14			7	11						8	5	3	1				
22				4				9	14	6"	11	12	2		7	10						8	5	3	1				
23		2		4				10"	9		11	6			7	12						8	5	3	1				
24		2		4					9		11	6			7	10						8	5	3	1				
25		2						14	9	11"	12	6	4		7	10*						8	5	3	1				
26		2		4					9	6	11"		12		7	10						8	5	3	1				
27		2	11	4				12	9	6					7	10"						8	5	3	1				
28	1	2	11	4				12	9"	6*		8			7	10						14	5	3					
29		2	11"	4				9		6		8			7	10						12	5	3	1				
30		2		4"		12		14	9		11	6			7	10						8*	5	3	1				
31		2							9	6	12		4	14	7	10						8	5*	3	1	11"			
32	1	2				10		9		6			4	14	7	11			12*			8	5"	3					
33	1	2	3			5		9	10"	6		12	4		7	11						8							
34	1	2				5		9		6		12	4		7	11						8		3			10"		
35	1	2				6		12		10			4		11	9						8	5	3				7"	
36	1	2				10		11		6	12	8"	4	14	7	9*							5	3					
37	1	2				10		11		6		8"	4		7	9						12	5	3					
38	1	2				10		11"	12	6		8*	4		7	9					14		5	3					
39	1	2				10		12	9	6			4		7	11"						8	5	3					
40		8						9"	10	6	11		4		7							2	5	3	1				12
41	1	8	3					9	10	6	11		4		7							2	5						
42	1	10	3			12		9		6	11"	8	4		7							2	5						
43	1	8	3			14		9		6	11"	7*	4	2	10	12							5						
44	1	8*	3			11		9	12	6		7	4	2	10"	14							5						
Apps.	33	42	15	27	1	18	1	27	33	41	23	16	26	5	42	35			6			28	28	23	11	1	1	1	
Subs		1	4			5		10	3		7	8	4	3		3	1	1	2	1	2	3							1
Goals		3				3		8	9	3	1	1	1		10	10						4		3					

Pos	P.	W.	D.	L.	F.	A.	Pts.
4th	44	21	12	11	59	37	54

League Cup

No.	Date	Opposition	H.T.	Res.	Att.	Goalscorers
2	26 Aug	Cowdenbeath	0-0	1-0	1561	Williamson
3	28	HIBERNIAN	1-1	2-3	6507	Campbell, McSkimming

No.	Geddes	McPherson	Reilly	Flexney	Burgess	Tait	Stark	Jack	Williamson	T.Burns	McSkimming	Porteous	Montgomerie	McStay	Mitchell	Campbell	McQuilter	Elliott	Callaghan	Brayshaw	Jenkins	H.Burns	Paterson	Black	Graham	Stephen	Clark	Reid	Roberts
2	1	2	3	5		6		12	9	10	11			4	7	8"													
3	1	2	3	5		6		12	9		11	10		4"	7	8													

Scottish Cup

No.	Date	Opposition	H.T.	Res.	Att.	Goalscorers
3	25 Jan	Meadowbank	0-0	1-1	2301	Mitchell
3R	4 Feb	MEADOWBANK	0-1	1-1*	4694	H.Burns

No.	Geddes	McPherson	Reilly	Flexney	Burgess	Tait	Stark	Jack	Williamson	T.Burns	McSkimming	Porteous	Montgomerie	McStay	Mitchell	Campbell	McQuilter	Elliott	Callaghan	Brayshaw	Jenkins	H.Burns	Paterson	Black	Graham	Stephen	Clark	Reid	Roberts
3		2				5			9	6	12		4		7	10		11"				8		3	1				
3R	1	2				5			9"	6			4	14	7	10			11*			8		3					12

* After extra time, Meadowbank won 4-3 on penalties

B&Q Cup

No.	Date	Opposition	H.T.	Res.	Att.	Goalscorers
1		Bye				
2	15 Oct	Morton	1-1	1-2*	2864	H.Burns

No.	Geddes	McPherson	Reilly	Flexney	Burgess	Tait	Stark	Jack	Williamson	T.Burns	McSkimming	Porteous	Montgomerie	McStay	Mitchell	Campbell	McQuilter	Elliott	Callaghan	Brayshaw	Jenkins	H.Burns	Paterson	Black	Graham	Stephen	Clark	Reid	Roberts
1																													
2	1	2	12	5		4			9	10	3	14			7	11			6"			8							

* After extra time

Killie assemble for the start of the 91-92 season. Back: C.Clark, Reilly, McStay, Brayshaw, Montgomerie, Smith, Callaghan. McPherson, Scott. 2nd Back: Hollas, Jack, Campbell, Flexney, Burgess, Geddes, Stark, Jenkins, McSkimming, Tait, Allan. 3rd Back: Elliott, Williamson, Coulston, McSherry, Burns, Fleeting, J.Clark, Mitchell, Porteous. Front: Hamilton, White, Reid, Plunkett, Sweetin, Wilson

SEASON 1992-93 First Division

No.	Date	Opposition	H.T.	Res.	Att.	Goalscorers	Geddes	H.Burns	Black	Montgomerie	Paterson	McPherson	Porteous	Skilling	Jack	Tait	Mitchell	Campbell	Reilly	T.Burns	Williamson	McCluskey	McStay	Furphy	Crainie	Wilson	Stark	McSkimming	Roberts	McCarrison
1	1 Aug	Morton	2-0	2-0	3274	Mitchell, Jack	1	2	3	4	5	6	7"	8	9	10	11	12												
2	4	Dumbarton	2-0	3-1	2109	Paterson, Jack, Tait	1	2	3	4	5	6	7*	8"	9	10	11	12	14											
3	8	RAITH ROVERS	0-1	1-1	4566	Mitchell	1	2	3	4	5		7"	8	9	10	11			6	12									
4	15	DUNFERMLINE	0-0	0-1	5347		1	2	3	4				8	9"	5	11			6	7	12						10		
5	22	Ayr United	0-0	0-2	5475		1	2	3	4				8	9	5	11	12		6	7"	14						10*		
6	29	MEADOWBANK	0-0	1-0	2821	Campbell	1		3	4	5	2"	12	8			7	9		6	10							11		
7	5 Sep	Clydebank	1-0	1-1	2216	Williamson	1		3	4	5	2"	8		14		7	9*		6	10		12					11		
8	12	Stirling Albion*	1-0	1-0	1441	Jack	1			4	5	2	8		9		7		3	6	10							11		
9	19	ST. MIRREN	0-1	1-2	5291	Williamson	1			2		8	10*	5	9"		7	12	3	6	14			4				11		
10	26	COWDENBEATH	1-0	3-0	2798	Williamson, Porteous, Jack	1			4		2	8	5	14		7	12	3	6	9	10*						11"		
11	3 Oct	Hamilton	0-0	1-1	2863	Skilling	1			4	5	2		8	12		7"		3	6	9	10						11		
12	10	MORTON	1-0	3-0	3991	T.Burns(2), McCluskey	1			4	5	2	12	8	14		7		3	6	9	10*						11"		
13	17	Raith Rovers	0-0	1-1	3718	Reilly	1			4	5	2		8			7	12	3	6	9	10						11"		
14	24	CLYDEBANK	1-0	3-3	3582	McCluskey(2), McSkimming	1			4	5	2		8			7		3	6	9	10						11		
15	31	Meadowbank	0-0	1-1	1104	McSkimming	1			4		2	8	5	12		7		3	6	9	10"						11		
16	7 Nov	Dunfermline	0-1	0-2	3924		1			4		2	8"	5	14		7		3	6	9	10			12			11*		
17	14	AYR UNITED	2-0	3-0	5709	McCluskey, Skilling, O.G.	1		3	4		8		5			7"	12		6		9				2	10		11	
18	21	St. Mirren	1-0	1-0	4686	Black	1		3	4		8		5				7		6		9				2	10		11	
19	28	STIRLING ALBION	1-0	1-0	3526	Skilling	1			4		2		5	14		12	7	3	6		9					10	8*	11"	
20	1 Dec	HAMILTON	1-0	1-0	3711	McPherson	1			4		8		5	11			7"	3	6		9				2	10		12	
21	5	Cowdenbeath	1-2	3-2	1176	Jack, Reilly, McPherson	1			4		8		5	11			7	3	6		9				2	10			
22	19	DUMBARTON	0-0	1-0	3591	Campbell	1			4		8		5	9		11"	7*	3	6	12				14	2	10			
23	26	DUNFERMLINE	1-1	2-3	5762	Stark, Reilly	1			4		8		5	9		14	7	3	6	12					2*	10		11"	
24	29	Morton	0-1	0-2	2822		1			4		8		5			12	7	3	6	9					2"	10	11		
25	2 Jan	Ayr United	0-0	1-0	8424	Porteous	1			4		8	7	5						6	11	9				2	10	3		
26	16	MEADOWBANK	4-0	5-0	3366	McCluskey(2),Porteous,Wlliamsn,McPhersn	1			4		8	7*	5			12			6	11	9"			14	2	10	3		
27	27	Hamilton	2-1	2-1	3106	Williamson, Porteous	1			4		8	7"	5				12		6	11	9				2	10	3		
28	30	RAITH ROVERS	0-0	3-0	7003	Porteous(2), Stark	1			4		8	7	5						6	11	9				2	10	3		
29	13 Feb	Dumbarton	0-0	0-1	2346		1			4		8	7"	5			9			6	11				12	2	10	3		
30	16	Clydebank	0-0	0-2	2107		1			4		2	7	5			12	8		6	11				9"		10	3		
31	20	COWDENBEATH	0-0	1-1	2928	Campbell	1	14	4			8	7	5			9"	12		6	11					2*	10	3		
32	27	ST. MIRREN	0-0	1-0	6555	McCluskey	1	2			4	8		5						6	11	9					10	3		7
33	6 Mar	Stirling Albion*	0-1	0-2	1386		1	2		4		8	14	5				12		6	11	9*					10	3"		7
34	9	MORTON	1-0	2-2	3407	Williamson, O.G.	1	2		4		8		5						6	11	9					10	3		7
35	13	Raith Rovers	0-1	0-2	4738		1	2		4	5	8	7					12		6	11	9"					10	3		
36	20	AYR UNITED	1-1	1-1	5660	Skilling	1			4	5			8				7		6	11	9				2	10	3"		12
37	27	Dunfermline	0-0	2-2	5224	Campbell, McSkimming	1			4	5	7		8				11"		6	12	9				2	10	3		
38	3 Apr	CLYDEBANK	4-0	6-0	3005	McClusky(2),Mtchll(2),McSkimmng,McPhrsn	1			4	5	7		8			14	11*		6	12	9"				2	10	3		
39	14	Meadowbank	1-1	1-1	1493	McSkimming	1			4	5	12		8			7			6	11*	9				2"	10	3		14
40	17	STIRLING ALBION	1-0	3-0	3852	McCluskey, Mitchell, McCarrison	1			4	5	2		8			7			6"		9			12		10	3		11
41	24	St. Mirren	1-0	1-2	8432	Mitchell	1			4	5	2		8*			7			6	12	9				14	10	3		11"
42	1 May	DUMBARTON	1-0	1-0	3793	McCluskey	1			4	5	2		8			7		6			9			12		10	3		11"
43	8	Cowdenbeath	1-0	3-0	2754	Stark, Crainie, McPherson	1			4	5	8					7		6			9			11	2	10	3		
44	15	HAMILTON	0-0	0-0	12830		1			4	5	8		2			7		6			9			11		10	3		
						Apps.	44	9	10	42	21	39	17	40	11	5	26	13	18	39	26	29		1	3	18	28	35	4	6
						Subs		1				1	3		7		6	11	1		7	2	1		6	1			1	2
						Goals			1		1	5	6	4	5	1	6	4	3	2	6	11			1		3	5		1

* Played at Stenhousemuir's ground

Pos	P.	W.	D.	L.	F.	A.	Pts.
2nd	44	21	12	11	67	40	54

League Cup

No.	Date	Opposition	H.T.	Res.	Att.	Goalscorers	Geddes	H.Burns	Black	Montgomerie	Paterson	McPherson	Porteous	Skilling	Jack	Tait	Mitchell	Campbell	Reilly	T.Burns	Williamson	McCluskey	McStay	Furphy	Crainie	Wilson	Stark	McSkimming	Roberts	McCarrison
2	11 Aug	Morton	0-1	3-2*	3454	T.Burns(2), Jack	1	2	3	4	5*		7"	8	9	10	11	14		6	12									
3	18	HIBERNIAN	1-0	3-1*	7495	McSkimming, McCluskey, Jack	1	2	3	4				8	9	5	11	14		6	7"	12						10*		
QF	25	ST. JOHNSTONE	0-0	1-3	8293	Campbell	1	2*	3	4	5				9	8	7	14		6	12	10"						11		

* After extra time

Scottish Cup

No.	Date	Opposition	H.T.	Res.	Att.	Goalscorers	Geddes	H.Burns	Black	Montgomerie	Paterson	McPherson	Porteous	Skilling	Jack	Tait	Mitchell	Campbell	Reilly	T.Burns	Williamson	McCluskey	McStay	Furphy	Crainie	Wilson	Stark	McSkimming	Roberts	McCarrison
3	9 Jan	RAITH ROVERS	2-0	5-0	7309	Williamson(3), McCluskey, McPherson	1			4		8	7	5				14		6"	11*	9			12	2	10	3		
4	6 Feb	ST. JOHNSTONE	0-0	0-0	9278		1			4		8	7*	5			12	14		6	11				9"	2	10	3		
4R	10	St. Johnstone	0-0	0-1*	7144		1			4		8	7	5			12			6	11	9"				2	10	3		

* After extra time

B&Q Cup

No.	Date	Opposition	H.T.	Res.	Att.	Goalscorers	Geddes	H.Burns	Black	Montgomerie	Paterson	McPherson	Porteous	Skilling	Jack	Tait	Mitchell	Campbell	Reilly	T.Burns	Williamson	McCluskey	McStay	Furphy	Crainie	Wilson	Stark	McSkimming	Roberts	McCarrison
1	29 Sep	CLYDE	2-0	2-1	2688	McCluskey, Mitchell	1			4		2	8	5			7	12	3		9	10"						11	6	
2	20 Oct	AYR UNITED	1-0	1-0	7122	McCluskey	1			4	5	2		8			7	12	3	6	9	10"						11		
QF	28	MORTON	0-0	1-2	4956	T. Burns	1			4		2		8	12		7		3	6	9	10		5				11"		

With a lucky mascot in their ranks & a new club badge, Killie await the start of a season which will end in triumph.
Back: T.Burns(player-Manager), R.Williamson, H.Burns, T.Black, C.Paterson, R.Geddes, S.McSkimming, G.McCluskey, W.McStay, R.Jack, W.Stark(player-assistant-manager).
Front: R.Montgomerie, A.Mitchell, A.McPherson, A.Squirrel, M.Reilly, I.Porteous, M.Skilling

SEASON 1993-94 Premier Division

No.	Date	Opposition	H.T.	Res.	Att.	Goalscorers	Geddes	McPherson	Black	Montgomerie	Skilling	Millen	Mitchell	Reilly	Brown	McCluskey	McSkimming	Crainie	Williamson	Roberts	Campbell	Porteous	Paterson	Stark	Burns	Lauchlan	McInally	Napier	McCloy
1	7 Aug	DUNDEE	0-0	1-0	8162	Brown	1	2	3	4	5	6	7	8	9	10"	11	12											
2	14	Aberdeen	0-0	0-1	13534		1	2	3	4	5	6	7"	8		10	11*	12	9	14									
3	21	MOTHERWELL	0-0	0-1	7555		1	2	3*	4	5	6	7	8"		10	11	12	9		14								
4	28	Rangers	0-0	2-1	44243	Roberts, Williamson	1	2	3	4	5	6	7		14	10"	11		9	8*		12							
5	4 Sep	HIBERNIAN	0-1	1-1	7727	McCluskey	1	2	3	4	5	6	7		12	10	11		9	8"									
6	11	ST. JOHNSTONE	0-0	0-0	5670		1	2*	3	4	5	6	7			10"	11		9	8		12	14						
7	18	Hearts	1-0	1-0	8309	Skilling	1	2	3	4	5	6	7	8		10"	11		9			12							
8	25	PARTICK THISTLE	1-0	3-1	7411	Black, Williamson, McCluskey	1	2	3	4	5	6	7	8"		10*	11		9	14		12							
9	2 Oct	Celtic	0-0	0-0	23396		1	2	3	4	5	6	7	8		10"	11		9	12									
10	5	DUNDEE UNITED	0-0	1-1	7034	Roberts	1	2	3	4	5	6	7	8			11		9	10									
11	9	Raith Rovers	0-2	2-2	4754	Mitchell, Williamson	1	2	3	4	5	6	7	8			11		9	10									
12	16	ABERDEEN	0-0	1-1	9108	Mitchell	1	2	3	4	5	6	7	8	10	12	11		9"										
13	23	Dundee	0-1	0-1	4537		1	2	3		5	6	7"	8	10	12	11		9				4						
14	30	Motherwell	1-0	2-2	7384	Mitchell, Roberts	1	2	3	4	5	6	7"	8	12		11		9			10							
15	6 Nov	RANGERS	0-0	0-2	19162		1	2	3	4	5	6		8	7		11		9	12		10"							
16	9	Hibernian	1-0	1-2	6441	Brown	1	2	3	4	5	6		8	7		11		9	12		10"							
17	13	CELTIC	1-1	2-2	16649	Skilling, Williamson	1	2	3	4	5	6		8	7		11		9	10"		12							
18	20	Partick Thistle	0-0	1-0	6437	Crainie	1	2	3	4	5	6		8			11	12	9			7"		10					
19	27	St. Johnstone	1-0	1-0	4576	Williamson	1	2	3	4	5	6		8	12		11	14	9*			7"		10					
20	30	HEARTS	0-0	0-0	6948		1	2	3	4	5	6		8	7"			11	9					12	10				
21	4 Dec	Dundee United	0-0	0-0	7100		1	2	3	4	5	6		8	7		11	12	9					10"					
22	11	RAITH ROVERS	1-0	1-0	6012	Brown	1	2	3	4	5	6		8	7			12	9					10	11"				
23	18	Aberdeen	0-1	1-3	10800	Skilling	1	2	3	4	5	6	10	8	7		11		9										
24	1 Jan	MOTHERWELL	0-0	0-0	10511		1	2	3	4		6	9	8			11	7		12		10"			5				
25	4	DUNDEE	0-0	1-0	7406	McSkimming	1	2	3	4		6	9	8	10		11	7*				14	12		5"				
26	8	Rangers	0-0	0-3	44919		1	2	3	4		6	9	8	10		11	7		5									
27	15	HIBERNIAN	0-0	0-3	7358		1	2*	3	4		6	7	8		10	11	12				9"		5		14			
28	22	Hearts	1-1	1-1	9204	McPherson	1	2	3			6	7	8		10	11	5	9				4						
29	5 Feb	ST. JOHNSTONE	0-0	0-0	6345		1	2	3	4		6	7	8	5*	14	11		9								10"	12	
30	12	PARTICK THISTLE	1-0	1-2	7511	Mitchell	1	2	3"	4		6	7	8	5*	14	11		9								10	12	
31	1 Mar	Celtic	0-0	0-1	10882		1	2	3	4		6	7	8"	5				9						10		12	11	
32	5	DUNDEE UNITED	0-1	1-1	7403	Brown	1	2	3*	4		6	7		8	10			9"						5		12	11	14
33	15	Raith Rovers	0-2	2-3	3585	Mitchell, McSkimming	1	2	3*	4		6	7	8	9		11		10									5	12
34	19	ABERDEEN	0-1	2-3	8544	Black, McCloy	1	2	3*	4		6		8	9	10"	11		12						5			7	14
35	26	Dundee	0-3	0-3	3485		1		3	4		6	7		9		11		10						5"		12	2	8
36	30	St. Johnstone	1-0	1-0	5513	McPherson	1	2	3	4		6	7	5	9"		11		10									8	12
37	2 Apr	HEARTS	0-1	0-1	8022		1	2	3	4		6	7	5		14	11"	10*	9									8	12
38	16	CELTIC	0-0	2-0	11576	Black, Brown	1	2*	3	4		6	7"	8	10	12	11		9				5					14	
39	19	Partick Thistle	0-0	0-1	7299		1	2	3	4		6	7	8	10	14	11		9*				5"					12	
40	23	RAITH ROVERS	0-0	0-0	7426		1	2*	3	4		6	7	8	10	9"	11		12								14	5	
41	26	Dundee United	1-0	3-1	8801	Williamson(2), McSkimming	1	2	3	4		6	7	14	10"		11		9						5*		12	8	
42	30	Motherwell	0-0	0-1	8185		1	2	3	4		6	7"		10		11		9					14	5		12	8*	
43	7 May	RANGERS	0-0	1-0	18012	Black	1	2	3	4		6		8	12	10	11		9"					7	5				
44	14	Hibernian	0-0	0-0	9975		1	2	3	4		6	7	8	9"	10	11								5			12	
						Apps.	44	43	44	42	23	44	34	37	26	16	40	6	36	7		7	4	6	12		2	10	1
						Subs								1	5	7		8	2	6	1	6	2	2		1	6	5	5
						Goals		2	4		3		5		5	2	3	1	7	2		1							1

Pos	P.	W.	D.	L.	F.	A.	Pts.
8th	44	12	16	16	36	45	40

League Cup

Round	Date	Opposition	H.T.	Res.	Att.	Goalscorers	Geddes	McPherson	Black	Montgomerie	Skilling	Millen	Mitchell	Reilly	Brown	McCluskey	McSkimming	Crainie	Williamson	Roberts	Campbell	Porteous	Paterson	Stark	Burns	Lauchlan	McInally	Napier	McCloy
2	10 Aug	MORTON	1-1	1-2	5118	Mitchell	1	2	3	4	5	6	7	8		10	11	9"		12									

Scottish Cup

Round	Date	Opposition	H.T.	Res.	Att.	Goalscorers	Geddes	McPherson	Black	Montgomerie	Skilling	Millen	Mitchell	Reilly	Brown	McCluskey	McSkimming	Crainie	Williamson	Roberts	Campbell	Porteous	Paterson	Stark	Burns	Lauchlan	McInally	Napier	McCloy
3	29 Jan	AYR UNITED	1-1	2-1	12856	Black, McSkimming	1	2	3	4		6	7	8	5	10	11		9										
4	19 Feb	Morton	1-0	1-0	7255	Williamson	1	2	3	4		6	7	8	5	14	11*		9"			12					10		
QF	12 Mar	DUNDEE	1-0	1-0	10446	Brown	1	2	3	4		6	7	8	9	10"	11		12						5				
SF	10 Apr	Rangers	0-0	0-0	35134		1	2	3	4		6	7"	8	10*	12	11		9				5				14		
SFr	13	Rangers	1-0	1-2	29860	Black	1	2"	3	4		6	7	8	10*	14	11		9				5				12		

Premier football returns to Rugby Park after ten years and these are the players who eagerly awaited the big kick-off. (Back): A.Jack,R.Williamson,D.Crainie,M.Skilling,C.Meldrum,R.Geddes,C.Paterson,M.Roberts,D.McCarrison,J.Plunkett. (Middle): G.Hollas(Stadium Man.), T.Brown,A.Kerr,D.White,S.Hamilton,G.Kelly,G.Matthews,P.Flexney,K.Doig,S.McCloy,I.Gallacher, D.Bagan, H.Allan (Physio), (Front): M.Reilly,S.McSkimming,G.McCluskey,T.Wilson,W.Stark(Asst.Man.),T.Burns(Manager),J.Stewart (Goalkeeping Coach), A.Mitchell, R.Montgomerie, T.Black, I.Porteous. (Gus McPherson is missing from the picture)

AFTERWORD

by ROBERT FLEETING

In December 1989 the present Board assumed control of Kilmarnock FC and I was elected Chairman. With my brother Jim as manager and the immediate signing of Tommy Burns, the elements were in place which would serve as a catalyst in transforming the club's fortunes. We knew that here was a club which was - potentially - the third biggest in Scotland. Yet we were entering the last decade of the 20th century with the team in the Second Division, playing in a largely pre-war stadium.

We escaped from the Second Division at the first opportunity but it is not an episode that I particularly relish and I can honestly say that, had we won the 2nd Division title, I would never have allowed the Second League's flag to fly over Rugby Park. Success for us here at Kilmarnock is not about promotion to the First or Premier Divisions, it is about returning to European football and that is our aim.

At the same time, I was always aware of the implications of the Taylor Report and the last 4½ years have seen a lot of time devoted to the construction of a ground suitable for the 21st Century. An all-seated ground holding ten or twelve thousand would have been no good to Kilmarnock FC. The Board left no stone unturned in our efforts to provide the spectators with a ground which would equal the pride they took in our improved performances on the pitch. The supporters themselves have played a large part in aiding the reconstruction of Rugby Park, with over £½m coming from them after the Board sought their involvement in the project.

Thanks to the fans, the Football Trust and my fellow directors, our new ground will shortly be a reality. The home game with Rangers in May 1994 was the last to be played in front of a pre-war terracing. By May 1995 we will be playing in an 18,000 all-seated, all-covered stadium here at our Rugby Park home. The decision to go ahead with the new ground is the most momentous in the club's recent history. A few good years on the pitch do not establish the long-term prospects of a football side just as a few bad years do not lead to its demise. I believe our future was secured by the decision of the Board at 9.00am on Friday April 1st 1994 to give the stadium the go-ahead. If we can leave a tangible legacy to those who will come after us, it is my hope that - come Kilmarnock's 250th anniversary - the supporters in the year 2119 will recognise the significance of that Board meeting in 1994

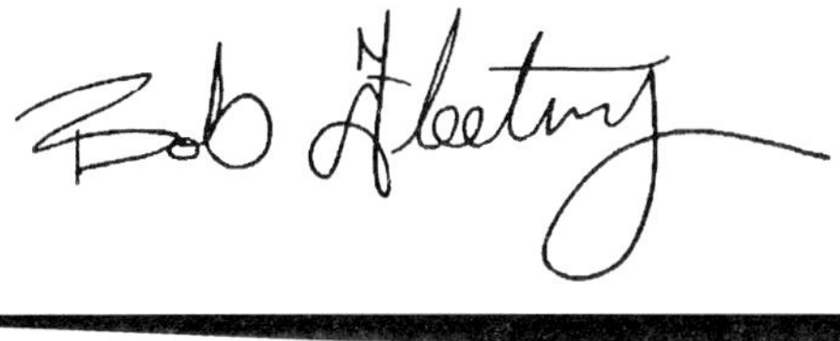

ADVANCED SUBSCRIBERS

Robert Fleeting Chairman, Kilmarnock

James Moffat Vice-Chairman, Kilmarnock
Laurel Chadwick Director, Kilmarnock
John Paton Director, Kilmarnock
Ronald Hamilton Director, Kilmarnock
Provost Daniel Coffey, Kilmarnock & Loudan District Council
Dr.Erich Stammberger Oberburgermeister, Kulmbach, Germany
Monsieur Alain Fabre, (Mayor), Ales, France

Kevin Collins Secretary, Kilmarnock
Tommy Burns Manager, Kilmarnock
Denny Martin Commercial Manager, Kilmarncok
Billy Stark Assistant Manager, Kilmarnock
Monsieur Jean Namotte, (Mayor), Herstal, Belgium
Mr. Nodar Khashba, (Mayor), Sukhum, Abkhazia
Senora Manuela De Madre Ortega,(Mayoress),Santa Coloma De Gramenet, Catalonia

Neil Ross, Middlesbrough, Clevelend
Ayrshire Districts Supporters Association
London & South-East Kilmarnock Supporters
David Ross, Dundonald, Ayrshire
Patrick Gardiner, Wytham, Oxford.
Richard Ross, Kilmarnock, Ayrshire
Brian Caldwell, Beeston, Leeds
Douglas & Iona Steveson, Lybster, Caithness
Stuart Ross, Dunbar, East Lothian
Gordon Allison, Girdle Toll
Richard Cairns, Kilmaurs, Ayrshire
William Ross, Hurlford, Ayrshire
John Livingston, Kilmarnock, Ayrshire
David Steele, Carlisle, Cumbria
Vince Harvey, Giffnock, Glasgow
Frederick Pegg, Ballingry, Fife
Eddie Dryden, Middlesbrough, Cleveland
Rab McLaughlin, Middlesbrough, Cleveland
Andy Croft, Middlesbrough, Cleveland
Philip Bentley, Lewisham, London
Peter Cogle, Aberdeen
Harry Kay, Yorkshire
David Keats, Thornton Heath
David Clow, Ardrossan
B. Hourston
N. Nicol, Derby
David Jowett
Colin J. Massie
Mark Tyler, Rayleigh, Essex
John Byrne, Barrhead
Graham Spackman
Richard Wells
Martin Simons, Belgium
Phil Hollow
G.D. Painter, Somerset
J. Ringrose
Derek Hyde
A.N. Other
Jonny Stokkeland, Kvinesdal, Norway
The Beautiful Game
Steve Emms
Raymond Shaw
Robert Smith
Geoffrey Wright
Andrew & Janet Waterman
Stewart Davidson
Duncan Watt
Bob Lilliman
Philip H. Whitehead
Christer Svensson, Sweden
W.D. Phillips
G.T. Allman
Allan Grieve
Andrew Hart
Gordon Simpson, Ashford, Middlesex
Peter Pickup
Carin Runciman, Glasgow
Alasdaiir Murray, Killie Exile
Gordon Wallis
Alan Runciman
Keith Coburn
George MacMillan 1994
David Lumb
Chris Hooker, Spurs Fan
Donald Noble, Dunkeld, Perthshire
John Treleven
Alan Davies
John Mungall, Jakarta, Indonesia

Derek Wheatcroft
W.B. Kilmurray
Ian Alexander Neil, Luton
Gordon Neil, Irvine, Ayrshire
F.J. Lee, Plymouth
Trevor Clydesdale
Dave McPherson, Colchester
John Draper - PNE Programmes
Trond Isaksen, Norway
Roland Hansson
Richard W. Lane, Newark
Les Butler, Rotherhithe, London
Alan Hindley
Willy Østby, Norway
Robert M. Barrett, Giffnock
Gordon McCreath, Irvine
John G. Farmer, Edinburgh
Jim Dumigan, Kilmarnock
Evelyn Cavens, Wardneuk, Kilmarnock
Gordon L. Smith, Irvine
Sandy Tyrie, Kilmarnock
John Archibald, Northampton
Colin M. Speirs, Hamilton
Tom Irvine, Beith
Sandy McCutcheon, Kilmarnock
John & Margaret McGhee, Kilmaurs
Gordon Edgar, Dundonald, Ayrshire
Alex Roan, Stewarton
Louise Mitchell, Mauchline
Douglas Lyburn, Rutherglen, Glasgow
James R. Miller
James McIntosh, Ardrossan, Ayrshire
Ronnie Malone, Kilwinning
Ian Robertson, Ardrossan
Ian Barr, Kilmarnock
George Forty Stirling, Kilmarnock
Harry Bennett, London Road
David D. Hunter, Kilmarnock
David & Frazer Murray, Troon
Roy Hair, Glasgow
William & Cameron Austin, Stewarton
Jackie Smith, Barassie, Troon
Fraser McInroy Ross, Barassie
Andrew B. Miller, Catrine
Liam Clarke, Kilmarnock
Clive Livingstone, Cumnock, Ayrshire
Mrs. Sharon Callaghan, Kilmarnock
Mr. Raymond Montgomerie, Saltcoats
Allan Wark, Dundonald Road
Malcolm MacInnes, Darvel
Andrew Hodge, Kilmarnock
Derek & Lorraine Cole, Kilmarnock
Jimmie McCrindle, Dreghorn
Neil Tyre, Ardrossan
Gordon W. Wyllie, Irvine
William E. Cush, Kilmarnock
Les Bagan, Kilmarnock
Ross MacKenzie, Kilwinning
William Gemmell, Kilmarnock
James Chalmers, Kilmarnock
Mrs. Elaine Shaw, Kilmarnock
Robert Muir, Kilmarnock
John G.M. Smith, Dalry
Robert Gilbert, Kilwinning
James Flannigan, Kilwinning
Kenneth Gordon, Rockford, Illinois
Tom Millar, Stewarton
Stuart W. Little, Kilmarnock

George Batton, Newmilns
John McRobert, Stranraer
James Strathearn, Girvan
Stuart J. Ferguson, Kelvinside, Glasgow
Charlie Bull, Glenrothes, Fife
Robert Martin, Alloway
Alexander Campbell, Glasgow
Alistair J. Campbell, Glasgow
Alan Muir, Kilmarnock
David Graham, Tokyo, Japan
Graeme Stevenson, Paisley
Hazel, M. Fergusson
Craig McAvoy, Ayr
Ian Freeland, Linlithgow
Graham Norman Orr, Aberdeen
James Baird, Marden, Kent
Campbell Howie, Kilmarnock
Alastair Harwell, Dundonald
Andy Wotherspoon, Kilmarnock
Jim Ellis, H.M.S. Sceptre
Kevin McWhirter, Onthank, Kilmarnock
Malcolm Smith, Stromness, Orkney
Malcolm Hunter, Troon
Iain M. MacInnes, Kilmarnock
David William Richardson, Kilmarnock
Jack MacKenzie, Beith, Ayrshire
John MacKenzie, Kilmarnock
James S.Gracie, Bottisham, Cambridge
Jonathan Kelly, Kilbirnie, Ayrshire
Allan Kerr Graham, Dalry
Brian Cassidy, Walton-on-Thames, Surrey
Liam McIlvanney, Kilmarnock
Dr. William Murray, Inverness
John Gilmour, Liff, Dundee
Gordon Walker, Winsford, Cheshire
Alistair Colquhoun, Saltcoats
Angus Begg, Pitmedden, Grampian
Gary Whitten, Chingford, London
Daniele Marcolini, Verona, Italy
Gordon Andrews, Fenwick
Paul Archer, Broomlands, Irvine
Adam L. Baird, Kilmarnock
Colin Armstrong, Kilmarnock
Derek Barclay, Forever Killie
Jill Barr, Dreghorn
Vincent Barrie
Steven Boyce, Stevenson
Willie Boyd, Kilwinning
Eric Brown, Kilmarnock
Alan Brown, Newmilns
Irene M. Brown, Newmilns
Camerson M. Brown, Houston
Gordon Brown, Bellfield, Kilmarnock
John A. Bryden, Ayr
Graeme W.B. Bryson, Sorn
Allan Burleigh, Shortlees, Kilmarnock
Ian Burnett, Kilmaurs, Kilmarnock
Richard Cairns, Kilmaurs
Michael Caldow, Kilmarnock
Iain Cameron, Glasgow Road
Ian Wallace Campbell, Kilmarnock
Steven Campbell, Dean Park, Renfrew
Ewan Campbell, Bearsden
David Ross Campbell, Kirkintilloch
James Campbell, Kilmarnock
James Bummer Campbell, Kilmarnock
Tom Clark, Newton Mearns
Ross & Iain Clark, Kilmarnock

Vic Coburn, Saltcoats
Bob Coburn, Ardrossan
William Lynch Coffey, Kilmarnock
Ross Mark Connelly, Kilmarnock
Kenneth Coull, Kilmarncok
Alastair & Sarah Crabb, Troon
John Craig, Tannockhill, Mauchline
Angus Craig, Kilmarnock, Ayrshire
Wilson Craig, Kilmarnock
David Crawford, Kilmarnock
15, Rosebank Crescent, Ayr
John Crombie, Kilmarnock
John Cunningham, Kilmarnock
John Davidson, Barassie, Troon
Kevin S. Dempster, Prestwick
Johnny Devlin, Crosshouse
Andrew Docherty, Dundonald, Ayrshire
Karen Dolinie, Galston
Ewan Donaldson, Dreghorn, Irvine
Bill Donnachie, Edinburgh
Gary Dougan, Luce Avenue
Denis Duke, Bourtreehill, Irvine
Nina & Justin Dumigan, Kilmarnock
Michael Dumsday, Knaresborough, Yorkshire
Brian Dunbar, Edinburgh
Andrew Dunlop, Stewarton, Troon
David Ellery, Finsbury Park
Ruaridh Ellery, Pitscottie, Fife
Eilidh Ellery, Pitscottie, Fife.
Hugh M. Ellis, Kilmarnock
Rohan Evans, Melborune, Australia
Christopher Ewart Kerr, Kilmarnock
James D. Ferguson, Whitecraigs, Glasgow
James Findlay, Wardneuk, Kilmarnock
Robert Finnie, Kilmarnock, Scotland
Stephen Fitzsimmons, Kilmarnock
Rodger Edward Forbes, Kilmarnock
Rony Galbraith
Peter Gemmell, Erskine
Peter Gemmell, Snr., Lochwinnoch
Alan Gibson, Bonnyton, Kilmarnock
Ben Gilmour, Kilmarnock
David Gordon, Kilmarnock
Janice Grant, Kilmarnock
Neil Grimmond, Newton Mearns
Andrew G. Hair, Kilwinning
William A. Hair, Saltcoats
Steven Hall, Irvine
Amanda Hamilton, Kilmarnock, Ayrshire
Tracey & Sharon Hamilton, Kilmarnock
Stuart Hamilton, Kilmarnock
Paul Hamilton, Kilmarnock
Duncan Hamilton, Kilmarnock
Gavin Alexander Hardie, Ayr
Andrew Hart, Kilmarnock
Robert A Harvey, Newmilns
Gerry Harwood, Kilmarnock
Andrew Hastie, Mauchline
Alistair Henderson, Dreghorn
David Hendry, Glasgow
Jim Hendry, Kilmarnock
Jamie Hewitson, Kilmarnock
Christopher Hewitt, Brussels, Belgium
Eric Hewitt, Kilmarnock
Paul Hogg, Newmilns
John Houston, Glenrothes
Alasdair G. Houston, Irvine
George Howe, Blantyre
Mary Hubble, To Mary from Dennis
Ian Hunter. Catrine
Jim Ingram, Bullsbrook, Western Australia
Jim Irvine, Aberdeen
Ian James, Branalea
Donald M. Jamison, Waterfoot, Eaglesham
Billy Jess, New Cumnock
Steven Johnston, Kilmarnock
Douglas Johnston, Killie Exile
Paul Johnstone, Irvine
Billy Kerr, Galston
John Kerr, Kilmarnock
Alan Kerr, Kilmarnock
Alan King, Saudi Arabia
Denham Graham Kirkpatrick, Kilmarnock
Andrew Lindsay, Troon
Ann Linn, Newmilns
Steven J. Love, Kilmarnock
Alison Elizabeth Love, Kilmarnock
Alistair Lyon, Stewarton
Joseph John Mabon, Stewarton
Ian Mason, New Cumnock
Graeme Mathie, Troon
David Mawson, Kirkintilloch, Glasgow
James Maxwell, Saltcoats
Boyd T. McCamon, St. Albans
John McCluskie, Kilmarnock
Robert Graham McCluslie, Kilmarnock
Hugh McClymont, Kilmarnock
Scott McCue, Kilmarnock
Ewan McDowall, Barnard Castle
Iain Stuart McEwan, Killie
Karen McGougan, Kilmarnock
Harry McGougan, Kilmarnock
J. McIlwraith, K.F.C.
John McIlwraith, Kilmarnock, Ayrshire
Peter McKelvie, Crosshouse, Kilmarnock
Robert A. McKerrell, Kilmarnock, Ayrshire
Stuart McLean, Glasgow
Gregory McLelland, Kilmarnock
Andrew McRoberts, Kilmarnock
Andy McSwiggan, Kilwinning
Ronald M. McWhirter, Alloway
Bob McWilliam, Kilmarnock
Rebecca Millar, Killie Kid
John B. Miller, Burnhouse
Hugh Miller, Brisbane, Australia
Raymond Montgomerie, Saltcoats
Jim Montgomerie, Saltcoats
Kerr W. Morton, Prestwick
David Muir, Kilwinning
James Alexander Murdoch, Kilmarnock
James McEwan Murdoch, Kilmarnock
Iain Murray, Mauchline
Iain Murray, Kilmarnock
Brian Niven, Kilmarnock
Adam O'Neill, Killie's Dribbler
Phil Osborne, Dumfries
Matthew Osborne, Ca Ayr
Tom Parker, Lethbridge Park, Australia
Robert Parker, Kilmarnock
Alan Paterson, Helensburgh, Dumbartonshire
Owen Quigley, New Farm
Brian J. Rankin, Dreghorn, Irvine
James Richmond, Kilmarnock
Jan. Richmond, Kilmarnock
Eddie Riley, Troon
Liz & Bruce Roberts
Alan Robertson, Newton Mearns
Ian, Alan, Paul Rogerson
Jim Ross, Fairlie, Ayrshire
Terence Ruddy, Galston
James Ruddy, Catrine
Guy Scott, Ardrossan
Iain M. Sherry, Kilmarnock
Paul Skilling, Kilmarnock
Dr. John Smith, Hamilton
Geoff Smith, Kilwinning
Ronald Smith, Kilmaurs, Kilmarnock
Richard Steele, Kilmarnock, Scotland
George M. Stevens, Girvan
Derek Stevenson, Dean Castle, Kilmarnock
Freddie Stevenson
Iain Stewart, Crosshouse, Kilmarnock
James Stewart, Bellfield, Kilmarnock
Harry Stewart, Ayr
Samuel Stowe, Mauchline
Roger Strain, Stretton, Killie
Kilmarnock Deaf Supporters Club
Margaret-Ann Sweetie, Kilmarnock
Andrew & Julie Tannock, Irvine
Scott Thomson, Irvine, Ayrshire
Innes Thomson, Dunoon, Argyll
Gordon Thomson, Troon, Ayrshire
George James Thomson, Kilmarnock
Alfred Troth, Kilmarnock
Kirk Tudhope, Kilmarnock
Ken Tudhope, Kilmarnock
Des Turnbull, Kilmarnock
Arthur Stark Walls, Kilmarnock
Neill Watson, Newmilns
Paul Whip, Larkhall
George Whiteside, Troon, Ayrshire
Iain Whitton, Northumberland, Morpeth
Charles Williamson, New Farm
Andrew Wilson, Kilmarnock
Jim Wilson, Kilmarnock
Mary Bicker Wilson, Kilmarnock
Kevin William Wilson, Kilmarnock
Brian Wright, Crosshouse
Blair Young, Brakpan, Transvaal
Blair Young, Lanark
Sam Young, Mauchline
Nimbley Family, Bellfield, Kilmarnock
Galbraith Family, Newton Mearns
P. Robinson (KFC/SWFC) Sheffield
Tommy Adams, Ayr, Ayrshire
Richard Allison, Kilmarnock
Matt Allison, Holmlea, Kilmarnock
Alan Blakely, Paris
Stuart Blakely, Irvine
Derek Brewer, Irvine
Iain Brewer, Irvine
Denis Brown, Giffnock
Ewan Brown, Perth
Alan Buchanan, Kilmarnock
James H. Campbell, Kilmaurs
Alistair Carey, Lower Largo
Allan Collins, Ex. Player
John Collins, Barassie, Troon
Peter Cormack, Edinburgh
Angus Craig, Kilmarnock
David Craig, Aberdeen
Matthew Ferguson, Mauchline
To Ian from Jim
Hugh Gillies, Blyth, Nottinghamshire
Alan Graham, Burnside, Glasgow
Derek Hannah, Lerwick, Shetland
Jacqueline Highet, Kilmarnock
Brian James Highet, Kilmarnock
Paul Hyde, Hyndland, Glasgow
David Hyde, Leatherhead, Surrey
Matthew Jackson, Bovingdon, Herts.
Jim Kerr, Linlithgow
Alex Knox, Kilwinning
Alistair Leslie, Edinburgh
James, Joanne, Stuart Love
To Jimmy Love Carol
Alan MacGregor, Dumfries
David McBride, Carnock, Dunfermline
Anne McGuire, West Acton, London
Scott McIntosh, Derby
Allan Ferguson McKay, Aberdeen
David A. McLean
Alastair D. McLean
Gregory McNally, of Troon
Anne McVey, Kilmarnock
Thomas Moffat, Catrine, Ayrshire
Hugh Morton, Darvel
Ian Mossie, Drongan, Ayrshire
Alex Orr, Crosshouse
George N. Rutherford, Aberdeen
Kevin Scoular, Derby
Tom Simpson, Galston
Mungo Sinclair, Furnace, Argyll
Brian Hugh Smith, Dunfermline
Ian Smith, Kilmarnock
Alan Speck, Newton Mearns
Andrew James Speirs, Larkhall
Richard Thomson, Kilmarnock
J. Gary Torbett, Irvine
James G. Torbett, Troon
Joe Walker, Drummondplace, Inverness
Robert Williams, Newmilns, Ayrshire
Andrew Wilson, Kilwinning
Archie James Fulton, Australia
Bill Lang, Gold Coast, Australia
Sandy Quail, Tuart Hill, Australia
Dolina & Gavin McClung
G.Park, Middlesex
Arran Matthews, Buckinghamshire

A SELECTION OF TITLES

From
'YORE PUBLICATIONS'
12 The Furrows, Harefield,
Middx. UB9 6AT

(Free lists issued 3 times per year. For your first list please send a S.A.E.)

REJECTED F.C. OF SCOTLAND - Vol. 1: Edinburgh and The South. *(By Dave Twydell)* The first of three volumes on the written and basic statistical details of the Scottish ex-League Clubs. The book is well illustrated, is a hardback and contains 288 pages. (Clubs covered - Edinburgh City, Leith Athletic, St.Bernards, Armadale, Broxburn United, Bathgate, Peebles Rovers, Mid-Annandale, Nithsdale Wanderers and Solway Star). Price £12-95 Plus £1-30 Postage.
Volume 2 - Glasgow and District. Same price with another 11 Clubs' histories: Abercorn, Arthurlie, **Beith**, Cambuslang, Clydebank, Cowlairs, Johnstone, Linthouse, Northern, Third Lanark, and Thistle. (240 pages)

REJECTED F.C. VOLUME 1 (Reprint) *(By Dave Twydell)* The revised edition of this popular book - now in hardback - this volume provides the comprehensive histories of: Aberdare Athletic, Ashington, Bootle, Bradford (Park Avenue), Burton (Swifts, Wanderers and United), Gateshead/South Shields, Glossop, Loughborough, Nelson, Stalybridge Celtic and Workington. The 288 well illustrated pages also contain the basic statistical details of each club. Price £12-95 plus £1-30 postage.

'GONE BUT NOT FORGOTTEN - PART 2' *(By Dave Twydell)* The abbreviated histories of a variety of defunct non-League Clubs and Grounds; the old Hillingdon Borough, Wycombe's Loakes Park, Oswestry Town and Shirley Town are included in this edition (Part 1 is now sold out). A particular merit of these books is the high illustrative content, and with details for readers to track down the sites of the Grounds - 64 pages. Issued every 6 months Price £4-95 plus 45p postage.
(Volumes 3 and 4 now available - same price)

DONNY - The Official History of Doncaster Rovers *(Tony Bluff and Barry Watson)* Written by two supporters of the Club, the full statistics (from 1879) and including line-ups (from 1901). The book is well illustrated, including many line-ups, and also contains the full written history of the Club. Hardback with full coloured dustjacket and 240 pages. Price £14-95 plus £1-80 postage and packing.

COLCHESTER UNITED - The Official History of the 'U's' *(Hal Mason)* With football involvement from the 1920's, the Author - a former journalist and Colchester programme editor - is well qualified to relate this complete history of the Club since its formation in 1937 (including complete statistics and lineups from this season). Large Hardback with dustjacket, 240 pages, priced £14-95 plus £2-70 postage.

AMBER IN THE BLOOD - History of Newport County: *(Tony Ambrosen).* The full written story of football in Newport from the pre-County days up to and including the recently formed Newport AFC club. The text is well illustrated, and a comprehensive statistical section provides all the results, attendances, goalscorers, etc. from 1912 to 1993 - the various Leagues and principal Cup competitions; additionally seasonal total players' appearances are included. A hardback book, containing 176 large pages is exceptional value at only £13-95 plus £2-60 postage.

FOOTBALL LEAGUE - GROUNDS FOR A CHANGE *(By Dave Twydell).* A 424 page, A5 sized, Hardback book. A comprehensive study of all the Grounds on which the current English Football League clubs previously played. Every Club that has moved Grounds is included, with a 'Potted' history of each, plus 250 illustrations. Plenty of 'reading' material, as well as an interesting reference book. Price £13-95 Plus £1-70 Postage.

THROUGH THE TURNSTILES *(by Brian Tabner)* This incredible book which provides the average attendance of every English Football League club, for every season from 1888/89 to 1991/92. (*'The best Football Book I have ever read. " At the bottom end of the price range for a quality book. "* - The Footballer Magazine) Well illustrated, and also relates the development of the game (angled towards attendances). Also details of the best supported 'away' teams, season ticket sales over the years, etc. Large format hardback and 208 packed pages. An excellent read at £13-95 plus £1-70 Postage.

COVENTRY CITY FOOTBALLERS (The Complete Who's Who)
By Martin & Paul O'Connor. One of the most detailed books of its type. Every Football (and Southern) League player has been included - around 700. Seasonal appearances of every player, brief personal details, 'pen pictures', together with very detailed information on the movements of the players to other clubs. Plus: around 100 photo's of the Club's most memorable men, and information on the principal players from the pre-Southern League days. A hardback book with 224 large pages. £13-95 plus £2-60 postage.

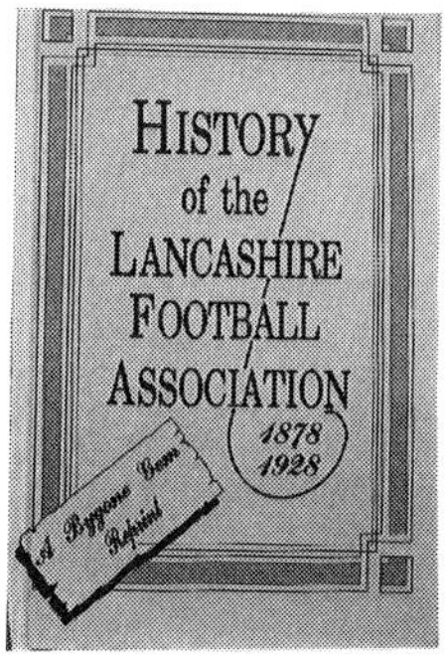

HISTORY OF THE LANCASHIRE FOOTBALL ASSOCIATION 1878-1928.
A rare historical and fascinating hardback reprint (first published in 1928). Contains the history of the formative days of Lancashire football. Sections within the 288 pages include the early histories of about 20 Clubs (Manchester Utd., Wigan Borough, Rochdale, etc.), Lancashire Cup competitions, Biographies, etc. For those interested in the development of the game, this is a 'must', and you will definitely not be disappointed. Price £12-95 Plus £1-30 Postage.

THE CODE WAR *(Graham Williams)*
A fascinating look back on football's history - from the earliest days up to the First World War. 'Football' is covered in the broadest sense, for the book delves into the splits over the period to and from Rugby Union and Rugby League, as well as Football (Soccer). Potted histories of many of the Clubs are included, as is a comprehensive index. 192 page hardback, price £10-95 plus £1-20 postage.

Available from:
TRANS VIDEO PRODUCTIONS
Regent House, 16 Old Road, Linslade, Leighton Buzzard, Beds. LU7 7RD
(Please add £1-00 P/P or obtainable from major video outlets)

REJECTED F.C. - The Video The video of the books (Rejected F.C. Volumes 1 and 2). Several hours of repeated entertainment. Includes extensive modern film shots, interviews with many personalities related to these teams, still shots to aid the telling of these Clubs' Histories... and an amazing collection of archive film (e.g. Ashington in 1924, pre-war New Brighton, Workington's last home League match, etc.). Every 'Rejected' club (from Accrington in 1888) is featured. Price £12-99 (incl. VAT), from major Video outlets.
FOOTBALL PHOENIX- The sequel to 'Rejected F.C. - The Video'. The stories on film of the five post-war League Clubs who became defunct and have successfully reformed (Gateshead, Accrington Stanley, Bradford P.A., Newport County and Aldershot). Film clips include all the goals from County's last game, and the Carl Zeiss match, plus Aldershot's last League game, and footage from 1970 of the new Stanley. 80 minutes of excellent entertainment at only £10-99.

YESTERDAY'S CIGARETTE CARD HEROES A video providing an insight of professional football in the 1930's to 1960's. A number of modern filmed interviews with famous players of 'yesteryear', including Tommy Lawton, Billy Wright, Roy Bentley, John Charles, etc. Their humorous stories, anecdotes, and other stories of their life in football. Includes cartoon strips illustrating their tales, archive action footage etc. 60 minutes of nostalgia! Price £10-99.
(Send a S.A.E. for full lists of Football and other specialist videos)